A New History of Social Welfare

FOURTH EDITION

Phyllis J. Day

Boston • New York • San Francisco • Mexico City
Montreal • Toronto • London • Madrid • Munich • Paris
Hong Kong • Singapore • Tokyo • Cape Town • Sydney

Series Editor: *Patricia Quinlin*
Editor-in-Chief: *Karen Hanson*
Series Editorial Assistant: *Annemarie Kennedy*
Marketing Manager: *Taryn Wahlquist*
Composition and Prepress Buyer: *Linda Cox*
Manufacturing Buyer: *JoAnne Sweeney*
Editorial-Production Coordinator: *Mary Beth Finch*
Editorial-Production Service: *Modern Graphics, Inc.*
Electronic Composition: *Modern Graphics, Inc.*

For related titles and support materials, visit our online catalog at www.ablongman.com

Between the time Website information is gathered and then published, it is not unusual for some sites to have closed. Also, the transcription of URLs can result in unintended typographical errors. The publisher would appreciate notification where these errors occur so that they may be corrected in subsequent editions.

Library of Congress Cataloging-in-Publication Data

Day, Phillis J.
    A new history of social welfare / Phyllis J. Day.—4th ed.
       p. cm.
    Includes bibliographical references and index.
    ISBN 0-205-36003-3
       1. United States—Social policy.   2. Social policy.   3. Public welfare—United States—History.   4. Public welfare—History.   I. Title.
HN57 .D33 2002
361.6'1'0973—dc21

                                                                    2002018552

Printed in the United States of America

10 9 8 7 6 5 4 3 2 1   07 06 05 04 03 02

Dedicated to
my Mother,
Nora Isabel Seymour Phelps,
1892–1957,
who loved unconditionally and taught me unconditional love.
And to all women
for their
wisdom, strength, courage, and endurance.

Contents

Preface   ix

1 Values in Social Welfare   1

Values in Social Welfare   2

American Social Values   4

Issues of Discrimination   12

Conclusion: Values and Power   23

Notes   24

2 The Institution of Social Welfare   27

The Meaning of Social Institution   27

Perspectives on Social Welfare   33

The Scope of Social Welfare   40

The Profession of Social Work   46

Conclusion: Social Work and Social Control   50

Notes   51

3 The Beginnings of Social Welfare: Political Economy and Early Societies   54

Prehistory and Social Welfare to 6000 B.C.   54

The Beginnings of History: 6000–3000 B.C.   57

Invasion, Conquest, and Patriarchal Religion   60

Moving into the Iron Age: 1200–400 B.C.   63

Greece, Christianity, and the Roman Empire   67

Conclusion: Beginnings of Charity and Control   78

Notes   79

4 *Feudalism and the Welfare State*   82

The Dark and Middle Ages   82

The Dissolution of Feudalism   92

Poverty Becomes a Crime   96

The Protestant Reformation: New Meanings for Work and Welfare   98

Social Welfare in England: The Tudor Period   103

The Industrial Revolution and the Emergence of Capitalism   109

Conclusion: Reifying the Values of the Past   114

Notes   115

5 *The Other Side of the World*   119

The Indigenous Peoples of America   120

The European Invasion   123

Social Welfare in the Colonies   135

Slavery in the Americas   142

Toward the Revolution   146

The New Nation and Its Constitution   147

Conclusion: Revolution to Status Quo   149

Notes   150

6 *America to the Civil War*   153

The First Civil Rights Movement   153

Private Philanthropy   158

Government Responses   163

Social Treatment in the 1800s   167

Nonwhite Minorities: Expendable Commodities in the New Nation   175

The Women's Movement in the 1800s   185

Conclusion: Working Toward Freedom   188

Notes   189

7 The American Welfare State Begins   192

The Civil War: A New Nation Emerges   193

After the Civil War   196

Postwar Political Economy   197

Population, Immigration, and the People   200

"True Womanhood"   207

Emerging Philosophies and Social Welfare   211

Public Welfare Efforts   221

Professionalization of Social Work   224

Conclusion: Moving Toward Reform   225

Notes   227

8 The Progressive Era, War, and Recovery   231

The Progressive Era   231

Population Movements and Immigration   234

Oppression of African and Native Americans   237

Labor and the Unions   240

Social Welfare in the Progressive Era   243

Women's Movements and Peace Protests   255

The Professionalization of Social Work   261

Conclusion: New Freedoms and Old Constraints   262

Notes   263

9 *The Great Depression and Social Security for Americans* 267

The Great Depression 268

Social Insurance in the United States 276

Programs of Social Insurance Based on the Social Security Act 279

Public Assistance Programs of the Social Security Act 282

The Professionalization of Social Work 286

World War II 288

The Resurgence of Social Work 297

Conclusion: Moving Toward the Future 301

Notes 302

10 *Civil and Welfare Rights in the New Reform Era* 306

The State of the Nation Under Eisenhower 308

Social Programs in the 1950s 309

Civil Rights Before Kennedy 312

Civil Rights in the Kennedy Years 318

Johnson and the Great Society 319

Civil Rights in the Kennedy–Johnson Years 325

Social Programs in the Kennedy–Johnson Years 329

Welfare, Civil Rights, and the Social Work Profession 336

Conclusion: Looking Back on the 1960s 338

Notes 340

11 *The Return to the Past* 343

A Retreat from the Welfare State 343

Social Programs in the 1970s 346

Civil Rights in the 1970s 356

Conclusion: Tightening the Reins   368

Notes   369

12   The Reactionary Vision   372

Biting the Conservative Bullet   372

Reaganomics: The Conservative Political Economy   374

The New Federalism   376

Pruning the Programs   380

Basic Needs Programs   387

Civil Rights Under Reagan and Bush   394

The Costs of Social Welfare   398

The International Element   399

Conclusion: Past Ideology in a Postindustrial World   400

Notes   402

13   The Synergistic Cycle   406

The New Synergy of Values   406

Economic Context of the 1990s   409

The Decline of Social Responsibility: Welfare as We Knew It   410

Supplemental Security Income   426

Social Issues   438

Affirmative Action and Civil Rights   442

Welfare for the Wealthy and Corporate Welfare   446

Conclusion: Futureword   455

Notes   458

Bibliography   467

Index   481

Preface

Traditionally, a preface is the place where we thank those who have contributed to the accomplishment that is a book. Throughout my life, people have touched me with their feelings, thoughts, and knowledge, and this book is, in a very true sense, a part of the part of me that was part of them. My teachers, my colleagues, my students, my friends, my family of origin and of marriage—all who participated in my life have contributed.

The book tries to answer the "why" of social welfare. In great part, it is a history of those involved in the social welfare institution not as wielders but as subjects/victims/recipients/clients. It seeks to redress in part the loss of history for women, nonwhite people, and other groups oppressed by social institutions, and to relate intimately the place of the labor force and working people with the social welfare institution. The breadth of the book ensures its failure to adequately cover its aspirations. I am well aware of much left undone, through lack of either space/time or knowledge. However, it is a beginning from which students and others can seek more deeply and, hopefully, fill in its blanks.

A New History of Social Welfare looks at the earliest forces for both aspects of social welfare: social treatment and social control. These themes are carried forward from a perspective that considers the synergistic relationships of economy, polity, religion, and social welfare and asks the "why" of treatment and/or control. To this end, I give attention to anthropological and archeological evidence of the ways people related to each other from as early as 20,000 B.C. to view the societal contexts of social welfare and the needs of society either to provide care for valued members or to ensure enough members for social tasks.

Because social welfare is so deeply affected by institutional racism, sexism, classism, and "otherism," the historical and evolutionary sources of these "isms" are given a great deal of attention. One of the results of institutional discrimination has been an "elimination" of history, or a selective compilation of a series of achievements of men who are generally Caucasian or Aryan and of the elite and/or warrior classes. This reading of history ignores or belittles the contributions of women, nonwhite people, and the poor laborers on whose backs history occurred. Although *A New History* cannot hope to redress all these issues, it provides much new or reinterpreted historical information to set events in a more unbiased social context.

Of particular import in this perspective is the analysis of humankind's relationships with deity—religions—both in providing charity and in elaborating on or perpetuating social control. This dichotomy of religiously legitimated charity and control underlies the development of social welfare in all its ramifications, the values that provide the *push* to helping or controlling "others," and the ways in which the profession of social work itself came into being and grew. Religions are synergistically related to other major institutions of society, whether we speak of European feudalism, the European invasions of the Western Hemisphere, colonial America, the Progressive movement of the early 1900s, the conservative backlash of the Reagan era, or the power of the Far Right and Religious Right to destroy the safety net of the poor in exchange for support for the wealthy in the 1990s. This synergism, then, is the key to the historical analysis of social welfare and the social work profession.

When I wrote the first edition of the book in the Reagan years, the conservative backlash occurring seemed to be just a glitch that sane and good-hearted people would soon overcome. In the 1990s, I understood that the Reagan years were part of a thirty-year trend that would ultimately reverse the social morality we had built with such anguish over the 300 years since North America was colonized. Now, under policies endorsed by the presidential administrations of George Bush, Bill Clinton, and George W. Bush, we have destroyed programs that underlaid social responsibility. We have not replaced them; we simply refuse to look at the consequences. Social responsibility and morality have taken a back seat to greed at both national and international levels. Our world has narrowed, but worse, we as individuals and as a nation have narrowed, condensed, and encapsulated ourselves. We have no space, no heart, for others, and this plays itself out in our social policies.

And now to thank those who helped me with this project. The greatest influence on the book and on my life was my mother, Nora Seymour Phelps, dead these many years. She gave me, from the beginning of my life, the courage to follow my convictions and search for reality no matter where the path led. Although her heart finally failed her, her spirit never did. Also, my sisters have contributed more than they know with strength, endurance, and courage throughout their hard lives: Avah, recently deceased, who always knew that "things will be better tomorrow"; Evah, who died as I was finishing this edition, with her gentle courage; and Lois, who never gave up and always faced the world with valor. Thanks also to my mentors, Rosemary C. Sarri, who serves as a model, however unattainable, for more women than she knows; and John E. Tropman, who always believed in me. My gratitude to my dear friends Joan Bowker, Keetjie Ramo, Mardell Nelson, Doug Yunker, and Harry Macy, all of whom have saved my life in ways they will never know. My former husband, Jerald R. Day, and my children—Jerry II, Nora Gaye, Merry Rose, Sean, and Joy Alyssa—helped and supported me in innumerable ways and brought gladness into my life.

For the first edition, I want to thank the editors and personnel at Prentice Hall, especially Nancy Roberts, Sociology Editor, and Marianne Peters, Production Editor. Also my thanks to my reviewers of all editions of this text, including Albert Roberts, Indiana University; George Siefert, Jr., Daemen College; Jack Otis, University of Texas—Austin, Patricia K. Cianciolo, Northern Michigan University; Paul H. Stuart, University of Alabama; Marcia B. Cohen, University of New

England; Nancy L. Mary, California State University–San Bernadio and Editor-in-Chief Karen Hanson of Allyn & Bacon. Thanks also to those who helped me prepare the third edition of the book, particularly Judy Fifer, ever patient and supportive; and Allyn & Bacon's Julie Cancio, Editorial Assistant, Jennifer Miller, Advertising Manager, and Marketing Manager Jacqueline Aaron; and Michael Granger of Modern Graphics. Thanks for the fourth edition go to Allyn & Bacon's Patricia Quinlin and Annemarie Kennedy; Marty Tenney of Modern Graphics; and the reviewers of this edition, James D. Stafford, the University of Mississippi; and Marina Barnett, Temple University.

I hope you like the new edition.

Phyllis J. Day

1

Values in Social Welfare

Once upon a time . . .

This is a book about love: of people helping others, of organizations that ease the way for people in trouble, and of people joining together to work for the benefit of others. Love—the idea of helping others—inspires each of us to enter the field of human services, to share our efforts, and to work for the well-being of humanity. Our first and best intentions are to care for others, to help the disadvantaged "live happily ever after." But love is not enough. Social welfare and the profession of social work are much more complex, and we must not let fairy tales blind us.

Love's dark side is power; society, through social welfare, uses that power to control. Both help and control are traditions of social work and social welfare, and through them we help to maintain society's structures of inequality. Despite society's investment in social welfare, our own commitment as social workers, or the willingness or ability of our clients, we will not be able to change those structures unless we understand both sides of social welfare. As it is, our targets for blame and change are misplaced. We blame our clients when they fail despite our efforts, they blame themselves for failure, and society blames both clients and social workers for wasted money and lost effort when poverty continues, deviant behaviors rise, and clients remain ungrateful and unrepentant. To understand this, we must throw away our fairy tales and begin to question the *why* of social welfare and social work.

Why is a good question, one we should ask more often. Why have our welfare rolls grown, and why is there hunger in America? Why is there more crime and delinquency? Why are so many people homeless? Why are mental health clinics doing a booming business? Why are there so many people with problems, and why are our prisons overflowing? Why do the costs of all forms of social welfare continue to rise? The answers lie in understanding society's institutions, how social welfare evolves from the interactions among these institutions, and what purposes social welfare really serves.

Our purpose in this book is to ask these questions. Our major theme is that synergistic evolution[1] of the institutions of polity, religion, and economy throughout time creates both social problems and their solutions, and that social

1

welfare and social work—its action arm—are the results. Synergy is "cooperative action of discrete agencies so that the total effect is greater than the sum of the effects taken independently."[2] We cannot study any of the institutions of society alone, for they are interdependent. We must look at their dynamic interactions to understand the institution of social welfare. Another theme is that society has rigid structures that maintain inequality, and that social welfare, because of its synergistic evolution, is a context for social control.

We must lay a groundwork for answering questions by looking at the place of social work and social welfare in society. First, we will look at American social values; second, at issues of poverty and classism; and finally, at institutional discrimination in American society. In the process, we will discover the synergistic sources and meanings of our values and their impact on perceptions and practices of social welfare. To do this, we must place some of our own beliefs and values in abeyance, for much of what we "know" is value. This is not an easy task, but it is essential.

Values in Social Welfare

Social welfare in any society has two major purposes: social treatment (helping) and social control. We easily agree with the helping purpose but are generally almost unaware of the social control function of social welfare because it is hidden in ideas about equality and what we consider our "right" to change our clients. Society needs certain social controls, for some behaviors must be regulated so that interdependent people can live and work together. However, not all such control is positive, and social welfare controls aim at our most vulnerable citizens. Because our clients need our help, they must meet our (and society's) demands. Seldom do they participate in social welfare decisions that affect their lives, and the price they pay for our help is often their personal freedom.

Our personal, societal, and social work values, therefore, are perhaps the most important factors in the practice of social work. Naomi Brill points out,

> We hold that all people are equal, but that those who do not work are less equal. . . . We hold that individual life has worth, but that only the fit should survive. We believe that we are responsible for each other, but that those who are dependent upon others for their living are of less worth.

She says further that human service workers are walking value systems, and that they must become aware of those values, evaluate them rationally, and change the irrational ones.[3] Paternalism, or the idea that we know what is good for others, is another problem. Because *we* have succeeded, we think we have the right to impose our values and decisions on those who have not. It implies that our clients lack something, that they are less than whole people who

> need to be brought up to our . . . levels. . . . [W]e, as experts and whole persons, have the ability, knowledge and the right to round out, remake, fulfill, or "pull

[them] up" . . . there is a "right way" which the expert knows, and a "wrong way" which the client does that underlies and colors the whole intervention process.[4]

Values permeate social welfare, whatever the perspective, culture, or period of history: what we "ought to" provide or how we "ought to" deal with deviants. Every perception or reaction is value-laden and value-based, and we can never be truly objective. Therefore, as social helpers, we have no right to impose what we believe on the lives of others. Our clients' life situations and life experiences are different from ours, and although we can empathize, we cannot understand their lives. To assume that we do, to make life decisions for them, is unethical. Society has a right to control dangerous or destructive behaviors, but most of social work does not involve those problems. Therefore, we should not enforce conformity to norms that may not be relevant to the life situations of others. In fact, doing so often creates or perpetuates their problems.

Our attitudes and values are often couched in religious, moral, or patriotic terms, and these attitudes and values are so much a part of our lives that we think they are facts rather than beliefs. A fact is the quality of being actual or having objective reality,[5] whereas a value is something intrinsically desirable.[6] In more practical terms, a fact is the way things are, and a value is how we wish they were.[7] We "know" both facts and values, but we may confuse them and base important judgments on what we wish rather than on what is. We should always test what we "know" by remembering that fact is something that has existed throughout history and in every culture. Everything else is value.

What Are Values?

In addition to being the way we wish things were, values have four identifiable characteristics, according to Hunter and Saleeby.[8]

- Values are *conceptual abstractions* drawn from immediate experience—from what we ourselves have learned about the world. Our unique experiences make each value unique to each of us (and to our clients).
- Values are *affectively charged for emotional mobilization;* that is, they make us want to take action or make us feel emotionally positive or negative about a situation. Racism, for example, makes us angry when we see it in others, and perhaps embarrassed or unhappy when we see it in ourselves, and we want to do something about the problem.
- Values are *criteria by which our goals are chosen.* For example, abortion is a tremendously charged value in our society. Almost every one of us takes a stand on abortion, based on whether we believe in the right of every fetus to survive or the right of every woman to control her own body. We set goals about abortion for ourselves and often work to set abortion standards for others.
- Values are *important rather than trivial concerns.* We may prefer the color blue, or to go to one university rather than another, but these issues do not stir us

to emotionally charged action. Rather, issues that involve basic questions of life, death, freedom, our rights as citizens or as workers, the concern we have for others—these are concerns that move us to anger, pride, fear, hope, or love and to actions to attain or resolve these emotions.

Miringoff and Opdycke say that values

are always in a state of change; sometimes they merge to form coherent systems, sometimes they have vague relationships, often they are in conflict. . . . [They] may be influenced by occupation, race, age, class position, or by external factors such as changing economic conditions and new norms of social behavior.[9]

Foundations of Charity and Control

To find where our values come from, or the reasons for the way we treat others, we must trace our way to two human characteristics so important that they are doctrines basic to society. The first is *mutual aid*; the second is *protection from others and otherness*. These characteristics are, respectively, the bases of values concerning social treatment and social control. Often contradictory, they have caused major dilemmas in the way our social welfare institution works. According to *Webster's Dictionary*, "a society is an enduring and cooperating social group whose members have developed organized patterns of relationships through interaction with one another."[10]

For early humankind, these included actions against predators (animal or human) and care for dependents (at first probably a mother–child bond). The need for defense resulted in fears of outsiders and otherness, whereas bonding was extrapolated into mutual aid in the wider society. As families bonded together to share food and protection, mutual aid expanded to include other cooperative efforts such as building, hunting, and farming. Care of children expanded to include caring for the helpless or valued members of the tribe, often the elders who had been instrumental in leadership or religious activities. In tandem with mutual aid, the abhorrence of otherness and defense against it meant protection of herds and homes from predators and, later, aggression to win more land and wealth from others. Eventually, fear and hatred of those outside the kin group were extended to in-group people who were "different" or posed a threat to tribal solidarity. A reluctance to share with others became firmly based, and today it is a reluctance to help those who do not "fit in."

American Social Values

Many values affect the human services, and all seem so positive that we rarely question them even when they contradict one another. However positive they may be for society in general, they can be intensely negative for certain groups in our society, such as women, children, the unemployed, and people of minority groups. Among the most basic values are

- Judaeo-Christian charity values
- Democratic egalitarianism and individualism
- The Protestant work ethic and capitalism
- Social Darwinism
- The New Puritanism
- Patriarchy
- Marriage and the nuclear family
- The "American Ideal."

Judaeo-Christian Charity Values

Judaeo-Christian charity values are based, first, on Judaic teachings of social justice and, second, on the teachings of Jesus as practiced in the early centuries of Christianity. They are *nonsectarian and social* rather than *religious,* and their major thrust is that those in need have a right to help and society has an obligation to provide for them. As society's primary social ethics, they are the bases for social altruism. Their prescriptions of love and charity are probably the reasons that people enter the human services.

Judaic prophets as early as Amos, in the eighth century B.C., enjoined people to charity as social justice and religious obligation. They believed that human relationships mirror those between deity and humanity, and that people must care for one another as God cares for them. Every person has intrinsic worth, and charity should be given without thought of self. Early Christian traditions reiterated and strengthened the prophetic Judaic teachings, adding ideas of equality for women. Jesus advocated for the poor and helpless, calling for justice for women, the poor, children, and other unfortunates. However, as time wore on, most of this advocacy position was lost.

If Judaeo-Christian values still underlaid social welfare, we would see a far different America. No one would be without enough food, clothing, or shelter. Every child would be assured of equal opportunity in the system, and society would take responsibility for the disadvantaged. Although work for self-support would still be encouraged, a person in need could seek help without stigma. Failure would not be blamed on the individual but on the social structures that prevented success. Oppression and exploitation would not exist, and success would be to invest in the lives of others rather than in personal wealth for oneself.

Social work *ethics* reflect Judaeo-Christian values, but social work *practice* owes more to other, more individualistic values. These distinctions help us to understand why our social programs are not always socially just and why our clients cannot succeed despite our "good works." Although we may have chosen social work as our profession because of its ethical Judaeo-Christian values, society's goals for social welfare are more accurately based on more restrictive values.

Democratic Egalitarianism and Individualism

Democratic egalitarianism was a primary tenet in the founding of the United States: All citizens are equal before the law, and no one has privileges based on class, heritage, wealth, or other factors irrelevant to citizenship. No citizen is better than any other, and all can share equally in societal decision making through either direct vote or representation. Although an equal share of resources is not guaranteed, the right to opportunities such as education and employment is.

Despite the ideal, in practice we do not have equality in America. Originally, the Constitution gave citizenship only to male property-holders, denying it to women, the propertyless, white ethnic immigrants, and people of color—primarily Native Americans, people of African descent, Hispanics, and Asians. Although all native-born men (except for Native Americans) became full citizens after the Civil War, women could not vote until 1918, and Native Americans gained citizenship even later. The rights of African Americans were denied by fiat until the Civil Rights Act of 1964, and women are still denied explicit equal rights under national law. In addition, custom restricts achievement opportunities for people of color, women, and other minority groups. Moreover, choice of candidates and policies often depends on wealth and power. Poor people have little power to choose and middle-class people choose among those selected by the elite. Still, our persistent belief in American equal opportunity has major impact on our assessment of client motivations and capability.

Related closely to egalitarianism is individualism: the ideal of individual effort and personal motivation by which any American can achieve success. It is a frontier ideology, coming from early days in America when anyone could win success in the new world of free land. Today, the value persists in the ideas that there are frontiers of the mind and that education, technology, and hard work can win wealth and success if only we try hard enough. We must be self-reliant—in control of and responsible for our own lives—and sheer effort will bring success. To ask for help from others is an admission of weakness, and failure to achieve—money, happiness, status, whatever—is the fault of the individual rather than society.

From this comes our tendency to blame the victim, to place the burden of failure on personal lack of effort. People are poor because they will not work rather than because of high unemployment. A person who is robbed or raped should not have been where such crimes could happen, or in some way "asked for it." The aged poor should have planned better for retirement, and poor children are hungry because their parents fail rather than because society does not provide social insurance. Our "blanket value" of individual responsibility exonerates society and confirms personal failure for those who cannot or do not reach "success."

Success has many meanings. Our responsibility is to help clients to achieve their own successes, not ours. Moreover, because American society is neither fully egalitarian nor democratic, we realize that institutional discrimination and class stratification keep some people from achieving success regardless of their efforts. Opportunities do not accrue automatically with citizenship, and blaming the victim does not overcome structural barriers to success.

The Protestant Work Ethic and Capitalism

The Protestant work ethic is the moral basis for American capitalism: an economic system in which profit through business enterprise is mostly uncontrolled by governments. Bonacich says,

> Capitalism . . . depends . . . on exploiting the labor of the [poor]. . . . For this reason, [they] have an interest in [poverty], since if there were no have-nots, there could be no one to work for them, no one to rent their buildings, no one from whom wealth could be derived. This . . . means that capitalist societies . . . can never rid [themselves] of poverty. Poverty is the basis of wealth. The dependency of the rich on the poor is the fundamental hidden reality of this system.[11]

A social rather than an economic creed, the Protestant ethic is a value accepted by most Americans regardless of religion. Its complex of values includes individualism, personal achievement and worth, the morality of wealth, and, for America, patriotism. Work for economic gain is the way to success, a sign of personal morality, and a moral obligation. Conversely, poverty and public dependency demonstrate immorality.

The work ethic springs from the mercantilist movement of the early Middle Ages and the Protestant Reformation. Martin Luther's belief in work as a calling and John Calvin's teachings on predestination came to mean that those predestined to salvation were identifiable by their wealth. If wealth showed morality, then surely poverty demonstrated immorality. With this line of reasoning, the wealthy justified both their wealth and their exploitation of workers to accumulate it; the rich felt they had a moral obligation to save the poor by making them work. Surplus production could then be sold and profits reinvested to make more profits—the "just rewards" of the wealthy.

Our definitions of "worthy" and "unworthy" poor come from that definition of the Protestant work ethic. The worthy poor are those who cannot work—the aged or disabled, for example. However, people who can work should, even if there is no work—they "can work if they want to" or "can support their families if they work hard enough." The doctrine of personal fault, then as now, relieved the wealthy of the economic burden of supporting the poor and gave them "religious credit" for not furthering the immorality of pauperism. We still believe that poverty is the result of laziness or degeneracy. The work ethic is so important a value in American society that we do not see who the poor are: young children, mothers who care for them, the aged, the disabled. Although changing technologies and government programs mean new unemployment and underemployment, because of the work ethic, we insist that anyone who wants to work can earn enough to live on.

Social Darwinism

Darwinism, a biological theory never intended to become economic, says that organisms unable to survive in an ecological niche will die out. In the nineteenth century, Malthus extrapolated the theory into a social and economic one: Population trends predicted, to him, a future teeming with poor people supported by "worthy" hard workers. This theory became known as social Darwinism, which said that state support of the poor was against the laws of "economic nature" and that the lives of people who were "economically unfit" should not be saved by giving them public assistance. Moreover, it claimed they were poor by choice because of moral degeneracy, and so *should* perish. Any society continuing to aid them would be destroyed by their immorality.

Today, social Darwinist attitudes infect all of society's institutions. Founded on the economic issue of support for the poor, stigma spreads insidiously to groups *likely* to be poor, legitimating discrimination and exploitation against them *regardless* of their economic situations. Politically speaking, this maintains the status quo for the power elite. The idea that "they are not as good as us" permeates society's institutions and is directed against, among others, people of color; those of "different" religions; homosexuals denied equal family or job benefits; people differently abled physically, mentally, or emotionally; elders neglected in nursing homes or abused by their caretakers; and, of course, the poor, particularly mothers and their dependent children. Sadly, the Temporary Assistance to Needy Families (TANF) program classes children in their parents' economic status, and after two years of public assistance, they too become "unfit" to receive society's help.

Although rarely espoused openly today, social Darwinism exists covertly in many welfare policies and programs and in the public idiom. Along with the Protestant work ethic, it opposes Judaeo-Christian charity values and helps to explain our society's loathing of "reliefers." Public assistance programs demonstrate the value clearly in low grants, stigmatization of recipients, insensitive and irrelevant eligibility testing, and attempts to put recipients to work regardless of wage or personal situations. We still believe that supporting the poor contributes to their immorality, although we are blind to the support we give to the wealthy through tax breaks and government support of and investment in corporations.

The New Puritanism

Arising from political, economic, and religious changes in the fourteenth century, New Puritanism now permeates American society. It is an essential political thrust of the Religious Right, a powerful lobby group for legislation to enforce compliance to the patriarchal and Puritan values of the past. Puritan values include chastity, particularly for women; honesty in dealing with others; abstinence from things defined by religion and custom as immoral, such as promiscuity, gambling, and the use of alcohol or drugs to excess; and "proper" behavior (that is, behavior that will not offend others). Puritan morality also emphasizes the sanctity of marriage and family and patriarchal authority in the home and condemns lifestyles such as communal living and homosexuality.

The New Puritanism is somewhat analogous to what David Wagner calls the "New Temperance," a peculiarly American ideology that obsesses on sin and vice. It particularly concerns substance abuse, sexual behaviors, food and fitness, and suspect freedom of speech issues such as pornography, lewd language, and the content of music, movies, and so forth.[12] He contends that this constitutes a culturally normative "consensus war" "primarily against the working class, ethnic and racial minorities, and poor people. . . ."[13] The result of this is to further the "otherization" of such groups and make them more subject to political control.

The Religious Right, made up primarily of Protestants with a sprinkling of Catholics and Jews, uses modern technology in its battles: Television brings the moral campaign into our homes and computer technology enables immediate contact with adherents on action issues. This New Puritanism has catapulted people from the radical Right into office, removed liberal incumbents, and sponsored laws and movements that reinforce religious beliefs on women's career and reproductive choices, prayer in school, and other moral issues. Militant on the side of domestic law and order, it advocates national insularity and military force to maintain it despite the interdependence of the world's nations.

Patriarchy

Patriarchy is a system in which power and authority are vested in men, whereas women and other powerless groups, such as children, workers, and slaves, are oppressed and often owned. More than the domination of women by men, it arose early in history when patriarchs (male heads of families) took absolute power over families and clans and began to conquer weaker groups. Religious legitimation of conquest bonded with patriarchy to produce a new kind of society, one based on male authority rights. Today, it is a worldwide system of exploitation by Western society of women (sexism), the poor (classism), nonwhite people (racism), and people and governments of developing countries (neocolonialism or imperialism).

In a patriarchal society, male authority permeates every institution: In the polity, men hold most appointed and elected offices and make laws, decisions, and policies; in the economy, men have control of capital, resources, and the production and distribution of goods and services; in religion, men hold the highest offices, dictating moral standards of society; and in the family, men make major decisions as "heads of the house." Under patriarchy, women suffer dual oppression: as women in male societies and as workers in patriarchal systems. They have been bought, sold, or married for political liasons, and laws control their sexuality, including reproduction, which is geared to produce children as workers or to carry on men's inheritances. In marriage, in the labor force, and in systems of public assistance, they and their children are economically dependent, and ultimately their subsistence and well-being depends on the largesse (or lack thereof) of men.

Because of sex-role socialization in the patriarchal model, men and women are believed to have natural or God-given "spheres of competence." Men are believed to be stronger, more capable in politics and economics, more logical, and more independent, and so should control all social institutions. Their primary role is to support their families through paid employment. Women are believed to excel in caring for and loving others, in homemaking tasks, and in helping the dependent. They are presumed to be more emotional, more intuitive and less logical, less able to deal with stress, more dependent, and more given to unruly or flighty reactions. In the home, women's proper role is wife, bearer and rearer of children, and homemaker for a nuclear family. Outside the home, they should be caregivers—social workers, nurses, housekeepers, secretaries, and teachers, especially elementary school teachers.

Patriarchy controls the dependency of women and the work roles of men. For women, questions of whether, where, and when they will be employed, the kind of work they are hired for, and their income depend on men who control the job market. They work in lower-paying, stereotyped jobs, or with lower incomes than men for equal or comparable work. Married women, even if they work, depend primarily on their husbands for economic support and share their economic status. Women are ultimately responsible for their children, and depend on man-controlled systems at all levels for support: husbands, the courts to ensure support if they are without husbands, social insurance, the employment market, or public assistance.

Men also are dependent on patriarchal structures but have more freedom because they are more "legitimate." Nevertheless, most men are workers, and they are constrained to the single role of family support. To lose their jobs is devastating, for their self-concepts are usually based on their work roles. Patriarchy can be brutal for men as well as for women.

Marriage and the Nuclear Family

Marriage is a social, sexual, and economic relationship in which a man and a woman are legally joined to found and maintain a family. In America, we believe strongly in the nuclear family—husband, wife, and a few children—within the marriage system. Even with the explosive divorce rate—about half of all marriages end in divorce—the goals and customs of courtship, marriage, and family persist, and "happily ever after" is still the ideal.

Patriarchy underlies our expectations for marriage and family. Both men and women should be married, but we stigmatize singleness for women, particularly older women, whereas single men have a certain glamour. Young women, expecting to be married, are seldom educated or trained for employment; young men, knowing they will support families, aim their educational goals at employment. Women who work after marriage are often considered to be "supplementing" their husbands' incomes, even though today both marriage partners usually work to support their families. Monogamy is both law and custom, and although serial monogamy is usual today (as people marry, divorce, and remarry), fidelity within marriage is demanded for women but often overlooked for men. Sexuality outside marriage is frowned upon, considered promiscuity for women but "sowing wild oats" for men. If pregnancy results, generally the woman is blamed, and before marriage, within marriage, or after marriage, custom demands that women take life responsibility for children. Married couples are expected to have children, and those who do not are criticized. "A man's home is his castle," and men are the final authority in their homes. They are the major liaisons to the outside world (in fulfilling work roles, building credit ratings, and making major purchases, for example).

If marriages fail, although the emotional consequences may be terrible for both men and women, the financial consequences are usually more severe for women. Even in the best cases, where men pay support conscientiously, there are now two families and two dwellings on a single income. Working women rarely can support their children alone because they are generally hired only in sex-stereotyped, low-paying jobs. Single women are more likely than any other group to sink into poverty, and woman-headed households—single mothers with children—are the fastest-growing type of family.

There are equally strong negative values based on marriage. Anti-singleness is one, particularly for women. Divorced and never-married women, with a few exceptions, are also stigmatized, and even widows undergo some social ostracism. Heterosexuality is required, and the fear and hatred of homosexual people (homophobia or heterosexism) is one of our strongest prejudices. Also, new family patterns, such as communes or extended families, homosexual couples, or nonmarried heterosexual couples living together without marriage, are generally stigmatized by society.

The "American Ideal"

Values about personal appearance, although they may at first seem trivial, interact with other attitudes in society and underlie our self-concepts. In a society that values the white Anglo-Saxon Protestant ideal, to be or look different is no small thing. We are socialized early in life to admire the white middle-class look: clothes we should wear and television-clean homes. Our early readers are of the "Dick and Jane" variety, and children's books and games favor pretty white children. Our history books tell us of intrepid Protestant white men who built a new world and their own fortunes; they tell us also of Native American *savages* and black *slaves*. "Looksist" advertisements in books and on television show how we "ought to" look, and there are hundreds of books and health centers that promise to help us achieve that look.

This set of values includes individualism, racism (in that white people are preferred), and male work ethic and female dependency stereotypes. Generally speaking, men are supposed to be white, tall, dark (though sometimes blond), and handsome. They are heroes—strong, young, virile, and independent. They are assertive and intelligent, able to overcome all odds in the pursuit of excellence. The ideal woman is young, slender but buxom, blonde, and blue-eyed, with delicate, beautiful features. She is dependent on men and is loving, caring, and devoted to attaining a storybook home and family. Both men and women radiate health, youth, and vitality.

An often not-so-subtle discrimination against those who look different works against people who are not "handsome" or "pretty," against short men and tall women, obese people, older people, those who are not fair-skinned, and differently abled people who, defined by society as "handicapped" or "disabled," do not reach our standards of physical perfection. We also see it in schools, where poor children may not be "clean enough," or their clothes may be too shabby or unironed. It is particularly tied to racism: For example, African American children prefer to play with white dolls, and may only "discover" they themselves are not white when they come up against prejudice in schools.

Besides not liking others who are different, we dislike ourselves if we are different. We are not thin enough, not tall enough, not short enough, too fat, too old, too dark, too clumsy, or too ugly. Moreover, people prefer proximity to the American Ideal among those they work with, their love partners, their friends, and their significant others, for it reflects well on people if they can attract beautiful others to their lives. Although this kind of value should have no bearing on our attitudes to self or others, in fact it does, and we need to understand that some negative reactions come not from what people are but how they look.

Issues of Discrimination

Our complex value systems legitimate social welfare as a helping process, but also set up expectations that can be negative and controlling. These negative and controlling expectations dominate both economic life and social welfare services, creating classism/poverty and institutional discrimination in the United States.

Classism and Poverty

Stratification and Wealth.   Despite our belief in egalitarianism, the United States is basically a stratified society. *Social* stratification considers issues of position in society, education, employment, income, and even social aspirations as indicators of social position. *Class* stratification is the division of society into strata based on economic resources and assumes that other social indicators depend on income. *Classism* is prejudice against the presumed immorality of those in lower economic classes, based on beliefs that they are lazy, unmotivated, immoral, promiscuous, stupid, or incompetent.

All societies have some system of stratification, and some argue that society needs to give rewards such as money, prestige, and status to ensure that necessary leadership positions are filled. "Higher" people are motivated toward leadership and power,[14] whereas the unmotivated take on the less pleasant tasks at lower positions. This "theory of social positions"[15] blames the poor personally for their lack of success, for their

> low motivation, alienation, pathology, low incentive, authoritarianism, inability to defer gratification, dependence, inferiority feelings, illegitimacy, fatalism, weak ego, matriarchal family structure, social organization, deep-seated distortion, marital instability, inability to interact with community institutions, superficial interpersonal relationships, suspicion of people outside the family structure, poorly developed voluntary associations, low levels of participation.[16]

Others believe that society constructs barriers to achievement for some people based on class, race, religion, and sex, and that social stratification is repressive and limiting.[17] These concepts posit that government and the economic elite maintain the status quo through legislative and administrative agreements on production such as unemployment levels, minimum wages, public assistance levels, training and education grants and opportunities, restricted housing, and school systems. This gives employers a constant pool of laborers seeking work, and they can pay them minimum wages, hire and fire them more or less at will, and deny them fringe benefits available for long-term employment.

The proportions of wealth and income for classes in the United States have remained fairly stable for the past sixty years. According to Census 2000 figures, the top 5 percent of the population now has 49.7 percent of the nation's aggregate income, and the top 10 percent has nearly 73 percent.[18] The lower three quintiles makes 27 percent of the aggregate income, whereas the lowest quintile makes only 3.6 percent.[19]

Polarization of income between the very rich and the very poor increased during the Reagan administration and onward. In 1990, the top 20 percent of families had 44 percent of all income, increasing to 55 percent by 1995; the top 40 percent (those above middle income) had nearly 70 percent of all income, leaving only 30 percent to be shared among the rest of us. Middle-class Americans, who constituted 71 percent of the population in 1969, made up less than 60 percent by 1995. The average income of families in the top 20 percent climbed 32.5 percent, and the richest 1 percent (2.5 million people) had an 87.1 percent increase in income.[20] Because wealth—real estate, corporate stock, bonds, cash deposits, notes and mortgages, trusts—is permanent property, it is even more indicative of class stratification than income. Wealth changed little until 1972: From 1910 until 1972, the richest 1 percent held about 21 percent of all wealth, although it rose to 36.3 percent in 1929 and was 29.2 percent in 1965.[21] A 1992 Federal Reserve study shows that the wealthiest 1 percent, who control the key economic corporations, now hold 40 percent of the nation's wealth; half of this elite group own over a third (45 percent if personal residences are excluded).[22] The top 10 percent hold

69 percent, leaving only 31 percent for the bottom 90 percent.[23] In comparison, the wealthiest 1 percent of Britons hold 18 percent of that nation's wealth.

Most of America's capital is owned not by individuals but by corporations, banks, insurance companies, and pension trusts.[24] Dye and Zeigler say,

> Formal control over the economic life of the nation is concentrated in the hands of a very few men: the presidents, vice presidents, and boards of directors of the nation's corporate institutions.[25]

Poverty and Welfare.   Class stratification is the basis for poverty, not the other way around. Life for earliest humankind was surely hard and meager, and subsistence depended on cooperation. Poverty, a social definition of relative differences in resources, was based on availability of food, prowess in gathering it, and ideals of mutual aid. Today, poverty is the result of uneven distribution based on inegalitarian economics rather than scarcity of resources.

Poverty and the poor have been continually redefined over time, but before medieval times social and economic conditions were thought to cause poverty and there was no personal blame in being poor. With the end of feudalism, poverty became first immoral and then criminal, and poor people were categorized into those whom society should or should not help (worthy versus unworthy poor). In the United States, women with children are the most stigmatized of public dependents, whether they are single, divorced, separated, or deserted. Their status—detachment from male authority—violates values of patriarchy, marriage and family, individualism, social Darwinism, and, because of their dependency, the Protestant work ethic.

Social welfare is based partly on the need to control the poor and keep workers available for low-wage work. Fortified by our value systems, in our society poverty is

- An *economic* issue, both to keep people working and to provide them with subsistence
- A *political* issue based on the power to command production of resources
- A *class* issue entailing the division of society in economic strata
- A *religious* issue, for religion legitimates differential accumulation of wealth and defines charity as a religious duty
- A *women's* issue because of women's vulnerability to poverty, their life responsibility for children, and their caretaking of the needy
- An issue of *social control*, for the poor are considered a social liability rather than a social obligation.

"Poverty levels" were first formulated in 1964, based on assumptions about the cost of a short-term emergency diet, the dietary needs of the aging poor, and the estimate that people generally spent about one-third of their income on food. To calculate the poverty level, the cost of a "market basket" of food for an emergency diet is multiplied first by number of people in household and then by three (experts estimate that only about one-fourth of families living on such a budget get adequate nourishment). A reality test in analyzing poverty-level income is provision of food. In 2000, the poverty line was $20,236 for a family of four.[26] The third-of-the-budget assumption, then, provides a daily food allowance per person of $4.57, or $1.52 for each person's meal. However, the average income for a family in poverty is about half the poverty line of $17,603, halving the food allowance to about 75 cents per person per meal.

The third-of-the-budget assumption is in error, however, because more than one-third of the nation's poor households spend more than 70 percent of their total income on shelter alone.[27] For these families, dividing the amount left for food by at least half, assuming no other expenses, leaves about 60 cents per meal for each person's food. Provision of public assistance is not based on the poverty level.

A modern redefinition of poverty is the "underclass": people, usually African Americans, in inner-city areas beset by poverty and crime.[28] Regardless of the intent of sociologist William J. Wilson when he created this appellation, it is now a derogatory catch-all, grouping and typing people in inner cities not on their characteristics or needs but on demographic factors of institutional poverty, deteriorating houses and neighborhoods, homelessness, joblessness, and crime. In fact, the definition itself creates a ghettoizing, or blocking off, and the aim of police power in such neighborhoods seems more often to be containment and subjection rather than service or protection.

The poor are not a homogeneous group; they differ in as many ways as any segment of our population. However, their differences are stigmatized by society and often compounded: They are poor *and* unemployed *and* public dependents *and* women, or discriminated against because of race or ethnicity, or age, or being differently abled, and so forth. Multiple differences make for increasing need for social control, and women have been more continuously vulnerable because of the overlapping of sex and class discrimination.

Institutional racism, sexism, and ageism are reflected in poverty statistics. In 2000, 9.4 percent of white families were poor, but African Americans had a

TABLE 1.1 *People Below the Poverty Level, 2000*

Characteristic	Number (thousands)	Percent of Characteristic Population
All	31,139	11.3%
White	21,291	9.4
African American	7,901	22.1
Hispanic	7,155	21.2
Age 65+	3,360	10.2
Children under 18	11,633	16.2

Source: Bureau of the Census, Current Population Survey, *Poverty in the United States: 2000,* Bureau of the Census (Washington, D.C., 2001), www.census.gov, Table A-4, p. 28.

22.1 percent poverty rate (see Table 1.1). In 1996, in an American population of almost 270 million, more than 36 million people lived below the federal four-person poverty level of $16,036.[29] This is approximately equal to the total combined population of the nation's four largest cities, is larger than the population of Canada (by about 10 million), and is twice the combined populations of the seven nations of Central America. There are four times more poor people than there are college students, six times more poor people than Jewish people, twenty times more poor people than there are writers, artists, entertainers, and athletes combined. There are more poor people in the United States than there are seconds in a year.[30]

According to the Children's Defense Fund, one in six children in the United States is poor, and 77 percent of poor children live with a family member who worked at least part of the year. Even when at least one person worked full time, one in three children is poor, the highest rate in the 26 years for which data exist. Almost one in three black children is poor (13 percent of white children are poor, and more than one in four Hispanic children are poor. Thirty-nine percent of families headed by single women are poor, whereas 8.2 percent of children in intact families are poor.[31]

We know from the past that every year of child poverty at current levels will cost the economy between $36 and $177 billion in lower future productivity and employment, to say nothing of remedial costs such as hospitalization and long-term care for the disabled. Poor children are two or more times more likely than nonpoor children to suffer a variety of health problems, including stunted growth, severe physical or mental disabilities, anemia, and fatal accidental injuries. They are three times more likely to die than nonpoor children from birth defects or because of low-weight births, four times as likely to die in fires, and five to six times as likely to die of infectious diseases and parasites. In addition, they are nearly three times more likely to be diagnosed with learning disabilities and are diagnosed with extreme behavior problems in school more than six times as often as nonpoor children. The U.S. Department of Education reports that the risk of a student falling behind in school increases by 2 percentage points for every year he or she spends growing up in poverty. Poverty's effects are separate from—and stronger than—those of race, region, having a teen parent, or living in a one-parent home.[32]

In the 1990s, the United States had the highest child poverty rate of most industrialized nations, falling behind Australia, Canada, Great Britain, Norway, Sweden, and Switzerland. Greenstein says,

> This nation cannot continue to compete and prosper in the global arena when more than a fifth of our children live in poverty and a third grow up in ignorance. Allowing this to continue will not only impoverish these children, it will impoverish our nation—culturally, politically, economically.[33]

Quoting statistics enables us to make comparisons among figures. Understanding the despair of people who cannot feed their children, or scavenge in garbage cans for their food, or live over heat grates in the streets is more difficult. Most of us believe that poverty does not exist in the United States, or that if it does, it is the fault of the poor. These are easy rationalizations, ways that permit us to maintain our own sense of well-being and keep our values about hard work and individualism intact. However, poverty does not "just happen." It comes from our social values and the systems they maintain, and it is the result of a class-stratified society. The gap is maintained through economic practices enforced by legislation that is deliberately intended to preserve the status quo.

With legislation and administrative decisions developed by people who confuse social values with facts, our system protects the wealthy and jeopardizes the rest of us. Altruism exists in such forms as grants and foundations, but only within the context of systems that perpetuate poverty and class stratification. As a society, we need major changes in social structures to end the disgrace of poverty, changes that require values oriented to the well-being of all rather than to the money privileges of the very few.

Institutional Discrimination

Institutional discrimination permeates American systems so deeply that we may not recognize it. Based on hostile attitudes reified in rules, regulations, and procedures, its forms—racism, sexism, ageism, homophobia or heterosexism, and "otherism"—deny equal rights and opportunities to groups even when no individual prejudice may be involved. Moreover, types of institutional discrimination interact with each other and with classism, enforcing the status quo of our society: People discriminated against are more likely to be poor, and if more than one discrimination is present, the likelihood of poverty is even greater. For example, an aged African American woman is in triple jeopardy of being poor because of her age, race, and gender.

Institutional Racism. Racism is prejudice with power against people of color: African Americans, Hispanics, Asian Americans, and Native Americans. Our American values make us assume that race determines human traits and capacities and that white people are inherently superior to people of color. This is directly related to our hatred of "outsiders," or people who are different, and to the Protestant work ethic. The Protestant religion of our forebears legitimated their pursuit of wealth, and the idea that people of color were not as "human" as Caucasians allowed their exploitation. Over 75 percent of Americans are white. The rest of us are about 12.8 percent African American, 12 percent Hispanic. The Asian-Pacific Islander population is 3.7 percent, and there are about 2.4 million Native Americans.[34]

Native Americans. Estimates of Native American population at the time of conquest range to nearly 10 million in North America and tens of millions in Central and South America. As a result of decimation by European weapons and disease, the number of North American natives fell to approximately 200,000–300,000 by 1850.[35] Today, Native Americans are the most impoverished people in America. Their unemployment is more than double that of whites, and employment is heavily concentrated in lower-paying jobs: farm labor for men and service work for women. One-third live in poverty, and housing and health care conditions are still worse for rural Native Americans than for any other group. Death rates are high, and people die young because of poor nutrition and lack of health care. Infant mortality is comparable to rates in poor developing nations.

Asian Americans. Both Japanese and Chinese immigrants lived in the severest poverty when immigration began in the middle 1800s. However, some managed to climb the economic ladder in America despite racism. Most are now in white-collar jobs, although in larger cities women are likely to hold low-status, low-income service jobs. Asian American women have less income than do white women, but median income for Japanese American families is slightly higher than that for whites. Chinese Americans have not been quite so fortunate, nor have the most recent immigrants from Thailand or Korea, who are still being harassed by white workers afraid of losing their jobs.

Hispanic Americans. Approximately 58 percent of Hispanic Americans are of Mexican origin, and 10 percent are of Puerto Rican heritage. Although the poverty rate of Mexican Americans is high, Puerto Rican Americans are the poorest ethnic group in the United States except for Native Americans. Hispanic unemployment rates remain nearly double the rates for non-Hispanics, and most Hispanic workers are concentrated at lower job levels.

African Americans. Even after 400 years in North America, African Americans have been unable to move into mainstream society because of racial discrimination. Their early slave status is not the determining factor; rather, unrelenting racism has kept them from education, jobs with good incomes, decent housing, and the many benefits available to most citizens. The unemployment rate for African Americans is about twice that of white people, and the rate among African American youth, in 1994, was 65 percent in urban areas.[36] With underemployment—no jobs, part-time jobs, and jobs at poverty wages—their median income has remained at 55 to 60 percent of white income since the 1950s. Intact African American families are twice as likely as white Americans to be poor, and woman-headed African American families are nine times as likely to be poor as families headed by white men.[37]

Racism and Poverty. Institutional racism has a circular relationship with poverty. For example, many African Americans are poor and, therefore, must live in rental units owned by white people not living in the area. Their homes have a low property tax base, leading to poorly funded and equipped schools. Given a choice, better or more experienced teachers will not work there. The lack of high-quality education and a high dropout rate limit future employment and income, which means they are trapped in high-poverty areas with poor schools. Even those who succeed may not be able to move because realtors and homeowners will not sell to them. In 1994, banks, savings institutions, and credit unions refused loans to 33 percent of African Americans who applied, 31.6 percent of Native Americans, 24.6 percent of Hispanics, 16.4 percent of whites, and 12 percent of Asian Americans.[38]

Effects of educational discrimination that keep African Americans in poverty are clearly evident. Every day 3,494 African American students are suspended from school, and African American children are 1.5 times more likely to drop out of school than are white children. On average, African American high school *graduates* are half again more likely to be unemployed than are white high school *dropouts*, whereas African American college graduates are more likely to be unemployed than white people with only high school educations. African American males in public schools are two times more likely than white males to be placed in special education as retarded (1 of every 34), 1.5 times as likely to be placed in programs for serious emotional disturbances (1 in 62), and 2.7 times as likely to be corporally punished.[39]

Institutional Sexism.   Sexism, probably our oldest prejudice, is gender privilege for men. Based on patriarchal values, it assumes the political, economic, intellectual, and spiritual inferiority of women based solely on sex and without regard to individual capabilities, and has resulted in oppression and exploitation throughout history. It permeates all institutions of society: family, economy, polity, religion, and social welfare. At home, men have control of women, sometimes even to physical abuse or death. In the economic arena, women more than men are subject to low wages, part-time employment, and limited benefits. In the courts, male gender privilege often means low and often uncollectible grants for child support. Low public assistance grants when there is no other help completes women's povertization. Laws and religions continually challenge women's right to control reproduction. In juvenile justice systems, young women are incarcerated for "status offenses," or noncriminal morality charges. Mental health programs often base treatment on needs of families rather than women clients. The number of women in public office remains small compared with men in those offices. Most religions continue to restrict high positions to men and to teach the "proper" roles for women: submissive and secondary to men.

Customs of education and training keep women ghettoized in low-paying, sex-stereotyped jobs. They hold 80 percent of clerical jobs, 78 percent of service jobs, and 43 percent of professional jobs (mostly teachers and nurses). Even professional jobs, if they are "women's work," pay less than do men's lower skilled work, and often women are paid less for the same professional job. Married women make up 55 percent of working women, and a family headed by a woman is four-and-a-half times more likely to be poor than an intact or man-headed family.

The myths of Cinderella and "the women's sphere" are so deeply ingrained in our society that women themselves help maintain them by not training for better jobs, accepting their secondary roles as natural, and relieving men of responsibility for their impoverishment. This is not to blame women for believing what society has taught them but to indicate the power of social values to inculcate oppressive attitudes even in the oppressed. Women will continue to be oppressed and exploited until our society clarifies sexist values and overcomes its sexist myths.

Institutional Ageism.   Ageism is a preference for youth over older people and manifests itself not only in disrespect and the shunting aside of older people, but in job discrimination against people over the age of about forty. Youth fits the American Ideal of active, assertive, future-oriented, and beautiful, and we see older people as ugly, doddering, unproductive, senile, or living in the past. Perhaps we fear our own aging, for we do not respect the wisdom and experience of our elders. Ageism is institutional in that, especially in economic issues but also in the family, older people are prevented from sharing in society. Many are poor despite Social Security, and we do little to ensure that they will be secure in their old age. Also, our nuclear family system and our dedication to individualism moves our elders out of the center of family life and into loneliness. By 2000, people over age sixty-five represented 12 percent of Americans, of whom 10.2 percent lived below the poverty level.[40]

Age is a stereotype. Some people chronologically in their sixties may be as active, productive, and capable as much younger people. On the other hand, people as young as thirty often have stopped learning and become resigned and rigid in thought and deed. *Old* is an artificial designation that, in America, coincides with the retirement age of about sixty-five. However, retiring people from work is relatively recent, beginning in about the last half of the nineteenth century, resulting from longer life spans and the demands that younger people be employed. When the Social Security Acts of 1935 were passed, the United States was in the middle of its greatest depression. Giving pensions to older men not only gave them minimal support but took them out of the job market so that younger workers with growing families could be employed in what jobs there were. Women's retirement was not really an issue: They were discouraged from taking jobs away from men, but a great number were employed outside the home anyway. With labor demands and Social Security, they were retired from the labor market along with men but continued their usual jobs working in the home. In 1994, more than 80 percent of people over age sixty-five were retired, even though they were intellectually and physically capable of working. Although some people may *want* to retire, *enforced* retirement indicates that society no longer has use for older people.

Aging is another complication for women *vis à vis* poverty. If they lose their husbands during their middle years, they are unlikely to find sufficient employment for family support because they lack current job training and experience. Social insurance payments end when their children reach age eighteen, and if they have no dependent children they cannot receive TANF. If they have dependent children, they may receive TANF, but the grants are inadequate. Women's average earnings decrease compared to men's as they grow older. Because of lower overall wages during their employment years, they will receive lower social insurance and fewer pension benefits.

Our societal emphasis on youth borders on geriatricide, in practice if not in intent. If Medicare funds are exhausted by lengthy illnesses, Medicaid, the public assistance program, is an option only if patients divest themselves of most of their assets to become eligible. Life expectancy today is about seventy-one years (for white women 77.7 years), and over three-fourths of the aged have at least one chronic health problem. Moreover, the elderly face personal and emotional stress—loneliness, loss of loved ones, lack of purpose in life, retirement, and change of living arrangements—and these compound and often cause physical problems.

Institutional ageism is not confined to the elderly. Prejudice against aging begins around the age of forty. Many businesses are unwilling to hire workers over this age, even though age discrimination is prohibited by law. Employers fear that older people will take too long to train and that their productivity will therefore be limited. Also, experienced workers must be paid more than new workers. Finally, medical insurance and fringe benefit costs paid by the company rise with the number of older workers. For these reasons, hiring at a later age and keeping people on after the age of fifty or so is discouraged, even though older workers

> have lower turnover rates, produce at a steadier rate, make fewer mistakes, have a more positive attitude toward their work, and exceed younger employees in health and low-on-the-job-injury rates.[41]

This was one of the most painful problems of the recession of 1981 to 1983, during which millions of blue-collar workers, young and old, lost their jobs. Unemployment for many became permanent, and, after unemployment benefits were exhausted, they found they could not get jobs because of company policies not to hire people over age fifty. Initially, this meant a lower standard of life, when they had been used to better. In the long run, lower or no income in years when highest levels of earnings were expected meant lower Social Security and pension benefits at retirement. Some found work in marginal industries, but not before their lifetime savings were lost. Those unable to find work were reduced, after having lived all their lives in "the American Way," to living on public assistance and food stamps.

Homophobia or Heterosexism.   This prejudice against or hatred of homosexuals—gay men and women—is a product of Puritan morality and patriarchal values. Because their sexual orientation is toward people of the same sex, homosexuals fall outside the pale of "normal" value systems: patriarchy, morality, and marriage and nuclear family. Aside from sexual preference, the actions of homosexual people are no different from those of other members of the population. Homosexuality has existed throughout human history and was often considered preferable to heterosexuality. Benford argues that it is an evolutionary strategy that helped preserve at least early societies. He notes that in kinship societies

> a gay man or woman [worked] for the betterment of his or her relations, laboring in the tribe as specialized labor, free of the burden of childrearing. . . . [Because] the gay brother or sister labors on, the tribe as a whole has a better chance of surviving. . . . It is preferred as a minority strategy by evolution of the hunter–gatherer hominids we once were . . . and still are.[42]

Some of our finest scholars, authors, and other highly productive people have been homosexual. However, in American society they have been forced out of jobs and personally persecuted. The profession of teaching is particularly forbidden because of the fear that children might be "seduced into homosexuality." Some denominations of religions have only recently allowed homosexuals among their clergy; most do not acknowledge homosexual love relationships. Foster care or adoption is very difficult for even the most stable homosexual couple, and homosexuals divorcing heterosexuals have great difficulty in maintaining custody of their children. Defamation, blackmail against those who keep their sexual preference secret, and even physical injury are part of the expectations of homosexual people in our society. Discrimination forbids them the protection of many laws that most of us take for granted.

Otherism.   This catch-all category refers to people who, because of physical or social differences, do not fit the American Ideal. They may be differently abled, unsighted, obese, unattractive, or "different" in innumerable other ways. Discrimination against them varies: Those whom society calls physically, emotionally, or mentally "disabled" are subject to more prejudice than are the obese or the unattractive. People with physical disabilities are probably the most discriminated against among the "different" in our society. One estimate numbers this group at more than 40 million people. Although they are guaranteed civil rights, especially with the enactment of the Americans with Disabilities Act in 1990, these rights are often denied in ways as simple as access to buildings. At the end of 1994, 20.6 percent of the population (about 54 million people) had some level of disability, and 9.9 percent were severely disabled.[43]

In addition to the physically disabled, there are 12.5 million temporarily injured, 2.4 million deaf, 11 million hearing-impaired, 1.3 million blind, and 8.2 million visually impaired people in the United States.[44] There are also nearly 1 million developmentally disabled people, and estimates of the seriously mentally ill range to about 2 million. Of the latter, about 200,000 are in hospitals and treatment centers, 26,000 are in jails and prisons, 300,000 are in nursing homes, another 300,000 are in foster care or boarding homes, 200,000 live alone, 800,000 live with their families, and more than 150,000 live in public shelters or on the streets.[45] Although in 1843 Dorothea Dix testified about the horrendous treatment accorded people who were "different," treatment today is, in some cases, as brutal: Foster care operators abuse and sometimes kill their charges, homeless people scavenge in garbage cans to eat, defenseless people are murdered on the streets, and others freeze to death when their newspapers or cardboard homes cannot keep them warm enough.

The pervasive distaste toward "different" people in our culture adds an edge to those discriminated against in other ways. For example, nonwhite people can never reach the standards set for American appearance: They are not white. Most women can never meet the American ideal of beauty, nor men of handsomeness. Obese people are constantly railed at, not only for health's sake but because fat is "ugly." These stereotypes of what people "should" look like may seem trivial in the face of more serious disadvantages. However, they are another part of a value system that honors certain people and demonstrates a social dislike of others.

Although some individuals overcome the barriers of institutional discrimination, many cannot. This has very little to do with their capabilities, will to succeed, or hard work but is institutional in nature—part of the value systems with which Americans are indoctrinated. Whatever the discriminatory situation, we must look critically at why certain groups in our society cannot succeed, work to change our own discriminatory values, and develop programs to overcome centuries of institutional discrimination.

Conclusion: Values and Power

When people seek the help of social workers, they admit they have lost control of part of their lives. However, they are *not* asking us to take over; rather, they need us to help them regain their own control. We must be careful not to impose our own values on them or to exercise our power over them. There are times, of course, when we must assert power—when people are a danger to themselves or others—but this is the exception rather than the rule. In most cases, the use of power is an abuse of people. Our most precious values may encourage this abuse.

In general, social workers come from middle-class backgrounds, where hard work is the way to success. We believe in and reflect values of work, education, and perceptions of family life and define deviance by those lights. These values are not "wrong" or "bad" for us, and we can use them in our own lives as we please. However, these values are not realities common to all societies and cultures but derive from our own history and cultural belief systems. Most of our clients share these values, but because all people are unique, so are their value interpretations; some differences are sure to occur because reality is different for each of us. Also, the life situations of our clients require that they make different choices from those we might. We can never be in "the same situation" and must learn to respect their rights to make the decisions best for them.

The provision of social services can be undermined by values in many ways. Although our primary mandate is to enable others, we may find ourselves placing unreasonable demands on their lives or seeking to control them. We become society's way of enforcing conformity to norms that may not be relevant to the problem at hand. Norman Goroff has called social workers "soft cops"[46] because our work often hides values that society, the agency, or we ourselves want to impose on clients. However, they quickly discover our hidden agendas and value biases, a discovery that may hurt them deeply or cause them justifiable anger.

We began this chapter speaking about love, but we have discussed values that seem anything but loving. Probably some of your deepest beliefs have been touched in ways you never expected. We may feel that because our work is inspired by love, it can have only good effects, but wisdom, not emotion, is the essence of the helping relationship. To help people to "fit in," if that is what they want, may be an appropriate task of social work. However, to aid them in understanding the institutions of society and to help them to use that knowledge in gaining their goals is probably the real gift of love to others.

Study Questions

1. Name one universal morality issue that is a fact rather than a value.

2. How is social work involved in social control?

3. What American values conflict with one another? How?

4. In what ways are Judaeo-Christian values nonsectarian and social rather than religious?

5. What is the present-day impact of institutional discrimination on social welfare?

Notes

1. Peter A. Corning has posited a theory of human evolution that he calls the synergistic hypothesis, in which biology and politics have interacted to create modern humankind and its social structures. Carrying this idea further, we posit that all human social structures, including that of social welfare, have evolved from the intimate and dynamic relationships among the polity, economics, and religion. The inclusion of religion is not a usual one, but we believe that humankind's relationship to spirituality and deity over time is primary in the consideration of both social treatment and social control aspects of social welfare. For further information on Corning's synergistic hypothesis, see Peter Corning, *Synergistic Hypothesis: A Theory of Progressive Evolution* (New York: McGraw-Hill, 1983).

2. *Webster's New Collegiate Dictionary* 8th ed. (Springfield, MA: Merriam-Webster, 1980), p. 1174.

3. Naomi Brill, *Teamwork: Working Together in the Human Services* (New York: J.B. Lippincott, 1976), pp. 12–15.

4. Phyllis J. Day, "Social Welfare: Context for Social Control," *Journal of Sociology and Social Welfare*, Vol. VII (March 1981), p. 42.

5. *Webster's Dictionary*, p. 406.

6. Ibid., p. 1282.

7. Beulah Compton, *Introduction to Social Welfare and Social Work: Structure, Function, and Process* (Homewood, IL: The Dorsey Press, 1980), p. 78.

8. Mary Ski Hunter and Dennis Saleeby, "Spirit and Substance: Beginnings in the Education of Radical Social Workers," *Journal of Education for Social Work*, Vol. 13, no. 2 (Spring 1977), pp. 60–67.

9. Marc L. Miringoff and Sandra Opdycke, *American Social Welfare: Reassessment and Reform* (Englewood Cliffs, NJ: Prentice Hall, 1986), p. 2.

10. *Webster's Dictionary*, p. 1094.

11. Edna Bonacich, "Racism in Advanced Capitalist Society: Comments on William J. Wilson's *The Truly Disadvantaged," Journal of Sociology and Social Welfare*, Vol. XVI, no. 4 (Dec. 1989), p. 43.

12. David Wagner, *The New Temperance: The American Obsession with Sin and Vice* (Boulder, CO: Westview Press, 1997), pp. 4–5.

13. Ibid., p. 8.

14. Kingsley Davis and Wilbert E. Moore, "Some Principles of Stratification," *American Sociological Review,* Vol. 10 (1945), p. 246. Quoted in Miringoff and Opdycke, *American Social Welfare,* p. 8.

15. Miringoff and Opdycke, *American Social Welfare*, pp. 9–11.

16. Ibid.

17. Melvin Tumin, "Some Principles of Stratification: A Critical Analysis," *American Sociological Review*, Vol. 10 (1953), p. 380. Quoted in Miringoff and Opdycke, *American Social Welfare,* p. 11.

18. Bureau of the Census, Current Population Survey, *Measures of Household Income Inequality*, Bureau of the Census (Washington, D.C., 2001), www.census.gov/hhes/www/img/incpov00/fig. 12.

19. Ibid.

20. Phyllis J. Day, "The New Poor in America: Isolationism in an International Political Economy," *Social Work: Journal of the National Association of Social Workers*, Vol. 34, no. 3 (1989), pp. 227–233.

21. Richard Pearsall, "Gap Growing Between the Rich and the Poor," New Jersey *Courier–Post* (June 19, 1995), p. B1.

22. Ibid.

23. Bonacich, "Racism in Advanced Capitalist Society," p. 44.

24. Bernard Sanders, "Clinton Must Go to the People," *The Nation* (June 21, 1994), p. 865.

25. Thomas R. Dye and L. Harmon Zeigler, *The Irony of Democracy* (Belmont, CA: Wadsworth Publishing, 1970), pp. 98–100.

26. Bureau of the Census, Current Population Survey, *Poverty 2000: Poverty Thresholds in 2000 by Size of Family and Number of Related Children Under 18 Years*, Bureau of the Census (Washington, D.C., 2001), www.census.gov.macro/032001/pov/new21_000.htm.

27. Randolph E. Schmid, "Poverty in America Tops 39 Million," New Jersey *Courier–Post* (Oct. 7, 1994), pp. 13–14.

28. William J. Wilson, *The Truly Disadvantaged* (Chicago: University of Chicago Press, 1987). Wilson's thesis was, in brief, that as African Americans became middle class they left the urban ghettos, leaving those who remained as a "culture" based on class rather than race. Lack of motivation, not discrimination, was the barrier to success. Although this was not Wilson's intent, his description of underclass is now taken to describe poor urban African Americans as deviant. This has created a new social Darwinism. In the most common rendition, *underclass* refers to chronic, concentrated, inner-city minority impoverishment accompanied by extreme social isolation and exceptionally high rates of social pathology of all sorts, according to Devine and Wright in *The Greatest of Evils.*

29. L. Lamison-White, *Poverty in the United States: 1996* (Washington, D.C.: U.S. Department of Commerce, 1997), p. A4.

30. Joel A. Devine and James D. Wright, *The Greatest of Evils: Urban Poverty and the American Underclass* (New York: Aldine de Gruyter, 1993), p. 30.

31. Children's Defense Fund, "Every Child Deserves a Fair Start" (Washington, D.C.: CDF, November 3, 2001), Wysiwyg:///52/http://www.childrensdefense.org/fairstart-faqs.ht. p. 1.

32. Children's Defense Fund, *Welfare Reform Fund Briefing Book* (Washington, D.C.: CDF, 1995), p. 34.

33. Testimony from Robert Greenstein, Director, Center on Budget and Policy Priorities, before the House Ways and Means Committee, March 13, 1991.

34. Bureau of the Census, *Profiles of General Demographic Characteristics 2000*, prepared in conjunction with the U.S. Department of Commerce, Economics and Statistics Administration, Bureau of the Census (Washington, D.C., 2000), Table DP-1, p. 1.

35. Joe R. Feagin, *Racial and Ethnic Relations*, 2nd ed. (Englewood Cliffs, NJ: Prentice Hall, 1984), p. 177.

36. Richard J. Barrett, "Lords of the Global Economy," *The Nation* (Dec. 19, 1994).

37. Rosemary Sarri, Elisabeth Cramer, and Virginia du Rivage, *Highlights: Socio-Economic Status of Women in Michigan and the United States* (Ann Arbor: The University of Michigan Institute for Social Research and the School of Social Work, 1983), p. 6.

38. James H. Rubin, "Study: Race Still Factor in Mortgage Denials," New Jersey *Courier–Post* (July 19, 1995), p. 12D.

39. Children's Defense Fund, *State of America's Children Yearbook 1995* (Washington, D.C.: CDF, 1995), p. 117.

40. Bureau of the Census, Current Population Survey, *Poverty in the United States: 2000*, Bureau of the Census (Washington, D.C., 2001), www.census.gov/hhes/poverty/poverty00/pov00hi.htm. Table A, p. 2.

41. Charles Zastrow, *Introduction to Social Welfare Institutions: Social Problems, Services, and Current Issues* (Homewood, IL: The Dorsey Press, 1982), p. 465.

42. Gregory Benford, "A Scientist's Notebook: Sex, Gender and Fantasy," *Fantasy and Science Fiction* (Sept. 1995), pp. 117–118.

43. J. M. McNeil, *Current Population Reports: Americans with Disabilities, 1994–95.* (Washington, D.C.: U.S. Bureau of the Census, 1997 (P70), pp. 1–19.

44. Ralph Dolgoff and Donald Feldstein, *Understanding Social Welfare* (New York: Longman Press, 1984), pp. 350–351.

45. E. Fuller Torrey and Sidney M. Wolfe, *Care of the Seriously Mentally Ill: A Rating of State Programs* (Washington, D.C.: Public Citizen Health Research Group, 1986), pp. 1, 5–8.

46. Norman Goroff, "Humanism and Social Work: Paradoxes, Problems, and Promises" (mimeograph) (West Hartford, CT: University of Connecticut School of Social Work, 1977).

2

The Institution of Social Welfare

The Meaning of Social Institution

A social institution is a set of interrelated and interlocking concepts, structures, and activities enduring over time that carry out the necessary functions of a society, such as socialization, childrearing, education, and commerce.[1] There are five major institutions of society (see Figure 2.1):

- The economy
- The polity
- The family
- Religion
- Social welfare (which in our definition includes education).

The polity and the economy are the major underlying macrosystems by which our government is separated from other nations and by which people in our nation relate to society. Family, religion, and social welfare, although they also have wider applications, are usually more oriented to the internal systems (microsystems) of the society. Although social welfare has existed in some form since human society began, it became a social institution only when responsibility for particular groups of people became a function of society itself. In early societies the extended family fulfilled all functions: economic and political needs, social control, and social integration. However, as families became communities and nations, and as work became divided and specialized, societal functions diversified into social institutions. Today, in most societies, they overlap one another, and social welfare overlaps them all.

The major functions of religion and the family are socialization and social integration. Socialization teaches us the norms, values, and ways of behaving in our society, and social integration helps us to fit in or be brought back into the fold after deviating in some way. Gilbert and Specht say that social integration

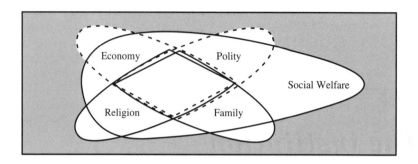

FIGURE 2.1 *Social Institutions*

has to do with the relationships among units in a social system. Members of a particular institution or of the system-as-a-whole must be loyal to one another and the system must achieve some level of solidarity and morale in order to function.[2]

Social integration makes us aware that we have stepped outside the bounds of the normal and points out how we can "change for the better." In addition, conformity to one's family, group, and society are taught more formally than is the case in socialization.

The Economy

The economy is all aspects of a society that relate to the production (making), distribution (meting out), and consumption (using) of goods and services. Production includes all outputs, from farm to manufactured goods, and capital (wealth accumulated in goods and profits and stored in stocks, bonds, sunk costs of manufacturing, savings, investments, and so on). Distribution is the marketing or meting out of products (goods and services). In America, we generally think that the market economy—what people buy and sell—is the major source of distribution; however, tax transfers are another major factor. They are monies taken from taxes and given directly, in cash, goods, and services, to select groups in society outside the labor market. For example, the poor receive money, food stamps, or subsidized housing, and the wealthy get tax breaks and subsidies such as farm price supports and land-bank monies or bailouts for industries or corporations in trouble. Consumption, which keeps production and distribution moving, is the using up of consumer goods and services, whether through the market or through tax transfers.

The economy also includes the organization of the workforce, employment, and planned unemployment to ensure sufficient production and consumption of consumer goods. In the United States, the Council of Economic Advisors suggests an unemployment rate of about 5 percent to ensure work force availability. The actual number of unemployed varies with the economy and with reporting because discouraged workers and the underemployed are generally not counted in unemployment statistics. Discouraged workers are those who have never been able to find work, those whose unemployment benefits have run out, and those who have been unemployed for so long that they have stopped searching for work. Underemployed workers are those who work full-time but earn so little that their families may live in poverty, or skilled workers who cannot find skilled jobs.

Capital, wealth, and the tax system are also part of the economy. Capital is money (or economic resources) accumulated through profit and devoted to the further production of goods or the accumulation of wealth. Profit is return on investment over costs of production, including labor, and surplus profit is that amount plus an excessive return for labor costs kept for private or corporate use. The American economy is monopoly capitalistic; that is, it is characterized by accumulation of capital invested for private or corporate gain. Wealth is the result of profit making and the retiring of resources from the market economy. Although wealth is generally less available for investment than is capital, if need arises it can be sold and transformed into capital.

The tax system is the assessment of and levy on income, production, and wealth by the government. Poor and middle-class people are taxed proportionately more than corporations and the wealthy because of tax write-offs, loopholes, and the ability of the wealthy to influence tax legislation. This results in an increasing class stratification as the wealthy reinvest saved tax dollars in new profit making while the poorer classes have decreasing amounts to invest even in their own well-being. There are several direct taxes, including property, sales, and income tax. Property and sales taxes are regressive, or taxed at a set rate regardless of the economic status of the taxpayer. Poorer classes, then, spend relatively more of their assets on these taxes than do the wealthy. Income tax is progressive; that is, those who earn more generally pay a higher rate on their taxable income. Taxes on corporate wealth depend on both the amount of wealth and its form: Wealth held in trusts or foundations may be virtually untaxable despite its benefits to those who control it. Indirect taxes are taxes placed on manufacturers that are then passed on in higher prices to consumers. Tax monies go to support the vast bureaucracies of the government; to provide for protection against other nations and negotiation with them; for public works such as roads, parks, and bridges; and for public well-being in programs for the public good, such as education, health care, and welfare programs.

The Polity

The polity is the exercise of power in a society. Any system—person, group, agency, organization, or wider system—that has legal or normative power, or in some instances nonlegal but coercive or customary power over other systems, is a part of the polity.[3] Among systems constituting America's polity are national, state, and local governments based on national and state constitutions, laws, legislative and judicial decisions; the political system and political parties, including elections and appointments to office; the criminal and civil justice systems; and administrative rules, regulations, and customs at all levels of government and in all government bureaucracies.

Polities can enforce behaviors or impose or prevent change, whether or not people or systems agree with their actions. On the international level, polities engage in wars or other demonstrations of strength to the point of conquests of other nations or people, taking political prisoners or slaves, and enforcing their own laws and policies on unwilling countries by use of embargoes or occupation. Examples include the near-genocide of Native Americans and the slavery of African-born people and their descendants in our own country, and imperialism and colonialism in developing countries today.

In the United States, the polity and the economy are so closely tied that it is difficult to see them as separate, for laws and regulations are based on the ideals of capitalism and the free market and much of the economy is politically supported. Higher socioeconomic classes often determine what legislation will be passed (through lobbying), who will be elected to office (through financial contributions), and what contracts (such as for defense) will be developed and awarded.

The Family

The family is an economic and social unit in which people live within a society and within which socially legitimated sexual relationships occur. In present-day America, the nuclear family—husband, wife, and children—is the normative ideal. In preindustrial times, the family was more clearly an economic unit, with members who worked at home farming, producing craft items, marketing, giving child care, and educating and training family members in all aspects of life. Today, the meaning of *family* is markedly different from what it was even two decades ago because of new kinds of extended and nuclear families. Examples include the commune (several heterosexual couples, married or unmarried, living with their children as a social and economic unit); unmarried heterosexual or homosexual couples living together as a family unit, sometimes with children and often with a contract to specify the rights and obligations of each partner;[4] and, very common today, the single-parent household, often woman-headed and with dependent children. These and other families exist today with varying degrees of legitimacy.

Religion

Religion is the complex of systems, organized or unorganized, by which people relate to deity and to their own existence with spiritual and moral values concerning personal life, work, and other people. Because of the interrelationships of the Protestant work ethic and Puritan morality with polity and economy, the United States has been called a Christian nation. However, although Christian religions are numerically predominant, other religions such as Judaism, Islam, the Baha'i Faith, Buddhism, Unitarianism, and forms of paganism also exist. Atheism and agnosticism, which either deny deity or allow for the possibility of deity, are also ways in which people relate to existence. Humanism, centered on a philosophy of the dignity and worth of people aside from consideration of deity, is another legitimate spiritual focus. Freedom of belief and the doctrine of separation of church and state are protected by the Constitution. Nevertheless, present-day conservative trends threaten this freedom as religious groups attempt to insert sectarian beliefs into the American legal system.

Social Welfare

There are many definitions of *social welfare*. Macarov tells us, for example, that in Poland social welfare is compensation for injuries suffered in great risks, such as war, that lead to inability to work. In Australia it is a public right that benefits both individuals and society as a whole. Sweden's social welfare goal is to redistribute income more evenly, and in Iran goals include bettering the quality of the work force and encouraging people to save.[5] To most Americans, *social welfare* means giving money to the poor—to people who cannot or will not work to support themselves and their families. However, that benefit, more properly called public assistance, is not the whole of social welfare, which encompasses almost every kind of service provided to members of society. Walter A. Friedlander says social welfare is

> [an organized] system of laws, programs, benefits, and services which strengthen or assure provisions for meeting social needs . . . basic for the welfare of the population and . . . the social order . . . to aid individuals and groups to attain satisfying standards of life and health, and personal and social relationships which permit them to develop their full capacities and to promote their well-being in harmony with the needs of their families and the community.[6]

The *Encyclopedia of Social Work* adds that social welfare is for the purpose of ensuring a basic standard of physical and mental well-being and providing universal access to the mainstream of society.[7] Others add that it provides for those who cannot cope by themselves, creates social change and the modification of social institutions, strengthens society while it helps individuals, and provides services outside the market economy for those unable to succeed within it.[8]

Two additional areas should be included in the definition of social welfare. First, social welfare now includes such new areas as *for-profit* services, including some nursing homes and day care centers; social services in business organizations, such as substance abuse counseling and day care for employees' children; and "natural" networks, the neighbors or parish priests who refer people to professional systems.[9] Second is the *welfare model* of deviance, which Peter Day says presents welfare problems as

> public [social problems] for which some remedial, correctional, or therapeutic intervention is required to alter, modify, or control the deviant and his [sic] behavior

... [as] a public responsibility. . . . First, it sees deviant behavior as a public problem existing outside the framework of normal social life; second, it considers this
behavior to be an expression of a deviant self different from that of the normal person; third, it promotes efforts to account for and correct this difference.[10]

This area of social welfare entails work with the delinquent, emotionally disturbed, or poor, among others. Although such social control has been a legitimate
part of American social welfare since its beginnings, some social work professionals have denied its existence as antithetical to individual freedom. However,
more recent perspectives clearly indicate that social welfare is, in many ways, social control.

For our purposes, American social welfare is the *social institution* that provides society's sum total of all goods and services

- To enhance the social and economic well-being of society's members or
- To ensure their conformity to current societal norms, standards, and ideologies.

It is based on society's values, whether altruistic, economic, or political; is legitimated by legislation or custom; and is carried out by public agencies, private not-
for-profit agencies, or agencies whose major goal is to enhance profit making for
their owner–investors. Social welfare has two kinds of functions:

- *Social treatment:* the provision of goods and services for the enhancement of
  human life
- *Social control:* generally, the provision of services to ensure conformity from
  deviants.

These functions determine the activities of human service professionals in carrying out society's mandates (laws and policies) regarding social services.

Most social welfare activities take place outside the market system; people
do not individually purchase or pay for services that may or may not be altruistic. For example, criminal justice programs require control of those we fear, businesses provide counseling or child care services as much to ensure optimum
productivity as to help their workers, and for-profit care homes, although they
give care, are obviously run for money. Some services cross the line between social treatment and social control; for example, education or recreational programs
such as Girl Scouts are aimed essentially at socialization and conformity but also
are life-enhancing. In any case, social welfare goods and services are provided
both for the benefit of individuals, families, and groups and to maintain order in
society.

Social welfare's tremendously broad scope includes provision of sustenance
(cash, food stamps, housing, and medical care); parts of the legal system, as in juvenile and criminal justice; education and educational services aimed at counseling or rehabilitation; mental health care; child, family, and marital counseling;

programs for special groups such as the aged or those who are developmentally disabled; substance abuse programs; and rehabilitative programs. Whenever other social institutions such as family, church, and economy do not provide a service, social welfare fills in the gaps. For example, public programs such as Social Security pensions now care for aged people who were once supported by the extended family.

Perspectives on Social Welfare

A perspective is a viewpoint based on values from which to look at a phenomenon. Our perspectives on social welfare come from diverse values that determine what we think social welfare should do and what its causes, purposes, functions, and results ought to be. Although we traditionally believe social welfare's causes to be altruistic, they are in fact interplays between altruism, the needs of the disadvantaged, and the desires of those in control. The purposes of social welfare are both to aid those in need and to maintain other structures and institutions of society, and these dual purposes reflect ambivalent goals and, hence, ambivalent programs, effects, and results. Their outcomes must be dually assessed on how well they serve clients and how effective they are for society's need to control. If assessed only on client benefit, most would be considered failures, for the lives of clients are not changed much by most social welfare programs. Looked at from the viewpoint of control, however, they may be very effective.

Our key to understanding this is *functionalism,* which is the usefulness of social welfare in maintaining certain of society's structures. For example, public assistance programs are functional in a number of ways. The low levels of support give some subsistence, but they also save tax money and provide a "work incentive" to get people off welfare. They relieve society of the burden of adequate support and provide employers with sufficient workers at low wages and minimum benefits. Public assistance programs also control sex-role behaviors by requiring that men work at almost any job and that women maintain "moral" sexual, economic, and childrearing behaviors (upon threat of losing their grants and sometimes their children). Other programs have other functions: For example, mental hospitals warehouse the unwanted, emotionally ill, or aged; low assistance grants maintain markets for substandard or used goods; and social welfare programs provide jobs in social work and human service fields. If programs are not functional, they will cease to exist, and the fact that they continue despite public outcry and lack of service effectiveness indicates their functionalism for society.

A program may have both manifest and latent functions. A *manifest function* is one that is evident, usually written into the laws, mandates, or organizational constitutions and bylaws of a program. *Latent functions* are unstated and either assumed or hidden. Because a function is latent does not necessarily mean it is bad, but it does mean that workers, clients, and relevant others may be unaware of its real purposes. For example, socialization to conformity in Girl or Boy Scouts is not written into the bylaws, nor is it particularly a bad thing, but it is a latent, or unadvertised, function. A more insidious example is that the control of women, through public assistance programs or mental health systems, functions to maintain a patriarchal society.

The Residual Perspective

The traditional perspective of social welfare is that, although society should help in emergencies, people in need are responsible for their own problems and should solve them with minimal societal intervention. This is called the *residual perspective*[11] and prescribes short-term, stopgap social welfare measures that last only until the social institutions normally providing help can resume their functions (the family or employment in the economy, for example). A major criterion is whether people are above a set level of money and assets, determined by *means testing* to ensure that applicants get no more help than they "should." Organizations and agencies have different eligibility levels or standards of need, but they are usually based on some relationship to the federal poverty level. Residual programs may also involve severe restriction of personal freedom (jail, long-term commitment to mental hospitals), short-term emergency care such as that offered by hospital emergency rooms, or 24-hour holds for people with acute or life-threatening psychiatric disturbances. In cases of emergency or personal detainment, danger to self or others, rather than financial resources, is the general criterion for eligibility.

To discourage the use of social welfare programs, services are often the least or smallest possible, aid is given grudgingly, and people who seek help are stigmatized by society. Control rather than treatment is often the goal. Means testing is used particularly in subsistence programs (those offering food, shelter, and clothing) but also in such programs as mental health or family planning and health facilities to determine a sliding fee, based on how much clients can afford. Closely related to means testing is "less eligibility," a concept arising with the Elizabethan Poor Laws of 1601. In this concept, no person receiving public aid should get a grant higher than the lowest wage in the locality. Even today "less eligibility" may be considered when setting maximum amounts for public assistance grants.

The residual perspective is the basis for the *medical model* of social work treatment, in which social services are intended to "treat and cure" people who deviate from "healthy society." This complex of ideas leads to blaming victims[12] as responsible for their problems and does not consider structural problems—such as lack of employment opportunities or special problems—as relevant. The most common example of a program in which the residual perspective dominates is public assistance. This perspective has kept public assistance limited in both eligibility and amounts of grants, often too little to maintain health and welfare. Few programs are so residual in nature, but many have residual elements.

To recapitulate, a residual perspective mandates that social welfare programs should give aid to people

- In emergency situations, when other social institutions fail
- On a short-term basis
- As a stopgap measure, until "normal" social institutions come back into play
- With eligibility usually determined by means testing
- In a way that encourages recipients to find other means of help, usually by stigmatizing them
- Begrudgingly, especially in assistance programs, where minimal aid is given.

Let us consider a concrete example of a mother applying for TANF:

- *Emergency.* She will be considered only if her income falls below state eligibility limits. It is assumed that as soon as possible she will become employed or find some other means of support (such as marriage or other family resources) and will leave the program.
- *Short-term.* The specified time limit to TANF is twenty-four consecutive months or sixty months lifetime limit.
- *Stopgap.* She will be allowed to receive TANF only as long as she has no other means of support. A major program goal is to move people off the rolls as soon as possible.
- *Means testing.* Her income and assets are assessed to ensure that they fall below the already low eligibility limits of TANF.
- *Stigmatizing.* Applying for TANF is demeaning because our American value system is so strongly opposed to public assistance. Also, the application process often entails speaking of intimate and personal details of one's life to a stranger, and permanent public records, though confidential, are made on the application.
- *Grudging and minimal.* Not only will she be subjected to the embarrassment of asking for public money, but the dollar amounts given are so minimal that they are known to be insufficient to maintain healthy subsistence on more than an emergency basis.[13]

The Institutional Perspective

The institutional perspective is at the opposite end of the continuum from the residual perspective. Its major criterion is membership in the society: Every person has a right to its services, without means testing or stigma. Programs are universal, that is, they cover every person within their designated mandate, whereas residual programs are selective in nature and apply only to a selected few or selected groups. The institutional perspective leads to the *structural or social model* of social work: Social problems are believed to come from oppressive or inegalitarian structures in society. Social problems are not based on personal fault, so solutions do not lie in controlling, punishing, or stigmatizing the individual; rather, they lie in root problems—such as classism, racism, and sexism—and their elimination.

Many programs of social welfare approach the institutional end of the residual–institutional continuum (see Figure 2.2). Public education, for example, is the right of all children in the United States, and Social Security ensures a retirement income for almost every person in the United States and supports surviving children of deceased workers. Mental health is one area that is now becoming institutional. Before the 1960s, the term used for people with emotional difficulties was *mentally ill,* and they were usually stigmatized for and ashamed of their problems. Now *mental health* is a social right. Although there is a sliding fee scale, private or public funds pay for services for those unable to pay, and no one is denied treatment because he or she is poor.

To recapitulate, then, the institutional perspective is a belief that

- Social welfare services should be available to all members of society who fit a program's mandates.
- There is no time limit for services, although there may be a time at which services can begin (such as school attendance or eligibility for Social Security pensions).
- If there is any means testing, it is to determine the amount people can pay rather than to deny services.
- There is no stigma for either applying for or receiving services.
- There is no societal pressure to leave the program.

We have been discussing perspectives of social welfare, not the programs presented as examples. However, we can place programs along a continuum from residual to institutional as long as we remember that few programs are either wholly residual or wholly institutional. Some programs have both residual and institutional elements. For example, juvenile probation has residual elements be-

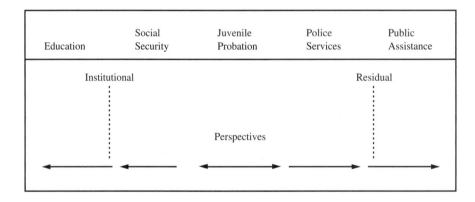

FIGURE 2.2 *Continuum of Perspectives, with Some Examples*

cause of the emergency nature of problems of children in trouble. However, institutional elements make protection under the system available to all children, including those who have suffered neglect and abuse. On the other hand, even though education is one of our most institutional programs, services of truant officers and some administrators in schools deal with emergency problems that are residual in nature.

Conflict Perspectives in Social Welfare

Although the perspectives discussed so far provide some prescriptions for social work practice, they are basically static and descriptive, dealing only minimally with policy analysis or problem causation. Newer perspectives based on sociological, economic, and feminist theories are now being applied to social welfare to assess its social history and suggest proactive and often radical models for human service work. More or less related to the institutional perspective and to structural models of practice, these perspectives view recalcitrant societal structures, rather than individual fault, as causes of social problems. They criticize these structures and prescribe social action and social change to a much greater degree than do present structural models.

Generally, the newer perspectives are based on *conflict theory:* They posit a conflict between those who control society's structures and those who are controlled and exploited by them. Piven and Cloward were among the first to develop these theories for social welfare, noting in their book *Regulating the Poor* that throughout history, whenever the disadvantaged rebelled against exploitation, welfare programs and benefits were expanded until the rebellion ceased.[14] Then, although benefits shrank, it was seldom to pre-rebellion levels and they were sufficient to keep people quiet for a time. Thus, expansion of welfare programs was not altruistic but political and economic: It quelled rebellions and, because benefits were always meager, it kept a quiescent workforce eager to take jobs with low wages and few benefits. This made labor costs cheap and profitable to producers.

James Rule says that redefining social conflicts as social problems changes their nature and enables people to believe that solutions can be found.[15] The redefinition places the burden for change on "deviants" and those hired to change them—social workers—and relieves society of the burden of changing its status quo. For example, if poverty is class conflict, the higher class must fight to keep its privileged position from those who would take away its benefits. If it is redefined as a social problem—poverty—powerless social workers "own" and must solve it. The upper class is satisfied because society remains stratified, the poor believe that solutions will be found, and social workers find solutions that usually do not work because the conflict elements remain. In the same way, if high unemployment among African Americans is defined as racism because of job discrimination, action to end it is implied, along with high risks and few rewards. However, if high unemployment among African Americans is defined as a social problem, the solution is job training programs, which are much easier to create than racial equality, even though they will not work because no jobs are available.

Seeing racism, sexism, and classism as social problems implies that solutions can be found in changing the victims rather than in changing society's exploitative structures. Because victims of society are not generally to blame for their victimization, only remedial, Band-Aid work can be done because the damage-causing structures remain. On the other hand, seeing the "isms" as conflicts implies action against society, but this does not mean that action will occur. In the first place, most Americans believe our society is egalitarian and democratic, and action against it means action against those principles. Second, although seeing "isms" as conflict issues might provide the right mind-set to work for change, restructuring of the system is too much for most of us to undertake.

Among the perspectives deriving from conflict theory are Marxian, socialist, socialist feminist, radical feminist, and feminist welfarist models. Marxian and socialist perspectives look at class stratification and exploitative behavior and perceive social welfare as helping to maintain inegalitarian structures. Rather than remedial treatment for the disadvantaged, eradication of the oppressive economic and political structures is advocated. Class advantages would be eliminated and profit sharing and a government based on worker control would redistribute wealth. Disadvantaged people would receive sufficient resources from the government to satisfy their needs. To a great extent, these perspectives ignore gender issues except to note that a different economic structure would eliminate gender stratification because it is based on worker oppression.

Socialist feminism's primary concern is the economic oppression of women, which began with the onset of private property and the loss of women's economic value to the family. In this view, women are doubly oppressed: first as workers in a capitalist economy and second as wives dependent on husbands who are in turn exploited workers. Women are involved directly in production at work, and at home in two kinds of reproduction that serve the capitalist economy: biological reproduction to supply a new generation of workers and maintenance of a home that offers surcease to the weary laborer and renews him for more productive work. A restructuring of class stratification and a redefinition of marriage and family roles—perhaps their elimination—would prevent both primary and secondary oppression. An altered economic system would provide new access for all kinds of social care, and social welfare's concerns should be social action and social change to give economic and political empowerment to women.

Radical feminism is concerned with political exploitation of women under a patriarchal system enforcing gender privilege throughout history. In this view, both class and gender exploitation began with the onset of private property and the loss of women's co-equal status. Patriarchal sex-role socialization keeps women in subordinate and powerless roles and increases their dependency on men and male systems (such as public assistance and mental health systems), so that women themselves believe in the "rightness" of male control and cooperate in their own subordination. Models for action include consciousness raising; values awareness; a reassessment of female roles in marriage, family, and society; and social action for empowerment even to the point of separatism, as in women's communities.

The feminist welfarist perspective is a critical analysis of social history that incorporates conflict theory, socialist and radical feminist perspectives, and the synergistic evolution of social welfare. It pays particular attention to economy, polity, and spiritual motivations concerning social treatment and social control. According to this perspective, value systems create a morally legitimate oppression for women and for the poor, and race privilege is superimposed on these. Its arguments are predicated on sex-role socialization to a patriarchal society's expectations: women as dependent, incompetent in money management, less mature, and given to emotionality. Men are also victims of patriarchal sex-role stereotyping and exploitation. Although they have more power than women, their most important sex-role identification is as worker, making them very exploitable in a capitalistic society.

A major issue from this perspective is the povertization of women. Public dependency for women arises from different causes than for men, yet public assistance programs are based on male models of need, that is, the idea that adults who can work should work (male pauper model). However, women are not simply capable workers, although they may be. They are socialized to family roles and away from lucrative employment by school and family systems, they have primary emotional and economic responsibility for dependent children, and the structures of society that deal with their dependence (courts and public assistance systems) do not provide adequate grants to lift them above poverty levels. Work itself is marginal and low-paying for most women, and few receive equal pay for equal or comparable work. To insist that work is their way out of poverty is a denial of the differential treatment accorded them throughout society's institutions.[16]

In addition, the needs of women as well as care by women create special problems for social welfare. Women are the majority of workers as well as the majority of clients in social welfare systems. They have little power or recognition, they cannot command resources because they are inadequately represented in welfare policy bodies, and their charity work is derogated by society's antipoverty values. Men in social welfare, on the other hand, have more legitimation because they traditionally have worked with employment programs (such as unions, job training, and social insurance). From this differential association with "undeserving" and "deserving" groups, neither women, social work, nor clients gain society's respect. Finally, social welfare itself contributes to the patriarchal control of women, the poor, and people of color. Established, financed, and directed by a white male political system, although women do much of its work, it is in general a male system, and it is oriented to maintaining the status quo of society.

To reiterate, conflict theory says that social problems

- Lie in the structures of society rather than the fault of the disadvantaged
- Are the result of attempts of an elite group to maintain the privileges they have accumulated through exploitation of other classes
- Will endure until the structures themselves are changed.

The feminist welfarist perspective is a critical historical analysis that

- Incorporates conflict theory and socialist and radical feminist perspectives
- Reconstructs social history to include perspectives of the poor, women, and races (and religions) other than the dominant white male system
- Sees social problems as the results of historical convergences of class privilege, race privilege, and patriarchal power
- Traces most social problems to structured inequalities primarily based on class, race, and gender
- Indicts social welfare as causative in great part of the maintenance of structured inequalities.

The Scope of Social Welfare

Social welfare ranges across all aspects of life, from birth to death, providing social services where other institutions fail or are inadequate.[17] Social services are activities that help or control, performed by people in the public (government) or private sectors, usually in social agencies formed around a particular social need, such as hunger, delinquency, or substance abuse. People who provide social services may be professional social workers with master's or bachelor's degrees; paraprofessionals (people indigenous to the client population who are trained by professional social workers but do not have professional degrees); laypeople, such as church volunteers; or people having little or no professional social work training but working in social agencies such as departments of public welfare, the juvenile division of the court system, and Social Security offices. Also, non-social-work professionals such as psychologists, psychiatrists, and members of the clergy provide counseling services. Finally, self-help groups with or without professional association and staffing provide emotional support and help to members; examples include Alcoholics Anonymous or women's consciousness-raising groups.

Public agencies are established by law on local (city or county), state, or federal levels and are administered by public officials according to legal mandates. Some have local representative boards, but power resides in the legislation. Private agencies are nongovernmental, although they may have government charters and often receive some funding from government bodies. They are often called *voluntary agencies* because they are established by voluntary groups, usually around a local need, and are funded substantially through private contributions. Some are developed by religious groups to provide social services specific to a religion's beliefs. Members of the community on volunteer boards make agency policy decisions, but staff and administration are often paid professionals. Although some still have individual fund drives, many are now part of United Way agencies, which run annual fund drives and apportion out contributions by locally established criteria to member agencies.

Some organizations offering social services are not social agencies but provide help to enhance their primary goals. For example, schools may provide counseling for children and their parents around the issues of absenteeism or lack of motivation, hospitals give social services to the families of dying patients or arrange extended care for aged patients, and churches carry out their religious mandates to care for the poor with food baskets and soup kitchens. Some social agencies provide a wide variety of services, some target only a few, and often services or clientele overlap.

There are certain generally identifiable fields of social services. They include

- Life necessity services
- Educational, recreational, or rehabilitative services
- Protective or custodial services
- Personal social services.

Life Necessity Services

Life necessity services supply food, clothing, shelter, and medical assistance. Public agencies provide the bulk of such services, although churches and such private agencies as the Salvation Army, Goodwill Industries, Volunteers of America, and Catholic Charities supplement such programs with grants or donations, or give temporary shelter. Food programs—lunch and breakfast or home-delivered meals—may be publicly or privately funded, and are carried out in schools, churches, and senior citizens' centers.

By far the largest public programs are those of the federal Social Security Acts of 1935 and their amendments. There are three major areas: Social Insurance, Public Assistance, and Maternal and Child Health (see Table 2.1). The largest program of social insurance is Old Age, Survivors, Disability and Health Insurance (OASDHI). Other social insurances include Unemployment Insurance and Workers' Compensation, both state programs with varying degrees of federal input. Public assistance programs include Temporary Assistance to Needy Families

TABLE 2.1 *Selected Government Programs for the Poor*

Social Insurance	Public Assistance	Maternal and Child Health
OASDHI	TANF	Family Planning
Medicare (the *H* in *OASDHI*)	Medicaid	WIC
Unemployment Insurance	SSI	Crippled Children
Workers' Compensation	General Assistance	Child Nutrition
	Poor Relief	
	Food Stamps	

(TANF), Supplemental Security Income (SSI), Medicaid, and general assistance or poor relief at state and county levels. The Food Stamp program is also considered public assistance, although it is a program of the Department of Agriculture. Among maternal and child health programs are the Crippled Children's program, school lunches, family planning programs, and Women's, Infants', and Children's Nutrition (WIC).

Social insurance programs are work related and directed to the "worthy poor." Originally the Social Security Acts established retirement pensions for aged workers and their spouses and pensions for the children of deceased workers (Old Age and Survivors Insurance, or OASI). Health insurance (Medicare) was added in 1964, and Old Age Assistance, Aid to the Blind, and Aid to the Permanently and Totally Disabled (which had been public assistance programs) were added in 1972. OASDHI is funded through the FICA tax. Workers' Compensation pays pensions or settlements for disabilities or death suffered by workers, and Unemployment Compensation provides benefits to workers laid off from regular employment for a limited time period. Both the latter programs are federally mandated but financed by employers (through taxes or private carriers) and are administered by the state.

Although social insurance is not means tested, public assistance programs are, and applicants are not accepted if they have income and assets over state-set levels. The Aid to Families of Dependent Children (AFDC) program was federally mandated but administered by states, with 50 to 75 percent federal financing and the remainder paid by the state. Before 1988, the program was specifically for one-parent families with children, although states could choose to fund intact families where the wage earner was incapacitated (AFDC-I) or unemployed (AFDC-UP). However, the Family Support Act of 1988 mandated AFDC-UP for all states, depending on the willingness of wage earners to engage in job training, "workfare," or job search. The Supplementary Security Income (SSI) program was financed by the federal government with state supplementation and administered by county departments of public welfare.

Most public assistance at the federal level was eliminated by the Personal Responsibility and Work Opportunity Reconciliation Act of 1996, specifically the Temporary Assistance to Needy Families (TANF) program, which replaced AFDC, SSI, Food Stamps, WIC, School Breakfast and Lunch Programs, and other benefit programs. Money formerly used for such programs was placed in block grants and given to states to administer at state and local levels. Federal requirements and standards, generally, no longer applied. Work and work training were TANF goals, and with some exceptions recipients who fail to find work within twenty-four months are removed from TANF rolls. There is also a lifetime recipient cap of sixty months on TANF.

Medicaid is a federal/state program providing health subsidies for most people, depending on the state, whose incomes fall below state-determined standards of need; it is administered by state and county welfare departments. Whereas the social insurance program Medicare pays for hospitalization and some extended care in nursing facilities (along with a few other benefits) for the aged or permanently and totally disabled, Medicaid—a public assistance program that varies on options from state to state—can pay many medical costs, including hospitalization, surgery, physicians' office calls, and prescription drugs. Depending on the state, it can also pay for hearing aids, prosthetics, eyeglasses, and the like.

Under the maternal and child health system, state public health departments can provide tuberculosis testing, immunization clinics, well-baby clinics, family planning programs, sexually transmitted disease testing and treatment, school health nurses, and control of communicable diseases, public health hazards, and epidemics. Other federal life necessity programs include subsidized housing in the form of loans, grants, or partial rent subsidies; railroad workers' and federal employee pensions; and medical costs for veterans (Veterans Administration). On the county and state levels, general assistance (GA) and poor-relief programs aid people who are not eligible for federal programs. Counties decide on the level of aid and administer the programs, with state matching funds (usually 60 percent state). Counties often have medical assistance programs for hospital care and burial subsidies for county indigents who are not covered by other programs.

There are also a variety of private organizations and brotherhoods (such as the Elks and Lions) that work to cure or control particular diseases or problems. Among them are the American Cancer Association, Crippled Children's Association, Muscular Dystrophy Association, March of Dimes Foundation, Epilepsy Foundation, Planned Parenthood clinics, and myriad others. They provide money for services, information, and education to the public; research; and prosthetics, eyeglasses, wheelchairs, and other equipment. The American Red Cross maintains a blood bank and provides a variety of health services to veterans and other citizens in times of emergency.

Educational, Recreational, or Rehabilitative Services

Educational, recreational, or rehabilitative services include job training, remedial education services, day care for children (custodial or educational), recreational programs and facilities, disability rehabilitation services, and educational and rehabilitative services for people in custodial care in prisons, mental hospitals, and juvenile detention facilities.

In addition to basic education, school districts often provide technical job training such as auto mechanics or typing. For young people no longer in regular school, "alternative schools" may offer basic education, training, personal or employment counseling, or remedial programs for literacy. General education degrees (GEDs) or technical certificates may be awarded. School social workers ("visiting teachers") counsel students, visit their homes to solve nonacademic problems, or undertake individual or group therapy with students or their families. Some may be "truant officers" or juvenile probation officers making sure that children attend school, stay out of trouble with the law, and are protected from neglect or abuse.

Several public programs offer job training and educational services for adults. TANF requires all public assistance recipients with children over age one to participate in work, job training, or public or private subsidized work in return for their grants. After two years, their public assistance ends, as do any kind of subsidized work or work training programs. Most War on Poverty job programs (such as the Manpower Development and Training Act of 1962, the Economic Opportunity Act of 1964, Job Corps for youth no longer in school, and the Neighborhood Youth Corps) were dismantled or severely cut by Reagan, Bush, and the 104th Congress. Programs previously written into public assistance were also cut (such as the Comprehensive Education and Training Act, the Job Partnership Training Act of 1981, and Job Opportunities and Basic Skills). However, state employment commissions still provide registration, testing, and counseling for jobs in addition to administering the unemployment compensation program.

Vocational Rehabilitation is a Department of Education program administered by state education departments (amendments of 1954 and 1973). It provides a full range of services to disabled people to train them for employment: medical testing to assess the extent of disability; medical and surgical services to lessen the extent of impairment; personal and rehabilitation counseling; education including college, depending on ability; vocational training in private or public schools; such special equipment as hearing aids, guide dogs, wheelchairs, canes, and prosthetics; special training in sign language or social adjustment; sheltered workshops; money for transportation and living expenses while training; and assistance in finding a job and essential equipment, such as licenses, tools, or stock.[18]

Prisons, mental hospitals, and other custodial care facilities also have rehabilitation and educational programs intended to provide released people with job skills that will enable them to earn a living once out of custody. Private agencies such as Goodwill Industries and Volunteers of America also give training and rehabilitation in sheltered workshops, where people unable to work in the general marketplace receive minimal pay for the work they are able to do.

Day care facilities for children may be financed privately or through TANF (to encourage mothers to enter the job force). Public welfare departments license and monitor private (approved) homes and private or public day care centers. Head Start, a War on Poverty program, provides educational care for children and other services to parents. Nursery schools offer early education and socialization skills to children in addition to day care. For adults with emotional, physical, or developmental problems, departments of education, mental health clinics, and private entrepreneurs provide day care, nursing home care, halfway houses, or extended care. These may also give social opportunities, counseling, or a variety of other services, as do programs and centers for senior citizens.

Recreational agencies give opportunities for recreation, training, education, social experiences, and socialization to normative beliefs and standards in America. They include day camps, summer camps, programs of the Young

Women's and Young Men's Christian Association or Hebrew Association (YWCA, YMCA, YWHA, YMHA), Boy Scouts, Girl Scouts, and their counterparts. Kahn says,

> In a major sense, social services exist to protect, to change, or to innovate with respect to many of the educational, child-rearing, value-imparting, and social induction activities once assumed by the extended family, the neighborhood, and relatives. The goal is socialization into communal values, transmittal of goals and motivation, and enhancement of personal development. Cognitive and emotional aspects of learning are encompassed.[19]

Protective or Custodial Services

Protective or custodial services include group homes and institutions for disturbed or delinquent children, programs for neglected or abused children and their parents, child guidance programs and school social work for troubled or troublesome children, foster care and adoption, homes for unwed mothers, mental hospitals or short-term group or custodial homes for emotionally disturbed people, and protective services and nursing homes for the aged or developmentally disabled. Rehabilitative work in prisons and juvenile institutions is included in this category, as are juvenile and adult parole and probation work. Public agencies offering such care are usually connected with either departments of public welfare or the juvenile or adult justice systems, but may include private for-profit institutions, such as nursing homes, or not-for-profit organizations, such as Crittenton Services and Salvation Army homes.

Protection for abused and neglected children and adults (particularly aged or developmentally disabled adults) was authorized by the Social Service Amendments to the Social Security Acts of 1935 (Title XX). Under this act, social workers from public welfare departments grant licenses to nursing homes, foster homes, and private care homes and deal with complaints of abuse by parents or other caretakers, including public or private institutions. At the local level, governments offer help for family violence through police department social workers, and private organizations are opening shelters for battered women and exploited children and runaways.

Personal Social Services

Personal social services offer

> brief, or intensive, personal help with environmental, situational, interpersonal, or intrapsychic programs. Frequently the goal is restoration of as much normal functioning as possible . . . [assuming control over] . . . dangerous or unacceptable deviance while help is rendered.[20]

It includes therapy for individuals or groups in such areas as child or marriage problems, substance abuse, and emotional difficulties related to divorce, death, and so on; psychological testing and psychiatric services; counseling on budgeting, credit, family planning, or employment; and access and advocacy services.

Although therapy and counseling are offered in some public settings—mental hospitals, for example—this has generally been the province of private social agencies. People intensively trained in clinical skills practice intervention techniques based on work by a number of theorists, including Freud, Adler, Jung, Rogers, Perls, Ellis, and Glasser. The techniques range across psychosocial casework, problem solving, task-centered therapy, psychoanalysis, client-centered therapy, Gestalt therapy, and behavior modification. Mental health clinics or family service agencies are among the primary providers of such care, but other organizations offer it as part of their services (Planned Parenthood, shelters for battered women, schools, group homes, probation offices, and juvenile and adult detention centers, for example). The relationship with the counselor and client motivation are essential elements in the counseling process.

Access services are a part of personal social services. They enable clients to find, understand, and use social services. Through information giving, referral, and follow-up, they help clients through the maze of bureaucracies and regulations that might preclude help. In addition, access services may help to locate gaps in service and coordinate agencies or develop new services to fill them. Advocacy services enable and empower clients to gain rights and services to which they are eligible or entitled under the law. Legal action, along with lobbying and influence, secures needed services, and clients are encouraged to undertake social action on their own behalf. Community action agencies, developed during the War on Poverty, were the forerunners in advocacy, but now most social agencies offer limited advocacy.

The Profession of Social Work

Some would argue that social work is not a profession. Although it is theoretically based, other professions share both theory and skills used in social work, and those skills are neither exclusive nor (in many areas) highly technical. Its professional culture includes undergraduate and graduate schools, apprenticeships, and professional associations (National Association of Social Workers and Council for Social Work Education). However, other schools and programs teach human services, especially on the interpersonal level. Nevertheless, society recognizes the expertise of social work as a profession, even though its ethical stance is often in conflict with major American values. In addition, social work has another problem: respect. Most of its practitioners are women and its clients are "deviants." Therefore, it is a "socially contaminated" occupation with little credibility. Finally, because its scope is broad and its targets many, it has no exclusive domain for practice.

On the continuum of occupations, social work falls near the professional end. Its general definition as a profession is the professional activity of helping individuals, groups, or communities enhance or restore their capacity for social functioning and creating societal conditions favorable to this goal . . . the professional application of social work values, principles, and techniques to one or more of the following ends: helping people obtain tangible services; counseling and psychotherapy with individuals, families, and groups; helping communities or groups provide or improve social and health services; and participating in relevant legislative processes.[21]

Social work is different from other helping professions in specific ways. Included in these are the overarching mission; the client system; the focus on client-in-situation; the target of practice; and the complex of values, knowledge, and skills that makes up the ethical stance of social work practice.

Social work intervention, although it may include intrapsychic therapy, goes far beyond personal problems of emotional or mental health. Social work's original mission was not personal but *social* intervention—reform of poverty and its causes. Although this has changed in many ways, the mission is still social in nature, dealing with elements beyond the individual client. These elements include not only mental health but financial security, employment satisfaction, marital health, elimination of inequality, and the attainment of civil and human rights for clients. Optimal social functioning in problematic areas of life is the goal of practice.

Unlike clients in other helping professions, the social work client may be an individual, a group, a family, an organization, a neighborhood group, or a political body. Moreover, the focus of practice is the client-in-situation (see Figure 2.3).

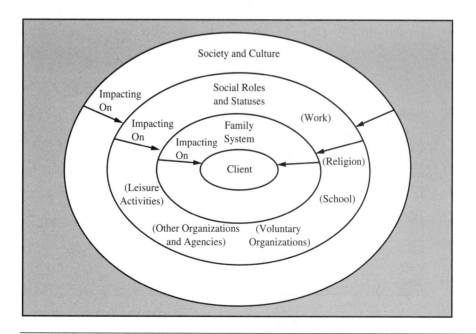

FIGURE 2.3 *Client-in-Situation*

The importance of the social environment in the helping process is a stated and formal criterion unique to social work, although other helping professionals surely deal with these relationships less formally. Social work considers the complex of systems that affect clients, influence their behavior, and may create and maintain their problems. Unlike such disciplines as medicine and psychology, which generally separate clients from the contexts of their lives, social work recognizes that individual change is based on the context of lives.

In addition, the target of social work practice is not the client, but the relationships and reciprocal interactions that instigate or perpetuate the problem situation (see Figure 2.4). To elaborate, the target of intervention for a depressed individual would be problematic relationships with spouse, children, employment, or other system. At a community level, it might be interactions among neighborhood groups and police, slum landlords, or public health officials. On the policy level, the target against which action might be taken would not be a legislator but the systems that keep poor legislation in place or prevent passage of a better law.

A final unique characteristic of social work as a profession is its carefully elaborated combination of values, knowledge, and skills. The attitudes, behavior, and commitment of its members are the defining elements of social work as a pro-

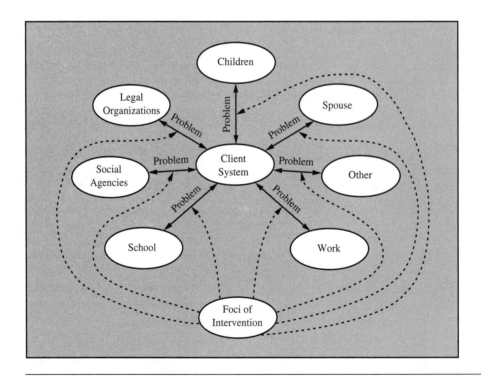

FIGURE 2.4 *Targets of Practice*

fession,[22] and these derive from social work's ethical stance (as defined in the National Association of Social Work Code of Ethics[23]).

The Emergence of the Profession

According to Peter Day,

> Social work was an evolutionary phenomenon with roots in social philosophies and ethical values . . . a spontaneous development, a manifestation of awareness of the need to create a means of protecting and helping those individuals adversely affected by changes which are reshaping society.[24]

Social work emerged in the United States during the Industrial Revolution in the middle and late 1800s, in great part a response to the needs of a rapidly expanding and poverty-stricken immigrant population. Also, it reflected changing family roles that freed middle- and upper-class single women from family responsibilities. No longer needed for teaching and child care in their families, these women became "friendly visitors" to the poor. Their mission, and that of the budding profession, was the elimination of poverty.

Social work derived from three movements with very different ideological bases: charity organization societies, child-saving, and settlement houses. Charity organization societies were developed by philanthropists to regulate the use of charitable agencies by the poor. Immorality rather than unresponsive social structures were to blame for poverty, and "friendly visitors" could "save" the poor by teaching them morality and good work habits. "Child-saving" developed around the time of the Civil War, when thousands of unsupervised children roamed city streets begging, stealing, and taking men's jobs at lower wages. Although early on child-saving acted more to rid the streets of young nuisances than to help children, it brought a new concept—childhood—that young people be viewed not as small adults but as needing special care because of their youth. Settlement houses, often developed by women, were based on the concept that people could work together for a common goal and change society to make it more relevant to the needs of the poor. In this view, the cause of poverty was not personal fault or immorality but unresponsive social structures, such as the economy and the polity. Grass-roots organization, education, and training, provided in supportive group settings and without moral stigma, were the means to success. New immigrants were the targeted clientele, but other people needing help were also welcome.

Early social workers soon realized that social structures were responsible for poverty, and they gathered data used to create social reforms. However, blaming the victim and the medical model remained in the public idiom. The medical model sees problems in the individual and seeks cures for the person rather than the society. The casework model of practice, emphasizing personal attention and individual work with clients, is a direct result of the charity organization societies' friendly visiting. On the other hand, group work, community action, and social action methods of social work developed from the settlement house movement; and adoption, foster care, and child guidance movements began with child-saving.

By the end of the nineteenth century, social work was no longer voluntary but paid employment and was given public recognition as an occupation. Still a women's job, the public looked on it as an extension of "women's sphere": home and family roles moved into the community. Formal training began in the early 1900s as the first step in professionalization, and social workers began to be acknowledged authorities on the needs of disadvantaged or deviant people. However, many practitioners have turned away from the mission of equality in order to accrue some of the benefits of a profession: status, better pay, and more authority in the community. A majority now enter middle-class, more status-laden mental health fields. Therefore, work with the poor or stigmatized disadvantaged is often left to people untrained in the knowledge, skills, and values of social work. Concern with social action and social change has, in great part, fallen by the wayside of professionalization, undercutting the historic mission of the profession itself.

The idea of a combination of skills, values, and knowledge is the underlying theme of practice at any level or in any style. We have already discussed the value base of social work; the knowledge base derives from many disciplines. For example, from psychology we obtain information on human development, mental health, and primary and secondary relationships; from sociology we learn of behavior in groups, societal values and norms, the place of person in organization, and the uses of power, status, class, race, and sex; from learning theory comes information on how people assimilate new ideas and their stages of mental development; and from history we become aware of the broad sweeps of economics, the polity, and religion in creating and changing the institution of social welfare.

Types of intervention techniques depend first on the purpose of the intervention—social treatment or social control—and are related to the needs of both the client system and society. Second, they depend on the client system type (individual, group, organization, or other). Third, the kind of technique depends on the theoretical base the worker is using. Therapists may use any of a variety of techniques, such as Freudian psychoanalysis, Gestalt therapy, confrontive techniques, principles of learning theory, and problem-solving models.

Conclusion: Social Work and Social Control

This overview of social welfare and social work particularly noted definitions of social institution, social welfare, and social work to provide common concepts. The perspective of social welfare as both social treatment and social control gave new insights into the political and economic purposes that maintain social problems and prevent disadvantaged people from attaining equality in our society. Social work is more than concern and care. It is also a political activity aimed at control. Peter Day says that

> social work acts have political implications . . . about the way that an organization or group is run, and therefore about who has the power to get things done.[25]

and

> [c]are and control can be seen as complementary aspects of public policy towards the poor and deviant . . . these two elements, originally separately institutionalized, have converged in the role of . . . social workers.[26]

Our discussion of perspectives demonstrated that social conflict may be the basis for social problems, and that redefining social conflicts as social problems is functional for continuing inequality and the status quo in our society. Newer perspectives arising from the conflict model give us useful ways to understand this. Finally, the feminist welfarist perspective further illuminates the social welfare institution and the status of social workers as often unaware tools of forces not oriented to benevolence: We may have become middle persons of social control for those we wished to help. As Hannah Arendt once stated,

> Compassion may itself be a substitute for justice . . . compassion always already signifies inequality. The compassionate intend no justice, for justice might corrupt current power relationships.[27]

Study Questions

1. What is the relationship of social welfare to the other institutions of society?

2. For your choice of social problem, what would constitute

   a. A residual perspective?

   b. An institutional perspective?

   c. A socialist or conflict perspective?

   d. A feminist welfarist perspective?

3. What are the elements of social work practice?

4. What is the definition of social welfare? Why does it include both social treatment and social control?

5. For your choice of social welfare program, explain the effect of the polity, the economy, and religion on the funding of the program. How do they affect the program's goals?

Notes

1. Compton quotes W. G. Sumner on the definition of an institution: "An institution consists of a concept (idea, notion, doctrine, interest) and a structure. . . . The structure is a framework or apparatus, or perhaps only a number of functionaries, . . . [that] holds the concept and furnishes instrumentalities for bringing it into the world of facts and action." In Beulah Compton, *Introduction to Social Welfare and Social Work: Structure, Function, and Process* (Homewood, IL: The Dorsey Press, 1980), p. 31. Neil Gilbert and Harry Specht say that an institution is a network "of

relationships that are generally accepted as the way of carrying out these essential social functions . . . human activities such as child-rearing and the production, consumption, and distribution of goods . . . raising and training the young," in *Dimensions of Social Welfare Policy* (Englewood Cliffs, NJ: Prentice Hall, 1974), p. 4.

2. Neil Gilbert and Harry Specht, *Dimensions of Social Welfare Policy* (Englewood Cliffs, NJ: Prentice Hall, 1974), p. 3.

3. As with the Ku Klux Klan or in situations of conquest over other polities. For example, the Ku Klux Klan influences and/or is part of the polity because it coerces behavior in American society. In war, a society coerces another society, taking power over it.

4. The Internal Revenue Service now has a special listing for Persons of Opposite Sex Sharing Living Quarters (POSSLQs).

5. David Macarov, *The Design of Social Welfare* (New York: Holt, Rinehart & Winston, 1978), p. 23.

6. Walter A. Friedlander, *Introduction to Social Welfare*, 5th ed. (Englewood Cliffs, NJ: Prentice Hall, 1961), p. 4.

7. National Association of Social Workers, *Encyclopedia of Social Work* (New York: NASW, 1977), Vol. II, p. 1503.

8. Klein (1968), Romansky (1971), and Martin Wolins (1976), discussed in Compton, *Introduction to Social Welfare and Social Work*, pp. 28–29.

9. Ralph Dolgoff and Donald Feldstein, *Understanding Social Welfare*, 2nd ed. (New York: Longman Press, 1984), p. 95.

10. Peter R. Day, *Social Work and Social Control* (London: Tavistock Publications, 1981), p. 12.

11. The concepts of residual and institutional social welfare are taken from Harold L. Wilensky and C. N. Lebeaux, *Industrial Society and Social Welfare* (New York: Free Press, 1965).

12. The phrase is taken from William O. Ryan, *Blaming the Victim* (New York: Pantheon Books, 1971).

13. The idea of minimal subsistence level for public assistance is based on the concept of poverty level developed by Mollie Orshansky in the 1960s.

14. Frances Fox Piven and Richard Cloward, *Regulating the Poor* (New York: Random House, 1971).

15. James B. Rule, *Insight and Social Betterment: Applied Social Science* (New York: Oxford University Press, 1978).

16. Diana Pearce, "Farewell to Alms: Women and Welfare Policy in the Eighties." Paper presented at the American Sociological Association Annual Meeting, San Francisco, Sept. 1982.

17. Although education and health services are part of the institution of social welfare, each has developed its own professional mandates and functions. For this reason, they will be discussed only in terms of the social services each provides rather than with their primary focuses of education and health care.

18. Charles Zastrow, *The Practice of Social Work* (Homewood, IL: The Dorsey Press, 1985), p. 375.

19. Alfred J. Kahn, *Social Policy and Social Services* (New York: Random House, 1973), p. 29.

20. Ibid., p. 30.

21. Dolgoff and Feldstein, *Understanding Social Welfare*, p. 285.

22. Ernest Greenwood, "Attributes of a Profession," in Neil Gilbert and Harry Specht (eds.), *The Emergence of Social Welfare and Social Work*, 2nd ed. (Itasca, IL: F. E. Peacock Publishers, 1981), pp. 231–240.

23. National Association of Social Work Code of Ethics. Taken from the NASW Code of Ethics as presented in Zastrow, *Practice of Social Work*, pp. 516–517.

24. Peter Day, *Social Work and Social Control*, from discussion paper #3 (British Association of Social Workers, 1973), p. 3.

25. Peter Day, *Social Work and Social Control*, p. 4.

26. Ibid., p. 16.

27. Hannah Arendt, *On Revolution* (New York: Viking, 1963), pp. 74–75. Quoted in David Wagner, *What's Love Got to do with It?* (New York: New Press, 2000) p. 1.

3

The Beginnings of Social Welfare
Political Economy and Early Societies

Prehistory and Social Welfare to 6000 B.C.

The political economy of any society is the way in which decisions are made (or power is wielded) to ensure the society's economic sustenance and survival. In our earliest history, it was tied inextricably to religion and sharing, for provision of food was the economy and the way food was shared was power. Obtaining food was the major task of early humankind and was intimately related to prayers to the gods of harvest and hunt to ensure an adequate food supply. Among our earliest archeological evidences, from about 25,000 B.C., are shrines and burial sites that show a communal life where all worked together to support the tribe. In prehistoric gathering and hunting societies,

> [S]ocial life is egalitarian. There is . . . no state, no organized government. Apart from religious shamans or magicians, the division of labor is based only on sex and age. Resources are owned communally, tools and personal possessions are freely exchanged.[1]

Men and women were apparently co-equal, although a division of labor existed based on women's childbearing and food-gathering tasks. Men began to work in stone to improve their hunting capabilities, and this work tied in neatly with the development of new foodstuffs, for

> polished stone tools correlated with the advent of agriculture. The grinding of tools was not unrelated to the grinding of grain. . . . [Moreover, this] corresponded to a sudden blossoming of all sorts of arts and crafts in Europe after about 40,000 B.C. . . . until at least 10,000 B.C.[2]

One of the most important of these crafts was cloth making. Whether for warmth, decoration, or trade, this skill was probably a major factor in the politics and economics of any early society. To begin, fibers were a by-product of the agriculture in which women engaged. Secondly, cloth making was an activity very amenable to the exigencies of pregnancy and childrearing: It was a sedentary activity, could be done in the home or, if necessity required, on the move, and was an important input into the economy of the society. Barber says,

> [N]eedles came into being around 26,000 B.C.; clearly sewing of beads on garments took place. Thread was invented from twisting fibers, and this led the way to inventions such as snares, fishlines, tethers, leashes, carrying nets, handles, and packages.[3]

Twisted fiber string and thread were available in the Paleolithic period and by 15,000 B.C. people possessed the skills for making cordage, which pushed forward the development of sailing boats and commerce.[4]

The importance of cloth making goes far beyond the obvious. Clothing was nearly as essential as food and had economic value that, in turn, gave women a kind of power in the society. When, in later ages, the accumulation of private property by men meant that women's products also belonged to men, cloth was merchandised throughout the whole known world. One of the main bases for trade, cloth spurred exploration, travel, and the development of tools and later machinery to produce more and better cloth products. Through the invention of machinery to produce it, women's labor in cloth eventually led to factories and banking establishments for international trade, and finally to their expulsion from cloth making except as paid employees or for hobbies.

Until recently, we assumed that men's hunting provided most of the food for their wives and families. However, archeological data and studies of present-day nonindustrial societies show that gathering and scavenging by women was the most stable source of food.

> The techniques of hunting were probably much later developments. . . . When . . . adult males brought back food to share, the most likely recipients would be first their mothers, and second their siblings . . . a hunter would share food *not* with a wife or sexual partner, but with those who had shared food with him: his mother and siblings.[5]

The greater number of female than male deity figures indicates a sacred status for women, probably because of their seemingly magical ability to bear children and because they were the primary gatherers of food. Women served as priestesses of shrines, the centers of tribal life dedicated to goddesses of fertility and the harvest. Moreover, because of their childbearing, cloth-making, and food-gathering functions, they probably invented the first tools: containers to hold food, slings to hold babies, and cultural inventions such as social organization and communication.[6] Food sharing between mother and children developed into a rudimentary social welfare: mutual aid and caring for designated powerless people (children, the disabled) and those who had benefited the tribe (the aged and sacred).

> [T]he act of sharing is so frequently a matter of polity as well as etiquette that even when food is scarce and hunger is acute generosity is more likely to prevail over hoarding simply because the maintenance or strengthening of social bonds is so important in rudimentary societies.[7]

During the Neolithic period, from 25,000 B.C. to about 6000 B.C., pastoral societies flourished all around the Mediterranean Sea and in the valleys across North Africa and Asia. Where mild climates, fertile soil, access to water, and a sufficient growing season occurred naturally, societies retained their sex- and class-egalitarian nature for millennia. Communal life existed even after the Ice Ages from 15,000 to 10,000 B.C. However, a new polity evolved when, to ensure a more stable food supply, women developed the science of horticulture and men turned from hunting to the domestication and herding of animals. No longer nomadic, their societies developed the crucial social invention of private property, with men "owning" herds and, later, their grazing lands. Thereafter, because they owned the land, they owned its products, and the communal nature of food production changed to private production under the ownership of men.

A change in religion legitimated both the secondary status of women and the accumulation of private property. Around the fifth to second millennium B.C., men became aware of the connection between coitus and childbirth. Women's creative functions ceased to be thought magical, and women lost sacred status and became dependent on the goodwill of the men who supported them. If male support ended—through death, desertion, or divorce—women had few choices. They could become public dependents, bond themselves to a new master through marriage or agreement, enter prostitution, eke out a living, or starve. In all but the last, they remained under the control of a man or men. Gender oppression began with women's double loss of economic input and sacred status, until eventually they also became the property of the male landowners. Coward says,

> [T]he explanations of the emergence of the paternal . . . [procreative] family were explanations for the emergence of individual property rights. . . . First, individual interests were conflated with . . . transmission from father to genetic offspring. Second . . . it became possible to "sex" property, assuming a natural division of labour between the sexes. Men created it, therefore property was masculine.[8]

As female power declined, male power grew. Although both male and female deities were worshipped well into the Bronze Age (1200 B.C.), as men took power, men's religions became preeminent. In turn, these religions legitimated men's accumulation of wealth and power and their "god-directed" aggression against other tribes and peoples. They conquered societies and confiscated lands, herds, wealth, and often the people themselves as slaves, becoming a new class elite with class stratification and division of labor. The poor, free or enslaved, worked to accumulate more for their masters. As religion legitimated the accumulation of wealth and personal power, the elite's allegiance to religion brought religion more power.

The Beginnings of History: 6000–3000 B.C.

During the centuries between 6000 and 3000 B.C., wave after wave of migration—some peaceful and some based on conquest—surged across the world. Freedom from constant nomadism brought permanent settlements in areas most conducive to agriculture—around the Mediterranean, in the fertile basins of the Tigris and Euphrates Rivers, in the high plateaus of India, and along the valleys of the Nile in Egypt and the Yellow and Yangtze rivers of China. To the north, in the colder mountainous regions of the Caucasus, settlements were later in coming, and nomadic and warlike tribes presented a constant threat to the established societies of the warmer south.

Sharing was no longer the only means of personal and tribal survival, for as some people sank into poverty, new forms of social care were established. Altruism played a part, but a more pressing purpose was the coordination of work and protection under the political control of patriarchs: flooding and irrigation, adequate pasturing for herds, and control of marauding nomads. Patriarchal religions based on the needs to control workers and women (to ensure heir legitimacy) evolved. Massive efforts to ensure an orderly system of flood control, irrigation, and crop distribution were undertaken in China and Egypt, and dynasties also arose in pastoral areas around the Mediterranean and in the valleys of the Tigris and Euphrates rivers. The patterns of patriarchal classist societies developed among all the peoples of the known world.

Africa and Egypt

There is a curious hiatus in our thinking and knowledge about Africa that is based on pervasive Western racism. Long before the Egyptian dynasties, black Africans led the world in civilization. Africans used iron tools and mathematics, cultivated grain, painted pictures and created pottery of great beauty, and worshipped gods. Egypt owes much of its civilization to the influence of people from the interior of Africa. Although we usually think of Egyptians as white or Semitic, they were black-, brown-, and yellow-skinned people. At least one-third of the people in ancient Egypt were black Africans. Many Egyptian soldiers were black, and "Black peoples toiled on the pyramids, offered prayers to the sun-god, and served with distinction in the state bureaucracy."[9]

Throughout the ancient world, Africans were honored for their intelligence, their beauty, and the extent of their civilization. Ethiopians were described as "the most powerful, the most just, and the most beautiful of the human race."[10] For more than fifty centuries, they fought, traded, and intermarried with Egyptians, and Egypt's history is theirs also. Many Ethiopian pharaohs were of African descent, including the beautiful and venerated Queen Nefertari. In the middle of the eighth century B.C., the Ethiopian kings Kashta and Piankhy conquered Egypt, and Ethiopians ruled benevolently for more than a century, rebuilding Egypt's fortunes, abolishing capital punishment, and renewing its religions.

In ancient Egypt before 5500 B.C., a strongly matriarchal system existed, and the royal successor was probably female. As patriarchy gained power, there arose a strong inducement for sister–brother marriage, and the ruler of the First Dynasty was expressly said to be male.[11] From then on, the ruling houses, called "pharaohs," slowly shifted to male rule until even the word *pharaoh* came to mean *male ruler*. "Poor laws" developed to provide for a reasonably healthy and constant work force, with administrative channels for the poor to take their complaints directly to the pharaoh. It was believed that God gave the poor the power to curse their oppressors throughout eternity, and those in power feared the curse. Therefore, Egyptian social welfare was based on both the economic need for workers and the religious need for life after death.[12]

The need to build dikes against the ever-threatening floods caused the development of the corvée in which every adult man owed the pharaoh one year's work out of every seven. This was not slavery (although there were slaves in Egypt), but for that year the person belonged to the pharaoh and could be used to the death in his service. After systems of irrigation and flood control were well established, corvée labor built tombs and shrines. A bureaucratic system directed by a grand vizier was responsible for labor projects, for harvesting, storing, and distributing grain, and for charity oriented to maintaining the strength of laborers for work.

From the Fourth through Sixth Dynasties (2700–2200 B.C.), peasants were owned by mid-level lords. Dutiful work was among the strongest ethics, as was the accumulation of personal wealth through trade. Supplies were centrally controlled, and when uprisings occurred or when food was limited, frontiers were closed so that

> the available harvest and supplies would suffice for the local population. . . . Thus centralized planning and coordination are not inventions of the modern age and, specifically, careful provision of food supplies was a fundamental social welfare effort directly tied to national intentions and needs.[13]

Mesopotamia in the Bronze Age: 3000–1200 B.C.

In the fertile valleys of the Tigris and Euphrates rivers, a more pastoral, more diverse, and more egalitarian set of societies evolved. Not dependent on mass labor as in Egypt, they were smaller and less monolithic. Wave after wave of migrants settled with and assimilated into the Semitic tribes of the region. By about 3000 B.C., most cities were walled against aggression and came under the protection of individual warlords, and private ownership in herds of sheep and goats had begun. Shrines still provided for the needy, and those especially designated for care were widows, orphans, disabled people, and "strangers at the gate," or foreigners.

The creation of accounting methods and the rudiments of written languages developed among the Sumerians who moved into Mesopotamia in about 3000 B.C. Driven from their homes in central Asia by drought, they settled peaceably among the indigenous Semites in the area that is now Iraq and some parts of Turkey and Syria. At first, Sumerian leaders were elected by vote based on strength and popularity, as occurred in most prehistoric tribes, and this evolved into a system of rulers and ruled. Gradually the Sumerians took over the land until their families and clans collectively owned about seven-eighths of it, the rest belonging to shrines where as early as 2000 B.C., widows, orphans, and the poor were protected by the goddess Nanshe.[14] Land could be sold only if all the prominent members of the family or clan agreed, and the new owners became the ruling class or nobility. The land was worked for them by poor, landless freemen.

Three principal classes developed: the noble (*awilum*), or full citizen; the ordinary freeman, or second-class citizen (*mushkenum*); and dependent freemen, generally called "clients." Slaves were a fourth class, mainly prisoners of war, and were not citizens but chattel. Only the wealthy were given education, possibly daughters as well as sons. Aside from officials, about one-fifth of the population were craftsmen and the remainder were laborers. Men, women, and children worked at herding and irrigating, and they were paid in corn, wool, clothing, wine, and oil, or they might be paid in part or in full in silver.[15]

Around this time, Semitic tribes began conquests resulting in a series of short-lived dynasties: The Akkadian dynasty, established in 2750 B.C., ruled for 500 years. The dynasty of Ur, characterized as an efficient bureaucracy, lasted from 2100 B.C. to 2000 B.C. Amorite warriors formed a third dynasty, and then Babylon ruled. The sixth ruler, from 1792 to 1750 B.C., was Hammurabi, a benign ruler noted for social justice. He codified current laws and practices in the Stele of Hammurabi, developed several centuries before Moses, whose laws were similiar.[16] It demonstrated the general way of life until Babylon fell to Persia in 539 B.C. and set down laws particularly to protect widows, orphans, and the weak. Kingdoms in Mesopotamia depended mostly on agricultural production and flocks of sheep and goats and, for a time, their kings dealt peaceably with one another to pasture or irrigate lands. When conditions were particularly bad, arrangements might be made with a neighboring ruler to allow the flocks to cross into better-provided territory. At times, kings joined together in armies to prevent raids on their cultivated lands by the nomadic people of the desert.[17]

Until about 2000 B.C., shrines continued to serve the poor, distributing food in times of need. However, as societies evolved, the shrines began to lend at interest rather than give aid. Free peasants who had no resources in hard times gave themselves and their children into ownership of the temples, and by 1000 B.C. the shrines owned many prisoners of war, slaves donated or bequeathed, and formerly free people. However, temples remained an important source of care. Dolgoff and Feldstein say,

> There are three noteworthy points to observe about this ancient culture: temples were important economic forces; governmental action was taken to relieve

economic burdens and pressures, probably to avoid serious conflicts; and temples served as "social welfare" agencies, anticipating major religious institutional functions to follow in later centuries.[18]

Note here the synergism of economy, polity, religion, and social welfare.

Invasion, Conquest, and Patriarchal Religion

Pomeroy says,

> Patriarchal religion . . . appeared in recognizable form in about 3000 B.C. and is clearly associated with invasion—the Cretes by the Greeks, the Mediterranean by people from beyond the Caucasus, and so on. This . . . [shows] the connection of a powerful male deity with invasion and war.[19]

The association of patriarchal religion with aggression reified economic stratification and the accumulation of private property. Where once strangers and foreigners had been treated benevolently and aided, they were now "outgroups," people who worshipped other gods. It became a religious obligation to conquer or destroy them.

In about 2000 B.C., warlike tribes swarmed across the Caucasus and Transoceana and invaded the Persian highlands south of the Caspian Sea. Of greater size and strength than the indigenous people, they mowed through them from Greece to India with a deadly new war technology: horse-drawn war chariots with sickles on their wheels. So devastating were these invasions that, after more than twelve centuries of written records, a complete interruption occurred.

> Egyptian inscriptions virtually disappear between 1730 B.C. and 1580 B.C.; after the fall of Babylon around 1530 B.C. inscriptions in Babylonia also disappear . . . and are not resumed until 1400 B.C. Assyrian records vanish between 1720 B.C. and 1400 B.C. Hittite inscriptions suffer the same fate for more than a century. In short, a catastrophic hiatus occurred throughout the Middle East, a sort of Dark Ages brought about by multiple invasions of iron-bearing, horse-drawn chariot-riding barbarians . . . these great invasions . . . wrecked countless states, kingdoms, and even empires, and destroyed more than one rudimentary civilization.[20]

The invaders settled, intermarried, and assimilated into the indigenous Semitic tribes of the areas (see Figure 3.1). Their male war gods became predominant and tribal warfare became a way of life. Communally oriented societies became stratified by class and gender.

The Israelite Influence

In the fourteenth century B.C., a few Semitic tribes formed the Twelve Tribes of Israel, a coalition based on spreading monotheism across the known world. Their

FIGURE 3.1 *Peoples of Africa, Europe, and the Middle East, 6000–1500 B.C.*

method, in common with like societies of the era, was conquest. Early Israelite society laid the foundations of Western civilization: looking at monotheism alone we see that pattern of human/deity relationship as a cornerstone of belief through the ages, and the concept of coalition is mirrored at every societal level today. As with others on journeys through social evolution, they committed terrible acts and wonderful acts. That they were Israelite does not lessen either the horrendous or wondrous nature of those acts: social evolution is social evolution.

Inspired by a male war god to spread monotheism, they ravaged Assyria and much of the Middle East for three centuries. Perhaps more deadly than their enemies because they believed that worshipers of other gods should be killed, they often slew every person and every living creature and burned every field in the kingdoms they conquered. (This pattern was not invented by the Israelites and persists in warfare today.) Because their enemies were polytheistic and did not worship the Israelite god, their deaths were perceived as inconsequential. Conquest and assumption of the land, wealth, and people of "outgroups" was a religious obligation. Their new wealth and power demonstrated again the synergism among economy, power, and religion.

The Israelites laid the religious bases of Western Judaeo-Christian society, influencing social welfare in many unrecognized ways. Both the positive elements of dealing with the poor and the negative reasons for their dependency are clear in the Old Testament of the Bible, which demonstrates that, *like all other tribes emerging from the Bronze Age,* our Israelite ancestors were warriors. Although many prescriptions exist for care of widows, orphans, strangers, and the poor, these occurred three centuries after the period of conquest and may have been necessary reactions to aggression and restrictive patriarchy as the society matured. Before this happened, the oppression of women, the poor, and "outsiders from the faith" had been *set into society as religious precepts* for Western civilization.

The outstanding characteristics of the ancient Israelite tribes were aggressive and warlike behaviors, differentiation into classes of ruling elite and dependent vassals, and male-dominant or patriarchal authoritarianism. Caring for others, as it had arisen from an interdependent desert existence, no longer existed as part of the natural order except within the tribes. Rather, aid became a necessary addition to a stratified society, to maintain allegiance and a work force. Warlords and priests became the elite upper classes. The lower classes were artisans and laborers (*gerim,* who belonged to the tribe, and *metics,* or foreigners). *Gerim* were personally free but ritually impure, had no political rights, and could not own property, although they were given shelter and grazing rights. After the Exile, they were allowed intermarriage and conversion to Judaism, yet class stratification and, often, debt slavery continued. *Metics* had no protection or personal rights under law unless they bonded themselves to a warlord.[21]

In addition, allegiance to a male deity reified the secondary status of women. Pagan women could be killed out of hand or forcibly "married" to their conquerors. However, the social and legal position of Israelite women also suffered.

> The Decalogue ranked a wife among her husband's possessions, and while he could repudiate her she could not ask for divorce, and she remained legally a minor all her life. Wives and daughters did not inherit, except in the absence of male heirs.[22]

Wives called their husbands *ba'al* (master) or lord, as slaves addressed their masters. Although wives in Egypt and Babylon at that time were heads of families and could acquire property, take legal action, and inherit, Israelite women had no legal status. If husbands died, women were remarried to the husbands' brothers or put under guardianship of a male relative. This protected them in the society, but the society itself made the protection necessary.

Matrilineal inheritance was the pattern in surrounding polytheistic religions, but in patriarchal Israelite tribes, male line inheritance required celibacy for unmarried women and monogamy for married women. Stone says,

> [T]he lack of concern for the paternity of children among people of the Old Religion, which allowed matrilineal descent patterns to continue . . . was the crux of the persecution of ancient beliefs. [If] a religion existed alongside their own, a religion in which women owned property, were endowed with a legal identity, and were allowed to relate sexually to various men, it would be difficult for the Israelites to convince their women that they must be property. . . . Each woman must be retained as possession of one man for the purposes of legitimizing their children.[23]

The admonitions against women written into the Deuteronomic revisions of the Jewish Book of Law clearly delineate the fate of Israelite women who disobeyed sexual prohibitions. Unmarried women had to remain virgin and were stoned or burned if they did not.[24] Unmarried women, if raped, were married to the rapist. After marriage, women had to be monogamous, although men might acquire any number of wives and concubines. Adultery was an offense against the husband's property, so both men and women taken in adultery could be put to death.[25] Women could be divorced at will by their husbands,[26] and daughters, like slaves, could be sold by fathers. Non-Israelite women could be killed outright or, if virgins, could be taken as wives or slaves.

Although later Judaic teachings redressed ancient Israel's aggressive behavior, three particular groups became more vulnerable to poverty. One group was the poor, as class stratification occurred; the second was women, whose fate became dependent on the goodwill of men; and the third was "outgroup people"—those who, because they served other gods, were considered expendable and exploitable.

Moving into the Iron Age: 1200–400 B.C.

A thousand years before Christ, the legendary black Queen of Sheba made her visit to Solomon, and the riches of the earth seemed assured to Israel. It was the era of Zoroaster's revelation and the Magi of Persia,

> the age of Confucius, Lao-Tzu, and the great Chinese schools of philosophy, the age of the Upanishads and the Buddha in India, of Socrates, Plato, and Periclean Athens; of the great Hebrew prophets in Palestine—Elijah, Isaiah, and Jeremiah.[27]

The skill of writing became common and oral traditions fell into disuse. In Greece, Homer began to write his epic poetry. During the Archaic period (700–400

B.C.), both Greek and Roman civilizations grew to prominence. In Africa, the Ethiopian pharaoh Taharka steadfastly resisted the attacks of Assyrians, became a hero in Greek poetry, and ensured Ethiopia's sovereignty for centuries.[28]

After its period of conquest, Israel's powers began to decline from about the eleventh century B.C. Eventually, the Israeli people were captured and enslaved in Babylon and the prophets began to exhort the Jewish people to altruism. New laws began to address the grievances of the poor and the problems of women. Judaic charity rested on a priestly influenced community of free peasants and herdsmen,[29] and was based on humankind's relationship with God and a God-ordered responsibility for self and others. Because all belonged to God, charity and giving without thought of self or salvation was one's responsibility to God.[30] Need was the only requirement for aid, and help was a duty and a human right. Responsibility for self meant to work for one's own support but, when necessary, to receive help without shame (Jeremiah). Charity, prayer, and repentance were the three pillars of the world.[31]

Dolgoff and Feldstein say that "Judaism bases its requirements for altruism on essentially two concepts: *Tzedakah* (or *tzaddakah*), a mixture of charity and justice; and *Chesed,* loving kindness." The word for charity means righteousness or justice, and so giving charity meant being just or righteous, or as God required one to be. There was no special effort or conscious behavior denoted as being charitable: Honor to the poor was honor to God, and oppression was blasphemy. These concepts became law around the eleventh century B.C. and were codified in the Talmud after the Persian king Cyrus freed Israel from Babylonian captivity (600 B.C.). The Talmud is a collection of laws and traditions completed between 500 and 400 B.C. when, with imperial Persian approval, it became law for the Israelite people. Even today, it constitutes authority on social welfare among most Jews.[32]

The Talmud and the Old Testament laid out laws for the treatment of the poor, widows, children, the sick, the old, and strangers. The hungry were to be fed, the naked clothed, and the stranger sheltered.[33] Farmers were forbidden to glean the corners of their fields or to pick up fallen fruit, so that those in need might have them.[34] The hungry were allowed to eat from the crops of others, but could not carry food away with them.[35] Harvests every seventh year were dedicated to the poor, and in every fiftieth year—the Jubilee—slaves were emancipated and property outside the walled cities was returned to its original owners. (This has been seen as an attempt to lessen the importance of private property but might have continued class stratification because of the earlier unequal distribution of land.) In fact, there was no record of starvation in peaceful times in Judaic culture.

The universal and institutional perspectives of Judaic social welfare are among its most notable characteristics, for charity was without stigma. For example, in early times people reached into the community charity box either to deposit money or take it out without others knowing which they did. Dolgoff and

Feldstein say charity was institutionalized in two important respects: expected behavior of the donor and nonstigmatization and entitlement of the poor.

> Essentially, a culture developed that valued enterprise but without categorizing the poor as evil or idle . . . the society and individuals in it would be judged on the degree to which they provided for the poor without demeaning them.[36]

In later centuries, Hebrew philosopher Maimonides refined charity into eight degrees, ranging from giving grudgingly to preventing poverty. These refinements and earlier Judaic laws concerning social welfare have been carried out for centuries in the daily lives of the Jewish people. They constitute a major basis for the institutional perspective on social welfare in society today: that members of society have a right to receive help.

In the theory and practice of present-day Jewish religion, many of the problems of class stratification legitimated by the religion of their early ancestors have been redressed by what Miringoff and Opdycke call temporizing values—those that place humanistic charity before such overriding values as individualism and the work ethic.[37] However, in early societies, *all* Western tribal societies, including the Judaic, were warrior societies in which male deities legitimated oppression. This was coincidental to the era but is a fact of Western history, and the religious values that legitimate oppression still underlie our society.

The Dynasties of China

China's history parallels that of Egypt, though at a later date. In early years, leaders were elected, but by about 1500 B.C., short-lived dynasties had developed. By 1000 A.D., the patriarchal Chou dynasty had overthrown the matriarchal Shangs[38] and male rule became hereditary. Although clans and families owned property in common, the patriarch's decisions were absolute. Development of a feudal society coincided with patriarchy, and in about 800 B.C. monarchy developed. Serfs were taxed as property, so many were emancipated because of major tax assessments between 600 and 400 B.C. Left to fend for themselves, many turned to the state for help.[39] Buddhism, founded in 500 B.C., inspired its priests, such as Mencius in the fourth century B.C., to exhort China's rulers to care for the poor, and poverty was redefined as a holy state. A meager system of welfare developed, providing only food and shelter.

As feudalism collapsed, the ruling elite instituted the first unified Chinese empire in 221 B.C.[40] The emperor, as Son of Heaven, was owed obedience and loyalty but obligated by God to provide for his subjects.[41] Local patriarchs became an intermediary level of privileged bureaucrats over common people, who had few rights and were conscripted for armies and the government workforce on coordinated systems of irrigation and flood control. The bureaucracy was hierarchical, with two senior officials roughly corresponding to prime minister and head of civil service. Below them were offices of astrology, records, court and imperial household superintendent, security, crime and punishment, foreign affairs, treasury, and taxes and work projects. Next were forty-two civil service posts. The officials had their own social welfare system: one day of rest in five, sick leave, education for their children (the next generation of civil servants), and often retirement pensions of money or textiles.[42]

The bulk of the population was working-class commoners. In return for service to the emperor, they received a subsistence level of support. Each adult man served one month per year on state building projects, and each spent two years in the army.[43] By the first century B.C., in times of natural disaster the government's relief policy enabled the poor to buy food from its granaries or, if they could not pay, to receive free grain. In addition, the poor were taken from ravaged areas and resettled on new lands. We know little about poor women, but the patriarchal precepts of Confucius, teaching the traditional roles of wife and mother, came to prevail completely during the Han dynasty (200 B.C.–200 A.D.),[44] so we can assume few benefits for women apart from those of their men.

There were also noncitizens or substandard people, without rights to citizenship or social welfare. Slaves, less than 1 percent of the population, had been prisoners of war or children sold into slavery by their parents in times of hardship. Their masters had rights to their labor but not power of life and death. Those owned by the wealthy fared far better than did free peasants, who were subject to drought, famine, and pestilence. Concubines of the wealthy—sisters or female servants of their wives—were another group of the substandard, and were usually released from concubinage into marriage. Convicts in the well-developed system of criminal justice were also substandard people. Punishment included head shaving (signifying loss of life after death), a maximum sentence of five years at hard labor, beheading, or cutting in two at the waist. Relatives of convicts also became noncitizens and were confiscated along with other goods. In extreme cases, family members were exterminated also.[45]

India and the Caste System

Great civilizations developed in India well before 2000 B.C. but collapsed during the great patriarchal invasions. Indian society rebuilt, reifying the Hindu caste system and immutably setting inequalities in social position. The caste system had different effects for social welfare than did Western class systems. Poverty was not a condition for personal blame, nor was it traceable to unjust structures of society; rather, it was the effect of *karma*, a spiritual belief in reincarnation that placed people in life positions so that they might atone for past lives or prepare for future ones. Because one's position in the next life (reincarnation) was determined by actions in the present life, an obligation prevailed to care even for the lowest caste, the "untouchables,"along with a fatalism about the inevitability of poverty.

Rulers were enjoined to care for the poor by religious beliefs, but as in all societies, social aid was modified by economic and political elements. Nevertheless, as early as 300 B.C., hospitals and shelters for both people and animals were endowed by Prince Asoka of India. Much interpersonal helping was carried out by clans and kin within castes. For women, the caste system produced a rigid structure of inequalities within inequality, although women seemed to have far greater freedom in early Vedic times, when female deities held sway and before social and political patriarchy triumphed.[46] However, although in both China and India Tantric Buddhism emphasized the basic metaphysical equality between the sexes, neither granted women real equality. The freedom of Indian women was increasingly curtailed. They were not allowed education, and widows could not remarry, thus forcing them into poverty or prostitution if no male guardian would protect them. In fact, the problem of widows was solved by the practice of *suttee,* where widows were burned with their deceased husbands (along with other possessions). Although it is commonly believed that they went willingly to death because of their sorrow, if they refused they were bound and thrown on the pyre anyway.[47] Islamic invasions dating from about 700 A.D. exacerbated the position of Indian women, and until only recently, historically speaking, India lay under severely misogynist governments.[48]

Greece, Christianity, and the Roman Empire

Greece and the City–States

At about the time ancient Judaism triumphed in the Middle East, the societies of Greece and Rome began to develop. In Greece, during the Bronze Age, raids and forays to gain slaves and booty were the way of life. Military preparedness was vital, and men served as warriors while women served as bearers of future warriors. Still, because upper-class wives maintained homes and businesses for husbands away at war, they acquired some wealth and power and had higher status at the close of this period (about 700 B.C.) than at any other time until the Hellenic period, about the time of Christ (see Figure 3.2).

From 700 B.C. until about 400 B.C., colonization was the goal of conquest. Population pressure was one reason: There was a rise in fecundity and a decrease in infant and juvenile mortality, although there were twice as many men as women because of female infanticide. The Greek city–states were established by about 500 B.C., and many farmers left the land to become a new poor working class, exacerbating the already-present class stratification. To the early Greeks, work was a curse that brutalized the mind and made it unfit for thinking about truth or practicing virtue, and because work was despised, so was the worker. The wealthy became an elite class based on the labor of slaves and poor citizens. Slaves, whether men or women, did much of the work of ancient Greece. However, their status could actually be higher than that of freedpersons, depending on the wealth of their owners, and many when freed stayed with their old masters rather than become part of the poverty-stricken underclass.

Upper-class women in Athens were at first confined to the home. As their activities became more visible they became less valued, particularly because they

FIGURE 3.2 *European Peoples and the Persian Empire, 500 B.C.–300 A.D.*

worked at tasks deemed appropriate only to slaves. There was a steady erosion of their legal status and matrilineal inheritance, and they could not inherit their husband's property or incur debt, nor were their legal actions binding. Although they were citizens, they were under the guardianship of men (fathers, husbands, or male next-of-kin). Fathers arranged marriages to secure political liaisons and material bonds among families, retaining the right to revoke marriages. Girls were first married at about age fourteen to men twice that age, and many died young in childbirth. Dying or divorcing husbands arranged new marriages for their wives. A wife's rape or adultery required divorce and such women became outcasts, although the only penalty for rapists was a monetary fine.[49]

Women in the city–states of Sparta and Gortyn, though under the same general laws, had more status than did Athenian women because they could inherit from their husbands, too often killed at war. In time, women owned half the wealth of the cities. In Sparta, both men and women belonged to the state, and marriages were arranged eugenically. Children could be killed at birth because of physical weakness or deformity, for the goal was to produce superior people. However, once breeding obligations were fulfilled, sexual freedom—heterosexual or homosexual—was permitted. Homosexuality flourished in Greece, for the love of men for men was considered sacred. The women of Sparta and Lesbos were particularly valued among both men and women, and both homoerotic and heterosexual relationships were formed with the approval of society.[50]

For *poor* women in all the city–states, life was more difficult, although their status as virtual possessions of men by 500 B.C. gave them some protection. Pomeroy says that the lives of women lacking such protection were truly pitiful, especially if they had children, for most of the work they could do was done by slaves. Their work was essentially an extension of women's work in the home; they were washerwomen, workers in the clothing industry, vendors in the market, midwives, or nurses for children. Some became prostitutes, and some of these, the *hetairai,* even acquired transitory wealth and influence (though denied civil rights). Few Greek women became rich, but some foreign women who engaged in large-scale financial transactions did.[51]

The ideals of philanthropy and democracy, both important to Western social welfare, arose with the Greek city–states. Democracy was only for the free citizen, man or woman. Slaves and foreigners were excluded. The concept of *democracy,* though limited, entered into Western political thought to influence ideas about human rights.[52] It exists today in our value of individualism, in ideas of equality, and in the representative structure of American government. *Philanthropy* meant, in that era, the benevolence of gods toward humankind, but by the fourth century B.C. its meaning had evolved to refer to the obligation of the powerful to help their subjects or dependents. Greeks sought honor by giving donations of food, money, or oil to the city treasury for emergencies and food shortages, to citizen mutual aid societies, or to people of elite status in financial difficulty. Volunteer service in public offices was another road to honor, as was help to the "worthy poor"—generally nobles or merchants—who were well reared and educated but had fallen on hard times. The "unworthy poor" were people at the bottom of society—workers and the unemployed—and philanthropic gifts were denied them; they were not "worth" help because their gratitude did not bestow "honor." The unemployed were considered lazy and were expected to get along any way they could. Slaves were not eligible for citizenship and could not receive help. Needy foreigners were expected to return to their homelands. Beggars were rounded up and sent away, for aiding them was thought to encourage their pauperism. Poor, landless, or unemployed citizens were recruited as mercenary soldiers or given shares of land to colonize in far-off lands.

Caring for the poor in Greek city–states was self-seeking rather than altruistic. Still, hostels and medical centers, the remnants of older religious shrines, were scattered throughout the country, and the Athenian state distributed grain during food shortages—but only to citizens. There were also allowances and pensions for the crippled, public distribution of grain in bad times, and institutions for the custodial care of various unfortunates.[53] Orphanages and pensions were provided for children of fathers killed in war, and other orphans were supported until their eighteenth birthdays. However, attitudes toward the poor were harsh. Contraception, abortion, and infanticide were encouraged, and Plato urged euthanasia for the disabled or aged. Slavery, concubinage, and enforced colonization were also considered welfare, for the well-being of state rather than individual was the primary goal. Macarov believes that, despite the fact that the concept of philanthropy originated in Greece, the *spirit* of philanthropy never existed there, for

> the nature of the society was such that the citizens *were* the state. . . . [This] may have arisen from a lack of religious commandments concerning charity. A concept of gods who competed with people, manipulated people, and behaved like people did not lend itself to divine commandments concerning people's actions. . . . Indeed, according to Plato's *Republic*, the aged and the handicapped were to be done away with.[54]

In 359 B.C., Macedonian conquerors under Alexander the Great brought an end to the Greek city–states. This gradually ushered in new laws for women in all social classes. Earlier antifeminist legislation was rejected, and women were no longer confined to their houses. Polygamy, especially in royal families, became common, and divorce was often anticipated in marriage contracts. Queens ruled jointly with kings, and although women in Greece might need a male guardian, those in Hellenized areas away from the Greek mainland and in Egypt did not. The birthrate declined drastically, exacerbated by the practice of putting unwanted children out to die and the lack of interest in maintaining family lineage.

In response to the need for a growing population, new doctrines glorifying wife and mother roles for women arose, promulgated by the Stoics. Marriage and childrearing were elevated to the level of moral, religious, and patriotic duty. The straight-line, rational thinking and logic so loved by the Greeks were carried over into Roman society, and the dualistic reasoning of man as mind versus woman as body was reemphasized, particularly in the period of Christianization.

Early Roman Society and the Beginning of Christianity

Social welfare in Roman society was political. Whereas in Judaism it was given from kinship and caring and in Greece for honor, in Rome in the early Republic it was given in the form of doles—irregular gifts, especially to free men and boys—to gain votes. Therefore, only minimal help (if any) was given women and girls. Even wealthy women gave to men, for men held the power.

> The doles were motivated not so much by humanitarian reasons as by political desires to keep men pacified and curry favor with the crowds. . . . Since women, although citizens, could not vote, and their hunger was not likely to drive them to revolution, there was little point in including them in the largesse. Moreover, including women would have meant reducing the portions of men, and the benefactor would not have won the good will of those he courted.[55]

The dole was only enough for one, so wives and children of poor men might starve. However, eligibility depended not on need but on voting power, so even if they received a dole men could work to support their families.

In the late Republic (450–150 B.C.), there were a number of assistance programs in addition to the dole: occasional distributions of food by rich Roman citizens, private food programs, and public feasts established by private benefactors. In addition, trade and craft groups organized as collegia, giving monthly contributions to a common fund for mutual aid.[56] Patronage by the wealthy supported dependent workers with food, clothing, shelter, and other necessities. Some children's assistance programs were set up in the early Empire (100 B.C.–100 A.D.) specifically for future recruitment of soldiers. Boys received more money than girls and were supported until age seventeen or eighteen. Girls were not supported as often—in one town, of 300 recipients, only thirty-six were girls—and their doles were at a lower level and stopped at age fourteen, when they were expected to marry. Female infanticide and neglect meant a higher death rate for girls, and if they lived, their life span was shorter by five to ten years than that of males because of poor health resulting from malnutrition and childbearing at an early age.[57] Life expectancy in general was short, about forty or fifty years for the elite class. Over half the wives of the poor died before age thirty, most between twenty and twenty-five.

Patriarchy was a major characteristic of both the late Republic and early Empire. The *paterfamilias*, or father of the family, had absolute authority (*manus*) over women and children, even to slavery and death. Only men had legal rights; women could not appear in court, buy or sell property, or inherit their husbands' estates. Husbands judged their wives for crimes and could sentence them to death even for misdemeanors, and certainly for infidelity. Priestesses and wealthy courtesans had some autonomy, as did freedwomen of guilds and crafts, who were not supervised by their husbands and seemed really to be free.[58] Most poor freedwomen, however, were working-class shopkeepers, artisans, domestics, woolworkers, or clothes makers. Slaves, men or women, could buy their freedom (*manumission*), but many stayed with their former owners rather than being released into the ranks of the poor to starve.

At the turn of the millennium, Greek, Roman, Jewish, Egyptian, and Eastern societies converged and blended, and Rome moved fully into the Empire to become ruler of the Western world (see Figure 3.3). Its territories expanded as far as the British Isles, and conquests amassed riches for the ruling class. Great wealth led to increasing corruption and even wider disparities between the rich and poor. The need for defense garrisons in far-flung lands and profligate spending by those in power led to huge tax assessments. Unbelievable poverty existed: By the second century A.D., despite dole and patronage systems, "of 1.2 million people, all but 150,000 heads of families in Rome needed to draw on public foods, and in Constantinople another 80,000 were receiving free food."[59]

The financial structure was based on a tax system in which the poor were assessed proportionately more, significantly increasing poverty and bringing even less money into the central treasury as former workers fell into bankruptcy. For centuries Rome had hired mercenaries to man troops, but now wealth was concentrated in individual estates rather than in the central government, and mercenaries could no longer be paid.

This destructive economic stratification was only one of the internal problems besetting the Roman Empire. Internal revolt arose on all fronts: slaves under Spartacus, for example, or the revolt of Palestine in 66 A.D., where, in retaliation four years later, Titus razed Jerusalem. Jews, whose laws and customs differed from Roman laws, sought new political power, and radical Jewish zealots agitated for religious freedom. Among non-Jews, the religion of Isis, spreading from Egypt, brought new hope to the poor and enslaved, inspiring revolt. Its primary converts were the disenfranchised—women and the poor—who gained little from the male dominant and class-stratified state religion of Rome (under the war-god Mithras). Roman religion denied religious office to most women and all slaves and freedpersons, but the cult of Isis allowed women as well as men, slave as well as freedperson, and poor as well as rich into its hierarchy. Each insurrection increased demands on the Empire's strained economy.

From the time of the late Republic, women were increasingly emancipated. New marriage laws took away the rights of the *paterfamilias* and set limits on the legal subjection of wives. Common-law marriages were usual, and a wife could retain her legal position by bearing three children or spending three nights a year away from her husband's home. After 195 B.C., women could administer their own dowries and divorce their husbands at will. By the end of the Republic, upper-class women were equal with men and owned much of Rome's wealth. In 18 B.C. Augustus brought marriage under control of the state because, as upper-class women refused to have children, Rome had increasingly fewer men to become controllers, officers, and bureaucrats in Rome's far-flung Empire. However, the birthrate among the lower class remained stable, producing ever more children born into poverty and more fuel for rebellion. At the same time, Teutonic barbarians began a series of increasingly successful border

FIGURE 3.3 *Roman Territory by 264 B.C.*

wars and raids against the Empire. Rome was beset from both within and without.

Jesus and the New Religion

Into this time Jesus was born, a revolutionary who opposed both class and gender oppression. He reminded Jewish society of its prophetic past and spiritual teachings regarding the poor and oppressed and decried the personal accumulation of wealth, emphasizing that unless their bounty was shared, rich men could not attain salvation.[60] Although Jesus and many of his associates were of the middle class, his appeal to the poor was immense. For a time, egalitarianism and communal sharing of resources and work were attempted, and leaders of the new religion encouraged the wealthy to take responsibility for the poor.

Jesus came from a patriarchal society (Judaism) that was very aware of class stratification but blind to the oppression of women. His awareness of gender oppression probably came from ideals of gender equality in Greek society and from the religion of Isis. Both women and men became his disciples, and one of his closest disciples was Mary Magdalene.[61] He overturned inequalities of punishment for sexual offenses,[62] revised marriage laws to give women protection against divorce,[63] enforced monogamy on men as well as women, and recognized women's spiritual status.[64] Although patriarchy reasserted itself in the new religion within three centuries of his death, Jesus' teachings on women's spirituality and equality were clear.

Two perspectives on women fought for primacy in Christianity in the following centuries. The Byzantine Church and movements such as Gnosticism and Montanism regarded both men and women as spiritual beings. Gregory of Nyssa, for example, postulated that both sexes have a spiritual and a bodily nature[65] and all have access to God through redemption. Rome's Paulist doctrines, advocated by Augustine (354–430 A.D.) and Tertullian (c. 130 A.D.), posited that men were beings of spirit and intellect whereas women represented earthliness and sin. Their ideas were based on women's (Eve's) original sin and on Paulist letters about women's proper place in home and church, that is, as secondary to husband in all matters sacred and secular.[66] Such teachings reconfirmed the patriarchy of Jewish and early Roman and Greek societies. By 300 A.D., the Roman Church had decreed Gnosticism heresy, disallowed teachings of the spiritual equality of women, and decreed that women, because of their deficient natures, could be redeemed only by their husbands or by renouncing their womanhood to enter convents. These doctrines became dominant in Western society and are transmuted today into societal sex roles, including women's dependency.

Christianity was a blending of Greek thought, Jewish teachings, and the resurgence of ideas on class and gender equality from the religion of Isis. Although we generally think of its center as Rome, in the early days the Roman Church was basically a small illegal enclave of Hellenized Jews and Greeks. Jesus was a Jew from Semitic Asia Minor, and his teachings were first and more enduringly accepted there. Until the fourth century A.D., when Christianity became Rome's state religion, most of the Roman clergy were recruited from the Eastern Church centered in Constantinople. The Latin Church did not have time to grow, for all Rome's energies, including those of the church, went to protect the city, the greatest prize of the Empire for invading barbarians.

> [T]he Latin Church was soon engulfed by the barbarian invasions and, with little time for pointless theological disputations, had to take over the main burden of preserving what was left of civilization during the Dark Ages.[67]

In the Eastern Church, an extensive system of relief developed. Christians pooled their possessions to provide a daily distribution of food. Both men and women were teachers and leaders, and women of wealth were instrumental in financing Christianity's growth and activities, establishing hospitals and monasteries, and working with the poor:

> [T]he Byzantines [were] a nation . . . characterized by . . . many works of practical philanthropy . . . a virtue not only of the rich and prominent, but of all organizations and classes of people.[68]

In both Eastern and Roman Churches, care for the needy became a major activity. In a sense, poverty was sanctified by Jesus, and early Christians based an "ethic of poverty" on his teachings.[69] To aid the poor was like having aided Jesus himself. Poverty, not wealth, was the way to salvation. The poor, slaves, widows, orphans, and those imprisoned, exiled, or working in mines as punishment for their Christian beliefs were aided. From the first, women were actively engaged in charitable works, opening the first hospitals and even the first monastic communities. Because Christians met in each other's homes, the concept of hospitality was elevated to religion.[70]

Ideas of work, private property, and wealth changed. Work was no longer degrading, as Christians worked to support themselves, to demonstrate their worth to nonbelievers, and to serve the needy. Private wealth was considered immoral by early Christians because it created class disparities, but the religion's leaders soon realized it was a permanent characteristic of society and developed a new doctrine on wealth. Now the wealthy "owed" the needy the excess products of their wealth. By the fourth century, the good that wealth could do and the salvation it would provide for the rich were major tenets of the religion. Salvation depended on how one treated the needy: the hungry, thirsty, strangers, those needing clothes, the sick, and prisoners.[71]

By the middle of the second century, Christian charity was organized, with each church member expected to give a regular donation, often weekly, to the poor box. In addition, contributions of bread and wine were collected at the Eucharist and a chosen officer, often a bishop, distributed the excess to the poor of the congregation.[72] Although at first this care was restricted to Christians, it was later extended to the poor regardless of religion. Christianity became legal in 313

A.D. and was declared the state religion of the Empire under Constantine in 361 A.D., with his personal conversion. He believed that religion should be responsible for the needy, and Christianity became the state agency for charity. State, church, and voluntary social welfare functions thereafter overlapped and the state was relieved of some of its burden regarding the poor. Privately endowed foundations, especially in Italy, invested capital in real estate mortgages, and interest was given to towns or state administrators for charitable uses. In Byzantium, clergy distributed assistance, and in Rome, a private voluntary group administered a state-supported social welfare system.[73]

State and Church in Rome

Chastising the rich in the third century, St. Cyprian said, "[They] add properties to properties and chase the poor from their borders. Their lands extend without limit or measure."[74] Although feudalism—in which serfs are hereditarily bound to the land and service to its lord—did not develop for centuries elsewhere in Europe, it began in Rome even before the fall of the Empire (about 476 A.D.) as Rome disintegrated under internal forces and repeated Teutonic barbarian attacks. Many of the poor traded their freedom to wealthy landowners for protection in walled "manors." Small freeholders placed their land under the lord's control and became tenant farmers. The urban poor, competing with slaves for scarce jobs, also bonded themselves into serfdom, along with runaway slaves, army deserters, vagabonds, tax-ruined farmers, and peaceful immigrants from barbarian tribes. Accustomed to hereditary service, by the fourth century these serfs were officially tied to the land.[75] Large Roman estates expanded considerably, and the lords were relieved of labor worries while their wealth was ensured.

Rome's ability to support itself and the Empire was dealt a fatal blow in 410 A.D. when Visigoths, under Alaric the Great, destroyed the city and pillaged nearly its entire wealth.[76] In such a weakened state, the Empire was easy prey for waves of Teutonic invaders eager for its fabled opulence. The whole central ruling structure collapsed and western Europe was left in disarray, reverting to localized tribes. Cities shrank and trade and communications diminished. Although several kingdoms followed the Roman Empire, none were able to hold the vast area together. Intermarriage between the invaders and the Roman senatorial and landowning classes took place in Gaul, Spain, and Italy, and from this sprang the feudal nobility that was to rule Europe. Angles and Saxons invaded Britain to be overthrown in turn by Danes and Normans. The process of barbarization became irreversible, plunging western Europe into the Dark Ages (see Figure 3.4).

As the Roman Empire fell, the power of the Holy Roman Church rose. It attracted the best administrative and political talents that the Western classical world had to offer and substituted its own bureaucracy for that of the collapsing imperial machinery. Roman civilization and culture now rested in the hands of the Church. The invading kings, respecting that culture, converted to Christianity. This legitimized the new royalty with the Catholic people of the conquered regions and demonstrated the power of the Church at king making. Whereas the

FIGURE 3.4 *Barbarian Invasions, 400–500 A.D.*

Church had been a creature of the state, now many states owed the Church fealty and its spiritual bond held the Western world together.

A synergistic spiral of power occurred: The conversion of conquerors to Christianity gave them power over the local populaces, whereas the right to crown kings bestowed political power on the Roman Church. Now political rulers could claim they ruled by divine right, and because Rome conferred this right on the many kings, uniting them in spirit, the Holy Roman Empire became the center of power throughout Europe. For example, in the fifth century, Clovis, the victorious king of the Salic Franks in Gaul, was baptized a Christian along with 3,000 Frankish warriors. He then allied with other Christians and defeated his Visigoth and Burgundian enemies. With his Christian wife, Clothilde, he subsequently turned Roman Gaul into what would become France.[77]

Conclusion: Beginnings of Charity and Control

In this chapter, we have considered the history of humankind and mutual aid, traveling across cultures, from Western to Eastern; across time, from prehistory to the beginning of the Holy Roman Empire; and across religions, from prehistoric, polytheistic deity worship through monotheism to the beginnings of Christianity. Through all this, the synergistic relationships of religion, economics, and politics that evolved class and gender stratification have been demonstrated, and we have seen social welfare change from communal mutual aid to a complex system that not only helped the poor but controlled their work behavior. Women's loss of economic and sacred power made them possessions of men, and class differentiation put the mass of workers under the control of a small male-dominated ruling elite. In every society, as humankind moved toward patriarchy and private property, a new political economy based on class stratification and gender oppression evolved, and religiously legitimated exploitation became commonplace.

The history of social welfare is also a history of societies and cannot be considered apart from them. The societies of our ancestors, whether Jewish, Greek, Roman, barbarian, or Christian, reified gender and class stratification even though their religions ostensibly relieved oppression. Within each, social welfare took on new meanings with new times. In Judaism, social justice and human need were the keynotes, providing an institutional perspective that underlies some aspects of our social welfare today. Greek society developed ideals of both democracy and philanthropy, although the meanings of those ideals were far different in those times than today. Roman society, a blending of many trends from the past, gave us political structures and processes that continue to affect our legal and social systems. Christian altruism as taught by Jesus is still part of social welfare today. On the other hand, in the following centuries, patriarchal church leaders continued patterns of oppression as well as aid. The Holy Roman Empire became a religio-political system of diverse kingdoms under the spiritual leadership of Rome, and a spiral of power between kings and church ensured the success of Christianity in the Western world and the success of royal lineages in the many kingdoms of feudal Europe.

Social welfare came full circle, for again religion was responsible for the poor, although its tenor had changed. Poverty was still considered the result of social and economic conditions (rather than personal fault) and was redefined as a holy state. Although the Holy Roman Church worked ceaselessly to alleviate the misery of the poor, through its benisons to kings and the ruling elite it also helped to maintain structures that perpetuated oppression. The poor remained subject to the whims and desires of ruling elites in their pursuit of wealth and power, and social welfare became a means by which such goals were achieved. In all, synergistic relationships created forces that, a few centuries after the birth of Christianity, would set the economic, political, and religious overtones for social welfare in the world today.

Study Questions

1. What were some of the reasons for prehistoric social treatment? Social control?

2. What is patriarchal religion? What was its effect on women, outsiders, and the poor after it became established in Western civilization?

3. Explain the similarities in social treatment and social control among such disparate dynasties as those in China, India, and Egypt. How did they differ from dynasties in the Near East?

4. What were the connections among polity, economy, and religion in the Holy Roman Empire?

5. What was the significance of cloth making to the status of women in prehistoric times? What was the significance of its change to male control in terms of the institutions of polity, economy, and family?

Notes

1. Kathleen Gough, "The Origin of the Family," in Rayna Reiter (ed.), *Toward an Anthropology of Women* (New York: Monthly Review Press, 1975), pp. 62–63.

2. Elizabeth Wayland Barber, *Women's Work: The First 20,000 Years* (New York: W.W. Norton and Co., 1994), p. 25.

3. Ibid., pp. 43–45.

4. Ibid., p. 53.

5. Sally Slocum, "Woman the Gatherer: Male Bias in Anthropology," in Rayna Reiter (ed.), *Toward an Anthropology of Women* (New York: Monthly Review Press, 1975), pp. 45–46.

6. Ibid.

7. Ralph Dolgoff and Donald Feldstein, *Understanding Social Welfare*, 2nd ed. (New York: Longman Press, 1984), p. 26.

8. Rosalind Coward, *Patriarchal Precedents: Sexuality and Social Relations* (London: Routledge & Kegan Paul, 1983), p. 67.

9. Lerone Bennett, Jr., *Before the Mayflower: A History of the Negro in America, 1619–1964* (Chicago: Johnson Publishing Company, 1966), p. 7.

10. Quoting Lady Flora Louisa Lugard, *Tropical Dependency* (London, 1911), in Bennett, *Before the Mayflower,* p. 5.

11. W. Flinders Petrie, *Social Life in Ancient Egypt* (London: Constable and Co., 1923), p. 110.

12. Max Weber, *Ancient Judaism* (New York: Free Press, 1952), p. 252; and Noel Timms, *Social Work* (London: Routledge & Kegan Paul, 1973), pp. 17–18.

13. H. W. F. Saggs, *Everyday Life in Babylonia and Assyria,* 2nd ed. (New York: G.P. Putnam's Sons, 1967), p. 29.

14. Taken from Samuel N. Kramer. Quoted in Dolgoff and Feldstein, *Understanding Social Welfare,* p. 30.

15. Saggs, *Everyday Life,* pp. 66–68.

16. Ibid., p. 138.

17. Ibid.

18. Dolgoff and Feldstein, *Understanding Social Welfare,* p. 30.

19. Sarah B. Pomeroy, *Goddesses, Whores, Wives, and Slaves: Women in Classical Antiquity* (New York: Schlocken Books, 1975), pp. 12–13.

20. Amaury De Riencourt, *Sex and Power in History* (New York: Dell Publishing, 1974), p. 76.

21. Weber, *Ancient Judaism,* pp. 32–33.

22. De Riencourt, *Sex and Power,* p. 87.

23. Merlin Stone, *When God Was a Woman* (New York: Harcourt Brace Jovanovich, 1976).

24. Deuteronomy 22:23–25; Leviticus 21:19.

25. Deuteronomy 22:23–25.

26. Deuteronomy 24.

27. De Riencourt, *Sex and Power,* p. 79.

28. Bennett, *Before the Mayflower,* pp. 10–11.

29. Weber, *Ancient Judaism,* p. 258.

30. Isaiah 58:5–7.

31. Walter Trattner, "The Background," in Neil Gilbert and Harry Specht (eds.), *The Emergence of Social Welfare and Social Work,* 2nd ed. (Itasca, IL: F.E. Peacock Publishers, 1981), p. 22.

32. Pirke Avit 3:8 and 1:2. In Dolgoff and Feldstein, *Understanding Social Welfare,* p. 32.

33. Deuteronomy 15:8.

34. Leviticus 19:9; Deuteronomy 24:19–22.

35. Deuteronomy 23:24–25.

36. Dolgoff and Feldstein, *Understanding Social Welfare,* p. 32.

37. Marc L. Miringoff and Sandra Opdycke, *American Social Welfare: Reassessment and Reform* (Englewood Cliffs, NJ: Prentice Hall, 1986).

38. De Riencourt, *Sex and Power,* pp. 170–174.

39. Dolgoff and Feldstein, *Understanding Social Welfare,* pp. 28–29.

40. De Riencourt, *Sex and Power,* p. 182.

41. Michael Loewe, *Everyday Life in Early Imperial China* (New York: Harper & Row, 1968), p. 30.

42. Ibid., p. 31.

43. Ibid., pp. 70–75.

44. Dolgoff and Feldstein, *Understanding Social Welfare,* p. 29.

45. Loewe, *Early Imperial China,* pp. 61, 68.

46. De Riencourt, *Sex and Power,* pp. 161–177.

47. Mary Daly, *Gyn/Ecology: The MetaEthics of Feminism* (Boston: Beacon Press, 1978), pp. 145–146.

48. De Riencourt, *Sex and Power,* pp. 77–78.

49. Ibid., p. 132.

50. Ibid., p. 156.

51. Pomeroy, *Goddesses,* p. 202.

52. Dolgoff and Feldstein, *Understanding Social Welfare,* p. 36.

53. Pomeroy, *Goddesses,* p. 228.

54. David Macarov, *The Design of Social Welfare* (New York: Holt, Rinehart & Winston, 1978), p. 76.

55. Pomeroy, *Goddesses*, p. 202.

56. Gerald Handel, *Social Welfare in Western Society* (New York: Random House, 1982), p. 225.

57. Pomeroy, *Goddesses*, p. 228.

58. Ibid., p. 198.

59. Marc Bloch, *Feudal Society: The Growth of Ties of Independence*, Vol. 1, translated by L. A. Maryont (Chicago: University of Chicago Press, 1964), p. 61. Quoted in Handel, *Western Society*, p. 31.

60. Matthew 7:30 and 9:24.

61. This is discussed in the Gnostic Gospels; De Riencourt, *Sex and Power;* and Michael Baigent, Richard Leigh, and Henry Lincoln, *Holy Blood, Holy Grail* (New York: Dell Publishing, 1982).

62. John 8:3–11.

63. Matthew 19:8–9.

64. Luke 8:2–54; Acts 9:17.

65. Galatians 3:28.

66. Timothy 2:9–15; Ephesians 5:22–24.

67. De Riencourt, *Sex and Power*, p. 154.

68. D. Constantalelos, *Byzantine Philanthropy and Social Welfare* (New Brunswick, NJ: Rutgers University Press, 1968), p. 11; and Macarov, *Design of Social Welfare*, p. 76.

69. Mark 10:25; Luke 6:20.

70. Dolgoff and Feldstein, *Understanding Social Welfare*, p. 36.

71. Handel, *Western Society*, p. 49.

72. Handel, *Western Society*, p. 48.

73. Ibid., p. 34.

74. Ibid., p. 35.

75. De Riencourt, *Sex and Power*, p. 41.

76. Ibid., p. 154.

77. Ibid.

4

Feudalism and the Welfare State

Many forces changed Western society, first to a feudal society and then to states in which laws regulated the treatment of laborers and the poor. Religion was one such force: The Roman Church completed the conversion of all barbarian peoples in Europe around 1000 A.D., legitimating kings and legitimated in turn by the new European rulers who appointed priests, bishops, and even popes. The Scientific Revolution and its growing agricultural technology was another, moving humankind from its organic relationship with nature and placing the power of production in the hands of an elite. Feudalism and church power changed as the Commercial Revolution brought the onset of capitalism and the Protestant Reformation. Social welfare became control rather than aid for the poor.

The Dark and Middle Ages

Between the fall of the Roman Empire and the creation of the Magna Carta in 1215, the Dark Ages descended on Europe. Without a unifying government, cities shrank and communication and travel were disrupted. But the world was far from "dark" in the sense of stagnant. New forms of polity, economy, and religion were fermenting to create the framework for Western society. Throughout Europe, would-be kings fought to maintain new territories, and the common people suffered as wars raged across their lands. The Christian religion continued its rise in the Byzantine and Holy Roman Empires, and Islam rose and conquered great swaths of the Middle East, Africa, and Europe, bringing with it new concepts of government and scholarship (see Figure 4.1).

In the Byzantine world, Constantinople remained the center of civilization until the thirteenth century (see Figure 4.2). More influenced than Rome by egalitarian philosophies and traditions, the Eastern church discouraged both class and gender stratification. In Asia Minor, Syria, and Egypt, peasants settled into

FIGURE 4.1   *Christianity, 600–1500* A.D.

small farms and villages as free farmers. Taxes were reasonable, and in hard times the government and church collaborated to buy products and ensure employment in the monasteries.[1] Whereas women in the Roman Church remained under the hard hand of patriarchy, Byzantine women were free under the famed Justinian Code of Laws (Justinian and Theodora, 527–565 A.D.). In the East, inheritance through women was retained, the penalty for adultery was reduced from death to life in a convent (although men were still subject to capital punishment), and rape became punishable by death, with the rapist's property given to the injured woman.[2] Women and men often reigned together, and by the seventh century a church-supported welfare state had developed in Alexandria, with maternity hospitals, medical facilities, and food rationing.[3]

In the seventh century, the new religion of Islam swept across Arabia and the Middle East, into Africa to the south, and to the Pyrenees Mountains in Europe. By the eleventh century, it had seized Hungary, Poland, and Prussia from the Byzantine Empire. An aggressive and militant monotheism, it followed earlier monotheistic traditions by wiping out old religions and eradicating the rights

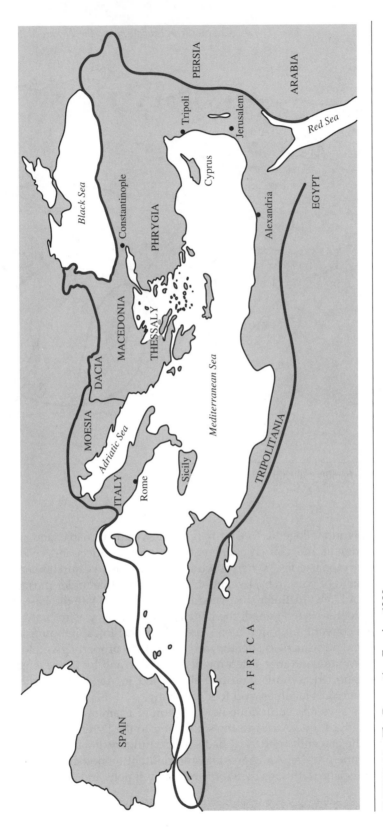

FIGURE 4.2   *The Byzantine Empire, 1200* A.D.

of women.[4] Although a few royal women retained power, most were totally sub-jugated and veiling, once a mark of honor, became required as women were iso-lated in homes and harems. Moral living and right conduct were at the core of Islamic belief, and it promoted an ethic of individual work and commercialism not unlike later Calvinist and Puritan beliefs. New sciences, including architec-ture and engineering, and new concepts of mathematics with Arabic numerals were developed by its scholars, and the concept of nation–state was instituted. By the twelfth century, Islamic hospitals were magnificently built and equipped and Islamic universities were the centers of scholarship and culture.

In Africa, the Sudanese kingdoms of Ghana, Mali, and Songhay, newly in-fluenced by Islam, rivaled those of Rome. The University of Sankore in Songhay's Timbuktu was the world center of learning for law, surgery, and history. Ghana reached its peak early in the eleventh century, and Songhay apexed in the fif-teenth century under the brilliant King Askia (1493–1512). He was said to be the equal of and superior to many European monarchs of the time,[5] and his realm, larger than all Europe, encompassed most of West Africa. The great Sudan em-pires ended in the seventeenth century, although states in East and South Africa, the East Coast, and Southern Rhodesia and Zimbabwe were centers of trade and culture into the eighteenth and nineteenth centuries.

In Europe, a hectic transition to a new kind of civilization began with the fall of the Roman Empire. Teutons, Franks, Visigoths, Angles, Saxons, and Celts warred across the continent, and about the time Justinian ruled the Byzantine Em-pire (527–565 A.D.), feudalism began its rise in France and Italy. Saxon kingdoms were established in England in the years 490–530, and in the eighth century the Viking Danes invaded England, to be defeated by Alfred the Great. In 800 Charle-magne was crowned by the pope as King of Italy, Germany, and France, founding the new Western empire, and two centuries later Macbeth murdered Duncan and usurped the throne of Scotland.

Normans and Saxons fought for control of England until, at the Battle of Hastings, William the Conqueror became king (1066). A short-lived feudalism came to England, ending in the thirteenth century with the signing of the Magna Carta by King John in 1215. The document granted civil rights to the people of England, but because it challenged the "divine right of kings," it was immediately annulled by the pope. Thereafter, it was reissued three times in modified form by Henry III (1216–1272). Toward the end of the Dark Ages, Huns and Poles repeat-edly invaded Russia, and Genghis Khan subdued the North of China in 1216. By 1236 Mongolians and Tartars under Batu Khan were invading Russia and Europe, burning Moscow in 1236 and ending Russian independence. By 1259, Kublai Khan had united China and built Peking as his capital.

Women had little status in Europe, except among the liberal Visigoths, under whose laws they jointly administered community property with their hus-bands and could claim a share of the land if the husband died first. In general, however, women were perpetual minors and possessions, to be bought and sold in marriage. Rape was a property crime against the husband, polygamy was common, and divorce or renunciation of wives and concubines was easy. Al-though there were queens and female warriors, most women were adjuncts to the male household and under feudalism belonged as well to the liege-lord and the estate. Marriage of feudal serfs involved a "bride price" to be paid to the lord. If the bride were comely, the price could be increased beyond the groom's means. By *droit de seigneur,* when the new price was defaulted, the husband could be thrown out and the wife raped by the lord, his knights, squires, pages, and possibly the chaplain. This was considered an honor for a mere peasant woman.[6]

Christianity enforced monogamy and decried divorce, and in this way brought a somewhat better life for women. By the eighth century, adult Frankish women were free of male guardianship, and by the tenth century Anglo-Saxon women had considerable power over property. Upon the husband's death, if there was no male heir, widows could inherit lands and title even if remarried, for the land belonged to family rather than individual. Also, in the rapidly growing cities, working women were freed from male domination of their earned property. Toward the end of the Dark Ages, married or single women could hold land, sell it, give it away, own goods, make a will or a contract, sue and be sued, and plead in the law courts in England and in Europe.[7] However, not until the eleventh century was a law written to forbid the selling of women.

The Feudal Society

Prefeudal Europe was a rural free-peasant economy counterpointed by great medieval cities in which the church and the rich held sway. Family and community constituted the fundamental economic units, although each farm family shared the natural resources of the territorial commons (forests, pastures, and water). Communal resources were regulated by elected or appointed officers. Women and men worked their freeholds and resisted the would-be kings warring across their lands. The European population between the Baltic and the Mediterranean, estimated to have been 27 million in 700 A.D., reached 60 or 70 million by 1200. The creation of a bourgeois class brought with it the emancipation of the rural masses.[8]

In the best of times the lives of peasants were in constant jeopardy; life expectancy for all people was no more than forty years or so. Harsh living conditions, poor health care, and poor nutrition made people weak, small in stature, prone to illness, and decimated by the plagues that periodically swept across Europe. Death by war was common for men, and childbirth a mortal hazard for women, rich or poor. Strayer and Munro say,

> While . . . there was much inequality in normal times . . . all [were] equally helpless in periods of misfortune. They all lived in unsanitary conditions; they had no doctors, and at times pestilence swept away whole communities. Few families could store grain; a year of flood or drought created terrible famines. The peasants could not defend themselves against heavy-armed feudal cavalry, and if their lord became involved in a war they were almost sure to see their fields ravaged and their houses burned.[9]

Feudalism did not come easily to Europe, for peasants dreaded the near slavery of serfdom, which was

> a degrading thing. . . . What men feared and resented . . . was not its subordination but its arbitrariness. The hatred of that which was governed not by rule, but by will, went very deep in the Middle Ages.[10]

Finally, however, force and the need for military security made peasants give up their lands and freedom and swear allegiance to local strongmen. They bonded themselves to a lord in return for protection and rights to land use (as tenants or in "commons"). Every person had an ascribed status: Roles were predetermined, inherited, and immutable (as opposed to being achieved through work or effort). According to Handel,

> Feudal society was the quintessence of hereditary aristocracy, privilege by birth instead of proved merit. A virtually impassable gulf separated the ruling class of lords and their fief-holders from the masses of peasants. Whatever their virtues or their vices, the rulers monopolized wealth, power, and prestige.[11]

Feudalism tied landhold with military service, and there was an "embeddedness" in the relationships among serfs, lords, and sovereigns. Nonfree peasants owed their lives and work to the lord, and he owed them protection and good management of the community so that, in hard times, they might survive. Lords had land, power, a stable workforce, the right to military conscription for their own battles and those of their sovereigns, and taxing power without redress. In time, the care of serfs by liege-lords became a kind of trust, a *noblesse oblige*, or obligation of honor, and in theory all were provided for. However, the lord's right took precedence over every right, need, facet of life, or desire of the serfs. Every man and woman was bound to the lord, and brutal treatment, up to and including rape and murder, was not uncommon.

As the centuries passed, the serfs won some concessions. Many "owned" their property and their heirs could "inherit" if each swore fealty to the lord. As population increased and agricultural technology changed, serfdom became economically infeasible for lords. They began to charge rents and fees for use of the land and a new money economy emerged. Ascribed status obligations vanished and poverty became rampant under contract labor. A new era of individualism and alienation began as lords were no longer obligated to support their serfs.

The Scientific Revolution

During the thousand or so years of the Dark and Middle Ages, new technologies changed industry, architecture, and agriculture, alleviated suffering, and enhanced life. Inventions included the spinning wheel, water mill, windmill, wheelbarrow, crank, cam, flywheel, rudder, compass, stirrup, gunpowder, lateen sail, padded horse collar, and nailed horseshoe.[12] The invention of new farming equipment was of primary importance: In particular, the padded horse collar could enormously increase the amount of land under plow. Because of the wars flying back and forth across Europe, the invention of new weapons such as the longbow and later the crossbow made conquest easier. In addition, the newly invented stirrup was the key to new armored warfare for lords and knights.

For women, cloth making took on added importance in commerce with the invention of the spinning wheel, and "piecing out" became a way of life for poor women (although nonpoor women continued in their cloth-making work, through guilds and crafts often owned by their husbands). Gies and Gies say,

> As in Roman times, linen and wool remained the principal textiles. The manufacture of cotton cloth, a Roman luxury import, was carried by the Arab conquest to Spain, Sicily, and Southern Italy as early as the tenth century, but it was not mastered by Christian Europe until the twelfth.[13]

Spinning never ceased, and the skill was universal, especially for women of the lower classes, who always had a spindle in hand. Spinning was so identified with women that the female side of the family was known as the "distaff side," or the "spindle side."[14]

As mechanization changed the way of life, the church developed a doctrine that intermingled religion and science and mandated stewardship of the earth by men. Nature, already equated with the female, now took on characteristics assigned to women, seen as passive, submissive, and controllable. This gynomorphic relationship was exacerbated as such church scholars as Thomas Aquinas posited a dual spirit/body approach to religion, in which mind and spirit were equated with men, and women (and the earth) were equated with body, earthiness, and evil. The persecution of women during the time of the Inquisition and Europe's ecological devastation during the Middle Ages were results of this equation.[15]

Until early feudal times, hand-hoeing and the three-field system, where land was allowed to lie fallow to increase its productivity, were the basic agricultural technologies. The invention of the oxen-drawn plow, although it put more land into production, kept an ecological relationship in which the number of acres needing manure and the number of animals supported on the manor were integrated. In times of good harvests, more oxen could be purchased to keep the land rich and to raise the subsistence level. However, as feudalism encroached, the new technologies and the demands of the lords altered the economy in significant ways. The invention of the horse collar began ecologically unsound production as more land was brought under cultivation in a shorter time (including fallow land), and fewer animals meant less manuring. The commandeering of horses and oxen for war and taxes exacerbated this practice and prevented reinvestment in animals to keep the ground fertile.

The Roman water wheel and handmills slowly spread northward from Italy, reaching the British Isles by the eighth century and Scandinavia by the twelfth. Lords took a monopoly on them, requiring payment for grinding grain, making cloth and paper, and sawing timber. People who kept illegal mills faced retribution in the form of higher taxes, higher mill costs, or destruction of property.[16] The draining of swamps, fens, and waterways for agriculture ruined local water and forest ecologies. By the thirteenth century, common use of woodlands was outlawed so that the elite could use wood as fuel in their homes and factories and for the building of the great sailing ships of the new international trade.[16]

The Enclosure Movement, from the twelfth century onward, was part of the social evolution that changed relationships between landowners and workers from an ascribed to a money economy. "Enclosure" meant the process of fencing, ditching, hedging, or barricading land formerly held "in common" by local villagers and peasants. In England, its legal basis began in statutes in 1235 and 1285 permitting landlords to enclose "wastelands," though this was conditional on leaving sufficient land for tenants. Most peasants and marginal people lived in villages having "common areas"—meadows, fields, forests, and water areas. There they planted small gardens, pastured their pigs and chickens, hunted and fished, and gathered firewood, reeds, fruits, and nuts to eke out their existence.

However, with the move to wage labor and the use of money as the preferred medium of exchange, high rent and taxes pushed peasants from their land. Those who had held the land by custom had no legally documented claim, and even those with legal rights could not afford the costs of enclosure, so many sold out and left.[17] Commons were declared "wastelands" and were seized for enclosure. Some were bought by wealthy farmers in need of larger tracts of land to support new agricultural technologies, but more often landowning lords made them part of their manorial holdings. Outside the jurisdiction of both city and guild regulations, the former common land was given over to the raising of sheep for wool for the international trade in cloth.

The Enclosure Movement reflected the continued growth of the textile industry in the fifteenth century, with improved spinning and weaving instruments and a proto-industrialization of the organization of work.[18] The "putting out" piecework system in Western Europe was gradually replaced by the factory system. In both home and workshop, "bells rang for the beginning and end of the working day as well as for meals, and inspectors regularly monitored all the workers."[19] It also reflected a loss of self-sufficient communities and an ever-widening international trade and economic system. Some have noted that the Enclosure Movement led to the creation of the wage-earning class by separating the workers from their land.[20] In any case, it was the end of an ascribed economic system and changed the face of land ownership, tenantship, and power. Though people fought enclosure, with land revolts in England in 1536, 1569, and 1607, it was a losing battle for the common person.

The Church and Social Welfare

The Roman Church was immersed in the politics of feudalism, a law unto itself, with governance, taxes, courts, and punishments. At its highest levels, corruption—the use of power for economic gain—was rampant. Any dissatisfaction or uprising to gain better treatment, such as the Magna Carta, was considered heresy. During the later Dark Ages, the Church established its own army, the Knights Templar, and its judicial arm, the Inquisition, to enforce its power both on foreign fronts (during the Crusades) and in Europe. Muslims and Jews were persecuted, as were non-Catholic Christians. For example, in 1209 a forty-year Crusade began against the Albigensian Christians in southern France. The whole of Languedoc was ravaged, crops destroyed, towns and cities razed, and the entire population put to death. In Béziers, at least 15,000 people were killed, many in the church sanctuary.

> When an officer inquired of the Pope's representative how he might distinguish heretics from true believers, the reply was "Kill them all. God will recognize his own."[21]

Lack of salvation and damnation to hell were overriding fears in the general populace, and to think or behave outside church mandates was nearly inconceivable. Coulton says,

> Medieval [thought] is characterized . . . by the convictions that each man has a soul to save, and that therefore, salvation is the main end of every human being, not a distant ideal but the most practical duty that is set before all . . . the last moment of life marked the man for an eternity of unspeakable bliss or of torment beyond all conception.[22]

Because both body and soul were charges of the Church, rulers did not need to give charity to control the populace. What little was given was, generally, either from whim or for salvation, often occurring on the ruler's deathbed and usually to relatives, immediate retainers, military leaders, or the Church.

Many manor lords were also Church bishops, receiving taxes as well as titles, donations, and legacies. Many used these for their own purposes rather than to help their parishioners. Although Rome had central authority in the distribution of charity, local Church authorities established their own regulations, and the lower levels of the Church remained dedicated to serving the poor. Priests collected money and distributed food and help throughout their parishes. Need was still considered the result of social, political, and economic forces rather than personal fault, although some Church fathers believed that indiscriminate giving was morally harmful to recipients. Generally, though, help was given anyone seeking it, even Muslims and Jews. The able-bodied were expected to work for their keep after a few days.

By the sixth century, both women and men had established religious orders whose primary duty was to care for the unfortunate. Their monasteries and abbeys evolved into the medieval hospital, which provided medical assistance but also housed and cared for travelers, widows, orphans, the aged, and the destitute.[23] By the eighth century, all Church members were required to tithe, at first to support diocese and bishop. In time, Church revenues supported four areas equally: the bishop; the parish clergy; church upkeep; and the poor, widowed, disabled, orphaned, and aged. In England in the tenth century under King Ethelred, support of the poor became a state law rather than a religious custom. As early as 800 A.D., Charlemagne's laws prohibited begging and fined those who gave alms to the able-bodied.[24]

Women were increasingly involved in services to the poor under Church auspices, and some conventual orders pioneered in nursing elderly and indigent patients.[25] Abbeys and convents also served as refuges to unmarried women, nonconformists, and female intellectuals, and most learned women of the Middle Ages were nuns (although the majority were barely literate).[26] Nuns came primarily from the nobility, although some were from gentry and merchant classes. Peasant girls, craftsmen's daughters, and serfs almost never became nuns, for the Church required dowries of lands, rents, or cash, and sometimes even clothes and furniture. The Church's view of the spiritual inadequacy of women limited nuns' activities and restricted them to convents, but some, under the direction of a few powerful and wealthy abbesses, served in communities. Semiconventual orders, such as the twelfth-century Beguines, took temporary vows and served the poor, ill, disabled, aged, and prisoners in both cities and rural areas.

In about 1140, the Italian monk Gratian compiled the *Decretum,* a set of laws made up of papal decrees, canons of church councils, and commentaries of church lawyers. It eliminated inconsistencies in canon law and distinguished between "voluntary poverty"—poverty for clerics, monks, or nuns—and the involuntary poverty of widows and orphans. It decreed that poverty was not a crime and that need alone obligated the Church to help the poor. Social justice was again the keynote, and the Church became increasingly critical of private wealth. By the beginning of the thirteenth century, the rich had to support the poor by law. These two interpretations of canon law—social justice and the obligations of the wealthy to the poor—set the institutional perspective on social welfare into Christian doctrine.

Forms of Private Welfare

Besides the overall responsibility of church and feudal manor for the poor, private welfare continued throughout this era. Care for fathers who turned over their trades to their sons in return for support in their older years was court-enforceable, as were deceased husbands' provisions for widows. Although in most places such women were encouraged to remarry, they also could continue to work their husbands' lands or receive a portion of the land until their deaths, when it reverted to the eldest son. Sons might also take their mothers into their households or purchase *corrodies* from local monasteries. A corrody was a daily ration of bread and ale and a dish of pottage from the monastery kitchen; a room, a servant, and firewood; and a new robe, shoes, and underlinen once a year. Candles and fodder and stalling for horses, or sometimes a house and garden, might also be included.[27]

In the cities, crafts and guilds—voluntary societies for the protection and mutual aid of their members—aided disabled workers or those unable to earn a living and gave pensions to survivors of deceased workers. Dowries for craftsmen's daughters might also be a part of the benefits.

> [Guilds] maintained hospitals, fed the needy on feast days, distributed corn and barley annually, provided free lodgings for poor travelers, and gave other incidental help.[28]

Women could become guild members, but often not as equals. Usually craftsmen could employ only their own wives or daughters, and women were paid less for the same work. Many eked out their income with prostitution or thievery, for which they were punished in stocks and pillory.

Finally, some kings, dukes, merchants, and lords provided alms or established hospitals or almshouses. Every major city in Europe and many of the smaller ones had hospitals. Between the twelfth and sixteenth centuries more than eight hundred were built in England alone (including those built by towns and craft and religious guilds). Private benefactors also underwrote almshouses for particular groups of people such as retired and disabled soldiers and sailors, old merchants, and fishmongers.[29] Funeral feasts or doles were given, often specifically to the working poor, at donors' funerals and on anniversaries of their deaths. The amount of donation was not as important as wide disbursement, for the purpose was to ensure the deceased's salvation. Charity demonstrated to all that the pursuit of wealth was justified and pleasing to God. Although they misrepresented their wares, gave short measure, or charged high interest, by giving charity they could "achieve" the best of both worlds: maximum financial gain on earth and salvation in the afterlife.[30]

The Dissolution of Feudalism

Agricultural production increased phenomenally with new technologies, but although many peasants became small landholders, the majority were pushed out of the agrarian economy. Increasing numbers of vagrants roamed the land, some looking for work, some on religious pilgrimage (during the Crusades), some as itinerant peddlers. Church provision for able-bodied beggars and travelers caused friction between the Church and the lords: lords wanted to keep serfs bound to the land, but Church policies supported them as they looked for better work. This threatened the lords' labor supply and increased the numbers of "rogues and vagabonds" who preyed on other travelers and townsfolk and poached on lords' lands and forests. Begging also became a problem and laws were established to control the poor. Increasingly, voluntary charity and the Church were blamed for supporting beggary and undercutting profits.

As crafts such as cloth making moved from home industry to organized production, people of all ages, including children, were hired as pieceworkers in their homes. The entrepreneur, a profit-making businessman, purchased wool in England, shipped it home, parceled it out to a family to clean, spin, card, and weave, took it back and gave it to another to full, then to another to dye, and to another to stretch, tease . . . and shear. Retrieving it for the last time, he gave it to an agent to sell.[31]

Work was from dawn to dusk, six days a week, with entrepreneurs controlling the lives of pieceworkers. They owned the houses in which workers lived and the stores where they bought goods and sat on city councils to make their laws. Workers could work only for their own entrepreneurs, and this protected entrepreneurs from market fluctuations, war, or other calamity, for they could simply leave workers with unsellable cloth. Workers often bankrupted themselves to avoid debtor's prison. Conflict often resulted—the first strike in the industry occurred in 1245, among the weavers of Douai—but strikes were put down with the force of law. Punishments ranged from cutting out tongues and banishing especially vocal protesters to seizing their goods.[32]

During this era, the booming textile industry brought enormous social changes. Lopez says,

> Perhaps most significant . . . was the advance toward modern business methods and organization. Unstinting credit was the great lubricant of the Commercial Revolution. The formation of large trading companies dealing extensively in credit transactions gave rise . . . to commercial banking dominated by such swiftly growing family-based institutions as the House of Medici.[33]

Cloth making was the only work that achieved the status of a large-scale commercial industry. Although its workers benefited little, the social changes it created were enormous. Cloth sails made travel for merchanting one of the most important means of achieving wealth and broadened the horizons of international travel. Large trading companies emerged that dealt extensively in credit transactions, with interest hidden in shipping fees to circumvent the admonitions of the Church against usury. These businesses were the precedents for transnational corporations that today rule the economic world.

Population increased slowly, held down by infant mortality, late marriages, early adult deaths, and abortion, infanticide, and available contraception. By the fourteenth century, the growth rate halted and began to decline. In 1315, because of the massive displacement of people from agriculture, food shortages became acute and waves of famine swept over Europe. The famines, exacerbated by ever-mounting war taxes, meant ever-higher prices. Thousands died of starvation.

The Black Death and the Witchcraze

An already weakened population was then devastated by recurring waves of the Black Death—bubonic plague—probably carried from India on flea-infested rats riding the great sailing ships of the new international trade. In 1348, plagues swept over Europe and England and 90 percent of those infected died. In some places, half the population succumbed.[34] A frantic populace demanded scapegoats for God's curse on the land, and they were found in "socially indigestible" people—those unwanted by society. Among these were Jews, Muslims, lepers, the disabled, homosexuals, and women.

In the late 1200s, hatred of "different" people began to rise, partly because of massive economic upheavals and the reification of Christian doctrine. Jews, for example, had to wear yellow stars or other distinctive dress, and there was missionary fervor against them, Muslims, and Christian heretics such as the Albigensians. Homosexuality, which was apparently widely accepted and practiced in twelfth-century Europe, was condemned by the Church by 1200 A.D., grouping homosexuals with arsonists, sorcerers, and Jews as criminals deserving execution. Women, always under the surveillance of the Church because of their sexuality, exceeded the population of men by 1300 A.D. and were persecuted particularly during the witchcraze, which began about that time. Accused women were often described as homosexuals or as practicing aberrant sexuality.[35]

Jews were accused of poisoning public wells, and in the hysteria that followed some estimate that 90 percent were massacred,[36] their wealth confiscated by Christians. Often, they were herded into wooden buildings that were torched or walled up in houses and left to suffocate or starve. Muslims were expelled in growing numbers, and their culture in Europe began to fall into ruin. In France, King Philip ordered every leper burned to death, and throughout Europe people who were "different"—diseased and mentally or physically disabled, for example—were accused of witchcraft and burned. Most massacres, except those of women, waned with the plague, ending by 1351.[37] The slaughter, along with the massive plague mortality, caused a great shift in wealth as survivors usurped the resources of the dead, becoming a macabre *nouveau riche*.

Beginning around the time of the first bubonic plague, women became more vulnerable to charges of witchcraft, and their treatment as witches became much more horrifying. Until this time, *malifice*, the belief that some people could cause sickness or kill cattle by curses, had been dealt with by local vendettas or vigilantes. Clergy were urged to counsel women out of the belief that they could curse. However, the belief in witches, often women who were healers or midwives, became conflated with fear of Satanism to become a virulent misogyny.[38] Over the next 300 years, hundreds of thousands of women were accused of witchcraft and killed. Only about 20 percent of the accused witches were men, but they do not seem to have been accused of deviant sexual relationships with the devil, as were women.[39]

At first the poor and old were accused of witchcraft, tried, and burned. However, as the witchcraze rose, women of every age, status, and class, and some men, were killed. The first description of sorcery appeared in 1337, when a woman was sentenced to burn by the famous legal authority Judge Bartolo.[40] Soon ordinary conjurers' tricks and women's work at healing were metamorphosed into witchcraft. A papal bull by Innocent VIII put the Inquisition in charge of witch hunting, and new and marvelous tests were created to try witches. If they died, they were innocent, but if they survived they were witches and had to be burned in the cleansing fire to save their souls.[41]

Accused women were often stripped, raped, and tortured before their trials, and estimates of the numbers killed range as high as 9 million.[42] Some towns were completely depopulated of women, and many women committed suicide rather than undergo the Inquisition. Women were burned before their children's eyes as examples, and often the children were then thrown in the fire as well. No woman was safe: Even the saintly Jeanne d'Arc, warrior woman and leader of the king's forces in France, was accused and burned at the stake in 1431, at the age of nineteen.

In most cases, women accused of witchcraft were single beggar women between the ages of fifty-five and sixty-five who had asked their neighbors for charity and had been denied. Klaits says,

> To exist by the charity of their neighbors was the only recourse of the propertyless and enfeebled. Giving alms to the poor was an everyday reality, not simply an abstract religious injunction. The beggar was the typical welfare case.... Her knock on the door to ask for a bit of bread, butter, or beer was entirely ordinary in a society that relied heavily on individual acts of charity to assist the needy.[43]

According to Thomas and MacFarlane,

> saying no to a request for neighborly charity may have inspired a considerable sense of guilt ... the emerging ethic of individualism may have been powerful enough to cause the denial of charity ... but the old medieval ideal of communal responsibility could still provoke guilt feelings over the refusal. A justified curse was thought always to work, and ... the ambivalent householder, later regretting his failure to give charity and thereby to forestall the domestic disaster that had subsequently occurred, suffered under a heavy burden of guilt.... Instead of blaming himself, the householder could project his guilt onto the charity seeker: she was the wrongdoer.[44]

Many witch accusations originated in charges against a quarrelsome neighbor, and midwives were often accused if the mother or infant died at childbirth, which was all too common. Poor widows lived on the margin of society, outsiders and newcomers aroused suspicion, and prostitutes, procurers, and tavern keepers, all of whom threatened family and community stability, were also among the extremely vulnerable groups.[45]

Politically, economically, and religiously the paranoia was reasonable. According to religious thought of the time, women without husbands were unqualified for salvation, were potential temptresses to sin, and often were consorts of Satan. Their life span had increased so that they outnumbered men, so many could not marry and widows often outlived their husbands. Thus, they became economic burdens to families and society, although there was some meager support for widows and children. Many became prostitutes to survive, reaffirming the Church's condemnation of women's sexuality. Those who supported themselves by healing—typical women's work in this era—were in growing danger as healing was redefined as a science. Because scientific education was available primarily to men through the Church, the skills of women who practiced it were believed to have come from Satan. There was often an economic incentive to an accusation of witchcraft: Canon law divided a witch's property between accuser and judge.

There were independently wealthy women in that era, such as those who had worked in guilds or developed their own businesses. Dowry law also returned women's marriage dowries to them on the deaths of their husbands, and this money could not be touched by others. Some used the money to begin commercial enterprises such as money changing, loans, surety in commercial activities for others, and speculations. Many gifted their daughters and other women so that they might be independent. This threatened patriarchal control of the economy, and where no other legal means could gain control of their wealth, the accusation of witchcraft immediately forfeited that wealth into the hands of men.[46]

The religious legitimation for gynocide allowed men to reaffirm religious and political power over women. In a social sense, the witchcraze rid society of an unwanted, perhaps threatening population: independent women. In the economic sphere, society no longer had to support excess women and their never-to-be-born children who might have added to unemployment and dependency.

Poverty Becomes a Crime

The Statute of Laborers

After the Black Death, a new "little Dark Age" descended on Europe. The devastation was so great that society seemed to stop, take a breath, and refocus on emerging needs and practices. The still agrarian-based economy was shattered by the phenomenal loss of labor, and in the cities the developing mercantile economy faltered without a needy and exploitable workforce. The diminished population created severe labor shortages and, as peasants' work became scarce and valued, their status increased. In places such as Germany, some reclaimed control of the land.

Until the fourteenth century, rulers had not been required to deal with issues of employment. Now, however, both nobility and the middle class (bourgeoisie) began to clamor for laws to control labor and vagrancy. Laws governing the right of people to come into cities, restrictive guild regulations, and city wage ordinances were enacted; in Paris, for example, wage raises could not exceed one-third of former level, prices were fixed, and profits of merchants were regulated. Workers were forbidden to organize for their own benefit.[47] England under Edward III gave Western society's most important response to the labor problem: the Statute of Laborers, enacted in 1349 and revised within two years for harsher enforcement and to ensure worker availability. Its intent was to bring employment under government control and to quell social unrest.[48]

The Statute of Laborers was the *first significant law on a national level aimed at the poor,* and it was not for their benefit but *to protect the interests of a commercially oriented government.* The statute regulated the movement of laborers to keep them where they were needed for production. Those found away from their own parishes were whipped, branded, sent to toil in the royal galleys, put into stocks, or given to anyone who claimed them. Able-bodied men and women under age sixty with no means of support were forced to work for any employer in need of their services, at no more than the prevailing wage, or be jailed. People who gave alms to the able-bodied or hired them away from their own parishes could themselves be fined and punished. During the 1350s and 1360s, fugitive laborers were declared outlaws and branded on the forehead with an *F.* Compton says,

> the essential notions . . . were that begging, movement, vagrancy, and the labor shortage . . . were essentially the same problem . . . begging was not a problem in destitution but a threat to the labor supply . . . [and could be solved] by fixing a maximum wage, by forcing any unattached person to work for anyone who needed labor, by forbidding alms, and by limiting the right of workers to movement.[49]

Treating the poor as criminals meant that poverty had become a crime in society's eyes.

The Statute of Laborers reified Charlemagne's seventh-century legal codes, classifying the poor as "worthy" and "unworthy," and ushered in the belief in personal rather than societal failure for poverty. It also began a gradual shift from church care for the poor to state control of labor by welding the nobility into an interest group in a *national* effort—for the first time—to dictate the future of labor. State and the elite classes would, from this time on, collaborate for their mutual good; labor was at the mercy of both, through state control of the movements, wages, and subsistence of workers and the unemployed. The statute did not completely reject the idea of charity: Those unable to work—the impotent poor—might still receive alms in their own communities. However, not until the end of the 1400s were such groups as pregnant women, the severely ill, or people over age sixty allowed charity.

As government control became more repressive, social unrest increased. Riots occurred throughout Europe: in France in 1358 and 1382, in Italy in 1378, and in England in 1381. To stem the tide in England, in 1388 Parliament enacted the Statute of Artificers. It required all people leaving their place of birth to have a *letter patent* telling their reasons for traveling, destinations, and date of return. Travelers without such documents might be returned home and indentured. Sturdy beggars—the able-bodied unemployed—transients, and those seeking higher wages were all treated the same, but the disabled or incapacitated were licensed to beg in their original home places.

Over the next century, the European population increased—by 60 percent during the 1500s and another 30 percent between 1600 and 1640—causing a massive glut in labor.[50] Small farms were enclosed by the nobility, pushing farmers from the land and causing vast unemployment and poverty. Because of fluctuating markets, an intermittent supply of raw materials, seasonal demands, rising prices and inflation, and the failure of wages to keep up with needs, about a third of England's population could not find work. The number of rogues and vagabonds in the 1500s was larger in proportion to the population than ever before or since, and fear of crime and disorder was rampant.[51]

The Commercial Revolution

Mercantilism, or a trade economy, became the predominant political economy of Western society during the Middle Ages. Laborers were pressed into service to produce trade goods for the new international markets. This, in turn, took them away from the production of their own food, especially with the enclosure movement, and turned them into a workforce dependent on the largesse of the mercantile class. Moreover, it ended the organic interrelationships of the old feudal society and moved people into cities and under labor contracts that could be broken at will by the upper classes. A new money economy began in which wealth was no longer in land and goods but in cash, a fluid asset enabling the accumulation of profits beyond the reasonable costs of materials, labor, and investment. This created interest-gathering investments where wealth could be stored rather than distributed, opening the era of capitalism.

In the early days of mercantilism, a paternalistic elite provided for the poor, much as had feudalism. Over time, however, mercantilist and national labor policies were influenced by foreign trade, in which cheap labor played the critical role. This created a new ideology about the poor: Low wages would make them work longer and harder, and low wages would also keep them from buying foreign products, thus keeping money within the nation and aiding the favorable balance of trade. Following this ideology, social welfare became an adjunct to labor policy rather than protection for the poor. Its purpose was to keep a viable labor force for mercantilists and the state. Increasingly, new ideas of "work morality" placed responsibility for the livelihood of the poor solely on their own shoulders, in a political and economic climate over which they had no control. By state policy, they were now merely units of production in the great national economy, dispensable commodities to be bought and sold or warehoused according to the economic decisions of others. Unemployment became a problem for employers only if workers became so debilitated by starvation that they could not work, and for the state only if poverty created social unrest that lowered production and upset the international balance of trade.

The Protestant Reformation: New Meanings for Work and Welfare

According to Gies and Gies,

> The fourteenth century ended on a somber note, the Black Death paying its return visits to a Europe that had not yet recovered from its earlier devastations. Popula-

tion, urban and rural, was still below its pre-plague level, the Hundred Years War smoldered in a precarious truce, and the Church was riven by the Great Schism, which enthroned rival popes in Rome and Avignon. Yet . . . Europe had advanced to a point where it at last rivalled Asia as a center of civilization . . . [in] power sources, industrial organization, architecture, shipbuilding, and weaponry.[52]

Under mercantilism, both church and state became supported by the moneyed middle class. New religions arose: In Germany Martin Luther began his Protestant Reformation in 1517, and England's Henry VIII instituted the Church of England in 1536. Klaits says,

> With the Reformation came the dissolution of the Catholic welfare organization . . . and the state assumed the burden of welfare. . . . As for the poor, in this capitalistic world they were losers, to whom winners need no longer feel any special obligation.[53]

Now landowners and merchants paid taxes to support welfare, making charity less incumbent on them and placing it into a governmental bureaucracy.

Lutheranism, Calvinism, and the Work Ethic

By far the most important event for the growth of mercantilism, capitalism, and ultimately social welfare was Martin Luther's break with the Catholic Church in 1517. Luther (1483–1546), a priest, protested Church corruption and deplored the selling of "indulgences" to ensure salvation after death. He taught that salvation could be attained only through the grace of God and that "right living" was the only means to salvation. One's vocation or work was a calling from God. Although Luther did not end poor relief and called for community chests to aid the needy, the implications of nonwork were clear. Those who accepted their calling through hard work obviously were more acceptable to God. John Calvin, one of Luther's followers, made these implications even clearer with new definitions of work and wealth. He taught that salvation was predestined—decided by God before one's birth—and that wealth in this life was the evidence of the grace of God. Therefore, the purpose of all human activity was not to attain salvation but to glorify God. Industry, thrift, frugality, and asceticism were the marks of true Christians, and frivolity, sentiment, and interest in comfort and luxury were deplored. Work was more than a requirement imposed by nature or as punishment, it was a spiritual discipline. Calvin's influence gave Protestantism an international appeal from which both capitalism and modern Western society developed. Its creed was essentially hard, stoical, and uncompromising in its demands.

A small ideological leap by Calvin's followers gave mercantilists religious affirmation both for their new wealth and for the exploitation of their workers to produce it. If wealth demonstrated morality, then surely poverty demonstrated immorality. Work as the means to wealth became the standard of the Protestant Reformation. Weber says,

> The pursuit of riches, which once had been feared as the enemy of religion, was now welcomed as its ally. The habits and institutions in which that philosophy found expression survived long after the creed which was their parent had expired . . . it ends as an orgy of materialism.[54]

The encouragement of work in others became a holy task and the financial benefit to those who reaped profits was a just reward for ensuring morality. Meanwhile, the poor were doubly damned by the necessity of making a living in an exploitative economy and by their newly defined immorality. The Protestant ethic became the keynote of Western society's policies in social welfare. Its psychological impact was phenomenal, for it fostered alienation from family and community, justified social stratification by income, became the model for self-concept, and made work the definition of spirituality. Poverty became moral degeneracy, and fault became centered in the self rather than in the structures of society.

Until this time, work had been considered at worst a punishment from God and, at best, a responsibility toward God and others. Before new technologies of storage and shipment, producing more than could be used was only wasteful. Ancient Jews had considered work a necessity by which, in partnership with God, they would advance civilization. For early Greeks and Romans, work was a degrading activity that took the mind away from its essential tasks of thinking and spirituality. Early Christians considered work a penance for original sin and admired the nobility of poverty, encouraging work not for its own sake but to support self and the needy and gain salvation. However, the needs of the mercantile society and the Protestant Reformation changed our attitudes completely. Weber says,

> this philosophy of avarice appears to be . . . the idea of the duty of the individual toward the increase of his capital, which is assumed as an end in itself. Truly what is here preached is not simply a means of making one's way in the world but a peculiar ethic. The infraction of its rules is treated not as foolishness but as forgetfulness of duty.[55]

Puritans joined businessmen in emphasizing the danger of pampering poverty, and giving charity meant abetting the immorality of the poor.

Women Under Protestantism

Protestantism also reified religion's harsh patriarchy. Luther did not believe in celibacy for the religious and closed down monasteries and convents, putting an end to their widespread charitable work. Although he married a former nun, his attitudes toward women were oppressive. Women's calling, and their proper role, was "church, kitchen, and children." He said,

> Take women from their housewifery and they are good for nothing. . . . If women get tired and die of bearing, there is no harm in that; let them die as long as they bear; they are made for that.[56]

Under Luther, marriage lost its status as a sacrament, for he agreed with some of his wealthy supporters that polygyny was not forbidden by the Old Testament. In fact, he recommended it to Henry VIII as a way out of his marriage difficulties. When Philip of Hesse requested a second wife, Luther married them secretly in 1540, in the presence of two eminent Protestant theologians. The scandal leaked out and although Luther withdrew from the position of bigamy he would not condemn it.[57] The early Anabaptists, following this lead, set up a system of "companion wives."

No less misogynistic were Calvin and the Scottish minister John Knox. The latter was eloquent in his condemnation of women rulers such as Mary Tudor, Mary Stuart, Elizabeth I, and Catherine de Medici. In 1558 he said their rule was

> contumely to God.... For who can deny that it is repugnant to Nature that the blind shall be appointed to lead and conduct such as do see ... that the foolish, mad, and phrenetic shall govern the discreet and give counsel to such as be of sober mind.... Woman in her greatest perfection was made to serve and obey man.[58]

Social Welfare and Work Morality

Protestantism and the work ethic swept over the world and, as the new standard of an emerging society, was reflected in all society's institutions, including social welfare. Mencher says,

> modern social welfare policy may be conceived of as commencing with the shift in the sixteenth century from the economic assistance programs of a declining feudal society to those of a rising commercial and secular world.[59]

Poverty as a crime was inextricable from vagrancy and begging, and work relief became a major innovation, setting people to work off their "criminal dependency" by such tasks as building roads and farming.

In 1525, Juan Luis Vives developed a prototype of present-day social welfare. A noted scientist, teacher of the daughters of Catherine of Aragon (a wife of Henry VIII), and a philosopher, he stressed individual and local investigation of the morality of the poor, dividing cities into parish quarters for a census of poverty. He advocated vocational training, employment, and rehabilitation for the able-bodied poor. Children were indentured for work training. Those incapable of work or the genteel poor were given piecework in return either for outdoor relief—support in their homes—or care in almshouses, for although outdoor relief was far less expensive, he believed it supported immorality. Parallel programs arose in Germany, Venice, France, Spain, and the Netherlands within the next twenty years. All centralized the distribution of voluntary charity in neighborhoods and communities and encouraged community chests and community responsibility.

Another prototype of service began with the Ladies of Charity, founded in 1617 by Vincent de Paul in France. A Catholic priest, he had been captured and sold as a galley slave. Upon his escape, he devoted his life to care for the poor and for prisoners, founding the Lazarites in 1618, an "association of priests organized to work among the outcasts of society and in the aid of prisoners."[60] The royal court of France helped to support his efforts, and the ladies of the court initially began to work with the poor. However, they lost interest and in 1663 the Sisters of Charity, a holy order with temporary vows, was founded. They did not wear habits or live in cloisters and tended to the aged, poor, sick, wounded, dying, and prisoners in the community. Following St. Vincent de Paul's ideals, the Conference of St. Vincent de Paul was organized in the 1700s by students Frederick Ozanam and Sylvain Bailly. They lived among the poor, visited them, and collected necessities for distribution. The pattern of anonymous giving, as well as the Society of St. Vincent de Paul, still exists.

Throughout Europe, social welfare activities of church and state were merging and the governmentalization of social welfare began. Early in the 1700s, Syndic Sillen devised a plan for Hamburg, Germany, in which public officials (burgomasters) were appointed to personally investigate the city's poor, so that "the deserving might be discovered and the undeserving rebuked." All charitable institutions were placed under a central bureau, and to prevent anyone from receiving unearned money the able-bodied were compelled to work and the unemployed were given public work.[61] People were placed in "work training"—given flax and yarn and taught to spin, and released after three months with a spinning wheel and a pound of flax.

The lack of good public health, which caused unemployment and poverty, was a major concern of the Hamburg plan. To combat illness and increase capability for employment, Hamburg built a hospital for incurables, free schools for children ages six to sixteen, and free day care centers for children of working parents. The programs were financed from a combination of public taxes, one-half of church poorbox collections, and weekly or annual citizen collections. Even children and servants had their own poorboxes at home, in which they put their pennies for the poor. Such programs became common in all of the European nations. In Bavaria, Count Rumford, a native Bostonian, recommended food and employment for every man, woman, and child and established a House of Industry that provided piecework and dinner. In Glasgow, Reverend Thomas Chalmers encouraged the formation of charity societies by districts and proclaimed that every boy be taught to read and every girl to sew.

However, it was soon apparent that normal channels of employment, private training, or state-created jobs could not solve the massive problems of poverty. Neither state nor employer took personal interest in laborers except to ensure that they would work, and employment and its converse, poverty, depended on the needs of the employer rather than the worker. According to Handel, idleness became a triple threat: to the order of the state, the productivity of capitalism, and the carrying out of God's will.[62]

Social Welfare in England: The Tudor Period

When Columbus voyaged into the New World, his first trip was delayed for a day by ships carrying Jews and Muslims away from Spain in their final exile. At the same time in England, the Tudors began their reign under Henry VII (1485). A contemporary of Luther and Calvin, he responded to the problems of the poor by putting beggars and idlers in the stocks, flogging them, and returning them to their place of origin. By the time of Henry VIII (1509–1547), social unrest, labor problems, and vagrancy were rampant, and in 1531 he required that all beggars be licensed. In 1536, angered by the pope's refusal to let him divorce, he founded the Church of England and confiscated most Catholic Church and monastery property. As had happened in Germany, the back of the church's care for the poor was broken, and great numbers of monks, nuns, and monastery workers were released to unemployment. Thereafter, major responsibility for poor relief fell on the state, and although private foundations, guilds, and donors continued to support some charities, state welfare was the new rule.

Also in 1536, the Act for Punishment of Sturdy Vagabonds and Beggars prohibited begging and casual almsgiving, with such severe penalties as branding, enslavement, and execution. Idle children from ages five to fourteen were taken from their parents and indentured. The English government charged church wardens and mayors to collect funds on Sundays, holidays, and festivals, for the first time paying them for their relief work and requiring accurate accounting. Although giving was still voluntary, the government was now involved in securing contributions. Funds from rich parishes were redistributed to poorer ones, instituting a kind of equity in poor relief throughout the kingdom, but poverty was so great that large-scale riots continued to occur.

In succeeding legislation under Henry VIII and Elizabeth I, the government moved from encouraged volunteerism to the imposition of taxes (compulsory giving) based on property and income. Refusal to pay or to serve as overseer of the poor if appointed by justices of the peace (for one-year terms) could mean imprisonment. The hoax of "voluntary giving" ended in 1572 with a general tax to provide poor relief. A community registration of the poor who had lived in the parish for three years was taken, and justices of the peace assigned them to private homes, paying their upkeep with the general tax. Over the next five years, a national system of welfare emerged in which, in one way or another, all people could have been provided for.

A new Statute of Artificers that regulated wages and hours was passed in 1583. Intended to control and stabilize the labor market, it forced vagrants, vagabonds, and beggars between ages twelve and sixty to work at hard labor or be indentured. Indenture lasted a minimum of one year, and release required approval of local justices of the peace. Both employer and employee had to give three months' notice, and workers could not leave without a certificate of lawful departure. Apprenticeship lasted seven years, with the minimum age at completion twenty-one or twenty-four. This served other functions besides learning a trade: It gave the master skilled labor, prevented young men from setting up competitive businesses, delayed marriage, and ensured control of the young and support of the old.

The Elizabethan Poor Laws of 1601

In the 1590s, between one-fourth and one-third of the populations of most English towns could not find work, and many starved or froze to death. Bread riots broke out in some parts of the country; and rioting, thievery, and social disorder were common. To maintain civil order, the English poor laws were recodified in 1597, authorizing every county to build civil (rather than religious) almshouses for the impotent poor and workhouses for the able-bodied poor. Responsibility for relatives became law: Parents were required to support their own parents and their children, grandparents their children and grandchildren, and capable children their parents and grandparents. Handel says,

> requiring family members to support one another involves a recognition of social change on the part of the Parliament . . . an awareness that the traditional feudal relationships, which assured the aged or disabled serf a livelihood, had substantially passed out of existence. The traditional manorial village was being replaced by . . . independent household units . . . a concept of the family as distinct and separable from the community.[63]

The famous Elizabethan Poor Laws of 1601, a recodification whose power has existed for nearly three centuries, legalized and formalized England's responsibility for the poor. The importance of these laws lies not in the amount spent for care of the poor, for it is estimated that public relief accounted for not more than 7 percent of the total in any one year for two generations after they were passed.[64] Rather, their importance is in *defining social welfare as part of the national labor policy,* placing it under the authority of the Privy Council. Never has the connection of social welfare to labor maintenance been so clear, setting the patterns of public assistance not only for England, but also for the United States. They included local investigation and administration of relief, work as a component of all assistance, and categorization of the poor into three groups: the able-bodied poor, or "sturdy beggars"; the impotent poor, those incapable of self-support; and dependent children (a new category). That same Parliament passed the Law of Charitable Trusts to keep trusts and endowments under government surveillance and control. Private donors, churches, monasteries, foundations, and guilds continued to support the charities of their choice under this umbrella, but they were restricted from giving so indiscriminately that the poor could leave local employment. The law resulted in a great outpouring of private money for education, outdoor relief, and the building of almshouses,[65] functions that abetted rather than contradicted national policies toward the poor; almshouses became the placement of choice.

The Privy Council's labor policy discouraged the mobility of laborers and encouraged permanent employment. Employers were exhorted to create new jobs, to employ workers even in hard times, and to purchase raw materials and produce goods for sale even when no market existed. Rents, prices, and wages were controlled, labor competition restricted, and marriage and the establishment of new households among the poor discouraged by the burning of available housing. Finally, the "normal" heavy punishments were given the unemployed or those who would not work for the "common wage": whipping and returning to place of residence, commitment to prison (or houses of correction), and in extreme cases banishment and death.[66]

At the local level, under the jurisdiction of the Privy Council, justices of the peace authorized the building of almshouses and workhouses, assessed taxes, and appointed tax collectors. They also appointed public overseers of the poor to ensure accountability for expenditures, to place more emphasis on labor than was common with church charities, and to be more efficient in the use of tax money. (Service was compulsory and refusal meant fines or imprisonment.) They set the amount of poor relief; made disposition of the poor to private homes, almshouses, or workhouses; and decided on removal of children from parents judged unable to care for them (for economic or moral reasons). Imprisonment was the punishment for both those who would not work and those who would not pay poor taxes.

New mechanisms for the differential treatment of categories of the poor were also clarified under the Elizabethan Poor Laws. Institutionalization was preferred because people believed that levels of support could better be set; costs for food, clothing, and shelter clearly determined; and "immoral" work behavior monitored. All institutional arrangements—orphanages, almshouses, workhouses, and prisons—had conditions in common. Many were little more than sheds divided into warrens of rooms with little heat or insulation. There were few if any sanitation facilities, and food was inadequate and often little more than watery gruel. Health and medical care were virtually nonexistent, and in most cases, well people were expected to care for those who could not care for themselves. Disease and infection ran rampant, and the bedridden or those chained in their places because of their behavior (the "insane," perhaps), were often left to live or die in their own excrement. House overseers or managers were usually given a flat fee for the support of their inmates and to buy materials for work, and they were allowed to keep what was not spent. If they could skimp on the amount of food, heat, clothing, and shelter allowed the inmates, they could make profits for themselves, and this was a common practice. Work done by the inmates was sold to private entrepreneurs or contractors, and the profits went to the overseer or the state rather than to the workers. Although some institutions were well run, most were not, and most eventually became undifferentiated dumping grounds for the unwanted.

Almshouses for the Impotent Poor

The impotent poor were those unable to support themselves (the aged, ill, disabled, and the genteel poor), those unequipped to work because of their upbringing, and sometimes pregnant women. Some outdoor relief was authorized for people able to stay in their homes, but this was always controversial because of the belief that it encouraged laziness and beggary. People were also assigned to live in private homes, and homeowners were paid at the "lowest bid" for their keep. All the poor had to do piecework to the extent of their capabilities. Women pregnant out of wedlock, however, were treated brutally, not only because of their sexual "immorality" but because their families, their communities, and the state feared the future dependency of their children.

Almshouses were usually mean buildings with little heat or insulation. Disease, lack of food, the cold of English winters, and lack of health care led to a high mortality rate, particularly among the aged and the sickly. The houses were usually out of the way, state supervision was rare, and being sent to an almshouse was often a sentence of death—again, an easy way for society to get rid of those who were no longer productive in the labor market.

Dependent Children

As social welfare became labor policy, *all its beneficiaries were considered past, potential, or present labor force.* Social welfare efforts were bent on ensuring that each category of the poor would fit into its proper "work niche." Therefore, dependent children—orphans, foundlings, unwanted children, or those removed from their parents—were considered either future laborers or, more often, future dependents, and their assigned treatment was often so uncaring as to be murderous. Often they were simply left by their mothers on the roadside to die. When the government assumed responsibility, their treatment was little better. They could be placed in foster homes, sold to the lowest bidder (the family that would require the least public support for them), placed into indenture, or put in state orphanages, where social reformer Jonas Hathaway estimated that 82 percent died in their first year.[67] Infants were also placed with paid wetnurses, but because nobody really wanted these children, few follow-up checks were made. Killing them or allowing their deaths was not uncommon and was, in a way, a service to the state, because they would not grow up dependent. Pay for their keep would continue until the officials discovered they were dead, often several months later. Fostering of older children or indenturing them to families was usually a means of getting work from them, and they were often worked to death. Those who survived were indentured to learn a trade (girls until eighteen or married and boys until twenty-four).

With the rise of the factory system, dependent children were contracted out to work in textile mills as early as age three or four, for their small fingers were nimble at looms and spinning jennies. They worked from daybreak until dusk, with a half hour for breakfast and an hour for lunch. If they fell asleep during their fourteen- to sixteen-hour workday, or if they had to relieve themselves, they were slapped or whipped back to work. A great number died before they reached their teen years, but neither their deaths nor their lives were important in the scheme of labor policy. Not until 1802 did the law limit children's working hours to twelve a day, also forbidding night work; however, this did not apply to children hired directly from their parents, for they could be worked without limitation. Under the Factory Act of 1833, children under age nine were prevented from work; by 1847, women and children under eighteen could work only ten hours a day in England.

Sturdy Beggars: The Able-Bodied Poor

Workhouses were another major aspect of the labor policy. The forerunners of the later factory system, they were modeled on the combination almshouse, workhouse, and penal institution of Amsterdam (1596), where inmates worked in fine textiles and lace. Going into the 1600s, England was in fierce competition with the Dutch in the textile business, and by 1650 workhouses were widespread. The goal was to make a profit for the state, and inmates were often contracted out to private merchants and entrepreneurs. Some workhouses were run fairly, with artisans in charge of production and fair wages paid to the inmates, but most were forced labor prisons. The Workhouse Act of 1696 put inmates to work at spinning, knitting, linen weaving, lacework, and the manufacture of nets and sails, but they could not compete with trained workers, and workhouses continued to lose money.

Any able-bodied man seeking public aid was required to leave his family and live in the workhouse. This was called the "workhouse test," for it was believed that only the "truly needy" would agree to it. Work tests were devised to demonstrate willingness to work—chopping wood or moving rocks, for example (and later, sewing tests for women)—even if the work itself was unnecessary, unimportant, or inefficient. Workhouses were considered essential both to maintain work behavior and to punish those who did not want to work. Tied to morality, they were maintained despite their high costs.

Although workhouses were first designed only for men, a revised Workhouse Act in 1722 put both men and women in workhouses, along with their children, adding a new category of the poor, able-bodied women, to the poor laws. Women were allowed to care for their children only at specified times during the day, and of the children forced to enter workhouses with their parents, only seven of one hundred survived the first three years.[68] Relief was refused to those who would not enter workhouses. Reformers Jonas Hathaway and Thomas Gilbert bitterly opposed workhouses, and Hathaway was able to push through a bill in 1767 that ruled that foster homes must be found for children under age six, rather than have them in workhouses. In 1782, Gilbert introduced a statute directing overseers either to find work for the poor in the community (rather than contracting them out to private entrepreneurs) or to maintain them on poor relief. This began a revival of outdoor relief, made national policy in 1795 as the poor were given the right to receive relief in their own homes.[69]

Prisons

Prisons were the final solution to the problem of unwanted people. They can be considered a part of social welfare because of the nature of the crimes for which people could be sentenced and the categories of people incarcerated. Poverty, nonwork, and even the inability to pay small debts might mean imprisonment. People were as likely to be imprisoned or hanged for stealing bread as for murder or highway robbery. Prisoners were forced to pay fees to their jailers for their upkeep, and they would not be released until they could; money was also extorted from their families. Men and women of all ages, criminals, debtors, the poor, the "insane," people with such diseases as epilepsy, prostitutes, pregnant women—all were thrown, willy-nilly, without segregation, into prisons. Conditions were worse than any other kind of institution, for the only law was that proclaimed by the jailer. People suffered from filth, cold, disease, attacks by other inmates, or the brutality of the jailers. Feeding, clothing, and caring for the ill was farmed out to the lowest bidder, and liquor was always available. Clubs and whipping were used freely, and excrement was left to accumulate in the sleeping cells.

Prison reform began in 1681, when philanthropist Thomas Firmin began to pay debtors' costs and fees to free prisoners of good character. (He also put the greater part of his fortune into building a model self-supporting workhouse.) Reformer John Howard, who had been himself imprisoned by a privateer and later became the sheriff of Bedford (1733), demanded that jailers guilty of extortion be dismissed. However, real reform did not begin until the Prison Act of 1877 transferred prison administration to a central authority.

Overview of Social Welfare in England

During the 1600s and 1700s, social welfare in England wavered from harsh enforcement of work and settlement laws to supporting workers in hard times. Police measures to control labor and prevent riots and revolutions were social welfare functions, and they favored employers and the entrepreneurial middle class. A new Settlement Act in 1662 kept laborers from seeking better jobs and could fine both worker and employer if higher wages than those set by the central authority were paid. Class interests continued to influence legislation, often in the guise of charitable intent. For example, in 1675 Parliament enacted a law providing poor relief from the public treasury

> to eke out the wages of the poor who received it—thus acting as a bounty upon the oppression of their employers . . . in weekly installments proportional to the number of children in the families . . . this acting directly as a bounty upon the increase of population.[70]

This enabled employers to pay low wages and refer their workers to poor relief for supplement while it paid a bounty for increasing the labor force. The 1675 act also gave authorities the ability to predict the future: It allowed them to eject people and families from the locality if they *might* become dependent. This was never well enforced because poor relief was cheaper than the ejection process, but it did give poor relief agents the power to declare certain people unwanted in advance. Those who could pay advance rent or put up a bond could stay, but by 1691 newcomers had to acquire a certificate to guarantee that they would not become dependent.

Policies in England continued to seesaw between restrictiveness and charity. One major revision was the Speenhamland Act, a wage supplementation program based on the cost of living. Justices of the peace paid subsidies to poor employed families and relief to dependent families in their homes, according to family size, when the cost of bread rose to one shilling, a kind of early consumer price index. As with the earlier law, however, the government thereby subsidized low wages. On the other hand, Speenhamland allowed the poor to work in sheltered workshops rather than being incarcerated in workhouses, urged employers to raise wages, and requested counties to set aside land on which the poor could grow food.

The Industrial Revolution and the Emergence of Capitalism

The Industrial Revolution is tied to the beginnings of cotton textile production (about 1760), when capitalism emerged, legitimated by the Protestant work ethic and tied to international trade and the new money economy. Government laissez-faire policies offered legal protection to employers in their exploitation of workers, a collaboration that benefited both employers and government. A new middle class of artisans, professionals, and managers arose from the undifferentiated laboring class. Social reformers addressed themselves to altruism in the sense of supporting the poor so that they might better labor and to the new ideals of socialism: the right of workers to share in the decisions and the profits of their labor. Capitalism was an outgrowth of political and economic mercantilist policies.

The Emergence of Capitalism

Keeping wages low increased the margin of profit, so low wages were necessary to the nation's political economy. So was poverty. The mercantilist society that had overrun feudalism was transmuted, at least by the 1700s, into a capitalist society where

> the primary motivation . . . is the drive for profit. Each capitalist enterprise must try to grow and to expand its profits. If it does not do so, then another, more aggressive capitalist enterprise will take that company's share of the market. . . . [It is] an economic system organized on the basis of competitiveness and competition . . . a value system and human behaviors which define a meaningful and successful life in the same terms.[71]

This had certain direct results for the poor. First, poverty was the most appropriate means, it was believed, to ensure a ready workforce and maintain profits, so wages were deliberately kept low. Second, poverty increased because wages either were kept too low for survival or, in times of economic depression, were nonexistent. Third, poverty's result for society was starvation, criminal activity, or social unrest. To control this and to maintain the economy, the government collaborated with the elite in controlling the poor.

Fourth, although the government ostensibly maintained a laissez-faire attitude—noninterference in business affairs—in reality it kept the workforce available through restrictive social welfare policies that took police action against workers or subsidized low wages. Thus, government actually rewarded its successful businesses with protection for such rapacious business practices as underselling, monopolization, and worker exploitation. Finally, capitalism led to a society highly stratified by economics: a wealthy elite primarily interested in maintaining wealth; an emerging middle class of artisans, professionals, and managers; and a vast majority of the poor—those in and out of unemployment whose labor was perceived as a commodity for the good of business and the nation.

A great many theorists appeared out of this Age of Enlightenment to analyze and rationalize the movement toward capitalism and industrialization. The first to precisely address the laissez-faire principle was Adam Smith, whose treatise *The Wealth of Nations* was published in 1776. He said,

> it is in vain . . . to expect . . . benevolence only. [Men] will be more likely to prevail if [they] can interest their self-love . . . and shew them that it is for their own advantage. . . . Give me that which I want, and you shall have this which you want, is the meaning of every such offer. . . . We address ourselves, not to their humanity but to their self-love, and never talk to them of their own necessities but of their advantages.[72]

Describing men's relationships in competition, he further said,

> men . . . feel so little for another with whom they have no particular connection, in comparison of what they feel for themselves; the misery of one . . . is of so little importance to them in comparison even of a small convenience of their own . . . they would, like wild beasts, be at all times ready to fly upon him; and a man would enter an assembly of men as he enters a den of lions.[73]

Philosopher John Locke supported capitalism and held that the most important human right was the right to hold property. Utilitarians Jeremy Bentham, John Stuart Mill, and Joseph Townsend supported the idea of laissez-faire because they believed that wealth was the primary source of happiness. The Utilitarian philosophy propounded the greatest good for the greatest number and espoused the equality of all members of society and their right to compete for their happiness. Education of the poor would help them safeguard their own interests rather than having the government do it for them. Although they believed that the unhappiness of some diminished the happiness of all, they felt that the government's efforts to redistribute wealth through poor relief would threaten the national economy. Therefore, they suggested a gradual elimination of poor relief.

Thomas Malthus's theories on population (1798) gave scientific support to the elimination of poor relief and the protection of wealth. He believed that population would outrun the world's ability to produce food and that poor relief encouraged paupers to have more children, thus prolonging the misery of their ultimate starvation. Moreover, because poverty and immorality were equated, Malthus and later social Darwinists believed that helping the poor would result in a population of moronic and immoral people because the poor reproduced more rapidly than did the wealthy "moral" and intellectual elite. Malthus and economist David Ricardo (1772–1823) believed that unfettered self-interest was the only way society could progress. Direct concern for the welfare of others, then, defeated the progress of society and was sure to result in failure.[74]

Karl Marx, Friedrich Engels, and their followers took the opposite view, criticizing capitalism for its exploitation of the poor and warning of the coming revolution of workers. Marx formulated the ideas of a class society or political economy in which the government was economically allied with and supported the elite, resulting in the constant oppression of the working force. This posited an ongoing class struggle that in time would cause the workers to overthrow the oppressive government. Then all would give according to their ability and be helped according to their need. Neither Marx nor Engels dealt in any depth with the problems of women in a capitalist society but recognized their double exploitation as both workers and "reproducers of labor." Although economic history has not demonstrated Marxist theories to be correct in all areas, the ideas illuminated both social reform and social welfare activism in that age and into the next century. Among such reformers was Robert Owen, a textile mill owner, who set up an ideal self-supporting industrial community and devised plans for cooperative agrarian organizations. His work became the model for English socialism.

The Industrial Revolution and the New Poor Law

In England and on the Continent, agricultural and industrial production revolutionized the social and economic bases of Western society as it moved into the 1800s. An extraordinary dislocation of people from their homes and employment occurred. People had moved to the cities for jobs, but now one machine could do the job of ten workers at less cost. Hundreds of new five- and six-story factories were built to use new labor-saving technologies, putting vast numbers of workers out of jobs. In many towns, workers destroyed and burned hundreds of machines and factories, as in the Luddite movement of 1811. Police power put down all such conspiracies, protecting the employers' interests. Fear of revolution, spurred by the American and French revolts, inspired antiworker legislation such as the Combination Acts of 1799 and 1800, which considered trade unionism to be conspiracy and treason.

The trend away from home industry was complete, and the family ceased to exist as an integrated economic unit. Now, each wage-earner—man, woman, or child—went out of the home to work hard in distant factories. The home became divorced from the workplace, for producing, selling, and consuming were relocated in different areas. Men could not support their families on such meager wages, so wives had to work at any kind of wage labor or in weeding and hoeing gangs on farms. Their competition with men for work kept wages for both sexes low. In the higher classes, women became "work useless," consumers of the goods others produced. It became "unladylike" to work, and idle wives were badges of social success for their prosperous husbands. Contract labor removed workers from the production of their own food and necessities, and they became parts of the work machine itself—often replaceable parts.

Among the rich, altruism toward the poor continued under new social philosophies whose leaders included Thomas Bernard, Hannah More, and John Wesley, the founder of Methodism. Bernard established a society for "bettering the conditions and increasing the comfort of the poor" in 1796, in which the rich were enjoined to serve the poor. More established charity schools (1801) so that poor children could be educated; and Wesley spoke out for just wages and fair prices based on social justice rather than the free market.

During the period between 1760 and 1820, real wages decreased by one-third[75] because of wars, rapid industrial change, poor agricultural years, and heavy taxes. Rents rose precipitously and governments destroyed homes to limit the increase in new families. By now, the Enclosure Movement begun so long before was complete, and poor people had no rights to common lands, pastures, or water. By 1830, widespread revolt had created a demand for new, harsher poor laws on one hand and a cry for social reform for the poor on the other. Middle-class professionals and artisans began to organize to provide mutual aid benefits, but poor workers had little protection. Capitalism, industrialization, and the restrictive social welfare that supported them were the clear victors in the battle for workers' rights.

In 1832, every county in England underwent a study by the Royal Commission on Poor Relief. Its conclusions, on completion in 1834, were that poor relief was responsible for "permanent paupery" and that poor taxes were used as subsidies for profit making by employers. The study resulted in the New Poor Law of 1834, which blamed the poor for their own poverty and declared public assistance no longer a right. In 1868, Benjamin Disraeli, one of the most eminent of Britain's prime ministers (1874–1880), said that it "announced to the world that in England poverty is a crime."[76]

According to the New Poor Law, the government would no longer take the responsibility for providing work. There would be no more outdoor relief except for the impotent poor and widows with small children. Two hundred new work-houses were built to house pauper families, where conditions were purposely so terrible that people went into them as an alternative only to starvation. Counties were coordinated into poor relief regions under a central board appointed by the king, and the principle of *less eligibility* was the guiding factor in meting out poor relief. From a work ethic and labor control point of view this makes good sense, for it provides an incentive to work. However, it enforces work at any wage, punishes those who cannot work or cannot find employment (and their dependents), and does not consider special needs such as illness or other emergencies that arise. Nevertheless, the idea of *less eligibility* is so popular it is still the standard of public assistance in the United States today.

In 1852, some outdoor relief, or aid outside institutions, was granted, and by 1854, 84 percent of paupers were on poor relief. By 1898, 216,000 people in England were in workhouses.[77] Reform in England continued, resulting in a more socialistic system than in the United States. Studies to determine the causes of poverty revealed that widespread illness and disease were major problems among the poor. Malnutrition and unsanitary living conditions were to blame:

> [P]eople lived in overcrowded quarters, and often adolescents and children of both sexes slept in one bed. This led to promiscuity, quarrels, delinquency, immorality, and rapid spread of contagious diseases. Many workingmen-boarders lived with families in the same room. Often seven to ten used one sleeping room, or lived in damp, dark cellars, without any ventilation. All over England the poorer quarters were without water supply and drainage; drinking water was often polluted in rivers or deficient pipelines. There were usually no outside toilets and no sewers. . . . Refuse was thrown into the public gutter, and the dead were left unburied.[78]

In the late 1800s, Edwin Chadwick, a Poor Law Board commissioner, appalled by the living conditions of the poor, developed plans for water systems, sewage, drainage, and free public vaccination for cholera, typhus, and smallpox. However, he was bitterly opposed and lost his position. Within a decade, and with better results, Florence Nightingale (1820–1910), a nurse in the Crimean Wars, began reforms of nursing, hospitals, and medical practice that would revolutionize England's public health system. Octavia Hill was also influential in the fight for the poor. With the help of philanthropist John Ruskin, she started rebuilding slums in London in 1864:

> She rented sanitary decent living quarters at low prices to working families who could not afford to pay higher rents . . . enlisted . . . volunteers who collected the monthly rents . . . and advised the families in economical home management.[79]

She was also one of the founders of the Commons Society, which built parks, gardens, and recreational facilities for the poor in London.

Among the most influential groups of this time was the Fabian Society, an English socialist group among whose leading members were Sidney and Beatrice Webb. They were primarily interested in practical reforms such as women's suffrage, wage and working hours legislation, housing projects, and education. Charity organization societies and the settlement house movements began in England about the same time. Edward Denison, a philanthropist, moved into a slum district to teach the Bible, history, and economics. He counseled the poor and became an advocate for them. Canon Samuel Barnett, a teacher, brought his students to his home in the slums at Whitechapel to serve the poor. Among his students was Arnold Toynbee, in honor of whom the first settlement house in the world, Toynbee Hall, was built. Its basic purpose was to bring educated men and women into contact with the poor, so that by common work and studies they might both learn.

Following that period, care for the poor took a different turn in England than in the United States. It is important to discuss English social welfare here because welfare in the United States was modeled on that of England, particularly in terms of the Elizabethan Poor Laws of 1601 and the New Poor Law of 1834. However, although English social welfare was softened by its exposure to the ideas of socialism and the activities of socialist reformers, welfare in the United States remained uninfluenced by and perhaps adamantly opposed to socialist influence. Without historical traditions of care for the poor, cut off from pre-Protestant Christian traditions, and influenced at a vulnerable state of development by a strict capitalist political economy, social welfare in the United States became "stuck" in its harsh antipoor, worker-exploitative past.

Conclusion: Reifying the Values of the Past

From the fall of the Roman Empire until the Industrial Revolution, the very basis of human existence was altered. Politically, small warring tribes became feudal estates and then nations, and social relationships changed from organic interconnections with family and community to alienated individuals whose primary concern had to be survival. Economically, a wealthy elite grew to control governments and to deal with the poor as cost units in production.

Vast changes in technology created the beginnings of mercantilism, and such ecological catastrophes as the Black Death and the destruction of balances of nature increased the difficulties of survival for the poor. Religion reified the secondary status of women and certain "outgroups"—Jews, homosexuals, and handicapped people—even to the point of killing them, and mutated in response to both polity and economy from supporting the poor in difficult times to justifying their exploitation.

Social welfare changed from ideals of social justice and charity as a right to redefinition of poverty as a crime, and its administration became civil rather than religious. It now controlled labor for the purpose of personal profit making by the new moneyed class. Although kind hearts and good deeds continued, the Protestant work ethic became the moral basis underlying the new political economy, and people of all religions picked up its secular ideas of work and wealth. With governments justifying exploitation based on the laissez-faire philosophy, capitalism became the major economic tenet of both Old and New Worlds. Whereas England and Europe progressed into new beliefs about social welfare despite primarily capitalist philosophies, the ideals of Protestantism and Puritanism as civil or state religion and capitalism as the morally appropriate economic system became a basic tenet of the United States.

Study Questions

1. What is feudalism? What kinds of help for the poor did it offer?

2. How did the Scientific Revolution affect feudalism? Social welfare?

3. What was the Enclosure Movement, and how did it affect land ownership policies in England? How did it affect employment and poverty?

4. How did poverty become a crime?

5. What impact did the Protestant Reformation have on social welfare? On women?

6. Of what importance to social welfare in North America were the Elizabethan Poor Laws?

7. In what ways are mercantilism, the Protestant Reformation, the Scientific Revolution, and capitalism intimately related?

Notes

1. Ralph Dolgoff and Donald Feldstein, *Understanding Social Welfare*, 2nd ed. (New York: Longman Press, 1984), p. 39.

2. Amaury De Riencourt, *Sex and Power in History* (New York: Dell Publishing, 1974), p. 156.

3. David Macarov, *The Design of Social Welfare* (New York: Holt, Rinehart & Winston, 1978), p. 97.

4. De Riencourt, *Sex and Power,* p. 194.

5. Lerone Bennett, Jr., *Before the Mayflower: A History of the Negro in America, 1619–1964* (Chicago: Johnson Publishing Company, 1966), p. 18, quoting Alexander Chamberlain.

6. Justine Glass, *Witchcraft: The Sixth Sense* (North Hollywood: Wilshire Book Co., 1973), p. 108.

7. Frances Gies and Joseph Gies, *Women in the Middle Ages* (New York: Barnes and Noble, 1978), pp. 27–31.

8. Frances Gies and Joseph Gies, *Cathedral, Forge and Waterwheel: Technology and Invention in the Middle Ages* (New York: HarperCollins, 1994), p. 109.

9. Joseph R. Strayer and Dana C. Munro, *The Middle Ages 395–1500* (New York: Appleton-Century Crofts, 1970), p. 130. Quoted in Dolgoff and Feldstein, *Understanding Social Welfare*, p. 41.

10. Richard W. Southern, *The Making of the Middle Ages* (New York: Dell Publishing, 1982), p. 50. Quoted in Dolgoff and Feldstein, *Understanding Social Welfare*, p. 42.

11. Herbert J. Muller, *Freedom in the Western World: From the Dark Ages to the Rise of Democracy* (New York: Harper & Row, 1963), p. 67. Quoted in Gerald Handel, *Social Welfare in Western Society* (New York: Random House, 1982), p. 32.

12. Gies and Gies, *Women in the Middle Ages*, pp. 1–16.

13. Gies and Gies, *Cathedral, Forge and Waterwheel*, p. 50.

14. Ibid., p. 51.

15. Carolyn Merchant, *The Death of Nature: Women, Ecology, and the Scientific Revolution* (San Francisco: Harper & Row, 1980), pp. 1–3.

16. Ibid., pp. 46–47.

17. *The Hutchinson Family Encyclopedia,* 195.152.156.15/encyclopedia/88/MOOO3688.ht, Helocon Publishing, 2000.

18. Gies and Gies, *Cathedral, Forge, and Water Wheel*, p. 269.

19. Ibid.

20. "Capital and Labour—Population: The Growth of the Proletariat," www.history.rochester.edu/steam/lord/3-1.1.

21. Michael Baigent, Richard Leigh, and Henry Lincoln, *Holy Blood, Holy Grail* (New York: Dell Publishing, 1982), p. 49.

22. G. G. Coulton, *The Medieval Scene* (Cambridge: Cambridge University Press, 1930), p. 1. Quoted in Handel, *Social Welfare*, p. 32.

23. Walter Trattner, "The Background," in Neil Gilbert and Harry Specht (eds.), *Emergence of Social Welfare and Social Work*, 2nd ed. (Itasca, IL: F.E. Peacock Publishers, 1981), p. 25.

24. Walter A. Friedlander and Robert Z. Apte, *Introduction to Social Welfare*, 4th ed. (Englewood Cliffs, NJ: Prentice Hall, 1955), pp. 9–10.

25. Gies and Gies, *Women in the Middle Ages*, p. 65.

26. Ibid., p. 64.

27. Ibid.

28. Dolgoff and Feldstein, *Understanding Social Welfare*, p. 43.

29. Merchant, *Death of Nature*, pp. 47–48.

30. Gies and Gies, *Women in the Middle Ages*, pp. 168–169, 181.

31. Ibid., pp. 157–161.

32. Ibid.

33. Robert S. Lopez, *Commercial Revolution of the Middle Ages 950–1350* (Cambridge: Cambridge University Press, 1976), p. 72. Quoted in Gies and Gies, *Cathedral, Forge and Waterwheel*, p. 169.

34. Merchant, *Death of Nature*, p. 48.

35. Joseph Klaits, *Servants of Satan: The Age of the Witch Hunts* (Bloomington: Indiana University Press, 1985), p. 21.

36. Ibid., p. 21.

37. Ibid., p. 37.

38. Ibid., p. 77.

39. Ibid., p. 52.

40. Nider's *Formicarium*, in De Riencourt, *Sex and Power*, pp. 252–263.

41. J. Sprenger, *Malleus Maleficarum*, M. Summers (trans.) (New York: B. Blom, 1970), pp. 112–121. Discussed in De Riencourt, *Sex and Power*, pp. 249 ff. Jacob Sprenger's rationale for this state of affairs is interesting and ingenious. After stating the exceptional vulnerability of the "fragile sex" and the eagerness of women for explanations on this topic, he elaborates:

> Now the wickedness of women is spoken of in Ecclesiasticus XXV: All wickedness is but little to the wickedness of a woman. . . . What else is a woman but a foe to friendship, an unescapable punishment, a necessary evil, a natural temptation, a desirable calamity, a domestic danger, a delectable detriment, an evil of nature, painted with fair colors! Therefore if it be a sin to divorce her when she ought to be kept, it is indeed a necessary torture . . . since they are feebler both in mind and body, it is not surprising that they should come more under the spell of witchcraft . . . they have slippery tongues, and are unable to conceal from their fellow-women those things which by evil arts they know; and since the natural reason is that she is more carnal than a man . . . she is an imperfect animal, she always deceives . . . a woman is beautiful to look upon, contaminating to the touch and deadly to keep.

It is significant that in England, where judicial torture was not allowed, witch hunting started much later. According to De Riencourt in *Sex and Power* (p. 254), in 1487 the University of Cologne gave its official seal of approval to the *Malleus Maleficarum* and stated that

> whosoever denied the reality of witches and witchcraft should be prosecuted for raising obstacles to the Inquisition's labors. It had the full support of public opinion, and on numerous occasions, the crowds, frightened by natural catastrophes, took matters in their own hands without waiting for official sanction and killed scores of unfortunate women . . . the Reformers themselves, Luther and Calvin at their head, entertained exactly the same beliefs regarding witchcraft as did Roman Catholics, and persecuted witches with as much fanati-

cism as their Catholic antagonists. Persecution started in earnest, however, to reach its climax, not under the relatively lenient Church of England, but under the fanatical Puritans; the number of Englishwomen who were burned without ever having been brought to trial will never be known but must have been considerable. King James VI was not far behind Pope Innocent VIII and Sprenger in his persecuting zeal.

42. Mary Daly, *Gyn/Ecology: The MetaEthics of Feminism* (Boston: Beacon Press, 1978).

43. Klaits, *Servants of Satan*, p. 89.

44. Keith Thomas, *Religion and the Decline of Magic* (London: Weidenfeld and Nicolson, 1971), p. 554; and Alan MacFarlane, *Witchcraft in Tudor and Stuart England* (New York: Harper & Row, 1970), esp. pp. 92–99; also see Klaits, *Servants of Satan*, p. 89.

45. Klaits, *Servants of Satan*, pp. 94–95.

46. Eleanor S. Riemer, "Women, Dowries, and Capital Investment in Thirteenth-Century Siena," in Marion A. Kaplan (ed.), *The Marriage Bargain* (New York: Haworth Press, 1985), pp. 59–79.

47. Dolgoff and Feldstein, *Understanding Social Welfare*, p. 46.

48. Gies and Gies, *Cathedral, Forge and Waterwheel*, p. 172.

49. Beulah Compton, *Introduction to Social Welfare and Social Work: Structure, Function, and Process* (Homewood, IL: The Dorsey Press, 1980), p. 153.

50. Dolgoff and Feldstein, *Understanding Social Welfare*, p. 46.

51. Gerald N. Grob, *State and Public Welfare in Nineteenth-Century America* (New York: Arno Press, 1976), p. 7.

52. Gies and Gies, *Cathedral, Forge and Waterwheel*, p. 235.

53. Klaits, *Servants of Satan*, pp. 90–91.

54. Max Weber, *Protestant Ethic and the Spirit of Capitalism* (New York: Scribner, 1976), p. 3.

55. Ibid., p. 54.

56. De Riencourt, *Sex and Power*, p. 261. Martin Luther as quoted in De Riencourt.

57. E. Lamy, *La Femme de Demain* (Paris, n.d.), p. 100. Quoted in De Riencourt, *Sex and Power*, p. 259.

58. John Knox (ed.), "First Blast of the Trumpet Against the Monstrous Regiment of Women," in Merchant, *Death of Nature*, pp. 146–147.

59. Samuel Mencher, *From Poor Law to Poverty Programs* (Pittsburgh: University of Pittsburgh Press, 1967), p. xvi.

60. Frank Dekker Watson, *The Charity Organization Movement in the United States* (New York: Arno Press and the New York Times, 1971), p. 15, originally printed by Macmillan, 1922.

61. Ibid., p. 23.

62. Handel, *Social Welfare*, p. 63.

63. Ibid., p. 96.

64. Blanche Coll, *Perspectives in Public Welfare: A History* (Washington, D.C.: U.S. Government Printing Office, 1971), p. 7.

65. Ibid.

66. Mencher, *Poor Law to Poverty Programs*, p. 30.

67. Ibid., p. 27.

68. De Schweinitz, *England's Road to Social Welfare* (1943), pp. 65–66. In Compton, *Introduction to Social Welfare*, p. 58.

69. Ibid., p. 73.

70. Grob, *State and Public Welfare*, p. 8.

71. Jeffrey Galper, *Social Work Practice: A Radical Perspective* (Englewood Cliffs, NJ: Prentice Hall, 1980), p. 25.

72. Adam Smith, *The Wealth of Nations* (New York: Modern Library, 1937), p. 14.

73. Adam Smith, *Adam Smith's Moral and Political Philosophy*, Herbert W. Schneider (ed.) (New York: Hafner, 1948), p. 25.

74. Mencher, *Poor Law to Poverty Programs*, pp. 67–68.

75. Ibid., p. 60.
76. De Schweinitz, *England's Road*, p. 24.
77. Handel, *Social Welfare*, p. 121.
78. Friedlander and Apte, *Introduction to Social Welfare*, p. 94.
79. Watson, *Charity Organization Movement*, pp. 13–14.

5

The Other Side of the World

The conquest of the Americas demonstrates decisively Western society's obsession with wealth. Although some early explorers were priests who came to convert Native Americans, most came for fortunes for themselves and the governments that supported them. Their religions, moreover, legitimated conquest and exploitation of others in the name of the now-moral quest for wealth. Protestantism, with its dour philosophies of labor and profit, changed the social, spiritual, and economic consciousness of the world, and Catholicism, responding to the economic imperatives of emergent mercantilism, did not seriously object. Persecution of women, Jews, and non-Christian people was common, and a papal bull issued in 1455 authorized Portugal to enslave all infidel people,[1] legitimating slavery even before the discovery of the New World. Such attitudes and behaviors in the colonization centuries (1500–1800) provided the basis for the political economy of the United States, including social welfare and the uses of the laboring poor.

Life in this era was bitter, exploitable, and cheap, and people were profit-making commodities. In Europe, the great mass of people lived in desperate poverty, fed or starved at the will of their masters. Plagues and disease were common to all classes, and famine killed thousands. Cities swamped with people looking for work meted out severe punishments for large or small transgressions as the poor eked out their meager living with crime and prostitution. They lived in hovels, under bridges, or in the streets, or were confined in almshouses or jails. Concern for the poor was almost always directed to increasing their ability to work or keeping them from rebelling, and their treatment depended not on humanitarianism but on the business decisions of others.

Europeans who came to the Americas found a new land ripe for economic plunder. Whether in the high cultures of Meso-America or the democratic societies of North America, gold, silver, land, and the greater commodity, human labor, were available for the taking. At first contact, there were more than two hundred distinctive Native American groups, with a population estimated at ten million in North America and tens of millions in the rest of the hemisphere.[2] In North America, they included

- Hunting, fishing, and farming societies of the East
- Great Plains hunters and agriculturists
- Fishing societies of the Northwest
- Seed gatherers of California and the Southwest
- Navaho shepherds and Pueblo farmers in Arizona and New Mexico
- Desert societies in Arizona and New Mexico
- The Alaskan groups.

These many societies were at greatly differing stages of development, some with highly diversified social and economic systems. In North America, most of those along the Eastern Coast and in the Midwest were agrarian, and most had national boundaries within which they farmed, fished, and hunted. Some Southwestern societies were nomadic; others were farming and herding societies. In Meso-America, the Inca, Maya, and Aztec peoples had hierarchical priest-king societies that rivaled those of Egypt, Greece, or Rome. These existed alongside slash-and-burn agricultural societies in the lowlands.

Although every society was different, they were unilaterally treated as one by the invaders; that is, they were forced to submit or die. Disease, forced labor, and the technologies of gunpowder, muskets, and cannon devastated the Native American population. Of the millions of Native Americans living in the Americas at first contact, by about 1850 only about 200,000 remained in North America, and the high cultures of Meso-America had been wiped from the earth.

The Indigenous Peoples of America

As early as 25,000 B.C., immigrants from the Far East crossed the Siberian land bridge to range downward and outward through the Americas (see Figure 5.1). By about 9000 B.C., Paleo-Indian big-game hunting societies stretched from the grasslands of the Pacific coast to the Rockies. Archaic cultures flourished, and after several millennia Woodland societies, with their invention of horticulture, emerged in the Ohio and Illinois valleys. Their stages of social development closely paralleled those of early Europe. They lived in dispersed villages, built huge burial mounds and earthworks, and demonstrated a highly developed religion and a system of social stratification with their grave goods. The Hopewell culture began about 300 B.C. and reached its peak in the early centuries after Christ, enduring until about 850 A.D. An extensive trading network developed among societies from the Rockies to the Great Lakes regions.

The democratic societies of North America counterpointed the hierarchical systems of the Incas, Mayans, and Aztecs in South and Central America. Here priests and kings, with their bureaucracies, ruled peasants and artisans through

FIGURE 5.1   *The First Immigration to the Western Hemisphere*

labor conscription, tribute, and taxation. Corvées farmed, worked in the royal mines, herded royal alpaca and llama, built roads, monuments, and temples, and warred and colonized; whole populations were moved to new territories to ensure common language and ethnic groups. Intensive agricultural systems, in which two-thirds of the population labored to provide food for the national granaries from which the people were fed, included both permanent and floodwater irrigation, permanent crop rotation, and fertilization. Great pyramids, statuary, and colonnaded temples graced cities that spread over hundreds of acres,[3] and vast engineering projects brought water to Peru's coastal valleys as early as 500 A.D. Ceramic crafts and textile manufacturing compared in excellence with those of Europe, and metallurgical techniques for bronze, silver, and gold were widespread.[4] The Mayan calendar was more accurate than that used in contemporary Europe, and long before the concept of the zero had become part of European mathematics, the ancient Maya used it in their calculations (see Figure 5.2).

FIGURE 5.2 *The People of the Western Hemisphere at the Time of Columbus*

In architecture, metallurgy, astronomy, and statecraft, the most highly developed of the native American states were fully comparable with Old World civilizations. For example, the supreme Inca controlled the lives of as many as six million people. Teotihuacán, the largest city in the New World, covered an area of some 2,000 acres by 800 A.D. Ten thousand people labored over a period of ten years to build its Pyramid of the Sun, and probably as many as 30,000 constructed the Incan Sacsahuaman fortress, where 300-ton megaliths were fitted together to form 30-foot-high walls. A vast network of roads and suspension bridges across ravines and rivers connected the Incan empire.[5] For all practical purposes, the Americas remained in the Stone Age because of the lack of large animals suitable for riding and traction.

> In the absence of traction animals, the wheel was not invented (except as a toy); consequently, the wheeled vehicle, the potter's wheel, the spinning wheel, and the waterwheel all remained unknown. The discrepancy in technological levels conditioned much of the relationship between the European discoverer–adventurers and the Native Americans.[6]

The Stone Age technology of the Americas was no match for medieval firepower and horse-warfare.

The European Invasion

Although Norsemen explored in the New World centuries before Columbus found the Caribbean Isles in 1492, the impetus for colonization awaited the social and technological innovations of the Middle Ages and the push for international markets. Within a few decades after Columbus's first voyage, Dutch, English, French, Spanish, and Portuguese began the expansion that would create European-controlled nations on the bones of indigenous New World societies (see Figure 5.3).

The French in the New World

The French in early America were perhaps the least exploitative of the European invaders, for they assimilated with rather than tried to change Native American cultures. Voyageurs and priests, looking for adventure, trade, and souls to convert, sailed the Atlantic Coast and the St. Lawrence Seaway. France's Verrazano explored the Atlantic shores to Nova Scotia in 1524, and in 1534, Cartier found the Iroquois in the St. Lawrence Valley. Marquette and Joliet, followed by LaSalle, journeyed across the Great Lakes, down the Mississippi to Louisville, and finally into the Gulf of Mexico in 1682. The French first settled, unsuccessfully, in Canada in 1541 and did not attempt settlement again until the founding of Quebec in 1608. France's occupation of Florida and part of the Gulf Coast began in 1562, and Jesuit missions were on the Great Lakes by 1633, ministering to the Five Nations—Mohawk, Oneida, Onondaga, Cayugo, and Seneca—who inhabited the

FIGURE 5.3 *European Invasions in the New World*

area north of Lake Ontario. However, "as they spread the gospel they also spread disease. . . . Half the Hurons in Georgia Bay died between 1634 and 1640."[7]

The primary interest of the French was to "harvest" beaver, and Native Americans responded by overkilling beaver, unravelling the fabric of their rituals of the hunt. The introduction of alcohol

> amounted to an additional epidemic. . . . They believed that liquor produced a welcome transformation of the personality and that they were not responsible for what they did when in an altered state . . . [including] men killing each other, husbands burning wives, wives dishonoring husbands, and fathers putting their children in cauldrons.[8]

In 1663, King Louis XIV took an interest in colonization. The French settlers lived on scattered farms, and the King sent troops to protect them. He also encouraged them to marry Iroquois women. Jean Talon was appointed first governor of new France in 1665, and he began colonization in earnest.

> The same year Talon arrived . . . the first shipment of "daughters of the king," from orphanages in France, also docked. . . . In fifteen days, all were married and in 1666 New France had a population of 3215, of whom 204 were men.[9]

The Spanish in the New World

Before the marriage of Ferdinand and Isabella (1469) united Aragon and Castile, a warrior class—the *hidalgos*—ruled the dukedoms that became Spain. Soldiers good with weapons and horses, they had fought the Moors for seven centuries and considered ordinary work beneath them. These were the *conquistadores* who came to America for riches for themselves and their monarchs. Catholic priests accompanied them to convert Native Americans to Christianity, and together they mapped the Caribbean, the Gulf of Mexico, Meso-America, much of South America, and the Southwest from the Rio Grande to California and Oregon. The first nonindigenous permanent settlers in what would become the United States were a group of African slaves abandoned by their Spanish owners in the area of South Carolina, in 1526.[10] The first permanent city in the New World was settled not at Plymouth Rock but by the Spanish at St. Augustine, Florida, in 1565.

Although the Spanish were not interested in colonization, Columbus wanted a governorship as his reward. On his second voyage, in 1493, he founded the town of La Isabela on the northern shore of the Dominican Republic and set up a system of forced labor to help settlers work the land. To "pacify" the rebellious Taino Native Americans, he sent 500 to Spain to be sold as slaves, and then began to raid other settlements to make up for labor shortages. Those who resisted being sent into underground mines had their arms cut off and were sent back to their villages as warnings.[11] A new governor, Nicolas de Ovando, was appointed in 1502. He regulated forced labor into a system called the *encomienda*, in which workers mined in return for wages, protection, and Christian instruction. If the Tainos ran, the *hidalgos* chased them with greyhounds fed on human flesh to make them better man-hunters. Within fifty years of Columbus's first voyage, the Tainos had been exterminated.[12]

Slaving expeditions and disease stripped the Greater Antilles and the Bahamas of its indigenous inhabitants by 1513, when Ponce de León raided Florida. Many who were enslaved committed suicide, others ran away, and a great number were simply worked to death. The decimation of Caribbean societies was abetted by the native peoples' lack of resistance to European diseases such as smallpox, measles, bubonic plague, and respiratory infections. Epidemics of monstrous proportions occurred all through the first centuries of contact: One-third of the population of the Tupinanba in Brazil was wiped out by smallpox in 1562, and Borinquén (Puerto Rico), which had a native population of 50,000 in 1493, was so reduced by 1530 that newly imported black slaves were the majority.[13] By the end of the 1600s, when sugar from the West Indies became the major import to Europe, most of the Caribbean's native populations had vanished.

De Soto landed in Tampa Bay in 1539, where Native Americans lived in large villages called chiefdoms. Following his arrival,

> [t]he enslavement of men and women, the many pitched battles, the destruction of villages, the psychological shock of defeat, the looting, and the epidemics destroyed a social system. . . . Fifty years later, the world of the chiefdoms—Apalachee, Ocute, Coose, Pacacha, and others—had vanished.[14]

The Spanish also plundered Meso-America, beginning with the Aztec nation's subjugation in 1519 by Hernando Cortés. Reigning rulers and bureaucracies were reduced to puppet governments, and the people were enslaved to work in gold and silver mines. By 1550, the fabulous silver mines of New Mexico had been discovered, giving Spain wealth untold in Europe, and within a century the indigenous population had been so drastically reduced that society could not be sustained, and blooming cultures rivaling those of Europe ceased to exist. Recent demographic studies of central Mexico during the sixteenth century reveal an astonishing decline in population, from some twenty million to one million in less than one hundred years.[15]

Coronado's expedition up the Rio Grande (1540–1542) found villages of whitewashed and frescoed three- to five-story buildings with thousands of hospitable Pueblo Indian inhabitants. They had cultivated fields of maize, beans, squash, and cotton, had domesticated turkeys and dogs,[16] and had stores of grain for the winter and seeds for future plantings. Within a few years, tributes demanded by the Spanish had wiped out their stores and mass starvation began. A particularly despotic crown-appointed governor, Oñate, ravaged the tribes to such an extent that his removal was demanded by Franciscan missionaries, who were then given control. By the 1600s there were 3,000 missionaries in the area, with a European Catholic system of welfare for now poverty-stricken people who, before the invasion, had fully supported themselves.

The Apache nations of the Great Plains, whose societies surrounded the Pueblos, were conquered by 1650. Spanish farms began to enclose their land, and disease and crop failures added to the distress already caused by massive tributes, leading to mass starvation and, finally, rebellion by both Apache and Pueblo Indians. Apache raids were common all during the 1600s and more frequent after 1650. In 1675, Juan de Treviño, the Spanish-appointed governor in what is now New Mexico, decided to stamp out native religious practices and arrested forty-seven shamans. Three were hanged, one hanged himself, and the others were whipped and released. In response, a Tewa shaman named Popé organized the Hopis in the Rio Grande valley, the Jemez valley, and the Zuni Basin in 1680. He developed a network of 6,000 warriors among the 25,000 Native Americans, outnumbering the Spanish almost three to one, and led a siege on Santa Fe. A predawn attack killed 300 of the besiegers but Santa Fe was abandoned.

> It was a triumph for Popé. . . . For the first and last time in North America, the native people had defeated and thrown out the colonizer, and the land was returned to its original settlers.[17]

Shortly thereafter, a massive retaliation ensued in which the Hopis, disheartened, surrendered without a fight, leaving the Spanish once more in control.

The Spanish Church maintained an essentially hands-off policy on slavery because it was profitable for both church and monarchy. Even priests owned both Native American and African slaves. However, Native Americans were considered subjects of the crown and church, and one of the express purposes of sending priests and missionaries to the Americas was to save their souls. This moral paradox resulted in Spanish laws in 1542 to protect Native Americans from exploitation. The church maintained that slaves had human and spiritual rights, and slavery in South America was looked on as a contract in which masters owned the slaves' labor but not their humanity.[18] The sanctity of marriage and family was upheld and spouses and children were unlikely to be sold away from each other, they could earn money for themselves after work for their masters was done, and they could buy freedom for themselves and their families. The possibility of freedom meant the development of a class of workers and artisans, which over time became a stable and free middle class. Moreover, the invading Spanish took wives among the Native Americans and the African slaves, beginning a unique Hispanic heritage in which priests and missionaries took an important leading role.[19] In the northern colonies, where not only the work but the lives of slaves belonged to the master, these possibilities did not exist.

Protestants in North America

Northern Europeans came to America from about 1522 and found Native Americans in permanent homes in palisaded villages, cultivating fields of corn, squash, and cucurbits. Eager for furs and for the fish abounding in the Atlantic waters, both Dutch and English set up joint-stock businesses, partly financed by merchants in Europe, and by 1632 the indigenous peoples had iron kettles, axes, arrowheads, and knives, although few had firearms.

The Dutch East India Company sought to expand its profitable international trade with resources from the New World by giving colonists patroonships (absolute ownership of huge tracts of land) in return for establishing a colony of fifty adults. Although Dutch settlers were at first scrupulous in their dealings with the Native Americans, land had a different meaning for Dutch and Native Americans, and before long the Dutch took advantage of this difference. According to Native Americans, Mother Earth could not be sold, so in return for insignificant amounts, the Dutch "bought" their lands from them. When Native Americans refused to move, the Dutch began to kill them, often wiping out whole villages. In 1642, the brutal Dutch governor William Kieft launched a five-year war against the Native Americans. Settlers noted that after a raid on Staten Island killed eighty Native Americans, some survivors "came . . . with their hands or legs cut off . . . and some holding their entrails in their arms."[20] Kieft also began the practice of bounties on scalps: The going rate was ten fathoms of *wampum*.[21]

From 1623 to 1626, New York, New Jersey, and part of Delaware were settled by Dutch Protestants. Their charter required that each settlement provide preachers, schoolmasters, and comforters of the sick and required pastors' assistants to give help and solace to the unhappy, ill, or disabled. These systems of welfare were undertaken from both religious and business perspectives. Vagabonds and beggars were "bonded" to patroons in return for their board and clothing, often for life. Deacons supervised by clergy gave outdoor relief gleaned from church collections and fines to the impotent, ill, and disabled. The church was the community conscience, encouraging neighborhoods to care for their own poor and to establish mutual aid associations. By 1664, ten of the twelve Dutch settlements had established schools controlled by church and court and supported by taxation, tuition, the Dutch East India Company, and the church. When the Dutch lost New Amsterdam to the English, English poor laws were substituted for Dutch community care.

The English in New England

English colonists came for many reasons: to escape the poverty of peasant life in Europe, to find fortunes or adventure, or, in the case of Pilgrims and Puritans, to escape retaliation by the newly restored monarchy; under Oliver Cromwell they had beheaded King Charles I in 1649. The depletion of England's own natural resources, especially its forests, made the New World a bonanza for materials increasingly scarce in England, such as potash, timber, pitch, tar, resin, iron, and copper. In addition, production of New World goods, particularly sugar, tobacco, coffee, and chocolate, made new fortunes. Adventurers, many of them second (or later) sons who could not inherit in England because of laws of primogeniture, came seeking legal or illegal fortunes and became pirates, lawbreakers, highwaymen, businessmen, and a new mercantilist elite. Some came not so freely, transported to America as an alternative to prison, kidnapped by ship captains or "Newlanders" who received a bonus for every man, woman, or child arriving alive in the New World, or enslaved by traders seeking free labor in the sugar plantations of the Caribbean or the cotton plantations of the South.

The first English colony was established at Roanoke, Virginia, in 1564, by Sir Walter Raleigh. It survived only three years, and the next colony, founded at Jamestown in 1607, was a commercial venture financed by the joint-stock Virginia Company and expected to produce a profit. The Massachusetts Bay Colony was settled in 1629 by Puritan businessmen. Pennsylvania was settled by Quakers who followed William Penn into exile from England. Georgia was the only New England colony not established as a religious haven or a business: England transported free people and gave them land and tools in return for a promise of military service should it be needed. Georgia also was the only colony to accept Jews as equals, and slavery was not permitted under its earliest charter.

At first the companies and colonists followed the Dutch lead in land purchase and relied on friendly natives to help them through severe winters. Soon, however, colonists simply took the land, killing or enslaving its inhabitants: During the mid-1700s, 5 to 10 percent of slaves were Native Americans, and as late as 1790, 200 of the 6,000 slaves in Massachusetts were Native Americans.[22] The colonists' brutality precipitated such wars as that against the Wampanoag in 1675, where the leader, King Philip, was drawn and quartered and his skull displayed on a pole until the 1700s. Quakers were the major exception to such genocide, continuing to deal scrupulously with the Native Americans, although they too had both Native American and African slaves.

Although resources were plentiful in the New World, labor was scarce, and a concerted effort to populate the colonies began. By 1640, there were thousands of English colonists in New England. Spanish immigration to the entire New World between 1509 and 1790 was only about 150,000 people, but between 1600 and 1700, half a million English moved to North America[23] to begin the hard life of subsistence farming. In the early days, caves or houses covered with bark served as homes because colonists had no tools for turning logs into lumber. All members of the family worked, both in domestics (cleaning house, making yarn, grinding and milling flour, sewing, and spinning) and in the fields as they were needed. Men, when their labor in the fields was completed, worked with their wives at spinning and weaving. Religion as well as necessity prompted the work, for idleness was, according to religion, a sign that Satan was at work. In Massachusetts, a wife's refusal to serve her husband by laboring obediently and frugally was considered grounds for divorce. Both boys and girls were taught household work, and both spent as much time in the workshop as in home or field. Many colonists, wealthy or poor, bound out their children as domestic help to others so that they might learn the value of work.

Whereas New England and Pennsylvania were settled by immigrant family groups, setting the stage for community democracies, the South was settled by people who transported the English manor system to the New World. They accepted the burden of *noblesse oblige*, taking on government and public responsibility, becoming justices of the peace and overseers of the poor. The ideal of lord and serfs was also imported, making the concept of slavery easy. Tobacco was the staple crop and was often used as currency, selling for three shillings a pound as early as 1614. Virginia became a one-crop colony, exporting 2,500 pounds in 1616 and more than one million pounds in 1628.[24]

The cultivation of this crop required a large workforce for planting, transplanting, topping, suckering, weeding, worming, cutting, curing, binding, and packing. At first, indentured servants were used, but they soon paid off their bonds and became landowners themselves. The first slaves were brought by the Dutch to Jamestown in 1619, and landowners began to acquire an all-slave labor force. There were several reasons for this, including an incipient racism: White workers disliked working with the slaves. Slaves were also more docile and cheaper to keep because they could not make demands for better food, shelter, and clothing. Moreover, they reproduced themselves and, because they had nowhere to go, did not run away.[25] For some time, small farmers remained in the tobacco industry, but large plantations soon took over. In the 1600s in Virginia, small farmers were about one-twentieth of the population, but by 1730 one-fourth of them had been squeezed out.[26]

The Practice of Indenture

Because labor was scarce and the cost of passage high, the practice of indenture arose, whereby the price of passage was advanced to settlers who agreed to work it off, usually in five to eight years. The first indentured servants to arrive in the New World were probably a group of twenty Africans, brought to Jamestown a year before the *Mayflower*,[27] and between 1619 and 1660 some Africans continued to enter the country as indentured servants. In addition, a quarter of a million people—probably one-half of all white immigrants, a third of them women— came as indentured servants.[28] For almost one hundred years, white indentured servants were the principal source of labor in the New England colonies. In 1683, white servants represented one-sixth of Virginia's population. Two-thirds of the immigrants to Pennsylvania during the 1700s were indentured, and in four years, 25,000 came to Philadelphia alone. In 1624 there were only twenty-two people of African descent in Virginia, at a time when several thousand a year were being brought into South America. After 1680, slaves began to arrive in increasing numbers, but not until the 1750s did they exceed 25 percent of the population.

A regular and profitable traffic developed in indentured servants, and between 1654 and 1685, 10,000 sailed from Bristol alone, chiefly for the West Indies and Virginia. To control this traffic, a Colonial Board was created in 1661. People of all statuses were involved in the trade, and kidnapping and "recruitment" by "Newlanders" was common, with a commission gained on each person delivered alive to the New World. The punishment for "man selling" was the pillory, a mild punishment considering the profit gained. In 1654, burgomasters of Amsterdam sent a cargo of nearly thirty poor children to Peter Stuyvesant at New Amsterdam; under English laws, any dependent children could be deported to the colonies. London took from its almshouses 300 to 400 boys and girls ages ten to fifteen to ship to the colonies.[29]

Convicts provided another steady source of white indentured labor. Three hundred capital crimes were recognized for which the choice of punishment was hanging or indenture, including pickpocketing more than a shilling or shoplifting five shillings, stealing a horse or sheep, or poaching rabbits on a gentleman's estate. In 1717, a law gave indenture of fourteen years to those sentenced to death. Lesser offenses meant seven years of indenture: stealing clothing, burning corn, maiming or killing cattle; engaging in trade union activity, or being a vagrant, rogue, idler, petty thief, gypsy, or frequenter of brothels.[30] Ship captains also bought indentures for the danger-fraught three-month trip across the Atlantic, giving each person a space of 6 feet by 2 feet. Food was very scarce because captains overbooked by double, and people fought with each other for the dead bodies of mice and rats. No one could leave the ships until their indenture was bought, and those without a buyer were put on the auction block. Parents were forced to watch as their children were sold, and husbands and wives were separated. Children under five could not be sold but were given away to serve until the age of twenty-one.[31] Male indentured servants were more valuable, so ships' masters were paid twice as much for men as for women.

Bonds were usually for five to seven years, but they often lasted longer because of debts to the master. Wages were room and board plus fare to America and "freedom dues"—a little extra to start off—at the end of indenture. These included clothing, food, a gun, and sometimes fifty acres. Lucky servants might get an additional wage, perhaps three pounds a year, or a suit of clothing at the end of service. Cash payments were rare; payment was often given in tobacco or other produce. Although the master controlled all personal affairs, indentured servants had legal rights and could sue. Usually marriage was forbidden, and childbearing was considered an interruption in work and an impairment of health and stamina. Nevertheless, about one in five women did have children, and both mother and father had to pay a fine to reimburse the master for loss of services during pregnancy or submit to another two years of indenture.

Political dissent was another cause for indenture. For example, when Ireland was conquered by England early in the 1600s, Irish peasants were pushed off their lands and were often shipped to the colonies to work for English colonials. About half were indentured at double the passage rate of others and for double the time—about twenty years, with extra years for debts to the master. Before the massive trade in Africans began, many Irish indentured servants were shipped to Caribbean plantations to replace Native Americans in the burgeoning sugar industry. In Barbados, they were used for

> grinding at the mills and attending the furnaces, or digging . . . having nothing to feed on . . . but potatoe roots, nor to drink, but water with such roots washed in it, besides the bread and tears of their own afflictions; being bought and sold still from one planter to another, or attached as horses and beasts for the debts of their masters, being whipt at the whipping post . . . for their masters' pleasure, and sleeping in sties worse than hogs in England.[32]

White servants and black slaves worked together in the West Indies for some time. Indentured servants, because they were not long-term property investments, were often more cruelly treated than were African slaves.[33] Africans were the better bargain because the same money that could buy a white laborer for ten years could buy an African for life.[34] However, indentured servants had some right to personal property, and their children were free, whereas children of slaves became the slavemaster's property.

By the 1700s, English migration had slowed considerably because overpopulation was no longer a problem and political dissent had lessened. Although indenture continued for some time, the vast numbers of migrants coming in by this means also declined, and kidnapping and illegal recruitment were no longer so common. Some say that colonization of America was the largest and most successful welfare program in history.[35] Certainly for England this was true. It removed from the country its overpopulation, the poor, criminals, and undesirables, and at the same time returned a vast profit to the mother country. According to Handel,

> The colonizing efforts . . . combined philanthropic motives with political motives. . . . James Oglethorpe, an activist in the English movement to free debtors from prison, had the idea of helping such men get a new start in a New World. The project was financed with money raised by Oglethorpe and a large contribution from the English government, which hoped that [the] project would help solve the problems of vagrancy in England.[36]

Women in the Colonies

Women constituted a third of the early immigrants to North America. Many were kidnapped to provide the new country with wives and laborers, and male colonists paid for wives from Europe; for example, the settlers at Jamestown ordered two boatloads of women in 1619, paying 120 pounds of tobacco each for their passage.[37] Once they arrived in the colonies, regardless of their status, women's scarcity made their lot better than that of their European counterparts; there were six men for every woman in seventeenth-century Virginia, for example. Most could marry if they wanted or had the leverage to refuse an unsuitable proposal.[38] To increase the population, young people had much freedom in choice of mate. Women married and died young in the colonies. According to Jacobs,

> [P]erhaps as many as four of every five of the first groups of women [died] . . . within five years. . . . [W]omen married early, sometimes at twelve or thirteen. . . . [There was] the common phenomenon of a man's outliving three or four of his wives.[39]

Childbirth was one of the most common causes of death, and women feared pregnancy because they knew they might have less than nine months to live. The average number of children was nine, but it was not uncommon for a woman to have twelve or fifteen, not many of whom lived to adulthood.

Marriage was considered the natural and desirable life for women; although they contributed equally to the economy, they were secondary to men both politically and religiously. Most sexual behavior was not disapproved if the couple planned to marry, but if not, sexual activity was taken very seriously. Women who bore children outside marriage could be taken to court and sentenced to public whipping, branding, and fines. Their children, if they could not support them or could not or would not name the father, could be taken and apprenticed to a tradesperson.[40] Moreover, ministers cautioned women to remain under husbands' control, and those who objected could be punished by both the husband and the town. Adultery was the worst crime a woman could commit, for it was an offense against men's property rights. Divorce and legal separation were possible for women, but grounds were very difficult, and there were no laws forcing a man to support a wife from whom he was separated. In a separation, the woman usually lost everything, even her children. A 1748 law allowed husbands to appoint guardians for their children and to apprentice them out to learn a trade, specifying that mothers were entitled only to their love and respect.[41] For most women, legal and religious ties could not be broken by men's adultery, abuse, or even desertion—only by death—and women alone seldom could find work that would free them from economic dependence on their husbands or the government.

Early in colonization, women had more rights than in later times, especially on the frontier, where their labor was so desperately needed. There, even married women could own property and sue in courts, and they were generally favored by judges who defended them against personal abuse, enforced conjugal rights, and recalled runaway husbands.[42] They could also receive land grants as heads of families. For example, Pennsylvania offered seventy-five acres to female settlers, and if they brought servants and children, the grants were larger. Women also could develop their own lands: Margaret Brent, the colonies' first female lawyer, arrived in Maryland in 1638 and built a fortune in real estate. However, because land enabled women to remain single, most colonies soon refused to grant them land and denied them the right to inherit it.

Women and their daughters spun cotton, flax, and wool, looked after livestock, made butter and cheese, baked bread, cleaned and cooked, and bore and raised children. They doctored and nursed their families and prepared their own medicines (salves, balms, ointments, potions, and cordials).[43] Some women operated sawmills, distilleries, and slaughterhouses and were newspaper publishers or printers and teachers. They opened schools for women and achieved status as midwives, physicians, and apothecaries at least until the mid-1700s, when men entered the field of obstetrics. Women with a little capital opened small shops, selling anything from pastries and dry goods to hardware and liquor. Women could more easily take on unconventional roles in the South than in Puritan areas, for Puritans attached particular importance to regulating female behavior.[44]

Under common law, never-married women had the same rights as men and could buy and sell property, own businesses, and sue in court (*femme sole*). Once married, however, women entered the state of *femme couverte*, their rights "covered" by those of their husbands. Husband and wife were one person, and that person was the husband.[45] Married women had no property and no money of their own. Even their clothing, jewels, household goods, livestock, and furniture belonged to their husbands, along with dowries and inheritances. In most instances, husbands could sell wives' property without consent or take all their wives' earnings and allow them to starve.[46] Spaeth says,

> The husband's absolute authority over his wife included the legal privilege of beating her . . . [to be interfered with] only if the husband was unduly brutal. At the beginning of the eighteenth century Elizabeth Wildy complained . . . that her husband not only whipped and maimed her but also held her in the fire until her clothes burned. The justices felt that in this case the husband had exceeded his right of "reasonable chastisement" and ordered him to appear in court and explain.[47]

Most American colonies granted three exceptions to these practices of common law. They upheld the wife's right to share her husband's home and bed, the right to be supported by him even if he abandoned her, and the right to be protected from his violence. However, if these happened there was not much recourse because married women could not sue in court.

Widows had the same status as *femmes soles* in business affairs, although eldest sons got the bulk of deceased fathers' real estate, and personal property was divided among all the children. In common law, when a man died without a will, his widow inherited one-third of her husband's real estate and a third interest in slaves and personal property; the real estate reverted to the eldest son at the mother's death. If a man left less than his "third" to his wife, the woman could sue; courts upheld the thirds custom because this reduced the chances that widows could become public dependents. Custom was more generous than law, and often husbands left more to widows than their thirds, especially if there were minor children. Also, they rarely deprived their widows of minor children by appointing a legal guardian. Poor widows, however, had to depend on poor relief or hiring out, often to churches, and many took on the jobs of their husbands— farming, running shops, and smithing—to support themselves and their children.

Because of their secondary spiritual status, women were generally forbidden to speak out on such important topics as religion. The dozens of Quaker women who came to the colonies seeking religious freedom in the 1600s were considered heretics and were fined, whipped, jailed, pilloried, and, in a few instances, hanged.[48] Because government and religion were so closely related, especially in the Puritan colonies, those who argued religion might be considered traitors. An example was Anne Hutchinson, charismatic and intellectual wife of a prosperous businessman, who came to Massachusetts Bay Colony in 1634. She taught that people could approach God through prayer rather than solely through the mediation of a minister (antinomianism). Brought to trial as a heretic before Governor John Winthrop, who was both judge and prosecutor, she was declared guilty before the trial and exiled from the colony. She then helped found

Portsmouth, Rhode Island, on the basis of religious freedom. When her husband died in 1642, leaving her without protection, she fled to the wilderness and was killed, along with several of her children, in an Indian raid.

As in Europe, the colonies had a morbid preoccupation with women's devilish powers. Accusations of witchcraft were used to eliminate bothersome women, and leaders popularized the idea that intellectual women were influenced by Satan. A clear example was Mary Dyer, one of Anne Hutchinson's followers. Accused of being in league with the devil, she was hanged in Boston Commons.[49] In another instance, in 1640 Ann Hibbens was excommunicated for complaining about poor work done in her home by carpenters. The magistrates said her complaints were really against godly authority, and sixteen years later, after her respected husband died, she was executed as a witch.[50] In Salem, 150 (mostly women) of the 200 people accused in 1692 were imprisoned. Fifty confessed and twenty-eight were condemned to die. Fourteen women and six men, one an ordained minister, were actually executed.[51]

By the late 1600s, there was an increasing market for textiles, and town councils saw home piecework for women and their children as a way to reduce public relief.[52] Merchants paid high prices for yarn, and by 1675 towns were providing the capital to set up woolen mills where poor women and their children were put to work at spinning. In Boston, where dependent women were very numerous, the town collected 900 pounds to build a workhouse. This was the first attempt to organize female labor under one roof.

> The widows for whom it was designed refused to go there, objecting to the indignity, to the rigidity of its rules, and to being cut off from friends and community.[53]

The town fathers finally opened it as a factory in 1750.

Home manufacture waned as factories were built in response to the cotton revolution. Soon there were hundreds of cotton mills throughout New England, and factory owners, citing philanthropy as well as economics, petitioned towns to send them poor women and children to work in their mills. By the late 1700s, many towns required overseers of the poor to bind out indigent women and children to the factories.

Social Welfare in the Colonies

Although the colonists adopted England's poor laws almost whole cloth, there were fundamental differences in their ideologies of poor relief practice. First, in England, there was an overabundance of workers in cities, the result of people being pushed off the land. Vast unemployment, pools of workers waiting to be hired, poverty, vagrancy, and crime were the issues social welfare addressed. In a subsistence economy of extreme scarcity, money was not available for the poor, even those obviously dependent because of disability. In the early days of colonial America, on the other hand, labor was scarce and, theoretically, everyone could work. In fact, wages in New England were 30 to 100 percent higher than in England.

Second, whereas in New England upward mobility was limited only by effort (at least in theory), class stratification was firmly set in England and *noblesse oblige* provided a system of private charity, including legacies, endowments, and bequests to provide substantial funds for hospitals, asylums, and orphanages. In the colonies, private charities played an insignificant role until the end of the eighteenth century.[54] Finally, religion, historically the bastion of last resort for the poor, now insisted on individual effort and decried poor relief as contributing to the spiritual degradation of the poor. People who did not abide by the idea of the work ethic were punished, driven out, deported, or even hanged.

Early American Poor Laws

As in European Protestant countries, there was a belief that wealth and condition were divinely ordained. Paupers were treated as morally deficient, and were required to take paupers' oaths and have their names exhibited in the city hall or marketplace or published in newspapers. In some places they were required to wear the letter *P* on their sleeves. The numbers of "worthy poor" were very slim; because everyone started with an "equal chance," few were considered worthy of government help. One group considered worthy from the first were veterans, along with their families or survivors, because of their service to the colonies in the Indian wars. As early as 1636, they received pensions—outdoor relief—as a right.[55] By 1777, all states except Connecticut had special provisions for veterans. People injured in Indian raids were also worthy, at least of short-term help, as disaster victims.

Keynotes in care of the poor were local responsibility, relative and community responsibility, and categorization. Even in earliest colonial times, there were many public dependents. Essentially, they were the unemployable (the aged, disabled, orphans, unwanted children, and widows with children). Another group needing public relief was children of mixed races and old slaves who were freed so their masters would not have to support them when they could no longer work. More public dependents came from the frequent wars with Native Americans; recurring epidemics of smallpox, dysentery, measles, yellow fever; poor harvests or bad weather in times when production of food depended on nature and natural disasters could mean starvation; uncontrollable fires; high childbirth mortality; and the hazards of life in a new country.

Local Responsibility.   By 1642, colonial towns had given township or parish supervisors authority to collect poor taxes, investigate applicants for poor relief to determine their worthiness for aid, and dispense poor relief. In addition to poor taxes, money for relief came from fines for refusing to work at harvest time, selling at short weight, not attending church, and illegally bringing a pauper into town. If a town would not collect poor taxes, local county courts were empowered to assess and dispense funds. By 1636, Plymouth and Massachusetts courts were placing out the poor in homes, and in 1642 Plymouth's first official poor law directed that every case of poor relief be discussed at town meeting. By 1662, the colonies had adopted the English Law of Settlement and Removal, and all colonial towns had to supply food, firewood, clothing, and household essentials for their own poor.

To qualify for poor relief, people had to own property or have lived in a town for a prescribed time (one year was established by 1700). In England, the unemployed had to stay in their home areas, but in the colonies, the unemployed and undesirables had to move on. As early as 1639, eight years after Boston was settled, the courts there had the power to send the poor to towns where they could be employed[56] or to deport them from the country. Strangers were not welcome: Newcomers or "foreigners," even if they came from other colonies, were given three years' probation in some communities. If they could not support themselves and their families within that time, they were sent back to their former places of residence or banished. By 1725, strangers could stay no more than twenty days in many towns without the council being officially informed, and by 1767 no one could move into a town without the council's permission. In 1789, residency laws required that people be in a town for two years or be age twenty-one and have paid taxes for five years. They could also become residents by town vote. By 1793, five years without being warned out was required for residency.[57] *Warning out* had two meanings. First, it warned outsiders that they were not welcome in the towns, were not eligible for poor relief, and might be subject to punishments that ranged from stocks and pillory, flogging, or tarring and feathering, to hanging. Second, residents themselves could be warned out, serving notice that if they stayed they could not expect poor relief and might be indentured if they were in danger of becoming public dependents.

Family Responsibility. Families had a unique importance in colonial poor laws because they provided social control for the religio-political governments. Their role was to ensure that their members would not become dependent on the government. Every person under age twenty-one had to live with a family, and county courts or administrators had the power to place any child or dependent person with a family. Families that could not maintain independence for their members were considered dangerous to the community both economically and morally. Axinn and Levin say,

> Despite the family's usefulness, the impetus to maximize individual and family well-being did not center on the individual as family member or on the individual family as a unit. When a family was in trouble, the concern was to save its potentially productive members.[58]

By 1675, relative responsibility was established by law: People had to be bonded by their families to move in, and diseased or poor people had to be cared for by relatives.

People were expected to care for their own as a matter of course, but when this was not possible the needy were placed with families with the understanding that they would work to pay their keep. The aged, disabled, ill, and infants were placed house-to-house for their care, with the town paying the family to tend to them. The poor—unemployed men and women, widows and their dependent children, and children who were orphaned, unwanted, born out of wedlock, or removed from their parents by order of the court—were auctioned off to the person who would charge the town the least for their care; indentured, so that their bonds were held by the family where they were placed; or apprenticed. Apprenticeship was usually reserved for children of the higher classes so that they might learn a trade.

Some outdoor relief was given to those who were more or less worthy, such as the aged and the ill, so that they could stay in their own homes. Guardians might be appointed for them to make sure they were properly cared for. However, the general rule was to place them. Some families made it a business to provide places for the needy and set up what today would be called private care homes to take in several people in return for pay from the town. These differed from the town poorhouses, which were built, supported, and administered by the courts or towns. Although almshouses and workhouses were growing in popularity in larger towns, most small towns could not support them.

Classification of the Poor.   Most people who were poor, regardless of their situations, were assumed to be morally unworthy and were classified as follows:

- Impotent poor, who were aged or disabled long-term residents who could no longer work or people with severe physical or mental handicaps
- Able-bodied poor, both men and women, who were employable in some capacity but still solicited aid from the community
- Dependent children, for whom the goal of towns and courts was to ensure that they did not follow in the degenerate footsteps of their pauper parents.

The Impotent Poor.   The *impotent poor* were considered burdens on family and community and were expected to work to their limits. If not, the family had control of their lives up to but not including murder, and care ranged from the loving care of relatives to being chained or locked in unheated sheds, at the mercy of the elements until they died. Dependent children were under the care of local governments rather than parents from the first; they could be taken from parents considered unworthy. Also, they included orphans and abandoned, unwanted, or out-of-wedlock children. Widows were unlikely to be considered worthy poor and were urged to remarry, but a significant number, those whose husbands had been poor or indentured, were left destitute and could not find new husbands. Single women were seen as a threat to the morality and economic security of the town. Both they and widows were often banished from the community if they could not eke out a living as servants or seamstresses and family or neighbors would not provide bond.[59]

The Able-Bodied Poor.   Men and women who were employable in some capacity were considered to be going against God's law when they asked for relief. Punishments for poverty were the same as those for offenses against the community: bonding, warning out, selling to the lowest bidder (auctioning off), flogging, branding, or jailing. By the early 1700s, there was a surplus of unwed and widowed women in New England. Inability to marry or find work meant that many were homeless and near starvation, and towns were unwilling to support public dependents. Warned out of towns, along with their children, they wandered the country seeking work, and many disappeared into the forests forever. Often, the able-bodied were put to work on public projects, but usually they were auctioned off. Because this led to brutal treatment, inadequate care, hunger, and exploitation, reformers demanded they be placed in almshouses, workhouses, or houses of correction.

In 1660, Boston built a house of correction in which all indigents were herded together, and in 1739 the city built a workhouse that was a combination penal institution and poorhouse for vagabonds, rogues, idlers, criminals, the poor, and the mentally ill. Grob describes almshouses:

> [C]leanliness is an unknown luxury, all is filth and misery and the most degrading, unrelieved suffering. The inmates, sane and insane, were found in many instances huddled together without discrimination of age, sex, or condition; conmingling in unrestrained licentiousness and with results shocking to all sense of decency and humanity.[60]

Children ranging in age from one month to fourteen years could be found in many such almshouses.

Idlers and vagabonds constituted threats to colonial self-sufficiency and safety, but any objectionable people—for religious, political, or moral reasons—could be brought before the local courts and judged "rogues." Punishment for both men and women was public whipping and deportation to their former residences or confinement in jail. Demented or maimed people were deported or sold into indenture and criminals and delinquents were driven from town. For lesser crimes they were flogged or mutilated, and for more severe crimes they could be executed. Debtors were imprisoned for owing as little as two cents, and they had to provide their own necessities while in prison or go without.

Dependent Children.   Colonial laws were particularly concerned that children should not follow the road into idleness and poverty. Poor families were requested to bind out their children to service, and as early as 1641 the courts had the right to take the children of the poor and indenture them to guard against the "contagion of parental failure."[61] A statute in Virginia in 1646 accused the poor of obstinacy in not binding out their children and ordered county commissioners to take two children from every poor family and bind them out to flax houses. The county also placed orphans, children born out of wedlock, and unwanted children. White children born out of wedlock "belonged" to the parish if fathers failed to support them, and they were bound out by church wardens until fathers reimbursed the parish. Children of slaves and indentured servants were also bound out.

According to parish records, one-third of all those bound out were orphans. The remainder were children whose parents apprenticed them to learn a trade. They then lived with the master and rarely saw their families, and masters were responsible by law not only for material welfare but for spiritual guidance. Apprentice masters, along with guardians of wealthy orphans and orphanage matrons, were required to teach boys reading and writing and give all children Christian training. Most boys were apprenticed to carpenters, shoemakers, blacksmiths, or planters, whereas girls became domestics, although some learned to knit, spin, and sew. Apprenticeship contracts were registered by the courts, and the practice ensured an ongoing supply of artisans and craftspeople for the colony.

Child labor was viewed as beneficial to both child and society, teaching the sanctity of work and the evils of idleness. Boston spinning schools opened in 1656, and children and other poor were placed in them and paid by the piece. This gave the town income at minimum expense and provided employment for society's potentially rebellious elements. Unlike apprentice masters, employers were not responsible for children's well-being or education, although often they had contracts supposedly to protect them. To promote the work ethic among the poor, in 1759 Boston opened a spinning school for girls, and in 1751 the Society for Encouraging Industry and Employing the Poor was established to promote the manufacture of woolen cloth and to employ indigent women and children.

The importance of education in America led to both public and private school systems. In 1647 Massachusetts required towns of over fifty households to have a teacher for elementary school, and if there were more than a hundred families in a town, high school was mandated. This system, paid for by fees and taxes, was not compulsory; however, town selectmen could investigate any home to see that children were adequately taught there. In New York and New Jersey, Dutch Reformed parochial schools allowed poor children to attend free and charged fees to those who could afford them.[62] New Jersey had the first land-grant schools, in which certain lands were set aside for support of schools, and New York and New Jersey in 1704 established private catechism schools for people of African descent. In 1787 New York City created the first free school for such children, and a New Jersey law in 1788 required that they be taught to read. In the South, education lagged because farms and plantations were scattered. White families had tutors for children or educated them in England, but children of African descent were, on the whole, denied education because it was thought to make them unruly.

Private Philanthropy

Despite the lack of money available for social welfare in the early colonies, there was some private philanthropy based on either mutual aid or the desire to provide work as a solution to pauperism. Quakers, for example, asked the needy—even non-Quakers—to present their problems to the group, and the meeting voted food, clothing, shelter, and coal. Friendly visitors called on those needing help. Voluntary giving rather than taxes supplied necessities, which often included employment or materials for home handicrafts.[63] Quakers also established almshouses, workhouses, and later penitentiaries, where the immoral could reflect on their misdeeds.

There were many craft or religious welfare societies, such as the Friends Almshouse in Philadelphia for poor Quakers, established in 1713, or the Boston Episcopal Society (1724). In New York, the Society of the House of Carpenters was established in 1767. Like many ethnic groups, free African Americans founded mutual aid societies to help both the free and slaves; for example, in Boston, a Masonic Lodge was founded by free African Americans in 1784, and in 1787 the Philadelphia Free African Society was founded to provide mutual aid for the sick and for widows and orphans, along with schooling and apprenticeship for children.[64]

Benjamin Franklin was a strong proponent of voluntary associations and self-help. He preached the gospel of industry, frugality, and sobriety as the way to individual freedom, and he believed in personal, social, and civic responsibility. To these ends, he established a library and a volunteer fire company, worked to ensure the paving of roads and the cleaning and lighting of Philadelphia, worked to establish a police force, and founded a hospital and an academy that became the University of Pennsylvania. As a founding father of our country, he epitomized the meaning of social welfare of the time.[65]

Religion, particularly the Evangelical movement, brought new concern for the poor, along with ethics of individual responsibility and social order. It claimed that the rich had a responsibility toward the poor, and that the poor owed gratitude and work to them. Another religious movement, the Great Awakening, brought two great preachers, George Whitefield and Johnathan Edwards, who led a series of religious revivals between 1730 and 1750. They preached a humanitarian ethic that transformed philanthropy from the province of the upper classes to a shared activity of all classes, appealing to both conscience and altruism.

In the century before the Revolution, great depressions created a need for social welfare that neither public nor private funding alone could handle. Joint funding, therefore, became the pattern, one that continued until 1935. Rather than giving money for explicit causes, private donors gave money to the government for charitable purposes, and government officials, such as overseers of the poor, asked churches to take up collections to be used for support of public dependents.

Slavery in the Americas

There were many Africans in the New World before the importation of slaves to the colonies. They were explorers, servants, and slaves who accompanied French, Spanish, and Portuguese in expeditions in both North and South America. One of these was Pedro Alonso Niño, who piloted one of Columbus's ships. Free African immigrants were not considered racially inferior in early days. They could accumulate property and testify in court, and they toiled in the fields and fraternized with white indentured servants.[66] However, with slavery came racism.

Racism, slavery, and jurisprudence were intimately entwined in slave laws,[67] even though in 1619, when Africans captured from a Spanish ship were brought to the colonies, there were no legal precedents concerning slavery. Within twenty years, in Virginia, legislation based on presumptions of black people's inferiority appeared, "uniquely excluding blacks from the normal protections [of] . . . the government."[68] Legal decisions after that time were consistent with the inferiority assumption. According to Judge A. Leon Higginbotham, Jr.,

> The inferiority of African Americans was given the standing of a natural principle embodied through the existing moral and social climate of the time. . . .[69]

Higginbotham writes that the interrelationship of race and the American legal process had two bases: the profitability of slave ownership and the fear of slave revolts. In 1659, statutes reduced import duties on slave ships from Africa, thus encouraging the slave trade's profitability. By 1660, statutory enslavement had begun.[70] The first major slave codes, from 1680 to 1683, prohibited slaves from carrying arms or leaving the owners' plantations without "certificates"; limited time slaves could be absent; and mandated lashing for slaves who "lifted their hands" against any white person. Runaway slaves were put to death because they deprived owners of their "rightful property."[71]

Other legal mechanisms of control included bounties for bringing in scalps and ears of runaway slaves and the right to threaten, beat, lash, and even kill slaves without retaliation. A Virginia court in 1669 decided that, because slaves could not be punished by extending their terms of servitude, threatening and beating them would increase their productivity. Harder beatings meant a greater chance of killing them, so courts passed legislation that slave owners would not be criminally prosecuted for the "casual" killing of slaves.[72] Legislation in 1699 made manumission impossible unless the freed slave was deported from the country within six months, on penalty of reenslavement. In 1705, Virginia statutes led the way in reclassifying black people from human status to "real property," such as land or houses. In South Carolina, they were declared chattel or personal property similar to sheep, horses, or belongings.[73] Higginbotham says that

> . . . the purpose of the legal system was to convince each slave he had no will of his own . . . [and that] the power of the master must be absolute to render the submission of the slave perfect.[74]

To ensure the understanding of black people's inferiority, interracial sexual relationships were carefully codified. By 1662, it was legally decided that the mother's slave condition (slave or free) determined the child's slave status. White women who had children by slaves could be punished by fining or putting them into indenture, whereas white men received no punishment and often profited by selling their own progeny as slaves. In interracial marriages, the white partner could be imprisoned for six months.[75] Even free blacks were controlled: In Pennsylvania in 1725–1726, statutes required that all children of free blacks be bound out for service until age twenty-one for women and twenty-four for men. If the parents were married, the black partner was to be sold into slavery and their children were put out to service until they were thirty-one years old. The white partner was not punished.[76]

Higginbotham cites the *Dred Scott* decision (*Scott v. Sandford,* 1857) as embodying these precepts of slavery jurisprudence. In it, Chief Justice Taney wrote that people of African American descent are a subordinate and inferior class that, whether slave or free, remain subject to the authority of the dominant and superior white race. "In effect, the Supreme Court's majority opinion in *Dred Scott* codified into law, at the highest level of the American legal process, the precept of black inferiority."[77]

Slavery as practiced in North America was a response to the Protestant religio-economic dictum that wealth demonstrates morality and to the even older dictum of fear and hatred of "outsiders." Because Africans did not worship the Christian God, their lives were insignificant compared to the mandate of wealth for their masters. Whereas South American slaves had human rights because of the intercession of the Catholic Church, North American slaves were considered less than human and were bred as livestock. Masters owned not only their work but their lives, and Protestantism did not forbid their use (or that of white workers) even to death. Wealth-producing work was an end in itself, dictated by God to the faithful, and therefore religiously legitimate. Although certainly some people detested slavery, the protests of the few were drowned in the approval of the many. For the most part, slavery was not seen as evil at all but almost a moral imperative because it "protected" slaves from destitution, put them to work, and led to wealth for God's chosen. These beliefs created a system of slavery unequaled in brutality and gave rise to the American brand of racism.

The Golden Triangle and the Triangular Trade

The slave trade was called the triangular trade, with Europe, Africa, and North America as the corners of the triangle. Beginning in Europe, ships and exports supplied by the English and French went to Africa to purchase slaves. From Africa the ships went to North America via the West Indies, where slaves produced sugar. The triangle was completed when raw materials—lumber, iron, sugar, and so on—were shipped to England for manufacture (with a stopoff in New England to make rum of the sugar).

In the early 1600s, many Caribbean farmers produced sugar themselves because the cost of passage for slaves from Africa was too high to be expedient. However, as coffee and chocolate became popular in Europe, sugar consumption skyrocketed, so that by 1700 it was the most valuable agricultural commodity in international trade. This had two results. The first was an economic dispossession of small farmers in the Caribbean as the wealthy plantation owners took over:

> Barbados in 1645 had 11,200 small white farmers and 5,680 Negro slaves. In 1667, there were 745 large plantation owners and 82,023 slaves. . . . The price of land skyrocketed. A plantation of 500 acres which sold for 400 pounds in 1640 fetched 700 pounds for a half share in 1648.[78]

Because of the sugar trade, Barbados, with its 166 square miles, was worth more to England in the 1700s and 1800s than the whole of New England, New York, and Pennsylvania combined. Second, African slavery became economically profitable.[79] White indenture in the Caribbean was dying down and Native American workers were dying out. One African was said to be worth five Native Americans because of resistance to European diseases and experiences as slaves in Africa. African slavery was the wave of the future, first with sugar plantations and then for cotton plantations in the South.

Most African slaves came from an area bordering the West Coast of Africa—they were Hausas, Mindinagos, Yorubas, Ibos, Efiks, Krus, Fontins, Ashantis, Dahomeans, Binis, and Sengalies.[80] First the Portuguese, then the Dutch, French, and English (under Elizabeth I) seized leadership in the slave trade. Slave raids throughout Africa, especially the West Coast, robbed the continent of as many as 40 million people, most in the prime of their lives.[81] The strongest and healthiest men and women survived the passage to the Americas; many of the rest either died in Africa during and after their capture, walking hundreds of miles to the coast to be picked over, branded, and chained or died on slave ships. During this Middle Passage, they were packed into holds and chained at the neck and feet, often with no more than 18 inches of head room each for the six to ten weeks of the passage. They died of suffocation, starvation, and epidemics of smallpox and dysentery. Some committed suicide or killed those they loved or those who had food. Those who died were thrown overboard, and sharks followed slave ships regularly. Some gave birth to children while still in chains. Young women and girls were often taken for the pleasure of the crew.

Occasionally, when a ship was seriously damaged or disease ran rampant, slaves were thrown overboard to make the ship lighter, or ships were deserted in mid-ocean, their cargo of men and women chained helplessly together below the decks,[82] for they were considered animal cargo. In 1783, short of water, the captain of the slave ship *Zong* threw 132 slaves overboard (they often did this with livestock such as horses). Damages were awarded the owners for property, and the idea that this was mass murder never occurred.[83] One African recorded his voyage:

> I was soon put down under the decks and . . . with the loathesomeness of the stench and crying together, I became so sick and low that I was not able to eat. . . . On my refusal to eat, one of them held me fast by the hands and laid me across, I think the windlass, and tied my feet, while the other flogged me severely. . . . One day, when we had a smooth sea and a moderate wind, two of my wearied countrymen who were chained together . . . preferring death to such a life of misery, somehow made through the nettings and jumped into the sea.[84]

There were 155 recorded slave uprisings on ships between 1699 and 1845. When they reached America, diseased slaves were left to die and the remaining sold either to dealers or directly to plantation owners. The price of slaves fluctuated with the market: George Washington bought a man in 1754 for $250 but ten years later had to pay $285. Slaves were available either for cash or for a small down payment with small monthly payments.

During the slave trade from 1502 to 1860, 9.6 million Africans were brought to the New World, 6 million of them in the 1700s, at a rate of 50,000 to 100,000 a year. Of the nearly 10 million taken, about three-fourths died in capture or transit. Most were sold in the West Indies and South America, with about half a million (6 to 7 percent) sold in North America. Of these, an estimated 345,000 were sold before 1800.[85] Aside from the disruption of cultures of those brought to the Americas, the societies of Africa, large and small, advanced or more primitive, were ruined as millions of the strongest and youngest were taken from their homes. Undoubtedly, this mass deportation of native Africans led to the ease with which colonialism was soon enforced on Africa itself.

In England after the 1700s, slaveowners dominated Parliament, and the founding of banks based on the triangular trade began in the late 1700s and early 1800s. England and Scotland also developed insurance houses—such as Lloyds of London, originally a coffee house that listed runaway slaves—to insure both slaves and slave ships, and thus began the property insurance system of the world.[86] The slave trade, of course, was not seen as inhumane. In a time when life was so cheap and poverty was so much looked on as personal sin, slavery was merely another, very lucrative business. Indeed, many English humanitarians were included in those who ran the slave trade. Edmund Burke was one such humanitarian, as was John Cary, who in England founded the Society for the Incorporation of the Poor. Bryan Blundell, a noted slave trader, was trustee, treasurer, chief patron, and most active supporter of a charity school. Slave traders, because of their wealth from the trade, often held high offices in the government of England.

By the time George Washington became president in 1789, there were 4 million people in the North American colonies. Approximately one of every four of them was a slave, of which about one-third were women.

Toward the Revolution

Economics was at the base of the rebellion against King George and England. English law forbade the colonies to manufacture goods from the raw materials they produced, and only English-built ships could be used to transport raw materials to England and the finished products colonists were required to buy back from England. To aid England's wool business, laws required that all slaves and servants wear wool, even in the Caribbean, and that the dead be buried in suits of wool. Colonists were required to eat fish caught from English ships on Fridays and Saturdays, and as early as 1615 England had a monopoly on refining sugar produced in the West Indies. Such laws galled the colonists, many of whom had come to America to find freedom and financial success, and they began to fight against forced purchase of goods more efficiently produced in America. In addition, English treaties with Native Americans kept them from legally exploring and settling the land beyond the Appalachians.

The northern colonies produced food for sugar workers because planters did not want to take the land out of sugar production. By supplying food, however, they were taking trade from England in return for sugar supplies. England therefore imposed the Stamp Act, which required a tax on sugar imports to the northern colonies, and Americans refused to pay or to ship food to the sugar islands. Because of this, 15,000 Jamaican slaves died of famine between 1780 and 1787.[87] Moreover, colonials began to manufacture and process the raw materials of America despite English bans. They especially began to trade in rum from Caribbean sugar, textiles from southern cotton, and iron from northern mines. American rum production competed with English spirits made from corn and gave Americans an edge in the slave trade. In 1770, New England's exports of rum to Africa represented over four-fifths of the total colonial exports of the time. Metallurgy also became important for making fetters, chains, padlocks, irons for branding, axes for clearing the colonial land, and guns.

Women in the Revolution

Because of the general status of women at the time of the Revolution, their participation in developing the new country was limited. For example, although in North Carolina fifty-one women proclaimed their right to participate in political activities, no women attended the Continental Congress or state congresses convened to argue the question of Revolution. Abigail Adams, wife of John Adams, was nearly alone in her outspoken insistence that men misused their political power when they denied women equal rights. She continually tried to encourage the inclusion of women's legal and civil rights in the new government, writing to her husband to

> remember the ladies . . . if particular care and attention is not paid to [us] we are determined to foment a rebellion, and will not hold ourselves bound by any laws in which we have no voice or representation.[88]

Mercy Otis Warren, sister of patriot James Otis, was among the major intellectual writers of the Revolution. An antifederalist, she wrote plays and published under a male name, corresponding on public questions with both Samuel and John Adams, John Hancock, and George Washington. John Adams and many other men were concerned with women's rights, for a spirit of equality permeated liberal thought. Thomas Paine wrote an impassioned plea for their inclusion in the Constitution, and Benjamin Franklin said the women were unequal only because of the limits placed on them by education and tradition.[89]

As many as 20,000 women went to war in the Revolution, on both the British and American sides. They were cooks, nurses, doctors, laundresses, guides, seamstresses, and porters. More British women were paid because American soldiers could rely on volunteer patriots to care for their needs. Women were not simply observers, as this account of the British entering Cambridge illustrates:

> Poor dirty emaciated men, great numbers of women, who seemed to be the beasts of burden having a bushel basket on their back by which they were bent double, the contents seemed to be pots and kettles, various sorts of furniture, children peeping through gridirons and other utensils, some very young infants who were born on the road, the women bare feet, clothed in dirty rags.[90]

Hundreds of women participated in Benedict Arnold's disastrous assault on Montreal, which began in late fall. Led by ill-informed guides, ill-equipped for the bitter winter, and unaware that game would not be available, many starved, died of pneumonia and typhoid, or became lost and froze to death.

The Daughters of Liberty formed to boycott British products, especially tea, and many women supplied the Revolutionary army with clothes, food, and other provisions. Some women fought as soldiers and were rewarded with army pensions for themselves and their families. For example, Deborah Sampson Gannett dressed as a man and became an infantry soldier at age eighteen. After the war she married, and when she died at age sixty-seven, her husband applied for and received a pension based on her military service. (Not until the 1970s was there another ruling, by the Social Security Administration, that the spouse of a working woman was entitled to a pension.) Other well-known women heroes were Mary Ludwig Hayes, who went with her husband and replaced him at the cannon when he was wounded, and Molly Pitcher, who carried water to the wounded men.

The New Nation and Its Constitution

It is ironic that one goal for which the Revolutionary War was fought was equality when in America women still had the status of children and idiots and the slave trade was still active. Both free and slave people of African descent fought during the Revolution, many for the English, for they were not welcomed in the Revolutionary army. However, after the winter at Valley Forge, Washington was willing to accept any fighting man, and approximately 100,000 runaway slaves joined the Revolutionary army and were freed.

In 1773, slaves in Massachusetts petitioned the legislature for freedom, and this petition was followed by eight others during the Revolutionary War. Slavery was effectively terminated in the North by 1777. Five of the original thirteen states emancipated their slaves before the federal Constitutional Convention met in New York in 1788. Partial antislavery measures were enacted by New York in 1788, with total emancipation in 1799, and New Jersey began to pass antislavery legislation in 1786.[91] Vermont was first to abolish slavery in 1777, followed by Massachusetts and New Hampshire in 1783 and Connecticut and Rhode Island in 1784.

Despite the new freedoms the Constitution guaranteed, it was a creation of its time. As such, it was an elitist document; that is, it was written by white male property owners and ensured their rights without due consideration of the rights of women, people without property, and nonwhites. Although there was some agitation to ensure the abolition of slavery, this was dropped to gain ratification by southern slaveholders. Slavery was given formal recognition by the Constitution in the determination that slaves were three-fifths of a white man for purposes of determining voter representation; in the fugitive slave section, which ensured that slaves would be returned to their masters; and in the permission to continue the slave trade until 1808.

In addition, the Constitution gave the vote only to property owners and men with certain levels of education, ensuring an elitist and mercantilist bent. For example, James Madison believed that the establishment of a national government was the most important protection for the elites against mass movements that might threaten property. Dye and Zeigler say,

> Men like Patrick Henry and Richard Henry Lee of Virginia vigorously attacked the Constitution as a "counter-revolutionary document" . . . the new government would be "aristocratic," "all-powerful," and a threat to the "spirit of republicanism" and the "genius of democracy." . . . [It sets up] . . . an aristocratic upper house and an almost monarchial presidency.[92]

In fact, the leaders of the Revolution had asked George Washington to be permanent president, and had even prepared a throne for him, but he refused. To counteract accusations of aristocracy, Congress provided a Bill of Rights at its first meeting.

Although four decision-making bodies were established by the Constitution, only one, the House of Representatives, was to be elected by the people. The Senate was to be elected by state legislators and the president by an Electoral College. The powers of government were almost unilaterally based on the protection of property rights. Congress was given power to tax, regulate interstate commerce, protect money and property, regulate communication and transportation, conduct military affairs, and protect the rights of slaveowners to their slaves.

The Constitution did not deal with the problems of the poor, although popular workers' movements demanded a federally controlled monetary system (rather than factory scrip), the abolition of debts, and an equal distribution of property. Congress was given the authority to provide for the common welfare, but common welfare was not social welfare. The theme of individual responsibility and individual achievement permeated the new government, and the upsurge of liberalism did not change the nation's perspective on the causes of poverty or the needs of the poor. Because the political economy of the times was elitist, so was the Constitution: Those who wrote it were involved in profit making through the labor of the poor. Factions seeking equality were either ignored or defeated in the battle, and the class stratification that had been custom in the New World became a legal part of American government. Those who had no voice before the Revolution were denied voice in the new nation.

Conclusion: Revolution to Status Quo

The Constitution does guarantee citizens certain freedoms and civil rights, whether or not its authors intended. Many such rights have been fought through courts of the land; the Constitution and its amendments, particularly as interpreted by the Supreme Court, have made it possible for these fights to be won. Since the Constitution was written over two hundred years ago, although the basic protection of property rights has been maintained, civil rights probably not believed possible at the Revolution have come to pass. The abolition of slavery was the first of many civil rights to be granted, with women's suffrage and equal opportunity in employment, education, and other areas of life to come later. Despite its elitist beginning, and despite the roadblocks put in the way of equality, the basic underpinnings of the Constitution and the democratic orientation of the people of the United States have slowly made inroads or our racist, sexist, and classist society. Although we may be impatient that the promises of equality have not been fulfilled, patterns of equality were set into law, traditions, and customs as the United States became a nation.

Study Questions

1. What kinds of social welfare existed in the early colonies? On what were they based?

2. What were the differences between slavery in North America and slavery in South America?

3. How did indenture and slavery differ, and how did those differences set patterns for racism based on color?

4. What impact did the Revolution have on the treatment or control of the poor?

5. How did religion influence the provision of social welfare for the poor? For children?

Notes

1. Eric Williams, *Capitalism and Slavery* (New York: G.P. Putnam's Sons, 1966), pp. 1–10.

2. Henry F. Dobyns, "Estimating Aboriginal American Population," *Current Anthropology*, Oct. 1966, pp. 395–416.

3. Marvin Harris, *Patterns of Race* (New York: W.W. Norton and Co., 1964), p. 3.

4. Ibid., pp. 7–10.

5. Ibid., pp. 8–10.

6. Frances Gies and Joseph Gies, *Cathedral, Forge and Waterwheel: Technology and Invention in the Middle Ages* (New York: HarperCollins, 1994), pp. 285–286.

7. Ted Morgan, *Wilderness at Dawn: The Settling of the North American Continent* (New York: Simon & Schuster, 1993), p. 102.

8. Ibid., p. 104.

9. Ibid., pp. 196–197.

10. Lerone Bennett, Jr., *Before the Mayflower: A History of the Negro in America, 1619–1964* (Chicago: Johnson Publishing Company, 1966), p. 101.

11. Morgan, *Wilderness at Dawn*, p. 48.

12. Ibid., pp. 52, 55–56.

13. Joe R. Feagin, *Racial and Ethnic Relations*, 2nd ed. (Englewood Cliffs, NJ: Prentice Hall, 1984), p. 298.

14. Morgan, *Wilderness at Dawn*, p. 75.

15. Harris, *Patterns of Race*, p. 15.

16. Carl A. Sauer, *Seventeenth Century in North America* (Berkeley, CA: Turtle Island Foundation, 1980), p. 230.

17. Morgan, *Wilderness at Dawn*, pp. 213–214.

18. Sauer, *Seventeenth Century*, p. 60.

19. Stanley Elkins, *Slavery*, 2nd ed. (Chicago: University of Chicago Press, 1968), p. 61.

20. Morgan, *Wilderness at Dawn*, p. 157.

21. Ibid.

22. Feagin, *Racial and Ethnic Relations*, p. 179.

23. Harris, *Patterns of Race*, pp. 80–82.

24. Morgan, *Wilderness at Dawn*, p. 121.

25. Ibid., pp. 121–122.

26. Williams, *Capitalism and Slavery*, p. 26.

27. Bennett, *Before the Mayflower*, p. 36.

28. Carole Hymowitz and Michaele Weissman, *A History of Women in America* (New York: Bantam Books, 1980), p. 8.

29. Beulah Compton, *Introduction to Social Welfare and Social Work: Structure, Function, and Process* (Homewood, IL: The Dorsey Press, 1980), p. 199.

30. Williams, *Capitalism and Slavery*, pp. 11–12.

31. Compton, *Introduction to Social Welfare*, p. 188.

32. L. F. Strock, ed., *Proceedings and Debates in the British Parliament Respecting North America* (Washington, D.C., 1924–1941), p. 249. Quoted in Williams, *Capitalism and Slavery*, p. 17.

33. From the *Calendar of State Papers*, Colonial Series, v. 229. Report of the Council for Foreign Plantations (August 1664). In Williams, *Capitalism and Slavery*, p. 18.

34. Williams, *Capitalism and Slavery*, p. 18.

35. Compton, *Introduction to Social Welfare*, among others.

36. Gerald Handel, *Social Welfare in Western Society* (New York: Random House, 1982), p. 67.

37. Morgan, *Wilderness at Dawn*, p. 122.

38. William Jay Jacobs, *Women in American History* (Encino, CA: Glencoe Publishing, 1976), p. 7.

39. Ibid., p. 3.

40. Hymowitz and Weissman, *History of Women*, p. 11.

41. Linda E. Spaeth, "More Than Her 'Thirds': Wives and Widows in Colonial Virginia," in Linda Spaeth and Alison Duncan Hirsch (eds.), *Women, Family, and Community in Colonial America: Two Perspectives* (New York: Haworth Press, 1983), p. 11.

42. Amaury De Riencourt, *Sex and Power in History* (New York: Dell Publishing, 1974), p. 308.

43. Julia Cherry Sprull, "Housewives and Their Helpers," in Linda K. Kerber and Jane de Hart Mathews (eds.), *Women's America* (New York: Oxford University Press, 1982), p. 26.

44. Alice Kessler-Harris, *Out to Work: A History of Wage-Earning Women in the United States* (New York: Oxford University Press, 1982), p. 13.

45. Hymowitz and Weissman, *History of Women*, p. 22.

46. Ibid., p. 23.

47. Spaeth, "More Than Her 'Thirds,'" p. 11.

48. Hymowitz and Weissman, *History of Women*, p. 21.

49. Jacobs, *Women in American History*, p. 14.

50. Kessler-Harris, *Out to Work*, p. 16.

51. Hymowitz and Weissman, *History of Women*, p. 128.

52. Kessler-Harris, *Out to Work*, p. 17.

53. Ibid.

54. Walter A. Friedlander and Robert Z. Apte, *Introduction to Social Welfare*, 9th ed. (Englewood Cliffs, NJ: Prentice-Hall, 1974), p. 62.

55. Compton, *Introduction to Social Welfare*, p. 198.

56. Gerald N. Grob (advisory ed.), "Maryland Report on Almshouses," in *The State and Public Welfare in Nineteenth-Century America* (New York: Arno Press, 1976), pp. 6–7.

57. Ibid.; a note in Senate Document 2, Jan. 1859, historical references taken from the New Colony of Plymouth and Massachusetts Colonial Acts, p. 38.

58. June Axinn and Herman Levin, *Social Welfare: A History of the American Response to Need*, 2nd ed. (New York: Harper & Row, 1982), p. 19.

59. Walter Bremner (ed.), *Children and Youth in America: A Documentary History* (New York: Arno Press, 1969; originally published in 1914), p. 12. Quoted in Kessler-Harris, *Out to Work*, p. 5.

60. Grob, *The State and Public Welfare*, p. 16.

61. Axinn and Levin, *Social Welfare*, p. 20.

62. Compton, *Introduction to Social Welfare*, pp. 201–202.

63. Ibid., p. 198.

64. Ralph Dolgoff and Donald Feldstein, *Understanding Social Welfare*, 2nd ed. (New York: Longman Press, 1984), p. 65.

65. Compton, *Introduction to Social Welfare*, p. 176.

66. Bennett, *Before the Mayflower*, p. 36.

67. A. Leon Higginbotham, Jr., *Shades of Freedom: Racial Politics and Presumptions of the American Legal Process* (New York: Oxford University Press, 1996), pp. 195–196.

Higginbotham says the assumption of inferiority of people of African descent in American Slavery Jurisprudence is based on ten principles:

1. Inferiority: presume, preserve, protest, and defend the ideal of the superiority of whites.
2. Property: define the slave as property, maximize the master's economic interest, disregard the slaves' humanity, and deny slaves the fruits of their labor.
3. Powerlessness: keep them submissive and dependent in every respect, not only to master, but whites in general. Limit access to justice and establish differential punishment for blacks and whites. Utilize violence and government power to ensure submission.
4. Racial purity: preserve white male sexual dominance.
5. Manumission and free blacks: limit manumission and minimize the number of free blacks, confining them as close to slavery as possible.
6. Family: recognize no rights, destroy family unity, deny the right of marriage, demean and degrade, condemn both for conduct and state of mind.

7. Education and culture: denied, do not allow literacy.

8. Religion: recognize no rights to define, practice, choose leaders, or worship with other blacks. Encourage adoption of white masters' religion. Use religion to justify inferior status.

9. Liberty or resistance: rebellion and flight punishable by death, freedom of movement restricted.

10. By any means possible: support all measures that maximize slavery's profitability, legitimize racism, and, by use of violence if necessary, [end any activity] that advocates slavery's abolition or white supremacy's domination (pp. 195–196).

68. A. Leon Higginbotham, Jr., *In the Matter of Color: Race and the American Legal Process: The Colonial Period* (New York: Oxford University Press, 1978), p. 32.

69. Ibid., p. 3.

70. Ibid., p. 34.

71. Ibid., p. 38.

72. Ibid., p. 36.

73. Ibid., pp. 114, 169.

74. Ibid., pp. 8–9.

75. Ibid., p. 44.

76. Ibid., p. 285.

77. Ibid., p. 67.

78. Williams, *Capitalism and Slavery*, pp. 23, 25.

79. Harris, *Patterns of Race*, pp. 13–14.

80. Bennett, *Before the Mayflower*, p. 38.

81. Ibid., p. 30.

82. Jacobs, *Women in American History*, p. 11.

83. Williams, *Capitalism and Slavery*, p. 46.

84. Olaudah Equiano, "The Interesting Narrative of Olaudah Equiano," in Thomas R. Frazier, *Afro-American History: Primary Sources* (New York: Harcourt, Brace, and World, 1970), pp. 18–20.

85. Feagin, *Racial and Ethnic Relations*, p. 213.

86. Williams, *Capitalism and Slavery*, p. 108.

87. Ibid.

88. Jacobs, *Women in American History*, p. 19, quoting Abigail Adams.

89. Ibid., p. 16.

90. Sally Smith Booth, *The Women of '76* (New York: Hastings House, 1973), p. 144. Quoted in Hymowitz and Weissman, *History of Women*.

91. Thomas R. Dye and L. Harmon Zeigler, *The Irony of Democracy* (Belmont, CA: Wadsworth Publishing, 1970), p. 42.

92. Ibid., p. 51.

6

America to the Civil War

The First Civil Rights Movement

After the Revolution, egalitarian ideals took second place to laissez-faire capitalism, industrialization, and expansionism. The Constitution and new state governments ensured elitist control: Only white male Christians had suffrage in most states, and some states had minimum property requirements (some as high as $5,000) for eligibility to vote or run for office. Not until 1856 could all white men vote in the New England states, regardless of property ownership, although frontier states usually gave suffrage to all white men.[1] Some territories came into the union with suffrage for women; for example, Wyoming would not enter the Union unless it was allowed to continue women's suffrage, and Utah insisted on women's suffrage in order to maintain polygamy for the Mormon Church against the voting power of newcomers.

Jacksonian democracy declared that every (white male) person could succeed with individual hard work. This was, according to Dye and Zeigler,

> by no means a philosophy of leveling egalitarianism. The ideal of the frontier [was] wealth and power won by competitive skill . . . [creating] a *natural aristocracy*.[2]

Laissez-faire capitalism expanded to the West, where a new elite developed. Money was federalized: Rather than state or company scrip, federal money was put in state banks, thus breaking the Eastern monopoly of economic and political power.[3] Uncontrolled industrialization moved work from agrarian households to the cities.

The proportion of wage laborers increased (from 5.5 percent in 1796 to 27 percent in 1855 in New York City, for example), enabling employers to lower wages and increase their profits. Men were hired from the crowds of unemployed on the streets for day or seasonal work, and irregular employment, vast unemployment, labor uprisings, and the growth of labor movements resulted.[4] The powerful Protestant orientation to work remained. Macarov says,

> Factories needed workers, and workers need jobs, not just to make money but also to be moral, religious, law-abiding people. Factory owners thus did people a favor by allowing them to work, and workers were expected to be grateful to the point of not . . . asking for higher wages or better working conditions. This was not only ingratitude but almost blasphemy.[5]

Mobility and industrialization weakened family structure and community ties. Churches, neighbors, friends, and relatives could no longer be depended on for help in need. As the family and the economy changed, surplus unmarried women became teachers and social reformers. The idle wife became a mark of status for wealthier men, who hired (or bought) lower-class women to do household chores. The latter, considered sexually available and usable by upper-class men, were thought of as the "sexual sewer" of the rich.

The 1800s brought massive social experimentation, with money, time, and energy available to indulge in such issues as the franchise for women, ending exploitation of children, emancipation of slaves, temperance, and moral reform of the poor. The altruism of the times was based on the ideals of the poor's immorality, work as the only moral source of income, and almsgiving as the path to immorality. Social responsibility for poverty was rejected even though social data convinced such eminent philosophers as John Stuart Mill and John Marshall that poverty was the result of social exploitation.[6]

Slave labor and the cotton gin, invented in 1791, made cotton easy and cheap to produce. By the 1820s, cotton textiles constituted more than half of American exports, and Southern plantation owners refused to relinquish their new near-aristocracy by ending slavery. In the North, the new industrial elite made fortunes from the labor of immigrants—men, women, and children as young as five years old—who produced textiles, made clothes, mined iron and coal, and built transportation and communication links across the nation and around the world.

Immigration and Migration

Shortly before the Revolution, America had some 2.25 million white settlers, and only five cities had populations of 8,000 or more. Within fifty years, the population had reached 10 million,[7] a quarter of whom, by 1820, settled beyond the Alleghenies on Native American lands. Coll says the tide of immigrants

> rose steadily from only 129,000 in the 1820s to 540,000 in the following decade . . . to a pre–Civil War peak of more than 1.75 million in the 1850s. Altogether, about 6 million immigrants crossed to the "land of opportunity" between 1820 and 1860—

roughly half of them from Great Britain and Ireland, about 2 million from Germany, and about 50,000 from the Scandinavian countries.[8]

For a short time, the move West averted a labor flood and maintained reasonable wages in the Eastern cities. Soon, however, destitute immigrants "were like an army encamped in the midst of New York,"[9] stranded, with little help either to move inland or to establish new lives.

Almshouses, which cared for the poor and ill, were often the first stop of immigrants sick from infections and the deprivations of the Atlantic crossing. By 1796, almshouse commissioners were complaining of the enormous expense from foreign-born immigrants, and not until 1847 did immigration authorities decide that immigrants were entitled to aid based on their payment for passage. The Board of Commissioners of Immigration collected taxes and imposed indemnity bonds on immigrants, crews, and ships arriving at New York ports. These funds supported arriving immigrants or reimbursed local communities for outdoor relief, medical help, education, transportation, and job placements. Ward's Island in New York City's East River became a hospital and refuge for unemployable people and a nursery and school for orphans and children born out of wedlock. By 1855 there was a central landing for immigrant processing at Ellis Island.[10]

While immigration exploded, migration from rural areas increased dramatically as people moved to the cities for work. The urban population grew at the rate of about 40 to 50 percent per decade, and cities became squalid warrens of people living in acute poverty, beset by plagues and death-dealing illnesses, unemployment, and starvation. Even minimal sanitation and safety were lacking: Garbage and refuse flowed through the streets in open drains. There were no bathing facilities and almost no indoor plumbing, and water was drawn from street pumps or hydrants.

> [S]ewage disposal and police and fire protection were often left to chance....
> Water supplies became polluted, and epidemics, gang wars, and street crime
> raged unchecked. Saloons, brothels, and gambling houses flourished in ethnic
> neighborhoods, confined there by authorities who would not tolerate their exis-
> tence in "better" neighborhoods, and patronized by people from all over the city.[11]

The slums were breeding grounds for tuberculosis, pneumonia, and diphtheria, and children often died of "some unknown disease"—starvation.

> Periodically ... the United States was ravaged by deadly plagues—yellow fever,
> cholera, typhoid, to name the most virulent—caused by filth, impure water, and
> other unsanitary conditions. The plagues struck with most force in the cities ...
> and here sickness and death claimed first—and in greatest numbers—the poor.[12]

The supply of housing and services never caught up with the need, and people lived in sheds, garrets, and dark and poorly ventilated tenements. One row of tenements could house 500 people, with up to 200 in a single building—

almost a thousand an acre.[13] Rooms were divided and redivided, and when there were no more rooms, people lived in cellars. In 1843 in Boston there were nearly 8,000 people in cellars, and in 1846, just three years later, there were 29,000. By 1850 one of every twenty lived in a cellar, the average number per room was six and the maximum twenty. Begging was widespread, and an estimated 10,000 abandoned, orphaned, or runaway children roamed the streets. Life expectancy after moving into the Boston slums was fourteen years.[14] Hymowitz and Weissman write,

> Though most immigrants were in the prime of life, between the ages of fourteen and forty-five, they died more readily than the native-born. Their children, and especially their babies, died even more frequently . . . In Chicago, before 1900, three of every five babies died before age five.[15]

Employment and Unionization

For a short while after the Revolution, most people did not depend solely on wages: They were artisans, small landowners, tenants, traders, and urban mechanics. Even in New England, where large textile mills had developed by the beginning of the 1800s, factories were considered temporary places of employment for the poor or for young women putting away savings for marriage.[16] Men found farm work and the ownership of land more profitable than factory labor, so unmarried women, children, older married immigrant men and women, and people who otherwise would have been on welfare became the logical factory labor force.[17]

> The ten- to twelve-hour work day of women and children was spent in factories and mills that were dirty, noisy, dark, smelly, and dangerous. Hundreds of workers were jammed together in dimly lit rooms that were stifling hot in summer, cold and drafty in winter. The moist, lint-filled air in the cotton mills bred tuberculosis. In other industries women breathed dangerous fumes of paint and naphtha, tobacco, and glass and brass dust. Materials were flammable, and factory buildings were firetraps. Machines were cleaned and adjusted while they were running . . . workers often lost fingers and even hands in accidents.[18]

By the end of the War of 1812, approximately two-thirds of all factory workers were women[19] and children, who got about a fourth of the wages earned by men for the same work. Their average week's pay was $1.50, the same as for women who did piecework at home. The factory day began at 4:30 A.M., even for small children, and ended at sundown,[20] a day of hard physical labor in dangerous settings. Children were "sold out" to labor, with parents and employers colluding, lying about their ages so they could work.

> Here is a little child, not more than five years old. . . . She has on one garment, if a tattered sacking dress can be so termed! Her bones are nearly through her skin, but her stomach is an unhealthy pouch, abnormal. She has dropsy.

It is eight o'clock when children reach their homes—later if the mill work is behind and they are kept over hours. They are usually beyond speech. They fall asleep at the table, on the stairs.[21]

Before the Revolution, mill work for women was socially acceptable and often closely supervised. Some mills, such as that established by Francis Cabot Lowell in Massachusetts, were model communities with limited hours, schools, and chaperoned dormitories. However, conditions deteriorated even here, and in both 1834 and 1845 women struck for the ten-hour workday and higher pay. In response, the state legislature upheld the employer, conducting hearings and then visiting

> for an on-the-scene investigation. The committee report rejected the workers' demands for a ten-hour day, noting the *special responsibilities that laborers owed to their employers.*[22] [Italics added.]

By 1831, mills employed nearly 19,000 men and 39,000 women; by 1850 women were 24 percent of the total number of workers; and by 1900, 19 percent.[23]

Families were often paid in liquor, tobacco, or company scrip, usable only in company stores or for company-owned housing. Company credit, necessary in layoffs, increased their indebtedness and dependency on the company and limited their job mobility. This was common in mines, construction, factories of all sorts, and handwork industries such as sewing. There were

> almost no pensions; few men left much in the way of savings when they died; and life insurance spread slowly, especially among the working class. . . . [F]actory production replaced the putting out system, and . . . contrary to popular stereotypes (which are based on the minority of young women who worked in mills), there was very little industrial work open to any women in towns and cities before the late 19th century and almost none to married women.[24]

Wars with France (1807–1809) and England (1812) depleted the economy and caused a severe depression (1815–1821). By 1819, 500,000 people were unemployed, and at times a third of the labor force was idle.

> In Philadelphia alone, of 9700 employed in thirty businesses, 7500 were fired. Properties of farmers and small businesses were taken over by creditors.[25]

Wages fell 30 to 50 percent, most New England factories closed, and whole families starved or froze to death.[26] The unemployed formed citizens' committees and marched on the government, and fighting, looting, violence, and employment riots were common. Few social programs could cope with the mass distress, and soup kitchens opened and newspapers ran ads calling for food, money, clothing, and shelter for the poor.[27]

Trade unions formed as early as 1790, demanding a family wage for men, that is, enough pay to support a family; free education for children and the curbing of child labor and apprenticeship abuses (both to help children and to keep them out of the labor market); free public lands for settlement; restriction on private use of prison labor, as when prisoners were contracted out for work, undercutting wages; the establishment of a ten-hour day; control of currency by the government (rather than scrip issued by employers); the right to organize; and public work programs to protect the unemployed.

By 1837 there were at least five national unions: cordwainers (shoemakers and leather workers), combmakers, carpenters, weavers, and printers; and two-thirds of New York's workers were organized, with women taking the lead in organizing the mills. Strikes became common, even though the police were brought in and workers were brutalized and killed. However, by the beginning of the Civil War the labor movement had collapsed. In part, this was because of the adamant opposition of businesses and the courts, because the Civil War made soldiers out of unemployed, and, finally, because the Homestead Act of 1862 made free lands available for Western settlement.

Private Philanthropy

Despite mass unemployment and wages so low that saving was impossible and illness or accident devastating, the rich continued their diatribe against the laziness and intemperance of workers. There was little separation of public and private interests: Private groups formed associations and worked for legislation, often later inspecting or administering agencies set up and funded by government. Private philanthropy, as meager as it was, provided primarily for white people. Others were of no concern to most charities. This remained true at least until the 1950s.

Religious Answers to Poverty

Protestant religious groups led the way in social reform with dual goals: to help the unfortunate and to win newly arrived, supposedly un-Christian immigrants to Protestantism. Such organizations as the New York City Mission Society and the New York Female Moral Reform Society distributed food and clothing along with religious tracts and advocated better housing and sanitation along with moral improvement.[28] The Protestant reform movement led to

> reform schools, mental hospitals, and new kinds of prisons. In cities, experiments with mass education began under private auspices . . . by the middle decades . . . public educational systems had started to appear . . . private philanthropists created YMCAs for young rural migrants to cities, other reformers founded specialized institutions for the deaf and dumb, blind, feeble-minded, and idiots . . . [and began] campaigns to alter the treatment of criminals, delinquents, the mentally ill, and school children.[29]

Jewish immigrants brought with them their heritage of charity and mutual aid. Although Sephardic Jews came to America as early as the 1600s, by 1800 there were still only 5,000 Jews in the United States. Although they contributed substantial monies to the Revolution, they were denied voting rights except in South Carolina. By 1790 they could vote in five states, but restrictions remained as late as 1869 (North Carolina) and 1876 (New Hampshire). Excluded, by and large, from American social welfare, they shared their resources with new immigrants through mutual aid societies, especially for education and work.

Catholicism supplied its traditional forms of charity both in the Hispanic Southwest and with the new immigrants from Ireland and Italy in the East. Despite the poverty of Eastern immigrants in the 1850s and 1860s, Catholics began a highly effective program of outdoor relief. Catholic Charities, St. Vincent de Paul Societies (1850), and Little Sisters of the Poor groups (1840) sprang up and, on the model set by Sisters of Charity as early as 1809, began to build orphanages, schools, hospitals, and other facilities for those in need. Katz says,

> Catholic spokesmen distrusted the [Protestant] . . . often militantly anti-Catholic bias. They viewed [for example] the Children's Aid Society . . . as an agency designed to place Catholic children in Protestant homes.[30]

Especially after 1860, the Catholic Church made heroic efforts to alleviate urban suffering, dependence, and sickness. For example, Catholics probably provided half the money for children's institutions in Buffalo near the end of the 1800s and probably spent more of their incomes on charity than did Protestants.[31] The Catholic Church also gave more attention to needs of African and Native Americans, particularly those of children, than did Protestant charity.

Social Reform Ideals

Coinciding with the great depressions of the 1800s, eminent philanthropists began to issue reports on poverty, blaming it on the poor: their idleness, ignorance, spendthriftiness, hasty marriages; their use of pawnbrokers, lotteries, and houses of prostitution; and their gambling.[32] The most intense criticism was aimed at intemperance (despite the fact that the poor were often paid in liquor): A report in 1817 estimated that of the 15,000 people on charity, seven-eighths were pauperized by liquor;[33] John V. N. Yates, New York's secretary of state, stated in his famous report in 1824 that intemperance was the cause of two-thirds of permanent dependency.

Yates also found that poor laws were inadequate, ripe for misuse, and inhumane, and that a ninth of poor relief funds were used in court suits to deny clients' eligibility rather than for the benefit of the poor. He noted the barbarity of farming out or selling the poor, particularly children, and deplored their treatment and lack of education in the local almshouses. People he called "idiots" and "lunatics," also put in almshouses, had no adequate care and were often brutally mistreated. Along with other philanthropists, Yates called for poor relief to be turned over to private charities, both to provide more humane treatment and to save money. He also claimed that present laws encouraged beggary and vagrancy, and called for provision of employment for the able-bodied poor in almshouses, where they could both support themselves and provide for other inmates unable to do so.[34]

Yet the Yates report concluded that only 27 percent of the poor could actually work. The rest were aged, blind, or ill, had mental or physical handicaps (35 percent), or were under the age of fourteen (38 percent). He recommended that every county have a poorhouse with education for children, farms for producing food, and facilities for hard labor for able-bodied inmates. In addition, he asked that no healthy male age eighteen to fifty be given outdoor relief, that street begging be punished, that attempts to return paupers to earlier places of residence be abolished as too costly, and that an excise tax be levied on distilleries to combat drunkenness.[35]

Plans for rehabilitation of the poor and poor relief administration were similar to those in Europe in the 1500s. The 1818 Report by the Society for the Prevention of Pauperism recommended the prevention of beggary and the restriction of saloons, the establishment of employment bureaus and savings banks, mutual aid and life insurance to deal with employment hazards, supplies for home industry, and cooperation among charitable agencies. It also recommended division of cities into districts, with poor relief administered by friendly visitors to give moral support on living without temptation to drink and other vices.[36]

Reform advocate Matthew Carey summed up the prevailing reform viewpoint, saying that

- Every man, woman, and grown child able and willing to work should be given employment.
- The poor should be able to support themselves by industry, prudence, and economy, without depending on aid.
- Their sufferings arise from their idleness, dissipation, and extravagance.
- To support the poor through taxes, charitable individuals, or benevolent societies leads to the fostering of their idleness and improvidences, producing or increasing the distress it is intended to relieve.[37]

Unitarian minister Joseph Tuckerman was among the most socially aware reformists. He argued against wages too low

> to supply even the bare necessities of life, and the frequent occurrence of periods, even of months together, during which numbers . . . find it impossible to procure any employment whatever by which to keep themselves from destitution and suffering.[38]

In 1832 Tuckerman began a "ministry at large" that anticipated almost every aspect of the later charity organization societies and the profession of social work. He found inadequate housing and urban problems instrumental in other problems and noted the radical importance of the "child problem" as a special charity issue.

[H]is most detailed report, written as agent of a State Commission ... advocates ... tests of work for the able-bodied, houses of industry worthy of the name for the more capable, and the refer[ral] of all temporary poverty [relief] to private relief. ... [He] was the first American not only to distinguish between pauperism and poverty but to advocate consistently the abolition of outdoor relief, the cooperation of all forces working on charitable problems, the principle of the registration bureau, and personal visitation or friendly visitation.[39]

The Association for Improving the Condition of the Poor

A bitter winter from 1837 to 1838, in the middle of a massive depression, broke the back of private charity, and starvation and death by freezing were once more common. By 1840, there were over thirty relief-giving agencies, and in 1843 the most notable was developed: the Association for Improving the Condition of the Poor (AICP), founded by philanthropist Robert Hartley in New York. His plan was the European model: division of cities into wards with local residents as advisory committees; planned rather than haphazard giving; trained friendly visitors to investigate poverty, distribute relief, and give counsel, encouragement, and advice; and the cooperation of all charities, including reciprocal referral. Casework—personal attention—was believed helpful in itself even without providing relief, and paid staff and volunteers should both be used.

The AICP's friendly visitors—usually women—were told:

> You become an important instrument of good to your suffering fellow-creatures when you aid them to attain this good from resources within themselves ... when [their] sufferings are the result of improvidence, extravagance, idleness, intemperance, or other moral causes which are within their own control; and endeavor ... to awaken their self-respect, to direct their exertions, and to strengthen their capacities for self-support. ... Avoid all appearance of harshness, and every manifestation of an obtrusive and censorious spirit.[40]

Less eligibility remained the primary tenet, and the AICP would not, at first, distribute alms, giving only a little money and small quantities of food and clothing.[41] Recipients were required to abstain from alcohol, send young children to school, and apprentice children of a suitable age for vocational training. Though based on Protestant ideals, the AICP did not limit its help to Protestants.

Soon the AICP became involved in social reform, acting against lotteries, Sabbath desecration, gambling dens, and intemperance. As it accumulated data on social conditions, its leaders became convinced that alcoholism, promiscuity, and child neglect came from the filth and overcrowding of the slums rather than personal fault. On this basis, it opened a model tenement and petitioned for the appointment of the first state legislative commission to investigate tenements. Concern for public health and personal hygiene led it to open two dispensaries for the indigent sick (1846), establish a hospital for crippled children, open a public bathhouse, and campaign for a law forbidding the adulteration of milk. For children, it demanded compulsory school attendance laws and was instrumental in passing legislation to provide for the care and instruction of idle truants and for the arrest and detention of vagrant children. In 1851, under AICP auspices, New York opened a juvenile asylum for such children.[42]

AICPs spread throughout the country, and by 1877 they had reversed their stand on almsgiving, which then became their major function. Although the AICP movement provided innumerable services to the poor, perhaps in the long run its most valuable contribution was in the compilation of data: the beginnings of social research about poverty and deviance and the framework for the profession of social work.

Special-Interest Charities

A number of other charities based on special needs or particular populations developed over the decades before and around the Civil War. Among them were the American Female Guardian Society, Homes for the Friendless, the Mission to Children of the Destitute, the Society for the Relief of the Ruptured and Crippled, the Association for the Relief of Respectable Aged and Indigent Females, the Home for Little Wanderers, and the American Temperance Society. Youth agencies and missions became common, the most noted of which was the Young Men's Christian Association, established in America in 1851 to protect young men coming to the city from the dangers of irreligion, intemperance, and immorality. It provided inexpensive living quarters with sanitary facilities, gave relief to poor families in the neighborhood, coordinated local welfare services, and surveyed needs. Jewish centers for both boys and girls were established in the 1840s. The first Young Women's Christian Associations opened in Boston in 1866 and New York in 1867. Boys' Clubs began about 1860 to give boys opportunities to participate in sports and activities in a Christian atmosphere. The Salvation Army, known for its charitable work with the urban poor, was organized by William Booth in 1865; Volunteers of America, providing shelter and some work for indigent male vagrants, was founded later by his son and daughter-in-law.[43]

Ethnic groups also formed mutual aid societies. By the 1830s there were more than a hundred for people of African descent. Chinese immigrants brought mutual aid societies based on family, territories in China, trade and guild associations, and mutual political groups. Immigrant women organized local and national mutual aid clubs such as the Finnish Cooperative Home and the Polish Women's Alliance. The latter was one of the largest women's groups to develop in the late 1800s, with ties both to Polish nationalism and the international feminist movement. Such groups raised money for ethnic churches and lodges, built orphanages and hospitals, formed health insurance and death benefit companies, and gave outdoor relief. Their leaders championed the rights of workers, especially women and children employed in the mines and mills, and supported women's strikes with food and money. The Polish Women's Alliance gave health insurance to women workers' families and death benefits to husbands and orphaned children.[44]

Government Responses

The American Revolution scarcely changed poor laws: Categorization into worthy and unworthy poor, local and relative responsibility, harsh treatment, and the work component remained virtually the same as in colonial times. The four basic treatment methods continued to be

- Workhouses or poorhouses (almshouses)
- Outdoor relief (alms to people in their own homes)
- Auctioning off the able-bodied
- "Selling" those unable to work to the lowest bidder.

However, two new trends began to influence social welfare. First was a gradual shift from local to state power, with states demanding that every county build a poorhouse. Whereas local authority and responsibility had been the keynote of care in colonial times, increasingly the states set policy and standards for poor relief in the 1800s. Second, both private and public charities came to believe that poorhouses were less expensive, more efficient, and more humane than outdoor relief, and institutionalization became a major goal in social welfare.

Institutionalization gathered momentum during the 1820s as increasing restrictions were placed on outdoor relief. In 1821 the general court of Massachusetts ordered Josiah Quincy (later governor) to lead a committee to investigate poverty. The committee concluded that

- Outdoor relief was wasteful, expensive, and destructive to morals.
- Almshouses were most economical because the poor could be forced to work in them.
- The poor should be employed in agricultural work.
- A citizen's board should supervise the almshouses, rather than leaving them to local contractors.
- Intemperance was the most powerful cause of pauperism.

Quincy said,

> [t]hat of all modes of providing for the poor, the most wasteful, the most injurious to their morals and destructive to their industrious habits is that of supply in their own families. . . . [T]he most economical mode is that of Alms Houses; having the character of Work Houses or Houses of Industry, in which work is provided for every degree of ability in the pauper; and thus the able poor made to provide, partially, at least, for their own support; and also to the support, or at least the comfort of the impotent poor.[45]

Such men as Yates, Quincy, Hartley, and others remarked on the inhumanity of auctioning off workers or selling the dependent poor, acknowledging that they were often tortured, forced to live in filth, ignorance, and disease, and literally worked to death. Children, the aged, and the ill were taken in only for the pittance paid by poor relief officials, and the money was used not for their support but as income for the caregivers. Infants given out for care (babyfarming) died early from starvation and neglect. Coll says,

> Whatever their shortcomings, almshouses were humanitarian as compared with the irresponsible, cruel systems of auctioning the poor or contracting for their care with persons who were often on the edge of dependency themselves.[46]

However, the real purpose of almshouses (poorhouses) was always to save taxpayers money. Katz says,

> Stripped of rhetoric, the goals of much nineteenth century reform can be reduced to a desire to lower property taxes and to keep the streets safe. Although some reform advocates claimed lofty social goals, by and large prosaic fears of crime and rising expenses for poor relief fueled the moral–social control tradition.[47]

Almshouses were forerunners of penitentiaries, for poverty was considered petty criminality except in times of epidemics or severe depressions.

By 1832 fifty-one of New York's fifty-five counties had poorhouses, and soon they were everywhere. Supervisors were political appointees whose pay came from inmates' work, either on the workfarm or contracted out to private businesses. "Savings" were accrued by holding down the costs of food, clothing, and heat. Supplies for poorhouses were also contracted out privately. A report on county poorhouses says,

> In two counties, the committee found that the poorhouses were supplied by contract, the contractor being allowed to profit by all the labor which he could extract from the paupers. In both counties, the contractor was a *superintendent of the poor;* in one, he was also *keeper of the poor house.* In one, the keeper received his compensation from the contractor; and in this case the food supplied was not only insufficient in quantity but consisted partly of tainted meat and fish. The inmates were consequently almost starved. They were also deprived of a sufficiency of fuel and bedding, and suffered severely from the cold. So gross and inhuman was the conduct of the contractor for this poor house that two female inmates (lunatics) were frozen in their cells (or rather sheds) during the last winter, and are now cripples for life.[48]

The committee spoke out against almshouses and for outdoor relief, saying that "half the sum requisite for their maintenance in the poor house would often save them from destitution" and that

Common domestic animals are usually more humanely provided for than the paupers in some of these institutions; where the misfortune of poverty is visited with greater deprivations of comfortable food, lodging, clothing, warmth and ventilation than constitute the usual penalty of crime. The evidence taken by the committee exhibits such a record of filth, nakedness, licentiousness, general bad morals, and disregard of religion . . . as well as of gross neglect of the most ordinary comforts and decencies of life, as if published in detail would disgrace the State and shock humanity.[49]

With each year poorhouse conditions deteriorated as overcrowding waxed and supervision waned. People with all kinds of problems were put in them together, without sanitation or privacy: orphans, foundlings, unmarried mothers, prostitutes, and criminals. Even the deserving poor—the aged, ill, or disabled—were confined in poorhouses,

the lunatic suffering . . . in a dark and suffocating cell in summer, and almost freezing in the winter . . . a score of children . . . poorly fed, poorly clothed, and quite untaught . . . the poor idiot . . . half-starved and beaten with rods because he is too dull to do his master's bidding . . . the aged mother . . . lying in perhaps her last sickness, unattended by a physician, and with no one to minister to her wants . . . a [mentally ill] woman . . . is made to feel the lash in the hands of a brutal underkeeper.[50]

In 1858 the Massachusetts State Charities Board appointed a special committee to investigate public charitable institutions. Its report found that

[i]n the month of May, 1858, there were in the State almshouses . . . a total of 2425; and of these 1176 were little boys and girls, 483 were on the sick list, 200 were insane or demented, and only 70 were able to do any kind of outdoor labor. . . . The entire proceeds for the labor is only $1.50 per head . . . [and] the average weekly support is 83 cents per person.[51]

Poorhouse inmates had little medical care and died quickly, often from malnutrition. According to that same report, in a poorhouse that accommodated 800 people, from May through October, thirty-nine adults and twenty-one children died, and in the previous six months, in the winter, forty-eight adults and forty-six children died. No more than 3 percent of children under the age of one lived.[52] The deaths were of "natural" causes—starvation—rather than contagion. The committee recommended that

- A permanent State Board of Charities be created
- The board be given powers of examination, power to transfer inmates from one institution to another, and power to pardon
- The local trustee/investigator system be maintained
- Trustees be appointed by the State Board to hold office for five years

- Harmless, mentally ill inmates be transferred to almshouses, where they could be kept more cheaply.

The committee also recommended that children placed in reform schools be given work or education, placed in foster homes where feasible, given privileges for good behavior, and that their parents be forced to pay for their keep. Finally, they spoke out against the administration of almshouses, saying that

> in fact, it has seemed to us . . . that the great problem to be resolved in regard to these institutions was not how the unhappy inmates can be made to pay their way, but how the swarms of officials we found in them could be made to earn their own salaries. . . . [T]he salaries of the overseers and officials absorb so much that no kind of labor, agricultural or mechanical, can be made profitable to the State when carried on in governmental institutions.[53]

One result of such studies was that churches and benevolent associations began to found institutions for specific groups. Another was that states rather than local counties began to take responsibility for certain classes of the distressed or deviant, such as the mentally ill and people with mental retardation.

In the early 1800s, women made up about 30 percent of all poorhouse inmates, rising to 40 percent by the Civil War and 47 percent during the Civil War. Short-term residency for all people was high: in the period between 1853 and 1886, 29 percent were there less than a week and 44 percent less than three weeks. About 20 to 25 percent remained about fifteen months, and the elderly and children remained for years. Until about 1850, whole families were incarcerated. Poorhouses were used more heavily during depressions, especially by young men who remained only until they found work. After 1875, children were no longer placed in poorhouses; the poorhouses became homes for the aged poor and for single mothers with infants. By 1900, 85 percent of the inmates were aged.[54]

Various institutions and organizations grew out of the poorhouse experience, including penitentiaries, the juvenile justice system, schools for people who are deaf or blind, general hospitals, and mental hospitals. It is ironic that the poorhouse idea—care in nursing homes, orphanages, and day care centers—arose again nearly two hundred years later as "privatization" under the Reagan and Bush administrations and the 104th Congress in 1995.

Outdoor Relief

Although institutionalization was intellectually a more popular solution for caring for the distressed and deviant, outdoor relief was more manageable, less expensive, and less likely to cause labor rebellions or the breakup of families. In the South, where *noblesse oblige* still existed, outdoor relief was both common and acceptable.[55] Still, in the North, it was increasingly discouraged (only Baltimore prevented it entirely). In New York, for example, between 1830 and 1860 temporary outdoor relief accounted for 34 to 50 percent of all expenditures for relief; in Boston in 1832, while 4,500 people were in almshouses, there were more than 1,500 families and nearly 400 individuals on outdoor relief.[56]

As politicians took over poor relief, graft and corruption became rampant. Administration was careless, extravagant, and corrupt. To combat this, stricter rules of eligibility were instituted and paid personnel were hired to administer aid. Private charities demanded that poor relief be returned to them, arguing that public charity was degrading to its recipients and that politicians could not be trusted with it.[57]

Social Treatment in the 1800s

Medical Care and General Hospitals

The first general hospital, for both the mentally and physically ill, was begun in 1755 by Thomas Bond and Benjamin Franklin, who solicited public monies matched by private funding. In Philadelphia a decade later, Dr. John Morgan established the first medical school at King's College (Columbia University). Marine Hospitals Service, the first federal program in public health, was set up in 1789 to care for seamen. However, the first public hospitals were really the county poorhouses, for every county was required to care for the medically indigent. In rural poorhouses, care, if given at all, depended on the other inmates, which is one reason so many died. However, by the end of the 1700s, larger almshouses set aside special medical wards where inmates occasionally saw a doctor. Urban poorhouses became teaching hospitals, where treatment was a combination of old remedies, guesses, and experimental treatment or surgery, for little was really known about the human body. Few healing medicines existed and smallpox, yellow fever, diphtheria, malaria, tuberculosis, and dysentery resulted in high death rates.

The dangers of childbearing had changed little over history, except that the use of forceps presented new dangers from infection and injury. For poor women, without adequate nutrition and forced to work during their pregnancies, the dangers were worse. Employers gave no time off for pregnancy or recovery from childbirth, and a day's absence from work could mean loss of the job.[58] For the poor,

> only those too far gone to protest would make the trip to a public hospital where inadequate nursing and unsanitary conditions actually diminished one's chance of survival.[59]

Those who could not avoid hospitals often paid for it in the coin of experimentation. This was especially true for women, as male doctors developed an interest in gynecology and reproduction after the discovery of the ovum in 1824. Although poor women and slaves rarely had the kind of "women's problems" that incapacitated upper-class women, their organs could be explored to determine why such problems occurred. If the experiments were successful, the treatment was extended to middle-class clients. By 1830, thirteen states had laws establishing that only "regular" doctors could practice, and in 1848 the American Medical Association was established.

During this era, women were increasingly being constrained to idleness or invalidism. An upper-class wife

> was the social ornament that proved a man's success: her idleness, her delicacy, her childlike ignorance of "reality" gave a man the "class" that money alone could not provide.[60]

A host of mysterious ailments rose, among them sick headaches, nerves, and hysteria; and doctors related them all to women's reproductive organs. "Ladies" were sickly and sickly was feminine: Normal female processes such as puberty, menstruation, pregnancy, childbirth, and menopause (the "death of the woman in the woman") were considered pathological. Possibly the fees paid by wealthy women increased the diagnoses of ill health. Perceptions of beauty for "ladies" also caused such illnesses:

> The fainting and swooning attributed to many nineteenth-century ladies was often caused not by an innate delicacy but by their constrictive underwear. The corset caused more than discomfort, when laced too tightly it could actually dislocate a woman's kidneys, liver, and other organs.[61]

The new gynecological specialists controlled women in many ways. Often female castration (ovariotomy) was prescribed for "taming" unruly women, education was discouraged, and women were told to cultivate their maternal feelings because "good" women had no sexual feelings.

Medical treatments were often worse than the problem. According to the earliest available records (circa 1912), patients had a fifty–fifty chance of coming away from treatment worse than when it began. Standard therapeutic approaches were bleeding, violent purges, heavy doses of mercury-based drugs, and use of opium. Treatments for "women's ailments" could be bizarre indeed: bleeding by leeches applied to the genitals or breasts to provoke menstruation, and

> in some cases leeches were even applied to the cervix despite the danger of their occasional loss in the uterus.[62]

Men generally controlled the medical field during the decades of the 1800s, but a few women were able to make inroads on their monopoly through alternative medical schools, which graduated women as well as men. Harriet Hunt, denied admission to Harvard twice, went to such a school and practiced medicine and her own brand of psychiatry with mostly women clients. Elizabeth Blackwell (1821–1910) was admitted to Geneva Medical College where, despite being ostracized and harassed, she graduated first in her class in 1849. Denied employment by hospitals, she opened a small dispensary in a slum district. Her patients were mostly women and children.

She was joined in 1858 by her sister Emily (1826–1910), who had graduated from the medical college at Western Reserve in 1854, and Dr. Marie Zakrzewska (1829–1902), a Polish immigrant who had received her medical training in Europe in 1856. The younger Blackwell began medical social work for patients in their homes, and she and Zakrzewska raised funds for the dispensary, incorporated in May 1857 as the New York Infirmary for Women and Children.

> Perhaps nobody, nowadays, can understand the willingness and devotion of the women who assisted me in . . . this primitive little hospital: who were willing to work hard, in and out of hours; who fared extremely plainly and lodged almost to uncomfortableness, yet who felt that a good work was being accomplished for all womankind. And this was true of all—students, nurses, and domestic help. . . . We had constant applications from students to share in the experience of practice.[63]

During the Civil War, Elizabeth Blackwell organized the Women's Central Association of Relief and the United States Sanitary Commission, selecting and training nurses. Later, she opened the Woman's Medical College within her infirmary. Emily Blackwell took over operation of both medical college and infirmary when her sister retired, and Zakrzewska, after having accepted a professorship of obstetrics in Boston, went on to found the New England Hospital for Women and Children in July 1862.

Mental Hospitals and Psychiatry

The first law for the treatment of the mentally ill was passed in Massachusetts in 1676, ordering selectmen to provide care and protect the community from them. In North Carolina in the early 1700s, church wardens were ordered to confine the "insane" in almshouses. Generally, however, the mentally ill and people with retardation were left with their families. Those who were violent were thought possessed by the devil, and they were often whipped, shackled in the marketplace, or kept in outdoor pens despite the weather. Many were locked in basements, attics, or outhouses, put in straitjackets, chained to walls, or jailed. The first colony-wide mental hospital was built in 1769 in Virginia, but most communities simply sectioned off rooms from other institutions; for example, in 1791 New York General Hospital appropriated its cellar for the mentally ill. In 1821 Bloomingdale Asylum was created in the New York General Hospital, but not until 1870 did Willard, the first state hospital for the mentally ill, open.

Benjamin Rush—statesman, physician, and educator—is considered the father of American psychiatry. Physician-general for Washington's forces in the Revolution, he opened the first free medical clinic in America during the early 1800s. Becoming interested in the treatment of the mentally ill, he studied under Phillippe Pinel of France, who advocated "moral treatment": paternal kindness, guidance, occupational therapy, and humaneness. Rush introduced moral treatment in a Pennsylvania hospital in 1783. His methods included cold and hot baths, heated and ventilated rooms, simple tasks for the patients, and training the staff for kindness. He also separated the sexes and separated the violent from quiet patients. His methods certainly surpassed earlier treatment for the mentally ill, yet by today's standards the techniques were inhumane: "scientific" experiments on patients who were perceived as objects and oddities rather than as human beings.

In the early 1800s, private asylums were established on Rush's model. The mentally ill were often treated in their own communities, where they could be visited by friends and family. The asylums became training centers for the new science of psychiatry and charged the public fees to see patients exhibited once or twice a week. People were committed easily and informally, with an application from a relevant other signed by a physician. It was particularly easy for husbands to commit troublesome wives.

While private care progressed, public care remained intolerable. A report from Maryland says,

> As you enter, the crash of bolts and clank of chairs are scarcely distinguishable amid the wild chorus of shrieks and sobs which issue from every department. The passages are narrow, dark, damp, and exude a noxious effluvia. The first common room you examine . . . is perhaps for females. Ten of these, with no other clothing than a rag around their waists, are chained to a wall, loathesome and hideous, but when addressed evidently retaining some of the intelligence and much of the feeling which in other days ennobled their nature. In shame or in sorrow one of them perhaps utters a cry; a blow which brings blood to temple and a tear from the eye, and additional chain, a gag, an indecent or contemptuous expression compels silence. If you ask where these unfortunate creatures sleep, you are led to a kennel eight feet square with an unglazed airhole eight inches in diameter [where] . . . five persons sleep. The floor is covered and walls bedaubed with filth and excrement; no bedding but wet decayed straw, and the stench so insupportable that you turn away and hasten from the scene.[64]

The push toward state care of the mentally ill began with the Boston Prison Discipline Society's study of conditions in public jails. This led to other investigations, including that of Dorothea Dix (1802–1887). Born in 1802 to a moderately wealthy family, Dix became interested in the mentally ill when she volunteered to teach Sunday School to women in a Cambridge, Massachusetts, jail in 1841. There she found a group of mentally ill women locked in unheated cells and suffering from gross neglect. Bettering the treatment of people with retardation and the mentally ill became her life's work. She visited every almshouse, workhouse, prison, and jail in Massachusetts, finding inmates in bare, filthy, and often unheated cells. Often the straw and chaff from their beds, cemented with their own excrement, was their only covering. Men and women were kept together, nude, with only male attendants. Whippings and beatings were common.

Dix maintained that the state had moral and legal obligations to the mentally ill and called on influential friends Horace Mann and Samuel Gridley Howe to help her mobilize the press and the public. Together they secured passage of a bill to enlarge Worcester Asylum (1843). Following this success, Dix investigated other states, but most were either unwilling or unable to fund adequate care for the mentally ill. She concluded that the federal government must take the responsibility and in 1848 submitted a proposal to Congress to reserve 5 million acres of land, its income to be used for the care of the indigent mentally ill. The Ten-Million-Acre Bill noted that precedents existed in land grants for public schools, schools for people who are deaf, and support for the private railroad industry. It was passed with more than she had hoped for: 10 million acres for the indigent mentally ill and 2.5 million for facilities for indigent people who were deaf and mute.

However, President Franklin Pierce vetoed the bill in 1851, saying that to support the indigent mentally ill would open the doors to federal care for any indigent. He was probably right: For the first time, aside from a few veterans' benefits, comprehensive federal legislation would have provided an incipient welfare state nearly a century before the Social Security Acts of 1935. Although Pierce is portrayed as the villain who delayed social welfare for eighty years, he was acting within the political economy of his time: strict adherence to precedent, prohibition of use of federal lands for big business and special interest groups, and states' rights.

Dix could not muster enough support to resubmit the bill after Pierce's four-year tenure, even though federal land was subsequently disbursed for such worthy causes as the Morrill Act, which established land-grant colleges, and the Homestead Act. Nevertheless, she continued her work for the mentally ill until the end of her life, forty years later.[65]

Education

Education as a way to individual achievement is a persistent American ideal. After the Revolution, particularly when industrialization produced a glut of workers, education grew from a desirable to a mandatory goal. Because agriculture no longer needed child workers, cities were flooded with them, unwanted, orphaned, abandoned, and neglected. To educate them would serve a multitude of purposes: help them get ahead, keep them from public dependency and crime, and preserve jobs for men whose wages their labor undercut. By 1802 overseers of the poor were required to provide education in Pennsylvania and in Washington, D.C., and had established schools for poor children by 1804. In 1812 New York required schools to stay open three months of the year to qualify for state funds. Although by 1831 education for children of African descent, even those who were free, was outlawed, the push for white education went on. In 1852 Massachusetts was the first state to require school attendance for children ages eight to fourteen, for nine months each year.

The first American educators included Anthony Benizet, who came to Pennsylvania in 1731 to teach both white children and those of African descent and to work for the rights of Native Americans and against racism and slavery, and Benjamin Franklin, who called for public education to combat poverty. However, women were the most instrumental in education, both for children and for themselves. Although high schools required college-educated male teachers, women with high school educations could teach in elementary schools (although they were paid two or three dollars a week compared to men who were paid ten or fifteen).[66] Frances Wright (1795–1852), a Scottish immigrant, traveled the country to gain support for free public schools. She opened an interracial school at Nashoba, Tennessee, but it failed. In 1833–1834, Prudence Crandall opened another school for girls of African descent in Canterbury, Connecticut, but after pupils and teachers were stoned, the well poisoned with excrement, the school doors smashed and broken, and the building set afire, she admitted defeat.[67]

Women leaders in education included Emma Hart Willard (1787–1870), Elizabeth and Emily Blackwell, Catharine Beecher, and Lucretia Mott (1793–1880). Their problems were many. For example, Willard was refused admission to Vermont's Middlebury College but later established the Academy for Female Education and, in 1821, the Troy Female Seminary, which offered a full high school education to girls: solid geometry, philosophy, science, and history. She wrote her own history and geography textbooks and became wealthy from their sale. In 1823, Catharine Beecher, sister of Harriet Beecher Stowe, established a teachers' seminary and unsuccessfully tried to start a chain of teachers' colleges. Oberlin College in Ohio, founded in 1833, was the first to set up a rigorous educational program for both women and men. Its original goal for women was to train them to become ministers' wives or intelligent mothers and homemakers, but it later became a center for antislavery and feminism.

Elizabeth Ann Bayley Seton (Mother Seton, 1774–1821) began parochial education in the United States. A convert to Catholicism after her husband died, she opened a Catholic free school in 1809 at Emmetsburg, Maryland, and later founded St. Joseph's College for Women.[68] In addition to her work in education, she established the American congregation of the Sisters of Charity and what would become the Gray Ladies in hospitals and orphanages. By the time of her death, the Sisters of Charity of St. Vincent de Paul had twenty communities of volunteers. Seton was beatified in 1963 and, in 1975, became the first native-born American to be canonized.

Care of Blind, Deaf, and Developmentally Disabled People

Children who were blind, deaf, or otherwise disabled were usually placed in almshouses. In 1810 Dr. John Stanford, a minister, became interested in teaching them. Later, Dr. Thomas Gallaudet traveled to Europe to learn how to teach deaf people and returned with a teacher, Laurent Clerc, to found America's first institute for people who are deaf in 1817. As state subsidies began, private asylums were built in Massachusetts and Connecticut in 1819, New Hampshire in 1821, Vermont and Maine in 1825, and Kentucky in 1826. Essentially, the treatment used rewards and punishments to develop internal control.

Drs. John Fisher and Samuel Howe traveled to France and Switzerland to observe how children who were blind or mentally retarded were taught. Returning to the United States, they established a facility for the blind: Perkins Institute, which became the Massachusetts School for the Blind (Thomas Perkins donated his mansion for the school). In 1846, Dr. Howe was given state funds to establish the Massachusetts School for Idiotic and Feeble-Minded Youth at Perkins.[69] By the time of the Civil War, there were schools for people with mental retardation in New York, Pennsylvania, Ohio, and Connecticut, all established under state rather than local auspices.

Social Control and Juvenile Justice Systems

In the cities, thousands of children of working parents were abandoned, orphaned, or left home alone with latchkeys. They committed petty crimes but were judged as adults, sentenced to adult jails and prisons without hope of probation or pardon, and whipped, mutilated, or hanged for stealing bread or shoes. Their age was not grounds for mercy, for there was no concept of childhood—children were simply small adults. However, the growing sciences of sociology and psychology, the lessened need for their labor because of new factory technologies, and the growing altruism of the times led to new concern for them. In 1823 philanthropists Thomas Eddy and John Griscom established the Society for Reformation of Juvenile Delinquents and, with an initial subscription of $418,000 from private donors, developed the New York City House of Refuge in 1825. It was a prison, factory, and school until 1932, when it merged with the New York State Vocational Institution. Boston opened a House of Reformation in 1836, Philadelphia in 1828. In 1847 a public state reform school for boys opened in Westboro, Massachusetts, and one in Lancaster for girls in 1854. The latter had small group cottages, no fences, and no barred windows. Courts had the right to commit children over the objections of parents on charges of vagrancy or incorrigibility. Not until 1869 were children given legal representation, and the first Juvenile Court was not established until 1899, in both Illinois and Colorado.

The reformatory movement was part of the burgeoning child-saving concern, and it went hand in hand with the development of new forms of penology. Reformatories were based on indeterminate sentencing—at the discretion of either the judge or reformatory administrator—and "organized persuasion" rather than "coercive restraint." The idea was to give the inmate control over his or her progress toward freedom through "industry and good conduct" and to keep delinquents safe from exposure to temptation. Zebulon Brockway recommended a series of graduated reformatory institutions. The first was a House of Reception, where the prison authorities took information on prisoners' ancestry, constitutional "propensities" (toward crime or poverty—part of social Darwinism), and early "socialization" to formulate a plan of treatment. The second was an Industrial Reformatory to train inmates for work; the last was an Intermediate Reformatory, where they worked and learned to live in society.[70]

Frederick Wines was appointed a special commissioner to the second International Penitentiary Congress in Stockholm in 1878 and returned to advise Congress on child legislation. Among his proposals were that children should not be punished but rather educated for work through moral training, religion, and labor; that reformatories should be segregated according to religious preferences; and that the number in each should be small enough for personal attention. The lives of the inmates were to include primary education and be characterized by simplicity in diet, dress, and surroundings. Reformatories were built away from the cities so children would not be distracted from their moral education. Manual labor was favored over intellectual education, to maintain a class bias, and children of African descent were taught to cook, wait on tables, and launder whereas white children were taught agriculture and factory work, maintaining the racist bias.

The Elmira Reformatory in New York, for male first offenders ages sixteen to thirty, was founded in 1870 and opened six years later. Intended as a model system to rehabilitate young people through education and training, it was soon so overcrowded that reform took second place to control. With only 500 cells, by 1899 it held 1,500 inmates. Discipline was an integral part of the "treatment" program: Military drill, "training of the will," and long hours of tedious labor were the essence of the reformatory plan.[71] Zebulon Brockway, its director, required inmates to

> observe regular army tactics, drill, and daily dress parade. . . . By means of the military organization . . . the general tone . . . changed from that of a convict prison to the tone of a conscript fortress . . . a convict community under martial law.[72]

In the 1890s, charges of brutality by Brockway prompted investigation, but Brockway's political influence cleared him and within a year divested the accusing Board of Charities of its authority to monitor prisons.[73]

Beginning with Elmira, reformatories were built across the nation. Despite the reformers' enlightened ideas, the reality was repressive: steel cages, maximum-security cell blocks, inmate feuds, and corporal punishment, often vicious. Many child-savers and reformers, including Homer Folks, began to advocate a "cottage system," where inmates were placed in small group homes on the reformatory grounds, presided over by a "Christian gentleman and lady who . . . hold the relation of father and mother toward the youth."[74] These medium-security cottage reformatories gradually replaced the jail-like large reformatories.

Adult Criminals and Penitentiaries

The adult criminal justice system rose from almshouses, jails, and prisons. In 1776 Quakers established the Philadelphia Society for Alleviating the Miseries of Public Prisons, on the principle that the best treatment was isolation and meditation in country settings, away from the temptations of city life. In 1823 they established the first penitentiary for the able-bodied poor, where prisoners—including debtors and vagrants—were confined only at night and worked in silence during the day in prison workshops. Older people were put in solitary cells and deprived of communication, whereas younger offenders were placed in dormitories. All were expected to work and meditate on their deviance and to pray for forgiveness, with the expectation that this would teach them the error of their ways. Penitentiaries were the beginning of the idea that criminals could be rehabilitated by treatment rather than punishment.

Other prisons not based on the penitent model but using some of their ideas were built: one at Auburn, New York, in 1816, followed by Sing Sing in 1825 and San Quentin in California in 1852. The two major systems of the reform era were the Auburn, or "silent," system characterized by enforced silence and group activities, and the Pennsylvania, or Eastern, system of solitary confinement. This latter "star model" had a central rotunda and seven cell blocks starring out like the spokes of a wheel, enabling guards at the center to observe inmate activities in all the cell blocks.[75] Although methods were more humane than the previous floggings, physical abuse, and incarceration without work or recreation, rehabilitation was rare. The inmate power system—a hierarchy among the prisoners based on force— taught criminality much more effectively than prison officials taught rehabilitation. Prisoners were neither penitent nor rehabilitated when released, yet the innovations remained because of the political power of the reformists. Officials also liked the rehabilitative methods for they gave them more power over inmates.[76]

Probation began with Isaac Hopper, a man who informally helped discharged prisoners find homes and jobs. In Boston in 1841, John Augustus agreed to supervise people who had committed minor offenses, to post their bail, and to report back to the court rather than have them put in prison. He used his own money for their rehabilitation, and his method was both more conducive to rehabilitation and much less expensive than prison. Thereafter, the practice grew throughout the criminal and juvenile justice systems. From this time forward, social workers were involved in probation work, surveilling probationers and helping clients stay away from criminal activity.

Nonwhite Minorities: Expendable Commodities in the New Nation

Galper writes,

> The genesis of racism in the United States is deeply rooted in capitalism. . . . Racial oppression, as the basis for generating an unpaid labor force, enabled this country to move from a relatively primitive agricultural state of economic development to

a more mature, heavily industrialized state. It provided a speedy way to accumulate the surplus that industrialization requires.[77]

Although white workers also were exploited, the effects were greater for people of color: genocide for Native Americans, the destruction of cultures and societies of Africans brought to America, and imperialism in the lands of Hispanics.

Native Americans: A Case of Genocide

Under English rule, Native Americans had the rights of independent sovereign nations, and this *ideal* continued after the Revolution. However, American independence was a catastrophe for Native Americans.

> When France, Spain, and England vied for the North American continent, the tribes could play the Europeans off against one another. After [1783] . . . America was dominant and the tribes were losers.[78]

Washington declared a policy of peaceful adjustment, and Supreme Court decisions and the Northwest Ordinance of 1787 upheld the rights of Native Americans to hold their lands. Under the ordinance,

> The utmost good faith shall always be observed towards the Indians; their land and property shall never be taken from them without their consent; and in their property, rights, and liberty, they shall never be invaded or disturbed, unless in justified and lawful wars authorized by Congress; but laws founded in justice and humanity shall from time to time be made, for preventing wrongs being done to them, and for preserving peace and friendship with them.[79]

Indian traders were licensed, and in 1796 government stores opened to give supplies on credit to Native Americans.

However, it was never suggested that Native Americans become citizens, for they were considered "incompatible" as

> pagan, preliterate, and nomadic. [White society] was Christian, literate, and agricultural. . . . There was no need to go to war to take Indian land when it could be bought for a pittance [after the whites had impoverished the Native Americans]. But the question remained of what to do with the Indians once their land had been acquired.[80]

The Northwest Ordinance applied to Native American lands and included the germ of *manifest destiny*—the belief that white people should own all of North America. It was, in fact, a political declaration of war:

> [T]he Indians shall never be invaded or disturbed, *unless in just and lawful wars authorized by Congress*. [Italics added.][81]

It warned the tribes that if they did not cede their lands by purchase, they would be forced off. All presidents after Adams gave tacit approval, and white people began to invade Native American lands. As Native Americans defended their territories, the invaders retaliated with murders, planned raids, and action by state and federal militias. Their rationalization was that the Native Americans had been British allies. Wars followed treaties followed wars, but no treaty made by whites with Native Americans was ever honored.

The diversity of the Native American nations generally prevented organized resistance against the invaders. Even so, the great Shawnee Chief Tecumseh, along with his prophet brother, Tenskwatawa, began to organize the diverse societies. However, when Tecumseh went south to recruit for his Shawnee Confederacy, Indiana Territory Governor William Henry Harrison marched against his Tippecanoe encampment with 800 militiamen. The Prophet led the defending Shawnees, promising that bullets would not hurt them, and most were slaughtered. That defeat, while Tecumseh was only days from bringing 50,000 men against the United States, ended organized resistance by the Shawnee Confederacy. Tecumseh joined the British in the War of 1812 and was killed in 1813.[82]

Under Presidents Monroe (1824) and Adams (1825), the Bureau of Indian Affairs was organized in the War Department (moving to the Department of Interior in 1849). Pressures to remove Native Americans beyond the Alleghenies increased as twelve states gained enough white population to be admitted to the Union between 1816 and 1848. Treaties were negotiated, honored, and broken as Native Americans were forced out of their lands east of the Mississippi.[83] Andrew Jackson, inaugurated in 1828, encouraged states to defy Supreme Court rulings that protected Native American rights, and their militias wiped out Native American protest or retaliation. Jackson's Indian Removal Act of 1830 authorized $500,000 to aid Native Americans in their "adjustment" to new territories and moved all but a handful of Eastern Native Americans west of the Mississippi along the infamous Trail of Tears.

About half the Creek nation died during the migration and the first years in the West. Oklahoma, already the home of the Five Nations of the Southeast, became "a vast concentration camp."[84] During the next ten years, more than 70,000 people were moved. Among them were the Sauk and the Fox, who made a desperate but doomed stand in Illinois, and the Ottawas, Potawatomies, Wyandots, Shawnees, Kickapoos, Winnebagos, Delawares, Peories, and Miamis. Only a few remnant groups were left, in New York, Florida, Maine, and Virginia, along with a large group of Cherokees in the Great Smoky Mountains who had resisted so strongly they were allowed to remain.

> Forced migration at gunpoint was the lot of some native groups after they had been defeated. Among the famous forced marches was the one imposed on thousands of Cherokees, Creeks, Chicasaws, Choctaws, and Seminoles, who . . . were forced to move to the Oklahoma Territory. . . . Other tribes in the West, such as the Navahos, were rounded up after military engagements and forced to migrate to barren reservations.[85]

The Indian Trade and Intercourse Act (1834) was supposedly intended to strengthen the federal government's aid to Native Americans, but white intrusion continued, ranging from honest treaty making to genocidal forays aimed at exterminating the "Indian menace." The discovery of gold in California in 1849 sent thousands of whites westward, and the Kansas–Nebraska Act of 1854 and the Homestead Act in 1862, which gave 160 acres of unoccupied government land to anyone (not Native American) who lived on it for five years, authorized white settlement of Iowa, Kansas, and Nebraska. Between 1840 and 1860, an estimated 250,000 white settlers migrated across the plains to the West Coast.[86] In 1869 the transcontinental railroad brought white hunters, who destroyed the bison-based economy of the Plains tribes.

Despite the media glamorization of the battles of white settlers against "savage" Native Americans,

> a total of only 362 white settlers and 426 Native Americans died in all the recorded battles between the two groups along wagon train routes. There is only one documented attack by Native Americans on a wagon train, in which there were two dozen casualties for the white settlers.[87]

White settlers, seen as victims of Native Americans and glorified as pioneers, in fact succeeded in massive territorial aggression. Their conquest refuted most religious and political doctrines of equality and personal freedom. Ironically, some of the democratic traditions of the United States probably arose from Native American cultures; for example, the statement that "all men are created equal, that they are endowed by their creator with certain inalienable rights" comes from the laws of the League of the Iroquois. These laws were also the model for state–federal relations, where the sovereignty of each nation balanced with that of the League; the processes for referendum and recall; and suffrage for both men and women.

The conquest reinforced two major doctrines: that of profit, and that "outsiders" or the "different in beliefs" are less than human. Though legitimated in the names of progress and Christianization, it was genocide: the trickery and deceit with which the conquest began; the murder and enslavement of Native American peoples; their removal person by person and nation by nation until the continent "belonged" to the white government; attempts to wipe out Native American culture by taking away their children, placing them on reservations, and denying them such essentials as food, clothing, and shelter; and the savage decimation of their remaining population by war and murder. It is a tribute to the persistence of their cultures and religious beliefs that they still survive.

Chinese in America

Chinese were among the first immigrants to North America after its rediscovery in 1492, when Spanish explorers moving up the coast toward Oregon before the 1600s hired them to build ships. However, few Chinese came to settle permanently because of strong family ties and religious needs to tend the spirits of their ancestors in their homelands. In fact, emigration from China was a capital offense. China had remained a self-sufficient feudal economy from the onset of the dynasties in 221 B.C. and did not take up world trade until European invasions in the middle 1800s. European demands caught China in its last dynasty (which lasted until 1917) with an emperor more interested in building monuments than in defense. In 1840 the British, Spanish, and Portuguese waged the first Opium War against China, opening it for trade. The second Opium War, from 1856 to 1860, ended China's unity and self-sufficiency.

Although Americans did not make war on China, they took advantage of the new China trade, including the trade in men. "Shanghaiing" became common, and the Portuguese based in Macao were the biggest traders in kidnapped Chinese. This "pig trade" sold Chinese men to Americans for the price of passage to work in mines and on railroads. Though nominally free, the Chinese began life in America in debt slavery to those who bought their passage. They were shipped in conditions similar to those of African slaves: chained, in 18-inch spaces, with minimal food, water, and health care. A high death rate during passage was common.[88]

The Contributions of People of African Descent

As the worldwide demand for cotton became insatiable, the price of slaves increased until it became cheaper to breed than to buy them. There were premiums on good breeders, and female slaves, because they could reproduce, became more valuable than male slaves. A breeding woman was worth one-sixth to one-fourth more than one who did not breed.[89] Infants could be sold away like calves from cows, and white men, who had free access to slave women, sold their own children. Virginia, which did not depend on the cotton industry, became a primary slave-raising state and Washington, D.C., was among the top slave markets until the 1850s.

> The price of a good slave for the fields increased from $300 in 1820 to over $1000 in 1860 . . . [and] the slave population grew from about a million and a half to nearly 4 million during this period.[90]

The Constitution authorized slavery in saying that a person of African descent was three-fifths of a white for representation purposes, requiring the return of fugitive slaves to their masters, and delaying the ban on slave trading until 1808, although slave trading continued into the 1850s. The last slave ship landed at Mobile Bay, Alabama, in 1859 (the same year that John Brown attacked Harper's Ferry, where thirteen white men and men of African descent were captured and hanged by Robert E. Lee). Nor were free African Americans in the North considered people: They could not vote except in a very few cases where they owned property, their children could not be educated in schools with white children, and they were segregated in housing, employment, transportation, and medical services. Employment was mostly limited to domestic service at extremely low pay for women, with little work available for men.

Slaveowner and Cotton Culture.   Fewer than one in four Southern families owned slaves, and nearly half the slaves lived on small farms worked by twenty or fewer. However, about seven thousand families owned fifty or more slaves, and these were the families who set the goals of the South. Slaves on small farms were sold away less often than were those of larger plantations, and those in the coastal South—Virginia, Maryland, Georgia, and the Carolinas—worked under better conditions than did those in Alabama, Mississippi, Arkansas, Texas, and Louisiana.[91]

The *cotton culture* existed from the Carolinas and Georgia into the Mississippi Valley, and every state had its own *slave code*. Slaves could not assemble in groups of more than five or so when away from their plantations and could not leave plantations without passes. Even free African Americans had to carry passports to prove their status. At first, religion was not allowed, but after a time, slaves were allowed to believe in the parts of the Christian religion that taught unquestioning obedience to their masters in return for happiness in heaven. Preachers could preach only what they were told, and religious meetings had to be witnessed by white people. Every white person had police power over every person of African descent, free or slave.

> [T]he slave, if slavery were to be successful, had to believe he was a slave. . . . Each slave was taught . . . that he was totally helpless and that his master was absolutely powerful . . . that he was inferior to the meanest white man and that he had to obey every white man without thinking, without questioning. Finally, if these lessons were learned, the slave looked at himself through the eyes of his master and accepted the values of the master.[92]

Plantation owners' wives were an integral part of slave life. They supervised work in the home, sewed clothes for slaves, and doctored them. These white women often treated the female slaves and their children with vicious cruelty if they knew of or suspected their husbands' sexual involvement with the slaves. The census of 1860 testified to the frequency at which masters exercised their sexual "privileges" on slave women: By that year there were nearly 600,000 children of mixed racial background.[93] Husbands of women slaves could take no action against white rapists on pain of death.

> The rape of black women was an attack on black men as well as on black women, who were warned not to call on their men for protection unless they wanted to see them lynched and raped. Rape was used to reinforce a sense of powerlessness in black men.[94]

Although some slaveowners earned a reputation for kindness and others for cruelty, most fell in between, taking some care of slaves as property but willing to resort to cruel punishments.

> Masters who were psychotic [or] sadistic . . . devised ingenious methods of punishment. And "kind" masters whipped the skin off slaves' backs and washed them down with brine.[95]

Slave Families.   Slaves were encouraged to marry and have families, and could often pick their own mates, for their owners felt that families and love relationships stabilized the slaves and kept them from running away. Monogamy was enforced, with adultery a major offense. If slaves married outside their plantations, the man was generally given a pass to visit on Wednesday and Saturday nights and all day Sunday. Children took their fathers' names and adoptions were permitted. However, family life depended on the grace of the master, and there was the constant threat of selling away children or spouses. In fact, rebellions often occurred because of this, and often whole families escaped together to avoid it.

Children were usually cared for in a communal arrangement, mothered and fathered by anyone who was near, because of the constant labor demanded of both men and women. Old women tended them in "children's houses," with older children helping until the age of eight or so, when they were given shoes and clothing other than gunny sacks and were set to work.

> Feeding slave children out of a common pot as though they were animals and ignoring their desire for modesty . . . was part of the attempt to condition slave children to view themselves as less human than whites and perhaps not human at all.[96]

There was sexual equality among men and women slaves, with both taking over the chores of the family after their work for the master was completed. Food was issued once a week, clothes twice a year.

Although slaveowners often lightened the work of pregnant women, the cumulative effect of malnutrition, hard work, and many babies was devastating. There were many miscarriages, babies were often sickly, and infant mortality was high. Some say that mothers often smothered their children to keep them from slavery, but more recent evidence indicates that the term *smothering* was used to record unexplained deaths. The incidence and timing of the deaths indicates a striking resemblance to sudden infant death syndrome, a reflection of extreme poverty, low birth weights, and poor post- and prenatal care. After emancipation, when women resisted gang labor and took lighter tasks through their pregnancies, the rate of "smothered infants" was only one-fifth of that before the Civil War.[97]

The Work of Slavery.   The plantation was a combination factory, village, and police precinct, complete with totalitarian regimentation. On large farms, work was organized either by tasks or by gangs. On the task system, when a job was done the slaves had free time for themselves, for gardening and the like. In the gang systems, field hands were worked by overseers paid for immediate production and "drivers" with whips given rewards for fast pace.[98] There were rewards for hard work, such as bonuses, prizes, and the opportunity for occupational mobility into skilled trades or manager positions. This was effective to the extent that, at the end of the Civil War, 83 percent of mechanics and artisans in the South were people of African descent.[99]

Seven out of eight slaves were field workers. Women were expected to work as hard as men in the fields and then do women's work in the slave quarters. Their third job was to reproduce. Davis says,

> Where work was concerned, strength and productivity under threat of the whip outweighed considerations of sex. In this sense, the oppression of women was identical to the oppression of men. . . . Expediency governed the slaveholder's posture toward female slaves. When it was profitable to exploit them as if they were men, they were regarded, in effect, as genderless, but when they could be exploited, punished, and repressed in ways suited only for women, they were locked into their exclusively female roles.[100]

Slave women were also used for hauling ore in Southern mines. House slaves in the South were treated as nonexistent, often sleeping in the same rooms as their masters. Urban slaves could be hired out a year at a time and had more freedom than did plantation slaves.

Slave Rebellions.   Slavery did not continue without resistance, which included nonviolent resistance, slowed working pace, feigned illness, and strikes. Violent resistance and rebellion were constant fears among plantation families, and at least 250 slave revolts are recorded. Southern families feared their slaves would copy the revolt in Haiti in 1791, where more than 100,000 of its half-million slaves joined with a voodoo priest named Boukman and for three weeks ravaged the white plantations.

> In an instant . . . 1200 coffee and 200 sugar plantations were in flames; the buildings, the machinery, the farmhouses, were reduced to ashes; and the unfortunate proprietors were hunted down, murdered, or thrown into the flames.[101]

Toussaint L'Ouverture took over leadership as governor of Haiti in 1801 but, betrayed by Napoleon on a state visit to France, he died in prison. His successor, Jean-Jacques Dessalines, continued to fight so persistently that in 1803 Napoleon gave up his dream of making Haiti the foothold of his western empire and ceded the Louisiana Territory to America for four cents an acre.

Rebellion in the South followed. In the early 1800s Gabriel Prosser gathered weapons and a force of a thousand slaves to march on Richmond. When heavy rains cut them off from the city, they were captured and at least thirty-five, including Prosser, were hanged. In 1811, near New Orleans, several hundred slaves attacked whites on plantations. Dozens were killed and the leaders executed, their heads displayed along the route to New Orleans. An 1822 conspiracy of several thousand armed slaves, led by Denmark Vesey against Charleston, South Carolina, was betrayed, and Vesey and thirty-six others were hanged.[102] The most famous rebellion was led by Nat Turner in 1831. It spread throughout Virginia and North Carolina, and whole white families died in their plantations. The Turner rebellion ended when the militia was called out, and although Turner escaped, he was executed several months later.

Harriet Tubman (1820?–1913) led another kind of resistance. Called the Moses of Her People, she escaped slavery in 1849, then returned time after time to lead others—more than 300—to freedom. Rewards for her capture reached $40,000. During the Civil War she served as scout, spy, and nurse for the Union forces in South Carolina, and after emancipation she settled in Auburn, New York, taking orphans and old people into her home. The Harriet Tubman Home for Indigent Aged Negroes was supported by former abolitionists and the citizens of Auburn. When she applied for a federal pension for her war service, she was awarded $20.00 per month (half that of white pensioners).

Free People of African Descent.   From the time of the Revolution, abolitionists of both races worked together. One such movement was the American Colonization Society (1817), which sought to settle freed slaves in Liberia. The American Anti-Slavery Society, formed in 1833 under the leadership of William Lloyd Garrison and Arthur Lewis Tappan, tried to educate free African Americans to gain U.S. citizenship. The most famous abolitionist was Frederick Douglass, a powerful orator and ex-slave, who spoke out for both abolition and women's rights.

In 1826 John Russwurm became the first man of African descent in America to graduate from college, at Bowdoin, and joined with Samuel E. Cornish to found the first newspaper for people of African descent, *Freedom's Journal,* in 1827. Their first national convention, chaired by Richard Allen, was held in 1830. In 1838 David Ruggles founded the first magazine for people of African descent, the *Mirror of Liberty.* Two colleges for men of African descent opened: Lincoln University in Pennsylvania and Wilberforce University in Ohio, founded by the African Methodist Episcopal Church. In 1855 John Mercer Langston became the first elected public official of African descent, a township clerk in Ohio.

The Missouri Compromise of 1829 divided the Louisiana Purchase along the Mason–Dixon line, ensuring that Southern states could continue slavery: Maine was admitted a free state and Missouri a slave state. In 1850 a new compromise admitted California as a free state, created two new territories in New Mexico, and added a drastic fugitive slave law to soothe Southern plantation owners. It also prohibited slave trade in Washington, D.C. The Compromises began to give way: In 1857 a Southern-dominated Supreme Court handed down the *Dred Scott* decision, claiming that slaves were personal property, to be protected for their owners. It also declared the Missouri Compromise unconstitutional because the federal government did not have the power to forbid slavery in any territory (the states' rights issue).

Before the Civil War, there were half a million free people of African descent in the United States (11 percent of the total population), half in the South. Many were well-to-do. They had churches, literary debating societies, fraternal organizations, and societies for mutual aid. Among the freed slaves, indigent or helpless people were supported by relatives, friends, neighbors, and relief associations, and free African Americans established schools and orphanages to aid children of African descent.[103]

Hispanic Americans

Hispanic Americans have a history divergent from that of Native Americans because, having been conquered by Spain, they became Spanish citizens. Their settlement of the Southwest dates from about 1530, when land grants were given to them by the Spanish crown. Mexico won independence from Spain in 1821, and Anglo-Americans almost immediately began infiltrating, at first by trying to purchase Mexico's northern border along the Rio Grande. There, several thousand Hispanics had a self-sufficient economy, with almost no poverty because the church and landowners found work for the indigent.

An estimated 4,000 white settlers were in the Texas area in 1821, but by the 1830s there were 20,000 Anglo immigrants.[104] In 1845 the United States simply annexed Texas, precipitating the Mexican War of 1846. In 1848 the Mexican government was forced to cede Texas for $15 million under the Treaty of Guadalupe Hidalgo, giving the United States most of northwest Mexico, including California where, before the Gold Rush, there were 7,500 Hispanic settlers. The Treaty guaranteed protection for Mexican land rights, along with personal property rights and religious freedom. However, white settlers moving into the Southwest ignored the guarantees. Anglo settlers sued against Spanish land grants and typically won in Anglo courts, for many Hispanics had lost evidences of title and had little money to fight the court decrees. The 1853 Gadsden Purchase gave white settlers even more Mexican land. Taxes were used to disinherit the Hispanics: The United States levied property tax rates at levels only the largest of Spanish landholders could afford, forcing small Hispanic entrepreneurs off their land and into low-wage labor.[105] Violence was common: In the 1850s, 2,000 white miners attacked Mexicans in Sonora, killing dozens and wiping out a community.

Lawlessness against Mexicans had a semiofficial status with the Texas Rangers, a kind of vigilante force created to terrorize and subordinate Mexicans. Numerous lynchings were recorded, and white settlers often became rich with the help of the Texas Rangers. An estimated 2.0 million acres of private land and 1.7 million of communal land were lost between 1854 and 1930 in New Mexico alone. A study in Texas found that from 1850 to 1860, one-third of Hispanic Americans were ranch- and farmowners, one-third skilled artisans or professionals, and one-third manual laborers. However, by 1900 the number of ranch- and farmowners had dropped to 16 percent, and two-thirds of the Mexican population had become manual laborers.[106]

As with Native American resistance, there are persistent myths about heroic battles of white settlers against Hispanics. The most popular is the myth of the Alamo, where 180 principled, presumably native-born Texans fought against Mexican bandits led by Santa Ana. However, the Mexican troops were a legal army and most of the "defenders" of the Alamo were ne'er-do-well newcomers and adventurers, brawlers such as James Bowie, William Travis, and Davy Crockett. The Alamo, in addition, was one of the best fortified sites in the West, with twice as many cannons, better rifles, and better training than the Mexican forces had. Many whites at the Alamo chose to surrender rather than be killed, and the

Hispanics were winning until General Sam Houston made a surprise attack from the north, wiping out most of the Mexican army.

The same myths persist about Mexican bandits attacking white settlers. However, these fighters were actually guerrillas resisting the takeover of Mexican land and wealth. There were numerous raids during the 1830s and 1840s, and Juan Cortina, a Mexican hero, fought for the poor in the Texas borderlands, clashing with local militia and Texas Rangers in the 1850s and 1860s. Far from being an uneducated and uncouth criminal, he issued formal statements of grievances detailing the stealing of lands and the bias of Texan legal systems. Colonel Robert E. Lee was sent to Texas to put down Cortina, but succeeded only in limiting his activities.

By the 1880s, manual labor was being used extensively on the railroad, and by 1900, American capital—railroads, agribusiness, and the federal government—owned the Southwest. In 1902 the National Reclamation Act brought irrigation to Southwest farms, and the Homestead Act was extended into that area. White farming population was insufficient to meet labor demands, and Mexican workers became the agrarian labor class.

The Women's Movement in the 1800s

Although the image of the strong and hardy pioneer woman persisted into the 1800s, new theories of human behavior placed women in a sphere that limited them to home, family, and economic control by husbands. "Feminine traits" became desirable and necessary for middle-class women. Poor women, of course, were not included in this image; they continued to labor in domestic and factory work and often took in sewing or laundry or kept boarders in their homes for extra money.

The two major issues of this era were abolition and suffrage. Suffragists recognized the economic ties among slavery in the South, economic exploitation of workers in the North, and the suppression of women. Although women were not owned in the sense that slaves were, they were

> almost treated like Negro slaves, inside and outside the home. Both were expected to behave with deference and obedience towards owner or husband; both did not exist officially under the law; both had few rights and little education; both found it difficult to run away; both worked for their masters without pay; both had to breed on command and to nurse the results.[107]

Women could not vote; could not practice law, theology, or medicine; could not sign wills or contracts without their husbands' consent; and could not serve on juries. All wages they earned belonged to their husbands, as did real estate and other property; laws of divorce favored the husband and husbands were awarded custody of children.

Among the first to note the connections between abolition and women's rights were Sarah and Angelina Grimke. The daughters of an aristocratic slave-holding family in the South, Sarah joined the Quakers and moved to Philadelphia in 1822, where Angelina joined her seven years later. They became active abolitionists, and Angelina became the first "respectable" American woman to speak in public, presenting the Massachusetts legislature with a petition signed by 20,000 women demanding an end to slavery. Her pamphlets were burned in the South, and both sisters were condemned by the clergy, who saw their public lobbying as an un-Christian assault on the social order and the sanctity of home and family.[108] (The 1837 pastoral letter of the Congregationist Churches, using the New Testament as a base, implied that feminists were antiscripturalists whom God would punish with the loss of ability to have children, degeneracy, and ruin for "taking the place of men.")

Other women also were active in the movement. Lucy Stone was an ardent feminist who worked with William Lloyd Garrison against slavery. She married Henry Blackwell (brother of Drs. Emily and Elizabeth), and both she and her husband agreed that she would be called by her maiden name. (Others who adopted the style were called "Lucy Stoners.") Ernestine Potowski Rose (1810–1892), a Polish immigrant in 1836, was a fearless abolitionist, speaking against slavery even in the South. She campaigned for property rights for women, women's suffrage, and easier divorce laws.[109] Lucretia Mott (1793–1880), a teacher and social reformer, helped to organize the Philadelphia Anti-Slavery Society. She and her husband, James, gave up a profitable cotton business because it was the product of slavery. In 1840 she attended the World Anti-Slavery Convention but was refused seating as a delegate because she was a woman. At the convention she met Elizabeth Cady Stanton, and the Motts and Stantons became close friends.

Elizabeth Cady Stanton married abolitionist Henry B. Stanton over her father's objections and became an ardent worker for women's suffrage. Along with Susan B. Anthony and others, including Frederick Douglass, she organized the Seneca Convention on women's issues in 1848, where the audience of 300 included forty men (but no people of color). The convention called for equal educational rights; fairer laws for marriage, divorce, and property ownership; the end of a double moral standard; the right to write, speak, and teach on a basis equal with men; and equal participation in the trades, professions, and commerce. All the resolutions passed immediately except Cady Stanton's demand for women's suffrage. Even her husband opposed it, but Frederick Douglass lectured in its favor and the resolution survived a close vote on the floor.[110]

Well before the Seneca Falls Convention, Susan B. Anthony (1820–1906) had joined Cady Stanton in working for women's suffrage. Cady Stanton did the theoretical work, including the ideals and language of the campaign for women's rights, and Anthony built the organizational machinery. The daughter of a prosperous mill owner, Cady Stanton took a job teaching when her father suffered reverses in his business. Astonished at the low pay she received as a teacher, she became a radical feminist. She arranged state and regional women's conventions, organized a petition campaign for a women's property laws that passed in 1860, and became a leader for Garrison's American Anti-Slavery Society.

Sojourner Truth, born as a slave around 1797, was as concerned about women's rights as with abolition. All twelve of her brothers and sisters and two of her children were sold before her eyes. One of her first acts when freed by New York's emancipation law (1827) was to sue, successfully, for the return of a son who had been sold away from her. She felt she had been touched by God to work for abolition and women's rights and became an evangelist and an abolitionist, walking and preaching throughout New York and Connecticut and later Ohio, Indiana, Missouri, and Kansas. She became known as a moving speaker on both topics, rivaling Frederick Douglass in eloquence, with whom she often shared the speaker's platform.

Between the Seneca Falls Convention and the beginning of the Civil War, there were some changes in the status of women. In 1848 New York enacted a law guaranteeing that women could keep the property they had before marriage, along with new bequests and gifts. Pennsylvania, California, and Wisconsin soon followed suit. (However, the intention was not completely altruistic—it protected the land of wealthy property owners who resented seeing land and riches pass out of the family through marriage.) In 1860 another bill in New York granted married women rights to wages, allowed wives to make contracts without the husband's approval if he were incompetent, and guaranteed inheritance rights after a husband's death. In addition, the Homestead Acts of 1860 and 1890 gave free land to both men and women: Husbands and wives together were given 640 acres, whereas single men and women received only half that amount.

The common interests between women and slaves bound them together until after the Civil War, when the Fourteenth Amendment specifically gave the right to vote to men, including men of African descent, but not to women. Even faithful supporters of women's rights such as Horace Greeley and Wendell Phillips would not support women's protests against the amendments. Frederick Douglass told women to be patient, for this was the Negro's hour, and race, not sex, was the issue because people of African descent were still being killed. The women's movement split bitterly: Lucy Stone and Julia Ward Howe led the American Women Suffrage Association, supporting freedmen's suffrage and seeking to work within the system and avoid "peripheral" women's issues. Cady Stanton and Anthony formed the more radical National Women's Suffrage Association and aligned themselves with all kinds of women's causes: the double standard in marriage, free love, labor unions, and the civil rights of prostitutes.[111] Anthony approached the issue in very racist terms, suggesting a trade-off in suffrage: educational but not sexual qualifications for voting. "Educated suffrage" meant gaining the votes of middle-class educated white women for politicians and writing off those of lower-class people of African descent and immigrants.

The National Suffrage movement probably had no more than ten thousand members at any one time and faced its greatest opposition in the South, whose people remembered suffragists as abolitionists. Western states very often offered state suffrage to women, for women were a scarce commodity, often outnumbered by men by twenty to one. Wyoming, Utah, Colorado, and Idaho all granted women's suffrage.

Conclusion: Working Toward Freedom

Between the Revolutionary and Civil wars, the United States fomented with so-cial reform and social change. The economy changed from colonial agrarian to massive industrialization, and because of the demand for cotton, America took its place in international trade. On both international and continental fronts, the United States became a power to reckon with: Both France and Spain gave up their rights to American territories; England ceded rights to the sea while Amer-ica sprawled and brawled across the continent, taking by force what it could not buy or gain by trickery. The structure of families changed, from extended to nuclear, isolated, and alienated. Fortunes were made in both the North and South on the exploitation of workers—immigrants, freedpersons, and slaves—who were helpless against the political, economic, and social control of the wealthy elite.

In social welfare, Protestant ideas of poverty and the morality of work con-tinued to direct the treatment of the distressed and deviant. Both private charity and public agencies called for institutionalization of those who could not care for themselves. This created almshouse and poorhouse conditions so horrendous that, with the growing social awareness of the century, new treatment was de-vised for special groups, such as the mentally ill, children, those who were blind or deaf, those with mental retardation or other disabilities, and juvenile and adult offenders. New methods of treatment and rehabilitation grew, some succeeding while others failed.

Finally, in the major social movements of the century, white women of all economic classes and all people of the laboring classes (slave or free) were the driving forces for change. Their formidable foes were the white male elite, bol-stered by church and government and determined to maintain the status quo of power and profit—the battle was slow. Incremental changes were inevitable, but even such a revolutionary change as the Civil War brought few increments in practice. The equality won for slaves, if only in the abstract, was not mir-rored in new rights for women, Native Americans, Hispanics, or Asians. Those freedoms, and true freedom for African Americans, were to be delayed for decades more.

Study Questions

1. What was the impact of urbanization and immigration on social welfare?

2. What were private and public responses to need before the Civil War?

3. What political influences surrounding the Dix bill prevented its passage? What might it have accomplished if it had passed?

4. Compare the treatment of Native Americans, Hispanics, and people of African de-scent in terms of colonialism, genocide, and their status as human beings.

5. How did the women's movement contribute to social welfare?

Notes

1. For example, Massachusetts and New York required male voters to have $300, up to $1,000 to run for Congress, $1,500 to $3,000 to run for the Senate, and $5,000 to run for governor. Pennsylvania allowed any man who paid taxes to vote or run for office and in 1812 New York allowed the same, even extending voting rights to some free property-owning African Americans. See Thomas R. Dye and L. Harmon Zeigler, *The Irony of Democracy* (Belmont, CA: Wadsworth Publishing, 1970), pp. 6–14; and Beulah Compton, *Introduction to Social Welfare and Social Work: Structure, Function, and Process* (Homewood, IL: The Dorsey Press, 1980), p. 218.

2. Dye and Zeigler, *The Irony of Democracy*, p. 65.

3. Ibid., p. 67.

4. Michael B. Katz, *Poverty and Policy in American History* (New York: Academic Press, 1983), p. 10.

5. David Macarov, *Work and Welfare: The Unholy Alliance* (Beverly Hills, CA: Sage Publications, 1980), pp. 234–235.

6. Samuel Mencher, *From Poor Law to Poverty Programs* (Pittsburgh: University of Pittsburgh Press, 1967), p. 167.

7. Ibid., p. 136.

8. Blanche Coll, *Perspectives in Public Welfare: A History* (Washington, D.C.: U.S. Government Printing Office, 1971), pp. 22–23.

9. Mencher, *From Poor Law to Poverty Programs*, p. 77.

10. Compton, *Introduction to Social Welfare*, p. 226.

11. Maxine Seller, *Immigrant Women* (Philadelphia: Temple University Press, 1984), p. 50.

12. Coll, *Perspectives in Public Welfare*, p. 24.

13. Carole Hymowitz and Michaele Weissman, *A History of Women in America* (New York: Bantam Books, 1980), p. 195.

14. Ibid.

15. Ibid., p. 198.

16. John A. Drout and Dixon R. Fox, *The Completion of Independence* (New York: Macmillan, 1944), pp. 373–374. In Mencher, *Poor Law to Poverty Programs*, pp. 133–134.

17. Coll, *Perspectives in Public Welfare*, p. 34.

18. Hymowitz and Weissman, *History of Women*, p. 236.

19. Edith Abbott, *Women in Industry: A Study of American Economic History* (New York: Arno Press, 1910, first published by *The New York Times*, 1909), pp. 48–62. Referenced in Compton, *Introduction to Social Welfare*, p. 228.

20. William Jay Jacobs, *Women in American History* (Encino, CA: Glencoe Publishing, 1976), p. 31.

21. Hymowitz and Weissman, *History of Women*, p. 238, quoting Marie Van Vorst, a wealthy woman who took a job posing as a poor woman in a South Carolina mill to investigate working conditions of women and children.

22. Jacobs, *Women in American History*, p. 32.

23. Compton, *Introduction to Social Welfare*, p. 228.

24. Katz, *Poverty and Policy*, p. 12.

25. Mencher, *From Poor Law to Poverty Programs*, p. 137.

26. Compton, *Introduction to Social Welfare*, p. 227.

27. Coll, *Perspectives in Public Welfare*, p. 34.

28. Seller, *Immigrant Women*, p. 162.

29. Katz, *Poverty and Policy*, p. 202.

30. Ibid., p. 115.

31. Ibid., p. 194.

32. 1818 Report of the Society for the Prevention of Pauperism, founded in 1817 by Thomas Eddy and John Griscom. Quoted in John B. McMaster, *A History of the People of the United States* (New York: D. Appleton, 1895), pp. 527–528; and John V. N. Yates, Secretary of the State of New York, 1824; and reported in Mencher, *From Poor Laws to Poverty Programs*, pp. 145–146.

33. David Scheider and Albert Deutsch, *The History of Public Welfare in New York State* (Chicago: University of Chicago Press, 1938), p. 212.

34. J. V. N. Yates, "Report of the Secretary of State in 1824 on the Relief and Settlement of the Poor," reprinted in the *34th Annual Report of the State Board of Charities of the State of New York, 1900.* Vol. 1, pp. 939–963.

35. Frank Dekker Watson, *The Charity Organization Movement in the United States* (New York: Arno Press and *The New York Times*, 1971), p. 690.

36. Compton, *Introduction to Social Welfare*, p. 236.

37. Quoted in Philip S. Foner, *History of the Labor Movement in the United States* (New York: International Publishers, 1947), p. 98. Reported in Mencher, *From Poor Law to Poverty Programs*, p. 144.

38. Watson, *Charity Organization Movement*, p. 73.

39. Ibid., pp. 75–76.

40. Coll, *Perspectives in Public Welfare*, p. 36.

41. Ibid., p. 37.

42. Mencher, *From Poor Law to Poverty Programs*, p. 83.

43. Compton, *Introduction to Social Welfare*, p. 287.

44. Seller, *Immigrant Women*, p. 179.

45. Coll, *Perspectives in Public Welfare*, p. 30.

46. Ibid., p. 22.

47. Katz, *Poverty and Policy*, p. 196.

48. Gerald N. Grob (advisory ed.), *The State and Public Welfare in Nineteenth-Century America* (New York: Arno Press, 1976), p. 3 of Senate Document D.

49. Ibid., pp. 6–7.

50. Coll, *Perspectives in Public Welfare*, p. 25.

51. Grob, *State and Public Welfare*, p. 9 of Senate Document D.

52. Ibid., p. 53 of Senate Document 2: "Massachusetts State Charities Report of the Special Joint Committee Appointed to Investigate Charitable Institutions of the Commonwealth of Massachusetts, 1858" (Boston: William White, printer to the State, 1859).

53. Grob, *State and Public Welfare*, p. 50 of Senate Document 2.

54. Katz, *Poverty and Policy*, discussing the Erie County, New York, poorhouse, pp. 66 and 217.

55. Coll, *Perspectives in Public Welfare*, p. 22.

56. Ibid., p. 31. Also, Philadelphia blamed inadequate almshouses for the growing need for outdoor relief and over ten years (ending in 1824) spent $621,000 for outdoor relief and $470,000 for almshouses. By 1857, Philadelphia preferred outdoor relief, with investigation and supervision by paid staff, as less expensive and more humane than almshouse care.

57. Robert W. Bruere, "The Good Samaritan, Inc.," *Harper's Monthly Magazine*, Vol. 120 (1910), p. 834. Referenced in Watson, *Charity Organization Movement*, p. 79.

58. Barbara Ehrenreich and Deirdre English, *Complaints and Disorders: The Sexual Politics of Sickness* (New York: The Feminist Press, Glass Mountain Pamphlet #2, 1973), p. 19.

59. Ibid., p. 48.

60. Ibid., p. 16.

61. Hymowitz and Weissman, *History of Women*, p. 68.

62. Ehrenreich and English, *Complaints and Disorders*, p. 33.

63. Seller, *Immigrant Women*, pp. 97–98.

64. Grob, *State and Public Welfare*, p. 13: "A Report on the Public Charities, Reformatories, Prisons, and Almshouses of the State of Maryland," by C. W. Chancellor, Maryland Secretary of the State Board of Health, July 1877.

65. Seaton W. Manning, "The Tragedy of the Ten-Million–Acre Bill," *Social Service Review*, Vol. 36 (March 1962), pp. 44–50; and Roy Franklin Nichols, *Franklin Pierce* (Philadelphia: University of Pennsylvania Press, 1958), p. 289.

66. Jacobs, *Women in American History*, p. 17.

67. Ibid., p. 25.

68. Ibid., p. 22.

69. Compton, *Introduction to Social Welfare*, p. 289.

70. Zebulon Brockway, *Fifty Years of Prison Service*, pp. 397–398. Discussed in Anthony M. Platt, *The Child Savers: The Invention of Delinquency*, 2nd ed. (Chicago: University of Chicago Press, 1977), p. 48.

71. Platt, *The Child Savers*, p. 73.

72. Ibid., pp. 67–68.

73. Compton, *Introduction to Social Welfare*, p. 289.

74. Platt, *The Child Savers*, p. 63.

75. Albert Roberts, in a preliminary review of Day, *A New History of Social Welfare*.

76. Grob, *State and Public Welfare*, p. 100.

77. Jeffrey Galper, *Social Work Practice: A Radical Perspective* (Englewood Cliffs, NJ: Prentice Hall, 1974), p. 51.

78. Ted Morgan, *Wilderness at Dawn: The Settling of the North American Continent* (New York: Simon & Schuster, 1993), p. 438.

79. Joe R. Feagin, *Racial and Ethnic Relations*, 3rd ed. (Englewood Cliffs, NJ: Prentice Hall, 1989), p. 179.

80. Carolyn Merchant, *The Death of Nature: Women, Ecology, and the Scientific Revolution* (San Francisco: Harper & Row, 1980), p. 28.

81. Morgan, *Wilderness at Dawn*, p. 427.

82. Ibid., p. 417.

83. Compton, *Introduction to Social Welfare*, p. 221.

84. Feagin, *Racial and Ethnic Relations*, p. 178.

85. Joseph Hraba, *American Ethnicity* (Itasca, IL: F.E. Peacock Publishers, 1979), p. 222.

86. Feagin, *Racial and Ethnic Relations*, p. 178.

87. Ibid., p. 181.

88. Jack Chen, *The Chinese in America* (San Francisco: Harper & Row, 1980), pp. 1–30.

89. Lerone Bennett, Jr., *Before the Mayflower: A History of the Negro in America, 1619–1964* (Chicago: Johnson Publishing Company, 1966), p. 84.

90. Dye and Zeigler, *The Irony of Democracy*, p. 57.

91. Ibid., p. 57.

92. Bennett, *Before the Mayflower*, p. 93.

93. Hymowitz and Weissman, *History of Women*, p. 62.

94. Jacobs, *Women in American History*, p. 12.

95. Bennett, *Before the Mayflower*, p. 75.

96. Hymowitz and Weissman, *History of Women*, p. 48.

97. Michael P. Johnson, "Smothered Slave Infants: Were Slave Mothers at Fault?" in Linda K. Kerber and Jane DeHart Mathews (eds.), *Women's America* (New York: Oxford University Press, 1982), pp. 102–105.

98. Hymowitz and Weissman, *History of Women*, p. 43.

99. Hraba, *American Ethnicity*, p. 43.

100. Angela Davis, *Women, Race, and Class* (New York: Vintage Press, 1983), p. 6.

101. Bennett, *Before the Mayflower*, p. 99.

102. Feagin, *Racial and Ethnic Relations*, p. 218.

103. Dye and Zeigler, *The Irony of Democracy*, p. 71.

104. Feagin, *Racial and Ethnic Relations*, p. 270.

105. Ibid.

106. Ibid., p. 272.

107. A. Sinclair, *The Emancipation of the American Woman*. In Jacobs, *Women in American History*, p. 12.

108. Hymowitz and Weissman, *History of Women*, p. 823.

109. Seller, *Immigrant Women*, p. 256.

110. Jacobs, *Women in American History*, p. 43.

111. Hymowitz and Weissman, *History of Women*, p. 173.

7

The American Welfare State Begins

The Civil War affirmed federal responsibility over states' rights and laid the groundwork for the United States to become a welfare state. The first evidence came in the Freedmen's Bureau, a federally legislated program that cut across state lines to care for people displaced by the Civil War. Massive economic problems, including major depressions, pushed responsibility for social welfare upward from local overseers of the poor, first to city or county welfare departments, then to states, and finally, with the Social Security Acts of 1935, to the federal government.

Three social welfare movements attained importance during the period from 1865 to 1900: the Charity Organization Society (COS) movement, the settlement house movement, and the child-saving movement. The first two led the developing profession of social work down two different paths, the COS toward individual casework and settlements toward grass-roots organizing for social action and social reform. Child-saving overlapped the others: It took children from their parents and placed them where they might learn the values of hard work, following COS beliefs in overcoming the genetic elements of pauperism, whereas settlement house movements worked on child labor laws, grass-roots aid, and education for children. The labor movement also became a social welfare issue, as COS workers tried to hold down social unrest and settlement house workers fought for reforms.

Both COS and settlement house movements were based on socio-religious ideals: the morality of work and wealth, the personal fault of the poor, and ideas of social justice. In addition, burgeoning new sciences—genetics, sociology, and psychology—had growing influence in both. Whereas COSs sought to contain change brought by immigrants from Southern and Eastern Europe, settlement work was a part of the wider reform movements that included socialism, populism, and the social gospel movement.

192

Although history looks on the emerging social work profession as a caring society's response to need, this was not wholly true.

> Welfare reform . . . served industrial capitalism in three ways: . . . it made relief increasingly humiliating and unpleasant and so provided an incentive to labor; . . . emphasized the parasitic and degraded qualities of the very poor, thereby reducing popular sympathy and justifying retrenchment and repression; and . . . divided the working class against itself . . . when labor militancy was growing.[1]

The class backgrounds of social welfarists and the political dynamics of the times demonstrated the presence of elite ideals in the developing profession. They quite intended

> to pacify an unruly, exploited urban proletariat through encouraging them to accept their class position as morally just.[2]

According to Saville, the welfare state is a result of the interaction of three main factors:

- The struggle of the working class against exploitation
- The requirements of industrial capitalism for a more efficient environment in which to operate and the need for a highly productive workforce
- Recognition of the price of political security.[3]

Piven and Cloward state the case more succinctly, saying that the provision of welfare arises from the need to quell rebellion among the poorer classes through provision of some but not all their demands to maintain a low-wage workforce.[4]

The Civil War: A New Nation Emerges

More than any other reason, the Civil War erupted because the Southern states tried to maintain economic control over their own production. The North, in international competition with England, sought high tariffs against foreign goods, but the South insisted on lower tariffs and adopted a *doctrine of nullification* in which they simply would not charge taxes they opposed. To fight this, Northerners and Westerners created the Republican party, and in the four-way presidential race in 1860, their conservative candidate, Lincoln, won 40 percent of the vote (98.6 percent of the Northern vote).[5]

Lincoln was not an abolitionist. In fact, he opposed civil and social equality for slaves, saying in 1858

> I am not, nor ever have been, in favor of bringing about . . . the social and political equality of the white and black races . . . of making voters or jurors of Negroes, nor

qualifying them to hold office nor to intermarry with white people . . . there must be a position of superior and inferior; and I as much as any other man am in favor of having the superior position assigned to the white race.[6]

However, he was a pragmatist who did not want to destroy the Southern elite on whom the manufacturing North depended. His goals were to restore orderly government, establish federal over states' rights, and prevent the disruption of the Northern manufacturing monopoly.

His election moved the nation toward secession and conflict. Within a year, South Carolina seceded from the United States, followed by ten other states within six months. Unable to tolerate the loss of economic control secession threatened, and pressured by liberals to abolish slavery, Lincoln declared war. Southern politicians left the government and Northern industrial capitalists took their place, changing the political emphasis of the nation from agrarian to industrial and plunging the South into economic depression. The North's economic diversification enabled it to profit immensely from the sale of armaments and provisions for soldiers and to continue its profitable international trade. Meanwhile, the South faced devastation and famine as it sought to produce food on cotton plantations and to buy arms for the war. Working people in the North feared an influx of freed slaves would take their jobs, and after the Draft Law of 1863, rioted in the streets of New York. The riot left hundreds of people of African descent dead and caused a million dollars' worth of damage.[7] At the onset of the Civil War, there were more than 500,000 free people of African descent in the United States, half in the South.

For the North, the Civil War was a poor man's war. The Draft Law gave upper-class men the legal right to buy their way out of the army for $300 or hire others to take their places. Poor men had no such escape, and their families became destitute, for soldiers' pay was about $13.00 per month, with no allotments provided for the families they left behind. Although in 1862 the government established a pension fund for disabled veterans and for the dependents of those killed in the war, along with orphanages and homes for the disabled, dependents of living soldiers went without help. They took jobs in textile mills and munitions factories in greater numbers than ever but were paid a fraction of what men had earned.

Most Civil War battles were fought in the South. Formerly pampered Southern white wives tried desperately to produce food for themselves, their families, and the Confederate troops and to supervise now unruly and rebellious slaves. Union soldiers, storming through the country, burned the fields and killed livestock so that Confederate soldiers could not be provisioned, and the meager supplies grown or hoarded by Southern women were destroyed. To survive, they looted stores and stole, and some few—Rose O'Neal Greenhow and Belle Boyd, for example—joined the Confederate forces as spies and saboteurs, blowing up bridges and communication lines used by Union forces.

The many slaves who sought to enlist in the Union forces were an embarrassment to Lincoln, who maintained that the war was a disagreement among white gentlemen that had nothing to do with slavery. When Northern freedmen tried to volunteer, he thanked them and sent them home, although liberals, abolitionists, and leaders of African American descent asked Lincoln to "hit the South where it would hurt the most: free the slaves and give them guns."[8] He insisted that his policy on slaves was to have no policy and for almost two years appeased slave-holding border states by allowing Union commanders to return fugitive slaves to their owners. Although the Emancipation Proclamation went into effect January 1, 1863, it did not apply to slaves in loyal border states or in sections under Union control in the South. Finally, Congress emancipated the District of Columbia and declared that escaped slaves were contraband rather than property and generals stopped returning them.

Soldiers of African descent were paid only half the salary of white soldiers, and many fought without pay. Overall, there were at least 186,017 of these troopers in the Union army, with losses of 68,178.[9] Their rallying cry was "Forty acres and a mule"—the same chances given white settlers. When captured by Southern forces, they were routinely killed. When Fort Pillow, Tennessee, was captured by Southern Major General Nathan Forrest, 300 people of African descent, including women and children, were slaughtered—shot, nailed to logs and burned, and buried alive.[10] Nevertheless, people of African descent fought bravely against their former owners and for freedom and the Union.

Charity in the Civil War

Of the 300,000 Union soldiers who died in the Civil War, two-thirds died from infections—typhoid, malaria, and dysentery—rather than battle wounds. The casualty rate on both sides was about 50 percent. The Army Medical Corps was unprepared for such carnage and had fewer than 150 surgeons, some of whom joined the Confederacy. Women stepped into the breech, at first with an interest in "moral regeneration" or "medical charity." Soon, however, at least 3,200 women were tending the wounded alongside doctors. Early in the war, such women, who actually handled men's bodies, were considered little more than prostitutes, but this changed because of the value of their work to the armies. Dr. Elizabeth Blackwell began to train women for combat work, and later Dorothea Dix supervised them as superintendent of nurses of the Army Medical Corps.[11] Clara Barton, who founded the American Red Cross after the Civil War (1881), organized a facility that secured medicine and supplies, searched for the missing, and nursed the wounded. In 1864 she was formally appointed superintendent of nurses for the Army of the James (River).

Middle-class Northern women concerned about the destitute dependents of soldiers established more than 20,000 female aid societies to relieve the poor and sew clothes for soldiers. Then, looking at conditions on the battlefield, a group of women from the wealthiest families in New York—Blackwell, Schuyler/Hamilton, Roosevelt, Astor, and Stuyvesant—formed the Women's Central Association of Relief to improve conditions on the battlefield. The group gained official Union recognition and evolved into the U.S. Sanitary Commission, a private agency.

Schools, newspapers, theaters, private donors, and a series of "sanitary fairs" contributed $50 million to support it. The commission inspected camps and hospitals, transported the wounded, provided food and clothing on the battlefront, and arranged special relief for dependents. It constructed new buildings to provide accommodations for bathing, washing, and the sanitary disposal of wastes, and developed new techniques to evacuate the wounded, including railroad cars with swinging bunks, operating rooms, and quarters for nurses and surgeons.[12]

It also set up an entire fleet of floating hospitals for coastal and river work and developed a massive campaign against scurvy by asking women to collect lemons, potatoes, dried fruit, onions, and pickled vegetables. Special projects helped the "walking wounded" by distributing paper and envelopes to write home, collecting vital statistics, obtaining back pay and removing false charges of desertion from records, and establishing soldiers' homes where transient soldiers could find food and lodging. Over the period of the war, the Commission served more than 4.5 million meals and furnished more than 1 million men with places to sleep.[13] It aided both Union and Confederate soldiers in prison camps.

After the Civil War

The Freedmen's Bureau

In 1862 10,000 slaves were left to fend for themselves when the Union defeated Confederate forces at Port Royal. To aid them, Lincoln authorized two volunteer organizations—the National Freedman's Relief Association of New York and the Boston Education Commission—to distribute food and clothing, rehabilitate abandoned and pillaged homes, establish schools for children of African descent, and use free labor in cotton cultivation. After the war, the Freedmen's Bureau was established on the Port Royal model. Located in the War Department from which it drew food, clothing, and medical supplies, it was the first federal welfare agency in the United States. In 1866 it was renewed for two years over President Johnson's veto, with an allotment of $6.9 million. Extended until 1872, it helped repair the damages of the Civil War for all the needy in the South, regardless of race or wartime loyalties.

Thousands of white southerners and freed slaves relied on the Freedmen's Bureau for relief, for need was the only criterion for eligibility. There were no residence requirements because of the great displacement caused by the war. A comprehensive family agency, it provided food, shelter, and clothing; counseling to restore family relationships; advocacy for children; and free medical care and employment services, including training. It also distributed land and building materials at minimal cost, established institutions for the orphaned and elderly, and opened more than four thousand schools for children of both races. Furthermore, it became an agency for civil rights advice and advocacy.

In its first three years, the bureau distributed 18.3 million rations, of which about 5.2 went to white people. By the end of its fourth year, 21 million rations had been distributed, with 6 million going to white people. The bureau either helped found or supported Howard, Atlanta, and Fisk universities, Hampton Institute, and Talladega College.[14] Its most important impacts for social welfare, aside from its overarching federal nature, were that it was a model for private and public cooperation and that it required high standards of accountability from its cooperating agencies.

Services for Veterans

Over 2 million men served in the Union forces, with a casualty rate of 43 percent. For them, but not for survivors of the Confederate army of 781,000 men (casualty rate 52 percent), the government undertook a wide range of services. In March 1865, Lincoln nationalized military and naval asylums for totally disabled officers and voluntary servicemen. Later, the government built and operated a group of national homes for veterans in economic distress because of wartime disabilities. Veterans' homes in the South served only Union veterans, whereas Southern states provided pensions, outdoor relief, and institutions for the disabled and for orphaned children of Confederate veterans.

Over the next twenty-five years, the federal government liberalized eligibility for veterans' services and increased the level of benefits. In 1866 it spent $15 million for veterans' pensions, increasing in 1882 to $30 million and in 1889 to $86 million. In 1890, Congress passed the Dependent Pension Act to keep Union veterans who had served at least ninety days (and their wives) from going to poorhouses or becoming public dependents. By 1898 expenditures for veterans had tripled, covering over 745,000 people, with federal and state governments providing cash payments, medical services, and homes.[15]

Postwar Political Economy

Before the war, states were almost independent nations, but the Civil War made each a unit of the Union. The victory reinforced economic domination by the industrial North, which now dictated its terms of production and blocked industrialization in the South. The loyal were rewarded: Union veterans got pensions, Northern manufacturers got tariffs, and the people of both West and North got free lands in the West (under the Homestead Act of 1864). Railroad promoters received land grants that tied West and North together and ensured that the flow of commerce would bypass the South.[16] Finally, the Constitution's Thirteenth Amendment freed people of African descent from slavery, while the Fourteenth Amendment granted them due process and equal protection under the law and rescinded the three-fifths clause to certify that they were fully equal to white persons. The Fifteenth Amendment granted universal suffrage to men of African descent, though not to women, but did not prohibit mechanisms to prevent voting such as poll taxes, literacy tests, and laws that forbade voting by men whose fathers or mothers were slaves. Not until the Civil Rights movement of the 1960s did questions arise about the implementation, not only in the South but also in the North, of these amendments.

The war brought wealth and power to Northern industrialists. New markets opened in the expanding West and the rebuilding South, and Eastern banks and stock markets established credit to aid in the accumulation of capital. Corporate pools, trusts, holding companies, and monopolies appeared, and free-market competition declined. V. O. Key says,

> as business became increasingly national in scope, only the strongest or the most unscrupulous survived. Total output and total capital investment increased while ownership became concentrated and small competitors disappeared. Monopolies emerged, and great family fortunes developed.[17]

Capital investment in manufacturing nearly quadrupled in the twenty years following 1879 (at $2.5 billion), to reach $11.5 billion in 1904.[18] Whereas in 1860 there were 140,000 factories and 1 million laborers in the workforce, by 1900 factories increased to 208,000 with a workforce of 4.7 million laborers. Manufactured products increased in value from $1.8 billion to $11 billion, and the gross national product nearly tripled ($6.7 billion in 1869 to $17.0 billion in 1900).[19] Taxes and tariffs protected the small wealthy elite of the nation.

The federal government tried to limit monopoly building by passing the Interstate Commerce Act (1887) in an effort to control railroad barons. By 1890 fourteen states and territories had antimonopoly laws, and thirteen states had antitrust laws. However, these laws and the Sherman Anti-Trust Act of 1890 were mostly ineffective. In 1884 the Bureau of Labor Statistics was formed to collect information on the subject of labor and its relationship to capital and earnings, and in 1889 problems of farmers led to the Department of Agriculture being upgraded to cabinet status.

The large low-wage labor force—immigrants, African Americans, women, widows, and children—aided national growth, although they profited little from it. Industrial workers, including women and children, worked a six-day week, twelve to fourteen hours a day, for one or two dollars per week. Periods of unemployment were common in cities, and agricultural workers faced floods, blizzards, and droughts. Two major depressions, in 1873–1878 and 1893–1898, threw hundreds of thousands of people out of work.[20] In the 1893–1894 depression, 40 percent of the factories in the country shut down. Fifty to 66 percent of working families were poor and 33 percent lived in abject poverty. Labor armies (such as Kelly's, 1894) marched on Washington to demand jobs.

Labor and Unionization

Women.   During the war, women entered the labor market in great numbers— almost 300,000 of them, earning about one-third the wages of men. The government hired many in post office and clerk jobs, where they earned an average of $300 a year less than men for the same jobs. They also sewed for the government, obtaining cut fabric from government warehouses and returning finished clothes for a fixed price.[21] By 1879, 70 percent of all women workers were domestics, and one-fourth of all nonfarm workers were women. By 1890 4 million women ages fourteen and up were employed—18 percent of the female population and 17 percent of the labor force. A decade later, 5 million were working, especially women of color and the foreign-born. Many were married. When the typewriter came into general use in the 1890s, women who had refused to work alongside immigrant women or in factories took jobs in offices, earning as much as $7.00 a week.[22]

Women were subject to many kinds of exploitation but seldom complained for fear of losing their jobs. In the garment industry, for example, bosses made "mistakes" in computing piecework; fined them for singing, talking, laughing, or washing; and charged for everything they used: machinery, electricity, needles, thread, drinking water, and washrooms. The price for needles was 25 percent more than bosses paid, and for electricity 20 percent more. They were charged 325 to 400 percent above the cost of materials, and often had to give sexual favors in return for the job, a raise, or a better position.[23]

Tramps.   One of the most problematic issues of the period was that of "tramps." Men out of work began traveling the country looking for jobs, asking for handouts, and staying temporarily in poorhouses. The Civil War had taught them that tramping was no worse than bivouac duty, where they had camped out and lived off the land. Although American generosity dictated that refusing food to a wanderer was the worst form of meanness, a massive fear of tramps began to shake the nation.

> It was the context as well as the quantity of population movement—increased labor, militancy, and the unmistakable emergence of an industrial proletariat— that prompted respectable citizens to transform unemployed, wandering, hungry, and perhaps often angry men into a new and menacing class called tramps.[24]

Professor Francis Wayland of Yale helped to legitimate public hatred of tramps by writing that tramping was not the inability to find employment but the unwillingness to work, and that tramps were labor agitators who stirred up discontent, preached revolution, and threatened the political and social stability of America. He called tramps "a disease, a virus of demoralization infecting the will of the working class."[25] In fact, working people were joining together in what might have become a revolution against the great corporations and monopolies. The abolition of outdoor relief and the call for imprisonment of tramps was related to the control of this union.

> Nineteenth century discussions of pauperism either omitted or rejected the impact of depressions, economic cycles, seasonal unemployment, and technological change on the ability of men to find work . . . [and] refused to acknowledge that most tramps were men on the road only a short time seeking work, not a permanent and dangerous class.[26]

Labor Unions.   Although labor unions had been agitating for labor reform from the early 1820s, the war and free land in the West had all but ended their activity. After the war, they began again to gain strength. The first National Labor Council was called by craft unions in 1866, and in 1878 the International Labor Union was formed (it ended in 1882). Farmers organized to prevent railroad robber barons from taking their lands, and by 1875 there were 30,000 local granges with a membership of 2.5 million. More than 1 million African American farmers organized the Colored Farmer's Alliance in union with the populist grange movement.

The Knights of Labor formed in 1869, gaining 50,000 members by 1883 and 700,000 by 1886.[27] It demanded an eight-hour day, equal pay for equal work, an end to child labor, and cooperation among workers. Teachers, farmers, and even housewives formed their own women's locals and sent delegates to the general assembly. Women were welcomed in the Knights of Labor, which accepted everyone but bankers, lawyers, gamblers, and owners of stock. In 1886 women constituted 10 percent of its 500,000 members, with 200 separate locals ranging from housewives and washwomen to farmers and factory workers. However, the Knights of Labor became identified with radicalism and, beset by internal turmoil, its membership dropped to 100,000 by 1890.

One of the most important unions for women was the Working Women's Protective Union, formed by women of all classes. Until 1894 it provided legal services for victimized women, built boarding houses and protective shelters for women, placed nearly 2,000 women in jobs each year, and collected unpaid wages for them.[28] African American women formed their own unions, which were welcomed into the National Colored Labor Union at its founding in 1869.

The American Federation of Labor (AFL), created in 1881, was a federation of craftsmen and artisans and welcomed neither laborers nor women. Although its national policy admitted women, locals generally did not, and the few that did would not seek equal pay. In fact, the AFL sought to get women out of the labor force through protective legislation, proposed in both 1892 and 1894. The AFL claimed that the eight-hour workday and the prohibition of female employment on foot-powered machinery were aimed at "protecting" weak women, but these rules actually were aimed at taking women out of better-paying jobs. Berch says,

> The leading figure in AFL's anti-women worker campaign was . . . president Samuel Gompers . . . [who contended] that "the wife as a wage-earner is a disadvantage economically considered, and socially is unnecessary."[29]

Population, Immigration, and the People

White Immigration, African American Migration

During the war, immigration was encouraged and immigrants were excused from military service to staff the factories or secure the West. From 1870 to 1900, the U.S. population more than doubled, from 31.5 million to 76 million. Nearly 14 million of this increase—a third of population growth—was from immigration.[30] Migration to the cities increased: In 1860, 20 percent of the population was in the cities, but forty years later 40 percent was urban. By 1900 nonfarm employment was substantially greater than farm employment: In a labor force of 29 million workers, 18 million were nonfarm workers.[31] The percentage of African Americans in the population remained stable: 13 percent in 1865 and 12 percent in 1900. Their in-migration to the North was limited during this period: In 1860 there were 156,000 in the East, 184,000 in the North Central states, and 4 million in the South. By 1900, there were only 385,000 in the East and 175,000 in the North Central states, but the southern African American population reached 8 million.[32]

The presence of new ethnic and religious groups, along with freed slaves, brought new dilemmas of racism, religious discrimination, and ethnocentrism or nativism. Immigrant Italian Catholics refused to adopt the new (Protestant) ways of America, keeping their language, religion, and native customs intact. Often, immigrants saved enough money to bring kin and even entire villages to America, where they developed their own churches and schools. Political exiles, such as Jews forced from their German, Russian, and Austro-Hungarian homelands, brought new and disturbing ideas of political freedom with them: socialism and the right of workers to share in profits.

Asian Immigrants

Chinese men began to immigrate to America in 1820, but women were rarely allowed in. Nearly all these immigrants came from seven districts in southern China, in the province of Kwangtung near Canton. The Chinese knew little about current wages and so were easy to exploit, but they were unwilling to return to China because poverty there was so desperate. Their immigration continued to be encouraged for a short time after the Civil War when the Central Pacific Railroad, finding itself behind the Union Pacific, began to hire them from Western mines and directly from China. During the 1870s Chinese men were almost one-quarter of the wage laborers in California.[33]

However, the United States was in the midst of a great economic depression in these decades, and the Chinese were perceived as taking jobs from white men. They were forced out of mining by whites and, after the intercontinental railroad was completed, lost construction jobs also. In a time of unionization, "anticoolie" unions were formed: the United Brothers of California and the Anti-Chinese Union of San Francisco in 1876 and the California Workingmen's Party in 1877. Samuel Gompers of the AFL declared that the Chinese worked for depressed wages and were beyond the pale of labor organization, and the International Workingmen's Association and the Knights of Labor advocated an end to their immigration. Republican candidate Rutherford B. Hayes put an anti-Chinese plank in his platform.

Violence marked anti-Chinese activities throughout the Civil War decade, but after 1870 it became sustained and coordinated. Laws were passed regulating Chinese shrimp catches, prohibiting the hiring of Chinese by corporations and municipal works, authorizing the removal of Chinese residents from city boundaries, prohibiting them from engaging in fishing, denying them licenses for businesses or occupations, prohibiting attendance at public schools, and finally stopping all Chinese immigration via the Exclusion Acts of 1882. In 1871 a massacre took place in Los Angeles in which twenty-two Chinese were killed and hundreds were driven from their homes. "Riot Night" in San Francisco on July 23, 1877, began when a crowd listening to labor organizers erupted into violence against the Chinese, and over the next three days burned Chinese laundries and homes, attacked a steamship company that brought Chinese to America, and did half a million dollars' worth of damage before police, army troops, the navy, and about five thousand citizens ended the riot.[34]

Between 1879 and 1882, Congress passed two bills suspending Chinese immigration, but both were vetoed because they violated international treaties with China. In 1882 the first Chinese Exclusion Act was passed, suspending immigration for ten years and barring Chinese aliens from citizenship. Renewed in 1892 and made permanent in 1904, it was not repealed until 1943, when the Chinese were America's allies in World War II. The Geary Act of 1892 and the McCreary Amendment of 1893 required all Chinese to carry certificates of residence with identifying photographs or be subject to arrest and deportation.[35] The Immigration Acts of 1924 virtually ended Chinese and other Asian immigration until 1968.

Social Darwinism, racism, and economic motivation made Chinese the targets of discrimination and violence from their first immigration. Local ordinances prohibited them from working in some areas, taxed them discriminately, and controlled them with mob violence: They were beaten, burned, shot, and lynched. By 1900, 57 percent of Asians in the United States, primarily Chinese, were in domestic service.[36] They became a middleman minority in the West, working in trade and commerce as agents, labor contractors, rent collectors, money lenders, and brokers—people with easily liquidated assets. Many invested in laundries, for there they owned businesses rather than having to sell their labor. Few white protectors or social reformers took their part, probably because reformers, if they cared, were in the East, and the frontier West had few laws to control violence.

The Chinese brought with them traditions of mutual aid: trade guilds that were both work and birthright associations giving fraternal welfare; Hui Kuans, or linguistic divisions; class or lineage clubs and organizations; and "tongs," voluntary associations based on mutual interests, primarily protection and the provision of illegal goods such as drugs and prostitutes. In great part, the welfare efforts were aimed at financing education for the young. Another Chinese welfare device was the Rotating Credit Association, where a core of participants each made a contribution and then each contributor got all or a part of the amount.

Native Americans After the War

Railroads were at the heart of American expansionism and created new elites of robber barons who took land from farmers and decimated the resources of Native Americans. By 1865 there were 35,000 miles of railroads, four years later the transcontinental railroad was completed, and by 1900 there were 175,000 miles of railroad across the United States. For Native Americans, the railroads often meant starvation as the great herds of bison were killed off for sport.

In 1871 the federal government in effect eliminated the political rights of Native Americans by declaring them wards of the federal government and refusing to recognize them as independent nations. It was cheaper to feed them than to kill them: A study in 1870 estimated that the cost per dead Native American was about $1 million. The Allotment Act of 1887, called the Dawes Act, further destroyed their cultures by dividing the land—approximately 140 million acres—among individual freehold farmers. Many quickly sold or were cheated out of their allotments, and some 90 million acres of the best land was transferred to whites, while 90,000 Native Americans were left landless.

The Bureau of Indian Affairs was responsible, through Indian Agents, for supplies, education, instruction in farming, and supervision of lands. They were also to distribute food when times were hard. However, by the 1880s Indian agents were notoriously corrupt and incompetent, withholding supplies to sell for profit. In some agency towns, agents were near-dictators, helping white settlers to take over Native American land. A member of the Assiniboine testified before a Congressional Committee:

> They gave us rations once a week, just enough to last one day, and the Indians they started to eat their pet dogs. After they ate all their dogs up they started to eat their ponies. All this time the Indian Bureau had a warehouse full of grub. . . . Early that spring in 1884 I saw the dead bodies of the Indians wrapped in blankets and piled up like cordwood . . . the other Indians were so weak they could not bury their dead; what were left were nothing but skeletons.[37]

Well-wishing reformers won government support to open boarding schools for Native American children, taking them from their parents and interrupting the childrearing process to "Americanize" them. In 1887 the government appropriated $1.2 million to the Bureau of Indian Affairs and to missionary groups for 227 boarding schools to enroll 14,300 children.[38] Placed there for four to eight years, the children were subjected to strict "moral" discipline, their hair cut to end their "heathen" ways, and not allowed to see their parents for months.

One result of the oppression and decimation of Native American societies was the rise of a new religion: the Ghost Dance. It was developed by a Paiute Messiah named Wovoka, also called Jack Wilson, who was possibly a descendant of Tecumseh's brother, the Prophet. It taught that white men would disappear and that living and dead Native Americans would be reunited. In 1889 there was a resurgence of the Ghost Dance, and it became more militant as the injustices of the white man were counted: the extermination of the bison, the removal West of the many Eastern societies, confinement on reservations where the people were at the mercy of Indian agents, and the theft of their land. Some Ghost Dance followers began to preach active resistance to the whites, and apprehensive white authorities alerted the military to stop their assemblies.[39]

In 1890 the U.S. Cavalry mistook a gathering of Sioux Ghost Dancers at Wounded Knee, South Dakota, for an Indian uprising. Nearly three hundred Sioux, including women and children, were massacred. The soldiers continued to kill until almost everyone was murdered. A survivor, Black Elk, said,

> Men and women and children were heaped and scattered all over the flat at the bottom of the little hill where the soldiers had their wagon-guns, and westward up the dry gulch all the way to the high ridge, the dead women and children and babies were scattered. . . . The snow drifted deep in the crooked gulch, and it was one long grave of butchered women and children and babies, who were only trying to run away.[40]

This was only one massacre. Abetted by the new technology of the Gatling (machine) gun, federal soldiers, vigilantes, and settlers set about genocide. Not until after World War I was any real thought given to the rights of Native Americans, and by this time, their lives, societies, and cultures were all but lost.

Emancipation and the Plight of the Freedmen

In the South, cities were in ruin, transportation lines destroyed, and fields barren. There was no money for seeds, machinery, or livestock, and near-famine occurred because of drought and the lack of organized workers. The first concern of Southern states was to get artificial limbs and cash payments to veterans so they could work, and the second was to provide for war orphans. States established central public welfare offices to distribute food and clothes to poor whites but gave nothing to the impoverished freedmen. As in fourteenth-century Europe as feudalism fell, former slaves were left without even the small protections of food and shelter in the winter.

Poor white laborers returned to the South to find themselves in competition for work with 4 million freedmen. Cotton mills came to the South, and a populist alliance of freed slaves and white laborers was in the making. However, because this threatened white elite political and economic control, Southern capitalists encouraged race hatred and pitted white worker against black. Many white laborers believed that emancipation itself was a plot of Northern capital to lower wages and enlarge its labor pool.[41] Entrepreneurs—carpetbaggers—coming from the North to help the freed slaves or to cheat them aggravated the situation.

For freedpersons, the change from slavery to wage-earning status meant that tens of thousands of people died from starvation, disease, and privation. For example, in the years immediately following the war, one-fourth of all infants in some communities died in their first year and life expectancy declined by 10 percent.[42] Before the war, the plantation had ensured stability; after the war, tenant farming, sharecropping, and the independent ownership of small farms became a tenuous way of life. African Americans from 1860 to 1900 never owned more than 6 percent of the land of the rural South.[43]

During Reconstruction (1867–1877) in the South, Senator Charles Sumner and House Representative Thaddeus Stevens were the strongest supporters of freedpersons. Bennett says, in fact, that slaves owed their freedom more to these two than to Lincoln.[44] Lincoln's plan for Reconstruction included giving free land to freedpersons, but his assassination left Reconstruction in the hands of easily influenced Andrew Johnson, who set out to appease plantation owners, first by pardoning them and then demanding that former slaves turn over their land to former owners. He refused to break up plantations and turned ex-slaves over to former masters with no protections against reprisals. Appalled, Stevens gained the support of Congress to put the South under military control until free elections could be held. Congress enacted the Fourteenth and Fifteenth Amendments, which granted citizenship and the right to vote to people of African descent and guaranteed their rights to life, liberty, and the pursuit of happiness. Because African Americans outnumbered whites in Mississippi, South Carolina, Louisiana, and Florida, they were elected as governors and lieutenant governors, secretaries of state, supreme court judges, and state treasurers. In their new positions they helped to formulate new state constitutions for the Southern states. Before long, however, their leaders were accused of corruption and of being led by Northern carpetbaggers and scalawags. At least five thousand leaders were killed. Bennett maintains that their greatest crime was the violation of the American caste system, saying "If there was anything Southern whites feared more than a bad Negro government, it was a good Negro government."[45]

Revenge became the keynote of the South. Retaliation against African American Union veterans was common. In Memphis in 1866, forty-six veterans were killed and seventy-five were wounded, five women were raped, and twelve schools and four churches were burned. In New Orleans, thirty-five veterans were killed and more than one hundred wounded. The Ku Klux Klan held its first national meeting in Nashville in April 1867, under the leadership of Nathan Bedford Forrest, of the Fort Pillow massacre. Soon the South was honeycombed with chapters: the Knights of the White Camellia, Red Shirts, White League, Mother's Little Helpers, and the Baseball Club of the First Baptist Church.[46] Many Ku Klux Klan members were well-known politicians and landowners in the community.

Any atrocity against African Americans was permitted, from raiding their holdings to raping the women, from castrating men to lynching and burning them. There was no protection from the Ku Klux Klan except submission, and often that was not enough. Members of the Klan legitimated their actions by swearing devotion to the Flag, to "racial purity" (particularly of white women), and to Christianity. One lynching took place every two days or so, approximately one hundred per year in the 1880s and 1890s.[47] Newspapers advertised lynchings in advance, and crowds came on chartered trains to see them. People also were roasted alive over slow fires and otherwise mutilated. Although there was some opposition to lynching, the violence and horror of this reign of terror left most people in too much fear to protest or even to flee.

The presidential race between Rutherford B. Hayes and Democrat Samuel J. Tilden was crucial in the treatment of freedpersons. Elections were disputed in South Carolina, Florida, and Louisiana. Although the Electoral Commission upheld Hayes's claim to the states, Democrats threatened to hold up election results past the day of inauguration, leaving the country presidentless, unless Hayes agreed to the South's demands for "home rule": the right to deal with freedpersons as they chose. Upon this agreement, he was elected. Federal troops were withdrawn from the South in 1877, and the racial caste system was established, excluding African Americans from nearly all trades except agrarian labor and domestic service, from education (*Plessy v. Ferguson*, 1896), and from the political process.

Soon new laws—Black Codes—were passed in all former Confederate states except Tennessee. They denied African Americans property rights, specified the work they could do, and forbade work as artisans and mechanics. Orphans or children whose parents were judged unable to care for them were apprenticed, often to their former masters, with no guarantees of food, clothing, or shelter such as white apprenticed children had. Every freedperson needed to carry a written labor contract or a license from the police. Whereas white unemployed workers were "unemployed," unemployed freedpersons were "vagrants" who could be tried and sent to prison. Other charges for which they could be imprisoned were idleness, quitting a job or making too much money, insulting gestures, or "disrespect": women who resisted sexual attacks by white men were "disrespectful." Although victims of these laws could appeal, in white courts they seldom won. Black codes were ignored by a federal government eager to pacify the Southern gentry.

Once convicted, African American men or women were likely to be sentenced to chain gangs, their labor sold to employers or factories or given for local government projects for leases of ten to twenty years. The convict lease system, first established in Georgia, was profitable to both employers and the state, and there came to be a "compelling economic reason for increasing the prison population."[48] Chain gangs were often used as "schools" for "undisciplined" young African Americans who had grown up since slavery. Chains welded to their bodies, men and women together (there was no sex discrimination in prison), they lived in unbelievable conditions, and 30 percent of those given over to state overseers died. Davis says,

> Whereas the slaveholders had recognized limits to the cruelty with which they exploited their "valuable" human property, no such cautions were necessary for the postwar planters who rented black convicts for relatively short terms. In many cases sick convicts are made to toil until they drop dead in their tracks.[49]

Bennett adds:

> After a study of Southern chain gangs, Fletcher Green, a modern scholar, concluded that they had no parallel except in the persecutions of the Middle Ages and the concentration camps of Nazi Germany.[50]

Those who learned to live under the Black Codes were, in a short time, once more subservient tenant farmers on land they had briefly owned. Seventy-five percent of African American farmers became tenant farmers, and although they were paid for the food or cotton they produced, the cost of seed, equipment, housing, and food purchased from the landowner kept them in debt, often for life. This indebtedness produced a new form of quasi-slavery.

Seeing the continued retribution against freedpersons and hoping to lessen it, Booker T. Washington, president of Tuskegee Institute (which he built), declared there must be some kinds of segregation. He used the parable of the open hand with separate but equal fingers, one that could close in a fist for common causes, and said that questions of social equality were extremist folly. This speech, called the Atlanta Compromise, asked for support for education, an end to killing, and economic opportunity for African Americans. Although his hoped-for benefits did not appear, his "separate but equal" appeal helped to justify enactment of Jim Crow laws throughout the South.[51] Upheld by the Supreme Court in 1875, such laws asserted that individuals, but not states, could legally discriminate against African Americans.

Jim Crow laws limited areas in which African Americans could live, and Jim Crow sections appeared in both Northern and Southern towns. In addition, housing, facilities, education, medical treatment, and burial became segregated. Literacy, property, and poll tax tests kept African Americans from voting, as did the *grandfather clause*, which denied the vote to people whose grandfathers had not voted. This ended the political power of African Americans; for example, in 1896 there were 130,344 African American voters in Louisiana, but in 1900, two years after the grandfather clause was passed, only 5,320 voted.

"True Womanhood"

After the Civil War, white middle- and upper-class career women formed a new generation of educated women. Seventy-five percent of college women who graduated before 1900 remained single, many moving into settlement work or casework. Freed by new homemaking technologies (washing machines, nonfire cookers, and vacuum cleaners) and new amenities that freed them from food preparation (canned food, bread cheaper to buy than to bake), middle-class women aspired to paid work, social reform, and college. Married women began to enter the labor force in great numbers, and by 1890 women made up 18 percent of the labor force.[52]

Puritan upbringings and Protestant beliefs still dominated American thought, and a moral outcry was raised against women who, by working outside the home, flouted the "natural order." Part of this was economic, for women now controlled their own money and undercut men's wages in the marketplace. However, a great deal had to do with the new definitions of the "virtuous" woman. The result was the "Cult of True Womanhood," which taught that women were more highly evolved spiritually than were men, as evidenced by their obvious lack of sexual desire,[53] that their unique attributes—compassion, nurturance, and morality—"unfitted them for competitive economic struggle."[54] Therefore, although their natural place was in the home, women—especially unmarried women—could move into the outside world, making it purer and more moral by attacking uncleanness and immorality. Moral issues such as prohibition, prostitution, criminality, prison improvement, pure food and drug laws, child labor, public sewers, corruption in government, and peace were the new province of "true womanhood."[55]

Across the nation, professional women, ethnic minority women, African American women, and working women began to form thousands of clubs, and by the late 1880s coalesced into national organizations such as the National Council of Clubs and the General Federation of Women's Clubs. By 1920 the latter had nearly a million members active in improving the social environment by investigating sanitation and government corruption; raising money for worthy causes such as hospitals, schools, and homes for the aged; and becoming involved in the labor struggles of wage-earning women. Wealthy women, free to use their money as they wished, often sponsored meetings and speeches and donated their money profusely to good causes, especially those involved in health care. (For example, between 1885 and 1889, five new nursing schools were created in Chicago, founded and funded by women.)

African American women's clubs supported the new class of working women by giving them places to live, a community of safety, and emotional and spiritual help. Of the 2.7 million African American women over the age of ten, a million worked for wages: nearly 39 percent in agriculture, 30.8 percent in domestic service, 15.6 percent as laundresses, and 2.8 percent in manufacturing.[56] Despite discrimination, they still managed to enter some professions. Charlotte E. Ray (1850–1911) became the first African American woman lawyer to practice in the United States, receiving her law degree from Howard University. When prejudice forced her from the practice, she turned to teaching. Caroline V. Still became a doctor, and Anna J. Cooper became a teacher in Washington, D.C. Fannie Barrier Williams founded the first school for African American nurses.

In 1874 the first truly national women's organization was born: the Women's Christian Temperance Union (WCTU). The union considered alcohol not only the downfall of families but the support of powerful political machines, because saloons were the meeting places of political bosses. Its major purposes were to protect women from drunken husbands and fathers and protect the sanctity of the home. In twenty years the WCTU gained more than 200,000 members and rose to prominence under the leadership of chief organizer Frances Willard (1839–1898), its president for twenty years (beginning in 1879). Called from the presidency of the Women's College of Northwestern University, Willard challenged WCTU's conservative leadership and linked suffrage and temperance, saying that women could stop the liquor traffic if they had the vote. She also fought the national drug trade from 1883 on, and any reform that would help women and children interested her. She lobbied for women's suffrage, recovery homes for alcoholic women, and reform schools for juvenile offenders. She helped to organize the General Federation of Women's Clubs in 1889 and laid the groundwork for the National Council of Women. By her death in 1898, WCTU had a membership of nearly a quarter million adults, with almost as many in youth groups.[57] At that time, a serious split developed between suffrage forces and antiliquor forces, and WCTU divorced itself from the suffrage issue.

Most women's issues were in some way connected with women's sexuality and men's attempt to control it. The Cult of True Womanhood, the arguments against women's suffrage, the extension of women's sphere into public service, and the fight against immorality—particularly sexual immorality—were both sexist and sexual in nature. Important influences at issue were the moral outrage against contraception and the spread of sexually transmitted diseases throughout the middle-class population.

Wives of the upper classes were "pure women," sexually passionless and dependent. They were proper wives, mothers, and moral social reformers. If they had to have careers, only those that spread their "womanliness" into society— charity work, teaching, and nursing—were acceptable. Even obvious signs of their sexuality—pregnancy and childbirth—were finessed away as "duty." On the other hand, lower-class women were considered passionate and sexual, and therefore immoral. Their sexual or economic exploitation was, therefore, legitimate.[58]

Although research by Dr. Clelia Duel Mosher (1863–1940), a pioneer in the study of women's sexuality, indicated that the perception of women as passionless was a male fantasy,[59] this belief was common and strong. For example, Dr. Theophilus Parvin said in 1883,

> I do not believe one bride in a hundred . . . accepts matrimony from any desire for sexual gratification . . . it is with shrinking or even with horror, rather than with desire.[60]

Nathan Hale, Jr., summed up his review of the sexual advice literature at the turn of the century with a similar conclusion:

> Many women came to regard marriage as little better than legalized prostitution. Sexual passion became associated almost exclusively with the male, with prostitutes, and women of the lower classes.[61]

Male doctors in this era were so convinced that "normal" women had no sexual interest that, if it occurred, they took drastic measures against it, such as clitoridectomy, ovariectomy, and incarceration in insane asylums. Gynecologists sought to alleviate all kinds of physical and mental conditions through ovariectomies: incurable or obscure pelvic pains, hysteria, weakness, and "temperamentalism." Wives who did not "behave" or submit to the control of their husbands were often subjected to such operations and, given that little anesthesia was available, became docile at even the threat of ovariectomy. When antisepsis and anesthesia made abdominal operations safer and surgeons became more skillful at their tasks, operations to rid women of their "hysteria" became even more common.

Before the discovery of the ovum in 1824, abortion was considered contraception, and there were few restrictions. By 1840, there was an upsurge of abortions, and until the Civil War, one-third of the states had no abortion laws. In states where abortion was against the law, doctors rather than women were punished. At the end of the Civil War, when the population of men was decimated, physicians instigated and carried out a campaign against abortion. Forty statutes were passed in the period 1860–1890 declaring any interruption of gestation a crime, with the woman considered at fault and acting against God and nature.[62] The severely declining birthrate among white upper classes was another reason for the campaign: Between 1860 and 1910, live births decreased by nearly one-third. The birthrate among African Americans remained high but still declined, and the birthrate decreased by 26 percent among immigrant women. This inspired more outcries based on social Darwinism and the duty of white women to produce children so that the United States would not be taken over by the "degenerate classes."

Contraception was also condemned, and women who practiced it were called immoral. As early as 1821, Dr. Charles Knowlton of Boston was prosecuted for writing a book on mechanical and chemical means of contraception,[63] but it did not really become a legal issue until after the Civil War. There was, in fact, a great deal of contraceptive information available—the rhythm method, use of condoms or sponges soaked in antiseptic solutions, and intrauterine stem pessaries—but doctors generally refused to discuss it with women. The advice to women who wanted to avoid having children without a good reason was

> Get a divorce and vacate the position for some other woman, who is able and willing to fulfill all a wife's duties as well as to enjoy her privileges.[64]

The Comstock Act in 1873 made it illegal to give contraceptive advice, and some physicians were prosecuted under the new law.

The declining birthrate was not solely because of contraception. Rather, much of the decline, as well as infant mortality and blindness and maternal morbidity and mortality, was caused by sexually transmitted diseases. Barren marriages and "one-child sterility" were often the results of gonorrheal infection, most often in wives infected by their husbands (because doctors colluded with husbands in hiding the infection). One physician, writing in 1910, argued,

> prior to 1850, just 2 percent of our native-born white women were sterile, whereas by 1900 the ratio had increased to one in five. Venereal disease . . . was behind this. . . . Other physicians presented figures purporting to show that from 20 to 75 percent of childless marriages were the result of venereal disease–induced sterility.[65]

German physician Emil Noeggerath stated in 1879 that most reproductive diseases were caused by gonorrhea. Others estimated that up to 75 percent of all major gynecological surgery was because of gonorrhea.[66]

Unfortunately, the attack against sexually transmitted disease became an attack against prostitutes. Prostitution was one way women could survive: It paid better than most low-wage jobs they could find, even though a prostitute's life expectancy was only four years. Many immigrant women, unable to find jobs, engaged in "casual prostitution" until they could find work. Many other women became unwilling prostitutes under the hard hands of their former lovers or white slavers who sold them in cities around the world. Seldom, if ever, were the men who frequented prostitutes blamed for carrying disease back to their wives; in fact, men were often encouraged to take sexual satisfaction elsewhere rather than to "bother" their "pure" wives. In 1874 Dr. Marion Sims, president of the American Medical Association, recommended national regulation and licensure of prostitution to control sexually transmitted disease. However, this was opposed by people who believed regulation would legitimate prostitution and open up legal red-light districts and by feminists who argued that women would be prosecuted for proliferation of disease rather than the men who used them.

Emerging Philosophies and Social Welfare

Two ideals influenced the development of social welfare after the Civil War. The first was social Darwinism, which defined the worthy and moral as those who succeeded economically. Charity Organization Societies followed this "scientific" ideal, relying also on the emerging sciences of genetics, sociology, administrative management, and psychology. The second ideal was the populist democratic/socialist movement influenced by the economic philosophy of Karl Marx and Friedrich Engels, the British Fabian socialist movement, and the social gospel movement. Marxism posited that the government was a tool of the economic elite in exploiting workers and the Fabians sought collective ownership of the means of production. The social gospel movement, led by Protestants, wanted social reform through a return to the basics of Christianity. From 1870 on, populism challenged capitalism, calling it "the science of extortion, the gentle art of grinding the faces of the poor."[67] Populism was one inspiration for labor unions, the grange movement, women's clubs, and, in social welfare, the settlement house movement.

Social Darwinism and the Charity Organization Society

Throughout the 1800s, some social reformers argued that poverty was caused not by personal deviance but by social and economic structures arising from industrialization. However, conservatism and work morality continued to have a greater impact than did social reform on employment practices and social welfare. New scientific knowledge about genetics and psychology provided "proofs" that, indeed, the causes of deviance (including poverty) lay in the individual. Social Darwinism taught that white Anglo-Saxons (preferably Protestants from northern Europe) were genetically better than people of other ethnicities. Moreover, a better world could be created by "containing" people afflicted with problems such as poverty; nonwhiteness; or mental, emotional, or physical disabilities. Nature should be allowed to take its course in ridding society of such defective people and to help them was against God's law. Therefore, science and religion joined in legitimating institutionalization, inadequate poor relief, taking children from families, and in the case of people of color, murder.

Herbert Spencer, an English philosopher with great influence in America between 1870 and 1890, became the spokesman for social Darwinism, saying

> If they are not sufficiently competent to live, they die, and it is best they should die. . . . The whole effort of nature is to get rid of such, to clear the world of them, and make room for better.[68]

He argued that poor laws provided for the

> artificial preservation of those least able to take care of themselves. The poverty of the incapable, the distresses that come from the imprudent, the starvation of the idle, and those shoulderings aside of the weak by the strong were "the decrees of a large far-seeing benevolence."[69]

The class bias is clear: Social aid takes people out of the labor market, makes them unavailable for work, and thereby undermines the God-given reward—wealth—of nature's fittest. The poor and needy,

> [u]nfit to survive . . . were nevertheless kept alive by humanitarian charity. Far from contributing to the development of mankind and society, they were dead weight—a drag on the movement to ultimate perfection. Consequently, pity for those afflicted with problems was replaced with blame, leading to the creation of an outcast class viewed and treated not with indifference but with contempt.[70]

Helping the poor or deviant went against the efficient operation of the "invisible hand" of the market. Not only were the poor to blame—so were those who helped them. This guilt-by-association works against the social work profession even today.

Social Darwinism became a major creed of the Charity Organization Societies, which began in London in 1869 and in Buffalo in 1877 under the leadership of the Reverend S. Humphreys Gurteen. By 1894 there were ninety-two COSs in the United States, and at the close of 1904, approximately 150. The vast majority were in large cities in the East and North—over fifty were in cities with populations of more than 60,000.[71]

The purpose of COSs was to organize all charities in an area so that needy people could be served but would not be able to get help from more than one charity. To do this, they developed central case registries and forums in which all agencies, including the police, could work closely together on cases. Paid staff investigated applications for charity, and volunteer *friendly visitors* personally interviewed applicants in what would become casework practice. Volunteer boards determined eligibility and set grants on a case-by-case basis. Systems of accountability were bureaucratized and COSs kept case records to collect social statistics on poverty, unemployment, wages, family expenditures, disease, and working conditions. Wealthy volunteers became difficult to find, and soon paid workers administered COSs in all major cities. By 1892 women workers far outnumbered men and thereafter dominated the leadership and development of the emerging profession of social work.

An explicit goal of the Charity Organization Society movement was to restore the "natural order" of class stratification. It was no coincidence that the movement began at a time of economic turmoil, with massive unemployment, low wages, and people displaced by the war. The burgeoning wealth of the upper classes was salt in the wounds of those without enough to eat, and social disruption was everywhere. The end of the Civil War brought war production layoffs at the same time the labor market was flooded with returning soldiers, new immigrants, war widows, and freed slaves. For the first time in history, unemployment was a national problem. Charity Organization Societies, developed and maintained by the elite classes, had more than altruism at stake.

Although heredity could not be changed, "moral" environments and treatment could alleviate some of the results of bad heredity. Casework consisted primarily of moral advice, although workers were told not to make moral judgments. Outdoor relief was given only as a last resort because it was material rather than spiritual and "demoralized the poor." Josephine Shaw Lowell (1843–1905), founder of the Charity Organization Society of New York and of many custodial institutions for the retarded, said,

> relief-giving ... seeks material ends by material means, and therefore must fail .... For man is a spiritual being, and, if he is to be helped, it must be by spiritual means.[72]

People were encouraged to work even when no work could be found, and severe work tests were given the able-bodied, although at fair wages. Gambling, intemperance, and vice were attacked as routes to the disease of pauperism.

COSs helped women and children only if the breadwinner died, and then only if the friendly visitor felt it better to keep the family together. Institutionalization was preferred: Mothers were sent to poorhouses and children to orphanages, to "train them away" from the heritage of pauperism. Drunkards' families were not helped unless the drunkard left; their wives were then considered widows. Deserted families, however, got no help for fear that it would encourage other men to desert. The aged were helped only if they were not to blame for their own destitution. If families were eligible for support, the COS first asked relatives, friends, churches, former employers, and fraternal societies to support them. If that did not work, private donors and charities were approached.

COSs also cooperated with police, directing their actions toward beggars, vagrants, and wayward husbands. Plainclothes officers often reported daily to the COS. On COS advice, vagrants were sent to houses of correction for two to six months, and then to state farms on indeterminate sentences with a maximum of two years.[73] In addition, COSs worked with public relief agencies, investigating applicants and at times handling the entire public outdoor relief system. Early COSs lobbied for housing reform and worked to bring disease-prevention techniques, such as vaccinations, into the community. They built tuberculosis sanitoriums and fresh air camps for slum children; provided day nurseries and sewing rooms; taught mothers thrift, better health care, and home economics; found employment for men; and lobbied for legislation to discourage vagrancy and vice.[74]

Josephine Shaw Lowell was a major force in the COS movement. During the Civil War, she had worked in the U.S. Sanitary Commission, later becoming chief fundraiser for the National Freedmen's Relief Association of New York. A member of the New York Charities Aid Association, she did research in 1875 on able-bodied beggars, and in 1876 became the first woman member of the New York State Board of Charities. There she reported on the conditions in and administration of jails, almshouses, hospitals, orphanages, and other public institutions. Her call for reform led to the nation's first custodial asylum for mentally retarded women (Newark, New York, in 1885) and a state training school for girls in 1886. She was one of the founders of the New York Charity Organization Society in 1882 and led in organizing the Consumers' League of New York in 1890. She also founded the Woman's Municipal League to mobilize politically conscious women to lobby for reform legislation and, in later days, became a strong supporter of organized labor and a frequent organizer for striker relief. Lowell set the standards for the COS movement. She believed the almshouse or workhouse would become the agency for moral regeneration and training and was instrumental in setting up COS eligibility guidelines.[75]

The most advanced thinking of the time on charity came from Amos G. Warner, a political economist who in 1894 wrote the book *American Charities*. Warner headed the Baltimore Charity Organization Society and the Public Charities of Washington, D.C. According to his analysis, poverty came not from personal willfulness but from the complex interrelationships of personal and economic factors. The most common causes for relief applications were bad health, illness, industrial accidents, and industrial diseases. Most dependents, he found, were not capable of work. Despite the fact that unemployment and illness caused almost half the poverty in cases he studied, he concluded with a list of causes of poverty that included "evil associations and unwise philanthropy—which caused indolence and a variety of unhealthy appetites."[76]

By 1900 COS goals and delivery of services had changed significantly. Although in 1895 a majority of COSs in principle had no general fund for material relief, by 1901, of seventy-five societies, all but six provided outdoor relief in urgent cases from either emergency or general funds. By 1904 about half of all COSs maintained funds for relief.[77] The careful data workers had collected demonstrated clearly that the causes of poverty were societal rather than personal in nature. Social work was becoming a profession, with casework practice and both personal and social diagnoses—the beginning of the person-in-situation focus of today's profession. Both United Funds and the Family Service Association came directly from the Charity Organization Society.

Private Interest Agencies

A multitude of other private agencies aimed at moral regeneration of the poor got their start or grew during the decades after the Civil War. By 1880 there were at least thirty nondenominational missions in city slums, along with orphanages, hospitals, homes for the aged, and homes or institutions to take in mothers or immigrants. Some aimed at religious conversion or help for tramps, among them the Salvation Army and Volunteers of America. Others, such as Crittenton Services, focused on the problems of women: unwanted pregnancy and prostitution.

William Booth founded the Salvation Army in London shortly after the Civil War. His daughter, Evangeline Cory Booth (1865–1950), grew up in Salvation Army work and in England became known as the White Angel of the Slums. In 1889, at the age of twenty-three, she took command of all Salvation Army forces in London and surrounding areas. Her older brother, Ballington, and his wife, Maud, commanded the Salvation Army in the United States. When they broke away to found the Volunteers of America, Evangeline took temporary leadership until her sister Emma Booth-Tucker and brother-in-law took charge. Evangeline took over the organization in Canada until Emma died (in 1904) and then returned to lead the U.S. forces, where she proved herself a fine administrator and efficient money raiser. She set up a disaster relief service following the San Francisco earthquake and later instituted hospitals for unwed mothers, a chain of residences for working women, and homes for the aged. During World War I, she set up canteens for soldiers, earning the Distinguished Service Medal for her work.[78]

Evangeline's sister-in-law, Maud Ballington Booth, joined the Salvation Army in 1882. After pioneering work in the London slums, she and her husband, Ballington Booth, moved to the United States and successfully established the U.S. Salvation Army. After being ordered by William Booth to another post, they resigned and organized the Volunteers of America (1896). While Ballington concentrated on the Volunteers of America, Maud organized the Volunteer Prison League to establish rehabilitation missions in prisons throughout the nation. In addition, she established welfare programs for prisoners' families, postrelease employment counseling, and halfway houses, all supported by contributions from her lecture tours.[79]

Crittenton Services began when Charles Crittenton opened four missionary homes for "fallen women" in California. Kate Harwood Waller Barrett (1857–1925), who was educated in the Florence Nightingale Training School in nursing and attained her medical degree from the Women's Medical College of Georgia in 1892, contacted him because of her interest in the plight of prostitutes and unwed mothers. She opened Crittenton homes for unwed mothers, moving them in the direction of vocational training and skills for motherhood rather than moral proselytizing. In 1895 she established the National Florence Crittenton Mission, and as its vice president was in charge of more than fifty semiautonomous homes. Invited to the 1909 White House Conference for Children, she later became a special representative of the Labor Department on a commission investigating moral grounds for the deportation of women aliens.[80]

Populism and the Settlement House Movement

Whereas COSs sought to differentiate between classes based on social Darwinism, settlement houses sought to reconcile class differences. The basic settlement house ideal was to have wealthy people move into areas where the poor and disadvantaged lived so that both groups could learn from each other. Canon Samuel Barnett, pastor of the poorest parish in London, established the first settlement house there in 1884. Toynbee Hall was based on the social gospel movement and attracted middle-class people to emulate Jesus by living among the poor. The first American settlement house was the Neighborhood Guild, established by Dr. Stanton Coit and Charles B. Stover on the lower east side of New York with the help of Dr. Jane E. Robers and Jean Fined. In 1889 Jane Addams founded Hull House and Vida Scudder founded the College Settlement, a club for girls, in New York City. Soon Lillian Wald established the Henry Street Settlement, where she taught nursing to immigrant women. A great number of public health services arose from the Henry Street experience, including the Visiting Nurses Association in 1893. By 1910 there were more than four hundred settlement houses in the United States, mostly in Eastern and Midwestern cities.[81]

Settlement houses were run in part by client groups, and they emphasized social reform rather than relief or assistance. Three-fourths of settlement workers were women, and most were well-educated and dedicated to working on problems of urban poverty.[82] Early sources of funding were wealthy individuals or clubs such as the Junior League, and at first their founders tried to provide "culture" to members, such as art, music, and lectures. When they found a need, they added new features such as playgrounds, day care, kindergartens, baths, and classes in English literacy. Other services included art exhibits, lectures, and classes in homemaking, cooking, sewing, and shopping, especially for immigrant women who were not used to the facilities available in the United States such as grocery stores and the products they offered (fresh bread, milk, and canned goods). Settlement workers tried to improve housing conditions, organized protests, offered job training and labor searches, supported organized labor, worked against child labor, and fought against corrupt politicians. Over time settlement houses became centers of social reform, and clubs, societies, and political groups such as the Socialist party used them as bases of operation.

The most famous settlement house was Hull House in Chicago, established by Jane Addams and her friend Ellen Gates Starr in 1889 on the pattern of London's Toynbee Hall. It attracted many powerful women in its work. Among them, Jane Addams stands out. In her early years, after graduation from college, she was plagued by ill health. Unable to work, she traveled with Ellen Starr to England in 1887 and there became interested in Toynbee Hall. Returning to Chicago, she established Hull House and began her work in social reform. She became the most famous woman in America, a model of feminine virtue. She was

> a gifted scholar, a brilliant administrator, a shrewd tactician, and a marvel of a businesswoman, who handled an annual budget of several hundreds of thousands of dollars. But people kept insisting she was a saint.[83]

Addams influenced Theodore Roosevelt to mount a progressive reform platform in his presidential campaign in 1912, and became a leader in the Progressive party, although she considered resigning when it exhibited racist tendencies. With her founding of the International Society for World Peace, she became a "serious threat to national security."[84] Although she won the Nobel Peace Prize in 1931, when she died in 1935 she was considered by the FBI to be the most dangerous woman in America.

Addams was greatly influenced in her work by Florence Kelley (1859–1932), who changed her from a philanthropist to a reformer. Kelley, a Cornell graduate who became a socialist, was divorced in 1891 and moved to Hull House. There she worked for labor and political reform, particularly for children and immigrants. In 1892 reform Governor John Altgeld appointed her to the State Bureau of Labor Statistics, and she began to investigate factories and sweatshops in Chicago, involving Hull House women in her work. She became head of the National Consumers League and lobbied for fair labor practices, maximum and minimum work hours, and minimum wages for women.[85]

Mary O'Sullivan (1864–1943) also came to Hull House, where she interested Addams in the problems of working women. A labor leader and reformer, she organized the Chicago Women's Bindery Union in 1889. She and Addams organized a cooperative apartment house for working women, and women bindery workers held their union meetings at Hull House. O'Sullivan became one of Florence Kelley's twelve investigators into conditions in tenements and factory "sweatboxes" in 1892. In the same year, she became the American Federation of Labor's first woman organizer.[86]

Julia Lathrop (1858–1932) was appointed by Illinois Governor John Altgeld to the Illinois Board of Charities in 1893. During her tenure, she personally inspected all 102 county almshouses and farms in the state, along with all Cook County's charity institutions. A strong advocate of community care for mental patients, she became a charter member of Clifford W. Beer's National Committee for Mental Hygiene. Concerned with children, she helped Lucy Flower, Addams, and others in their fight for the first juvenile court system in the world, and Lathrop was the first woman to head a federal bureau: the Children's Bureau. There she instituted studies on child labor, mothers' pensions, out-of-wedlock births, juvenile delinquency, nutrition, and mental retardation.[87]

Lucy Flower (1837–1921), with Dr. Sarah Stevenson and others, helped found the Illinois Training School for Nurses in 1868. In 1886 she drafted legislation for a state industrial school for dependent boys, and although her bill was defeated, a private agency for that purpose was organized in 1889. She helped organize the Chicago Bureau of Charities, the Cook County Juvenile Court, the Protective Agency for Women and Children, and the Lake Geneva Fresh Air Association for poor urban children. Appointed to the Chicago Board of Education in 1891, she introduced kindergartens and manual and domestic training classes. She was the first woman to hold a statewide elective office in Illinois, as trustee to the University of Illinois.[88]

Grace Abbott came from work at Hull House to become director of the Immigrants' Protective League. With her sister, Edith Abbott, she joined the faculty of the Chicago School of Civics and Philanthropy, one of the first schools of social work in the nation.[89] Appointed to the staff of the federal Children's Bureau, she succeeded in having clauses prohibiting child labor written into all government war contracts during World War I. In 1921 she was named its head, succeeding its first director, Julia Lathrop.[90]

Dr. Alice Hamilton studied medicine at the University of Michigan, specializing in bacteriology and pathology. At Hull House she developed a well-baby clinic, and then went to the New England Hospital for Women and Children in Boston. There her interests in bacteriology led her to study medical problems of women in tenements and houses of prostitution. Later, she became a pioneer in industrial diseases.[91]

Hannah Greenbaum Solomon (1858–1942) became the first Jewish member of the Chicago Women's Club in 1877 and helped to establish the National Council of Jewish Women and the Illinois Federation of Women's Clubs (1896). In 1899 she was elected treasurer of the National Council of Women, and with Susan B. Anthony and May Wright Sewall, represented it at the International Council of Women in Berlin in 1904. Working with Jane Addams and other social reformers on child welfare concerns, she helped to rehabilitate the Illinois Industrial School for Girls.[92]

Hull House and the many settlement houses throughout the nation provided forums and centers for women reformers. They led the way to community organization and group work practice within the profession of social work. Yet the settlement movement and the profession itself were primarily concerned with the white population. In fact, when Jane Addams tried to include African Americans in her work with settlement houses, she faced such opposition that a separate settlement house had to be opened for that group.

Child-Saving

Child-saving took impetus from the COS and settlement house movements. Whereas the settlement house movement worked diligently for child protective labor laws, COSs believed that poverty was inherited but that adult pauperism could be prevented by taking children out of bad environments. Before the 1870s, children were regarded as small adults, and childhood did not exist. From this perspective, their work was not exploitation but their duty to family, society, and God. As a result, children were required to work as soon as they were able, often in the mills by the age of three. They were also charged with adult crimes, tried as adults, and generally expected to maintain themselves. Even laws that required poor and dependent children to be taken from their parents and placed in foster homes or indentured were not for the benefit of the child's happiness—indeed, many would have probably preferred to remain with their families regardless of poverty—but to ensure good and moral work behavior throughout their lives.

Several trends changed this common perspective toward children. First, after industrialization child labor was not so necessary. Indeed, much of the concern of labor unions about child labor was not that the children were being exploited but that, hired in place of men, their wages held down those of adults. Second, with the decline in birthrate, children became more valued, especially among the upper classes, whose concern for their own children led to concern for all children. Also, this coincided with their growing interest in "saving" the lower classes. Third, the social reform movements of the 1800s began to redefine children as different from adults and protect them from abuse, neglect, and dependency. New knowledge available in psychology, sociology, and learning theories also contributed to a new perspective on the rights of children, and child welfare became a field in itself, as did juvenile justice.

Many would date the onset of the idea of *parens patriae* (the government taking the place of parents) from this time, but in fact the state had continuously intervened in child care, though usually to put children to work or keep them from becoming state dependents. Child protection became a new standard for social reformers, although the first action to protect a child came when the Society for Prevention of Cruelty to Animals sued to have an abused child taken from her foster parents (*Mary Ellen* case, 1875). Embarrassed that there was no such protection for children, both public and private agencies moved to organize. Adequate food, shelter, clothing, and medical care—part of the growing reform movements for all people—were more easily justified on altruistic grounds for children.

Benevolent societies formed to provide nurseries and day care for children of poor and working women, where before the only recourse for these women had been to put their children in orphanages. The earliest day care center in the United States opened in New York City in 1854, and enough more opened in the next three decades to found the National Federation of Day Nurseries in 1898. Private philanthropies also opened orphan asylums, such as the Benevolent Ladies Association Home, a facility for children whose mothers had died during birth or poor children whose mothers worked. Homeless mothers of good character could also be sheltered there. The idea was to isolate children from outsiders, including parents, to rehabilitate them through discipline and obedience to authority.

Children of African descent presented a special problem, for only a few people really cared about them. In Philadelphia in 1822, the Quakers founded an orphanage for the Care of Colored Children, followed by orphanages in 1835 in Providence and in 1836 in New York. White mobs burned Philadelphia's orphanage in 1838 and, during the Draft Riot of 1863, 500 white men burned the New York asylum. An orphanage in Albany indentured such children at the age of twelve. Here, a trust fund was established in payments of $100 per year by the indenturer, and given to the child at age twenty-one.[93]

"Contamination" by poverty was a major concern of both public and private child-savers. Therefore, taking children away from poor mothers was common practice, and outdoor relief and mothers' pensions were discouraged.

> Reformers . . . argued that it was better to break up a poor family than to risk accustoming children to life on the dole, which was so inherently demoralizing that it would transform them into lifelong paupers.[94]

Ironically, public agencies were more willing to give outdoor relief to mothers than were social workers, who argued that such aid should be given only if the mothers were closely supervised.

Until the 1870s, most children were placed in catch-all almshouses, their numbers doubling between 1856 and 1868. In 1875 the New York Board of Charities reported that 9 percent of all inmates were children (593) and nearly 300 over the age of two were "intelligent and in need of training." Following this report, New York passed a law prohibiting children's placement in poorhouses unless they "were defective, diseased, deformed, idiots, epileptics, or paralytics," that is, unfit for reform because they could never become self-supporting. In 1883 Pennsylvania passed a similar law.[95]

The orphanage movement was under way. Some states started statewide orphanage and placement systems; others required counties to provide them. The orphanages, however, were run on the almshouse model, with overseers earning their wages by saving on supplies. Mortality rates were about 20 percent.[96] Work morality was the major emphasis: rigid discipline, work schedules, and harsh punishments for rule infractions.

Perhaps the best known child-saver was Charles Loring Brace, who began the Children's Aid Society in 1853 (a national private agency that merged with Family Services in the 1960s). Brace believed that pauper families should be prevented from getting any kind of relief that would keep them together. His solution was to relocate children with families in the West, where they might learn the benefits of hard work in an untouched environment. For twenty years, haphazardly and without follow-up, often simply "taking" (kidnapping) children they felt were in need, agents loaded children on trains and shipped them to cities in the West, where they were "picked over" and chosen by families. Unfortunately, many families just wanted the extra help and badly mistreated the children. Many simply disappeared, either running away, getting lost, or dying. More than 50,000 children over a twenty-five-year period were shipped to the West, from 4,000 a year in the 1870s to about 500 in 1892.

The first Children's Aid Society was established in New York, with Boston in 1864 and most major cities following. Children's Aid Societies became adoption agencies with high standards for placement, requiring extensive knowledge of the child and his or her needs, a comprehensive study of available homes, and consistent supervision by the agency. Counseling and rehabilitation of parents were intended to keep families together, and this had priority over foster home placement. Adoption, which had been a simple agreement by the parties, began to require legal evidence of transfer of children similar to a registration of deeds. However, as early as 1851 Massachusetts required a judge to determine whether adoption was in the best interests of the child, along with consent of the natural parents.[97] By the late 1800s, orphanages, foster homes, and adoption were common.

Child-saving cut across all fields of reform, from public dependency to the establishment of juvenile justice systems. The first juvenile court law in the nation was drafted by the Illinois State Conference of Charities in 1899 and strongly influenced by such women as Jane Addams, Florence Kelley, and other Hull House workers. It was called "An Act to Regulate the Treatment and Control of Dependent, Neglected, and Delinquent Children," and dealt with children under age sixteen. The law provided a special juvenile courtroom and a separate record-keeping system and allowed for the appointment of juvenile probation officers. Within ten years, there were similar laws in twenty-two states, and by 1919 all states except Connecticut, Maine, and Wyoming had juvenile court laws.[98]

Undoubtedly much child-saving sprang from altruism, but other motives included the fear of pauperism, children's wages that lowered men's salaries, and the need to get children off the streets and out of criminal activity. For whatever reason, the public good required that children be "rescued," and as the movement progressed toward the twentieth century, there was a tacit acknowledgment, perhaps spurred by the new science of psychology, that children had special needs.

Public Welfare Efforts

Although social welfare history usually stresses private philanthropy, in the late 1800s public welfare actually touched more people. Asylums, orphanages, workhouses, almshouses, and outdoor relief provided the necessities of life to the poverty-stricken. The Civil War brought greater centralization and more coordination to bear on the nation's massive needs, and in the 1880s, governments slowly withdrew from subsidizing private organizations. They began to build their own service systems, especially in income maintenance, corrections, and institutional care for people with mental illness, retardation, or physical disabilities. Private charity interests continued with special groups of the deviant or distressed—unwed mothers, prisoners, immigrants, and children—but turned from income maintenance to professionalized casework. Gradually, their services were offered as additions to public services rather than in place of such services, and two systems of welfare developed.

Whereas private charities insisted that outdoor relief was more costly to society and more degrading to recipients, public bureaucracies, through their studies and statistics, noted that institutions cost society more in money, shattered families, longer-term care, and unhappiness. In addition, they were more difficult to supervise humanely. The public sector moved toward outdoor relief, although public monies continued to subsidize some private agencies, particularly those serving women and children. By the 1890s, few agencies except those serving the aged were subsidized. Instead, public monies were given to county boards of supervisors to provide outdoor relief. Cash grants ranged from $5 to $30 per month, but the more common kind of support was in food, clothing, or shelter.

During that period, poverty was severe even for those still employed. For example, in Lawrence, Massachusetts, the average salary was $500 a year in 1875, but a small family needed more than $600 simply to pay for essentials. Tenement rents in 1893, when wages dropped below $300, were often $200 a year. With depressions, or when people were injured or killed on the job, or when employers decided to lay off workers for any reason, disaster struck the common family. Added to this, massive immigration and the large "army" of tramps roaming the country necessitated a centralized and coordinated government system for adequate care of the poor, although "adequacy" was seldom achieved.

By the end of the century, the average wage in the United States was between $400 and $500 per year for a ten-hour day, six-day week, and poverty began at about $460 for a family of five. There were no employment benefits and unemployment was common. Women and children had to work, for men could not support their families alone. Almost 40 percent of the population lived in cities, and women made up 20 percent of the workforce.[99] Ten million people, or 12 percent of the total population, lived in poverty, and 4 million people received public assistance.[100] Almshouses in New York City gave outdoor relief to 209,092 people, compared with the 30,560 people aided in 1900 by private societies.[101]

Because the poor were so often ill, public health became an issue. The discovery of germs made public officials realize that some highly infectious diseases could be prevented through vaccination, aseptic treatment conditions, and better nutrition and sanitation among the poor. Although only a start was made in this era, the federal government moved toward national action. In 1878 foreign quarantine became the responsibility of the Marine Hospitals Service (forerunner of the Public Health Service). Emergency funds to prevent epidemics were appropriated in 1883 and a hygienic laboratory was added in 1887. The service took over foreign and interstate quarantine in 1893.

Public welfare monies were often used by politicians to buy votes. Immigrants used to the *padrone* system of their native countries were easily persuaded by money, food, and help in finding jobs. Officials gave special services to voters, but nonvoters such as women and children, regardless of need, went unaided. Friends and relatives of politicians were often financed from the public coffers, and politicians helped themselves; for example, in New York during the 1873–

1878 depression, Boss Tweed stole $100 million from the New York City treasury. Serious irregularities in the Department of Public Charities and Corrections led to the complete suspension of outdoor relief from July 1874 to January 1875, and private agencies were flooded with desperate people seeking aid. Public relief was only partially resumed, primarily in distributing coal and giving aid to the blind. In 1876 and 1877, funds were allotted to be distributed through voluntary agencies.[102] In graft-infested Brooklyn, a municipal reform movement cut all outdoor relief in the winter of 1878, a period of depression and labor conflict, and desperate citizens rioted.[103]

The separation of private and public welfare continued as control moved from local overseers to state governments. Centralization brought the creation of state boards of charities and corrections, later to become state departments of public welfare. The first was in Massachusetts, in 1863, under the directorship of Dr. Samuel Gridley Howe (president for ten years), who emphasized the importance of keeping families together whenever possible and recommended humane treatment for those in institutions. The board's primary goal was to control and coordinate private and public agencies and to ensure legal standards of care.

Howe instituted a study in which board members inspected mental asylums, state hospitals, almshouses, industrial schools, and charitable institutions to which the state gave aid. From the survey, Howe developed a plan of inmate classification and regulations for administration. Because of concern for children, in 1869 a "state visiting agent" was appointed to attend the court trials of juvenile delinquents and to assume care for children not committed to reform schools—a forerunner of the juvenile probation officer.[104] In 1885, the state board of Massachusetts became the first to supervise charitable, medical, and penal institutions. Other states soon followed: Boards formed in Connecticut, New York, Wisconsin, Rhode Island, Pennsylvania, Michigan, Kansas, and Illinois. By 1897, sixteen states had state boards of charity.

The major results of such boards were better care and protection of dependent children because they were removed from poorhouses and placed in licensed children's asylums or foster care homes, more uniform and efficient administration of local public relief, a decrease in urban pauperism through the protection of immigrants, and improved care for the mentally ill. The state boards also gave a nationwide voice to social welfare by establishing the American Social Science Association (1865), which later became the National Conference on Social Welfare.[105]

National organization was next, and Massachusetts, Connecticut, New York, and Wisconsin met in 1874 to form the Conference of Boards and Public Charities, a national network of private and public charities. In 1879 voluntary agencies were invited to participate in the conference's annual meetings. (The 1874 conference officially condemned outdoor relief in the middle of the 1873–1878 depression for demoralizing the workforce.) Within ten years, COSs dominated the conference, although it remained a forum for current thought and new policy. For example, in 1886 Frederick H. Wines questioned the pseudoscientific statistics that showed individuals to be the cause of poverty and crime, urging that the Conference look at the invention of labor-saving machinery, aggregation of capital in large and wealthy corporations, aggregation of population in urban centers, and the emancipation of women.[106]

At the seventeenth conference in 1890, Josephine Shaw Lowell argued that people should be given aid only "when starvation is imminent." Poverty or non-work, in the majority's view, was a threat to a sound and moral economic system. She mentioned the obvious failure of public relief: the rising populations of poorhouses and mental hospitals and the growing number of unemployed vagrants. In rejoinder, Franklin B. Sanborn, secretary of the Massachusetts State Board, made a plea for outdoor relief or "family aid," saying that outdoor relief statistics often included medical care and burials and so were overstated. He concluded that except in hard times few able-bodied people were in poorhouses and that there would never be enough institutions for all the poor. He also deplored the idea that separating families was the best way to prevent dependency. As the century waned, private charities began to support government relief efforts. Many recommended mothers' pensions to keep families together, and most supported the move by the court system to create a juvenile justice system. By the end of the century, these trends had solidified. Public and private charities were clearly separated, and centralization of public welfare and outdoor relief had been accomplished.

Professionalization of Social Work

Another post–Civil War trend was the professionalization of social work. In 1882 the newly formed Children's Aid Society of Pennsylvania began a training program, and in 1894 the New York Society conducted a course of twelve lectures on practical social problems. By the later 1890s, the Boston Associated Charities were paying workers to learn COS techniques and giving lectures on social and philanthropic topics. Mary E. Richmond (1861–1928) was instrumental in the profession's development. In over forty years of practice she defined casework and the importance of person-in-situation.

Richmond began her social work career as an assistant treasurer in the Baltimore Charity Organization Society and rose through the ranks to become its general secretary. She developed a consistent and coherent social work philosophy based on professional training and social research, and maintained that both personal casework and social action were necessary to practice. In 1893 she began a series of educational conferences for friendly visitors, using social histories as case material; in 1897 she developed a plan and curriculum for a "school of philanthropic training." Both Edward T. Devine, executive secretary of the New York Charity Organization Society, and Robert de Forest, its president, supported her efforts, and in 1898 sponsored a course in applied philanthropy based on her ideas. This developed into the New York School of Philanthropy in 1901, offering a full academic year of classes for beginners in social services. The school, which depended on community agencies for field training, changed its name to the New York School of Social Work in 1919.

In 1899 Richmond published *Friendly Visiting Among the Poor* and, after numerous articles and lectures expounding her method, she published *Social Diagnosis* in 1917. The latter became the basic casework text for social work education. It taught the importance of social investigation before diagnosis and the need to base treatment on both insight and social action.[107] In 1909 Richmond was named director of the Charity Organization Department of the new Russell Sage Foundation in New York City, where she directed social research and developed further the methodology of social work. As the rift between tax-supported relief and private casework efforts developed, Richmond took the latter view, arguing that outdoor relief, especially mothers' pensions, could not give the caring supervision that private social work practice provided. In addition, she noted the possibility of graft and unaccountability in public welfare and believed that private agencies would be more careful of how money was spent.[108]

In the same period, the Chicago School of Civics and Philanthropy was instituted under the direction of Hull House worker Julia Lathrop and Graham Taylor of the Chicago Commons Settlement. It became the Institute of Social Sciences in 1903–1904, under the Extension Division of the University of Chicago, and later the Graduate School of Social Service Administration, emphasizing research and social planning. Both it and the New York School were tied to city agencies for field placement instruction, a practice considered essential in the budding profession.

The profession of social work continued on its two courses: that begun by the COS movement (which looked to individual casework to "cure" the distressed and deviant using the "medical model") and that following the settlement house movement (based on community action, group work, and social action and reform against structural problems of society, or the "structural model").

Conclusion: Moving Toward Reform

As society and social welfare entered the 1900s, the underlying motivations for aiding others—work ethic and Puritan morality—remained the same or became strengthened by new pseudoscientific reasoning. The Civil War's upheaval ensured federal supremacy over states' rights, but where it suited the purposes of the elite, states continued to act as they had, oppressing African Americans and exploiting child labor for the profits of the rich, for example. Social welfare had moved from the direction and influence of private philanthropists to centralization and bureaucratization, in both public and private sectors, and the two finally became separated. Yet the philosophies of blaming the victim, the morality of work, and the control of the poor by state, alone or under the direction of an economic elite, remained.

Social work moved from volunteer friendly visiting to a professional career, with goals, training, and an elaborate methodology of social diagnosis and social casework. It lost its elitist character as it split into two philosophies—the Charity Organization Society and the settlement house movements. Social reform movements still tried to control the poor and to teach Puritan and work ethic morality. Philanthropy, though it still existed, had distanced itself from social problems and was involved in "higher" issues such as the provision of public libraries, the endowment of colleges, and the funding of new social research.

The underlying issues of sexism, racism, and classism continued to direct the economic and political system of the nation. Social Darwinism, new scientific theories and information about diseases and medical practice, Freudian ideas about psychology, the new discipline of sociology, and the Cult of True Womanhood all gave legitimacy to the exploitation of minority groups, including immigrants, women, and working people. Although labor unions were gaining power, they were also increasingly exploitative, especially of women and nonwhites. The Gilded Age, a period of immense accumulation of wealth for a very few, provides a showcase of exploitation. Although it freed some people so that they could begin social reform, that freedom—in suffrage, labor reform, social welfare, and political reform—came on the backs of others.

Social treatment progressed in new government and private agencies as the developing social work profession provided new methods and careful research on the causation and remedy for many social ills. Yet social control was an inextricable part of social welfare, advanced as much by the new technologies as was social treatment.

It was visible and explicitly stated: in new regulations and procedures, the exploitation of workers, inattention to the needs of nonwhite people, and the repression, once more, of women. Prostitutes were blamed for sexually transmitted disease, woman workers were subject to low pay and terrible working conditions, married women were at the economic mercy of husband and society, widows were threatened with removal of their children, and professional women, under the guise of nurturing society, participated unknowingly in the control and exploitation of other women.

Study Questions

1. How did the Civil War affect social welfare for women? For nonwhite people? For the poor?

2. What were the major contributions of the Freedmen's Bureau to American social welfare?

3. What were the major social welfare movements during the late 1800s? Compare and contrast their treatment of the poor.

4. What is Social Darwinism? How did it apply to new immigrant groups? What was its effect on social welfare?

5. What was the status of women before, during, and after the Civil War? What factors contributed to the change in status?

6. What was the status of people of African descent after the Civil War? How was their freedom blocked?

7. What was the status of Native Americans and Hispanic Americans after the Civil War?

8. How did the economy, polity, and religion contribute to the treatment of nonwhite people up to and after the Civil War?

Notes

1. Michael B. Katz, *Poverty and Policy in American History* (New York: Academic Press, 1983), p. 130.

2. Marvin B. Gettleman, "Charity and Social Classes in the U.S., 1874–1900," *American Journal of Economics and Sociology,* Vol. 22 (April–July 1963), pp. 313–329. Reported in Jeffrey Galper, *Social Work Practice: A Radical Perspective* (Englewood Cliffs, NJ: Prentice Hall, 1974), pp. 427 ff.

3. J. Saville, "The Welfare State: An Historical Approach," in E. Butterworth and R. Hobman, *Social Welfare in Modern Britain* (Glasgow: Fontana-Collins, 1975). Referenced in Peter Day, *Social Work and Social Control* (London: Tavistock Publications, 1981), p. 14.

4. Frances Fox Piven and Richard Cloward, *Regulating the Poor* (New York: Random House, 1971).

5. Thomas R. Dye and L. Harmon Zeigler, *The Irony of Democracy* (Belmont, CA: Wadsworth Publishing, 1970), pp. 69–70.

6. Ibid., p. 79.

7. Carole Hymowitz and Michaele Weissman, *A History of Women in America* (New York: Bantam Books, 1980), pp. 148–149.

8. Lerone Bennett, Jr., *Before the Mayflower: A History of the Negro in America, 1619–1964* (Chicago: Johnson Publishing Co., 1969), p. 67.

9. Joseph Hraba, *American Ethnicity* (Itasca, IL: F.E. Peacock Publishers, 1979), p. 266.

10. Bennett, *Before the Mayflower,* p. 168.

11. William Jay Jacobs, *Women in American History* (Encino, CA: Glencoe Publishing, 1976), pp. 96–97.

12. Ibid., p. 98.

13. Ibid.

14. June Axinn and Herman Levin, *Social Welfare: A History of the American Response to Need,* 2d ed. (New York: Harper & Row, 1983), p. 94.

15. Ibid., p. 92.

16. Ibid.

17. V. O. Key. Quoted in Dye and Zeigler, *The Irony of Democracy,* pp. 79–80.

18. Katz, *Poverty and Policy,* p. 130.

19. Blanche D. Coll, *Perspectives in Public Welfare: A History* (Washington, D.C.: U.S. Government Printing Office, 1971), p. 40.

20. Ibid., p. 41.

21. Axinn and Levin, *Social Welfare,* p. 97.

22. Alice Kessler-Harris, *Out to Work: A History of Wage-Earning Women in the United States* (New York: Oxford University Press, 1982), p. 146.

23. Angela Davis, *Women, Race, and Class* (New York: Vintage Press, 1983), p. 137.

24. Kessler-Harris, *Out to Work*, p. 91.

25. Hymowitz and Weissman, *History of Women*, p. 240.

26. A nineteenth-century discussion of pauperism, in Hymowitz and Weissman, *History of Women*, pp. 240–241.

27. Jacobs, *Women in American History*, p. 107.

28. Kessler-Harris, *Out to Work*, p. 91.

29. Bettina Berch, *The Endless Day: The Political Economy of Women and Work* (New York: Harcourt Brace Jovanovich, 1982), pp. 40–41.

30. Axinn and Levin, *Social Welfare*, p. 131.

31. Coll, *Perspectives in Public Welfare*, p. 40.

32. Ibid.

33. Hraba, *American Ethnicity*, p. 305.

34. Jack Chen, *The Chinese in America* (San Francisco: Harper & Row, 1980), pp. 136–142.

35. Ibid., pp. 162–164.

36. Hraba, *American Ethnicity*, p. 302.

37. Joe R. Feagin, *Racial and Ethnic Relations*, 2d ed. (Englewood Cliffs, NJ: Prentice Hall, 1984), pp. 194–195.

38. Ibid., p. 199.

39. Ibid., p. 201.

40. Ibid.

41. Hraba, *American Ethnicity*, p. 216.

42. Bennett, *Before the Mayflower*, pp. 92–93.

43. Ibid., p. 202.

44. Ibid.

45. Ibid., p. 217.

46. Ibid., p. 197.

47. Hraba, *American Ethnicity*, p. 278.

48. Bennett, *Before the Mayflower*, p. 197.

49. Davis, *Women, Race, and Class*, p. 89.

50. Bennett, *Before the Mayflower*, p. 239.

51. "Jim Crow" was a name made famous in a comedy in the early 1700s. It became synonymous with African Americans.

52. Kessler-Harris, *Out to Work*, p. 185.

53. Hymowitz and Weissman, *History of Women*, p. 205.

54. Kessler-Harris, *Out to Work*, p. 185.

55. Hymowitz and Weissman, *History of Women*, p. 220.

56. Davis, *Women, Race, and Class*, pp. 87–88.

57. Jacobs, *Women in American History*, p. 144.

58. Hymowitz and Weissman, *History of Women*, p. 299.

59. Dr. Clelia Duel Mosher studied the sexual habits of married women as a student at the University of Wisconsin before 1892. The project spanned twenty years, with 70 percent of the women born before 1870. Most were more highly educated than poor, with twenty-seven teachers. They were upper-middle or middle-class women rather than members of a leisure class and, despite a high level of education knew little about sex before marriage.

60. Carl N. Degler, "What Ought to Be and What Was: Women's Sexuality in the 19th Century," in Judith Walzer Leavitt (ed.), *Women and Health in America* (Madison: University of Wisconsin Press, 1984), pp. 40 ff.

61. Ibid.

62. Pamela Johnson Conover and Virginia Gray, *Feminism and the New Right: Conflict over the American Family* (New York: Praeger Publishing, 1983), pp. 4–8.

63. Beulah Compton, *Introduction to Social Welfare and Social Work* (Homewood, IL: The Dorsey Press, 1980), p. 298.

64. James Reed, "Doctors, Birth Control, and Social Values, 1830–1970," in Leavitt, *Women and Health,* p. 127.

65. Ibid., p. 201.

66. Mark Thomas Connelly, "Prostitution, Venereal Disease, and American Medicine," in Leavitt, *Women and Health,* p. 201.

67. Sidney Fine, *Laissez-Faire and the General Welfare State* (Ann Arbor: University of Michigan Press, 1964), p. 173. Referenced in Gerald Handel, *Social Welfare in Western Society* (New York: Random House, 1982), p. 213.

68. Dye and Zeigler, *The Irony of Democracy,* p. 73.

69. Coll, *Perspectives in Public Welfare,* p. 42.

70. Piven and Cloward, *Regulating the Poor,* pp. 165–166. Paraphrased in Macarov, *Design of Social Welfare,* p. 197.

71. Frank Dekker Watson, *The Charity Organization Movement in the United States* (New York: Arno Press and *The New York Times,* 1971), p. 281.

72. Mrs. Charles Russell Lowell, "The Economic and Moral Effects of Public Outdoor Relief," *National Conference of Charities and Corrections Proceedings,* 1879, p. 203. Quoted in Coll, *Perspectives in Public Welfare,* pp. 44–45.

73. Watson, *The Charity Organization Movement.*

74. Compton, *Introduction to Social Welfare,* p. 286.

75. Coll, *Perspectives in Public Welfare,* p. 61.

76. Watson, *The Charity Organization Movement,* p. 324.

77. Ibid.

78. Robert McHenry (ed.), *Famous American Women: A Biographical Dictionary from Colonial Times to the Present* (New York: Dover Publications, 1980), p. 44.

79. Ibid., p. 45.

80. Ibid.

81. Handel, *Social Welfare in Western Society,* p. 70.

82. Hymowitz and Weissman, *History of Women,* p. 224.

83. Ibid., p. 232.

84. Ibid., p. 233.

85. Ibid., p. 228.

86. McHenry, *Famous American Women,* p. 234.

87. Ray Ginger, "Women at Hull House," in Linda K. Kerber and Jane DeHart Mathews (eds.), *Women's America* (New York: Oxford University Press), p. 272.

88. McHenry, *Famous American Women,* p. 135.

89. Ibid., p. 1.

90. Ibid.

91. Ginger, "Women at Hull House," p. 272.

92. McHenry, *Famous American Women,* p. 387.

93. Bennett, *Before the Mayflower.*

94. Katz, *Poverty and Policy,* p. 193.

95. Gerald N. Grob, *The State and Public Welfare in Nineteenth-Century America* (New York: Arno Press, 1976), p. 145.

96. Compton, *Introduction to Social Welfare,* p. 298.

97. Senate Bill 2 (Boston: William White, printer to the State, 1859). Quoted in Grob, *The State and Public Welfare,* p. 137.

98. Axinn and Levin, *Social Welfare,* p. 146.

99. Dye and Zeigler, *The Irony of Democracy,* p. 79.

100. Coll, *Perspectives in Public Welfare,* p. 64.

101. Katz, *Poverty and Policy,* p. 190.

102. Coll, *Perspectives in Public Welfare,* pp. 43–44.

103. Katz, *Poverty and Policy,* p. 233.

104. Walter A. Friedlander and Robert Z. Apte, *Introduction to Social Welfare* (Englewood Cliffs, NJ: Prentice Hall, 1974), p. 80.

105. Ralph Dolgoff and Donald Feldstein, *Understanding Social Welfare*, 2d ed. (New York: Longman Press, 1984).

106. Axinn and Levin, *Social Welfare History*, p. 102.

107. McHenry, *Famous American Women*, pp. 346–347.

108. Ibid.

8

The Progressive Era, War, and Recovery

The Progressive Era

The Progressive Era—the period between 1900 and World War I—was a time of prosperity for the United States. For the general population, conditions of life improved as technologies changed the way of life: better roads and communication systems; electrification; better housing, water supply, and waste disposal systems; more amenities in terms of food, clothing, and other goods; and better hospitals and medical technology. The democratic thrust of the Progressive Era meant more citizen participation and an increase in government responsiveness and honesty, leading to secret ballots, direct primaries, and direct election of senators (the Seventeenth Amendment in 1914); civil service reform; regulation of campaign expenditures; accountability in government; the initiative, referendum, and recall; and local rule under city commission and city manager forms of government. New social legislation included antitrust laws, the Children's Bureau, child labor laws, and health and safety laws. The progressive income tax gave the federal government the means with which to govern on a national basis.

Questioning government policies and control of the economy by the elite became possible; for example, Louis Brandeis pointed out that low-paying industries and those who controlled them were subsidized by employees, families of employees, and society as a whole.[1] The radical voice of reform became strident as "muckraking" newspapers exposed big business, city bossism, graft, and corruption. Progressive reform was sought by a many-sided coalition of small businessmen, writers, settlement house workers, social workers, lawyers, clergy, farmers, labor reform movements, unions, women reformers and suffragists, middle-class clubwomen, men and women of African descent, and politicians. Many of the nation's intellectuals were members of this coalition: John Dewey, Paul Douglas, Jack London, Walter Lippmann,[2] and Charlotte Perkins Gilman. The growth of the Socialist party became one indicator: It had fewer than 5,000 members in 1900, but nearly 120,000 by 1912. Eugene V. Debs, its chair, ran for president in 1912, winning 6 percent of the popular vote—900,000 of 15 million votes cast—on a platform calling for government takeover and regulation of private industry.[3] In that election, more than 1,000 socialists were elected to public office.

The progressive movement was also a reaction against big business and corporate profits. Under pressure, the government tried to intervene by enforcing the Sherman Anti-Trust Act in 1902, when the Supreme Court ruled against further incorporation of railroads by the Northern Securities Company. In 1906 the Interstate Commerce Commission (ICC) was given power to fix rates for railroad storage, refrigeration, and terminal facilities and for sleeping car, express, and pipeline companies. Telegraph and telephone companies were brought under ICC regulation in 1910.[4] In 1909 a 1 percent tax on corporate incomes over $5,000 was imposed; in 1913 the states ratified the Sixteenth Amendment, imposing progressive taxes on personal income.

Great trusts and monopolies formed or became stable, including Standard Oil, Consolidated Tobacco, and U.S. Steel. By 1914, supercorporations dominated coal, agrimachinery, sugar, telephone and telegraph, public utilities, iron and steel, railroads, oil, tobacco, and copper.[5] Between 1899 and 1929, total output of manufacturing increased by 273 percent,[6] and the gross national product had increased sixfold (see Figure 8.1). By 1910, 5 percent of the population owned nearly half the nation's property,[7] and in 1919, not quite 4 percent of all industrial organizations employed half the nation's workers and contributed more than two-thirds of the gross national product.

Poor laborers, whether men or women, were kept "in their places" by interlocking mechanisms of business, courts, social work, and government. "Protective legislation" based partly on social values that women were incapable of heavy work kept them in low-paying marginal jobs and gave employment to men who could work when and where women could not. Social Darwinism legitimated the eugenics movement, which advocated that all "inferior" people be ster-

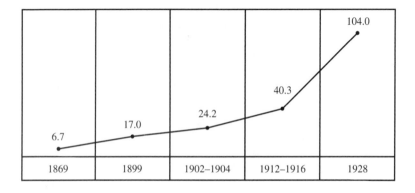

FIGURE 8.1 *Gross National Product (billions of dollars)*

ilized so that their children would not "infect" society: immigrants not of Anglo-Saxon or Germanic stock, who were often English-illiterate; nonwhite people; criminals and prostitutes; and the physically, mentally, or emotionally impaired. By 1915 twelve states had adopted sterilization laws based on the eugenics movement.[8] Dr. Harry Laughlin, a geneticist in the Eugenics Record Office, said in 1922:

> We in this country have been so imbued with the idea of democracy, or the equality of all men, that we have left out of consideration the matter of blood or natural inborn hereditary mental and moral differences. No man who breeds pedigreed plants and animals can afford to neglect this thing.[9]

By 1932, the Eugenics Society could boast that at least twenty-six states had compulsory sterilization laws and that thousands of "unfit" people had been prevented from reproducing.[10] In 1939 the Birth Control Federation planned a "Negro project" that, though not formally carried out, can still be observed in the "voluntary" sterilization of poor women—particularly African Americans and Hispanics—that occurred during the 1960s and 1970s.

By the early 1900s, the United States had fulfilled its "manifest destiny" to control much of the continent. Now, in an era of worldwide imperialism, it began small imperialisms: Hawaii, Puerto Rico, Guam, and the Philippines were annexed in 1898, Cuba was made a protectorate in 1901, the Panama Canal Zone was in effect annexed by treaty in 1903, and the Virgin Islands were purchased from Denmark in 1917. Internally consolidated by railroads, the telegraph, and the telephone, northern European nations were engaged in wider imperialism: England and France peacefully divided up the African continent, and Russia, looking eastward, fought its losing battle with Japan. Landlocked Germany, surrounded by other nations eager to expand, began plans as early as 1903 to prevent the encirclement it feared from surrounding nations.

The new activities, new technologies, expansionism, and reforms that burgeoned after the Civil War burst into the twentieth century fueled by the Industrial Revolution. Speed became the new master of societies; gone were the leisurely agrarian settings that fostered extended families, time for local reforms, or even world diplomacy. Communication and transportation technologies made local emergencies national and even international; for example, the San Francisco earthquake in 1906 mobilized help from agencies all over the nation and brought scientists from Japan to help with the crisis. The quake and its fire destroyed nearly 30,000 buildings and ravaged the downtown area. About 200,000 people were left homeless and damage was estimated at $500 million, yet within a year, the city was back on its feet.

On June 28, 1914, Archduke Ferdinand, heir to the Austro-Hungarian throne, was assassinated. This brought a flurry of telegrams, telephone calls, threats, and pleas, and in the critical period between July 23 and August 4

> there were five ultimatums with short time limits, all implying or explicitly threatening war. . . . In the final days the pressing requirements of mobilization time-

tables frayed the last shreds of patience. And even before mobilizations were formally announced, armies prepared for war, making a shambles of the efforts of diplomats . . . as time and the peace slipped away.[11]

Suddenly the world was at war, and neither time nor distance protected countries: Some people predicted that enemy air forces would bomb New York City. The country quickly adjusted to war conditions: Work in the munitions and supply business, in transportation, and in the production of steel led to such high profits that unemployment almost disappeared. African Americans from the South were recruited to work in northern factories, and the immigration of Mexicans was encouraged. More than 2 million African Americans came north, and more than 70,000 Mexicans entered the United States. In 1918, the same year that Czar Nicholas and his family were executed, Woodrow Wilson proposed the Fourteen Points on which the League of Nations was founded. For his work, he won the Nobel Peace Prize in 1919. However, in its new isolationism, the United States refused to join the League when it was formed in 1920.

After World War I, peace and prosperity returned for many. The average family could earn enough to live comfortably, particularly with credit now being offered for consumer purchases. Although the recession in 1921 brought widespread strikes, especially among dockworkers and steelworkers, standards of living continued to improve, and with higher profits and sales came high employment and a rise in real wages. A new belief in the "invisible hand" of the marketplace once more brought harsh reaction against public dependency.

Those who continued to help the poor or to work for social reform were considered un-American, and a "Red Scare" resulted from fear that the people's revolution in Russia might spread to the United States. It brought accusations of Bolshevism against socialists, suffragists, labor reformers, pacifists, settlement house workers, and social workers, and this encouraged many to get out of poor relief and into casework practice. Criminal syndicalism laws made it a felony to advocate violence for political change, and twenty-four states passed laws threatening jail for anyone displaying a red flag (350 people were jailed). Vigilantes attacked unionists and "reds," and loyalty oaths were instituted for teachers and other public employees. On one night in 1920, U.S. Attorney General Mitchell Palmer arrested 4,000 people in thirty-three states for being "radical aliens," and great numbers were deported.[12] People advocating political positions different from those in power were persecuted. For example, in 1918 Eugene Debs was sentenced to ten years (commuted in 1921) under the espionage and sedition laws, and Marcus Garvey, a Black Nationalist leader, was deported on trumped-up charges of mail fraud.

Population Movements and Immigration

During the first two decades of the twentieth century, the U.S. population rose from 46.8 million to more than 100 million, with more than half living in the cities.

Between 1920 and 1930, another 6 million moved from farms to cities.[13] Reasons for urbanization included immigration, a general migration to the cities, and an increase in migration of Mexicans and southern African Americans into unskilled nonfarm jobs. Urban industrial growth and incorporation made possible the undercutting of small businesses by large corporations, and in rural areas new agribusiness put tenant farmers and small owners off the land because they were unable to afford new high-production technology.

From 1900 until the Immigration Acts of 1921 and 1924, more than 19 million immigrants entered the United States,[14] of whom more than 75 percent came from Southern and Eastern Europe. By 1910, less than 20 percent of the population of New York City was native born.[15] Nearly two-thirds of the population was poor, and a third lived in desperate poverty. Women and children worked at lower wages than men, and men working full-time averaged between $400 and $500 per year, although it was estimated that the average family needed at least $600 to $800 to survive.[16] Wages were about 60 percent of basic subsistence.

Immigration Acts

Spurred both by the labor glut and social Darwinism, Congress passed the Immigration Act of 1907. Amended in 1910, it charged a head tax of $4.00 on each immigrant and listed those to be excluded: "idiots, imbeciles, the feeble-minded, insane, paupers, those likely to become paupers, people with contagious diseases, criminals, anarchists, children under sixteen unless accompanied by an adult, and laborers under short-term work contracts."[17] Quota restrictions passed in 1924 (in effect until 1965) were first based on national origin and the numbers of nationals in the United States according to the 1880 census, and then, in 1929, according to the 1920 census data. This effectively limited all Far Eastern immigration and greatly limited immigration from any Southern or Eastern European country.

Asian Exclusion.   Although the Oriental Exclusion Act of 1880 was written primarily against the Chinese, it applied also to the Japanese, who came despite its restrictions and prospered. Their mutual benefit societies offered jobs to newcomers and education for children, and with their greater skills in horticulture they were able to compete with white farmers despite the high cost of the barren land they bought. To control this, Congress passed an alien land bill in 1913 forbidding Japanese aliens to own land. The Japanese circumvented it by incorporating with white partners or deeding it to their American-born children until 1920, when another amendment forbade this practice.

Japanese immigrants faced a rabidly racist American population. By 1905, newspapers, unions, the American Legion, and the California Farm Bureau were campaigning against the "Yellow Peril." Attacks on Japanese people and businesses became common: Even the Japanese scientists coming to help after the San Francisco earthquake were beaten. However, as a world power fresh from its victory over Russia, Japan could offer some protection to its nationals. Therefore, rather than banning Japanese immigration, President Theodore Roosevelt signed the infamous "Gentlemen's Agreement" with Japan in 1907, "voluntarily" limiting immigration to former resident aliens and their immediate families.

Because Japanese women could not immigrate unless they had relatives in the United States, Japanese men simply arranged marriages by proxy with women in Japan, but in the 1920 immigration amendment, Congress also forbade importation of "mail-order brides." By 1922, the Japanese had been declared "aliens ineligible for citizenship" (*Ozawa v. U.S.*, 1922), and the Oriental Exclusion Act of 1924 almost completely stopped their immigration until 1968. They remained a small group prospering in agriculture and service occupations: By 1919, they ran 47 percent of all hotels and 25 percent of all grocery stores in Seattle, for example.[18] By 1941, they raised 42 percent of California's truck-farm crops. However, at the onset of World War II, much of their wealth was seized and they were incarcerated in concentration camps.

Hispanic Immigration.   Hispanic immigration, legal or illegal, has always been encouraged by U.S. business interests, despite the overt public outcry against it. In 1902, when the federal government passed the National Reclamation Act that watered the Southwestern deserts, white farmers could not meet the growing labor demands in truck and cotton farming, railroad construction, mining, and maintenance. They recruited Mexicans, who soon made up about two-thirds of the labor force. However, new agricultural technologies pushed them out and they moved up the California coast and into the Midwest as migrant workers. Another major recruitment era was World War I, and after the war agribusiness encouraged their immigration; in the 1920s, 500,000 workers and their families immigrated. Mexicans were specifically exempted from the Immigration Acts of 1921 and 1924.

With the Depression, Mexicans were no longer needed for farm work and the Immigration and Naturalization Service (INS) created a border patrol to stop their illegal entry, making it a felony in 1929. Still, in the crop season, businessmen openly recruited them to the United States. After crops were in, neither their employers nor the law felt any obligation to return them to their homes. The company store system kept them in debt to their employers, and thousands were stranded without food, shelter, or clothing, and with no claim on schools, hospitals, or welfare. Their own mutual aid societies provided very limited help at times, and often the Mexican government itself appropriated funds to help its nationals stranded in the United States.

Between 1931 and 1940, only 22,000 Mexicans immigrated. Often they moved to cities, where they became strike-breakers in the great labor movements of the era and were subject to violence from other workers. Even those legally in the country had little protection from such attacks, and a movement to "repatriate" them began. Approximately half a million Hispanics unable to prove citizenship were deported, although the majority were in fact American citizens. Texas and California deported the largest numbers, but in Illinois and Indiana fully half of all Hispanics were "repatriated."

After World War II another Hispanic group, the Puerto Ricans, began to move slowly into the United States along the Eastern Seaboard. They, however, were American citizens, because Puerto Rico had been ceded to the United States at the end of the Spanish American War and its people given citizenship in 1917 (Jones Act). As their island was slowly taken over by white landowners, they began to move to mainland cities. Although in 1899 they had owned 93 percent of their land, by 1930 absentee companies owned 60 percent.

Oppression of African and Native Americans

Although social reformers took on nearly every other cause in the Progressive Era, the civil rights of African Americans were ignored. Over the history of the National Conference of Social Welfare, for example, only two programs were held on racial minorities.[19] Some settlement houses recognized their problems as they began to migrate to cities, but the few that actively tried to recruit African Americans found that their other clients refused to come. A few moderately successful settlement houses developed in large cities, but on the whole, African Americans were subject to rigid segregation or were blocked from even the meager social services that were provided other poor people. They were excluded from unions and from employment, although women found it easier to work, as domestics, than did men.

In 1900 nine-tenths of all African Americans lived in the rural South, but a new "enclosure movement" of their lands began after the Civil War, making them tenant farmers of their former owners or pushing them to Northern cities. Two million migrated: The largest number, 87,000, came to Washington, D.C., but Baltimore, New Orleans, Philadelphia, and New York each gained more than 60,000 African American citizens.[20] In 1913 African Americans owned 550,000 homes, operated 937,000 farms, managed 40,000 businesses, and held $700 million in funds, even though more than 70 percent were literate. They had 40,000 churches, thirty-four colleges in the South, 35,000 teachers, and 1.7 million students in public schools,[21] although rigid segregation was still maintained in all facilities.

World War I brought thousands of African Americans to Northern factories. Thousands more entered the Army—370,000 soldiers and 1,400 officers went into race-segregated units. More than half fought in France, often assigned to the French Army. Among them, Henry Johnson and Needham Roberts were the first Americans cited for bravery, although African Americans were usually assigned menial chores. An official order from General Pershing in 1918 reinforced segregation: The prevention of contact between French and African American officers was ordered so that white soldiers would not be offended, and contact between French women and African American soldiers was forbidden. White officers could not eat, shake hands with, initiate conversations with, or commend African Americans.[22]

A great outpouring of hatred against African Americans took place during and after the War, related to the fear that they would take "white" jobs. In 1916 there were fifty-four lynchings, and despite a "silent march" of 20,000 protesters in Washington organized by the National Association for the Advancement of Colored People (NAACP), violence escalated. In East St. Louis on July 12, 1917, white workers drove nearly 6,000 African Americans from their homes and killed between 40 and 200. In 1918 there were sixty-four lynchings, and in 1919, with returning veterans seeking jobs, eighty-three African Americans were lynched and eleven burned alive. The Ku Klux Klan was revitalized: A rally at Kokomo, Indiana, drew 200,000 people. One of every eight white men belonged to the Klan at its height, and their terror was directed not only at African Americans, but also at Hispanics, Jews, and Catholics. Klan membership included senators, representatives, judges, sheriffs, and other government officials.

No African American could escape persecution, as the following account from 1918 demonstrates. Mary Turner, a pregnant woman, was hanged, doused with gasoline and motor oil, and burned.

> As she dangled from the rope, a man stepped forward with a pocketknife and ripped open her abdomen in a crude caesarean operation. Out tumbled the prematurely born child. . . . Two feeble cries it gave—and received for answer the heel of a stalwart man, as life was ground out of its tiny form.[23]

The following summer, 1919, was called the Red Summer because of its violence. Over twenty-six riots broke out across the country: In Washington, Chicago, Omaha, and Knoxville, 170 African Americans were killed and 537 injured. They defended themselves and some whites died, as did whites who tried to help them. For example, in Omaha, a mob lynched and burned a man and hanged the mayor who tried to prevent his lynching.

African American Leaders

Booker T. Washington was considered the "quintessential black" to white leaders: For example, Andrew Carnegie donated $600,000 in U.S. Steel bonds to Tuskegee with the stipulation that $150,000 be used to support Washington and his family so that he could continue his great work. He was invited to dine at the White House by Theodore Roosevelt, and some say that Roosevelt's defeat in 1912 had to do with his friendship with Washington, which alienated the South. Washington practically ruled "Black America" from 1895 to 1915,[24] sending annual messages to "his people" and having the final word on their political appointments. A strong advocate of vocational education, he urged them to seek economic rather than political advantage.

Among the more radical leaders was William Edward Burkhardt (W.E.B.) DuBois, a Harvard graduate. He returned to America in 1894, having studied at the University of Berlin, but was appalled at the submissive attitudes of his African American students. He and another Harvard graduate, William Monroe

Trotter, organized a strategy-planning meeting in 1905 at Niagara Falls to demand civil, political, and social rights. This meeting, attended by Jane Addams, laid the groundwork for the NAACP, of which DuBois became the only African American officer as director of research and publicity. In 1909 the First National Committee on the Negro met officially to form the NAACP; Florence Kelley and Lillian Wald were present. Trotter went on to form the more militant leftist National Equal Rights League. It consistently opposed segregation in such facilities as YMCAs and settlement houses and established the African American press as a dominant force in the protest movement. The National Urban League, formed in 1910, had as its goals economic opportunity and civil equality through persuasion and conciliation. Its first executive officers were George Edmund Haynes, the first African American to receive a degree from the New York School of Social Work, and Eugene K. Jones. The league's welfare component served as a channel for contributions from white benefactors to African Americans in need.

Marcus Moziah Garvey was the first radical nationalist of African descent in the twentieth century. His Negro Improvement Association advocated nationalism and a separate nation in Africa. The association's platform of racial separation, racial pride, and worldwide political liberation attracted millions of followers, mainly urban working-class African Americans. Garvey's goal was a united Africa under Africans, and in 1921 he declared himself provisional president of the new Republic of Africa. Raising more than $10 million, he organized cooperatives, factories, a commercial steamship venture, and a private army. In 1925, accused of mail fraud, he was deported to his native Jamaica, and died in London in 1940.[25] Amy Jacques Garvey, his second wife, played an active role as secretary, colleague, and leader in her own right in the organization.

African American women were also leaders in the Progressive Era. Mary McLeod Bethune (1856–1913), the daughter of slaves, was perhaps the most influential woman of her time. Educated by missionaries, she started a girls' school in 1904 in Daytona Beach, Florida. Her class of five paid 50 cents each for tuition, and in two years she had 250 students. She paid her regular teachers $15 to $20 a week and relied heavily on volunteers. Later, she organized Bethune College, buying a former dumpsite for $250, and in 1922 amalgamated her girls' college with Cookman College, the first higher education institution for African American men in Florida. Because its students were served unwillingly and inadequately in white hospitals,[26] Bethune–Cookman College had a fully equipped twenty-bed hospital on its campus.

Ida B. Wells Barnett (1862–1931), also a daughter of slaves, was a journalist and activist. Educated at Rust and Fisk Universities, she began her teaching career in 1884 at age fourteen. However, when she criticized the quality of education, she lost her job. Later, she bought an interest in the *Memphis Free Speech* newspaper and began an antilynching campaign. A protester against segregation, she sued the Chesapeake and Ohio Railroad for forcibly removing her from an all-white railroad car. Moving to Chicago, she organized local women in various causes and served as secretary of the National Afro-American Council. In 1910 she founded and became president of the Negro Fellowship League. From 1913 to 1916, she served as a probation officer in the Chicago municipal court. Although she took part in the 1909 meeting of the Niagara group, she refused to become involved in the NAACP because of its conservatism.[27]

Clubs such as those formed by Wells Barnett became the backbone of help for African American women and families in the cities of the North. Darenkamp and colleagues say,

> . . . the formation of black women's clubs represent a notable historical movement of this time. Along with fighting for equality for blacks and providing companionship, the black reform societies helped black women find employment, set up day nurseries and kindergartens, and established homes to protect young black women from sexual abuse. Like most middle-class white women of the era, black club women were middle class and educated but unlike many of their white counterparts the vast majority worked outside the home.[28]

Although African Americans were still subject to public social welfare controls such as juvenile and criminal justice, for all practical purposes these women's clubs and mutual aid societies took over the functions that social work provided for white people.

Native Americans

Native American activism, though repressed by the government and the Bureau of Indian Affairs, still existed in the Progressive Era. The Pan-Indian Society of American Indians was founded in the early 1900s to develop pride and a national leadership and to encourage educational and job opportunities; only a fourth of Native American children were being educated. A new religion also rose and was incorporated in 1919 as the Native American Church. Its sacramental use of peyote was thus protected from attacks by Christian missionaries.

Native Americans who fought in World War I were rewarded with citizenship, and in 1924 all became citizens, but they remained wards of the government. In 1928 appropriations for education were increased, and by the mid-1930s some boarding schools were replaced by day schools under the Johnson–O'Malley Act, which gave aid to states that provided public education to Native Americans.

Labor and the Unions

The economy of the Progressive Era did not rise smoothly. There were depressions in 1907, 1910, 1919, and 1920 before the major crash in 1929. Each depression was accompanied by labor riots, strikes, and counteractions by police and courts. The depression of 1907–1908 paralyzed the country but led to the formation of such unions as the International Ladies' Garment Workers Union (ILGWU). Major strikes, often led by women, broke out in 1909 when charities reported double the number of applicants in winter and quadruple the number in the spring.[29] In the depression of 1914–1915, a conservative estimate said 2 million people were jobless. In New York City, relief recipients increased by 23 percent in 1913 and 57 percent in 1914,[30] but charity expenditures increased only 14 and 17 percent, respectively. The New York Association for Improving the Condition of the Poor (AICP) paid men $2.00 a day for a maximum of three days for working for the city because the city could not afford to give them relief. In 1919 a vast wave of strikes broke out across the nation, and on Memorial Day in south Chicago police fired on a peaceful demonstration of workers, supporters, wives, and children, killing about thirty people, most of whom were shot in the back.[31]

Trade union membership declined throughout the early 1900s, from 3.2 percent in 1900 to a low of 1.5 percent in 1910. By 1920, it had surged upward to 6.6 percent.[32] Women were among the most active union organizers because the highly touted "protective legislation" proposed by unions and reformers benefited women far less than it did men. It stressed their inability to do hard labor or work long hours and cut back work hours, night work, heavy work, and overtime hours and reserved those jobs for men. If women won equal pay through their union activities, jobs went to men, who were preferred as workers for the same price. Protective legislation was first tested in 1908 in Oregon, where it set a national precedent for government intervention for women and children in the labor market. It also set a precedent for legal discrimination against women in terms of the jobs they could hold and the wages they would be paid, and contributed to channeling women into the rapidly expanding white-collar sector.[33]

In 1900 the average workweek for organized laborers was fifty-seven hours, whereas those in the building trades worked a forty-eight-hour week.[34] Unorganized laborers, such as steelworkers, worked a twelve-hour day and an eighty-four-hour workweek. Women and children often worked more than fifteen hours a day, at wages of about $1.50 for the day; for example, in 1905 a group of laundry workers in Illinois were hospitalized from exhaustion after working sixteen to twenty hours a day in the heat and dampness of steam-filled plants. Women were told that if they did not work on Sundays they need not come in at all.[35]

Women and Unions

Over 5 million women were employed in 1900, making up one-fifth of the nation's total workforce. By 1910, women comprised 25 percent of the labor force. A Women's Bureau survey during that period showed that 90 percent worked for economic reasons and that 25 percent were the principal wage earners of their households. By 1920, 25.6 percent of working women were in white-collar jobs, 23.8 percent in manufacturing, 8.2 percent in domestic service, and 12.9 percent in agriculture. A typical commercial laundry worker worked more than forty hours a week and took home less than $15.00 a month. In the same year, 75 percent of African American women worked in agricultural labor, domestic service, and laundry work. In factories, they were paid less than were white women and up to a third less than men. The workforce was rigidly segregated, and amenities such as lunchrooms, cloakrooms, fresh drinking water, and clean toilets were provided only to white women.[36] In the 1920s less than 2 million of the 8 million wage-earning women were married, but by 1930 more than 3 million were married. Employers often refused to hire married women and often fired them when they married. Twenty-six states had laws prohibiting the hiring of married women.

Women were among the most active unionists because of the low pay and terrible conditions under which they worked. Industry-bred diseases were common, and women workers had a mortality rate more than double that of non-working women and a third more than working men. In 1903 women founded the National Women's Trade Union League (NWTUL), which sought equal pay, an eight-hour workday, minimum wages, and full citizenship rights for women. The NWTUL was part of the American Federation of Labor (AFL), which tolerated but did not wholly support it, as AFL president Samuel Gompers vehemently fought both women's labor and "socialist movements."

Partly in response to AFL's refusal to help women and partly because of the socialist reforms taking place at the time, in 1905 radicals formed the Industrial Workers of the World (IWW), which advocated complete abolition of the wage system and the employing class. In the first five years of the century, it waged 13,964 strikes and 541 lockouts.[37] One such strike was against the mills in Lawrence, Massachusetts, where the governor sent 1,400 militiamen to back up police and state troopers. They were directed to "strike the women on the arms and breasts and the men on the head."[38] Strikers sent their starving children to strike supporters in other cities rather than end the strike, and the children aroused such sympathy that Lawrence mill owners refused to let any more leave.

> [T]roopers surrounded the railway station, clubbed the children and their mothers, and then arrested them. The mothers were charged with "neglect" and "improper guardianship."[39]

In 1909, when general strikes shook the nation, the NWTUL called a strike among garment workers against Leiserman and Company's Triangle Shirt Waist Factory. At the time, 80 percent of the garment workers were women, 70 percent were between the ages of sixteen and twenty-five, 65 percent were Jewish, and 26 percent Italian. Twenty thousand struck against the company. The police beat and clubbed them and threw them in jail. According to one judge who tried a young woman striker, "You're not striking against your employer . . . you're striking against God."[40] Yet every day up to fifteen hundred women joined the union. Middle-class women who had never before considered the plight of working women contributed money for bail and for relief.

This strike led to the founding of the International Ladies' Garment Workers Union, which by 1914 was the third largest unit in the AFL. In 1913 the ILGWU signed the famous "protocol" contract, limiting work by gender. Only men could be hired as cutters and pressers, and the lowest-paid men had to earn more than the highest-paid woman, even for the same work. Cutters were paid $27.50 a week and finishers, examiners, and sample makers—jobs reserved for women—were paid $9.50, $11.50, and $13.00, respectively.[41] Modest gains of the strike included a fifty-two-hour workweek and limited overtime.

However, some of the most important demands for health and safety were ignored, and two years later the Triangle Shirt Waist factory caught fire. The factory, which had 500 workers, was on the top three floors of a ten-story building. Fire exits were kept locked to make sure employees did not steal from the company, and fire hoses were left unconnected. There was little chance for escape. Some women burned to death, others jumped from the windows, falling like "bundles of burning cloth" to their deaths. In all, 146 workers died. The judge fined the owners $75.00 for negligence.[42]

Among women important in the union movements were Bessie Abramovitz, Harriet Stanton Blatch (daughter of Elizabeth Cady Stanton), Elizabeth Gurley Flynn, Rose Schneiderman, Agnes Nestor of the glovemakers, Mary Kenney O'Sullivan of the bookbinders, and Leonora O'Reilly. Abramovitz helped organize the Amalgamated Clothing Workers of America, one of the first unions to provide health care, housing, adult education, scholarships, and day care centers. Blatch organized the Equality League of Self-Supporting Women in factories, laundries, and garment shops. At its height it had 19,000 members. Flynn, a socialist, participated in twenty strikes and was arrested fifteen times between 1906 and 1926. Schneiderman organized for both the NWTUL and the ILGWU, becoming president of the latter. She also organized summer schools for working women, served as chairperson of the industrial section of the Women's Suffrage party, became secretary of the New York State Department of Labor, and was an unsuccessful candidate for the U.S. Senate. Franklin D. Roosevelt named her a member of the Labor Advisory Board in his administration.[43] Despite women's activities in the labor movement, they did not achieve top positions even in occupations they dominated.

Social Welfare in the Progressive Era

Several important changes took place in social welfare in the early 1900s. First, settlement house workers were progressively excluded from the profession of social work. Second, professionalization took the form of Mary Richmond's social diagnosis and casework method, which, although it considered the impact of environment on distress, remained oriented to personal rather than structural change. Third, bureaucratization and the use of scientific management techniques created new organizational structures and processes for accountability in the profession. Fourth, social workers, although they still protested that private charities could provide better psychic care to the distressed, formed new coalitions with public agencies that provided the funds for relief. For example, in 1914 they developed the Association of Public Welfare Officials in New York. Finally, although business interests were not altruistic, welfare became increasingly a business issue, and businesses encouraged welfare as a part of municipal reform to defuse political agitation and bypass political machines.[44]

In 1910 Kansas City organized the first Board of Public Welfare, followed in 1913 by Cook County in Chicago. In 1917 Illinois instituted a State Department of Public Welfare, and other states followed suit, with governors appointing heads of welfare. This innovation from traditional political appointments took public welfare out of politics except through the governor. Coll says,

> The reform spirit in which many social workers interpreted their role in the early twentieth century marked a departure from concern about pauperism to concern about poverty and a corresponding turnabout from the doctrine of personal fault to stress social and economic conditions as prime causes of hunger and squalor.[45]

After World War I, social reform was overwhelmed by a sense of prosperity and the belief that work would provide the final triumph over poverty. Spiraling prices and freely available credit increased profits and led the economy upward. The United States was the richest country in the world: By 1925, it was producing 55 percent of the world's iron, 66 percent of its steel, 62 percent of its petroleum, 52 percent of its lumber, 60 percent of its cotton, 80 percent of its sulfur, and 95 percent of its automobiles.[46] Demands for social insurance and public relief were considered a betrayal of the American way, and public dependents and social workers were seen as parasites or subversives. Settlement houses were believed to be hotbeds of radicalism, and gradually they became traditional social agencies, losing their autonomy as they took money from newly developing community chests. Professional casework, with its emphases on individual blame and middle-class morality, became the byline of the profession.

A new split in services for the needy emerged. The first cohort comprised professional social workers disassociating themselves from the "unworthy" poor through casework practice; the second was made up of public welfare bureaucrats, often political appointees without training. These latter were the "moral descendants" of overseers of the poor and were often chosen precisely for their antiwelfare stances. Poor relief remained extremely discretionary, based on personal values and beliefs relegitimated by the booming economy. Only the "morally deserving" were aided—often the aged, sometimes the handicapped, and white widows who could subject themselves to moral investigation.

Religious, ethnic, and class differences continued to influence the provision of welfare. Protestant mission societies demanded church or Sunday school attendance as the price of assistance, and many new immigrants, particularly Catholics and Jews, avoided all church-related agencies, even nonevangelistic ones such as the YMCA. Language was also a barrier, and immigrants were stereotyped as ignorant, slovenly, stubborn, and "inert" if they did not want, or could not afford, a middle-class lifestyle. Middle-class workers in both ethnic and mainstream agencies considered themselves better than those they helped, making them pay in the coin of humiliation for food, shelter, and clothing.

An enormous expansion of public education coincided with the great immigrations at the turn of the century. Kindergartens, vacation schools, extracurricular activities, and vocational education and counseling were offered by schools, and corporations, unions, churches, YMCAs, YWCAs, and settlement houses co-sponsored Americanization classes for immigrants.[47] Some states experimented with home teachers who took women to clinics, instructed them, and advised them on personal problems, housekeeping, and child care—the beginning of school social work. These *visiting teachers* paid little attention to girls, who were expected to stay home to help with housekeeping and younger children, but encouraged boys to stay in vocational education programs. Less money was spent for girls' education than for boys, and girls dropped out much more often.

Home economics classes were considered particularly important for immigrant women; however, few attended classes either because they had little time or because their husbands forbade it. For example, the immigrant population in Chicago in 1920 was over 300,000, but only 400 women attended "mothers' classes," and of these only 240 were regular students. Vocational education was highly supported for men. The Smith–Hughes Act of 1917 allotted 42 percent of its grants to schools of agriculture and 28 percent to trade or industrial schools. Seven percent went for general education and 23 percent for home economics courses for women. By 1920, most states had compulsory education to age fourteen, with a greatly lengthened school year. By 1923 there were sixty-eight land-grant colleges, twenty-four state universities, and seventeen colleges for African Americans.

Reforms for Children

At the turn of the century, one out of six children was gainfully employed—7 million children between the ages of ten and fifteen. No one knows how many under the age of ten worked, especially African American children on southern farms, but 60 percent of farmworker children were employed by people other than their parents. Children worked in cotton, woolen, and silk mills, clothing and tobacco sweatshops, and coal mines and iron mills; up to 2.5 million worked in street trades.[48] Underage children working illegally were taught to hide when inspectors came. In 1900 Pennsylvania reported 120,000 children working in mines and mills, and New York reported some 92,000 employed who were under fifteen years old.[49] As textile mills moved south, employment of children increased until they made up 30 percent of all textile mill workers.[50] New labor laws and compulsory education began to make inroads on child labor: By 1910, only 2 million were working, by 1920, 1 million, and by 1930, about 667,000.

One of the most outspoken advocates against child labor was Irish immigrant Mary Harris Jones, known as Mother Jones (1830–1930). She fought for labor all her life, in the 1877 Pittsburgh railroad strike, the Haymarket riot of 1886, the Pennsylvania coal miners' strike in 1900, and the garment and streetcar workers' strikes in 1909. First an organizer for the Knights of Labor, she also organized for the United Mine Workers and the IWW. While supporting a textile mill strike in Pennsylvania in 1903, she found that 10,000 of the 75,000 mill workers were children, many of them maimed by machinery. She publicized their plight, speaking of

> Eddie Dunphy, a little fellow of twelve, whose job it was to sit all day . . . handing in the right thread to another worker. . . . Eleven hours a day . . . with dangerous

machinery all about him . . . for three dollars a week. And . . . Gussie Ragnew, a little girl from whom all the childhood had gone. Her face was like an old woman's . . . little boys with their fingers off and hands crushed and maimed. . . . Philadelphia's mansions were built on the broken bones, the quivering hearts, and drooping heads of these children.[51]

Mother Jones marched her "children's army" to President Theodore Roosevelt's summer home, from Philadelphia to Long Island, feeding them with donations from people along the way. Although the president refused to see them, the nation became aware of the "crime of child labor," and shortly thereafter Pennsylvania passed a child labor law setting a minimum age of fourteen for child employment. Often beaten and jailed, Mother Jones continued until her death to "fight like hell" for children and the rights of labor.[52]

National intervention in child labor was prohibited by the Constitution, so reforms were fought out state by state. Although thirty-four states eventually passed child labor laws, they had so many loopholes that they were, for the most part, ineffective. The paradox is clear. Labor would benefit from the restriction of child labor, giving more jobs to men. However, labor standards for children would raise wages and reduce profits; therefore, although altruism won the day in law, loopholes and overlooked violations of the laws nullified the victory in favor of factory owners.

Child Labor and Social Reform.   In 1902 Lillian Wald and Florence Kelley called a meeting of representatives of thirty-two settlement houses in New York City to discuss child labor, and in 1903 the group secured passage of a law regulating street trades. A national child labor committee was formed in 1904 as a clearinghouse against child labor, with such members as Edgar Gardner Murphy, Lillian Wald, Felix Adler (a crusader for housing reform), New York COS director Edward Devine, New York COS president Robert DeForest, and Jane Addams.[53] This committee influenced President Roosevelt to call the 1909 White House Conference on Child Dependency, which was attended by 200 prominent men and women. The conference went on record as favoring home care for children rather than institutionalization and recommended the creation of a public bureau to collect and disseminate information on children and child care.

In 1912 the Children's Bureau was established by William Howard Taft as a permanent part of the Department of Commerce and Labor. Its primary purpose was to protect children from early employment, dangerous occupations, and diseases. It advocated a minimum work age of fourteen in manufacturing and sixteen in mining, with documented proof of age, an eight-hour workday, and prohibition of night work. The first fifteen social workers ever employed by the federal government were hired to staff it, with Julia Lathrop as its director.[54] The bureau investigated and reported on all matters pertaining to child welfare and child life: infant mortality, birth rates, children's institutions, juvenile courts, desertion, dangerous occupations, accidents and diseases, child labor, and children's legislation. Its initial appropriation of about $25,000 was doubled, but was still far less than the money spent for animal research—$1.25 million.[55] The mortality rate for young animals at that time was lower than that of children.

All child labor reforms were called Bolshevik plots to "nationalize" children and families and were consistently declared unconstitutional. The Keating–Owens Bill to control child labor came to Congress in 1916 but failed to pass the courts; then an attempt to place a 10 percent tax on interstate commerce using child labor was outlawed. Finally, in 1924 a constitutional amendment was proposed, but was defeated by a lobby of manufacturers and Catholics, who called it a threat to family life. Nevertheless, by 1930, all states and Washington, D.C., had enacted child protection laws.

Mothers' Pensions.   The most important social welfare reform of the Progressive Era was the granting of mothers' pensions—outdoor relief—to poverty-stricken widows. Social workers consistently opposed this measure, claiming that outdoor relief would spread the contagion of pauperism to the next generation. They favored institutionalization: A study in New York found that COS workers had committed 2,716 children to orphanages solely because their mothers were poor, and almost another thousand whose mothers were ill.[56] However, this practice was increasingly questioned by settlement workers and judges in juvenile courts for, as Grace Abbott noted, mothers' child-caring contributions far exceeded their earning power in the marketplace.[57] Florence Kelley, speaking in favor of mothers' pensions, said,

> No money earned in the United States costs so dear, dollar for dollar, as the money earned by the mothers of young children.[58]

State after state chose to give mothers' pensions without consulting social workers. Faced with *faits accomplis,* they demanded the right to investigate and administer the pensions with social casework, to prevent recipients from "expecting relief as their right," and to "redeem" recipient families. They claimed that casework would ensure moral homes and proper upbringing for poor children. Convinced by their arguments as professionals and by the omnipresent public hatred of outdoor relief, states gave social workers the tasks they asked for. Their investigations were

> . . . thorough if not humiliating. If accepted for aid—and the rejection rate was very high—the mother was assumed to be in need of "supervision." . . . Why was a mother presumed to be competent to rear her children without caseworker supervision as long as the breadwinner was in the home but presumed to be incompetent when deprived of the breadwinner's support? . . . The growing profession of social work would doubtless have considered such a question impertinent.[59]

By 1911, twenty states provided mothers' pensions, and within ten years forty states allowed them. The first statewide law began in Illinois in 1911 as an addendum to the Juvenile Delinquency Code called the *Funds to Parents Act.* Wisconsin was next. The bills aimed at both providing for destitute children and establishing "moral" homes for children via a contract between the mother and the courts. If the agreement was violated by the mother, her children could be placed in foster homes or institutions. The programs were selective in the families they served, for there was still a strong reluctance to give outdoor relief. Recipients, therefore, were required to be of good moral character, widows, and white. Bell notes,

> Blacks were rarely admitted to this elite program for fatherless families, and as late as 1922 social workers reported that "low-type" families . . . Mexicans, Italians, and Czechoslovakians were seldom helped. If they were they usually received lower grants than "high-type" Anglo-Saxons.[60]

Most early laws confined aid to widows in the belief that assisting deserted mothers would encourage more desertion. By 1926, however, only five states still limited aid to widows. At local discretion, divorced mothers and those with husbands totally incapacitated, physically or mentally impaired, imprisoned, epileptic, or in an institution for the mentally ill were also included. Six states (Alabama, Georgia, Kentucky, Mississippi, New Mexico, and South Carolina) had no mothers' pensions. Coll says,

> In all states mothers' aid was not mandatory but at the option of county or municipality. So they were maintained only in a few towns. Ratios of children aided per 100,000 . . . ranged from 1.4 to 331 in 1926. A few—Arkansas, Indiana, Texas, Tennessee, Virginia—aided less than 20 per 100,000. . . . By 1934, about half the aid to mothers . . . [went] to cities of 50,000 or more.[61]

In 1926 maximum grants ranged from $70.00 a month in states such as California, Michigan, Indiana, and Ohio to $30.00 in Illinois, Iowa, Louisiana, Missouri, Montana, and Nebraska. In others, grants were made individually by administrative decision and according to need, although they could not exceed the cost of institutional care.[62] In California, women receiving mothers' pensions were called "gilt-edged widows," but in reality the payments were so low that welfare mothers still had to work, often as domestics or laundresses. In Chicago, where mothers' pensions began, Judge Pinckney's average award to mothers was $262 per year, and he was one of the most liberal judges.

Child and Maternal Health.   The health of women and children was a primary concern of the Children's Bureau. Findings in 1909 indicated an unusually high infant and maternal mortality rate, higher for women than any cause except tuberculosis. The maternal death rate was 6.7 per 1,000 live births and more than 250,000 infants died before the age of one (10 percent). Poor clinical and obstetrical training were blamed, for at least half of all maternal deaths were considered preventable. Nearly 40 percent were caused by puerperal sepsis (bacterial infection caused by the delivering physician's dirty hands), toxemia, pelvic disproportion, and hemorrhage. As head of the Children's Bureau, in 1918 Julia Lathrop drew up a bill (later called the Sheppard–Towner Act) to establish public health clinics and hospitals. The bill was labeled a Bolshevik plot and an infringement on physicians' privileges, and opponents ridiculed its writer as an unmarried nonmother who presumed to instruct mothers on child care. Missouri Democrat James Reed went so far as to ask Julia Lathrop if she had ever been a mother to give her the right to talk about children. She replied, "No, sir, have you?"[63]

In 1921, after three years of lobbying, the Sheppard–Towner Act passed. Lathrop retired immediately before its passage, and Grace Abbott, newly appointed to direct the Children's Bureau, was given a five-year $1,252,000 grant to administer it. The program served nearly three thousand child and maternal health centers in forty-five states, and infant and maternal mortality dropped so significantly that the grant was extended for another two years. After the 1929 crash, a congressional committee ruled it too expensive, and although Congress dropped it, the program was reconstituted as part of the Social Security Act of 1935.

One of the most important new health programs was the Kentucky Committee for Mothers and Babies (renamed the Frontier Nursing Society in 1928). Mary Breckinridge, a nurse, developed the program in 1925 to train nurse midwives in order to cut the alarming infant and maternal mortality rates in doctorless rural areas. Breckinridge hoped to gain federal Sheppard–Towner funds, but the director of Kentucky's Bureau of Maternal and Child Health Care stonewalled the federal grant application on the grounds that Kentucky's 2,500 practicing midwives, rather than outside nurses, should be trained. Breckinridge withdrew her federal proposal and raised money through women's committees to carry out her program.[64]

Medical and Psychiatric Social Work

As early as 1879 the National Conference on Charities and Corrections discussed mental illness and organized the National Association for the Protection of the Insane and the Prevention of Insanity. Its goals were research and education for better hospital policies and conditions, but it was opposed by hospital administrators and therefore failed after seven years. Psychiatric social work began on an organized basis in 1895, and New York State Hospital Services established its Pathological Institute in Albany in 1902 with a treatment program for the mentally ill. In 1905 Dr. Adolf Meyer was named chief of the New York State Hospital's Pathological Institute and moved it to Manhattan State Hospital. Meyer and his wife, a social worker, saw mental illness as maladjustment, and as Mrs. Meyer began to collect case histories, social workers became part of the mental health team. By 1906, the New York COS had established privately supported aftercare programs in each state hospital, and medical social work began to proliferate.

In 1905 the first social service department in a hospital was organized in Massachusetts General Hospital in Boston. Social workers went into the community to see patients in their homes and to investigate social conditions that had sent them to hospitals or to which they had to return. Bellevue in New York City was established soon thereafter, and in 1907 Johns Hopkins established a social work outpatient section in 1907. In 1921 Johns Hopkins began a two-year program to train medical social workers. Between 1905 and 1917, more than a hundred hospitals in thirty-five cities hired hospital social workers, and in 1918 the American Association of Hospital Social Workers formed.

The mental hygiene movement began when a former mental patient, Clifford Beers, voiced his distress at his treatment over three years in mental hospitals (in his book *The Mind That Found Itself*). He founded the National Committee for Mental Hygiene (NCMH) and supported it himself, going deeply into debt, until in 1912 Henry Phipps donated $50,000 to the association. The Rockefeller Foundation and Russell Sage gave further support, and the NCMH began to look at broader concerns than mental hospital reform, over Beers's objections. The broadened mental hygiene movement focused on

- Issues of the role of mental hygiene in education, criminology, and economic dependence
- Programs of "preventive" mental health and mental health treatment
- Research to define the "normal" personality (especially through improved childrearing and education and the early detection and treatment of "abnormality")
- Training a new generation of mental health professionals.[65]

Training mental health professionals referred especially to social workers, whose schools, professional associations, and journals were funded by the Russell Sage Foundation, the Commonwealth Fund, and the Laura Spelman Rockefeller Memorial Fund. Soon hospitals, private mental hospitals, and universities were establishing their own psychiatric care units. The mental hygiene movement led to the development of an alternative method to explain psychological problems, which had before been considered almost genetic in nature. This meant that mental disorder or deviance became a disease that could be prevented, detected, and treated. New diagnoses included the "maladjusted," the "psychopathic personality," and the "borderline patient." According to a text in use in the 1920s, people with personality disorders included paupers, prostitutes, misfits, criminals, drug users, bashful people, gypsies, old maids (by choice), unskilled laborers, dreamers and artists, deep thinkers, radicals and agitators, chronic grouches, peace-loving pacifists, and the over-studious.[66]

Veterans' services also had impact on the new mental hygiene movement. "Battle fatigue," a problem of soldiers returning from World War I, presented a different problem to the helping professions. No longer were the poor or deviant the only appropriate subjects for mental health care. The National Committee on Mental Hygiene and the Boston State Hospital collaborated to set up an intensive training program for social workers at Smith College in 1918. This program later became the Smith College School for Social Work, a model for psychiatric training for social work professionals.[67]

As early as 1896, Lightner Witmer developed the first psychological clinic in the United States (at the University of Pennsylvania) to introduce scientific knowledge about children and to train teachers, social workers, and psychiatrists. In 1907 he opened a hospital school for residential treatment of children with learning disabilities, and in 1909 Jane Addams and Julia Lathrop served on the advisory committee that established the Institute of Juvenile Research in Chicago. From these beginnings, Child Guidance Clinics began to open, funded in 1921 by the Commonwealth Fund for Prevention of Juvenile Delinquency. The Commonwealth Fund provided monies for many offshoots of the mental health movement: research on the causes and prevention of delinquency, establishment of an experimental system of school social workers, programs of direct public education, and the Child Guidance Clinics, which were actually demonstration projects.

The clinic personnel set up the first clinic in St. Louis and, when it became self-supporting, moved on to other cities throughout the nation. The clinics were oriented to providing "proper" childrearing practices; that is, they stressed giving advice to parents and working with them, along with schools and courts, to prevent juvenile delinquency. Such clinics gave a tremendous impetus to the social work profession by stressing the need for trained caseworkers; they also set new standards for child care, based on new mental health knowledge and middle-class standards. A particular kind of conformity in childrearing was intimated across class lines, and once again social welfare practices legitimated *parens patriae*, this time through mental health rather than poor relief.

Veterans' Welfare

Before the outbreak of war in 1914, veterans' pensions cost $174 million annually.[68] However, the war's terrible devastation made the nation eager to expand benefits for its survivors. In 1917 President Wilson appointed a Council of National Defense to review and recommend veterans' benefits, and a new benefit—the offer of readjustment and rehabilitation services for psychiatric problems such as shell shock—was added. Compulsory allotments were voted for families, at first paid by soldiers but later by the government. The War Risk Insurance Act was expanded to include voluntary insurance against death and total disability, medical and surgical hospital care, prostheses for those injured in service, and vocational rehabilitation.

By 1918, of the 4,744,000 in service, 116,000 had died and 204,000 were wounded, and by the mid-1920s, the Public Health Service had to increase its beds to 11,639 to accommodate veterans. Congress also authorized the use of beds in army and navy hospitals and in sixty national homes for disabled veterans. Because veterans' benefits were fragmented among the Bureau of War Risk Insurance, the Rehabilitative Division of the Federal Board for Vocational Rehabilitation, the Public Health Service, and the Armed Services, President Harding appointed a board (the Dawes Commission) in 1921 to establish the Veterans' Bureau. Benefits were further expanded in 1925, including the use of veterans' hospitals for veterans whose disabilities were not service-connected.[69]

During the war, the Red Cross provided canteens and clubs for servicemen, gave social services to men in military hospitals, and provided services to servicemen's families to help them cope with wartime separation. Although social work services had been previously provided for the nonpoor, they had been in assigned special categories, such as the mentally ill. The use of social work services for problems of "normal" (but stressed) people who were not poor gave a new impetus to the casework method in professional social work.

Aid to Blind People and Aid to People with Disabilities

Social workers objected to giving home relief to blind people because, they argued, flat grants did not take into account the degrees of need, discouraged industry, and made no provision for rehabilitation.[70] However, aid to blind people was approved by most people, and this was the first group to receive outdoor relief as a right, in Ohio in 1898. In 1915 Illinois required counties to grant $365 annually to blind people with incomes of less than $465 a year, and by 1925, twenty-seven states had aid to the blind programs.

Some states also had aid to the disabled programs such as the employment bureau opened by the New York COS to place the physically, mentally, and socially disabled in employment where their disabilities would not interfere with their work. After two years, the number of applicants averaged a hundred a month, and placements averaged eighty a month.[71] Vocational rehabilitation to help all categories of disabled people was established in 1920 in the Department of Education. The need continually outpaced the available federal funding, so not all in need were served.

Old Age Assistance

Pensions for the aged were one of the last reforms to be made, probably because society believed people should save for their old age or that relatives should support their aged parents. However, with new medical technologies and better nutrition people lived longer. Supporting them often went beyond the means of their children, and their small savings could not stretch through their longer old age. Many groups, including social workers, demanded that industry provide pensions, but they refused to do so voluntarily. Even if they had been willing, many aged people would have fallen outside their pension plans, such as women who had not worked, domestic workers, farm workers, and day laborers.

By 1905, the Massachusetts Bureau of Statistics had noted the problems of the aged poor and recommended pensions as the only humane way of dealing with them (although Massachusetts decided against pensions in 1910). Both the National Conference on Charities and Corrections and the Progressive Party endorsed social insurance in 1912, including old age insurance. However, by 1914, only Arizona and Alaska had even limited plans, and fewer than 1 percent of workers were covered by private plans. After the war, pensions for the aged were tied to health insurance by such groups as the Consumers League, Women's Trade Union League, and American Association for Labor Legislation. This measure was fought by both employers and the American Medical Association, and old age pensions were lost in the battle.

As increasing numbers of the aged sank into poverty, dependence on public assistance grew, and by 1923 states were moving toward old age pensions. They helped "only persons of good character," however, and excluded people who deserted wives or husbands and those who had been tramps or beggars. Some states required fifteen years of residency and had limits on earned income and assets. Many also placed liens on recipients' property, to be claimed after death.[72] Montana, Nevada, and Pennsylvania passed limited voluntary bills in 1923, and the first mandatory bill was passed by California in 1929.[73] By 1929, eleven states had bills to provide pensions for the aged, and between 1929 and 1933, nineteen more enacted them.[74] Laws passed after 1929 were compulsory for the entire state. However,

> In 1929 only a little over 1,000 elderly persons received assistance, at a total cost of $222,000; by 1932 more than 100,000 persons were receiving OAA [old age assistance] at a total cost of $22 million a year.[75]

Most states set age eligibility for assistance at sixty-five, required that relatives support the aged if possible, set residency requirements, required recipients to be U.S. citizens, and ordered recipients to exhaust their savings before application.

Unemployment Insurance and Workers' Compensation

John R. Commons and John B. Adams of the University of Wisconsin led the fight for unemployment compensation, public employment offices, and regulation of industry. Although bills were introduced in a number of states, none passed until Wisconsin made unemployment compensation voluntary in January 1932 and compulsory in June of the same year. On the federal level, a bill was proposed to be administered by the Children's Bureau under a Federal Board of Unemployment Relief. It would have provided $125 million for the first six months, with another $250 million for the second. This bill also failed to pass, and not until the Social Security Act of 1935 was unemployment dealt with.

Workers' compensation, to help those injured on the job or the survivors of those killed at work, was first discussed at the American Sociological Association Conference in 1902 and again in 1905 and 1906. Despite the horrendous rate of industrial accidents at the time, Samuel Gompers and unions vehemently opposed workers' compensation, for they wanted welfare to be a union function and feared state intervention in union affairs.[76] However, the nation moved inevitably toward workers' compensation. Every year, half a million workers were injured in industrial accidents and 15,000 were killed. Employers blamed this on workers, saying that they knew the risks of the jobs when they took them. Courts generally supported this claim, although some states, including Massachusetts and Illinois, recommended industrial insurance to factory owners.

In 1906, under Theodore Roosevelt, the Federal Employment Act was passed, providing a minimum workers' insurance for federal employees, and in the same year the National Conference on Charities and Corrections appointed a committee on the issue. A National Conference on Workers Compensation was called in 1909, and shortly thereafter a major study was undertaken in Pittsburgh. This study, a comprehensive survey of all labor conditions in the entire city, was one of the most important social research efforts of the era. It was funded by the Russell Sage Foundation, and members of its committee included Paul Kellogg, a social worker; William H. Matthews, head of Pittsburgh Settlement House; Robert Woods, settlement house worker; Florence Kelley, director of the National Consumers' League; and John R. Commons, a well-known economist. The study looked at wages, hours, conditions of labor, housing, schooling, health, taxation, fire and police protection, recreation, and land values.

In 1910 Crystal Eastman published the final report of the study, "Work Accidents and the Law," arguing that the high rate of industrial accidents would continue as long as employers were not held responsible. After the Eastman report, thirty states investigated safety conditions in industry.[77] Ten states enacted workers' compensation laws in 1911, and by 1920, forty-two states had adopted her suggestions into law. Generally, they included compensation for workers and their survivors based on economic loss due to industrial accidents, employer responsibility for all accidents regardless of fault, and a voluntary insurance pool under public administration. Although many people were not covered and benefits were limited, it was a beginning.

Reformers tried to include health insurance in workers' compensation, but heavy opposition came from the medical profession, insurance companies, employers, Christian Socialists, superpatriots who saw all social insurance as "made in Germany," and, strangely enough, labor unions. Because of this, health coverage was dropped from consideration (except in some maternal and child health cases) until the major reforms of Medicare and Medicaid in the 1960s. Supporters of health insurance during the Progressive Era believed that illness was a more important cause of poverty than industrial accidents. They claimed it would not increase costs of medical care in the long run and that it would prevent poverty as it prevented illness. However, once more came the cry of Bolshevism and progress toward health insurance ceased. Katz says,

> In their struggle against social insurance measures opponents deployed the old American ideology of voluntarism, condemning the interference for the state, praising the efforts of private philanthropy, and stressing the importance of individual achievement. In place of voluntarism they held out the menace of social and racial degeneration, the destruction of the moral basis of American society, and the victory of other social systems, that is, socialism and Bolshevism.[78]

Juvenile and Criminal Justice

By the Progressive Era, the juvenile justice system had significantly changed the lives of poor children. *Parens patriae* influenced juvenile laws, new children's codes, the control of child labor, and mothers' pensions. Foster care, adoption, and protection for abused children were instituted by this time, as were separate facilities for delinquent children or probation under local courts for children committing federal crimes. The Federal Bureau of Prisons, organized in 1930, set up a national training school for boys, two detention centers, and federal prison camps.

For adults, the criminal justice system made much more use of probation, parole, and rehabilitation. In 1910 the New York COS led the way to a system of probation and fines for drunks so that they would not be incarcerated. For long-term offenders, commitment to a farm colony and hospitals for care and cure was recommended.[79] Federal prisons were established in 1890, and after riots in 1919 their conditions improved considerably. The Department of Justice introduced parole services and began probation investigations in 1925. In 1930 the Federal Bureau of Prisons expanded its services to include vocational training, recreation, and educational facilities, medical and dental care, and religious and cultural activities, and set up reformatories and correctional facilities for minor crimes and short-term sentences. A medical center was established for the physically and mentally ill.

Women's Movements and Peace Protests

Women continued their reform movements in the Progressive Era, encompassing labor reform and children's welfare, the suffrage movement, the peace movement, and reforms related to sexuality. The areas of struggle, though often carried out by different groups, were related both by content and by interlocking memberships.

Suffrage

The suffrage groups that split after the Civil War coalesced in the 1900s into the National American Women's Suffrage Association (NAWSA). After a brief presidency by Carrie Chapman Catt (1849–1947), who succeeded Susan B. Anthony in 1900, Dr. Anna Howard Shaw (1847–1919), a Methodist minister and physician, became president. Although Shaw was an eloquent orator, she had almost no administrative skills and little tact. She consistently alienated men in power by attacking their politics, thus undermining their political support for women, and left NAWSA's administration in a shambles, with many of its staunchest supporters, such as Florence Kelley, resigning. Shaw resigned in favor of Jane Addams in 1911, and in 1915 the presidency was resumed by Carrie Chapman Catt.[80]

Catt, a tireless lobbyist, built NAWSA into a strong organization at both state and federal levels. She developed a "Winning Plan" of support and influence for legislative leaders in return for their favorable votes on women's issues, such as voting rights in party primaries and federal elections. During World War I, although Catt joined Jane Addams in forming the Woman's Peace Party, she supported Wilson's war policies. As reward, he threw his weight behind both suffrage and temperance movements. The prohibition amendment was passed in 1919 and suffrage ratified in 1920. Its major goal attained, NAWSA became the League of Women Voters. In 1925, Catt founded the National Committee on the Cause and Cure of War and served as chair until 1932. She was also active in support of the League of Nations, for relief of Jewish refugees from Germany, and on behalf of the child labor amendment.

Politicians, unsure of the effect of the new women's vote, established the Women's Bureau in the Department of Labor in 1920 and passed the Sheppard–Towner Act for maternal and child health in 1921. Changes were also made in the civil service system, making it fairer to women, and in consumers' rights systems for pure food. However, women continued either not to vote or to vote with their husbands, and soon their effect on the national structure was discounted. After 1924, with the election of Warren G. Harding, the nation reverted to conservatism in terms of women's issues.

A more radical suffrage movement existed alongside that of NAWSA, merging into a peace movement that opposed Wilson's war policies. Among its leaders were Alice Paul, Lucy Burns, Rose Winslow, Crystal Eastman, and Mary Ritter Beard. Alice Paul (1885–1977), a devout Quaker, studied at the New York School of Social Work and lived at the New York College Settlement. She became disillusioned as a social worker and in 1906 went to England to work in settlements there. She joined the British suffrage movement led by Emmaline and Christabel Parkhurst, a radical group that practiced nonviolent resistance, including blocking roads and picketing homes and government buildings, and was jailed three times. Returning to the United States in 1910, she joined NAWSA but became impatient with its timid policies.

In 1913 Paul and her radical cohort formed the Congressional Union for Women's Suffrage.[81] It adopted a stance of active interference, including a spectacular suffrage parade in Washington, D.C., on the day of Wilson's inauguration in 1913. The parade became a riot, and troops were brought in to put down the crowd that was beating the women. The sympathy they aroused was short-lived, however, and in 1914 NAWSA withdrew its support of Paul. Although the suffragists never committed acts of violence, violence on a new scale was committed against them. Uniformed soldiers attacked women pickets blocking the White House, and by June 1917, they were being arrested. At first, the charges were dropped, but gradually the courts began to convict and jail them for up to six months. More than two hundred women from twenty-six states were arrested for blocking the streets, and ninety-seven were sent to the District of Columbia jail or the infamous Occoquan workhouse, where "the rats were so big dogs were afraid."[82] They were beaten at random, Alice Paul was tortured by being kept awake, and the authorities responded to hunger strikes by force-feeding the women by tube until their noses bled. Rose Winslow wrote,

Yesterday was a bad day for me in feeding . . . vomiting continually. . . . The tube has developed an irritation somewhere that is painful. Never was there a sentence like ours for such an offense as ours, even in England. . . . Don't let them tell you we take this well. Miss Paul vomits much. I do too, except when I'm not nervous . . . we are making this hunger strike that women fighting for liberty may be considered political prisoners. . . . God knows we don't want other women ever to have to do this over again.[83]

The Congressional Union joined with the Woman's Party in 1917 to become the National Woman's Party, and Paul became its major spokesperson and organizer. After passage of the Suffrage Amendment in 1920, she drafted the first equal rights amendment in 1923. When it failed, she turned crusader for the League of Nations and founded and represented the World Women's Party at its meetings in Geneva. She continued as chair of the National Woman's Party from 1942 until her death in 1977, still seeking an equal rights amendment to end a societal sexism nearly untouched by the suffrage amendment of 1920.

Women and Health

The public health movement came at a time when women were still mostly excluded from regular medical practice. In 1920, for example, only 40 of 482 general hospitals accepted women as interns, and from 1925 to 1945 there was a 5 percent quota on women admitted to medical schools.[84] It was also a middle-class women's movement perceived as "cleaning society" as women cleaned their homes. Its financing was often justified with classist arguments about costs to the middle class of sickness among workers, absenteeism due to illness, and relief for orphans. Public health was closely related to the police; in fact, in earlier years it had been a police function, and public health workers continued to call on the police to enforce their mandates. Raids on tenements were commonplace, as police sought out disease carriers, including prostitutes, and such problems as typhoid were seen as visitations from God against sin.

Prostitution and Sexually Transmitted Disease.   One major goal of the public health movement was to conquer sexually transmitted disease, and the method was to control prostitutes. Their health was not the issue, despite their high mortality rate after entering the field. The concern was to keep middle-class wives "clean" from infection by their husbands who used prostitutes. The men, however, were never blamed; the prostitutes were. Both men and women in the movement agreed on fighting prostitution, especially when "fallen sisters" obviously preferred prostitution to the back-breaking, low-paying jobs available to them.

A small minority of immigrant women prostitutes first caught the public eye, confirming social Darwinist, sexist, and nativist stereotypes. Women immigrants outnumbered men by the early 1900s, and many were young single women without family or friends, trying to survive in a new culture. The Immigration Bureau entered the battle to deport such "immoral" people as part of its sexually transmitted disease control program. Its commission found prostitution in virtually all ethnic communities but failed to note the power of poverty and the double standard in perpetuating it. Grace Abbott, then director of the Immigrants Protective League of Chicago, believed that poverty, loneliness, ignorance, and a desire for romance made immigrant women particularly vulnerable to sexual exploitation.[85] She condemned America's moral double standard and advocated that the Immigration Service pay less attention to keeping "immoral" women from immigrating and more to helping them to survive in America.[86]

Men transmitted such diseases across all class lines. In 1904 Prince Morrow, the chair of a committee investigating sexually transmitted disease, estimated that 60 percent of the adult male population would have either syphilis or gonorrhea within their lives (an estimated 450,000 new infections per year).[87] In 1910 a new estimate stated that 80 percent of urban males had sexually transmitted diseases and 60 to 75 percent of "marriageable" men had gonorrhea.[88] Syphilis caused sterility—for both men and their wives (as well as prostitutes)—and general paresis, a deterioration of the brain. Eight to 20 percent of insanity cases were linked to sexually transmitted diseases.

Children also suffered: In 1905 research showed that between 25 and 40 percent of all congenital blindness in infants was caused by gonorrhea from infected mothers,[89] and one of every four babies was blind. Wives were infected because doctors often colluded with husbands to keep sexually transmitted diseases secret even after they became detectable (for syphilis, with the Wasserman blood test in 1906) and curable (a 1910 arsenate compound destroyed the syphilis spirochete). Alexander Fleming's discovery of penicillin dropped the infection rate dramatically. Medical control was possible, but social ideologies prevented it. Many physicians would not discuss sexually transmitted disease, especially in public, for "by its nature it besmirched them." As early as 1903 the American Medical Association formed a standing committee on sexually transmitted disease, but because of its "dirty" nature, many hospitals would not admit sufferers as patients.

A study in 1914 estimated that between 28 and 100 percent of prostitutes had sexually transmitted disease[90] and that infection of men was in most cases directly traceable to prostitutes. A later study by Dr. Howard Woolson, of the Bureau of Social Hygiene, estimated that there were at least 200,000 prostitutes in "a regular army of vice" and that 60 to 75 percent carried sexually transmitted diseases. An estimated 25 to 35 percent of the adult population was infected. He also noted that there was considerable shuffling back and forth between prostitution and low-paying jobs.

Legislatures took action to protect innocent wives: In Washington in 1909 and Wisconsin in 1913, laws required men to have physical exams before marriage, and by 1921 twenty states had similar laws. Sexually transmitted disease control was added to the U.S. Public Health Service in 1918, and by 1922 all forty-eight states had some kind of legislation requiring the reporting of sexually transmitted disease.[91] However, hiding the disease made the laws ineffective. Also, because wives were perceived as victims, they were not examined, so clandestine affairs or previous sexual liaisons continued to spread the disease. Finally, exams were not given carefully or the results examined because of doctors' belief in the morality of their clients, and therefore much disease simply escaped notice.

Police efforts severely reduced prostitution, and its regulation became a major issue. Because prostitution was considered "essential" for men, the men could not be regulated, but women could. One camp advocated moving all prostitutes to a particular red-light district under medical control. A wide variety of people opposed this, some feeling that medical regulation would give moral legitimation to the trade and others believing it was an infringement on the rights of freedom of women. Such eminent people as Theodore Roosevelt opposed the opening of a "tenderloin" district, calling for a war on commercialized vice rather than its regulation. Feminists and social workers such as Jane Addams and Maude E. Minier opposed such regulations because they controlled the lives of women but not the men who used them. Antiregulationists could also point to a study of European regulation by Dr. Abraham Flexner, who reported in 1914 that such containment and supervision was simply ineffective.[92]

In addition to wage-earning prostitution, there was a worldwide active "white slave trade"—women kidnapped and sold into prostitution. In 1873 Congress had passed an act aimed at breaking up this trade, and the Immigration Law of 1903 particularly excluded "prostitutes and persons who procure or attempt to bring in prostitutes or women for the purpose of prostitution." The law was strengthened in 1907 so that women immigrants who became prostitutes within three years could be deported. In 1904 a worldwide conference was held on white slavery, and in 1910, following its mandate, the United States made procurement of immigrant women for immoral purposes a felony. In addition, alien women living in a house of prostitution or employed in a place frequented by prostitutes could be deported.[93]

Abortion and Contraception

Abortion and contraception were also public health issues. Both were looked on as vice, and this closed the only avenues open to women who feared death in childbirth or the added burden of more and more children. Poor women still frequented abortionists, paying in pain and death, but middle-class women could arrange for "legal" abortions because of their "delicate conditions." In 1904 a symposium on abortion in Chicago, along with the Chicago Medical Society, came out against abortion. For a short time this influenced newspapers to drop their thinly disguised abortion ads and doctors to cut back on the number of abortions they performed. However, by 1908 the ads were back, producing an estimated $50,000 a year in revenue, and doctors resumed their profitable illegal practice on which city officials took protection payoffs.[94] It is estimated that after 1900 between 5,000 and 10,000 women died every year from botched abortions,[95] and by the mid-1930s, there was one abortion for every four pregnancies,[96] with about a million illegal abortions a year.

The fight for contraception was a fight against abortion, death in childbirth, and poverty. Pioneers included the socialist Emma Goldman (1869–1940), who as a midwife saw the desperate need for birth control and believed that women's control of their own reproduction was among their most important rights. Goldman gave the first public lecture on contraception, for which she was jailed. (Goldman also spent two years in jail for speaking out against the draft, and when the red scare hit the nation after the war, she was among 248 leftists deported to Russia, in 1919.)[97]

Another leader was Margaret Sanger (1883–1966), one of Goldman's students and founder of Planned Parenthood. A nurse among New York's immigrants, she saw her own mother die young from bearing too many children and like Goldman believed that women's emancipation began with control of their own bodies. She saw the terrible problems rising from lack of such control: too many children and the effects of illegal or homemade abortions. She wrote,

> I heard over and over again of their desperate efforts at bringing themselves "around"—drinking various herb teas, taking drops of turpentine on sugar, steaming over a chamber of boiling coffee or even turpentine water, rolling down stairs, and finally inserting slippery-elm sticks, or knitting needles, or shoe hooks, into the uterus. . . . Life for them had but one choice: either to abandon themselves to incessant child-bearing, or to terminate their pregnancies through abortions.[98]

Attending a woman who nearly died from an abortion and whom another pregnancy would kill, she heard her beg the doctor for contraceptive information. The doctor replied "Tell Jake to sleep on the roof." Three months later the woman was dead.

Sanger began her campaign for contraception by distributing handbills, some through the mail. She was arrested under the Comstock Act for sending out "obscene materials" and fled with her family to Europe. In Holland, she found that state-dispensed diaphragms had reduced maternal mortality by half. She returned to the United States in 1916 with more knowledge of contraception and opened the Brownsville Clinic in New York, conducting a house-to-house canvass to inform possible clients. Police closed her clinic and arrested Sanger and her sister, Ethel Byrne. Byrne was sentenced to thirty days in jail and began a hunger strike. After she went 103 hours without food, Commissioner of Corrections Lewis ordered her force-fed. Dangerously ill from the effects of the force-feeding, she was released on the promise she would not speak again of contraception.[99]

In Sanger's next clinic, which opened in 1917, physicians dispensed diaphragms smuggled in from Europe only to women whose medical history indicated that another pregnancy would be a health hazard. Other women were referred to sympathetic doctors.[100] Unable to get a license, Sanger turned over her Birth Control Research Bureau to physician Robert Layton Dixon, but he was also unsuccessful at obtaining a license. By 1927, Dr. Hannah Stone, the clinic's medical director, could demonstrate and prescribe diaphragms, but not until 1936 were doctors allowed to distribute contraceptives. The Depression, with its skyrocketing welfare costs, made contraception less socially offensive.[101] Although the American Medical Association in 1937 recognized that contraception was an important medical topic, it remained illegal until 1938, when a court ruling allowed physicians to import, mail, and prescribe devices. Even so, the under-the-counter racket in contraception remained a $250-million-a-year business because doctors were still unwilling to prescribe contraceptives.

The Professionalization of Social Work

A professional association for social workers developed from community social work clubs affiliated with the Conference on Charities and Corrections, and the Intercollegiate Bureau of Occupations organized a separate social work bureau in 1913. In 1917 a National Social Work Exchange was organized; anyone who believed she or he was eligible was accepted as a member. By the end of World War I, there were seventeen schools of social work, and in 1919, under the leadership of Porter Lee, school representatives agreed on a standardized curriculum with casework as the major method. This group evolved first to the Association of Professional Schools of Social Work and then into the Council on Social Work Education. In 1921 the Conference on Charities and Corrections became the American Association of Social Workers—later the National Association of Social Workers—and members were required to have four years of experience or academic and professional training.

Professionalization also came through the fundraising community chests of charity organization societies. The first of these came in 1900, when the Cleveland Chamber of Commerce organized a Committee on Benevolent Institutions to accredit charities and evaluate methods for collecting and accounting for money. Altruism was only part of the goal, for the Hollis Amendment to the income tax law just before World War I provided tax loopholes for donors up to 15 percent of their income. In addition, those who supported community chests could decide which agencies would live and which would fail, and community chest boards, made up of locally prominent people, achieved great power over budgets and programs for member agencies.

Community chests became today's United Fund or United Way, whereas the service portion of charity organization societies evolved first into the American Association of Charities and then the Family Welfare Association of America. In 1946 these organizations confederated into the Family Services Association of America. Settlement houses also became member agencies of United Way, losing their autonomy by accepting funds from community chests and losing their impetus for reform in the bureaucratization and professionalization of social work. During the same period, public welfare workers went from being overseers of the poor to county-level government bureaucrats in charge of investigating and doling out money to the "worthy poor." Thus the two historic themes of welfare—public and private charity—merged in the early decades of the century and parted in the 1930s to become public welfare and family casework services. Social reform movements that stressed that poverty was caused by economic and social issues solidified into the settlement house movement; this movement lost its voice for reform in the newly prosperous nation.

By 1929, there were 4,600 social workers belonging to forty-three chapters of the American Association of Social Workers (founded in 1921). Almost as many belonged to the American Association of Hospital Social Workers and the American Association of Psychiatric Social Workers. Twenty-five programs led to master's degrees in social work (MSW) and a new professionalism that would legitimate social work and gain support from state legislatures, foundations, and philanthropists. Psychoanalytic casework was the method of choice, and social workers could now come to the profession equipped with learnable skills as well as goodwill. New human behavioral theories became the knowledge base of the profession, which subsequently moved away from its historic mission of care for the poor. Veterans' services, the mental health movement, child guidance clinics, the growth of an organized theory of social development, the growing interest in psychology, and Freudian psychoanalysis became the threads that bound the profession together. At the Milford Conference of 1929, social casework was proclaimed the generic method of social work in both purpose and methodology regardless of practice setting.

Conclusion: New Freedoms and Old Constraints

From the Progressive Era and World War I to the stagnation and Depression of the 1920s, social reform and social work took separate paths. Social reform had virtually ended by 1920, and social work had become a middle-class profession. The government's reform legislation had bureaucratized county and state departments of public welfare, with more regularized funding and more accountability. The move away from institutionalization of the poor was almost complete and pensions, though far from adequate, were the trend of the future.

Although we often think of this era as one of increasing equality, in reality America had lost little of its classism, racism, or sexism. The gains made by labor unions were primarily for men, and women's secondary status in the job market was confirmed in most states by law. The polarization of classes had increased, and the great wealth of the few insulated and isolated them from the problems of the poor. By 1929, 5 percent of the population owned half the nation's wealth, and 42 percent of all families earned less than the $1,500 required for minimum health and decency for a family of five.[102] Racism based on economic problems and exacerbated by attitudes of social Darwinism existed as though the Civil War and Emancipation had never happened.

In this era, each social movement contributed to the new definitions of deprivation, dependency, and public and private social welfare responsibilities. Social reform also set forth *ideals* of equality for workers, people of color, and women and laid the bases for future civil rights action. Finally, the era clearly crystallized the scope and method of professional social work and set it apart from social reform. Concern with poverty, whether for the benefit of the needy or to maintain a low-wage workforce for business, became the domain of government bureaucrats. The new domain of social work became casework—mental health, psychiatric casework, school social work, medical social work, and so on—for people who could afford such services or were entitled to them as members of society.

As the government under Herbert Hoover continued to support big business as a right, unemployment began to push the economy into its downward spiral toward the stock market crash of 1929. Despite the many warning signals, the nation continued to operate as if economic realities did not exist: The "invisible hand" of the marketplace would set everything right, and the new profession of social work would, through casework, set to rights the growing number of the unemployed and poor. Suddenly, however, the bubble burst, and the United States faced a crisis that could destroy it.

Study Questions

1. What were the major targets of social welfare in the Progressive Era?

2. Who were the most powerful women of the Progressive Era? What did they do?

3. How did treatment of children, the aged, and the poor change during the Progressive Era?

4. What roles did the emerging profession of social work play in changes in the treatment of children, the aged, and the poor during the Progressive Era?

5. Discuss some of the shortfalls of the Progressive Era.

6. What were the major women's movements? What were their outcomes?

7. What other reforms and new knowledge set the bases for today's social welfare? Today's social work profession?

Notes

1. June Axinn and Herman Levin, *Social Welfare: A History of the American Response to Need*, 2d ed. (New York: Harper & Row, 1982), p. 134.

2. Beulah Compton, *Introduction to Social Welfare and Social Work: Structure, Function, and Process* (Homewood, IL: The Dorsey Press, 1980), pp. 350–352.

3. John Ehrenreich, *The Altruistic Imagination: A History of Social Work and Social Policy in the United States* (Ithaca, NY: Cornell University Press, 1985), p. 37.

4. Axinn and Levin, *Social Welfare*, p. 135.

5. Blanche Coll, *Perspectives in Public Welfare: A History* (Washington, D.C.: U.S. Government Printing Office, 1971), p. 63.

6. Axinn and Levin, *Social Welfare*, p. 129.

7. Ibid., p. 128.

8. Angela Davis, *Women, Race, and Class* (New York: Random House, 1983), p. 212.

9. Joseph Hraba, *American Ethnicity* (Itasca, IL: F.E. Peacock Publishers, 1979), p. 18.

10. Davis, *Women, Race, and Class*, p. 214.

11. Stephen Kern, *The Culture of Time and Space: 1880–1918* (Cambridge: Harvard University Press, 1983), p. 260.

12. Ehrenreich, *Altruistic Imagination*, pp. 45–47.

13. Axinn and Levin, *Social Welfare*, pp. 128–129.

14. Coll, *Perspectives in Public Welfare*, p. 63.

15. Compton, *Introduction to Social Welfare*, pp. 322–323.

16. Coll, *Perspectives in Public Welfare*, p. 66.

17. Compton, *Introduction to Social Welfare*, p. 322.

18. Hraba, *American Ethnicity*, p. 321.

19. Compton, *Introduction to Social Welfare*, p. 349.

20. Axinn and Levin, *Social Welfare*, pp. 128–129.

21. Lerone Bennett, Jr., *Before the Mayflower: A History of the Negro in America, 1919–1964* (Chicago: Johnson Publishing Co., 1966), p. 287.

22. Ibid., pp. 292–293.

23. Ibid., an account by Walter White, p. 294.

24. Ibid., p. 277.

25. Ibid., pp. 296–297.

26. Linda K. Kerber and Jane DeHart Mathews (eds.), *Women's America* (New York: Oxford University Press, 1982), pp. 261–262.

27. Bennett, *Before the Mayflower*, p. 284; and Robert McHenry (ed.), *Famous American Women: A Biographical Dictionary from Colonial Times to the Present* (New York: Dover Publications, 1980), pp. 434–435.

28. Angela Darenkamp, John McClymer, Mary Moynihan, and Arlene Vadum, *Images of Women in American Popular Culture* (New York: Harcourt Brace Jovanovich, 1985), p. 343.

29. Samuel Mencher, *From Poor Law to Poverty Programs* (Pittsburgh: University of Pittsburgh Press, 1967), p. 382.

30. Ibid., p. 385.

31. Ehrenreich, *Altruistic Imagination*, p. 45.

32. Alice Kessler-Harris, "Where Are the Organized Women Workers?" in Kerber and Mathews, *Women's America*, pp. 226–241.

33. William Jay Jacobs, *Women in American History* (Encino, CA: Glencoe Publishing, 1976), p. 140.

34. Axinn and Levin, *Social Welfare*, p. 141.

35. Compton, *Introduction to Social Welfare*, p. 337.

36. Alice Kessler-Harris, *Out to Work: A History of Wage-Earning Women in the United States* (New York: Oxford University Press, 1982), p. 238.

37. Ibid.

38. Carole Hymowitz and Michaele Weissman, *A History of Women in America* (New York: Bantam Books, 1980), pp. 254–259.

39. Ibid., p. 259.

40. Pauline Newman, "Triangle Shirt Waist Fire," in Kerber and Mathews, *Women's America*, p. 224.

41. Maxine Seller, *Immigrant Women* (Philadelphia: Temple University Press, 1984).

42. Newman, "Triangle Shirt Waist Fire," p. 224.

43. McHenry, *Famous American Women*, p. 136.

44. Michael B. Katz, *Poverty and Policy in American History* (New York: Academic Press, 1983), pp. 226–227.

45. Coll, *Perspectives in Public Welfare*, p. 74.

46. Axinn and Levin, *Social Welfare*, p. 127.

47. Seller, *Immigrant Women*, p. 198.

48. Compton, *Introduction to Social Welfare*, pp. 331–332.

49. Hymowitz and Weissman, *History of Women*, p. 239.

50. Compton, *Introduction to Social Welfare*, p. 332.

51. Mother Jones, *The Autobiography of Mother Jones*, 3d rev. ed. (Chicago: Charles H. Kerr, 1977), pp. 138–139.

52. Jacobs, *Women in American History*, p. 124.

53. Compton, *Introduction to Social Welfare*, p. 332.

54. Ibid., p. 364.

55. Ibid., p. 360.

56. Coll, *Perspectives in Public Welfare*, p. 77.

57. Winifred Bell, *Aid to Dependent Children* (New York: Columbia University Press, 1965), p. 6.

58. Axinn and Levin, *Social Welfare*, p. 160.

59. Coll, *Perspectives in Public Welfare*, p. 79.

60. Bell, *Aid to Dependent Children*, p. 21.

61. Coll, *Perspectives in Public Welfare*, p. 80.

62. Ibid., p. 79.

63. *Social Service Review*, 1951, p. 384. Quoted in Compton, *Introduction to Social Welfare*, p. 364.

64. Nancy Schrom Dye, "Mary Breckinridge, The Frontier Nursing Service, and the Introduction of Nurse-Midwifery in the United States," in Judith Walzer Leavitt (ed.), *Women and Health in America* (Madison: University of Wisconsin Press, 1984), pp. 327–344.

65. Ehrenreich, *Altruistic Imagination*, pp. 65–67.

66. William Sadler, *Theory and Practice of Psychiatry*. Discussed in Mary Shea, "The Ideology of Mental Health and the Emergence of the Therapeutic Liberal State: The American Mental Hygiene Movement, 1900–1930," Ph.D. diss., University of Illinois at Champaign–Urbana, 1980; in Ehrenreich, *Altruistic Imagination*, pp. 65–67.

67. Ehrenreich, *Altruistic Imagination*, p. 67.

68. Axinn and Levin, *Social Welfare*, p. 155.

69. Ibid.

70. Gerald Handel, *Social Welfare in Western Society* (New York: Random House, 1982), p. 131.

71. Frank Dekker Watson, *The Charity Organization Movement in the United States* (New York: Arno Press and *The New York Times*, 1971), p. 369.

72. Handel, *Social Welfare in Western Society*, p. 131.

73. Axinn and Levin, *Social Welfare*, p. 145.

74. Coll, *Perspectives in Public Welfare*, p. 81.

75. Ibid.

76. Katz, *Poverty and Policy*, p. 225.

77. Axinn and Levin, *Social Welfare*, p. 137.

78. Katz, *Poverty and Policy*, p. 222.

79. Watson, *Charity Organization Movement*, p. 372.

80. Jacobs, *Women in American History*, p. 213.

81. Dale Spender, *There's Always Been a Women's Movement This Century* (Boston: Pandora Press, 1983), p. 16.

82. Ibid., p. 22.

83. Doris Stevens, *Jailed for Freedom* (New York: Boni and Liveright, 1920), pp. 187–189. Referenced in Seller, *Immigrant Women*, pp. 269 ff.

84. Seller, *Immigrant Women*, p. 117.

85. Ibid., p. 130.

86. Compton, *Introduction to Social Welfare*, p. 338.

87. Mark Thomas Connelly, "Prostitution, Venereal Disease, and American Medicine," in Leavitt, *Women and Health*, pp. 196–221.

88. Ibid., p. 200.

89. Ibid., p. 201.

90. Ibid., p. 197.

91. Ibid., p. 203.

92. Bettina Berch, *The Endless Day: The Political Economy of Women and Work* (New York: Harcourt Brace Jovanovich, 1982), p. 45.

93. Seller, *Immigrant Women*, pp. 130 ff.

94. James C. Mohr, "Patterns of Abortion and the Response of American Physicians, 1790–1930," in Leavitt, *Women and Health*, pp. 117–123, esp. p. 119.

95. Ibid.

96. Hymowitz and Weissman, *History of Women*, p. 293.

97. Jacobs, *Women in American History*, p. 191.

98. Kerber and Mathews, *Women's America*, p. 312.

99. Ibid., p. 318.

100. Hymowitz and Weissman, *History of Women*, p. 296.

101. James Reed, "Doctors, Birth Control, and Social Values, 1830–1970," in Leavitt, *Women and Health*, p. 131.

102. Ehrenreich, Altruistic Imagination, p. 49.

9

The Great Depression and Social Security for Americans

The years between the complacency of the 1920s and the social revolt of the 1960s taught us many lessons. Although society clung to work ethic traditions, the Great Depression of the 1930s demonstrated that social and economic forces rather than individual fault created poverty, hitting both the wealthy and poor laboring classes. The Social Security Acts of 1935 were the most important social legislation in American history, though retaining ideals and traces of legislation predating the Elizabethan Poor Laws of 1601. Among these were definitions of worthy and unworthy poor, a low-wage workforce kept in line by social programs, the influence of the elite in the programs to prepare future workers, and the dedication to work as morality.

As the federal government assumed care of the poor, the social welfare system effectively split into two sections: the private sector, staffed by professionals inspired by psychoanalytic and social development theories, who treated middle-class clients with emotional problems; and the public sector, which provided income assistance to the poor. The public sector was further split: local public relief offices, staffed by people hired by political appointees, and the state and federal bureaucracies, staffed with more highly educated civil servants and often administered by professional social workers.

The Social Security Acts provided a safety net for many, but some still fell through. Racist attitudes among welfare workers discouraged minorities from public assistance programs for which they might qualify. People in intact families unable to support their families through work did not qualify for Social Security's Old Age and Survivors Insurance program, unemployment insurance, or public assistance. County poor relief and general assistance programs were usually their only recourse. Mothers with dependent children, already suspect because they were disattached from a male breadwinner, were increasingly devalued when they sought public assistance. Although war efforts and unionization could lift most white male laborers from poverty, these other groups remained stigmatized and needy.

World War II changed the economic system of the United States from consumer to military production as demands for war materiel brought more prosperity. It was immensely profitable because it was ultimately consumable—as fast as weapons were produced they became outdated, and if used were destroyed. Moreover, war production was capital-intensive, rather than labor-intensive, so as more sophisticated automation developed, workers and their demands became less important in profit making. Hard-won unionization became increasingly oriented to management's needs once basic rights were secured. During the war, women and people of minority groups went into the labor force and, for the first time, made good wages. They created a new middle class and taught their children to reach for equality. When the war ended, women displaced by returning veterans went back to childbearing with a vengeance, producing the generation of children known as the "baby boomers." Many minority people kept their jobs because of unions and because, remembering the lessons of World War I, the nation kept many veterans out of the labor market by financing their educations. This newly created middle class changed the demographic face of America as they took higher-level jobs, moved to the suburbs, and left the inner cities to the poor.

The Great Depression

The Great Depression did not crash full-blown on the economy in 1929. There were many warnings: high unemployment, lack of consumer buying, loss of homes and farms as mortgages failed, and strikes and riots when workers could no longer earn a family wage. However, the business boom in the early 1920s led to faith that the economy would right itself. In fact, President Herbert Hoover urged companies to high production and high prices in a "supply-side" economics: Provide the goods people want, they will buy, and once more the economy will rise. This essentially conservative wait-and-see philosophy could not deal with the deepening depression. Different from former depressions, it was based on "paper money": stocks and bonds for the rich and easy credit for the poor. Workers—the vast underpinnings of any economy—had scant real money to purchase goods. A 1929 study by the Brookings Institution showed that although $2,000 per year was needed for basic necessities, almost 12 million families, or nearly 40 percent of the population, had annual incomes of less than $1,500, and another 30 percent made less than $3,100 per year.[1] Credit lent a false sense of security because payments could be delayed "until things got better," but as consumers lost their jobs, creditors foreclosed.

The whole economic structure collapsed in October 1929. A spiral of falling sales, rising unemployment, declining income, further production cuts, and more unemployment began. In some cities, unemployment reached 40 percent and in some counties, 90 percent. The gross national product, at an all-time high of $103 billion in 1929, fell to $55.6 billion in 1933, and did not reach pre-Depression levels until 1941.[2] By 1933, manufacturing was 20 percent below its 1929 level. Average weekly wages were down 35 percent and aggregate corporate profits, which had hit a record $8.7 billion in 1929, dropped to minus $2.7 billion in 1933.[3] Unemployment increased in nine months from nearly 3 million to over 4 million; three months later, in May 1930, it was at 4.6 million, and by September 1930, over 5 million were unemployed. By the spring of 1931, over 8 million were jobless, and by 1932, one of every four people formerly in the labor force was unemployed and one of every five was on welfare.[4]

The first people laid off were Hispanic and African American men. By 1932, 56 percent of all African Americans were unemployed, and by 1933, nearly 18 percent of African American family heads were certified for relief.[5] Next to go were African American women, as white women displaced them in domestic labor. White blue-collar men lost their jobs next, and finally white women working in food and garment industries. White-collar workers and people in sales managed to hold on into the 1930s.[6]

By 1935, 30 percent of African Americans were on relief rolls,[7] twice the relief rate for whites, even though nonwhite people were less likely to receive relief and the grants were lower. It was worse in the South: In Atlanta, 65 percent were on relief and in Norfolk, Virginia, 81 percent were. In some areas, a de facto slavery returned; in others, communists began to organize African Americans into cells by offering to help them deal with white employers, renters, and welfare agencies. Lynchings nearly doubled in the South as white unemployment worsened, and African Americans in the North lived in absolute squalor. Men rarely found work, and women worked at any jobs they could find. Domestics made an average $6.17 per week and did white families' weekly washes for 50 cents each.[8]

Wage-earning women in 1930 numbered more than 10 million. Because of the protective legislation of the Progressive Era, they worked primarily at "women's jobs" rather than in heavy industry. As husbands lost jobs, wives went to work in the expanding clerical and human services sector—jobs men refused to take because of low pay.[9] Minimum wage levels for women rose dramatically; in New York in 1934, for example, they climbed 16.6 percent in eighteen months while men's rose only 3.4 percent. However, their wages were still so low that employers preferred to hire women over men.[10] Ninety percent of women who worked did so for economic reasons and 25 percent were the family's principal wage-earners. In 1920 only 23 percent of married women worked, but the numbers increased to 28.9 percent by 1930 and 36.7 percent by 1940.[11] Fewer than a third of all employed women were married.[12] The Depression destabilized the family: The marriage rate per 1,000 unmarried women declined from 92 in 1920 to 68 in 1930, and the birthrate went from 27.7 per 1,000 in 1920 to 21.3 in 1930 and 18.4 in 1933.[13] Although divorce rates showed no appreciable change, suicides and desertions increased.

Problems were compounded by a massive drought all the way from Virginia to Arkansas. Moreover, new farm technologies threw tens of thousands of workers off farms, forcing them to cities and adding to unemployment and dependency there. Because the Depression was worldwide, the market for farm exports dropped to $2.5 billion in 1932, less than half that of 1919. Individual farm incomes dropped from $945 annually in 1929 to $379 per farm in 1933, although farm production fell less than 5 percent.[14]

Not until 1931 did Congress enact the Wagner–Rainey Bill over Hoover's veto. It authorized the Reconstruction Finance Corporation to make loans to tide companies over this "self-limiting" crisis. Believing in the power of private sector charities, Hoover instituted a national voluntary fundraising drive through the Emergency Committee on Employment to ensure cooperation among private and public charities so that no one would be cold or hungry. However, the committee became merely a clearinghouse for correspondence, advice, and encouragement and gave little real aid.[15] Public relief expenditures skyrocketed to $54 million by 1931. Seventy-four percent of relief expenditures ($31 million) came from public funds during 1929 while in 1930 all relief expenditures doubled, with 75 percent ($51 million) coming from public funds. States tried to meet the demand: In 1931, New York, under the governorship of Franklin D. Roosevelt, disbursed funds to cities and counties for outdoor relief and work projects, and seven more states followed suit before 1932.[16]

Charities struggled valiantly to turn the tide of poverty and to prove the value of private casework methods to counsel people out of poverty. However, by 1931 they had given up and placed responsibility for relief on the federal government. Family welfare associations (formerly COSs) and the National Federation of Settlements argued that poverty was societal rather than personal failure, and for all practical purposes the social work profession gave over income maintenance to public welfare. Between 1929 and 1932, public relief expanded eightfold but still provided less than an average of $30 per recipient a year.[17]

Social Revolt and Temporary Relief

Demonstrations, strikes, and riots occurred nationwide as the Depression worsened. In March 1930, more than a million people demonstrated in dozens of cities, demanding relief. Some forty workers were killed in strike-related incidents, and between 1933 and 1934 troops were called out in sixteen states.[18] Petition drives, at least three with more than a million signatures each, demanded government action. Unemployment councils fought against evictions, protested cutbacks in what little welfare there was, and demanded a massive program of relief. The New York Unemployment Council, for example, claimed to have prevented 77,000 evictions between 1930 and 1934. Across the nation, 2 million people were involved in unemployment movement actions, with thousands jailed or hurt and fourteen killed.[19]

In 1932 between fifteen and twenty thousand World War I veterans marched on Washington, demanding early receipt of the bonuses they had been promised by 1945. They and their families erected shacks across from the White House, but after a month Hoover dispatched soldiers to burn "Hooverville." Hoover vetoed the early bonus bill but Congress overrode the veto, granting half the "adjustment compensation certificates" to be paid to veterans in 1937. When the Federal Economy Act cut veterans' pensions and benefits, veterans marched again in 1933 and 1934, and the protest became so severe that in 1934 Congress rescinded the act. More than 10,000 veterans stranded in Washington were assigned to work camps in the Civilian Conservation Corps, and another 7,000 were sent either to special work camps if they were disabled or to the Works Progress Administration. The bonus payment, made in 1937, put nearly $3.5 billion into the hands of veterans.[20]

Workers turned to the left: Communists played a major role in San Francisco's longshoremen's strike, in Toledo independent radical socialists demonstrated, and in Minneapolis the Trotskyite Social Workers party led a general strike.[21] Six million workers organized in three years. Other citizens took political action. A retired California physician named Townsend started a movement to give federal pensions to every worker over age sixty-five—$200 per month, returnable to the government if unspent and financed by a sales tax. By 1935 he had 25 million signatures and 3 million people in Townsend clubs across the nation.[22] In 1935 Huey Long, the reform governor of Louisiana, set up the Share the Wealth party, with 27,000 clubs around the nation and a mailing list of 7 million names. Long unsuccessfully challenged Roosevelt's presidential candidacy and was assassinated in 1935.[23]

As governor of New York, Roosevelt, with social worker Harry Hopkins, had provided benefits and work projects for the unemployed. As president, understanding that only emergency measures would quell the growing social unrest, he sent Labor Secretary Frances Perkins to Europe to study social programs that had staved off revolt there. The 1934 landslide victory of Democrats in Congress mandated a restructuring of the economy, and Roosevelt's subsequent actions strengthened the executive branch of the government enormously in the area of economic security. He expanded the cabinet and doubled the number of civilian government employees during the Depression years.[24]

Roosevelt's Emergency Measures

Roosevelt's wealth predated the Civil War and he did not have social Darwinistic "training." He believed in social justice and felt that the government was obligated to help the distressed.[25] His Federal Emergency Relief Act, administered by Harry Hopkins, was based on the belief that relief from unemployment was a right, and that any work, even digging holes and refilling them, was preferable to direct relief.[26] The Roosevelt administration determined to give the estimated 70 percent of those without work jobs until they could be reabsorbed into private employment.[27]

Roosevelt believed that Keynesian economics—demand-side consumerism—was the key to economic health. This meant, briefly, that putting money in the hands of consumers would increase buying and begin the upward spiral of the economy. Roosevelt intended to do this by saving farms and homes, reducing farm production, hiring out the unemployed in public works, and supporting manufacturers so that they could hire the unemployed. His temporary measures, the Federal Emergency Relief Act (FERA) and the National Industrial Redevelopment Act (NIRA), were passed in 1933. Both were declared unconstitutional and were replaced, respectively, with the Social Security Act of 1935 and the Works Progress Administration. However, during the time they were in operation, they reduced unemployment; controlled savings, investment, and consumption; and developed mechanisms to keep people out of the labor market.[28]

Federal Emergency Relief Act (FERA).   Roosevelt gave Harry Hopkins almost unlimited authority as director of FERA, with $500 million in grants to disburse for direct relief. Hopkins took office in May 1933, and by the end of the next month had paid out $51 million to forty-five states, Washington D.C., and Hawaii, putting about 20 million people on the relief rolls. By the end of the year, $324.5 million had been distributed. Half ($250 million) went to states on a matching basis—one federal dollar for every three state dollars—and another $250 million was distributed on need alone. No more than 15 percent of the total could go to any one state, and although states had to bear part of the cost, there was no formal plan for determining "shares." States that raised the most got the most.

To qualify for FERA funds, each state had to establish an emergency relief authority to receive and disburse federal monies on estimates of need, using means testing.[29] Rents and medical care expenses were paid directly to landlords and health providers. FERA provided direct relief to both individuals and families, but work relief was encouraged. Discrimination against people of color was "to be avoided" but was not forbidden: A disproportionate amount of FERA money went to rural areas in the South. One of FERA's most far-reaching effects was to legally end the distribution of federal funds through voluntary or private agencies, adding impetus to the profession's move away from poverty work. Aubrey Williams, a social worker and deputy administrator of the Works Progress Administration, said,

> the sooner social work as a profession can turn its back on direct relief as a valid form of social treatment, the better off will be the nation and the higher the standing of social work.[30]

No set guidelines for relief giving existed except for means testing, so FERA workers' discretion determined eligibility, grant amount, and work relief. They checked real property and bank accounts; conducted interviews with recent employers; canvassed families, relatives, friends, and churches for other support; and visited recipient families once a month. Work relief was supposed to be paid in cash but was often in-kind.[31] In the three years of its existence, FERA spent over $3 billion.

National Industrial Recovery Act (NIRA). NIRA instituted federal control of production, prices, and the rights of workers in industry. Its codes were intended to end cutthroat competition, raise prices, limit output, and provide for reasonable wages. It also reaffirmed the 1932 Norris–LaGuardia Act restricting federal courts from issuing injunctions against unions engaged in peaceful strikes, thereby legitimating unions and collective bargaining. For the first time, courts supported workers rather than employers. Unionization, which had been in a decline since 1920, began to pick up, and by 1935 unions had 3.7 million members.

Within half a year the ten largest industries in the nation agreed to come under NIRA.[32] Although it was declared unconstitutional in 1935, in its two years of existence it set standards for 2.5 million employers and 16 million workers. In that time, employment rose by 2 million, production rose from 62 percent to 79 percent of 1929 levels, and the gross national product increased from $55.6 billion to $72.2 billion.[33] Yet in 1935, 20 percent of the labor force was still unemployed.

Title II of NIRA created the Public Works Administration (PWA) with $3.3 billion given to industry for public improvement. Part of its budget—$400 million—went to the Civil Works Administration (CWA), but neither PWA or CWA used the money to increase employment. The Works Progress Administration (WPA), successor to both, hired the unemployed directly, setting a precedent for government as employer of last resort. NIRA developed a National Labor Board to mediate labor policies but, fought by large corporations, it was replaced by the National Labor Relations Act (NLRA) of 1938, also known as the Wagner Act.[34] Passage of the Wagner Act was aided by the excesses of industries *vis à vis* workers: more than $9 million spent between 1933 and 1936 on strikebreakers, labor spies, and munitions; a General Motors executive proposal offering a general force of 500,000 men to overthrow the government;[35] and Republic Steel's arsenal of 352 pistols, 64 rifles, 245 shotguns, 143 gas guns, and 2,707 gas grenades to be used against strikers. The Wagner Act outlawed company-dominated unions, heard unfair labor practices, and gave the Labor Relations Board power to determine bargaining units and petition courts to enforce its decisions.[36] It set a minimum wage (25 cents an hour, increased to 40 cents by 1945), a forty-four-hour workweek (forty hours in three years), and a minimum age of sixteen for child labor in industries of interstate commerce.[37]

Massive unionization of unskilled workers followed, joining together in 1937 to become the Congress of Industrial Organizations (CIO). By 1939 there were 10.6 million members in organized labor: 5 million in the CIO and 4.6 million in the AFL. African American workers were welcomed into the CIO, but the Wagner Act allowed discrimination against women. Although NIRA administrator Hugh Johnson, Secretary of Labor Frances Perkins, and Eleanor Roosevelt opposed differential wages for men and women, about a quarter of the codes, covering nearly 17 percent of all workers, allowed lower wages for women.[38] The Walsh–Healy Act of 1936 abolished child labor and set standards for workers in industries with sizable federal contracts. In 1939 twenty-one states still had no minimum wage laws for women, and thirty states still lacked eight-hour workday laws.

The Works Progress Administration (WPA).   Roosevelt's first job program was the Civil Works Administration, established in 1933 under the direction of Harry Hopkins. Workers were paid at regular rates for civil works already in progress, but the program lost money, and along with PWA, the CWA became the Emergency Work Relief Program under FERA. Roosevelt's Grand Design, however, envisioned a better program, one that paid money directly to the employee, and on this basis he instituted the Works Progress Administration in 1935 to hire workers until the economy revived or until the Social Security Act became operative. WPA was funded at $4.9 billion, but in its short lifetime spent $10 billion. WPA paid less than did regular employment, but wages were higher than poor relief, and by 1936 WPA employed one-third of all unemployed Americans at minimum security wages in nearly 8 million jobs. From 1935 to 1941, more than 2 million men per month were on WPA payrolls, with a peak of 3.25 million in November 1938. WPA financed more than 250,000 projects and spent $11 billion in the construction of roads, bridges, libraries; painting of murals; cultural projects for unemployed artists, actors, writers, and musicians; and myriad other works.[39] Macarov notes,

> work relief during the depression was more expensive than direct relief would have been . . . whether the work accomplished was worth the extra cost is debatable, but that it would have been cheaper to give out checks is hardly questionable.[40]

Other New Deal Programs.   Between 1930 and 1934, more than 4,000 banks failed because unemployed home and farm mortgage holders defaulted. Although banks foreclosed, they could not recoup their losses because they could not resell the homes. "Runs" on banks by depositors trying to get back their savings occurred, and Roosevelt declared "bank holidays," forbade gold payments and exports, and established penalties against banks that hoarded gold. His emergency banking bill led to the Federal Reserve Bank system, enabling the Treasury Department to regulate the banking industry.[41] The Federal Deposit Insurance Corporation (FDIC) was instituted to provide federal insurance against loss of depositors' savings.

More than 250,000 families lost their homes in 1932, and in every month in 1933 a thousand more lost theirs. To combat this, Roosevelt set up the Home Owners Loan Corporation, through a Federal Housing Authority, to give insured loans for home repair, to refinance mortgages in danger of failing, and to grant new mortgages for prospective home purchasers.[42] A later bill, the 1937 Housing Act, provided for federally subsidized housing.[43]

As farm income fell, farmers threatened a nationwide strike. In response, Roosevelt authorized the Agricultural Adjustment Act (AAA, 1933) to provide money for the purchase of new farm technology and limit farm production by paying farmers to slaughter their animals and leave their fields empty. However, only large farmers could afford the new technology, and marginal and tenant farmers, particularly African Americans, lost their land. The number of tenant farmers decreased by 303,000, with African Americans constituting 56 percent of the decrease. Not until 1935 were farmers receiving federal help required to keep the same number of tenants, and by then the move to the cities was nearly complete. The AAA also bought surplus food under the Federal Surplus Commodities Corporation, which it then distributed to the poor.

By 1935, Roosevelt had instituted the Farm Credit Administration (FCA) to administer all federal agricultural agencies, including the AAA. Farm income rose from $2.5 billion in 1932 to more than $5.9 billion in 1935. Although in 1940 there were about 6 million farms, this was a loss of nearly 200,000, almost entirely in farms of African Americans.[44]

Youth Programs.   Roosevelt established programs with the dual purposes of removing young people from the job market and giving them work training. The National Youth Authority (NYA) kept young people in high schools or colleges by giving them jobs to support them during their education. The Civilian Conservation Corps (CCC) employed young people to work in the preservation of natural resources in conservation camps. Young men between the ages of eighteen and twenty-five from relief families worked on reforestation, soil conservation, and flood control. They were given board and room and $30 a month, of which $25 was sent to their families. More than 2.75 million participated during the life of CCC, which was terminated in 1942.

Eleanor Roosevelt and Women in the New Deal

Eleanor Roosevelt (1884–1962) worked in settlement houses in the early 1900s and at age eighteen joined the National Consumers' League to work in the labor movement. She married her cousin Franklin in 1905 and provided constant support to him in his political career, particularly after his crippling attack of polio in 1921. While rearing six children, she continued her interest and activities in social causes and public affairs. She worked at Red Cross canteens for soldiers during World War I, encouraged the appointment of Frances Perkins first as New York's state industrial commissioner and then as U.S. Secretary of Labor, and was instrumental in such forward-looking social legislation as the National Youth Authority. She also worked to improve conditions for the mentally ill, coordinated the League of Women Voters' legislative plans, and was an active member of the Women's Trade Union League and the Democratic Party. She also developed (with Franklin) the national polio center at Warm Springs, Georgia, and taught sociology, economics, and government at the Todhunter School in New York City, of which she was part owner.

Eleanor brought an unprecedented number of women into Roosevelt's administration: Ellen Woodward, Hilda Worthington Smith, and Florence Kerr, all of whom held WPA appointments, and Lorena Hickok, a social worker who researched the impact of the New Deal programs. Eleanor also encouraged the rejuvenation of the women's division of the Democratic party under the leadership of Molly Dawson.[45] Because of the president's disability, Eleanor did much of the ceremonial and public relations work of the presidency, including the inspection of government works projects. She actively supported civil rights legislation and helped to financially support the NAACP. She publicly resigned from the Daughters of the American Revolution after it denied African American operatic soprano Marion Anderson permission to sing at Constitution Hall, arranging a concert at the Lincoln Memorial that was attended by 75,000 people. She argued for ending discrimination in the armed services and defense employment, supported student socialist groups, provided a forum for women's causes, defended social welfare programs, and served as advocate for Jewish refugees, especially when the president refused admission of Jewish children to the United States during Hitler's pogroms. She brought poor southern textile workers, northern garment workers, African American civil rights workers, and student activists to dinner at the White House so her husband could hear them, although he seldom acted on their issues.

After her husband's death, Eleanor continued to be the most effective woman in American politics. She encouraged Truman to push forward with civil rights and to maintain the temporary Fair Employment Practices Commission. As American delegate to the United Nations in 1945, she was the fundamental author of the Universal Declaration of Human Rights passed by the General Assembly in December 1948. A commissioner of the U.S. Commission on Human Rights in 1953, she spoke out against the McCarthy communist hunts. Retiring in 1953, after Dwight D. Eisenhower became president, she continued to work in the American Association for the United Nations. Her last official position was a chair of President Kennedy's Commission on the Status of Women, to which she was appointed in December 1961 and held until her death in 1962.[46]

Social Insurance in the United States

European social insurance programs began with Germany's Chancellor Otto von Bismarck's plan (1879) to subvert growing socialist influences. It provided workers in mines and factories insurance against illness, job accidents, and old age and disability. By 1889, the program required contributions from workers, employers, and the government. By the 1900s, all European countries had some form of social insurance based on commitment to full employment. Bell says,

> As European nations adopted comprehensive social welfare programs, they also made a commitment to maintain full employment . . . [reflecting] a conviction that everyone should have the right and opportunity to work. . . . Nowhere is the difference in values between other industrialized nations and the U.S. more striking than around the issue of full employment.[47]

The American social insurance movement began in 1906, when the American Association for Labor Legislation (economists and political scientists) began to investigate labor conditions. Its main tenet, based on evidence indicating poverty as structural rather than personal, was that social insurance was not charity but a basic human right, and that problems arising from poverty, age, sickness and accident ought to be guaranteed by the state rather than relying on either private charity or the benevolence of employers.[48]

In 1912 delegates to the National Conference on Social Welfare endorsed social insurance, and it became a part of Theodore Roosevelt's 1912 presidential platform. A 1913 study by Isaac M. Rubinow showed that between 80 and 90 percent of all wage-earners earned less than they needed to support families. The first state social insurance law was passed in Arizona in 1915, but was declared unconstitutional. Massachusetts passed the first state worker's compensation law in 1916, but the first unemployment insurance law was not passed until 1932.

By 1935 thirty states already had their own Old Age Assistance Programs, twenty-seven had Aid to the Blind programs, and a few had Aid to the Disabled. The federal Vocational Rehabilitation program was set into the Department of Education in 1920. In the private sector, corporations began to expand social insurance as a good investment because it kept people on the job and loyal, decreased their tendency to strike, and led to more satisfactory job performance. Pension plans also made possible the retiring of elderly workers and the hiring of younger, quicker, and cheaper workers.[49]

However, during the Depression, massive nationwide needs could not be met by any local organization, public or private. National action was required. Rather than a reactive program, however, Roosevelt envisioned a proactive Grand Design for national income support, with social insurance for the *worthy* poor (related to work participation) and public assistance for nonworking yet dependent people (the aged, dependent children), categories still considered *unworthy* poor. The Grand Design intended that no citizen should be deprived of the basic necessities of life, yet it was not completely altruistic. Its social control elements included "raising children up properly," maintaining a low-wage work force, and controlling the rebellious needy. Nevertheless, it was a major ideological step toward social morality and government responsibility.

In June 1934, Roosevelt instituted the Committee on Economic Security. Its members included the secretaries of labor, the treasury, and agriculture; the attorney general; and Harry Hopkins, administrator of FERA, with Frances Perkins, Secretary of Labor, as chair. The committee's charge was to build a "Grand Design" so that no citizen would go "ill-housed, ill-clothed, or ill-fed." In defense of his proposal, Roosevelt addressed Congress to this effect in 1934:

> People want decent homes to live in; they want to locate them where they can engage in productive work; and they want some safeguard against misfortunes which cannot be wholly eliminated in this man-made world of ours. . . . The complexities of great communities and of organized industry . . . [compel us] to employ the active interest of the nation as a whole through government in order to encourage a greater security for each individual who composes it.[50]

To avoid the charge that the "Design" was unconstitutional, Perkins suggested that the Social Security Acts (SSA) be financed through the taxing powers of the federal government, a ploy upheld in court despite arguments against it.[51]

Although inclusion of a health insurance plan was considered, the American Medical Association opposed it so strongly it was dropped, so it would not threaten the entire program. Aid to Dependent Children, originally intended to be placed under the Children's Bureau to give aid to all poor children, including those in intact families, was given at the last minute to the Department of Labor. Unfortunately, this removed the focus from children, placing it instead on mothers' morality and work ethic considerations.

Submitted in 1935, the Social Security Act was amended and became law in August 1936. It set a precedent for final federal responsibility for citizen well-being not seriously questioned until the 1990s. A revolutionary act in itself, SSA borrowed heavily from the past, expecting many of the Depression needs to "wither away" as the "invisible hand" of the market revived. It continued to categorize the poor as worthy (those who had been connected with the labor market) and unworthy (those peripheral to it).

> Frances Perkins . . . and Edwin Witte . . . who guided the 1935 law through . . . believed that open-ended government handouts to citizens must be avoided. In their view temporary "relief" payments to unemployed people, and minimal "public assistance" programs for dependent children and old people, had to be kept separate from "social insurance" programs that workers would earn as a matter of right through regular tax contributions from themselves or their employers.[52]

The SSA left many gaps: no provision for unemployed able-bodied workers, time-limited unemployment benefits, no health insurance, neglected disabilities, coverage of only certain kinds of employment (thus excluding millions), and extremely low benefits.[53] Galper says it was an extension of state activity into the social welfare arena to meet corporate needs, used to socialize the costs of production to government rather than elite. Such costs included

- Preparing (through job training) and maintaining the labor force
- Subsidizing low or irregular wages
- Stimulating consumer purchasing power by an influx of cash benefits during periods of high unemployment or recession.[54]

However, it filled the immediate needs of those needing help, both poor and rich, and set into law national provisions for citizens in need.

The Social Security Act set up two systems: federal social insurance for people connected in some way with the labor force, and federal/state categorical public assistance. The former provided direct payments from the federal government to retirees and their survivors or dependents; and the latter gave grants partly financed by the federal government but administered on state and local levels. Each state submitted a proposal to qualify for SSA funds, which had to include merit hiring, sound administrative procedures, fair hearings, and adequate records on which to compile annual reports. Categories eligible for aid were the aged (over sixty-five), blind, surviving children, and dependent children. Under separate titles, the Social Security Act provided for crippled children and their vocational education, maternal and child welfare, and the administration of the unemployment compensation laws.

The act was actually two separate pieces of legislation: a payroll tax and a pension plan. Harry Hopkins, its first director, said,

> I have never liked poverty. I have never believed that with our capitalistic system people have to be poor. I think it is an outrage that we should permit hundreds and hundreds of thousands of people to be ill clad, to live in miserable homes, not to have enough to eat; not to be able to send their children to school for the only reason that they are poor.[55]

Now he had the power to do something about it.

Programs of Social Insurance Based on the Social Security Act

Although the politics of the era changed part of the shape and intent of SSA, it passed as the basis for federal services for the "general welfare." Thus, its impact went beyond income transfer:

- It legitimated both state and federal income redistribution.
- It established local *federal* Social Security offices for administration of redistribution to the worthy poor.
- It established federally mandated *state* Bureaus of Social Aid for administration of categorical assistance to the "unworthy poor." These later combined with county offices for public welfare to provide all public assistance services.
- It ended most federally funded income redistribution by private agencies.
- It mandated the establishment of state offices for employment services and workers' compensation.
- It provided public health services for the poor and established guidelines for state-administered county health departments.

SSA established two insurance programs for the deserving poor (those who had worked or were working): Old Age and Survivors Insurance (OASI) (Title II) and Unemployment Compensation (Title III). Workers' compensation, provided to workers injured on the job or their survivors, developed state by state rather than being part of the national act. However, it is another program of social insurance.

Old Age and Survivors Insurance (OASI)

Originally this Title provided only for retirement pensions for people over sixty-five, along with their spouses, and was designated Old Age Insurance (OAI). Because it was not means tested, social work services were not required, so it was outside the purview of the social work profession. Monies collected from both employer and employee were paid into a reserve fund, with amounts originally based on actuarial tables developed by the secretary of the treasury. In 1937 employers and employees paid 1 percent of the first $3,000 earned, with no benefits over $85. A death benefit was also established. Most workers became eligible by working forty quarters (three-month periods), but farm and domestic workers, casual day laborers, and officers or crew of sailing vessels, federal or state employees, and charity employees were not eligible at all.[56]

Survivors' insurance (OASI) was added in 1939, providing pensions for widows and children of deceased workers. Disability coverage was not added until the 1950s (OASDI), and health insurance (Medicare) was added in 1965 (OASDHI). Most worker categories, including the self-employed, were added in the 1950s, and now coverage is nearly universal. Although at first workers could not earn income and still collect their pensions, this was relaxed. Retirees under age seventy are allowed to earn a small amount, and at age seventy could earn any amount and still receive total benefits.

The program was placed in the newly created Social Security Administration, with about 1,250 offices located across the country and with a central record office in Baltimore. The Treasury Department collects taxes paid by workers and employers through payroll taxes (FICA, the Federal Insurance Contributions Act, and SECA, the Self-Employment Contributions Act for the self-employed), prepares checks, and maintains the trust fund. Disability determinations are made by state agencies and reviewed by the Social Security Administration. Although it was set up as a trust fund (actually, three separate funds) to receive monies, the fund itself is basically a bookkeeping function. Via federal borrowing from and payback to the fund, monies have flowed more or less freely between it and general revenues since Truman's time.

To gain support, OASI was presented as an insurance program, on the quasimyth that benefits would be based on actuarial models of contributions. However, rather than insurance, it is a tax, bearing most heavily on the poor because the rate takes an equal percentage of a set amount from all employees. Although participants are viewed as "investors," the relationship of benefits to monies paid in is tenuous at best. OASI pensions have both a minimum and maximum grant level, and because people are taxed on an upper limit of income, the tax is regressive: Those making over the maximum taxable amount pay nothing more.

The system is inequitable in many ways, particularly for women. Families with two wage-earners get two benefits, yet the work of wives at home is ignored: When the wife stays at home, social insurance entitles the family to benefits for only one and a half people. Housewives, although they contribute to workers' earning ability, receive only the lower "dependents'" benefits. Women divorced after less than ten years of marriage (originally twenty) cannot claim survivor's insurance, although their children do. If the mother remarries she loses her survivor's benefit, and when the children reach majority at age eighteen, the mother loses survivor's benefits until she reaches age sixty-two. Those who cannot earn good wages because of institutional discrimination—people of color and women—therefore have inadequate social insurance. Finally, workers today are paying for the Social Security of the already retired rather than investing in their own retirement, and the children of today will pay Social Security for present workers.

Medicare, the health insurance program, was established under the Social Security Act in 1965. It has two programs: a regular contribution (Part A), taken from FICA Medicare to provide basic hospital services, and Part B, an optional contribution by participants to cover even more medical expenses.

Unemployment Compensation: Title III

The Social Security Act of 1935 mandated that states and employers provide insurance for workers unemployed through no fault of their own. Four million dollars was appropriated for this title for 1936 and $49 million for each fiscal year thereafter to *administer* state programs. Unemployment *grants* are paid out by states through taxes on employers. Federal administration funding is based on state estimates of the labor force, and if a state denies a substantial number of claims, it could lose that funding. Employers may offset taxes by paying the amount (up to 90 percent) directly into the state unemployment fund.

Within a short period after passage of the Social Security Act, all states established such funds, along with agencies to administer the state programs and provide employment services (now called state Employment Security Commissions). One purpose was to prevent layoffs, so employers with stable employment records pay reduced taxes: Employers hiring eight or more people for twenty months or more pay a 3 percent tax on their payrolls. Excluded from this tax originally were farm and domestic employers, the government, railroads, and non-profit organizations, although most are now included. Railroad employees were covered in 1938 by a special railroad retirement plan, and federal government employees were brought into the program in 1954. In 1956 the program was amended to cover four, rather than eight or more, employees.

The Unemployment Insurance program is based in the Employment Security Administration of the U.S. Department of Labor, and taxes are collected by the U.S. Department of the Treasury. However, states administer their own programs and these vary state to state. Unemployment insurance provides regular cash benefits for a limited time to people who have worked a base period and then been let go from regular employment. At first the base period for coverage was forty quarters, or the equivalent of ten years. As of 2002, earning $250 is considered to constitute a quarter of covered employment. Unemployed workers must file for benefits and must be willing, able, and available for work, but benefits cannot be denied for refusal to accept work where conditions are below those prevailing in the community or if the job does not meet the applicant's qualifications. Amounts of grants have some relationship to the amount formerly earned by the employee but also take into account number of people in the family. In any case, the grant is always much less than former wages.

Workers' Compensation: State Social Insurance

Workers' compensation came state by state rather than through national legislation. Most states set up their programs under state Departments of Labor or independent workers' compensation boards through private insurance agencies. Employers almost always fund such programs, although some states contribute funds and some employees might contribute to medical care. States may also impose a penalty against employers that do not have insurance. Premiums are based on company size and nature of risk. Many states still exclude agricultural workers, domestic workers, and workers in casual employment.

Workers' compensation provides benefits to victims of work-related accidents and illnesses regardless of fault, although workers must prove that their injuries were not from gross negligence, willful misconduct, or intoxication. Benefits for disabled workers or the survivors of dead workers reflect the worker's wages at the time of injury or onset of illness. They are given in cash and without means testing to spouses until they remarry and to children until they reach a state-set age. Benefits can be limited by time, amount, or extent of disability (temporary or permanent). Many states pay for the total length of the disability, including life, and some pay medical benefits. Some have a maximum number of weeks for temporary disability. Medical services, rehabilitation, and job training may be provided, although some states limit this liability.

In 1970 the National Occupational Safety and Health Act (OSHA) began to set standards for safe and healthy work conditions and authorized the National Commission on Workers' Compensation Laws to evaluate situations. The commission recommended compulsory coverage, no exemptions for small firms and government employees, coverage for all types of workers, coverage of all work-related diseases, and weekly cash payments at two-thirds of the gross wage up to a weekly benefit equal to 100 percent of the average weekly wage in the state. Also, it recommended no limits for permanent total disability benefits or for medical services and physical rehabilitation.[57] The interest of the federal government in occupational safety demonstrated that more federal intervention might be forthcoming. However, both the Reagan and Bush administrations and Republican-led Congress of the early 1990s limited the financing, standards, and scope of OSHA.

Public Assistance Programs of the Social Security Act

Although social insurance is considered an entitlement, public assistance is generally for those considered undeserving because they have not made the most of opportunities to work or save. The public assistance provisions of the Social Security Act set up categories of the unworthy poor, much as in the Elizabethan Poor Laws of 1601. The categories were Old Age Assistance (OAA, Title I), Aid to the Blind (AB, Title C), and Aid to Dependent Children (ADC, Title IV), which in 1940 added the caretaking parent to the grant (Aid to Families with Dependent Children, or AFDC). The categories were instituted as temporary measures that would "wither away" as the market provided jobs and income or as social insurance benefits took over. Recipient grants were based on federal–state sharing, and states determined both needs and the grant levels on which the federal share was based.

Eligibility, based on means testing and home investigations, was at the discretion of workers, which meant that they could make value judgments as to who deserved help. Blaming the poor for their poverty was still a keynote of assistance, even among the most forward-looking reformers. Harry Hopkins said,

> The means test is our one way of keeping panhandlers off the rolls. It calls for the most detailed prying into the lives and habits of every applicant for relief.[58]

Needs and grants for aged, blind, and disabled people were set low and those for children were set even lower. Public assistance categories were first placed under the Social Security Administration until Truman put them into the Department of Health, Education, and Welfare (DHEW). During the Reagan administration, the Department of Education was made a separate office and DHEW became the Department of Health and Human Services (HHS).

Old Age Assistance (OAA)

OAA was set up to provide an income for people over age sixty-five who did not have enough savings for retirement or had never worked. Until health and nutrition lengthened our lives, these people had not been much of a problem. They either died or their children took care of them. However, children with families of their own could no longer support their aging parents, and the poorhouse seemed costly and inhumane. Therefore, OAA was established as a form of outdoor relief for the elderly.

Under the original act, the federal government paid half the grant amount in any quarter up to $30 per month, along with 2.5 percent of the costs of administration. Eligible people were all those over sixty-five who fell below state grant levels and were ineligible for OASI. Federal age eligibility was sixty-five, but until 1940 states could set it as high as age seventy. No citizens could be excluded, and states could not demand that people reside in the state for more than five of the preceding nine years. OAA was a partial answer to the Townsend Movement, but was not as ubiquitous or generous.

Aid to the Blind (AB) and Aid to the Disabled (AD)

AB was for people judged legally blind by medical authorities. Again, the federal government paid for half the grant up to $30 per month and for 5 percent of administrative costs. AD was added to the Social Security Act in 1956. Later it was called Aid to the Permanently and Totally Disabled (APTD), with state-appointed doctors deciding eligibility. At first disability meant only physical disability, but the definition was later amended to include mental and emotional disability.

AB, APTD, and OAA were moved to Social Security in 1971, redefining these groups as "worthy poor." Because OASDI paid less than had some states, given their standards of need, those states moved to reduce their benefits to OASDI levels. However, the government required them to supplement the federal grant up to their former standards of need so that recipients would not lose income because of the move. With the establishment of Supplemental Security Income (SSI) in 1972, a federal floor was set for aged, blind, and disabled people, providing a basic guaranteed annual income (GAI) not necessarily connected with work history for all people in this group. Although SSI remained a public assistance program (means tested), as were the preceding categories, the Social Security Office administered distribution of benefits.

Aid to Dependent Children (ADC)

ADC was the most controversial categorical program of the Social Security Act. Originally, the Children's Bureau was expected to administer it, and provision was to be made for all needy children, including those in intact families. However, for political reasons it was taken from the Children's Bureau and restricted to

> children under age sixteen who were deprived of parental support or care by reason of the death, continued absence from the home, or physical or mental incapacity of a parent, and who were living with father, mother, grandfather, grandmother, brother, sister, stepfather, stepmother, stepbrother, stepsister, uncle or aunt, in a place of residence maintained by one or more of such relatives as their own home. (Title IV, 55A 1935)

Mothers were not included in the grants until 1950, when the program became AFDC and was moved to the Department of Health, Education, and Welfare when it was established.

The wording of the bill designates dependent children as those deprived of "parental support" rather than those in need. This allowed for worker discretion in deciding the definition of *support,* and in some states it came to mean the presence of a father figure available for "emotional support," rather than financial need. Thus, if welfare workers suspected that a woman was involved with a man, whether or not he contributed financial aid, the family could be put off the program. This gave rise to "suitable home" and "substitute parent" policies in which welfare workers could take away grants if they considered the home "immoral." Moreover, because "unsuitability" was often equated with neglect, it gave workers power to remove children from mothers they considered unworthy. Eligibility determinations often excluded out-of-wedlock children, those from divorced parents (because the mothers were considered sexually immoral), and African American children, because of the racism of workers who believed African Americans "always manage to get along."

Appropriations for 1936 were $24,750,000 and as much as needed thereafter, with the federal government paying up to one-third of the first $18 for the first child and up to one-third of $12 for each succeeding child per month. (Contrast this with the federal input of half of $30 for aged and blind adults.) ADC had to be given across each state at the same grant level, and a one-year residence requirement was allowed (later struck out as unconstitutional). Although ADC allowed mothers to care for their children at home, only those judged "fit and proper" by investigators were allowed to do so. The rest had to find jobs or alternative means of support, voluntarily give up their children, or have them taken away under neglect statutes. Local administrators could require eligible mothers to work as a condition for the grant.

Federal financing for ADC was probably enacted only because it was tied to other, more popular bills. Although some believe that disinterest led to ADC's meager provisions, intentional neglect because of institutional sexism and racism was the more likely cause. By November 1936, while forty-two states were receiving money for Old Age Assistance, only twenty-six were receiving ADC monies, although it had been legislated in all but three states (Alabama, Georgia, and South Carolina) by the end of 1935.[59] In 1936, 162,000 families received $49.7 million in benefits, or about $307 per family for the year.[60] The basic eligibility requirement for ADC was need, set by state standards and determined by needs testing. Although now fewer children were placed in orphanages, and to that extent ADC was a positive step, grants were always low and the threat of removal of children always present.

AFDC became a federal–state program, with the federal government contribution based on a formula depending on state-set levels of need. The program was severely cut back under the Reagan administration but continued until 1996, when it was replaced by the Temporary Assistance to Needy Families (TANF) program under the 104th Congress's Personal Responsibility and Work Opportunity Reconciliation Act.

Maternal and Child Welfare Act: Title V

Title V under the Social Security Act set up preventive and remedial health care for children, providing

- Child welfare services for the care of homeless, dependent, and neglected children, and those in danger of becoming delinquent. Money would be given to states on plans developed jointly by state departments of public welfare and the Children's Bureau.
- Vocational training and rehabilitation for crippled and physically handicapped children.

- Programs for maternal and child health, including prenatal and birthing care for mothers, and eventually some contraception, school nurses, public health programs, and the Women's, Infant's, and Children's food program (WIC).

This title was placed in the Children's Bureau. In 1936, $3,800,000 was approved, with grants to be given under the authority of the chief of the Children's Bureau, the secretary of labor. Each state was allotted $20,000 plus part of $1,800,000, depending on the proportion of state-to-national live birthrate. Another $980,000 was available for grants according to financial need of the states. State health agencies were required to administer these programs, with states contributing funds on a matching basis.

The Professionalization of Social Work

Because the Social Security Act moved federal funding from private to public agencies and most professional social workers were with private agencies, it fostered the split between professional social workers and public welfare. Public assistance was delegated to two parallel agencies: county welfare offices, which distributed general assistance, poor relief, and various residual programs of medical and burial assistance; and state Bureaus of Social Aid. Workers in the first were hired by local directors, who often were political appointees. Bureaus of Social Aid were established at the county level under a central state administration to administer Old Age Assistance, Aid to the Blind, Aid to Dependent Children, and later, Aid to the Permanently and Totally Disabled.

In effect, then, the United States had three parallel programs of income redistribution: OASI (under the Social Security Administration) and two public assistance programs (Bureaus of Social Aid and county welfare offices). Neither the Social Security Administration nor county offices required professional social workers, though for different reasons: OASI was an entitlement program, needing no personal investigation or surveillance, and county welfare offices required only a high school diploma or two years of public work for its workers. (See Table 9.1 for a summary of programs.)

A new breed of activist arose to champion the cause of the poor: the workers in Bureaus of Social Aid. Typically, young college graduates staffed the new federal offices: teachers, salesmen, and engineers unsocialized to "professionalism" and deeply critical of it as a defense of status and a tool of oppression. They became the rank and file of new social services unions, which gained 15,000 workers in the 1930s.

As early as 1931 workers of the Jewish Federation in New York City organized the New York Association of Federation Workers, and a little later the first strike in social work history occurred. This laid the groundwork for social work trade unions in the public sector, the first of which was the Home Relief Employees Association (December 1933). By 1938, 14,500 people belonged to social work

TABLE 9.1   *Parallel Income Maintenance Programs: Social Insurance and Public Assistance*

Social Insurance	Public Assistance	
Federally Mandated	*Federal/State Funds*	*State/County Funds*
Social Security	*Categorical Programs*	*Poor Relief, General Assistance*
OAI: Old Age Insurance 1935	ADC: 1935	
OASI: Add Survivors 1950	AFDC: Add Parents 1940	Medical Assistance
OASDI: Add Disabled 1956	*AB: Aid to Blind 1935	Burial Assistance
Medicare (HI): 1965	*OAA: Old Age 1935	Medicaid: 1961
Workers Compensation: 1935	*AD: Disabled 1951	
Unemployment Compensation	SSI: Supplemental Security Income 1971	
	TANF: 1996	

*Moved to Social Insurance (OASDI) in 1972.

locals, and the American Association of Social Workers included an estimated 10,560 of the 60,000 social workers in the nation. Eighty-three percent of those unionized were in public agencies.[61] Though concerned with their own job issues, they were also aware of the needs of their clients. Within a year, their successes had encouraged new unions in Chicago, Cincinnati, Cleveland, Detroit, Minneapolis, Newark, Philadelphia, and Pittsburgh.[62]

However, red-baiting campaigns in the late 1930s and the McCarthy witch-hunts after World War II brought the downfall of social work unions and activists. Many social workers were in fact communists or socialists, including Mary Van Kleeck, who attacked the New Deal because of its commitment to the needs of the elite rather than the needs of the poor at the May 1934 meeting of the National Conference of Social Workers. Bertha Capen Reynolds, a graduate of Smith, identified with both communism and the rank-and-file movement, saying that "caseworkers were employed to see that society was not troubled by [the economically unsuccessful]."[63] Although she was deeply respected in the profession, she never worked again as a social worker after the McCarthy red scare. Today a progressive branch of the social work profession bears her name: the Bertha Capen Reynolds Society.

"Professional" social workers turned to social casework, usually based on psychoanalytic models or new developments in family–child relationships. By 1937, child services and family agencies were merging because of the similarity of their practice base and middle-class clientele. Freudian psychosexual development theories and an emphasis on "inner self" created a ripe field for casework practitioners and gave "scientific" support to personal blame theories. These "prescribed" psychoanalytic treatment as "cures," lending more credence to the medical model of social work than the social/structural model. Ehrenreich says,

> social workers more and more became psychotherapists ... concerned with the life cycle problems of the middle class, their theoretical base widened ... behavior modification and learning theory, existentialism and humanist therapy, transactional analysis and gestalt therapy, systems theory and "social ecology" and a dozen varieties of family therapy and group work joined. ... Freudian psychodynamic theories as part of many social workers' armamentarium of approaches and techniques. What was "social " about these techniques few ever asked.[64]

From the psychodynamic perspective, the *presenting* problem was not the *real* problem. Requests for help, such as paying bills or dealing with authorities, were believed either to mask emotional problems or be indicative of psychological inability to cope with such problems. Disposing of the immediate problem, such as heat turnoff or need for food, was seen as

> unprofessional, potentially destructive, and [creative of] even further dependency. All casework services have to be ... "constructive" parts of a "plan." ... [T]he coercive aspects of the casework relationship ... stemmed from the structural position of the agencies which gave them enormous power over clients. ... They were extensions of other authoritative agencies—the police, the schools, the health agencies—or the key to desperately needed benefits.[65]

Freud's dictum "happiness is to love and to work" reinforced work as therapy for troubled souls. Moreover, Freud's differential psychosexual development theories for men and women reinforced women's secondary status in work and in the home. It also gave society scapegoats for the perceived growth of juvenile delinquency—mothers who put their own needs over those of their children by remaining in the labor market.

World War II

Although the Social Security Act alleviated some basic subsistence problems, war was the real reason for the end of the Depression. War came to Europe when Germany invaded Poland in 1939, but its gestation was much earlier. Germany was brought to its knees by World War I, and the "democratic" government of the Weimar Republic, imposed by its victors, collapsed in 1927. As the worldwide depression intensified, the German economic situation worsened, precipitating Hitler's rise to power. Although a 1923 coup d'état failed, by 1930 his Nazi party had gained 107 seats in parliament, and by 1931 the Nazi party had 800,000 members. In the next election, Hitler won 11 million votes against Hindenburg's 18 million, and in 1933, with 96 percent of the vote, became chancellor with dictatorial powers. In 1935 he formed a Rome–Berlin Axis with Mussolini's fascist regime, and in 1936 Germany and Japan, under Emperor Hirohito, signed the Anti-Comintern Pact, and Japan declared war against China.

The United States was an ally of Britain and Poland but had signed a Neutrality Act in 1937. Furthermore, it was involved in its SSA program development, a new recession, and strikes by half a million workers. However, by 1939 Roosevelt had to acknowledge America's European alliance as Germany invaded Poland. Still, not until Japan attacked Pearl Harbor on December 7, 1941, did the United States finally enter the war in an uneasy alliance with China and communist Russia.

Internment of Japanese Americans

As the United States went to war, its selective racism showed on many fronts. One of the most crucial was the internment of Japanese Americans. The first action against the Japanese took place on state and local levels: The legislature of California passed a bill denying elections of Japanese Americans to state government, state and federal police raids intensified, and more than 2,000 people of Japanese descent were arrested.[66] Most such cases were thrown out for lack of evidence, but this, according to California Attorney Earl Warren, merely "reflected the cunning of the Japanese." Japanese businesses were forced to close and citizens illegally detained, evicted, and fired. At least three dozen violent attacks were documented.

In 1942 Roosevelt proclaimed western California, Oregon, Washington, and southern Arizona as areas where no Japanese, German, or Italian aliens could reside. A War Relocation Board moved a small number of Japanese, German, and Italian aliens from "sensitive" military areas and restricted their movements.

Because Italy's fascist government had joined Nazi Germany in the "Axis alliance," about 10,000 Italians the FBI suspected of being "fifth-columnists" were stripped of their constitutional rights; hundreds were arrested, forced to carry special identification cards, observe curfews, or face internment. Among those targeted were Joe Dimaggio's father and Ezio Pinza, the opera singer.[67] However, only Japanese Americans as a group were pressured to resettle. The Federal Reserve Bank was ordered to protect their property, but most sold it at low prices, and businesses and farms went at losses.

Japanese Americans were detained and then transported, without any semblance of trial or due process, to barb-wired concentration camps. By fall 1942, more than 112,000 people, two-thirds of them citizens, were interned in ten camps under military guard. Allowed few personal possessions, they were housed in partitioned-off barracks with inadequate supplies. Small monthly wages were paid to those who would work. Local camp governments were established under the direction of the War Relocation Authority, with a council selected from the prisoners. The internees underwent constant political screening to ferret out disloyalties, and their demonstrations and riots were generally fruitless. A few thousand students and workers in special agricultural assignments were released, and many joined the army, in which their segregated unit was the most decorated in World War II. Some 6,000 renounced their U.S. citizenship. In 1943 more than 10,000 relocated to the East.

In 1944 one-third of the prisoners were allowed to leave the concentration camps, and in late 1944 the order to hold them was rescinded. Most returned to the West coast and over the next two years 800 returned to Japan.[68] The cost to the United States for the evacuation was about $250 million, and Japanese American losses have been estimated at $400 million or more. The internees formed the Japanese American Citizens' League to formally protest the evacuation and its losses to them, and by 1946 it was pressing for compensation. By 1950, nearly 24,000 were filed, totaling $132 million, but the government paid only $38 million, less than 10 percent of the estimated losses. In 1980 the Commission on Wartime Relocation and Internment of Civilians recommended that 60,000 survivors should receive $1 to $2 million,[69] but this was still minimal in the face of Japanese American losses from the internment.

The War Years

The federal government had refused since 1932 to hire married women whose husbands were already employed (Federal Economy Act, married person's clause) and fired 1,600 of those whose husbands held federal jobs. At the same time, 77 percent of the nation's school systems refused to hire married women as teachers, and half dismissed those who married. In Texas, women who worked in railroad companies were fired if their husbands earned over $50 per month. As late as 1939, legislatures in twenty-six states were considering bills to bar married women from all employment. A live-in domestic in New York earned $34 per month, and the Women's Bureau thought $6 per week was an adequate salary for a seventy-two-hour workweek.[70] Because of the recession, both government and private employers began to fire women. Norman Cousins, echoing the public sentiment of the day, said in 1939,

> There are approximately 10 million people out of work in the United States today ... There are also 10 million or more women, married or single, who are jobholders. Simply fire the women, who shouldn't be working anyway, and hire the men. Presto. No unemployment. No relief rolls. No depression.[71]

When the Japanese attacked Pearl Harbor, the United States had already been gearing up for war for two years. More and more people were being recruited to factory work: African American men from the South, Puerto Ricans, Mexicans and Mexican Americans, women, and even young people. Factory recruiters paid high school principals to send them students, and the minimum age for employment was reduced from eighteen to sixteen. Military and civilian demand pushed the economy upward. In 1940 the gross national product was $99.7 billion, and in a total population of 132.1 million, the number of workers in the labor force was 55.6 million, with 540,000 people in the armed services and civilian employment at 47.5 million. The unemployment rate was 14.6 percent, or 8 million workers. Sixty-four percent of the working population made annual wages of under $2,000 and 84 percent were under $3,000.

With the Selective Service Act of 1942, factories were left inadequately staffed to produce sufficient amounts of goods and war materiel. More than 16 million men were transported for military reasons; women, wives, and family followed them. Another 16 million moved for job reasons.[72] When war employment soaked up the residue of unemployed men, employers turned to women. They were recruited not only into the "women's" labor market, but also into war production plants. The War Manpower Commission estimated that only 29 percent of America's 52 million adult women had jobs and told them they were shirking their patriotic duties if they did not work. During the first two years of war, twenty states and Washington, D.C., enacted emergency laws to extend maximum daily or weekly working hours for women. Laws against night work were modified in eight states, and in four states various occupations previously covered by protective legislation were exempted. By February 1943, *Fortune* magazine suggested drafting women if they did not come forward to work.[73]

Nearly 11 million women had jobs before 1940 and 3 million were looking for work.[74] By 1940, nearly 16 million women of a total female population of 50.1 million were working full-time despite discrimination, lower pay, and segregated job classifications. Of the female workforce before the war, 48.4 percent were single, 36.4 percent were married, and widows and divorcees made up 15.1 percent. Labor force participation of women over age fourteen increased from 25 to 36 percent.[75] During the war, the percentage of single women workers decreased to 40.9 percent, while those married rose to 45.7 percent. Two million women went to work in offices, half in the federal government. By 1945, the wartime peak, 19.5 million women were employed, excluding those in the Red Cross and military service. By 1950, women were 32 percent of the labor force.[76] Three-fourths of new women workers were over thirty-five, 60 percent were married, and the majority had children of school or preschool age.[77]

Before the war, 40 percent of African American women—1.5 million—worked (compared with 25 percent of white women). More than half were in service occupations such as domestic employees (72 percent) and 20 percent were farm workers. By war's end in 1945, 2 million African American women were working, with 18 percent in factories and the greatest increase in manufacture of metals, chemicals, and rubber. Their numbers as factory workers quadrupled, and there was a noticeable and permanent decrease in their employment as domestic workers.

Pay for women changed with war employment as the federal government endorsed equal pay for equal work in government and war-connected jobs, and unions fought for equal pay so that men's pay would not be reduced. Union membership for women, which had been 500,000 in 1937, reached 3,500,000 by 1940. By 1944, more than 3 million women constituted 22 percent of trade union membership.[78] Still, in many jobs women received lower pay even when equal pay clauses were written into labor contracts. The National War Labor Board defended employers against women on the grounds that they would leave the labor force with the end of the war. Although some 700,000 workers received industrial training in the last half of 1941, only 1 percent of these were women.

The presence of women in factories led to improved working conditions in many ways, including company cafeterias, a few day care centers, transportation facilities, rest breaks, and some shopping and banking facilities on plant sites. In 1942 the federal government allotted $400,000 to assist local communities in funding child care, and the 1943 Lanham Act authorized money for day care centers, but few communities came up with matching funds to build them. Day care centers were expensive (up to $6 per child) and inconveniently located, and their hours open did not consider the travel needs of working women. Thus, they operated at only a quarter of capacity and were too cost-ineffective to continue. With the end of the war, the issue of day care centers as needed facilities faded away, replaced by the feeling that, at best, day care centers made it easy for mothers to be neglectful and, at worst, they were part of a leftist plot to destroy the American family. A 1945 bill asking for $30 million to continue day care centers failed, with some congressmen arguing that "women should be driven back to their homes." Although a bill for $20 million to continue centers through 1946 did succeed, it included no money for expansion and soon all federal support for day care ended.[79]

By 1943, unemployment had virtually ended, with a rate of 1.2 percent—about 1 million unemployed. Twenty-four percent of all women of working age were in the labor force. By 1945, with a population of 105.5 million, the gross national product was $211.9 billion, and civilian employment rose 11.1 percent, reaching 52.8 million.[80] Total employment in 1946 was 56.7 million, of whom 15.8 million were women.

The War and People of Minorities

Although many nonwhite people shared in the benefits of the Roosevelt years, the country still maintained a racist bias. For example, the Civilian Conservation Corps had a racial quota that limited participation; Federal Emergency Relief, National Industrial Recovery, and Agricultural Adjustment Act monies were given discretionarily according to race; the National Labor Administration had codes with discriminatory pay rates; and government employment was discriminatory and offices were segregated. Roosevelt, in political debt to the Southern aristocracy, refused to support antilynching laws and would not endorse a broad civil rights program.[81] Although he appointed more than one hundred African Americans to federal positions between 1933 and 1940, it was always at lower levels. William Hastie was appointed to the third U.S. Circuit Court, the highest African American judicial appointment up to that time; Robert C. Weaver was given a post in the Department of the Interior; and E. K. Jones took a post in the Commerce Department, Laurence Oxley in the Labor Department, Ira D. Reed in the Social Security Administration, and Mary Bethune in the National Youth Authority.[82]

The 1928 Merriam Survey gave impetus to major changes in Native American affairs under Commissioner Charles J. Rhoads. In 1933 Roosevelt appointed John Collier as commissioner (a post he held until 1946). Collier, who had been active in supporting Native Americans since the 1920s, instituted major changes under the Indian Reorganization Act of 1934 (the Wheeler–Howard Act), and most Native Americans had the right to decide whether they would participate in the changes. The act stopped allotment of Native American lands to white people and ended the forced assimilation of their cultures, allowed Native Americans to develop their own constitutions and elect tribal councils, created a fund to provide credit for agriculture and industrial projects so that Native Americans could develop tribal business corporations, and gave them over a million acres of new land. Health and school services were improved. The act also allowed for preferential hiring in the Bureau of Indian Affairs to Native Americans. The Secretary of the Interior, however, could still veto constitutions and make rules for tribal elections, and he also continued to supervise expenditures and regulate land management. Almost 25,000 Native Americans entered the armed services, most as draftees, and almost twice as many left reservations to work in war industries.[83] They came back as veterans entitled to such services as rehabilitation, education, housing, and jobs, and became the fathers of the generation that rebelled in the 1960s.

Before the war, partly in response to Roosevelt's New Deal, African Americans began to become Democrats. (He received about one-fourth of their vote in 1932, but in 1940 received 53 percent.) In 1944 the Supreme Court ruled that they could not be barred from primaries in Southern states, and by the late 1940s an estimated 600,000 African American voters were registered. By the time of World War II, they had become more vocal in their demands for equality. They had migrated to urban areas, become educated, and participated in the Works Progress Administration, the National Youth Administration, and vocational training. Their victories were few but steady: By 1940, 73 percent of African American men in the labor force had blue-collar jobs, despite tremendous resistance to their employment, and despite resistance to their induction, more than a million men and women of African descent served in the armed forces, though in segregated units. For the first time, they could enter combat units rather than be assigned to menial chores, and they could now enter the Army Air Corps and the Marines. Although African American officers were commissioned and sent to integrated officers' training schools, segregation continued for the regular soldier in living quarters and in training and recreation.

On the home front, their activism continued. In 1940 the Urban League had a membership of 26,000 in 46 branches, and the NAACP had 481 branch offices and 85,000 members nationwide. The latter's attention focused on the South, pushing for antilynching laws and laws to end quasi-peonage and debt slavery, for educational and employment opportunities, for equitable treatment in courts, for equal pay for work equal to that done by white workers and access to labor unions, and for the fair distribution of public education funds and the end of segregated facilities.

In 1943 the Congress of Racial Equality (CORE) began to challenge segregation in restaurants, swimming pools, and municipal facilities in Northern and border states and staged its first sit-in at a restaurant in the Chicago Loop. CORE was inspired by the Gandhian tactics of nonviolence and by the militancy of a new leader, A. Phillip Randolph. Randolph, son of an African Methodist minister, had won recognition for the Brotherhood of Pullman Car Porters after twelve years as a labor organizer. Protesting unfair labor practices, he threatened Roosevelt with a march on Washington by 50,000–100,000 black workers. In efforts to dissuade him, Roosevelt asked him, Walter White of the NAACP, and T. Arnold Hill, acting executive of the Urban League, to end plans for the march, but Randolph was adamant. In response to the threat, Roosevelt wrote an executive order barring discrimination in war industries and the armed services on June 25, 1941, and Randolph called off the march.[84]

This first Fair Employment Practices Committee met widespread defiance and was ineffective because it lacked power to punish offenders. Its institution touched off, in 1943, the worst series of riots by white workers since 1919. In a Mobile, Alabama shipyard, African American workers were promoted and white workers rioted until troops were called in to quiet them. There were riots in Harlem and in Detroit thirty-four people died in job riots. Because African American labor was necessary to the war effort, both the National Defense Advisory Committee and President Roosevelt spoke out against discrimination. This, along with the growing protest movements, fostered a second Fair Employment Practices Commission (FEPC) in 1943. Soon African American workers held 1 million factory jobs, union membership increased to 500,000, and their number in government increased from 50,000 in 1939 to 200,000 in 1944. The proportion of African Americans in war-related industries increased from 3 to 8 percent during war years, but layoffs at the end hit them much harder than whites. Since then, their unemployment has remained consistently double that of whites.

Not until the war ended did President Truman abolish segregation in army units, and at the same time ended discrimination in firms doing business with the federal government. As the war ended, however, racism once more took its toll. White people mobbed and attacked neighborhoods where African Americans lived and lynched returning veterans. Truman refused to recant his civil rights stand, however, and set forth a civil rights platform for the 1948 presidential election. Although he won the election on the African American city vote, it cost him the Southern vote and his proposed civil rights bill failed in Congress, which continued to refuse legislation to protect voting rights. Not until 1951 was lynching finally made a federal offense.

Social Welfare Services: The War and After

During the war, Roosevelt turned to problems of dislocation and distress related to the war itself. In November 1940 he named the administrator of the Federal Security Agency as coordinator of the Office of Health, Welfare, and Related Defense activities. This office provided services for training camps and their civilian communities. In 1941, he placed the Office of Civilian Defense in the Office of War Management to integrate servicemen's health, welfare, and recreation services with defense activities. By 1943, these had been integrated into the Office of Community War Services under the Federal Security Agency, serving both armed forces and the civilian population.

The Community Facilities Act of 1941 (Lanham Act) provided federal funds for construction of houses, schools, day care centers, hospitals, water and sanitation plants, and recreational facilities in communities affected by the loss of defense jobs. Routine physical health care was encouraged: During the war years, the Emergency Maternal and Infant Care program (1943) served more than 1.2 million military wives with 230,000 infants. Inoculation programs for all children were undertaken through public health services.

Education became a major service goal when Army examinations showed an illiteracy rate of one in five among inductees. The U.S. Office of Education was expanded to make federal aid available for elementary and secondary education and for agricultural extension services in rural areas. In addition, it awarded enormous government contracts for research in engineering, science, and civil aeronautics; education in defense industries; management; and the Reserve Officers Training Corps (ROTC).[85]

More than 16,535,000 servicemen went to war. The death toll for Americans was 292,000 in action and 114,000 from other causes. Nearly 700,000 were wounded. While the servicemen were gone, some never to return, the government concerned itself with helping the families who had given up fathers, sons, and husbands to the national need. The Servicemen's Dependent Allowance Act of 1942, under the War Department, provided family allotments. At first paid half-and-half by the serviceman and the government—by 1943, $797 million—by 1945, allotments totaled $3 billion, with the government paying $2 billion.[86]

After the war, major social legislation centered on veterans, both because the nation believed they deserved reward for services to their country and in order to avert a major economic catastrophe. We had learned from World War I: The release of millions of soldiers into the job market when millions were laid off as the war economy declined would have produced a massive depression. Although the Selective Training and Service Act of 1940 provided that inductees be reemployed at the end of service in positions of like seniority, status, and pay, the government took steps to keep veterans out of the labor market. The first was the 52–20 Plan, which provided veterans $20 each week for a year, whether or not they were disabled or involved in battle.

The second was the Servicemen's Readjustment Act of 1944, called the G.I. Bill of Rights. Its only eligibility requirement was that the veteran had served during a specific time. It provided stipends to support veterans and their families while the veterans went to school for vocational education or higher education, paid for tuition, and subsidized home loans, business and farm loans, unemployment insurance payments, and veterans' employment services. G.I. Bill expenditures were $3.4 billion in 1946 and $9.3 billion in 1950—23 percent of that year's federal expenditures.[87] In addition to averting a depression, the G.I. Bill upgraded the quality and earning power of the American workforce for a generation. The National Mental Health Act of 1946, in response to the mental health needs of veterans, began to fund research and training in mental health and to establish community mental health services. This led to even more programs and agencies for social work professionals.

Women After the War

The nation made a radical turnabout regarding women's work at the end of the war. Within two years, 14 million veterans returned to civilian work, and the number of women working as operatives and craftspeople dropped by over a million. Where they had been recruited and had won many gains for all workers because of the labor shortage, now it became their patriotic duty to leave the factory and return to marriage and family roles in the home. The Selective Service Act of 1942 contained a tacit assumption, because it guaranteed veterans the jobs they had held before the war, that women would want to go home. Frances Perkins, secretary of labor, insisted that their war effort was only temporary and they would return to the home when men came back. However, this did not acknowledge that many women had to work and that, for the first time, they had been paid reasonable wages. Many did not want to give this up. In a UAW poll asking if women would work after the war if jobs were available, 98.5 percent of single women, 100 percent of widows, and 68.7 of married women said yes.[88]

Unions helped little in retention of women's jobs after the war: In Detroit, for example, the AFL–CIO had between 300,000 and 350,000 women members by war's end. Yet when layoffs occurred, 41 percent of men laid off were offered new jobs at 8.5 cents lower per hour (the average wage of Willow Run workers was $1.23 an hour), but less than 3 percent of women were offered other jobs, and those who were lost more than 48 cents per hour. Layoffs for women were always higher than for men, with the old excuses of "heavy work," late hours, and women needed at home. A clause in a contract between United Steel and Wire and Local 704 said,

> When a man is the youngest employee in a classification involved in a reduction of force . . . he shall be permitted to bump any woman filling a job designated as a man's job . . . in case of plant-wide layoffs, women employees holding duly designated men's jobs will be laid off before any man employee. . . . A woman employee is not permitted to bump a man employee off a man's job.[89]

Women protested and picketed, but in general to no avail. In the two months following VJ Day (Victory over Japan), women were laid off at rates of 75 per 1,000, twice that of men. By the end of 1946, 2 million women had been fired from heavy industry, and some companies reinstated old policies of not hiring women.[90]

In 1946 the Women's Bureau held a conference on union contract provisions affecting women. The majority of the recommendations were for equal treatment rather than protection of women because of their "frailty." The bureau held that pregnancy should not be grounds for dismissal and that women returning after maternity leave be given their former jobs at current salary. Job classification and wage rates should be set by job, not by sex, and no new employees should be hired if women were available for upgrading.[91] A 1947 bureau report showed that 1 million fewer women were employed, and that although half were actively seeking work, there was an obvious shift to unemployment insurance and later to the welfare rolls. By 1953, 1 million women were seeking jobs, of whom African Americans made up the largest percentage.[92]

Women as workers faced increasing hostility after the war, fired by the growth of the social sciences and the social work profession's casework emphasis. The new information on child development, the Freudian interpretation of the roles of women and psychosexual development, and an intense concentration on the problem of juvenile delinquency blamed absent mothers for all kinds of problems. "Latchkey children"—given keys to get into their homes while their mothers were at work—were investigated by welfare departments, juvenile justice systems, and the growing number of family and children's agencies. The family and children's agencies, though unlikely to serve poor children whose mothers had to work, researched the problems of juvenile delinquents in terms of parent–child relationships and the "mental illness" of women who worked (that is, took on male roles). Their conclusions were very useful to a government trying to reduce the labor force and to men returning from war to their previous roles, indicating that the working mother was an affront to the rights of children for "good parenting" and the American way of life.

Although it is likely that the concentration on juvenile delinquency came from new reporting, new casework theories, and the fact that young people could not get jobs because veterans were returning to employment in a time of economic downswing, the whole issue was used to influence women to return home and participate in the baby boom. Women who entered male fields after the war—law, mathematics, physics, business, industry, technology—were discriminated against[93] because the "psychic maladjustment" that made them want to leave home made them poor business risks. Fewer than half of both men and women believed that women should have equal chance at jobs, even if they were sole breadwinners.[94] It was said that

> feminism represented a neurotic reaction to male dominance and a deep illness which encouraged women to reject their natural sex-based instincts.[95]

This made the case against women in the workforce on moral, political, economic, and "scientific" grounds.

Three million fewer women were employed in 1946 than at wartime peak, and between 1945 and 1947, 2.7 million women were removed from industrial employment.[96] However, by 1950 female employment neared its top wartime level. Need for money was still the main reason women worked: In 1947, 31 percent of all families still had incomes below $2,000 and 50 percent earned less than $3,000.

The Resurgence of Social Work

Shortly after the war, the economy began to pick up because of the massive backlog of demands for consumer goods. The return of veterans; the almost forcible reduction in the female labor force; and the ideology that women ought to be in the home, with babies and supported by husbands, led to an increase in marriages and a baby boom that meant a new market. Soon after the war ended, the birthrate reached a high of 26.6 births per 1,000.[97] As people could afford to move into the suburbs because of G.I. Bill home loans, the isolation of women from one another began, contributing to their loneliness and depression. Moreover, as they moved far from their mothers, the normal channels for learning about homemaking and child care were closed off. Once more, social professionals took over, and all "failures"—misbehaving or unhappy children—were the mothers' fault.

Treatment continued to be skewed by the idea of woman as dependent, nonassertive, and emotionally immature. Women who wanted to work were judged mentally ill, or worse, to be destroying their families and children. Although social workers believed deviance arose from the environment, the environment in question was not social and economic conditions, but home, early training, and how children dealt with authority, especially around the learning of toilet training and eating. These produced different disorders that could be "cured" by social work treatment.

The fear of juvenile delinquency began to alter the national consciousness as well as that of the profession. Between 1940 and 1960, the number of cases rose from 200,000 to 813,000, and Cloward and Ohlin's idea of a "deviant subculture," in which children learned criminal behavior from their peers, began to obfuscate the structural and economic reasons for delinquency. The profession of social work expanded and grew on this new emphasis of mental illness—called an epidemic—and by 1955 some 558,000 people resided in psychiatric hospitals, with about 200,000 new admissions a year.[98] Mental health clinics had 300,000 more clients, and the community mental health program began.

In addition to juvenile delinquency, social work's interest turned to drug abuse. During the first two decades of the century, alcohol consumption had been the "morality issue" of social welfare. This ended with Prohibition, but Prohibition itself created two massive organizations devoted to crime management: organized crime, which provided alcohol to those who wanted it, and enforcers of the Prohibition amendment, the bulk of whom were in the Treasury Department as "revenuers." When Prohibition was rescinded in 1933, both organizations turned to the business of newly illegal drugs (marijuana, cocaine, and heroin). Where previously drug abuse had been a medical problem, with relatively low costs for society, now it was a legal problem and a mental health problem, and the costs skyrocketed.

The number of social workers expanded in the 1930s from 31,000 to 70,000. The number of professional organizations also expanded: By 1930 they included the American Association of Medical Social Workers, the National Association of School Social Workers, the American Association of Psychiatric Social Workers, and the American Association of Social Workers. Members of these organizations made up less than 25 percent of social workers; the remainder were not affiliated or were in public assistance jobs and organizations.[99] By 1939, the American Association of Schools of Social Work required two-year Master of Social Work programs. In 1946 the National Council on Social Work Education was formed, and in 1952 it became the accrediting body for American and Canadian schools of social work until 1970, when Canada set up its own council.

Fees for service and private practice began: In 1943, Jewish Family Services in New York began to charge fees, and other family agencies followed suit with sliding fee scales. Now community centers and organizations for young people such as the Girl Scouts and YWCAs set up paid "memberships" for participation. The profession moved away from service and into support by middle- and upper-class clientele. Though parents could learn about child development and the skills of parenting from experts, lower-class clientele were not welcome, for they were not "treatable." By 1960, 9 percent of social work clients were in the upper socioeconomic class and 48 percent were in the middle class.

Group work practice was professionally recognized in the 1930s. Early settlement work led the way to its development, but group work developed primarily from the work of Mary Follett (1868–1933). Follett, a theorist in the field of organization and bureaucracy, adapted Frederick Taylor's scientific management to humanistic management. From 1908 to 1920, she developed community centers within neighborhood schools and worked for minimum wage legislation. Her 1924 book *Creative Experience* detailed her theory of *humanistic management* and posited a new form of democracy based on spontaneous organization, or grass-roots development through the creative interaction of people and groups. Group work was legitimated with the Association of Group Workers and the Social Work Research Association (1949). Near the same time, the Association for the Study of Community Organization was also formed, based on Follett's theories and settlement house experiences.[100]

While social work continued on its course, a split arose. On one side were the proponents of psychosocial casework, defended by such eminent social workers as Gordon Hamilton and Florence Hollis. On the other were "functionalists," who believed that although psychosocial investigation might be interesting, social work practice belonged in the here and now, and psychosocial practice's demand for long-term relationships, differential diagnosis, and setting of long- and short-term goals controlled rather than served clients. Among functionalists, Jessie Taft argued for a process model of helping, and Ruth Smalley argued against client control. Virginia Robinson's presentation, "A Changing Psychology in Social Work," written in 1930, was heavily influenced by Otto Rank and challenged Freud's paternalistic models. Robinson said that casework should focus on the relationship between client and environment, the client should be central, and the worker–client relationship was to strengthen rather than control clients. John Ehrenreich says,

> The functional school sustained a serious and coherent effort at dealing with the welfare state and its implications for social work theory, practice, and professional status. . . . It sought to rethink radically the relationship between the social environment and the individual. But it never convinced more than a minority.[101]

The debate between the functional school and psychosocial casework grew bitter and threatened to end all the professional gains made. Although the debate has never really ended, Helen Perlman's eclectic problem-solving model, which focused on systems and could incorporate either type of casework, helped to bridge the gap and reunited, however uneasily, the casework profession.

Reorganizing Federal Social Welfare Efforts

After the war, President Truman asked former President Hoover to head a commission to study the federal bureaucracy and make recommendations. From this study, the Federal Security Agency and several other domestic agencies were formed into a single cabinet-level department, the Department of Health, Education, and Welfare (HEW),[102] which then housed the Social Security Administration. Some new legislation was passed: the national school lunch program of 1946, the Housing Act of 1949, a special milk program for poor children in 1954. The Housing Act authorized 135,000 public housing units per year, but only 25,000 to 40,000 per year were built in the following decade. The houses built under this act, the public housing act, and the G.I. Bill promoted the movement of middle-class whites to the suburbs, while people of color and poor people moved into the central cities. Most social legislation other than for veterans took the form of incrementing existent programs after the war, including new provisions added to laws, expanded eligibility, and increased payments in both public assistance and social insurance.

The American Dream

After World War II, flush with the victory of democracy over fascism, veterans returned to a G.I. Bill of Rights that promised them their former jobs, higher education, and new homes—under the Veteran's Administration (VA). They stepped back into good jobs newly enhanced by unionism or could realize their dreams of education and profession. Even groups formerly discriminated against benefited: They had their taste of good wages supported by unions and could develop more stable home lives based on their better incomes. The middle class expanded, and it seemed that the American Dream was coming true.

The boom in consumerism produced by new higher wages and the move to the suburbs was joined by the "war business." "Corporate statesmen"—leaders of national corporations appointed to public offices during the War—grew in influence as the economy swung upward. What was good for business was assumed good for the nation, and war was extremely profitable—war materiel either became obsolete or was blown up. These business leaders, along with government officials and war advisors, came to be known as the "military-industrial complex." Support of war in other countries, in the guise of "saving the world from communism," became a goal of our corporate-influenced government, and wars backed by the United States exploded—in emerging countries in the Near

East, South and Central America, and the Far East. A "shadow government" began to dictate foreign policy for the United States.

Conclusion: Moving Toward the Future

As the nation moved into the 1950s, a new configuration to life and to social welfare began. The social legislation of the 1930s and the nation's adaptation to the war had created a welfare state, however minimal its provisions, for most of the needy groups in society. Poverty was changing: Now the workforce had some power to demand living wages, but groups without the capability for unionization were little better off than before. People of color, inspired by their earning power during the war and the advances they had achieved with little if any help from social institutions, were also demanding rights.

However, backlash soon emerged in race riots, the communist hunting of the McCarthy era, and the recalcitrance of both county relief and the Bureaus of Social Aid to extend benefits to those who were eligible but who were not "morally correct." During the next decade, the profession of social work would have little to do with issues of reform but would continue to firm up its psychological intervention techniques. Although researchers were well aware of the problems of people oppressed because of poverty, race, and sex, their work had little impact on society's orientation to the poor—still blamed for their poverty— or the distressed, now mentally ill rather than disadvantaged.

The children who reached adulthood during the 1950s have been called the Silent Generation, yet this may be only in comparison to the eruption of mass social movements in the 1940s. Surely the problems were there, and recognized, throughout the 1940s and 1950s: the unrest of people of color, the baby boom, the white flight to the suburbs, and growing urban unrest. Perhaps this generation taught its children that life did not have to be unfair. People of color and women for the first time had been treated equally, and they learned despite the postwar attempts to suppress them. They had money and could earn more, protected by fair employment laws. They became educated and vocal, and taught their children that their oppression was not only immoral but illegal. Automobiles gave them physical mobility and television widened their perceptions to the world rather than the neighborhood. The accent on education helped them to question not only local political situations, but those of the world.

The causes of gender and civil rights were nurtured during World War II, and many of the changes in social welfare sprang from changes during the war and its aftermath. The G.I. Bill made money available to a great number of people and created a new middle class. In addition, new technologies made the world smaller in both physical and mental senses, adding to the immediacy of new social welfare programs. The profession of social work had altered nearly completely from the provision of income maintenance for the poor to an accent on mental health for the middle class, and social workers had become professionals rather than reform voices crying in the wilderness. New services to children, veterans, and the middle class; new research into developmental theories and the knowledge bases of sociology, education, psychology; and an elaboration of skills and techniques via social casework and group work legitimated the profession as a part of American society.

Study Questions

1. What were the causes of the Depression? What effect did the Depression have on the rich? On the poor? On women? On minority people?

2. What were the underlying values of Roosevelt's Grand Design?

3. What effect did the Depression and the Grand Design have on the provision of social welfare? Explain the split between public and private agencies.

4. How did the profession of social work react to the onset of World War II? What were the changes it made in services?

5. What was the status of women before, during, and after the war? How did this reflect on the provision of social welfare services?

6. What happened to minority people before, during, and after the war, and what consequences did this have for civil rights?

7. Explain how the G.I Bill changed the face of the middle class.

Notes

1. June Axinn and Herman Levin, *Social Welfare: A History of the American Response to Need*, 2d ed. (New York: Harper & Row, 1982), p. 175.

2. Ibid., p. 176.

3. John Ehrenreich, *The Altruistic Imagination: A History of Social Work and Social Policy in the United States* (Ithaca: Cornell University Press, 1985), p. 86.

4. Thomas R. Dye and L. Harmon Zeigler, *The Irony of Democracy* (Belmont, CA: Wadsworth Publishing, 1970), p. 83.

5. Axinn and Levin, *Social Welfare*, p. 192.

6. Carole Hymowitz and Michaele Weissman, *A History of Women in America* (New York: Bantam Books, 1980), p. 303.

7. Frances Fox Piven and Richard Cloward, *Regulating the Poor* (New York: Random House, 1971).

8. Hymowitz and Weissman, *History of Women*, p. 307.

9. Alice Kessler-Harris, *Out to Work: A History of Wage-Earning Women in the United States* (New York: Oxford University Press), 1982, pp. 257–260.

10. Ibid., p. 264.

11. Axinn and Levin, *Social Welfare*, p. 187.

12. Ibid., p. 202.

13. Kessler-Harris, *Out to Work*, p. 256.

14. Axinn and Levin, *Social Welfare*, p. 181.

15. From Albert U. Romasco, *The Poverty of Abundance—Hoover, the Nation, and Depression* (New York: Oxford University Press, 1965), p. 147. In Gerald Handel, *Social Welfare in Western Society* (New York: Random House, 1982), p. 134.

16. Axinn and Levin, *Social Welfare*, p. 190.

17. Ehrenreich, *Altruistic Imagination*, p. 87.

18. Joe R. Feagin, *Racial and Ethnic Relations*, 3d ed. (Englewood Cliffs, NJ: Prentice Hall, 1989), p. 280.

19. Ehrenreich, *Altruistic Imagination*, p. 88.

20. Axinn and Levin, *Social Welfare*, p. 189.

21. Ehrenreich, *Altruistic Imagination*, p. 89.

22. Ibid., p. 93.

23. Ibid., p. 95.

24. Ibid., p. 97.

25. Dye and Zeigler, *The Irony of Democracy*, p. 83.

26. Joseph Heffernan, *Introduction to Social Welfare Policy* (Itasca, IL: F.E. Peacock Publishers, 1979), p. 194.

27. Axinn and Levin, *Social Welfare*, p. 194.

28. Ehrenreich, *Altruistic Imagination*, p. 96.

29. Axinn and Levin, *Social Welfare*, p. 214.

30. Ibid., p. 204.

31. While Heffernan, *Introduction to Social Welfare Policy*, p. 199, says that all benefits were to be paid in cash, Axinn and Levin, *Social Welfare*, p. 214, say that most often benefits had to be worked off on public property.

32. Axinn and Levin, *Social Welfare*, p. 184.

33. Ibid.

34. Ibid., p. 185.

35. Ehrenreich, *Altruistic Imagination*, p. 93.

36. Axinn and Levin, *Social Welfare*, p. 186.

37. Ibid.

38. Kessler-Harris, *Out to Work*, p. 270.

39. Gerald Handel, *Social Welfare in Western Society*, p. 136.

40. David Macarov, *Work and Welfare: The Unholy Alliance* (Beverly Hills, CA: Sage Publications, 1980), p. 209.

41. Axinn and Levin, *Social Welfare*, p. 181.

42. Beulah R. Compton, *Introduction to Social Welfare and Social Work: Structure, Function, and Process* (Homewood, IL: The Dorsey Press, 1980), p. 414.

43. Axinn and Levin, *Social Welfare*, p. 180.

44. Ibid., p. 182.

45. William Jay Jacobs, *Women in American History* (Encino, CA: Glencoe Publishing, 1976), p. 238.

46. William H. Chafe, "Eleanor Roosevelt," in Linda K. Kerber and Jane DeHart Mathews (eds.), *Women's America* (New York: Oxford University Press, 1982), pp. 344–353; and in Robert McHenry (ed.), *Famous American Women: A Biographical Dictionary from Colonial Times to the Present* (New York: Dover Publications, 1980), p. 354.

47. Winifred Bell, *Contemporary Social Welfare* (New York: Macmillan, 1983), p. 7.

48. Michael B. Katz, *Poverty and Policy in American History* (New York: Academic Press, 1983), p. 221.

49. Samuel Mencher, *From Poor Laws to Poverty Programs* (Pittsburgh: University of Pittsburgh Press, 1967), p. 306.

50. F. D. Roosevelt, "Message to Congress," June 8, 1934, 73rd Congress 2nd Session (Washington, D.C.: United States Government Printing Office, 1934), pp. 10, 770. Quoted in Mencher, *Poor Law to Poverty Programs*, p. 333.

51. *New York Review of Books*, February 28, 1986, p. 7, reviewing Gosta Esping-Anderson, Martin Rein, and Lee Rainwater (eds.), *Stagnation and Renewal in Social Policy* (New York: M.E. Sharpe, 1986).

52. Andrew W. Dobelstein, *Politics, Economics, and Public Welfare* (Englewood Cliffs, NJ: Prentice Hall, 1980), p. 29.

53. Ehrenreich, *Altruistic Imagination*, p. 99.

54. Jeffrey Galper, *Social Work Practice: A Radical Perspective* (Englewood Cliffs, NJ: Prentice Hall, 1980), p. 77.

55. Harry Hopkins, quoted in Robert E. Sherwood, *Roosevelt and Hopkins* (New York: Harper & Row, 1948), p. 297.

56. Axinn and Levin, *Social Welfare*, p. 220.

57. Ralph Dolgoff and Donald Feldstein, *Understanding Social Welfare,* 2d ed. (New York: Longman Press, 1984), pp. 180–181.

58. Harry L. Hopkins, in Josephine Chapman Brown, *Public Relief, 1929–39* (New York: Henry Holt, 1940), p. 396. Quoted in Handel, *Social Welfare in Western Society*, p. 138.

59. Axinn and Levin, *Social Welfare*, p. 202.

60. Macarov, *Work and Welfare*, p. 52.

61. Ehrenreich, *Altruistic Imagination*, p. 111.

62. Galper, *Social Work Practice*, p. 169.

63. Ehrenreich, *Altruistic Imagination*, p. 118.

64. Ibid., p. 207.

65. Peter Day, *Social Work and Social Control* (London: Tavistock Publications, 1981), p. 86.

66. Feagin, *Racial and Ethnic Relations*, p. 329.

67. "Italians: Acknowledge Our Internment," *Quad-City Times* (Davenport, IA), October 27, 2000, p. 3A.

68. Feagin, *Racial and Ethnic Relations*, pp. 329–330.

69. Axinn and Levin, *Social Welfare*, p. 231.

70. Ibid., p. 135.

71. Norman Cousins, "Will Women Lose Their Jobs?" *Current History and Forum*, Vol. 41 (Sept. 1939), p. 14. Quoted in Kessler-Harris, *Out to Work*, p. 246.

72. Kessler-Harris, *Out to Work*, p. 276.

73. *Fortune* poll, cited in Sheila Tobias and Lisa Anderson, "Rosie the Riveter: Demobilization and the Female Labor Force," in Kerber and Mathews, *Women's America*, p. 299.

74. Ibid., p. 357.

75. Ibid., pp. 354 ff.

76. Kessler-Harris, *Out to Work*, p. 278.

77. Hymowitz and Weissman, *History of Women*, p. 313.

78. Kessler-Harris, *Out to Work*, p. 291.

79. Tobias and Anderson, "Rosie the Riveter," p. 369.

80. Axinn and Levin, *Social Welfare*, p. 230.

81. Ehrenreich, *Altruistic Imagination*, p. 99.

82. Compton, *Introduction to Social Welfare*, p. 438.

83. Ibid., p. 440.

84. Discussed in Feagin, *Racial and Ethnic Relations*, p. 229, and Lerone Bennett, Jr., *Before the Mayflower: A History of the Negro in America 1619–1964,* rev. ed. (Chicago: Johnson Publishing Co., 1966), p. 304.

85. Axinn and Levin, *Social Welfare*, p. 242.

86. Ibid.

87. Ibid., p. 243.

88. Ibid., p. 244.

89. Tobias and Anderson, "Rosie the Riveter," p. 361.

90. Ibid., p. 364.

91. Hymowitz and Weissman, *History of Women*, p. 313.

92. Tobias and Anderson, "Rosie the Riveter," p. 371.

93. Ibid.

94. Kessler-Harris, *Out to Work*, p. 297.

95. Chafe, "Eleanor Roosevelt," p. 443. Quoted in Compton, *Introduction to Social Welfare.*

96. Ehrenreich, *Altruistic Imagination*, p. 147.

97. Axinn and Levin, *Social Welfare*, p. 233.
98. Ehrenreich, *Altruistic Imagination*, p. 153.
99. Compton, *Introduction to Social Welfare*, p. 143.
100. McHenry, *Famous American Women*, p. 136.
101. Ehrenreich, *Altruistic Imagination*, p. 135.
102. Dobelstein, *Politics and Welfare*, pp. 84–85.

10

Civil and Welfare Rights in the New Reform Era

After the upheavals of the 1930s and 1940s, the nation entered the next decade almost with a sigh of relief. War hero Dwight D. Eisenhower was elected president in 1952, and on the surface, prosperity reigned. However, there were troublesome undercurrents. First there was the fear that the Soviets would obtain the atomic bomb and threaten the peace of the world. Next came a backlash against the Social Security Acts as a "communist plot," and a new red scare exacerbated by the Korean conflict. Finally, there was an increasing ideological frustration that the promises of equality of the 1930s and 1940s were still unfulfilled in the fifties.

On Truman's order, the atomic bomb eliminated Hiroshima and Nagasaki even though surrender talks were in progress. The Chinese communists under Mao Tse-Tung flexed their muscles in Korea and defeated U.S. forces at the 38th parallel. Renewed fear of communism led to the establishment of the Federal Employee Act and the House Un-American Activities Committee (1947), under leadership of Senator Joseph McCarthy, who charged the Roosevelt and Truman administrations with "twenty years of treason" because of their social programs. The committee launched a hunt for communists, and the Internal Security Act (McCarran Act) passed Congress, establishing six concentration camps to house political prisoners and allowing imprisonment without trial for those suspected of treason.

By 1953, a great number of dissidents were in jail or in hiding, for everyone was suspect. Thousands of teachers, social workers, journalists, screenwriters, government workers—guilty of usually nothing more than organizing unions, belonging to the communist party during the wartime alliance of the United States and Russia, attending a radical meeting, or supporting liberal causes—lost their jobs for refusal to cooperate with investigatory committees. Under pressure of investigation, the labor movement pulled back from radical action, liberals renounced their social programs, libraries removed controversial books, and books teaching communism or socialism were banned. Ethel and Julius Rosenberg were executed for giving the secret of the atomic bomb to Russia. Schools, universities, and many public organizations required loyalty oaths as criteria for employment. As welfare workers resisted the label of "soft" or "pink," eligibility regulations tightened and benefits were withdrawn from recipients.[1]

By 1954, McCarthy's accusations became so outrageous that he was censured by the Senate and removed from the committee. However, by then Federal Bureau of Investigation procedures were firmly in place. Anyone voicing differing opinions might be investigated. Great numbers of dossiers went into FBI files, including those of civil rights activists such as Dr. Martin Luther King, Jr.

Roosevelt's emergency relief measures during the Depression, new educational opportunities, unionization, and veterans' benefits opened up new resources to nonwhite minorities. During the war, they earned wages competitive with white people to support their families. Now they were unwilling to give up those gains. New political channels opened to them through voting, their presence in unions, and legislation and court cases that supported their citizenship. However, their frustration and that of the poor was invisible, for it did not affect the lives of the upwardly mobile middle class. Tension grew as those who had shared, however briefly, in economic equality in unions, labor, and the war effort taught their children to expect equality. The struggle became ideological as well as economic.

Unionization and veterans' benefits had empowered white laborers in the 1930s; now those winnowed out of success—women, the aging, and people of color—began to fight. Television added a new dimension: "Around the world" became next door as Americans watched famines, wars, riots, oppression, and death over evening meals. We saw people dying in Korea, the justice system manhandling peaceful demonstrators, and poverty in a society of affluence. We saw war becoming the basis for economic prosperity: From 1945 to 1970, the federal government spent 69 percent of its total budget on defense ($1 trillion). In the Kennedy–Johnson era, the defense budget increased dramatically, and by the end of the 1960s, 10 percent of all jobs were tied to the defense budget.[2] We saw young people's lives traded for monetary profit and foreign countries invaded in the name of economic prosperity. And we began to ask why.

As we found answers, social revolution erupted. Students rioted and people of minority groups staged demonstrations demanding equality. Women, joining civil rights groups, saw class and race hatred compounded for them by sexism. Welfare and economic rights became intimately related with civil rights in the new ideological struggle. Idealists and pragmatic politicians developed new social programs and expanded civil rights: Presidents John F. Kennedy and Lyndon B. Johnson joined the battle, claiming that the United States, having the power to create a great society, should do so. But the bubble of idealism lasted less than a decade. The internal political stresses of the War on Poverty and the disastrous and expensive Vietnam War led to a conservative backlash that undermined the 1960s-inspired movements, and all too soon welfare cutbacks and civil repression returned.

The State of the Nation Under Eisenhower

Dwight D. Eisenhower became president in 1952, a respected war hero in a time of reasonable prosperity for middle and upper classes. The gross national product rose from $100 billion in 1940 to $286.5 billion by 1950, and by 1960 it was $400 billion.[3] Unemployment reached only 4.5 percent in the early 1950s, and although it rose to nearly 7 percent in 1958, it returned to 5.7 percent in the next decade.[4] A series of mild recessions occurred between 1961 and 1963, and nearly 2 million people were added to the unemployment rolls. By 1960, almost 40 million people, or 22.4 percent of the population, lived below the poverty line of $3,022 for a family of four.[5] Urban unemployment was exacerbated as a displaced farm population moved to the cities. Between 1940 and 1969, the number of farms owned and operated by African Americans decreased by 87 percent, from 680,000 to 90,000.[6] Within three decades, 16 million white people and 4 million African Americans moved to the cities, and by 1950, 64 percent of the U.S. population was urban.[7]

With the population changes, patterns of family life altered as drastically as during the Industrial Revolution. New middle-class families began to move to the suburbs, leaving inner cities with a poor and increasingly African American population. Consumerism boomed as more people could afford a "home in the country," and the baby boom meant even more buying. By 1960, the U.S. birthrate nearly equaled that of India. The age of marriage lowered: 14 million women were engaged by the time they were seventeen (1960) and the average age at marriage for women was below twenty. Sixty percent of all college women dropped out to marry before they earned their degrees.[8]

Although consumerism and mobility increased material goods, "personal good" suffered. The community bonds of family and friends ruptured, and the separation of poor from wealthy, white from nonwhite, grew. Young white mothers, in the suburbs far from their older women relatives, became isolated and depressed. Mental health and parenting programs overtly aimed at helping women find happiness as wives and mothers. Poor women were increasingly defined as mentally ill or deviant on two counts: poverty and "unwomanliness" because they worked. "Pockets of mental illness" were found in low-income areas, especially after the Joint Commission on Mental Illness and Health reported in 1960 that stress-creating situations such as poor health, poor housing, unemployment, and poverty should be considered in planning for mental health.

After World War II, emotional problems took on new meaning. Where *mental illness* had been stigmatized and hidden, now *mental health* became the right of every American. The social work profession argued that all social problems could be solved with casework treatment and psychoanalytic techniques, and the power of the profession increased synergistically with new mental health funding. Two innovations moved the focus of treatment from mental hospitals to the community: The use of tranquilizers became widespread after 1954, and the federal government declared mental illness a disability, making patients eligible for up to half their community care under OASDI. A study by Alfred Stanton and Morris Schwartz (1954) demonstrated that the mental hospital itself made people sicker, and the exodus to community care began. Despite more people being admitted to mental hospitals, the mental hospital population showed a definite decrease by 1957.[9]

Tranquilizer use was particularly problematic for women. Any doctor could prescribe them for any reason, and women were increasingly vulnerable as they became more isolated and depressed. Sex roles predicted they would be happy with their suburban homes and families, and those who were not were often labeled mentally ill and in need of medication. Tranquilizers became a panacea for unhappiness, and their misuse often resulted in emotional dependency, addiction, or ongoing and irreversible physical or emotional damage. The mental health movement and the excessive use of tranquilizers also put a great number of people under surveillance and paved the way for a more subtle behavioral control.

Social Programs in the 1950s

Few new social programs were instituted under Eisenhower, but eligibility and benefit levels of public assistance were expanded. Theorists and researchers concluded that, except for some "pockets of poverty" and personal "case poverty," America's poverty problem was solved. Concern for the aged provided a constant pressure, and conferences on aging in 1950 and 1951 kept the nation aware of their need for services. Private benefit plans expanded under pressure from unions: By 1962 their expenditures were more than 11 percent of the total expended for workers' pensions and health care ($9.8 billion).

Social Insurance

Increasing numbers of people became covered under social insurance until, by 1961, 90 percent of the potential population was covered.[10] By 1950, wives or divorced mothers with entitled children—to age eighteen, or twenty-one if still in school—were included in survivors' grants. In 1956 disability insurance was added to OASI (now OASDI), and mentally ill people were classified as disabled. In 1957, people disabled before the age of eighteen became entitled to their own, rather than survivor's, benefits.[11] The age of eligibility was reduced to sixty-two for retiring and sixty for dependent spouses (age fifty if disabled). Dependent spouse survivors' benefits were increased to 82.5 percent of the deceased worker's entitlement at age sixty-two, or for young spouses caring for children, to 75 percent of the entitlement plus an equal amount for the children.[12] The income subject to social insurance taxes reached $3,600 in 1951 and was $7,800 by 1967, with a tax increase from 2 percent to 6.65 percent.[13]

Public Assistance

During this same period, while costs for social insurance increased from $47.0 billion in 1950 to $123.9 billion in 1960,[14] public assistance expenditures increased from \$2.3 billion in 1950 to \$3.3 billion ten years later. Although the number of aged recipients (OAA) decreased from 2.8 million in 1950 to 2.2 million in 1965,[15] numbers of recipients on the whole increased by 13 percent. The AFDC population boomed along with the baby boom. By 1960, AFDC rolls had increased to more than 3 million people, and expenditures by 92 percent to more than \$1 billion. During 1961, the first year under Kennedy, the number of AFDC recipients rose another half million, and expenditures rose another \$2 million.[16] However, structural rather than personal reasons caused the increase:

- Simple population growth, especially with the baby boom, accounted for many of the new cases. Between 1940 and 1970 the nation's population increased over 50 percent and the number of children under age fourteen increased by 80 percent.
- The number of divorces doubled between 1935 and 1970. Whereas in the 1940s 60 to 70 percent of families were eligible because of death or incapacitation of the father, by 1971, nearly three-fourths of all applicants were separated, divorced, or unmarried, and 5 percent of fathers had deserted.[17]
- The out-of-wedlock birthrate tripled between the beginning of World War II and 1968, from one in twenty-five births to one in ten. Of the fathers absent from home, 28 percent were not married to mothers of children being served.
- Legislation and court decisions extended coverage to needy children without regard to the marital status of their parents. In 1950, in addition to adult caretakers of dependent children, states could also choose to include incapacitated breadwinners in grants (AFDC-I). In 1961 states could choose to add unemployed parents to the rolls (AFDC-UP), although only half did so (the family was dropped when the breadwinner worked more than 100 hours per month).[18] Thus, parents and nonworking adults became part of the AFDC population. To society, this meant that women were "rewarded" for not having a husband's support and men were "rewarded" for not having jobs. Two of the strongest values in society were violated.
- Ideas about employability changed. One reason for the Social Security Act's ADC program was to remove women from labor force competition with men. Another was the rationale that a mother could care for her children more cheaply and more competently than could day care or institutionalization. But wives and mothers worked during and after the war, so AFDC became increasingly difficult to justify on those grounds.[19]
- The great displacement of agricultural workers to the cities added thousands of women, many of them African American, to AFDC rolls, and racist hostility toward the program increased.

To "contain" AFDC, states restricted eligibility, reduced need levels, restricted residency requirements, and tried to embarrass recipients and new applicants by publishing their names or closing entire caseloads, forcing the needy to reapply. Fewer applications were accepted: In 1948, 66 percent were accepted, compared to only 54 percent in 1958.[20] Especially in the South, families might be put off public assistance when it was assumed they could find work in the fields. Mandell says,

> The welfare system has been used as an instrument of economic exploitation by communities and states that needed cheap labor. This has been especially true in the southern states. For example, the farm policy adopted by Arkansas in 1953 required able-bodied mothers and older children to accept employment whenever it was available. This policy was responsible for 38.6 to 58.6 percent of all closings between [19]53 and [19]60.[21]

A classic example occurred in 1961 when the city manager of Newburgh, New York, closed all cases and allowed them to reopen only under grossly stigmatizing conditions: Applicants had to prove they had applied for city jobs and had not left other jobs voluntarily, and they had to reapply at police offices. All new cases had to be reviewed by the city manager and active ones by the city attorney. All able-bodied men had to work and vouchers rather than cash were given. Upon appeal, the state welfare board would not allow the new regulations, but the months they were in effect were painful for many.[22]

The greatest hostility was directed against women because of their "sexual immorality," the "great numbers" of out-of-wedlock children, and, again, the implication of mothers in causing juvenile delinquency. Part was a racist attack against the burgeoning nonwhite welfare population (in 1948, 31 percent of the recipients were nonwhite, and by 1974, 48 percent were nonwhite).[23] States gave their workers wide discretion in defining the "suitability" of the home, and the higher the rolls, the more stringent the requirements became. "Suitable homes" meant homes where no out-of-wedlock children lived and women had no men friends—no "men in the house." In further refinement of dependency, "need" became lacking a "father substitute" rather than needing money. Thus, children of women with men friends were not considered needy even if the friends contributed nothing economically. Violation of either suitable home or substitute parent policies, or even the accusation of such violation, could mean loss of grants.

In 1960 twenty-three states had "suitable home" rules, and such policies allowed Louisiana, in 1960, to remove 22,000 out-of-wedlock children from the rolls, 95 percent of them African American.[24] In Arkansas, Governor Faubus proudly asserted that "8,000 illegitimate children were taken off the welfare roles during my term of office." In Florida, AFDC applicants with unsuitable homes were told to place their children in foster care or institutions or face court action to have them taken away. Only 186 of 2,908 families complied; the rest withdrew their welfare applications,[25] which is what the department really wanted anyway. Handler says,

> Sexual promiscuity, men in the house, divorce, remarriage, and so forth . . . patterns of sexual behavior outside of conventional moral standards are tolerated by the public as long as the public is not called upon to support those who engage in such activities. The poor must stay married or become celibate. . . . As the price of

survival, the poor are required to engage in certain behavior not required of the rest of society or to forego amenities and pleasures enjoyed by others.[26]

AFDC workers were "investigators" whose purpose was to find ways to reduce rolls. They investigated employers, banks, credit agencies, and often neighbors; such a practice

> assumes dishonesty ... and applicants ... [must prove their] statements. The punitive administration of intake is, ostensibly, to protect the public by excluding applicants who do not qualify. It also protects the welfare rolls by using stigma as a rationing device.[27]

Investigations could take place at any time of the day or night, often with the cooperation of police. Workers "raided" women's homes looking for evidence such as men's shoes under the bed or clothes in the closet and assets that would not be purchasable on AFDC grants. These "midnight raids" continued even after the Supreme Court declared them unconstitutional in 1967. Investigators also kept information from recipients: amounts of grants, rights to fair hearings, and other programs. Clients asking for their rights were perceived as "challenging" and might lose their grants or their children—risks they could not afford. Although every kind of documentation was needed to qualify for AFDC, disqualification required very little, perhaps only an anonymous report from a neighbor.

Suitable home rules, farm work provisions, and residency requirements were disproportionately applied to African American families moving north.[28] The removal of grants from the homes of out-of-wedlock children halted in 1961 when Arthur Fleming, secretary of the Department of Health, Education, and Welfare under Kennedy, ruled that support could not be removed unless the welfare department found new "suitable homes" for the children. "Substitute father" or "man in the house" requirements were eliminated in 1968, under the *King v. King* decision, and residence requirements ended in 1969 with the *Shapiro v. Thompson* decision.

Civil Rights Before Kennedy

In 1948 the Dixiecrats in Congress—Southern Democrats led by Strom Thurmond—successfully challenged the Democratic party's support of civil rights when it defeated Truman's bill to reestablish the Fair Employment Practices Commission, eliminate segregation in public transportation, and outlaw poll taxes. Hostility to civil rights continued throughout Eisenhower's administration (although a federal antilynching law was passed in 1951). Segregation was deeply ingrained in both North and South: seventeen states and Washington, D.C., required it, and four states—Arizona, Kansas, New Mexico, and Wyoming—authorized it at local option.

Economic and political oppression meant that the nonwhite median income was 51 percent that of white families in 1947 and 56 percent in 1962. In 1952, 5.4 percent of African Americans were unemployed, compared to 3.1 percent of white workers, and in 1970, African American workers had 7.2 percent unemployment versus 4.5 percent white unemployment.[29] Generally, African American unemployment remained double that of white unemployment in spite of the poverty programs of the late 1960s.

The NAACP's policy of taking grievances to court increased the legal rights of people of minorities. Thurgood Marshall, Walter White, and William Hastie led the battles against segregation, along with Charles Hamilton Houston, Vice Dean of Howard University Law School.[30] In three court cases in 1950, the Court struck down segregation in schools and dining cars, saying that unequal rights were more than physical facilities, and in 1954 it ruled in *Brown v. Topeka Board of Education* that separate educational facilities were inherently unequal. This overturned the separate-but-equal doctrine of *Plessy v. Ferguson* and became the turning point in the civil rights movement. However, it also revitalized the white backlash by the Ku Klux Klan, White Citizen's Councils, and vigilante groups.[31]

Elected police and justice officials refused to enforce the federal rulings, and African Americans realized that legal victories were not enough. In Little Rock, young people tried to enter Central High School, and as white adults attacked them, Governor Orbal Faubus proclaimed that they would never enter white schools. His resistance finally provoked President Eisenhower to send federal troops to enforce the ruling. Still, ten years after the *Brown* decision, only about 2 percent of segregated schools had been integrated, and fifteen years later almost 80 percent of African American youth were still in segregated facilities.[32] Dye and Zeigler say,

> the *Brown* decision meant nothing to the overwhelming majority of Negroes, whose frustrations were intensified by the discrepancy between the declarations of the Supreme Court and the behavior of the local officials. Legally they were victorious, but politically they were impotent, since the South stubbornly refused to abide by the decisions of the Court.[33]

Segregationists renewed social Darwinist arguments against school integration with new "scientific" proof from researchers Arthur Jensen and Richard Hernstein, among others. They argued that inherited intelligence differences among racial groups required different educational techniques and that the national IQ would be lowered by higher African American birthrates. However, the tests they used showed a white cultural bias. New tests indicate that better economic and learning environments improve test scores; for example, African American children in the North may have higher scores than white children in the South.

Militancy increased with the evidence of the ineffectiveness of court action. The Congress of Racial Equality (CORE), founded in 1942, began a series of sit-ins in the North in 1955. Black Muslims, a religious group advocating separatism, became more vocal under the charismatic Malcolm X, who led African Americans to reexamine their oppression by whites and be proud of their African heritage. However, the key to mass civil rights activity came in December 1955 in Montgomery, Alabama, when Rosa Parks, a woman who had been a political activist for many years, refused to give up her bus seat to a white man and was jailed. This triggered a decade of protests and demonstrations, beginning with a year-long municipal bus boycott led by the young minister Martin Luther King, Jr. Although King and his coworkers were subject to threats, violence, false arrest, and imprisonment, they persevered, and after thirteen months the buses were desegregated.

King was a student of the nonviolent tactics of Indian leader Mahatma Gandhi. Educated at Morehouse College, Howard University, and Boston University, he preached a new social gospel. Adding religion to resistance, he gave spiritual and civil leadership to people of color and the white liberals who fought alongside them. After the Montgomery boycott, he helped to organize the Southern Christian Leadership Conference (SCLC) in Atlanta, which became the central organizing body for passive resistance. During one of his imprisonments, King won the Nobel Peace Prize, accepting it in the name of all those working for equality.

Young people in the South became increasingly active in demonstrations and sit-ins, but there was little organization among these student groups until 1957, when Ella Baker, a graduate of Shaw University and long-time civil rights activist, organized an SCLC youth conference attended by about two hundred delegates from Southern communities in twelve states. The group subsequently met monthly to coordinate student demonstrations across the South. In 1960 it became the Student Non-Violent Coordinating Committee (SNCC) and organized demonstrations across all color, age, and income lines, with the ideals of nonviolence and passive resistance.

SNCC then organized "freedom rides"—busloads of activists going to Southern communities to register voters and support civil rights activities. In 1961 at Anniston, Alabama, the first freedom bus was burned. Later, riders in Birmingham were attacked by white mobs. By September of that year, freedom riders had worked in more than a hundred cities in twenty states. At least 70,000 students of all ethnicities participated, with 3,600 students arrested and 141 students and 58 faculty members expelled from their universities for political action.

Television brought an immediacy to civil rights as, for the first time, people far removed from such problems viewed firsthand the paradox of freedom denied in a free country, police brutalizing the innocent, and the efforts of elected officials and the police in defense of, often the cause of, violence. Through television, citizens observed the gentleness and firm resolve of Martin Luther King, Jr., and the pacifism of young people as they were beaten, set upon by police dogs, and even murdered without official response. The image of the police became for many Eugene "Bull" Connor directing firehoses and police dogs against children, women, and old men. For some, this was the end of innocence and belief in the American system. The civil rights struggle was no longer "somewhere and someone else": It was a national disgrace.

Other protests began among Native Americans, Hispanics, the young, welfare activists, and women. Most protests were modeled at first on King's nonviolent example. Social workers were far from the forefront in this movement; generally, they argued caution rather than activism.

Native Americans

In 1949 Congress began to turn Native American programs over to state governments to rid itself of the "Indian problem." In 1953 it began the process of "termination," ending federal supervision of the tribes and freeing Native Americans from government wardship. Termination gave certain states the right to overturn or replace laws of the 1934 Reorganization Act. Supporters of termination included land-hungry whites and members of Congress seeking to cut costs, along with some tribal members. Between 1954 and 1960, several dozen tribes were terminated from federal guardianship.[34]

Ostensibly, termination gave Native Americans the same privileges and responsibilities as other citizens. In fact, many necessary support programs were abandoned through termination. The problems Native Americans had are exemplified in the case of Wisconsin's Menominee tribe: The state created a county from the former reservation and immediately billed Native Americans for property taxes. They were unable to pay, and lost sanitation services, police and fire protection, and highway maintenance. Their tax base was too small to support adequate schools and health services, and their sawmill and forest holdings were endangered. Many lost their homes and life savings.

Some tribes, such as the Klamath in Oregon, were not treated so harshly—they were given interim financing, transportation and moving costs, and help with jobs and housing. However, from the Native American perspective, termination was another kind of oppression. Native American groups such as the National Congress of American Indians (founded in 1944) worked vigorously against it. Nevertheless, between 1954 and 1960 several dozen groups were terminated. Although President Kennedy ended termination, it had become a rallying point for activism. In 1961 the National Indian Youth Council was created, with a Red Power ideology, and in the next decade, 194 instances of protest or civil disobedience occurred. Of these, 141 were legal suits and formal complaints, and the rest were protests such as delaying dam construction, occupying government facilities, picketing, and sit-ins.[35] The economic status of Native Americans grew increasingly worse. By 1960 unemployment had risen to 38 percent, compared to 5 percent for all males.[36]

Hispanic Americans

Traditionally, Hispanics in the United States have been agricultural workers. In the general social unrest after World War II, when the average annual income of Hispanic Americans was $2,600 (1956), Mexican Americans (Chicanos) began to organize for political action. During the next decade, when Hispanic income had increased about a third—still less than half that of white people[37]—more organizations were formed: the Mexican American Political Association, the Association of Mexican American Educators, the Mexican American Legal Defense and Educational Fund, and the Political Association of Spanish Speaking Organizations, a coordination council. However, they were all relatively ineffective.

Excluded from labor unions, Hispanic agricultural workers were continually denied economic advancement until Cesar Chavez organized the National Farm Workers Association. Some small strikes brought victories, but in 1965 police began harassment and brutality in California, while the hated Texas Rangers were brought in to enforce the growers' demands in Texas. Strikers and their leaders were imprisoned. Despite Anglo violence, Chavez kept the movement nonviolent and joined in 1966 with the Agricultural Workers Organizing Committee to form the United Farm Workers Organizing Committee.

More militant groups formed in the civil rights years: the paramilitary Brown Berets and the Chicano Moratorium Committee, La Raza Unida (California, South Texas, Colorado, California), the United Mexican American Students, and finally, a more violent group, the Chicano Liberation Front in Los Angeles, which claimed credit for a number of bombings of Anglo institutions. Under La Raza Unida in Denver, Corky Gonzales organized school strikes and action against police brutality. La Raza ran as a third party, undercutting Democratic strength in the area, and although it was unsuccessful in the elections, it helped Hispanics to become recognized as a united political force.[38]

The most militant of the Chicano groups was the Alianza Federal de Mercedes, formed in 1963 by Reies Tijerina, who in 1966 took his grievances to the New Mexico government at Santa Fe. At the same time, another group of Chicanos made citizens' arrests of forest rangers for violating old land boundaries, but Tijerina's group was arrested and tried for civil disobedience. In 1967 Tijerina was arrested at an Alianza meeting and taken to the courthouse at Tierra Amarilla, where later a group of armed Chicanos tried to arrest the district attorney. Some officials were wounded and in retaliation a number of Hispanics camping at a nearby picnic ground were detained without adequate shelter or water by armed police and hundreds of national guards, who claimed that Tijerina planned to take over northern New Mexico. Tijerina was charged with insurrection but acquitted for lack of evidence. However, he was jailed in 1969 because his wife had burned two national forest signs (government property).[39]

Until the 1930s, Puerto Rico was an agricultural colony based on sugar production, with the amount of land natives could own determined by the U.S. government. Massive strikes against U.S.-dominated business led to the Independence Party, under the leadership of Harvard-educated Pedro Albizu Campos. In March 1937, government officials massacred marchers in Ponce, and police raids led to armed revolt in five cities, with hundreds killed and 2,000 arrested for advocating independence. In 1948 Puerto Rico was given permission to elect its own government, and it became a commonwealth in 1952. Soon after,

Operation Bootstrap began to industrialize the island and help it pull itself out of the poverty U.S. ownership had created. Possible investors were promised cheap labor and no taxes, and soon U.S. agribusiness had taken over so much land that Puerto Rico had to import food. By 1970, 80 percent of all industry in Puerto Rico was owned by U.S. corporations.[40]

Increasingly, Puerto Ricans were moving to the mainland, especially along the East Coast. By 1940 there were 70,000 Puerto Ricans in the continental United States, and from 1946 to 1955, 406,000 entered. In the next decade, immigration dropped drastically, but in 1966 alone, 121,000 Puerto Ricans came to the Midwest and West.[41] During the 1950s, one-fifth of the Puerto Rican population left the island, encouraged by the government to migrate both to relieve unemployment on the island and to work on the mainland as cheap labor. In the United States, when they could find work, they became concentrated in blue-collar jobs, with women in sales and clerical jobs.[42] During the civil rights years, the Puerto Rican average income decreased from 71 percent to 59 percent of the national average.

Although the civil rights demonstrations of Puerto Rican Hispanics were less noted than were others, they did occur, particularly under the leftist-leaning Young Lords in Chicago. During the Johnson years, such groups were active in organizing programs for school breakfasts and lunches and providing protection against police brutality and advocacy assistance against social welfare agencies.

Chinese Americans

During World War II, China became an ally of the United States, and in 1943 Congress repealed the Chinese Exclusion Act. After the war, Chinese war brides were taken out of the regular immigration quota and Chinese began to immigrate, about 90 percent of them women. Thirteen thousand Chinese Americans had served in the armed forces, 17 percent of the Chinese American population. On their return as veterans, they took advantage of such benefits as the G.I. Bill. Barred from laboring jobs by the anti-Chinese attitudes of unions, they became educators, researchers, doctors, lawyers, accountants, nurses, ministers, white-collar workers, and social workers. By 1970, 24 percent of all Chinese American men had college degrees, double the U.S. average and higher than any other ethnic group.

However, the McCarthy red scare soon lit the fires of anti-Chinese racism again, especially after the Chinese Revolution that made China a communist state in 1949. The political situation of Chinese Americans worsened during the Korean conflict (1950–1953), when China supported the North Koreans against U.S. forces. McCarthy and people with his perspective urged that Chinese Americans be incarcerated, as had been the Japanese, because they were a danger to the U.S. war effort. Although this did not occur, Chinese in the United States were once more suspect.

Many, especially the elderly, lived in poverty. Because of Chinese traditions of family and benevolent associations, only about 25 percent of those eligible for public assistance actually received it; whenever possible, the Chinese took care of their own. As the nation entered the War on Poverty, some civil rights agitation did occur, especially in the great Chinatowns of California and New York. Mostly this centered on housing needs, for 60 percent of Chinese American dwellings were substandard. In the past, the Chinese Consolidated Benevolent Associations (CCBA) had served as the Chinese voice for civil rights and welfare, but now they were joined by more activist groups: the Chinatown Park and Recreation Committee, Chinatown Coalition for Better Housing, and the Chinatown Neighborhood Improvement Resource Center, a coalition of several activist groups.[43]

Civil Rights in the Kennedy Years

When John F. Kennedy won the presidency in 1960, people took his victory as a sign of a new era of liberalism. His Democratic party had lost power in the South, where white Dixiecrats opposed social programs that would benefit people of color, and among white urban workers, who had traditionally been Democrats because of Roosevelt's social insurance programs. Now African American urban Democrats were competing for jobs with white erstwhile Democrats, and the balance of power was shifting. If the Democrats helped the African American urban poor, they would alienate both the white urban workers and the Southern aristocracy.[44]

Because Kennedy needed Southern support, his response to the needs of African Americans was politically difficult. For two years he temporized, but by the summer of 1963 he could not ignore the facts his own investigators brought him: Poverty was widespread in America, and nonwhite people were systematically discriminated against in all facets of American life. Although he urged people to ask what they could do for their country rather than what the country could do for them, he began to understand the responsibilities a country had to its people, particularly a country that had the power to end poverty and discrimination.

In 1963 there were prolonged demonstrations and riots throughout the South. In Mississippi, Air Force veteran James H. Meredith tried to enroll at the University of Mississippi but was stopped by Governor Ross R. Barnett himself. Twelve thousand federal troops, marshals, and national guardsmen were rushed to campus to put down the riots.[45] However, the key demonstrations were in Birmingham, Alabama, where in a massive voter campaign African Americans marched to the registrar's office to demand registration. An escalation of white violence brought Martin Luther King, Jr., to lead the demonstration, and he was arrested and jailed by "Bull" Connor. Eight white church leaders of all faiths—Catholic, Jewish, and Protestants—denounced King and chided the African American community for following him. President Kennedy alerted Attorney General Robert Kennedy that intervention might be needed, and upon King's release April 20, violence began again.

By May 1, nearly a thousand people had been imprisoned. King called on African American children to march on May 2, and although Bull Connor held off for a day he finally attacked them, some no more than six years old, with fire-hoses, clubs, and dogs.[46] More than 2,000 people participated in subsequent demonstrations. Kennedy sent a mediator to intervene, and after six days of riot-ing, on May 10, Birmingham agreed to desegregate lunch counters, restrooms, fit-ting rooms, and drinking fountains. The city officials acted in good faith over the next three months, setting up a biracial committee, desegregating public facilities, and releasing 2,400 demonstrators from jail. However, on May 11—the day after the agreement—the Ku Klux Klan retaliated, bombing King's brother's home and the motel housing King's temporary headquarters, and a counter-riot ensued.

More riots broke out in Virginia, Maryland, and Georgia. Cambridge, Mary-land, was under limited martial law for more than a year. In Mississippi, Medgar Evers, a World War II veteran, led a demonstration of 700 people. He was assas-sinated on June 12.[47] Until then, Kennedy had pursued a "sophisticated to-kenism," but on the eve of Evers's death he began to compile a civil rights bill that guaranteed equal accommodations and gave the attorney general power to file suits to enforce the Fourteenth and Fifteenth Amendments. It remained bottled in Congress, and unrest grew worse: An estimated 1,412 demonstrations took place in the summer of 1963.

On August 28, King led a march of 250,000 people, including 60,000 white people, on Washington; standing before the Lincoln Memorial, he spoke of his dream of peace and civil rights. Eighteen days after the march, a church was bombed in Birmingham and four children were killed and twenty-one injured. This was the twenty-first bombing of establishments or homes of African Ameri-cans, and the twenty-first time the bombers were not apprehended. Over the year, there were more than 10,000 racial demonstrations, and more than 5,000 African Americans were arrested for political activities.[48]

Kennedy was assassinated on November 22, 1963, and although they mourned, African Americans continued their demonstrations, including a school boycott in Chicago involving 220,000 children. White resistance escalated, and demonstrators were arrested and confined for "insurrection" under Truman's McCarran Act. However, Kennedy's death gave the nation and Congress the moral thrust to attend to his civil rights bill that, along with the War on Poverty, became the legacy of democratic action in the 1960s.

Johnson and the Great Society

Lyndon B. Johnson assumed the presidency with a belief that the people had mandated a new day, one in which social welfare and civil rights were intimately connected. He called for a War on Poverty, and with his advisors—a liberal intel-lectual elite—drew up a coordinated attack on the many fronts of discrimination. Johnson's philosophy was "not a hand out but a hand up" and linked personal change with social reform. Although the poor were still considered "unmoti-vated," new theories pointed out the structural reasons for their lack of employ-ment, and both personal rehabilitation and change in opportunity structures became the cornerstones of the War on Poverty. The job-related poverty programs focused on men; the poverty strategy for women was to secure their right to welfare, not to get them into the labor force.[49] The many-pronged attack on poverty began with the passage of the Civil Rights Act in July 1964. In November Johnson was reelected by a landslide, and Congress passed his Economic Opportunity Act the same year and the Voting Rights Act in 1965.

The Civil Rights Act and Continued Protest

Black Protest. The Civil Rights Act of 1964 was the first significant entry by Congress into the civil rights field since the Civil War. The bill was still opposed by the Dixiecrats, and as a joke or as a last-ditch effort to defeat it, Howard V. Smith, a Virginian congressman, attached an amendment to the bill outlawing sex discrimination. In the ensuing discussion, Representative Martha Griffiths and Senator Margaret Chase Smith fought to have it retained.[50] The bill passed both houses by more than a two-thirds vote with the amendment intact. By its provisions:

- It became unlawful to apply unequal standards in voter registration or to deny registration for irrelevant errors or omissions on records or applications.
- Discrimination and segregation became illegal in places of public accommodation and in all establishments whose operation affected interstate commerce or whose discriminatory practices were supported by the state.
- The attorney general was authorized to undertake civil action on behalf of people so denied. Those who refused to abide by the law were considered in contempt of court and subject to fines or confinement without trial by jury, thus circumventing local politics.
- The orderly desegregation of schools was called for.
- A congressional committee was to study deprivation of the right to vote and to inform the president and Congress of its actions.
- All federal agencies and departments were required to end discrimination in order to receive federal funds. The withdrawal of federal grant money was an innovation in enforcement.
- Discrimination in employment or labor unions with twenty-five or more people was forbidden.[51]

The Civil Rights Act made all discrimination illegal on a federal, and therefore nationwide, basis. It forbade discriminatory employment practices based on race, color, religion, sex, or national origin and created the Equal Employment Opportunity Commission (EEOC) to enforce civil rights.

Racial demonstrations became, if anything, more violent after the act passed in July, perhaps because masses do not revolt until they perceive the possibility of actually bettering their lot in life, while at the same time perceiving that their attempts to do so are being thwarted.[52]

White resistance was overwhelming. The summer of 1964, when the bill was passed, was a Red Summer equal to that of 1919, and the summer of 1965 was known as the long hot summer, with riots in Watts (in Los Angeles), in Newark, New Jersey, and in Detroit. As late as 1970–1971, there were 250 race riots of various sizes in the nation.[53] The murder of white civil rights workers such as Viola Liuzzo, Michael Schwerner, Andrew Goodman, and James Chaney shocked the nation. Although an FBI agent witnessed Liuzzo's murder, the Southern jury refused to convict the murderer, who was finally convicted in federal court of depriving her of civil rights. He was imprisoned but released after ten years.

Because African Americans could not participate in the Democratic party's delegate selection in Mississippi, the Student Non-Violent Coordinating Committee sponsored its own election of delegates to the National Democratic Party Convention in 1964, under the name of the Mississippi Freedom Democratic party. Their delegates were denied seats and SNCC lost faith in the whole process of peaceful demonstration. It removed white people from its leadership in 1965 and from its membership in 1966. Stokely Carmichael became its chairman, and "Black Power" became the password. Its leaders—including Carmichael, H. Rap Brown, and John Lewis—defined Black Power as

> political and economic power and cultural independence of black people to determine their destiny individually and collectively, in and out of their own communities.[54]

Much of the theoretical underpinning of Black Power came from Malcolm X, of the Black Muslims. After having visited Moslem countries in Africa, he determined that liberation required political organization and involvement. Early in 1965 he founded the Organization of Afro-American Unity (OAAU) in Harlem, a united front organization to encompass all liberation groups and organizations (but no white groups). Malcolm X was assassinated in February 1965, but his teachings were passed on to other separatist/nationalist organizations.

James Farmer charted the new direction for the Congress of Racial Equality on Malcolm X's insights. His major target was African American economics, and he urged the development of cooperatives in the South and community programs for self-help in Northern ghettos. Farmer could not support Black Power within CORE and so stepped down, leaving the directorship to Floyd B. McKissick, a graduate of Morehouse College in Atlanta and the Law School of the University of North Carolina. In 1968 Roy Innis succeeded McKissick, with policies of self-help, government aid to African American capitalists, and private business involvement.

Huey Newton and Bobby Seale organized the Black Panthers in Oakland, California, in 1966, rallying around Malcolm X's statement that self defense and freedom by any means were the ways to equality:

> We should be peaceful, law-abiding, but the time has come to fight back in self-defense whenever and wherever the black man is being unjustly and unlawfully attacked. If the government thinks I am wrong for saying this, then let the government do its job.[55]

Armed Black Panthers monitored police who used unnecessary force, protested rent evictions, informed welfare recipients of their legal rights, taught classes in African American history, and demanded school traffic lights in a street where several African American children had been killed while crossing.

Eldridge Cleaver, author of *Soul on Ice*, became their minister of information, and the Black Power movement took another turn. Cleaver believed that destruction of capitalist imperialism was necessary to gain power for people of color. Under his leadership, Marxist–Leninism became the new ideology, and Black Panthers formed alliances with communists, the Student Democratic Society (SDS), and the Young Lords—a Chicago-based Puerto Rican militant group—and shifted its emphasis to internationalism.

Women's Protest.   By 1960, 40 percent of all American women were working in full- or part-time jobs and made up about a third of the labor force. Sixty-eight percent were in blue-collar or traditional female professions. Nearly half were mothers of school-age children, and many were middle class. Their individual freedom was still secondary to the needs of their husbands, however. In 1962 a Connecticut court ruled (*Rucci v. Rucci*) that

> a wife must both be a solicitous helpmeet and perform her household and domestic duties . . . without compensation therefore. A husband is entitled to the benefit of his wife's industry and economy.[56]

Kennedy appointed the first Presidential Commission on the Status of Women in 1961, chaired by Eleanor Roosevelt. The commission deplored the trend to blame women for juvenile delinquency and confirmed in 1966 that the EEOC should take action against sex discrimination.[57]

Women had worked actively for civil rights and against the war in Vietnam. In those battles they learned the rhetoric of equality and methods of political action, and also that men did not consider them equal partners even in those activities. In both the SDS and SNCC, for example, they were rarely allowed to speak and continued to perform "women's work"—making coffee, taking notes, and doing secretarial labor. A famous quote from Stokely Carmichael was that "the only position women had in the movement was prone." Realizing that their issues were a part of the larger struggle, women argued that patriarchy was the oldest and most basic form of oppression. When their voices went unheard, many split off from men-dominated groups to form protest movements of their own.[58]

Betty Friedan's systematic look at women's oppression added support to women's struggle. She talked of the romanticization of domesticity, the infantilization of women, and the transformation of the suburban home into a comfortable concentration camp. In 1966, 300 women and men organized the National Organization for Women (NOW), and Friedan was named its president. Its goal was to bring women into full participation as equals in American society. In 1967, NOW adopted a Bill of Rights urging the Equal Rights Amendment, joined the Women's Commission in calling on the EEOC to enforce antidiscrimination legislation, and worked for equal and unsegregated education, maternity leaves that preserved job security and seniority, tax deductions for child care, inexpensive day care centers, reform of the welfare system, and equality of benefits.[59]

Discussion of abortion as a woman's right began in the early 1960s, and NOW picked up the issue, advocating the right to contraceptive information and devices and safe legal abortions. Health care organizations also advocated legalized abortion as a medical issue, and laws were passed to permit it in certain instances. The War on Poverty established family planning programs and clinics, and Medicaid began to pay for abortions for poor women.

Youth Protest.   The youth movement was one of disenchantment from the "establishment"—groups and institutions that made the rules and laws many young people considered immoral. Young people demonstrated against colleges and universities, the Vietnam War, and the draft. Their protests were often brutally repressed by police, and university authorities denied the right of students to speak out. Demonstrations against the invasion of Cambodia in May 1970 and the killing of student protestors at Kent State (Ohio) and Jackson State (Mississippi) Universities virtually closed down the country's college and university system.[60] Youth became heavily involved in Senator Eugene McCarthy's bid for the Democratic presidential nomination in 1968. He made the war in Vietnam and the youth movement his causes and hundreds rallied to him. During the Chicago nomination convention in August 1968, confrontations between the police and the thousands of young people there became violent. Many were arrested and jailed, and for some imprisonment, in both prisons and mental hospitals, continued for years.

The youth movement was, in essence, a protest by middle-class young people against the materialism of their elders. Its concerns were the nation's continued injustices against the poor and people of color and the government's involvement in the internal affairs of other nations for profit. Young people turned from materialism and sought new ways of life offering freedom and creativity in such forms as communal living and, later, involvement in drugs as a way to heightened awareness. By 1973, the youth movement had crumbled. No longer looking outward to change the world, young people turned increasingly inward. Their search for new awareness and freedom was far from selfish in the beginning. That what they sought could not be found in an unresponsive government is, perhaps, one of the shames of our society. Other than some success in their protests against the war in Vietnam and the lowering of the voting age, few real benefits emerged from their struggle. However, Nixon's administration did end the Selective Service Act (draft) in response to their protests.

The Gay Liberation Movement.   Human social evolution has produced many sexual styles, socially acceptable or not, according to societies and times. Until after the Civil War, the few state regulations that applied to homosexuality were generally based on religious or moral grounds and referred to sodomy, prostitution, indecent exposure, and so on. According to William Eskridge, this social construction of sex and gender categories reflected a reification of the roles of men and women returning to "normalcy" after the Civil War. He says this

> . . . arose out of increased social and economic opportunities for women, which fueled not only a robust feminist movement, but also a reaction that emphasized rigid gender lines and roles. Faced with the newly independent woman, middle-class men grew obsessed with cultural reinforcements for manliness.[61]

Homosexuality, along with other sexual alternatives, became identified as "sexual perversion" during the Victorian era—the time of the "pure" wife on the pedestal versus the prostitute; "Women's Sphere" in social work, education, and nursing; the Comstock Law outlawing the mailing of birth control information as pornography; "red lighting" city districts to control prostitution; and so on. By the turn of the century, there were major subcultures of homosexuals in most big cities, along with new definitions for those "deviating" from male or female roles: sexual degenerates and psychopaths. Homosexual activity was generally labeled sodomy, indecent exposure, or "a crime against nature," and police action and enforcement targeted at homosexuals stimulated the creation of new laws to regulate same-sex intimacy.[62]

In the 1930s, child molestation became a national hysteria, and legal control of sexuality shifted from female corruption, such as prostitution or birth control, to male sexual aggression. Policing became increasingly aggressive, and penalties for homosexual activity included prison sentences and/or castration, called "asexualization." As medicine and psychiatry bloomed, it became fashionable to view alternate sexuality as mental illness, and offenders sent to mental hospitals received medical solutions: prefrontal lobotomies, massive injections of male hormones, electroshock, and other aversion therapies.[63] By the 1940s, antigay laws were used to arrest homosexuals, censor homoerotic publications, close down meeting places such as gay bars, and exclude gays from the Armed Services. National security was the rallying cry, claiming that homosexuals could be blackmailed for information. Under-Secretary of State Sumner Welles, despite his friendship with Franklin D. Roosevelt, was removed from his post because of his homosexuality, and accusations of homosexuality, true or otherwise, became key tools in prosecuting America's antiespionage campaign.

From 1947 on, the FBI under Director J. Edgar Hoover triggered unprecedented homophobia under the "national security" banner. Between 1946 and 1961, as many as a million lesbians and gay men were redefined as sexual psychopaths and given criminal punishments.[64] In 1953 President Eisenhower, in an executive order, added the homosexual category as grounds for investigation and dismissal from federal employment, and within two years more than 800 federal employees resigned or were terminated. Because the government shared its military and police records with companies contracted by the Defense Department, by the 1960s, over 2 million private sector employees were blacklisted.[65] In addition, gay people with jobs requiring a license were denied their licenses and their livelihoods—doctors, teachers, pharmacists, and so on. Interestingly, the American Civil Liberties Union (ACLU) upheld such actions on the basis of the perceived security risk.

Gay Liberation had its tentative beginnings in the late 1940s and early 1950s with the founding of the Mattachine Society in Los Angeles and the Daughters of Bilitis in New York and San Francisco. Generally, these organizations remained hidden because of the illegality of homosexuality in many areas and the threat of persecution. Mostly social groups, they devoted themselves to research and education rather than the active repeal of antigay laws. However, in 1961, Franklin Kameny, reduced to poverty because of license laws, organized the Mattachine of Washington Society to promote political activism. In 1964, when the Civil Rights Acts were being passed, he said:

> I do not see the NAACP and CORE worrying about which chromosome and gene produced black skin or about the possibility of bleaching the Negro. I do not see any great interest on the part of B'nai B'rith Anti-Defamation League in the possibility of solving the problems of anti-Semitism by converting Jews to Christians. In all of these minority groups, we are interested in obtaining rights for our respective minorities as Negroes, as Jews, and as homosexuals. Why we are Negroes, Jews, and homosexuals is totally irrelevant, and whether we can be changed to white Christians or heterosexuals is equally irrelevant.[66]

Active resistance began when, on June 27, 1969, New York City police raided the Stonewall Inn, a gay bar, and patrons fought back. The "Stonewall Riot" incident is widely accepted as the beginning of Gay Liberation, of which the major group is the Gay Activist Alliance. The alliance uses a nonviolent but militant strategy to persuade homosexuals to perceive themselves as an oppressed minority. The two major legal bases for the struggle of gays to reclaim their civil rights are the Constitution's First Amendment Freedom of Speech clause and Title VII of the Civil Rights Act of 1964. Three struggles overlap: to protect private gay spaces (homes, cars) against prying and intrusion by the police; to assert control over the institutions of gay subculture (gay bars, restaurants); and for equal gay citizenship—"public equality and equal treatment on their merits as employees, soldiers, immigrants, and parents."[67]

Civil Rights in the Kennedy–Johnson Years

The Voting Rights Act and New Legal Rights

The Voting Rights Act of 1965, along with Johnson's Affirmative Action Order in 1968, effectively ended legalized segregation. Almost a million Southern African

Americans registered to vote within three years, and by 1970, nearly 70 percent of eligible voters were registered.[68] Local sheriffs and judges who had been instrumental in denying civil rights to African Americans became vulnerable to the new voting blocs. In 1964 there were only about 100 elected officials in the nation who were of African descent, but in 1965 approximately 70 more were elected and by 1968 there were 248. By 1980, there were more than 4,900 elected African American officials in offices ranging from county clerks to mayors and judges. The first to serve in a presidential cabinet was Robert Weaver, in 1967, named the secretary of Housing and Urban Development (HUD), and Andrew Brimner became the first to serve on the Federal Reserve Board. Thurgood Marshall was appointed to the Supreme Court and Patricia Harris became the first ambassador of African American descent.[69]

One of the most important legal decisions during the Kennedy administration was the *Gault* decision. Before then, because of the tradition of *parens patriae* in juvenile justice, children had no real legal rights. Even minor offenses such as shoplifting or status offenses could mean years of detention in children's institutions, often to age of majority. The *Gault* decision secured due process for juveniles and gave young people the same rights as adults in the justice system, including adequate notice of charges and rights to counsel, to confront accusers, to avoid self-incrimination under the Fifth Amendment, and to cross-examination.

Under Johnson, new legal rights included the assignment of counsel to those unable to afford attorneys and, in 1966, the *Miranda* decision, which mandated clarifying a suspect's rights before his or her arrest. The *Miranda* decision began to be circumvented immediately with the 1972 decision denying the right to counsel in police lineups. Judicial and administrative decisions also strengthened the rights of the aged, mentally ill and developmentally disabled people, prisoners, and juveniles.

The Economic Opportunity Act of 1964

The Economic Opportunity Act of 1964 (EOA) was overtly aimed at calming riots and providing job training and employment for the poor and people of color—those most likely to rebel. Several programs led the way to or enhanced the programs of the War on Poverty. One was Kennedy's Manpower Development Training Act (MDTA) in 1962, designed to deal with institutional causes of unemployment by training people for better jobs. Johnson incorporated both the funding and the ideals of MDTA into the Title I and IV programs of the Economic Opportunity Act. Another Kennedy program, the Area Redevelopment Act of 1961, gave financial and technical aid to depressed regions by luring new industries to areas of regional unemployment and expanding industries already there. Johnson built on this program with Titles III and V of the Economic Opportunity Act of 1964 and the Economic Development Act of 1965, funding industries in depressed areas in Appalachia, New England, the Coastal Plains, the Ozarks, the Upper Great Lakes region, and a poverty-stricken sector in the Southwest.[70]

Title I included Job Corps training centers for out-of-school and unemployed youths, Work Training programs to help young people stay in school, and Work Study programs to enable them to go to college. Unfortunately, job training programs were often run by white middle-class people who believed that lack of motivation, rather than unavailability of jobs, caused unemployment. Participants came because they were paid for their attendance, but many perceived the programs as childish and inauthentic, teaching people to use alarm clocks and public transportation, for example, or filling out job applications when there were no real jobs available.

Unlike Roosevelt with his Works Progress Administration, Johnson did not attempt to create new jobs. According to Ehrenreich, this would have implied

> a direct government role in corporate investment decisions, a step that Johnson-era America was not ready to take and that the poor never gained enough power to demand.[71]

Although jobs became increasingly available at the same time as the training programs,

> it was the war in Vietnam, not the war on poverty . . . that both stimulated the economy and provided "jobs" (although often fatal ones) for many of the poor.[72]

Title III provided grants and loans to buy or improve real estate, reduce debts, construct buildings, operate family farms, and participate in cooperative associations, particularly in rural areas. Title IV targeted especially African American-owned businesses and investment opportunities by providing small business loans for African American entrepreneurs, although others could qualify.

Title V, Work Experience Programs (WEP), permitted businesspeople to use funds from the MDTA (1962) and Vocational Education Act (1963) to hire low-income and minority people, including AFDC recipients; money was channeled to the workers through the businesses. WEP also established Volunteers in Service to America (VISTA) to work in programs for Native Americans, migrant workers, or people in need in Washington, D.C., Puerto Rico, Guam, American Samoa, the Virgin Islands, and the Trust Territory of the Pacific Islands. VISTA volunteers also worked in agencies for the care and rehabilitation of mentally ill and developmentally disabled people.

Title II, Community Action Agencies, was the most controversial. It gave money directly to grass-roots public or nonprofit agencies established by the poor, bypassing the traditional channels of state and local governments, United Ways and social agencies, and political parties, although many traditional agencies also shared in the funding. A key term was *maximum feasible participation* of the poor. There were very different interpretations of how much "maximum participation" was feasible. To liberals and the poor, it meant that they had to be represented in developing goals and policies and in maintaining the programs receiving federal funds by administering and working in them. To mayors, governors, and traditional social agencies, it meant that people whom they had previously controlled now had massive funds and needed neither advice nor control. The Office of Economic Opportunity (OEO), which administered the programs, was under attack from the first by mayors and political machines, and legal suits were filed against its programs.

Community Action Programs (CAPs) were the local arms of OEO. Their services included advocacy against public and federally funded private agencies that discriminated or withheld services; job training and employment services; Head Start, a nursery school for deprived children; Upward Bound, teaching remedial educational skills so that young people might enter college; day care centers for employed parents; neighborhood recreation centers to enhance the lives of children in poverty; and neighborhood health and family planning centers. The New Careers Program trained tens of thousands of indigenous paraprofessionals to work in social agencies, increasing the numbers of social workers but threatening the profession's argument that only highly trained social workers could give services. It provided career ladders, increased on-the-job experience, and gave in-service training and release time for college. Legal Services Organizations (LSOs) provided class actions against established agencies: By 1968 there were approximately 250 LSOs, with 1,800 lawyers initiating more than 25,000 cases per year against schools, welfare departments, mental hospitals, police, city administrations, and courts. Other programs included mental health family-centered care, adult basic education, information and referral centers, police relations programs, and volunteer programs.

Although a manifest purpose of the EOA was to enable social agencies that qualified for OEO funds to be innovative and responsive to the needs of their clients, this rarely happened. Rather, agencies took the federal money and used it to expand their clientele in poverty areas while they maintained the same attitudes and intervention modalities: belief in personal fault and the efficacy of casework. For example, community mental health centers expected to pioneer new services remained attached to their entirely conventional outpatient services, although they now offered them in poor communities.[73] Funds intended to create neighborhood health centers were captured by hospitals for institutional expansion. School systems took the funds but did not use them to innovate. Ehrenreich says,

> in the end, despite the successful reorganization of many agency practices and attitudes, the poverty program failed to reform the service delivery system, much less to eliminate poverty.[74]

The fight against OEO was effective. In late 1966, Congress cut back and restricted the scope of the CAPs, and legislation in 1967 required OEO funds to be channeled through the offices of mayors. The fight went out of the OEO movement. Many mayors already had political control, or the agencies were so innocuous as to not matter anyway.[75] President Johnson, sensing the failure of the War on Poverty and concerned about his loss of support, abandoned OEO to throw the nation's resources behind the war in Vietnam. The most important immediate reason for the failure of OEO was the false assumption that "no one had a vested interest in maintaining poverty"[76] when in fact many people found it functional. Moreover, indigenous leaders of the civil and welfare rights battles were co-opted by the good government pay, and this loss of leaders devastated both movements. Furthermore, a major tenet of OEO was to train the disadvantaged to take jobs in society. As with other such programs, this "work ethic" basis was inauthentic, for the jobs simply did not materialize no matter how effective the training. Finally, OEO did fulfill its latent purposes and so was no longer needed: It quelled the rebellious by giving them some benefits, co-opted the leaders, and put control back in the hands of those who needed a cooperative low-wage workforce.

Social Programs in the Kennedy–Johnson Years

Poverty was easier to deal with than civil rights. The Social Security Administration's reports on poverty from 1959 census data, Attorney General Robert Kennedy's firsthand reports, and books such as Michael Harrington's *The Other America* (1962) and Dwight MacDonald's *Our Invisible Poor* (1963) pointed out the hidden pockets of poverty in the cities, among the aged or disadvantaged, or in rural areas such as Appalachia that existed even in this time of affluence.

President Kennedy's 1962 plans were modest: some advances in public assistance, the extension of unemployment insurance and liberalized OASI benefits, an increased minimum wage and an increase in AFDC benefits, a new housing act to create more jobs in construction, some training bills, and financial and technical aid for depressed regions. To stimulate consumer buying and corporate investment, he also cut personal and corporate income taxes.[77] He sought prevention rather than cure when possible: In 1963 alone, the Department of Health, Education, and Welfare (DHEW) spent $130 million for basic and support services, personnel training, research, construction of residential facilities, income maintenance, and maternity and infant care programs, including health screening programs, especially in high-risk populations.

Kennedy's Social Security Amendments

The most important changes for social welfare by far were those of the Social Security Amendments of 1962, called the Service Amendments. In 1961 Kennedy appointed a twenty-five-member Ad Hoc Committee on Public Welfare with members from both public welfare and private social work. They were charged to recommend methods leading to adequate financial assistance, efficient administration and organization of public assistance offices, research into the causes of dependency and family breakdown, and provision of rehabilitation services by trained personnel. The guiding ideals were still that

- People would not work if they could get welfare.
- Rehabilitative services by social workers could return recipients to the workforce.

The committee gave full support to social work's claim that casework and psychoanalytic intervention could "cure" the problem of motivation and strengthen the family, and that this would cause a drop in welfare rolls. Its major recommendation was that schools of social work receive enough funding to train new workers to "rehabilitate" AFDC families. Other recommendations included

- Support for unemployed and incapacitated parents
- Research and demonstration projects on out-of-wedlock births, dependency, and family breakdown
- The removal of residence requirements for public assistance
- New funding for day care
- Vouchers rather than cash for recipients who could not manage money
- Money earned by children to be exempted when figuring family eligibility or grant levels.

Kennedy's message to Congress in 1962 dealt solely with public dependency, reiterating the "blame the victim" and work ethic stances of most public assistance rhetoric. He called for a "new" approach to dependency:

> a return to seeking causes within the individual, buttressed by job training and employment services for the dependent and those who might become dependent.[78]

To carry out this new approach, the Social and Rehabilitative Service (SRS) was established in the Department of Health, Education, and Welfare.

Massive funding was provided to schools of social work and new standards were set to ensure that workers could provide adequate services: caseloads of no more than sixty (patently impossible as rolls continued to rise), one supervisor for every five caseworkers, home visits to improve family functioning, homemaker services, a "service plan" for every child, and guardians when AFDC funds were misused. Group homes grew rapidly in this period, and many children were removed to such homes or to foster care. Institutionalization was also an option: There were approximately 306,000 children in institutions at the time. Of these, 23 percent were labeled neglected and dependent, a third were adjudged juvenile delinquents, and a little over a third were in homes and schools for children with mental and physical disabilities.[79]

Employment was the most important goal, and AFDC recipients who refused training without good cause were removed from the grant (although their children remained recipients). Success of the amendments was measured in terms of the new financial independence of former recipients, but unfortunately, the rolls continued to expand, now faster than unemployment rates, and "services" became increasingly suspect. Whereas in 1955, 3 percent of all children were receiving AFDC, in 1970, 8.5 percent were on the rolls.[80] Although the numbers of people in poverty dropped by nearly half from 1960 to 1969, AFDC rolls more than doubled, from 2.9 million to 7.3 million. Expenditures tripled in the same period, from $1 billion to $3 billion, and by 1972 had increased tenfold, to $10.3 billion.[81] In 1961 in real dollars, the average monthly AFDC payment was $117 per family. A decade later, it was $183, or about $49 per person (compared with per capita income of $307 in the general population).[82] Levitan, Rein, and Marwick say,

> There is no evidence that the provision of social services for welfare recipients has induced labor force participation. . . . The failure of social services to "rehabilitate" welfare recipients led to a new emphasis on concrete programs related to employability. The emphasis shifted to day care, family planning, manpower training, and compensatory education.[83]

Under Johnson, the Social Security Act was further amended, first with the massive health programs of Medicare and Medicaid in 1964 (operationalized in 1965) and then with further AFDC amendments in 1967.

Medicare. Medicare was added to social insurance (OADSI), making it Old Age, Survivors, Disability, and Health Insurance (OASDHI). Medicare is an insurance-like system with two programs (Part A and Part B) to provide health care for people over age sixty-five and people with disabilities on Social Security. Part A is compulsory, and a "premium" is automatically deducted from monthly OASDHI checks, and Part B is optional, with an added premium for expanded services. General revenues, rather than the premiums, pay most of the cost. The program is operated through private mediaries such as Blue Cross/Blue Shield, to which the government pays a 2 percent administrative fee.

Part A pays for part of the costs of hospitalization, with deductibles paid by patients according to length of stay: skilled nursing home care for up to 100 days, 80 percent of outpatient diagnostic tests, and up to 100 home nursing visits per year following hospitalization. Part B has a higher yearly deductible plus monthly premiums and pays 80 percent of "reasonable" expenses for physicians' and surgeons' services, more home nursing visits, mental health care, and a number of medical appliances and diagnostic tests. For hospital stays of more than ninety days, a patient can draw on a sixty-day lifetime reserve, and hospice care for the terminally ill is provided.

Medicare does not pay for such needs as eyeglasses, dentures, hearing aids and batteries, prescription drugs not given by health professionals, and home care for fragile, nonambulatory, or senile people when other adults in the family work. Recipients get no money: Vouchers go directly to the health services. Because Medicare pays only "reasonable" costs, patients must pay all "unreasonable" or overcosts. When Medicare is exhausted, recipients pay their own way, relying on private insurance plans, or, having sold their assets, turning to public assistance (Medicaid).

Medicaid. Medicaid's forerunner was the Kerr–Mills Bill of 1958. A means-tested public assistance program rather than social insurance, it was administered through state departments of public welfare or public health. Like Medicare, Medicaid is a voucher program, with payment going directly to health care providers. Funded through general revenues, it was given on an open-ended basis to the participating states depending on per capita income, with grants-in-aid of 50–83 percent of Medicaid costs. The Health Care Financing Administration (HCFA) administers Medicade under the Department of Health and Human Services (formerly Department of Health, Education, and Welfare).

Medicaid's primary target is people on public assistance, although others below the poverty line may be covered if states so choose. States also must give Medicaid for people in other selected categories, such as children under twenty-one in foster homes or institutions for whom public agencies provide some financial support. In general, Medicaid pays for all costs of hospitalization, doctor's services and calls, prescriptions, diagnostic testing, emergency services, doctor's visits, and extended nursing home care for the aged or those with long-term disabilities who have exhausted other payment alternatives (including Medicare). Also, depending on different state guidelines, Medicaid might pay for eyeglasses, hearing aids, dental care, false teeth, prostheses, appliances, and other equipment. Medicaid funds were also paid to train professional medical personnel and facility inspectors, and for administrative needs such as information systems. By the end of 1964, thirty-nine states had Medicaid programs, five were establishing them, and six had decided not to. In 1982 thirty-four states chose to provide for the medically needy (in addition to public assistance recipients), but still only about three-fifths of poor households were covered.

Because health care providers understood that Medicaid was guaranteed by the government, highly inflated medical costs, not only for Medicaid recipients but also for the general public, occurred. Ironically, many health care services and physicians will not take Medicaid clients, leaving them to rely on a limited number of physicians and hospital emergency rooms rather than the preventive health care envisioned by those who developed the Medicaid program.

Social Security Amendments of 1967. During 1967, the Department of Health, Education, and Welfare underwent reorganization. One of the most interesting changes was the creation of an Assistance Payments Administration in AFDC. This divorced income maintenance functions from social services functions and split public welfare departments into two sections: social services, whose workers provide counseling services and services to neglected, abused, or dependent children and older people; and assistance payments, whose workers determine eligibility and set amounts of grants based on state levels of need, number in family, and their own discretion. Purchase of services from the private sector, for such treatment as mental health care, drug abuse, or family services, was also authorized.

The social work community had been for some time arguing that services to the poor should not be connected with whether or not they received financial aid. The National Association of Social Workers (NASW) supported the split in services as clients' right to self-determination, acknowledging that need did not necessarily call for services.[84] However, the split in services caused some unfortunate consequences. Services personnel were required to have bachelor's degrees (in any field), but assistance payments (AP) workers needed no more, generally, than a high-school education. Therefore, less-educated workers, often with harsh values regarding work and sexual morality, were AFDC's gatekeepers and had real power over subsistence issues. Services workers could only suggest to AP workers that clients' financial needs (beyond grants) be filled—more food, for example, or the purchase of a refrigerator or bedding. In effect, the split in services made the more-educated workers powerless except in an advisory capacity, and caused dissension within departments of public welfare.

Social services for children included protective services for the abused and neglected; licensing of foster homes, day care centers, and institutions; and placement services (foster care, institutionalization, or adoption) for children who could not remain with their biological parents. Workers were required to maintain contact with both biological and foster parents for the duration of need, and they could also request permanent termination of parental rights. In 1968 state and local departments provided services for 656,000 children, or 80 of every 10,000, and private agencies served another 219,000 children. In fiscal year 1968, child care cost $499.7 million, a 13 percent increase over 1967. Of that, only 9 percent was federal money, with over half coming from the state and the rest from the local level. Day care took the most—more than 60 percent.[85]

The sexual morality of single mothers remained an intense issue among AFDC policymakers. One result was a freeze on the number of out-of-wedlock or deserted children who could receive aid; however, this was overturned in 1969 because it punished needy children.[86] In 1970 there were 5.6 million children on AFDC, an increase of 900,000 from 1969, and family planning program services under Medicaid began to be offered to AFDC clients. Some, especially African American men, perceived this as race genocide, but in general women hailed it. Workers, whether services or AP, continued to believe society's sex and race stereotypes of their clients: that "most welfare mothers are promiscuous" and that "black women are worse (in sexual immorality) than are white women."[87]

Some states also chose to provide protective services to dependent aged or disabled adults, for many were subject to "granny beating" or mistreatment from those with whom they resided. Also, service workers in some states licensed nursing homes for elderly or disabled people and day care or group homes for developmentally disabled adults. Guardians were assigned as needed for either child or adult dependents.

The 1967 amendments made employment and training top priorities. The major AFDC work program was the Work Incentive Program, first called WIP, an appropriate name, soon changed to WIN. It required AFDC parents with no children under the age of six to register for work training and job placement. Any adult who refused to enroll, unless incapacitated or needed at home, was disqualified for benefits (although the children still received their portion of the grant). Children out of school and over age sixteen also had to register or be disqualified. WIN was a joint Public Welfare and Labor Department program that in the long run cost more, with fewer long-term benefits than simple grants would have. New work incentives developed and day care monies became reasonably generous. Work expenses, such as payment for uniforms and transportation, were paid by the Departments of Public Welfare. Very importantly, the "$30.00 and a third" disregard was instituted: that is, working parents could keep the first $30.00 they earned, along with a third of the remainder of their income, without a deduction in AFDC benefits.

Other Kennedy–Johnson Social Programs

Food Programs.   On his first day in office, Kennedy doubled the Surplus Commodity Program (reactivated by Eisenhower in 1957) by which the Department of Agriculture bought surplus food from farmers and distributed it to the poor. Concerned that this was a "white" diet—white flour, white rice, white lard—without nutrition, he instituted in selected counties a Food Stamp Program through the Department of Agriculture (aimed also at supporting farm prices). Under the Food Stamp Program, people purchased "vouchers" including a "bonus" amount determined on family size and assets beyond the dollar value of the stamps. Stamps were redeemable for any U.S.-grown foodstuffs, but no alcohol, tobacco products, or cleaning or paper products were allowed. Because the whole amount had to be purchased at one time (later twice a month), poor families often could not afford to buy them from their meager AFDC or general assistance allowances.

Johnson formalized the Food Stamp Program, extending it to all states that wanted it (although at first only twenty-two elected to have it). Over the next two decades, the benefit levels rose and coverage was increased from only those on public assistance to those qualifying as needy under state guidelines. In addition, food stamps became free rather than having to be purchased, increasing their use among eligible people. He also revamped the National School Lunch Program and the Special Milk Program and made money available for school breakfasts and lunches to Community Action Agencies, schools, and groups such as the Young Lords or CORE.

Mental Health and Developmental Disability.   Concerned very personally with the lack of services for his sister, who was developmentally disabled, in 1962 Kennedy appointed a mental health panel that presented the Mental Health Act to Congress in 1963. Though not passed until after Kennedy's death because of resistance from the American Medical Association, the act provided for construction of mental retardation facilities and community mental health centers, comprehensive services, and education and consultation to upgrade the nation's services. It also provided funding for the training of more social workers. Although Johnson's administration aimed at more practical aid, such as job training and housing, he did agree on the training of new social workers and continued their educational funding under the Social Security Amendments of 1967.

Housing. In the 1940s and 1950s, federal grants for housing averaged $2 billion a year, increasing in the 1960s to $7 billion. In 1961 Kennedy proposed to desegregate all federally funded housing, and in 1962, the government spent $820 million for housing for the poor (although it allowed $2.9 billion in subsidies for middle- and upper-income levels). An array of agencies administered the programs directed primarily at middle- and upper-income families on the assumption that the poor would take over housing vacated by them. In 1966 the many agencies dealing with housing were consolidated into a superagency, Housing and Urban Development (HUD), and expenditures reached $16 billion for construction guarantees and another $12 billion for mortgage guarantees. HUD administered

- Urban Renewal, to construct middle-class housing and tear down slums
- Mortgage guarantees for all income classes
- Public housing
- Housing for special groups, such as the aged and disabled.

HUD also brought housing programs up to date. The 1949 Federal Housing Administration was modified to help lower-income families, and new public housing and housing for special groups was constructed. Urban Renewal was a mixed blessing, giving money to rid cities of slums but displacing many of the poor those slums had sheltered. So many African Americans were left homeless that Urban Renewal was often called "Negro Removal." In the period between 1949 and 1964, an estimated 177,000 family dwelling units and 66,000 individual family units were razed by Urban Renewal, which replaced only 68,000, of which only 20,000 were for low-income people.

In 1966 the Model Cities Program began under HUD, its goal to provide assistance to cities to coordinate their welfare activities in "a massive and comprehensive effort to rebuild or restore entire sections and neighborhoods of slum and blighted areas."[88] In 1968 HUD was authorized to provide 6 million new dwellings for low- and moderate-income groups, with a budget of $2.6 billion, of which $412 million was earmarked for Urban Renewal. By 1971, it approached $10 billion, excluding loan insurance and guarantees, whereas Model Cities was budgeted at about $390 million a year.[89]

Specialized Programs. The Older Americans Act of 1965 developed from the National Conference on Aging (1950), the Committee on Geriatrics (1951–1956), and the 1961 White House Conference on Aging. These conferences created the Administration on Aging to fund community planning services and training, establish state agencies on aging, support research and demonstration projects to study the status of the elderly, and provide grants for community service programs. Amendments in 1967 extended the provisions and increased funding for community planning and innovative demonstration projects. It gave State Aging Offices the responsibility for statewide coordination and planning. Under Nixon in 1973, the Older Americans Comprehensive Amendments established a National Clearinghouse on Aging, increased grants for State and Area Agencies on Aging, gave training and research money for multidisciplinary centers of gerontology, and established multipurpose senior centers. It also provided for community service employment for the elderly, administered by the Department of Labor. The Retired Senior Citizens' Program and Foster Grandparents program were created, and nutrition programs were authorized in senior citizens' centers.[90]

The Elementary and Secondary Education Act (ESEA) of 1965 offered grants and services to schools serving low-income areas including inner cities, bilingual communities, and Native American schools. Before the act, such schools had low property tax bases and therefore lacked new and high-quality educational materials and facilities. They were very often staffed by teachers fresh out of college (because older, more experienced teachers often had the right to fill vacancies in newer suburban schools), who were unable to provide new and innovative teaching materials or could not cope with the needs of these children. ESEA money helped to provide better buildings, better teaching materials, and more experienced teachers attracted by the chance of creating innovative educational experiences. For Spanish-speaking children, ESEA provided bilingual classes.

Another Kennedy program, the Juvenile Delinquency and Youth Offenses Control Act, was funded at $10 million a year for three years. It researched the social causes of delinquency and developed innovative empowerment programs such as Mobilization for Youth (MFY), on the Lower East Side of New York City. MFY offered comprehensive services to youth gangs to break the cycle of delinquency and crime and organized the groups themselves to search out and provide services to young people. Under Johnson's Economic Opportunity Act, such innovative programs continued. One of the best known was Haryou—Harlem Youth Opportunity program—which offered supportive services and self-help and training classes for the youth of Harlem.

Welfare, Civil Rights, and the Social Work Profession

Only after 1964 did social work interest turn to social action and civil rights, especially in schools of social work. With an influx of activist students, often supported by government grants, schools became more flexible and varied, offering tracks in community organization, administration, and policy. Courses on ethnic minorities were established and enrollments of people of minority groups soared. By the early 1970s, almost 25 percent were nonwhite students, and many civil activists had joined the schools as students.[91] This new generation worked to empower rather than change their clients. At the same time, in Community Action Programs, paraprofessionals who served clients with great skill and care overturned the professional social work belief that only highly trained social workers could deliver human services.

In 1967 a new challenge confronted traditional service orientation. Under the leadership of Dr. George Wiley, a chemist turned advocate, welfare workers, welfare recipients, civil rights workers, members of the Student Democratic Society, poverty program workers, and a large number of VISTA volunteers met to establish a National Coordinating Committee of Welfare Rights Groups to plan welfare demonstrations. In the summer of 1967 they formed the National Welfare Rights Organization (NWRO). By 1969 NWRO had more than 22,000 dues-paying members in 523 local groups, the most members it ever had, which was around 2 percent of adult recipients of public assistance.[92]

NRWO's members militantly demanded publicity about welfare rights and benefits, information heretofore kept classified, and after extended struggles prepared and distributed handbooks on client rights to welfare mothers. They continued to demonstrate: In Philadelphia, when the welfare department refused requests for school shoes for their children, welfare mothers went en masse to a blood bank to sell their blood and purchase shoes. Of the twenty-seven who came, twenty-five were rejected because of anemia resulting from poor nutrition.[93] In 1969 NWRO, the Association of Black Social Workers, the radical student-based Social Welfare Workers Movement, and a newly formed women's organization, Women of the American Revolution, took over the National Conference on Social Welfare. Doors were barred and they demanded that the conference donate $35,000 to NWRO and the conference attendees another $25,000. Those demands went unmet, but negotiators agreed to seek an increase in minority membership and to focus the following annual conference on poverty and racism. At the 1970 National Conference on Social Welfare, Johnnie Tillmon, an AFDC mother from Watts and 1970 NWRO chair, told the assembled social workers

> If it hadn't been for you people who administer social services, we would have no organization. We organized because we were tired of being beat around by social workers.[94]

NWRO lobbied for a minimum guaranteed income of $6,500 for a family of four, the poverty level at the time, but was generally ignored. The idea of single mothers supporting families on welfare was an important challenge to key values of marriage and the work ethic, but NWRO argued that

> work in the home is a valuable aspect of the nation's productive efforts and that women have a right to be paid wages for caring for children in their homes.[95]

In the long run, NWRO was unsuccessful in lobbying for increased benefits or increased coverage. Although the idea of a guaranteed annual wage was seriously considered by President Nixon, Congress refused the Family Assistance Plan that would have instituted it.

Although some welfare workers organized in support of welfare clients and the new young activists took their part, mainline social workers remained conservative and casework-oriented in their approach. They cautioned the National Welfare Rights Organization, felt threatened by proposals to use paraprofessionals in their agencies and to train bachelor's level people in social work, and feared the new people they now had to deal with—Hispanic and African Americans, welfare department staffs, community action agency personnel, and poverty agencies.

Conclusion: Looking Back on the 1960s

Near the end of his second term, Johnson, worn down by the demands of the War on Poverty and the failure of the war in Vietnam, decided not to seek reelection. White backlash, protests by people of color, and failure in Vietnam meant his defeat on both international and domestic fronts. However, his dedication to the Vietnam War (1969–1975) was much higher than to the War on Poverty: Vietnam cost the federal government $120 billion, whereas the Economic Opportunity Act of 1964 spent only $15.5 billion from 1965 to 1973, less than a tenth of the amount spent on the war.

The civil rights movement splintered: Militancy and Black Power movements, along with Red Power movements among Native Americans and Brown Power movements among Hispanics, ruled the day. In 1966 there were riots in forty-four cities, and in the 1966 elections, Republicans gained forty-seven seats in the House of Representatives. Reagan became governor of California.[96]

> The angry mood of the public was also reflected in Congress, where President Johnson's proposal of a federal open housing law was killed by a Senate filibuster. In the same session, limits were imposed upon the authority of DHEW to divert funds from schools failing to desegregate . . . a trend toward repressive legislation directed against those who were responsible . . . urban violence.[97]

Although the Open Housing Law passed in 1968, it was probably in response to the slaying of Martin Luther King, Jr. rather than a liberal action.[98] The backlash against civil rights and welfare rights continued throughout the election year of 1968. Both Democrat Hubert Humphrey and Republican Richard Nixon moved their rhetoric closer to the conservative side. Status quo and law and order were the keynotes of this election year.

Neither the Social Service Amendments of 1962 nor the Economic Opportunity Act of 1964 reduced welfare rolls, nor did they quell civil unrest. However, social justice prevailed more during that time than since the 1930s, and perhaps since before the 1300s. The idea of service as a right, even though translated through the work ethic ideology, brought more people into programs and helped more than ever before. Relief programs came under federal standards that shared their costs even though "need levels" were determined by the states. In addition, thousands of new social workers were trained and thousands of paraprofessionals were given jobs in the social service system.

Looking back, we found benefits in the increased level of social insurance through OASDI and Medicare. Coverage was extended to over 90 percent of the population, but it still excluded federal government employees, railroad employees, irregularly employed farm and domestic workers who did not have minimum income for coverage, and self-employed people earning less than $400 annually. Benefit levels came under indexing; that is, they rose with the cost of living. Medicaid underlaid social health insurance for the nation. Civil rights legislation became a permanent part of the polity. Perhaps the greatest benefit of this was the emphasis on education and the movement of minority group persons, however slowly, into better and higher-status jobs.

Gains from the War on Poverty were few. Although community action agencies still exist, their major efforts are tied very securely into local governments. Head Start and Upward Bound programs continue, but at lower funding levels and with far less autonomy and innovation. Maximum feasible participation became a thing of the past, many programs were severely cut, and public assistance programs remained stigmatized. Poor people remain in the secondary labor market and in the secondary welfare system—marginal jobs and inadequate public assistance.

We learned many things from the 1950s and 1960s. Perhaps the most enduring lesson is that the threat of rebellion engenders accommodation, but when its force is dissipated, denial of services recurs. Moving into the Nixon years, control of the poor and other minorities tightened. Even during the Carter administration gains for social justice were few and, during the Reagan years, repression again became society's goal, fulfilled in the Clinton administration. However, the Decade of the Dream—of freedom and social justice—did happen. The shame is that, unless repression becomes severe enough to cause rebellion, it may not happen again.

Study Questions

1. What were the trends that led to the civil unrest of the 1960s? Who were the important leaders of the time?

2. Why was Kennedy unable to achieve civil rights and social reforms during his tenure? Why was Johnson able to do so?

3. What civil rights were achieved under Johnson?

4. What social reforms were achieved during the Kennedy–Johnson years?

5. How did the 1960s change the social work profession?

Notes

1. John Ehrenreich, *The Altruistic Imagination: A History of Social Work and Social Policy in the United States* (Ithaca, NY: Cornell University Press, 1985), p. 140.

2. Beulah R. Compton, *Introduction to Social Welfare and Social Work: Structure, Function, and Process* (Homewood, IL: The Dorsey Press, 1980), p. 437.

3. *Social Security Bulletin*, Vol. 46, no. 7 (July 1983), p. 95.

4. June Axinn and Herman Levin, *Social Welfare: A History of the American Response to Need*, 2d ed. (New York: Harper & Row, 1982), p. 230.

5. The "poverty line" was developed early in the 1960s by Mollie Orshansky. It was the amount of the budget that constituted a short-term emergency diet times a factor of 3, because it was estimated that a family should not have to spend more than one-third of its budget on food.

6. Ehrenreich, *Altruistic Imagination*, pp. 148–149.

7. Axinn and Levin, *Social Welfare*, p. 235.

8. Carole Hymowitz and Michaele Weissman, *A History of Women in America* (New York: Bantam Books, 1980), p. 326.

9. Compton, *Introduction to Social Welfare*, p. 479.

10. Ibid., p. 253.

11. *Social Security Bulletin*, Vol. 49, no. 2 (Feb. 1986), p. 38.

12. Compton, *Introduction to Social Welfare*, p. 446.

13. *Social Security Bulletin*, July 1983, p. 13.

14. Ibid.

15. Gerald Handel, *Social Welfare in Western Society* (New York: Random House, 1982), p. 139.

16. Axinn and Levin, *Social Welfare*, p. 245.

17. Sar Levitan, Martin Rein, and David Marwick, *Work and Welfare Go Together* (Baltimore: Johns Hopkins University Press, 1972), p. 6.

18. Compton, *Introduction to Social Welfare*, p. 454.

19. Martin Rein, "The Welfare Crisis," in Lee Rainwater (ed.), *Social Problems and Public Policy* (Chicago: Aldine de Gruyter, 1974), p. 50.

20. Levitan, Rein, and Marwick, *Work and Welfare*, p. 12.

21. Betty Reid Mandell, "Welfare and Totalitarianism: Part I. Theoretical Issues," *Social Work* (Jan. 1971), p. 24.

22. Axinn and Levin, *Social Welfare*, p. 246.

23. Levitan, Rein, and Marwick, *Work and Welfare*, 1972, p. 9; Rein, in "Welfare Crisis," pp. 89–102.

24. Winifred Bell, *Aid to Dependent Children* (New York: Columbia University Press, 1965), pp. v and 137.

25. Ibid., p. 121.

26. Joel P. Handler, *Reforming the Poor* (New York: Basic Books, 1972), p. 139.

27. Ibid., p. 26.

28. Dorothy C. Miller, "AFDC: Mapping a Strategy for Tomorrow," *Social Service Review* (Dec. 1983), Vol. 57, pp. 599–613, esp. p. 601.

29. Thomas R. Dye and L. Harmon Zeigler, *The Irony of Democracy* (Belmont, CA: Wadsworth Publishing, 1970), p. 297; Axinn and Levin, *Social Welfare*, pp. 231–232.

30. Lerone Bennett, Jr., *Before the Mayflower: A History of the Negro in America, 1619–1964* (Chicago: Johnson Publishing Co., 1966), p. 303.

31. Ibid., p. 313.

32. Compton, *Introduction to Social Welfare*, p. 482.

33. Dye and Zeigler, *The Irony of Democracy*, pp. 296–297.

34. Joe R. Feagin, *Racial and Ethnic Relations*, 2d ed. (Englewood Cliffs, NJ: Prentice Hall, 1984), p. 515.

35. Ibid., p. 190.

36. Joseph Hraba, *American Ethnicity* (Itasca, IL: F.E. Peacock Publishers, 1979), p. 227.

37. Feagin, *Racial and Ethnic Relations*, p. 274.

38. M. Barrera, C. Munoz, and C. Ornelas, "The Barrio as an Internal Colony," in Harlan Hahn (ed.), *Urban Affairs Annual Review,* Vol. 6. (Beverly Hills, CA: Sage Publications, 1972), pp. 465–498.

39. Feagin, *Racial and Ethnic Relations,* p. 188.

40. Ibid., p. 299.

41. Ibid., p. 303.

42. Ehrenreich, *Altruistic Imagination,* p. 152.

43. Jack Chen, *The Chinese in America* (San Francisco: Harper & Row, 1980), pp. 201–260.

44. Bennett, *Before the Mayflower,* p. 323.

45. Ibid., p. 338.

46. Ibid., p. 344.

47. Dye and Zeigler, *The Irony of Democracy,* p. 299.

48. Bennett, *Before the Mayflower,* p. 327.

49. Miller, "AFDC: Mapping a Strategy," p. 602.

50. Hymowitz and Weissman, *History of Women,* p. 343.

51. Dye and Zeigler, *The Irony of Democracy,* p. 300.

52. James C. Davies, "Toward a Theory of Revolution," *American Sociological Review,* Vol. 27 (Feb. 1962), p. 318. Cited in Dye and Zeigler, *The Irony of Democracy,* p. 309.

53. Feagin, *Racial and Ethnic Relations,* p. 226.

54. Raymond Hall, *Black Separatism and Social Reality: Rhetoric and Reason* (New York: Pergamon Press, 1978), pp. 165–167.

55. Ibid.

56. Leonore J. Wietzman, "Legal Regulation of Marriage: Tradition and Change," *California Law Review,* Vol. 62 (1974), p. 1187. Quoted in Lisa Peattie and Martin Rein, *Women's Claims: A Study in Political Economy* (New York: Oxford University Press, 1983), p. 42.

57. Alice Kessler-Harris, *Out to Work: A History of Wage-Earning Women in the United States* (New York: Oxford University Press, 1982), p. 305.

58. Hymowitz and Weissman, *History of Women,* p. 327.

59. Jane DeHart Mathews, "The New Feminism and the Dynamics of Social Change," in Linda K. Kerber and Jane DeHart Mathews (eds.), *Women's America* (New York: Oxford University Press, 1982), p. 408.

60. Ehrenreich, *Altruistic Imagination,* p. 182.

61. William N. Eskridge, Jr., *Gaylaw: Challenging the Apartheid of the Closet* (Cambridge, MA: Harvard University Press, 1999), p. 1.

62. Ibid., p. 18.

63. Ibid., p. 42.

64. Ibid., p. 63.

65. Ibid., p. 69.

66. Toby Marotta, *The Politics of Homosexuality* (Boston: Houghton Mifflin, 1981). Quoted in Lisa Langenbach, "Modern and Traditionalist Issue Groups in the American Party System: An Examination of the Realigning Potential of Cultural Issues in Changing Cleavage Structures" unpublished doctoral dissertation, Purdue University, West Lafayette, Indiana, Aug. 1986, pp. 75–76.

67. Eskridge, op. cit., p. 45.

68. Compton, *Introduction to Social Welfare,* p. 439.

69. Feagin, *Racial and Ethnic Relations,* p. 238.

70. Axinn and Levin, *Social Welfare,* p. 246.

71. Ehrenreich, *Altruistic Imagination,* p. 178.

72. Ibid.

73. Ibid.

74. Ibid., p. 177.

75. Ibid., p. 179.

76. Ibid., p. 161.

77. Ibid., p. 179.

78. Ibid.

79. Compton, *Introduction to Social Welfare*, p. 473.

80. Frances Fox Piven and Richard Cloward, *The New Class War: Reagan's Attack on the Welfare State and Its Consequences* (New York: Pantheon Books, 1982), p. 14.

81. Levitan, Rein, and Marwick, *Work and Welfare*, p. 8.

82. John E. Tropman, Alan Gordon, and Phyllis J. Day, "Welfare Codebook," unpublished manuscript developed 1971, based on data from *Statistical Abstracts of the United States 1971* (Washington, D.C.: U.S. Government Printing Office, 1972), p. 312; and *County and City Data Book 1964* (Washington, D.C.: U.S. Government Printing Office, 1960), p. 4.

83. Levitan, Rein, and Marwick, *Work and Welfare*, p. 46.

84. Axinn and Levin, *Social Welfare*, p. 261.

85. Compton, *Introduction to Social Welfare*, p. 134.

86. Axinn and Levin, *Social Welfare*, p. 260.

87. Phyllis J. Day, "Sex Role Stereotypes and Public Assistance," *Social Service Review* (March 1979), Vol. 53, pp. 106–115.

88. Robert Morris, *Social Policy of the American Welfare State* (New York: Harper & Row, 1979), p. 101.

89. Ibid., pp. 101–104.

90. Wilma Doyle, Leonard Z. Breen, and Robert Eichhorn, *Synopsis of the Older Americans Act*, Revised (W. Lafayette, Indiana: Department of Sociology and Anthropology, Purdue University, 1976), pp. 4–10.

91. Ehrenreich, *Altruistic Imagination*, p. 198.

92. Michael B. Katz, *Poverty and Policy in American History* (New York: Academic Press, 1983), p. 231.

93. Ehrenreich, *Altruistic Imagination*, p. 195.

94. Hall, *Black Separatism*, p. 164.

95. Jan Mason, John S. Wodarski, and T. M. Jim Parham, "Work and Welfare: A Reevaluation of AFDC," *Social Work* (May–June 1985), pp. 197–202.

96. Dye and Zeigler, *The Irony of Democracy*, p. 304.

97. Ibid., p. 302.

98. Ibid., p. 303.

11

The Return to the Past

A Retreat from the Welfare State

The 1960s were a time of flower children, psychedelics, free love, and rock and roll, when everything was touched with beauty, and love was the key word; when dreams grew into possibilities and possibilities could come true. We did not know how precious this time was until we lost it, but we knew with finality it was over when our children, demonstrating against U.S. involvement in Cambodia in 1970, were shot at Kent State University. That the killings were accidental is unimportant. The government was there with its show of force in the National Guard, and the guns were there to back up their power. Death by our own hands was the result. Others had died in the 1960s, but they died for the dream. With Kent State, the dream died.

As Johnson withdrew from his failures at home and abroad, the backlash that plagued him in his second term of office accelerated. The election of President Richard M. Nixon began the retreat into conservatism. Increasingly severe recessions racked the economy during the 1970s, with that of 1975 equal to the Great Depression, leading to an even greater economic crisis from 1981 to 1982. By 1970 manufacturing had declined to 25 percent of all employment, 17 percent of employment was in service occupations, and the government employed 18 percent of all workers.[1] The gross national product grew during the 1970s from $982 billion to $2,369 billion, but because of inflation, real median family income grew only 5 percent. In May 1980 the overall unemployment rate stood at 7.8 percent, with the rate for African Americans twice and the rate for teenagers three times the overall rate.

Despite its failure to end poverty, the Kennedy–Johnson legislation had a significant effect in reducing it. Although the Office of Economic Opportunity received less than $6 billion in all—not even 1 percent of the federal budget—from 1965 to 1968, 20 million people rose above poverty levels by 1969. Yet as OEO programs ended, poverty began to climb and by 1982 had jumped to 15 percent of the population. One notable exception was among the aged: Social Security increases (OASDI) were tied to cost-of-living adjustments (COLAs) in the 1970s, and poverty among the elderly fell by about one third, from 35.2 percent to 24.5 percent. It then decreased by another third, leaving only about 12 percent of the aged in poverty by the 1980s.[2]

Nixon's tenure, supported by a conservative backlash, moved the nation away from citizen and individual rights and toward the monolithic power of the transnational economy. On the domestic side, he dismantled most Great Society programs and gave their control over to states. This, soon to be called the New Federalism by Ronald Reagan, continued with revenue-sharing programs in which money formerly used for national social programs was given directly to states in block grants. To combat civil dissidence and growing social unrest, Nixon poured funds into law enforcement (Law Enforcement Assistance Administration, LEAA) and, suspicious of radical dissidents, authorized the COINTELPRO (counter intelligence program). Using the Federal Bureau of Investigation, his administration investigated and infiltrated dissident groups,[3] and by his reelection in 1972 most civil and human rights movements had ended (although the women's movement remained strong). Moreover, believing his executive powers placed him above the law, he used illegal activities to root out the intentions of his political enemies. This led to his forced resignation and the trial and imprisonment of his top aides, although he was pardoned when President Gerald Ford took office.

On the international level, Nixon used the Central Intelligence Agency (CIA) to keep the United States embroiled in the internal affairs of other nations. Although the Vietnam War ended in 1975, pressures from the military–industrial complex—corporations with interlocking memberships in the government and military—involved the United States almost immediately in Cambodia. U.S. foreign policies supported covert activities and overt weapons sales in nations ripe for revolt, such as Chile and Brazil, providing a profitable market for U.S. war materiel. In addition, his administration added to the power of transnational corporations through investments and tax breaks that depleted the general revenue and increased the flow of jobs to foreign countries.

The oil crisis of the 1970s provided a political/economic impetus to reunite the nation against "the world." The world, however, was now the market for transnational corporations that owed allegiance to no country or government. During the 1950s, massive industrial conglomerations began, and between 1965 and 1974, just under 13,000 companies merged. In 1973 transnationals invested more than $165 billion in foreign companies, and the share of taxes they paid to the United States declined from 30 percent of federal revenues in the 1950s to 16 percent by 1978.

Nixon's New Federalism revenue sharing cut up general revenues and distributed them directly to the states. This actually channeled more money to cities than had the Johnson programs, but it made social agencies compete with each other and with other urban programs for a share of the federal pie. Most programs suffered cutbacks, although Nixon expanded the Food Stamp Program and provided funds for child nutrition and rent subsidy programs. Food stamp expenditures rose from $550 million in 1970 to $4.4 billion in 1975—a sevenfold increase—and more than doubled again by 1981, to $10 billion. Public assistance became increasingly restrictive about work and training even though jobs were growing scarcer. As the middle class became more vulnerable to runaway inflation and as jobs closed down, the outcry against the poor led to taxpayers' revolts, most notably Proposition 13 in California, which set an upper limit on the amount that could be used for social spending (including even police and fire departments).

Nixon continued to support civil rights, but not with Johnson's fervor. Three important changes were enacted: The Equal Employment Opportunity Commission was given power to sue firms that discriminated, the Office of Federal Contract Compliance Programs (OFCCP) could impose sanctions against federal contractors for not hiring people of color, and the Fair Housing Act was amended to prohibit sex discrimination. The EEOC, OFCCP, and the Justice Department increased their activities against institutional discrimination.

Democrat Jimmy Carter was elected in 1976, following Ford's uneventful term. Both Ford and Carter maintained holding patterns, although Carter tried to move the nation toward social progress with a new welfare reform bill aimed at a guaranteed annual income, inflation reduction, and more jobs. Carter's federal appointments reflected his civil rights stance: Of the 298 federal judges he appointed, 23 percent were minorities, 15 percent were women, and many had records of sympathy toward civil rights and equal opportunity.

After the 1960s, the social work profession began its own retreat to conservatism, with social action declining and staid professionals thoroughly ensconced in the mental health movement. The defeat of the War on Poverty brought a mood of indifference, passivity, and resignation, leading to fewer enrollments in action programs in schools of social work.[4] However, the National Association of Social Workers (NASW) tried to encourage professional action by adding two lobby arms: in 1970 the Educational Legislative Action Network (ELAN) and in 1976 the Political Action for Candidate Selection (PACE) lobby.

The Council of Social Work Education (CSWE) began to accredit baccalaureate programs in 1971, and the NASW began to admit their graduates to membership. By 1976, NASW membership was 70,046, or 17,000 more than in 1970, and in 1975 schools of social work granted more than 43,000 MSW degrees. Between 1970 and 1976, social work jobs increased by 79,000. Caucuses also formed to represent minority interests. In 1968 new associations included the National Association of Black Social Workers, the Association of Puerto Rican Social Service Workers, the Asian American Social Workers (in California); in 1971 the Association of American Indian Social Workers formed.[5] By 1982 there were 384,000 social work jobs, with 88,000 in professional associations. Two-thirds of these were held by women and 19 percent were held by non-whites.[6]

Social Programs in the 1970s

Although President Ford did not tackle welfare reform, presidents Nixon and Carter expanded social insurance incrementally. In addition, each proposed basic guaranteed annual income (GAI) plans to provide a national minimum income through benefits and tax credits. Nixon's Family Assistance Plan (FAP) would have replaced Aid to Families with Dependent Children (AFDC) and unemployment insurance for every family with at least one child. Incentives would have been paid to encourage parents to enter the workforce, with job training programs and day care facilities greatly expanded.[7] FAP failed in the Senate on its first submission (1969) but seemed likely to pass when reintroduced in 1971, despite its GAI aspects. However, Nixon's Watergate problems left it to die in Congress.

President Carter's Better Jobs and Income Proposal was a negative income tax plan for all poor people regardless of family status. To be administered by the Internal Revenue Service, it would have consolidated AFDC, Supplemental Security Income, and Food Stamps under one cash benefit plan. Carter's plan was similar to FAP in provision for a federal minimum income guarantee, benefits with work incentives, job training, and child care. Under the program, those "expected to work" would have received at least $2,300 per year, with increasing benefits for family size and a possible basic yearly income of $6,100 before any disregards. The "not expected to work"—the aged, blind people, people with disabilities, and parents with children under age seven—would have received a minimum of $4,200 for a family of four. Federal monies disbursed to state and local governments would have created 1.4 million public services jobs and training slots for training useful in the private sector.[8] The proposal failed in Congress.

Social Insurance

Old Age, Survivors, Disability, and Health Insurance (OASDHI). There were two major policy changes in social insurance in the 1970s. The first was the legislation in 1972 that granted cost-of-living adjustments based on the Consumer Price Index, which rose 27 percent from 1970 to 1974 and another 15 percent by 1976. Thus, with every increase in cost of living, additional benefits were paid to recipients. The second was the transfer of all adult public assistance categories from public assistance to social insurance in 1971. This meant that recipients of Old Age Assistance, Aid to the Blind, and Aid to the Permanently and Totally Disabled were placed under the OASDI programs, with the effect of drastically increasing the number of entitled people without regard to work history. This led to the creation of Supplemental Security Income (SSI), a public assistance program in the Department of Health and Human Services (HHS).

The Social Security Amendments of 1978 changed the method by which coverage was determined so that, rather than counting quarters of the year for coverage, workers were credited with a quarter year of employment for each $250 of earned income. Fully covered workers could now retire at age sixty-two, though with reduced benefits. Surviving spouses could collect benefits at age sixty-two or, if disabled, at age fifty. Surviving unmarried children would collect benefits until age eighteen (or nineteen if still in school), and children born out of wedlock qualified as survivor dependents. Children with continuous disabilities would qualify to age twenty-two, when their own OASDI benefits would begin. For disability coverage, people had to be permanently unable to work and not yet sixty-five years old, and to have worked for a certain period before disablement.

Social welfare expenses boomed during the 1970s because of new entitlements and inflation. In 1970 expenditures reached nearly $146 billion, about 17 percent of the gross national product, and then almost doubled, to $290 billion, in 1975. With private expenditures included, 28 percent of the GNP went to social welfare in 1970. By 1976, social insurance accounted for 44 percent of welfare expenditures, increasing to 52 percent by 1983.[9] More than $55 billion a year went for retirement, with another $28 billion in benefits to disabled workers, dependents, and survivors.[10]

The federal share of expenditures for social programs increased: By 1970, it was somewhat more than 50 percent, but by 1978, it was 61 percent.[11] By 1983, total expenditures hovered at about 19 percent of the GNP. Wildavsky suggests that inflation caused between 35 and 45 percent of the increase between 1965 and 1975.[12] Food stamp benefits were also tied to the Consumer Price Index, and therefore increased proportionately with inflation.[13]

Income maintenance varied widely by geographic area and type of program. (In 1979 in Mississippi, for example, a family of four on AFDC received $101 monthly whereas an OASDI family received $580.) Social Security for a retired couple paid $431 a month, and Supplemental Security Income paid between $189 and $284. Unemployment benefits averaged about $350 monthly, including dependent allowances in the few states that paid them. In a number of states, maximum benefits payable to survivors or workers killed on the job were lower than those for temporary disabilities.[14] As of 1980, no family could receive more than 150 to 180 percent of the former worker's benefit, so the greater the number of children, the less per capita was received.

One reason for the generosity of Congress in OASDI payments was that, early in the 1970s, the program had surpluses not since matched. In 1970 OASDI collected $35 billion in taxes and paid out $32 billion. However, the worsening economy changed the surplus situation by 1975, and in 1979 benefits of $104.3 billion exceeded contributions of $103 billion. The deficit increased in the early 1980s, and prices increased faster than wages. Because they were COLA-indexed, OASDI benefits rose faster on average than workers' take-home pay—19 percent faster by 1980. In 1981 OASDI paid out $145 billion while collecting only $140 billion.[15]

Most people receive much more than they put into the Social Security system, and pensions depend on current legislation rather than on legislation at the time the person becomes eligible. Benefits are paid from current funds rather than the so-called trust or reserve fund, and funds collected from people now being paid are being contributed by workers today.

> The Social Security system in America made its first payment on January 31, 1940, to a retired unmarried woman who died thirty-five years later at the age of one hundred . . . for a total tax contribution of about $22.00 she received more than $20,000 over the thirty-five-year period. Her payment in 1940 was $22.54, and in 1974 was $109.20.[16]

Unemployment Insurance.   The recessions of 1969–1971 and 1974–1975 were moderated by the expansion of unemployment benefits. The period of eligibility was extended and offices were kept open nights and weekends. People are eligible for unemployment insurance if they have worked for a base period, which varies by state. Most states restrict benefits for students, pregnant women, and people unemployed because of marital or family obligations. Also, people fired from jobs for misconduct or refusing suitable work are treated differently: The waiting period for unemployment insurance is delayed. Most states figure benefits on base pay, with minimum and maximum levels, and a few states add extra for dependent children.

Approximately 20 percent of the population is not covered by unemployment insurance, although more than 90 percent of jobs are covered. Employers with fewer than four employees are not covered, and people looking for first jobs or having only brief employment do not qualify. Moreover, many employers do not hire full-time or let employees go before the base period is covered so employers need not pay unemployment insurance taxes. This secondary labor market, providing neither social insurance nor company fringe benefits, is a prime employer of young people, women, and people of color.

Public Assistance Programs

Public assistance after the Johnson years had several themes: the promiscuity of welfare mothers; the laziness of recipients; and fraud, including secret jobs; use of money to support communes; lying; and cheating. Heffernan says,

> The personal fault theme was supplemented by a belief that current welfare programs . . . encouraged withdrawal from the labor force, family splitting, and migration . . . for the purpose of receiving aid.[17]

Social Darwinism was still active. For example, in 1974 William Shockley, a Nobel Laureate in physics, advocated paying the "unfit poor"—those who did not pay income taxes—for eugenic sterilization at the rate of $1,000 for each point they fell below IQ 100. The bonuses, placed in a trust fund, would be doled out over the individual's life span. He noted that

$30,000 put in a trust for a 70 IQ moron potentially capable of producing twenty children might return $250,000 to taxpayers in reduced costs of mental retardation care.[18]

Obviously, his greatest interest was in control of women, for men can father many more children than twenty. He also established a sperm bank for contributions from men of "genetic superiority."[19]

Supplemental Security Income.   The move of adult categories—blind, aged, and disabled adults—out of public assistance and into OASDI meant that these groups were finally recognized as "deserving poor." The change had two major results. On one hand, it channeled even more hostility toward "undeserving" AFDC recipients. On the other, the new SSI program gave the nation a guaranteed annual minimum income except for AFDC recipients. The move meant that grants were less in some states than people received under the categorical programs (AB, AD, and OAA). This was particularly true for disabled people because of stricter federal medical certification for disability. To remedy this, SSI, a federal public assistance program funded through general revenue and tied to COLAs, was legislated in 1972 and put into effect in 1974. Means testing and social services were provided through local departments of public welfare.

With SSI, people falling below states' standards of need received an additional cash grant beyond OASDI grants. For eligibility and grant determinations, recipients were allowed no more than $1,500 in liquid assets ($2,250 for a couple), homes had to be worth less than $25,000, and cars worth less than $1,200. Referral to vocational rehabilitation was required for blind and disabled people under age sixty-five. Spousal or child income was counted as resources, but the first $65 earned and $20 per month of income were disregarded. States had to provide supplements up to state levels of need until SSI payments exceeded the total spent on former OAA, AD, and AB, when the federal government picked up the extra costs.

Aid to Families with Dependent Children: The Work Incentive and Absent Fathers Programs.   Despite the social protest movements of the 1960s, gains for AFDC families were soon lost. The National Welfare Rights Organization had made two proposals that were given serious consideration by the legislature. The first, cost-of-living increases, succeeded as a joint legislative–welfare reform effort in 1967. However, states would not give up their rights to set standards of need and the Supreme Court upheld their position.[20]

The second proposal, eligibility by declaration (1969), allowed welfare departments to rely solely on applicants' statements without in-depth verifications. New York City used it with apparent success for some time, but in general it was so modified at the local level that it was ineffective.[21]

In the 1970s, hostility increased toward AFDC recipients. Slippage of civil rights—the rights to privacy, equal protection under the law, and due process—continued apace. Searches for "men in the house" and midnight raids continued in spite of Supreme Court decisions,[22] and other regulations were ignored or finessed. For example, residence requirements, though unconstitutional, were used under the guise of "inappropriate housing" and decided at the discretion of welfare workers. Welfare workers again had free discretion to remove those not meeting their standards from AFDC rolls. AFDC grants continued to be minimal: In constant dollars, between 1970 and 1981, average benefits declined by almost 20 percent, and even with food stamps, benefits dropped by 9 percent.[23]

The Talmadge amendments of 1971 made participation in the Work Incentive Program (WIN) mandatory for all adult recipients with children age six or over. Because there were not sufficient spaces in the WIN training programs, "creaming" took place because administrators wanted good success records. In 1971 more than half of those in WIN programs were white, and 40 percent were men.[24] That WIN did not work seemed beside the point: It was required not for its effectiveness, but because of the desire to punish those who did not work. Senator Russell Long said,

> Of 250,000 welfare referrals found appropriate and referred to the Work Incentive Program during its first twenty-one months, less than 60 percent were enrolled in the program . . . and out of the 145,000 who were enrolled, one-third subsequently dropped out. Only 13,000 welfare cases have been closed following participation in the . . . program.[25]

The total appropriation to the "WIN funnel" was $500 million, with the following success rates of 2,664,000 assessed (through 1971):

- 627,000 were found appropriate
- 493,000 were referred to WIN
- 286,000 were enrolled
- 170,000 left, and
- 36,000 completed successfully.[26]

This meant a cost per person of about $13,900.

Child Support and Dependency Programs.   In 1972, Title IV.D. of the Social Security Act was enacted for child support enforcement. Officially called Notice to Law Enforcement Officials (NOLEO), it was more often called the "absent pappy" law. It required AFDC mothers to file suit against their children's fathers to collect back support. As early as 1960, Kaplan concluded that

> absent fathers of needy children, like their families, tend to be poor, and even the most vigorous law enforcement does not create income. Collections from fathers are grossly inadequate to meet their families' needs. The unemployment and underemployment of men, particularly . . . [African American men], appear to be the most pressing problem.[27]

Mothers, often against their will, became instruments of the law in compelling support from fathers, under threat of the loss of their AFDC benefits. Some had to sign warrants or complaints with the district attorney, others had to swear out paternity suits, and some had to submit to lie detector tests.[28] The law also opened Social Security and income tax records to help the new Offices of Child Support locate absent parents and permitted garnishment of federal wages and stipends to pay delinquent support orders.

In 1978 there were five times more mothers above the poverty level than below not receiving court-ordered payments, and of men ordered to support, two-fifths rarely paid anything and one-tenth paid only sporadically. In 1979, 34.6 percent (2.5 million) of 7.1 million children under twenty-one received child support payments. Over one-third of all fathers were not required to pay anything because of limited earning ability, and the amounts ordered bore little relationship to the man's income. After a year or two, in most cases, noncompliance was the rule rather than the exception. On the average, African American fathers are more conscientious about child support payments, and the poor are at least as conscientious as are middle- or upper-class fathers.[29]

Social Services (Title XX, 1962).   This open-ended act provided federal reimbursement to states up to 75 percent of costs for new programs for the disadvantaged. Ninety percent of social services money had to be spent for people on public assistance, with the remaining amount to be used for child care and family planning services, and for services to people with developmental disabilities; drug addicts, alcoholics, and children in foster care. State welfare departments saw it as a way to gain more federal dollars. Instead of developing new services, states began to charge the government for services they had traditionally provided. "Purchase of services" grants to private agencies were unusually generous, stimulating the growth of the "personal social service" industry—casework treatment—and encouraging social workers to enter private practice or organize private consultant firms.[30] States were reimbursed 50 percent of the cost in 1956, 75 percent in 1962, and up to 90 percent in 1975.

By 1972, to control flyaway costs Congress capped the program at $2.2 billion through the Revenue Sharing Act. The "open invitation" policy ended. With federal money limited, newly developed services deteriorated and purchase of services from private agencies—for mental health counseling, drug abuse, child care—dropped abruptly. Therefore, in 1974, legislators created Social Security Act "block grants" for which agencies competed, with costs capped at a "permanent" ceiling of $2.5 billion (raised to $3 billion for 1982). Now *only 50 percent was required to be spent on services for the poor.* Block grants were allocated to states on the basis of population, with state matching required, usually at 75:25 ratio. Some services qualified for a 90:10 ratio, especially administrative and staff development and social work education.

In the new block grant system, states had to plan comprehensively to develop social services. Each service had to have at least one of the following goals:

- Reduce the dependency of clients.
- Help them gain economic independence (get off the welfare rolls).
- Prevent or remedy the neglect, abuse, or exploitation of children and adults unable to protect their own interests, including the preservation, reuniting, or rehabilitation of the family system (leading to family preservation programs).
- Provide for the least intrusive care, usually community-based or home care rather than institutional care.
- Secure institutional care when other kinds are inappropriate and provide services to those so placed.

About 10.6 million people received social services in 1978, of whom about 30 percent were AFDC clients, 37 percent other people in poverty, and 13 percent people receiving services not related to income level. Child day care was the most costly item, totaling $732.3 million, and $324.8 million went for homemaker services, although only 11 percent of homemaker services went to AFDC families.

Because of the caps, mental health agencies withdrew many mental health services, cutting some of the most frequently provided: counseling, day care, child protective services, health-related services, homemaker services, transportation, and family planning. In addition, community mental health services neglected the great numbers of mentally ill being released from hospitals. The result was a national shame: homeless men and women wandering the streets of large cities without food, clothing, or shelter, living and often dying with nobody to care.

Concern for children, especially those born out of wedlock, came to the fore again in the 1970s. Programs to combat child abuse and neglect continued to receive increased funding, and in 1971 Congress passed the Comprehensive Child Development Act to provide funds for comprehensive high-quality day care. However, President Nixon vetoed it on the grounds that it would destroy the family, duplicate already existing services, and establish communal child-rearing against American values.

One unanticipated consequence of block grants was the move toward taking children from parents not considered "adequate." New institutions, foster care, and group home situations proliferated, with higher funding than for in-home preventive services. During this period, about 700,000 children were placed away from their parents, about 400,000 in various types of foster care and another 300,000 in institutions. One-third of the latter were placed in corrections facilities.[31] Thus, rather than giving support to intact but unstable families, millions were spent for child placement after families had disintegrated or deteriorated. Looking at yearly costs per child by type of care, homemaker services, family day care, and day care centers cost between $2,000 and $3,000 per child. For remedial care, $5,200 per child was spent yearly for foster home care, $15,400 per child for group home care, $18,600 for each child in group residences, $34,000 per child in general institutions, and $42,100 for each child placed in secure detention facilities.[32]

Institutional classism, sexism, and racism are all evident in such placements: There are more poor children and children of color placed in institutions, and boys and girls are placed differentially, girls more often for status offenses and boys for offenses that would be criminal if committed by an adult.[33] (Nearly half were locked up because of running away from home, being truant, or not being wanted at home.)

Other Social Welfare Programs

Food Stamps. Food stamp expenditures were $35 million in 1965, $550 million in 1970, more than $4.4 billion by 1975, and $10 billion in 1981.[34] In 1977 recipients were no longer required to buy food stamps, and "bonuses" figured on income level and number in household were simply given to eligible recipients. Still, many eligible people did not receive food stamps because, among other problems, they were not informed about the program or their eligibility, certification requirements were too difficult, offices were inaccessible, and using stamps was embarrassing to proud people. During the late 1970s, eligibility levels were changed several times, resulting in a 2.5 million drop in users between 1976 and 1978. Worsening economic conditions still pushed the number of food stamp users to new heights before the 1980s began.[35] In 1979 the average monthly grant per person was $34, so that $1,638 would be added to the purchasing power of a family of four over a year, still about $960 below the poverty threshold.[36]

Comprehensive Education and Training Act (CETA). CETA arose from the Manpower Development and Training Act of 1962, the Economic Opportunity Act of 1964, and the Emergency Employment Act of 1970. Nixon's administration established the program in 1973 to provide entry-level jobs in the private sector for young urban minority people and the chronically unemployed. In 1977, for example, five-sixths of CETA employees were school dropouts averaging below sixth-grade reading ability. One-half were from single-parent families, their family sizes were nearly twice the national average, and their family's per capita income was less than one-third of the total population's average. Eighty percent had previous arrests and 75 percent prior convictions. More than one-third had never held a twenty-hour-a-week job for longer than one month.[37]

State and local governments determined the extent of the program by how much they spent in matching funds. In 1974, however, a severe recession added millions to the unemployment rolls in the private sector and eliminated the competition for jobs there. In response, CETA became an employment agency for temporary public service jobs, in government and social agencies, that were to be picked up with local funding when CETA subsidies ended. However, almost two-thirds of the 6 million CETA jobs, which cost the federal government nearly $24 billion, ended when federal subsidies terminated. From 1974 to 1979, CETA was one of the largest government agencies, and spent $55 billion during the eight years of its operation.[38]

Education and Youth Programs.   The remnants of OEO, including Head Start, Upward Bound, Talent Search, and Job Corps, were moved to other agencies and continued with varying success. There is substantial evidence that Head Start had a positive effect on nearly every aspect of early childhood development, including the inhibition of serious educational and behavioral problems.[39] Disadvantaged children were less likely to be in special education classes, more likely to be in their regular grade at school, and more likely to graduate from high school, enroll in college, and obtain a self-supporting job. They were also less likely to be arrested or on welfare when adults. In 1983 Head Start served 400,000 children at a cost of $907 million, and reached about 20 percent of four- and five-year-olds from disadvantaged homes.[40]

Upward Bound and Talent Search programs encouraged young people to continue their education. Nearly 60 percent of Upward Bound students entered college and remained at least two years, and in 1976 Talent Search placed between 75 and 90 percent of its students in postsecondary institutions. Job Corps was not so successful, with only 30 percent completing vocational training from the corps. Nevertheless, in 1977 those who did earned $1,250 more annually ($1,500 for women) than young people in the same life situations who were not in Job Corps, and they generally obtained jobs with higher status and better working conditions. Trainees also were more likely to attend college and were 35 percent less likely to engage in criminal activities.[41]

In 1965 the Education for All Handicapped Children Act was added to the Elementary and Secondary Education Act (ESEA). It mandated that school districts provide appropriate educational opportunities for educationally impaired children. The act aimed for basic skills improvement, consumer education, bilingual education, and the acquisition of instructional materials and equipment. It was revised and extended in 1975 (Developmentally Disabled Bill of Rights Act), before which students with physical or mental handicaps could be taught in classrooms separated from the conventional classroom. With the revision, every child was required to have an individualized program in the least restricted feasible environment—the regular classroom where possible—with teachers specifically trained in special education. The federal government paid a substantial portion of the added costs to school districts. Because the federal government has no direct legal authority over public schools, the law was passed to protect the constitutional rights of disabled students.

Five-sixths of all ESEA funds were designated for educationally deprived and disadvantaged children, and grants were allotted according to the number of children from low-income families in the school district. Special grants were also given for migrant, neglected, and delinquent children. ESEA was credited with eliminating over 40 percent of the difference in reading achievement between nine-year-old white and African American children after 1965. In 1982, 10 percent of monies for bilingual programs were cut from ESEA by the Reagan administration, with another 50 percent to follow in 1983. For remedial instruction and related services, however, $3.5 billion was provided in 1984.[42]

Housing.   Nixon, Ford, and Carter did little in the area of housing. The Model Cities Program, along with public housing and Urban Renewal, was deemphasized by the Nixon administration in 1973 and effectively terminated by the Housing Act of 1974, which shifted federal resources to revenue-sharing strategies. Low-rent public housing, home loans for low-income families, and rent supplement programs were made available to the poor, along with special Department of Housing and Urban Development programs for the aged (HUD Title 8). The U.S. Department of Agriculture also gave home loans to farmers, and HUD administered the Office of Indian Housing. Most such programs are means tested, with the exceptions of Veteran's Housing Assistance and guaranteed mortgage loans from the Federal Housing Administration and HUD.[43]

Juvenile Protection and Adult Corrections.   In 1974 Congress amended the Juvenile Justice and Delinquency Prevention Act. Secure institutions and jails were overused and had became "schools of crime" for children institutionalized for noncriminal and minor delinquencies. There were almost no rehabilitative programs, and children in such institutions were often subject to physical abuse.[44] Another reason for the legislation was increasing estimates of child abuse in the home—between 60,000 and 2 million cases per year. Estimates indicated that half of the approximately 2 million children who ran away from home annually were physically and sexually abused by relatives and other adults, and that at least six children were beaten to death by adults on an average day.[45]

The Child Abuse and Treatment Act (1974) accelerated the development of state programs to aid the mistreated child, established the National Center for Prevention and Treatment of Child Abuse and Neglect at the University of Colorado Medical Center, authorized runaway shelters and hotlines, and promoted research and professional training in the areas of child abuse and protection, although funds were not allocated until Carter's administration. The Child Welfare Act of 1980 provided funds and federal regulations to alter the pattern by which children were removed to foster care, of whom there were 500,000 in 1980.

Attention to violent crimes during the Nixon years led to the Law Enforcement Assistance Administration (LEAA) in the Department of Justice in 1968. It conducted and funded research, promoted efforts to improve personnel in the field of corrections, and encouraged demonstration projects. Between 1969 and 1972, its budget rose from $60 million to $700 million,[46] providing impetus to the training of people to work in criminal justice.

Society has great faith in the justice system, but the fact is that it perpetuates institutional racism and classism. A study of the legal and social characteristics of 2,419 consecutive felony probation cases found that those most likely to be labeled as felons were defendants who were older, nonwhite, and poorly educated, had prior records, and were defended by court-appointed attorneys. These groups also are more likely to receive severe punishments such as imprisonment or death for rape and murder. Former Attorney General Ramsey Clark says,

Racial discrimination is manifest from the bare statistics of capital punishment. Since we began keeping records in 1930, there have been 2,066 Negroes and only 1,751 white persons put to death. Hundreds of thousands of rapes have occurred in America since 1930, yet only 455 men have been executed for rape—and 405 of them were Negroes. There can be no rationalization or justification of such clear discrimination. It is outrageous public murder, illuminating our darkest racism.[47]

Lesser punishments also show bias: Parole often depends on the value judgments of parole board members, corrections officers, and others in power. The safest risk, according to their biases, are middle-class white educated men, with white-collar rather than skilled or unskilled job training. African Americans have about one-half the chance of early release of whites at the same educational level.[48] The growing numbers in prison seem to validate our beliefs in the growing crime rate, but it is the reporting of crimes that is increasing. Because of racist and classist bias, there is a winnowing out of white, middle-class, white-collar men, and those left are generally people of color, especially African American men, and the poor.

During the 1980s, there were about 5,000 city and county jails, 400 state and federal prisons, and a variety of other detention centers. In some states, the cost of imprisonment for one inmate was above $20,000 per year, not including the cost of his or her family's support if they went on AFDC. On an average day, about 1.3 million people were confined. Spending for prisons and jails rose 50.9 percent during the first half of the 1980s, and in 1983, $10.4 billion was spent on corrections, up from $6.9 billion in 1980. Spending for police, courts, and prisons came to $39.7 billion in 1983.[49] The number of correctional officers more than doubled, to nearly 100,000.[50]

Civil Rights in the 1970s

Although the 1964 Civil Rights Act brought some lasting benefits to people of color and to women, the Equal Employment Opportunity Commission was unable to keep up with complaints in the 1970s. In 1974 nearly 57,000 people filed complaints that took more than two-and-a-half years to resolve, leaving a backlog of 100,000 cases by 1980. By 1982, the backlog was 5,000 to 10,000 cases.[51]

Native Americans

Native American protests became more radical after the Civil Rights Act of 1964, for although the War on Poverty brought some benefits in temporary jobs and training, systematic discrimination continued. Literacy tests and the gerrymandering of district lines, especially in Western states, was rampant, although more Native Americans began to serve in government office. (From 1900, only two dozen had served in state legislatures and only a handful in the U.S. Congress, although Charles Curtis, born in 1869 on the Kaw reservation, served as representative for fourteen years, senator for twenty, and vice president under Hoover.)

During the 1960s and 1970s, tens of thousands of Native Americans were encouraged to leave reservations for the cities. One-half to three-fourths of urban relocatees returned to reservations after a few years because of continued poverty and discrimination in jobs and housing. Still, by 1980, half of all Native Americans lived in metropolitan areas. In 1968 the government acted to attract industry to some reservations, and by 1972, there were 200 factories there, though only half the jobs went to Native Americans. By the late 1960s, the gross income from agriculture on reservations was $300 million, of which Native Americans received only about $100 million.[52]

With the beginning of the Indian Health Service in 1955, the health of Native Americans improved markedly. Mortality rates declined and life expectancy increased: Between 1955 and 1971, the infant death rate decreased by 56 percent and the maternal death rate by 54 percent, and deaths from tuberculosis, gastritis, and influenza pneumonia declined by 86, 88, and 57 percent, respectively. Still, Native Americans die younger than any other group, and infant mortality on some reservations is comparable to that of undeveloped countries.[53] In 1970 two-thirds of all the U.S. population sixteen to twenty-four years old had finished high school, compared to 50 percent of Native Americans in urban areas and 25 percent in rural areas.

The American land-grab of Native American lands continued: Until Native Americans abandon use and occupancy of land they have aboriginal title to it, and as recently as 1971 Alaskan Natives held aboriginal title to nine-tenths of Alaska. Therefore, in 1970 a judge held that an oil pipeline could not be laid across the Yukon until permission was obtained. However, "on December 14, 1971, Congress took note of the Alaskan Natives' aboriginal title and extinguished it."[54] In return, Congress gave the Native Americans a business corporation for each of their 220 villages to manage the land they would be allowed to take back from selected areas. It also agreed to pay them something less than a billion dollars from North Slope Oil revenues, but there is no deadline for payment. Eighty thousand Native Americans were affected by the act, so each would have 1/80,000 of a share in the corporation; however, their shares could not be sold until 1991, so they realized very little from the agreement. The only tangible benefit was a cash dividend, which in 1974 amounted to about $181 each.[55]

In 1973 the American Indian Policy Review Commission, the first top-level investigative commission in Indian affairs since the Merriam Report in 1928, was formed. Its members were five Native Americans and seven senators and congressmen, the majority from states with large Native American populations. In 1975 they ruled that tribes are sovereign political bodies with power to enact and enforce their own laws, and that a special trust relationship still exists between them and the U.S. government.[56] In 1977 their full report was issued:

> From the standpoint of personal well-being, the Indian of America ranks at the bottom of virtually every social statistical indicator . . . the highest infant mortality

rate, the lowest longevity rate, the lowest level of educational attainment, the lowest per capita income, and the poorest housing and transportation in the land.[57]

Of all men in the United States in 1977, 74 percent were employed, but only 56 percent of Native American men worked. Native American women averaged less than $400 a year for their employment. Rural residents lived in greater poverty than did those in cities. Thirty-four percent of Native Americans had an annual income of $4,000 or less, as compared with 15 percent of the total population; only 22 percent earned $10,000 or more, compared with 47 percent of the general population.[58]

Forced assimilation of Native Americans still exists. A prime example is the taking of Native American children from their families as part of the general discretionary trend of welfare and mental health workers,

> placing these children in white foster homes or institutions. In some areas 25 to 40 percent of all children are taken from their homes. Social workers argue the homes of poor Native Americans are not "fit" places for children. . . . [T]he poverty and "dirt" in the lives of Native Americans are fundamentally the result of the destruction of Native American resources . . . over hundreds of years of colonial oppression.[59]

Among Native American protest groups, the most radical was the American Indian Movement (AIM). In 1969, after student protesters occupied the no-longer-used prison island of Alcatraz, a hundred AIM members replaced them, arguing that their treaty rights guaranteed them unused federal lands. They were forcibly removed in 1971. In 1973 AIM led an armed occupation at Wounded Knee on Pine Ridge Reservation, arguing that the tribal government was dominated by whites. Federal agents and disguised army units occupied the reservation with an armed struggle that lasted seventy-one days, with two Native Americans killed and two federal officials wounded. Up to 300 Native Americans were involved. Illegal wiretapping and paid witnesses led to the defeat of the suit against AIM, but a dozen suspicious murders and accidents later happened to AIM members, with few arrests or convictions for the crimes. The Eighth Circuit Court of Appeals reversed a lower court's dismissal of complaints that their constitutional rights had been violated when the military intervened in a domestic problem with Air Force planes for surveillance and high-ranking military officers on hand, under the direction of Alexander Haig, vice chief of staff under Nixon. The court decided that

> the use of military forces to seize civilians can expose civilian government to the threat of military rule and the suspension of constitutional liberties.[60]

In 1974 a group of Mohawks occupied a forest preserve in New York's Adirondack State Park, claiming its 600 acres, along with 9 million additional acres in New York and Vermont. In September the state went to federal court seeking to evict the Mohawks, and they countered with a suit charging that the land had been usurped by fraud. On appeal, they were granted rights to considerable land in the state. Furthermore, in 1975 armed Menominees occupied the Alexian Brothers' novitiate building, and as a consequence, a committee was formed to supervise contacts between Native Americans and police, which was successful in improving police behavior. In 1979 the Supreme Court upheld a 1974 decision that treaties reserved fishing rights for Native Americans differently than for whites and recognized tribal rights to fishing resources. However, this led to a significant backlash of congressional bills aimed at breaking treaties, overturning court decisions, and exterminating land claims.[61]

In the 1970s, three dozen tribes created the Council of Energy Resources (CERT) to protect their interests. They hired a former Iranian oil minister to help them with contracts because they rarely received the correct royalties in dealing with white Americans for the development of coal, oil, and other resources. CERT obtained several million dollars of grants for technical assistance and reservation industrialization. Throughout this time, however, the government tried to co-opt CERT because Native American lands included one-third of the strip coal mining resources of the West and half the uranium outside public lands.[62]

Feagin says,

> Native American lands have been taken for dams, reservoir projects, national parks, and right of ways for roads. The sale of lands to private lumbering and mineral interests—200,000 acres in 1970—continues. . . . Large proportions of the usable land in reservations have been leased to whites.[63]

By 1973, some 300 land claims had been heard and over $300 million awarded to Native American societies. However, this represents less than 4 percent of the amount claimed. In New York and Maine, the Oneida society's claims against the government have returned some illegally taken land. An agreement providing for the acquisition of 300,000 acres to be held in trust for Native Americans was developed, and a $27 million trust fund was signed by Jimmy Carter in 1980.[64] In 1984 appropriations included $254 million to the Bureau of Indian Affairs for the operation of Indian-controlled boarding and day schools, and an additional $69 million went to the Department of Education to support the education of Native American children in public schools.[65]

Reaganomics hit Native Americans hard. After 1980 average unemployment on reservations jumped from 40 percent to a devastating 80 percent, and in some societies average income fell to $900 per year for a family of four. Because Native Americans receive no state or local aid, they have had to rely on the federal government for help, yet programs that benefited them, such as CETA, the Economic Development Administration, Housing and Urban Development, and Health and Human Services, were cut drastically.

Japanese Americans

Although Japanese Americans suffered personally and economically from their internment during World War II, they soon began to recoup their losses. In 1950 Japanese American activities in Hawaii led to statehood, and Daniel Inouye, a war hero, became the first Japanese American in the House of Representatives. Spark Matsunaga was second in 1962, and Inouye then became the first Japanese American senator in 1964. Patsy Takemoto Mink became the first Japanese woman in Congress. Whereas these congresspersons came from Hawaii, in 1976 Samuel Hayakawa was the first Japanese American senator from the mainland, reelected in 1982.[66]

In 1970 there were 591,000 Japanese Americans in the United States, with the heaviest concentrations in Hawaii (217,307) and California (213,280). Their median family income was $12,500 (all incomes median $9,600), although Japanese American women earned much less than men, at $5,880 (compared to $5,122 for white women). Only 7.5 percent lived below the poverty level. By this time their education level was higher than any other population group: Nearly all had finished high school and over half the men and one-third of the women were college graduates. By 1980 Japanese American median family income was $22,025.[67]

Japanese Americans continued to protest their illegal internment during World War II. In January 1983, Gordon Hirabayashi, who was jailed in 1943 for arguing against internment, sought to have his conviction set aside (along with that of Fred Koromatsu) on grounds that government lawyers had concealed important evidence at his trial: a naval intelligence report contradicting the army's claim that widespread disloyalty among Japanese Americans required their evacuation and internment. The "proof" that convicted them was a decoded intelligence statement suggesting that Japanese Americans working in aircraft plants had cabled production figures to Tokyo—figures printed ten days before in the *Los Angeles Times*. A star witness could not connect those cables to a single American citizen of Japanese ancestry. The U.S. Court of Appeals for the District of Columbia heard a $12 billion damage suit brought on behalf of all surviving internees. A federal district court judge dismissed the suit on statute of limitations grounds, but the Circuit Court finally reversed the dismissal and granted compensation to plaintiffs.

A resurgence of racism against Asians across the country was evident in the 1980s recessions. Peter Irons says,

> From California to Boston, violence against Asians has spread, as the "Rambo syndrome" and "Japan-bashing" have become respectable. The murder of Vincent Chin in Detroit and the wave of attacks on Vietnamese and other Indochinese refugees testify to the ugly strain of racism the Reagan Administration has done little to counter.[68]

Other Asian Americans

In 1970 there were 435,000 Chinese and 343,000 Filipinos in the United States. During 1973, immigration brought in approximately 21,700 Chinese, 30,000 Filipinos, and 5,500 Japanese. There were 1.5–3.5 million Asian immigrants from 1970 to 1980, and by 1980, Chinese had surpassed Japanese as the nation's largest Asian group. One-half million Indochinese immigrated to the United States in

1970, of whom two-thirds were from Vietnam. This last group was particularly threatened when they settled around the Gulf of Mexico, with incidences of burning in effigy and harassment of fishermen by the Ku Klux Klan.[69]

Mexican Americans

In 1970 Mexican Americans numbered more than 4.5 million, with almost 80 percent living in Arizona, California, Colorado, New Mexico, and Texas. Their median family income was $6,972 (though substantially lower in Texas), whereas that of all families was $9,600.[70] One-quarter of the Mexican American population lived below the poverty level. Approximately 17 percent of all children in the Southwest were Mexican Americans, but only 4 percent of the 325,000 teachers in the Southwest were Mexican Americans. Significant provisions were made for bilingual education under ESEA (1968), and in 1974 the *Law v. Nichols* decision determined that schools could not ignore the language problems of non-English speakers, yet we continue to weaken bilingual programs. In 1979 more than 50 percent of Mexican American children did not finish high school, and one-quarter had less than an elementary school education. In 1982 the Supreme Court ruled that all children, including illegal aliens, had to be provided schooling without tuition in U.S. schools.[71]

Little real progress was made to ensure equality for Mexican Americans, partly because of lack of differentiation between Mexican American citizens and illegal immigrant Mexicans. Officially, legal immigration was limited: There were new restrictions in 1960, and in 1965 the Immigration Act limited immigration from the Western Hemisphere to 120,000. In 1976 an immigration cap of 20,000 was placed on Mexico. However, whenever more labor is needed, growers support illegal immigration. Four to seven million undocumented Mexican laborers—*braceros*—entered the United States between 1920 and 1980. Whole families came to the United States, where they had no legal protection. Despite abuses, even death (for example, a truckload of Mexican laborers were left in a locked truck to die in the desert early in the 1980s), they are afraid to go to authorities for help. Because workers picking crops are often paid by the basket, their children work in the fields too, without adequate shelter, food, or health care. Although hiring of American children is prohibited by law, Hispanic children—whether illegal immigrants, legal immigrants, or Hispanic Americans—rarely have such protection. Major canneries and food producers do not bother to ask who has picked the baskets of food turned in for pay.[72]

In the mid-1970s, nearly all employers of Hispanics refused government help in finding American workers to replace Mexican workers who had been caught. There are no legal penalties against employers who knowingly hire undocumented workers, and although a 1982 Senate bill would have imposed fines as high as $10,000 and jail, it failed in the House. It was widely condemned by supporters of agribusiness based on Hispanic labor: A Heritage Foundation report said that imposing sanctions on employers who hire illegal aliens would cause significant economic disruption and that immigrants, both legal and illegal, have been "net contributors to the nation's economy." It recommended increased enforcement efforts by the U.S. Border Patrol, an increased quota for immigrants, and the establishment of a legal guest program rather than fines for growers. Only 1–2 percent of Hispanic workers are illegal aliens, considerably lower than the 5 to 10 million official estimate.[73] The Reagan administration passed an immigration bill in 1987 that allowed 350,000 "guest workers" into the United States at any one time and granted amnesty to those who entered the country before January 1, 1980.

Hispanics were always targets of hate groups such as the Ku Klux Klan and the Aryan Nation, especially in towns bordering Mexico. Overt action, however, always becomes more common as unemployment worsens. Most Americans would not work at such hard labor and low pay as do Hispanic farm workers, yet this is only a rallying cry to stir up hatred and action against those who are "different."

Puerto Ricans and Cubans

The 1974–1975 recession that brought cutbacks in the petrochemical industry left the island of Puerto Rico, a commonwealth of the United States, in permanent recession. *Puertoriquenos,* pushed out by the recession and encouraged to migrate to the mainland, came in great numbers. However, life was little better for them: In 1976 over 16 percent of Puerto Rican men and 22 percent of Puerto Rican women were unemployed. Except for Native Americans, Puerto Ricans are the poorest of all citizens in the United States. In 1980 when there were 2 million *Puertoriquenos* on the mainland, their median income was $9,900, one-half the national average.[74]

Puerto Ricans faced discrimination in more than employment and housing. For example, a federally funded survey by the Hispanic Health Council found that of 153 Puerto Rican women in Hartford, Connecticut, fully half have been sterilized. Women told interviewers they had signed consent forms without understanding them. The rate of sterilization in Puerto Rico has been between 30 and 35 percent for many years, encouraged by the government as a means of controlling population and welfare costs.[75] Sterilization for poor women of all ethnicities is a pervasive, though usually undocumented, reality of welfare life. Puerto Rican activist groups include Aspira, which tries to provide educational opportunities for young people, the Puerto Rican Legal Project, the Puerto Rican Defense Fund, the League of Puerto Rican Women, the Puerto Rican Teachers Association, the Puerto Rican Forum, and the Puerto Rican Family Institute.

A more recent group of Hispanic people came to the United States from Cuba after Castro's revolution. The first wave were professional and monied classes fleeing from nationalization of their wealth, so they were extremely conservative. In 1980 a new influx began of people poorer and less educated.[76] Unable to find work, they swelled the welfare rolls and competed with Miami's African American low-wage workers. Tensions between the two groups were severe, sometimes resulting in riots: In 1980 a major riot broke out in Miami, with three days of extensive burning and looting. It left sixteen dead and 400 injured, and caused $100 million in property damage.[77] In Miami alone, by 1982 Cubans constituted 39 percent of the population as compared to 44 percent white and 17 percent African American.

African Americans

Although significant gains were won for people of color in the 1960s, enforcement of civil rights remained problematic. A major issue during the 1970s was school busing to enforce desegregated education. In 1971 in the *Swann v. Charlotte-Mecklenburg Board of Education* decision, the Supreme Court upheld busing. However, white people opposed it as being against the "neighborhood school"—a thin veil for racism, because at least 44 percent of all children, regardless of color, ride buses to school, and fewer than 4 percent are bused for the purposes of desegregation.[78] Some school districts quietly and effectively integrated their schools, but many continued the battle into the 1980s, where it disappeared not because schools were integrated, but because of little enforcement under the Reagan administration.

The same lack of civil rights enforcement is evident in employment. African Americans, despite educational gains, remained unemployed and underemployed at far greater rates than white people; their unemployment rates are consistently double those of whites. In 1970, 56 percent of young African Americans twenty-five to twenty-nine years of age were high school graduates, and 10 percent had college degrees. In 1979, 75 percent had high school diplomas and 21 percent had at least some college. By 1980, the African/Caucasian differential in years of school had effectively ended. However, this did not significantly increase their chances of employment.[79] In recessions, they lose jobs at twice the rate of white workers—last hired, first fired. Official estimates of unemployment seriously underestimate real joblessness, subemployment, and underemployment. Those not counted, according to a nationwide study in 1980, were discouraged workers taken off the official unemployment rolls because they stopped trying (3.5 percent), part-time workers (5.4 percent), and full-time workers at poverty wages (9.5 percent). This brought the real unemployment rate significantly above official levels. In the 1981–1983 recession, African American unemployment generally went above 20 percent and, in some areas, for young men between ages seventeen and twenty-five, it soared to over 50 percent.[80]

Although few African Americans reached political eminence, a few became leaders, including Barbara Jordan, congressperson from Texas; Shirley Chisholm, who in 1972 declared her candidacy for presidency; Andrew Young, formerly an aide to Martin Luther King, Jr., the U.S. representative to the United Nations, and then mayor of Atlanta; and Reverend Jesse Jackson, who launched an unsuccessful bid for the presidency in 1984 under the banner of the Rainbow Coalition. African American mayors have included Marion Barry of Washington, D.C., Tom Bradley of Los Angeles, and Richard Hatcher of Gary, Indiana.

Violence against minority groups continued partly because of a resurgence of the Ku Klux Klan. Although by 1970 Klan membership dropped to an esti-mated 2,000, by spring of 1976, it was reinvigorated, growing, and engaged in ac-tivities

> such as protesting busing in Boston and Louisville, joining the textbook fight in Charlestown, West Virginia, creating a scandal in the New York state prison sys-tem, burning crosses from California to Maryland, going to court to sue and be sued, and appearing on national talk shows.[81]

Estimates of Klan membership in the late 1970s ranged from 2,000 to 10,000 mem-bers, with 30,000 to 100,000 sympathizers. The Klan's racial hatred is based on be-lief in white supremacy, fear of loss of jobs to people they believe to be inherently inferior, belief in "pollution" of the national "gene pool," and hatred of African Americans and Jews as matters of religious and economic ideologies. Their most potent belief is a fundamentalist Christianity, although they espouse no particu-lar denomination. They do espouse traditional values for women, the importance of home and family life, and male supremacy, but they began to admit women (and Catholics) to their membership in the 1970s.[82]

White supremacy groups include the Klan, the Aryan Nation, and neo-Nazis. Although some authorities believe they are essentially harmless, others feel that violence by the Far Right is a real danger in the United States. One group of the Aryan Nation—the Order, the Sword, and the Arm of the Lord—has robbed banks and killed. The dirty work of the Aryan Nation is often done by young "skinheads" who are preparing for a race war. Paramilitary camps span the coun-try and include significant numbers of neo-Nazis as participants or trainers. Some have "security forces," run national book services, distribute paramilitary train-ing manuals, and publish books on making bombs, explosives, and other weapons. The United Racist Front, formed in 1979, is a coalition of the National Socialist (Nazi) Party of America, the National States' Rights Party, and the Fed-erated Knights of the Ku Klux Klan. It was implicated in a 1979 Greensboro, North Carolina incident at which American Communist party members and union officials were slain at an anti-Klan rally.[83] Raphael Ezekial, a professor of psychology, says that hate groups

> have very dangerous things to tell us: . . . that racism has deep roots, that terror is widespread in this country, and that more people than we like to think can be moved by unsophisticated ideas.[84]

Women

The women's movement during the 1970s became more politically aware, if more fragmented, its values based on a deep-seated conviction that personal problems of women, such as poverty and low-wage work, spring from political causes. The National Organization for Women remained the strongest group. By the late

1970s, membership was nearly a quarter of a million. NOW worked for two major goals: passage of the Equal Rights Amendment (ERA) and the rights of women to control their reproduction through birth control and abortion. ERA was the overt issue, and although there has been much controversy over it, the amendment stated simply that

> Equality of rights under the law shall not be denied or abridged by the United States or by any State on account of sex.

In the 1960s, ERA was endorsed by presidents Johnson and Nixon. In 1972 the Senate joined the House in approving ERA, and sent it to the states for ratification. Twenty-one ratified it quickly, but by the spring of 1973, a significant counterattack had begun, stalling it three short of the needed three-fourths approval. In response to the backlash, some states even began rescission processes. For all practical purposes, ERA is now a dead issue for the United States, though many states have their own ERAs.

Foes of ERA insisted that it would bring a military draft for women, unisex toilets, and enforced Lesbianism, and that it would force women dependent on men into the labor market. To counteract women's liberation movements, antifeminist organizations began. For example, Happiness for Women (HOW), created in 1971, boasted 10,000 members within a year and 15,000 by 1981. It was "dedicated to the preservation of the family, preservation of the masculine role as provider, and preservation of the feminine role as wife, mother, and homemaker." Members supported

> God's divine plan, the family structure, removal of Communist and Socialist teachings from the schools, removal of radical elements of Women's Liberation Movement teachings from the schools, teaching the joys of womanhood to young girls, preservation of femininity, restoration of morality, elimination of drug abuse, return to patriotism, and the election to government of men and women dedicated to God, Family, and the Country.[85]

It was one of the organizations leading to the Moral Majority, which claimed that feminism was the primary cause of breakdown in family and marriage patterns because it takes away women's "right" to stay in the home. Moreover, it claimed feminism to be anti-God because it rejects male supremacy and so must be eliminated to restore traditional values. Abortion was a major issue because it concerned the sacredness of life. Ironically, many in the Moral Majority supported both the death penalty and massive arms buildups and opposed public assistance, on the basis that the latter encouraged out-of-wedlock births and interfered in the rights of the church to care for its own. The Moral Majority was the forerunner of the Christian Coalition.

Teenage pregnancies were also an important issue to women in this period. Between 1963 and 1978, premaritally conceived births increased 25 percent for white teenagers and 50 percent for African American teenagers. Out-of-wedlock births represented nearly 11 percent of all live births in 1970 and 15.5 percent in 1978. Although rates for African Americans declined, they remained about six times those for whites. During the 1960s, white unwed teenagers began to keep their babies rather than giving them up for adoption, as many as 76 percent in 1976, increasing to 93 percent by 1978, creating a real shortage for white adoptive parents.[86]

Despite the religious backlash against birth control programs, many were funded: The Bureau of Indian Affairs made family planning available in 1965, the Children's Bureau began to support family planning through state health departments in 1966, the 1967 OEO amendments included family planning funds for the parents' division of Head Start, and in 1975 the Office of Child Development initiated research and demonstration projects. Under Medicaid and through family planning clinics such as Planned Parenthood, funds came from Title XX or Title X of the Public Health Act. Sixty-three new fertility-related laws were passed in 1981, the largest number since 1973.[87] In 1983, influenced by pressures from far-right groups, the Department of Health and Human Services proposed that family planning clinics receiving Title X funds should be required to notify parents before prescribing contraceptives for teenagers. This "squeal rule" triggered some 65,000 protests, four to one against the regulation, but it was passed and implemented in many states.

The abortion issue struck at the heart of the reactionary religio-political system of the United States. Although abortions are less dangerous than is carrying a fetus to term, especially for teenagers, legal abortions became increasingly restricted. In the 1950s and 1960s, many states had reformed abortion laws to permit it in certain instances, particularly in the first trimester. Still, laws restricted abortion until the *Roe v. Wade* decision in 1973 upheld women's rights to decision in the first two trimesters of pregnancy, declaring that the interest of the woman was paramount in the first three months. The court explicitly rejected the idea that life begins at conception and that the fetus is a person protected by the Fourteenth Amendment.

After *Roe v. Wade*, legal abortions approached one-third of all pregnancies. New programs developed to help women with their abortion decisions, the most useful of which was probably that Medicaid would pay for abortions for poor women. However, the conservative backlash increased, and in 1976 a constitutional amendment banning abortion was proposed: the Hyde, or Human Life, Amendment. Although it was defeated, Congress imposed increasingly strict limits on the use of federal funds for abortions. In the 1980 *Harris v. McRae* decision, the Supreme Court ruled that states were no longer required to use Medicaid funds for abortions for otherwise eligible women except in cases of rape or cases where the pregnancy endangered the woman's life. However, government standards for what constitutes proof of rape are so narrow as to render this exception almost useless. The number of Medicaid-funded abortions dropped from 300,000 in 1977 to 17,983 in 1981.[88] Since the Reagan administration, there has been increasing political momentum to overthrow *Roe v. Wade* and make all abortions illegal, even for pregnancies that result from rape or incest.

Gay Liberation

The gay liberation movement took on greater national significance with the formation first of the Lambda Defense and Educational Fund in 1972 and the National Gay Task Force in 1973 (now the National Gay and Lesbian Task Force). The Lambda Fund defended civil rights of homosexuals in employment, housing, education, child custody, and the administration of justice, working solely through the court systems. It paid for legal representation on behalf of homosexual clients and maintained a national network of attorneys willing to take cases pertaining to homosexual rights. In 1986, Lambda counted over 7,000 people as regular contributors. The National Gay and Lesbian Task Force, a clearinghouse for federal legislation affecting homosexuals, coordinates the activities of local homosexual groups, works with the media to facilitate a more accurate portrayal of homosexuality, and assists foundations and associations working with the homosexual community. It was the prime organizer of the October 1979 March on Washington for Lesbian and Gay Rights, attended by just under a quarter of a million people.[89] Although few gains have been made for homosexuals, since 1983 most of the larger U.S. cities have enacted gay rights laws and more than half the states have repealed sodomy statutes.[90]

In New York City in 1970, the police raided a gay bar (the Snake Pit) and arrested 167 patrons. One was killed in the melee. Enraged by the raid's brutality, even mainstream politicians, including Congressman Ed Koch, argued for change. Gay groups gained access to police chiefs, mayors, and human rights offices. When Koch became mayor in 1978, one of his first acts was to prohibit discrimination based on sexual orientation in all municipal agencies, including the police department. Similar access and results were gained in Washington, D.C., and Los Angeles.[91] In San Francisco, gay political power increased with the election of Harvey Milk as supervisor and George Moscone as mayor in 1978. Both were assassinated, but by 1981, San Francisco had integrated openly gay police officers into their troops and gay-bashers were being prosecuted.

Gays pursued equality in the courts based on First Amendment rights and the Civil Rights Act of 1964 (Section VII). In 1972 the Supreme Court decided that the First Amendment allowed students to form Student Democratic Societies, and based on that precedent, in 1974 the University of New Hampshire was required to recognize a gay student group. In 1973 the Civil Service Commission notified federal agencies they could no longer deny jobs to homosexuals (*Scott v. Macy,* 1965). Whereas the Ninth Court of Appeals ruled that an openly effeminate man, a gay man, and a Lesbian couple had no sex discrimination in employment claims under Title VII because they were harassed for sexual orientation rather than sex (*De Santis v. Pacific Telephone & Telegraph,* 1979), later Title VII decisions applied by the Equal Employment Opportunity Commission (EEOC) makes gender stereotypes irrelevant to job decisions and protects workers against gay bashing in places of employment.[92]

As the Religious Right grew in strength, so did heterosexism and hostility. The epidemic of acquired immune deficiency syndrome (AIDS) is a case in point. Despite the fact that its consequences are always fatal, not until it began to infect heterosexuals did the national government begin to fund research adequately. In fact, AIDS among homosexuals has been labeled as God's curse against their sins and trivialized with jokes reaching as high as the presidential level.[93] A quote from Senator Jesse Helms exemplifies this:

> The government should think twice about spending much money fighting a disease brought on by deliberate, disgusting, revolting conduct.[94]

This is despite the fact that, more and more, AIDS has become a heterosexual disease. It is the number-one cause of deaths for all Americans age twenty-five to forty-four.[95] No discussion of bigotry and AIDS is complete without mention of the Reagan administration's role in suppressing information about the disease. Surgeon General C. Everett Koop was pressured to downplay the existence and spread of AIDS as well as the role of condoms in prevention; pressure on Koop mysteriously eased up after Reagan was reelected. The treatment of Surgeon General Joycelyn Elders and attempts in the mid-1990s to eliminate the office of Surgeon General altogether reflect the Far Right's desire to place public health decisions in the hands of politicians who lack even a basic understanding of epidemiology.

Conclusion: Tightening the Reins

Throughout the 1970s, conservatism increased. Where legislation could not be denied, as in the case of civil rights, it was supported. However, in dealing with women, children, people of color, and the poor, programs became increasingly more restrictive and even hostile. The hostility was augmented with the upsurge of groups devoted to male supremacy and their own brands of morality, ranging from such physically violent groups as the Ku Klux Klan and neo-Nazis to ideologically violent groups such as the Religious Right.

The election of Ronald Reagan in 1980, and his reelection in 1984, should have been no surprise to those watching the reactionary trends so evident in politics. With the overt backing of the Far Right and the Moral Majority, he saw his election as a mandate to enforce certain ideological beliefs, among them the Christianization of American politics, the return to patriarchal marriage and family norms, the breakup of social programs that supported people outside marriage and outside the work ethic, and the retreat from civil rights. In addition, his adherence to a war ethic—a "refusal to blink"—is "reasonable" given the reactionary trends of the 1970s. To intervene in sovereign nations for the sake of the economy or to end the world in defense of a principle, is not beyond the pale of such beliefs.

Study Questions

1. What is OASDHI? SSI? AFDC? Explain who is served by each program and what kinds of income maintenance they provided in the 1970s.

2. What was Title XX of the Social Services Act? How did it provide for the poor? What were some unanticipated consequences of this act for the social work profession? Why was it called the "double cross"?

3. What effects did the Nixon, Ford, Carter, and Reagan administrations have on the civil rights gained in the 1960s? How did these administrations affect people of color? Women? Gays?

4. Explain the evolution of the status of women from World War II into the 1980s.

5. What changes occurred in the social work profession in the Nixon, Ford, and Carter years? What effect did these social work changes have on social welfare? How did they affect AFDC?

Notes

1. June Axinn and Herman Levin, Social Welfare: *A History of the American Response to Need*, 2d ed. (New York: Harper & Row, 1982), p. 236.

2. Ibid., p. 289.

3. John Ehrenreich, *The Altruistic Imagination: A History of Social Work and Social Policy in the United States* (Ithaca, NY: Cornell University Press, 1985), p. 202.

4. Ibid., p. 203.

5. Beulah Compton, *Introduction to Social Welfare and Social Work: Structure, Function, and Process* (Homewood, IL: The Dorsey Press, 1980), p. 496.

6. Ralph Dolgoff and Donald Feldstein, *Understanding Social Welfare*, 2d ed. (New York: Longman Press, 1984), p. 272.

7. Andrew W. Dobelstein, *Politics, Economics, and Public Welfare* (Englewood Cliffs, NJ: Prentice Hall, 1980), pp. 150–151.

8. Gerald Handel, *Social Welfare in Western Society* (New York: Random House, 1982), pp. 152–153.

9. Axinn and Levin, *Social Welfare*, p. 289.

10. "Current Operating Statistics," *Social Security Bulletin*, Vol. 46, no. 7 (Washington, D.C.: U.S. Government Printing Office, July 1983), p. 20.

11. Ibid.

12. Aaron Wildavsky, *Speaking Truth to Power: The Art and Craft of Policy Analysis* (Boston: Little, Brown, 1979), p. 106.

13. Francis X. Russo and George Willis, *Human Services in America* (Englewood Cliffs, NJ: Prentice Hall, 1986), p. 242.

14. Winifred Bell, *Contemporary Social Welfare* (New York: Macmillan, 1983), pp. 170–171.

15. Russo and Willis, *Human Services*, p. 244.

16. Handel, *Social Welfare*, p. 194.

17. Joseph Heffernan, *Introduction to Social Welfare Policy* (Itasca, IL: F.E. Peacock Publishers, 1979), p. 238.

18. Bell, *Contemporary Welfare*, p. 157.

19. Ibid.

20. Joel P. Handler, *Reforming the Poor* (New York: Basic Books, 1972), p. 58.

21. Robert Morris, *Rethinking Social Welfare* (New York: Longman Press, 1986), p. 246.

22. Bell, *Contemporary Welfare*, p. 130.

23. Sar A. Levitan and Clifford M. Johnson, *Beyond the Safety Net* (Cambridge, MA: Ballinger Publishing, 1984), p. 78.

24. Ibid., pp. 36–37.

25. Senator Russell Long, quoted in Dobelstein, *Politics, Economics, and Public Welfare,* p. 129.

26. Levitan and Johnson, *Beyond the Safety Net,* pp. 36–37.

27. Saul Kaplan, "Support from Absent Fathers of Children Receiving ADC," Public Assistance Report #41 (Washington, D.C.: U.S. Government Printing Office, 1969). Quoted in Bell, *Contemporary Welfare,* p. 214 footnote.

28. Handler, *Reforming the Poor,* p. 32.

29. Bell, *Contemporary Welfare,* pp. 133–135.

30. Ibid., p. 22.

31. Ibid., p. 224.

32. Ibid.

33. Rosemary Sarri, *Under Lock and Key* (Ann Arbor, MI: National Assessment of Juvenile Delinquency, 1974).

34. Axinn and Levin, *Social Welfare,* p. 289.

35. Bell, *Contemporary Welfare,* p. 169.

36. Ibid., p. 105.

37. Levitan and Johnson, *Beyond the Safety Net,* p. 124.

38. Frances Fox Piven and Richard Cloward, *The New Class War: Reagan's Attack on the Welfare State and Its Consequences* (New York: Pantheon Books, 1982), p. 31.

39. Levitan and Johnson, *Beyond the Safety Net,* p. 118.

40. Ibid.

41. Ibid., p. 125.

42. Joe R. Feagin, *Racial and Ethnic Relations,* 3d ed. (Englewood Cliffs, NJ: Prentice Hall, 1989), p. 303.

43. Dolgoff and Feldstein, *Understanding Social Welfare,* pp. 201–202.

44. Kenneth Wooden, *Crying in the Playtime of Others* (New York: McGraw-Hill, 1976).

45. Russo and Willis, *Human Services,* p. 65.

46. Compton, *Introduction to Social Welfare,* p. 513.

47. Ramsey Clark, *Crime in America: Observations on its Nature, Causes, Prevention, and Control* (New York: Simon & Schuster, 1970), p. 335.

48. D. Stanley Eitzen, *In Conflict and Order: Understanding Society,* 3d ed. (Needham, MA: Allyn & Bacon, 1985), p. 213.

49. From the Justice Department's Bureau of Justice Statistics, reported in the *Lafayette (Indiana) Journal and Courier,* July 26, 1986, p. A4.

50. From the American Correctional Association, reported in the *Lafayette (Indiana) Journal and Courier,* Sept. 12, 1986, p. A7.

51. Feagin, *Racial and Ethnic Relations,* p. 234.

52. Ibid., p. 195.

53. Ibid., p. 199.

54. Eric Treisman, "The Last Treaty," *Harper's Magazine,* Feb. 1975, pp. 37–39.

55. Ibid., pp. 37–38.

56. Feagin, *Racial and Ethnic Relations,* p. 193.

57. Ibid.

58. Ibid., p. 198.

59. Ibid., p. 205.

60. *Lafayette (Indiana) Journal and Courier,* AP report, Sept. 17, 1986, p. A1.

61. Feagin, *Racial and Ethnic Relations,* pp. 190–193.

62. Ibid., p. 196.

63. Ibid.

64. Ibid., p. 191.

65. Levitan and Johnson, *Beyond the Safety Net,* p. 119.

66. Feagin, *Racial and Ethnic Relations*, p. 333.

67. Ibid., p. 340.

68. Peter Irons, "The Return of the 'Yellow Peril,'" *The Nation*, Oct. 19, 1985, p. 316.

69. Feagin, *Racial and Ethnic Relations*, p. 362.

70. Ibid., p. 275.

71. Ibid., p. 265.

72. Ibid., p. 264.

73. Ibid., p. 265, and *Lafayette (Indiana) Journal and Courier*, Aug. 22, 1985, p. B3.

74. Feagin, *Racial and Ethnic Relations*, p. 303.

75. Carol Giacomo, "Sterilization Count Higher Than Expected," *Hartford (Connecticut) Courant*, Oct. 13, 1980, pp. A10 and A12.

76. Feagin, *Racial and Ethnic Relations*, p. 351.

77. Ibid.

78. Ibid., p. 245.

79. Ibid., p. 243.

80. Ibid., p. 232.

81. Lisa Langenbach, "Modernist and Traditionalist Issue Groups in the American Party System: An Examination of the Realigning Potential of Cultural Issues in Changing Cleavage Structures," unpublished doctoral dissertation, Purdue University, West Lafayette, Indiana, Aug. 1986, p. 128.

82. Ibid., pp. 138–140.

83. Ibid., quoting the Anti-Defamation League report, 1981, p. 66.

84. Kate Kellogg, "The Far-Right Fringe," *Michigan Today*, June 1987, p. 6.

85. Katherine Gruber, *Encyclopedia of Associations* (Detroit: Gale Research, 1981). Cited in Langenbach, "Modern and Traditionalist Issue Groups," p. 164.

86. Bell, *Contemporary Welfare*, p. 124.

87. All figures are Ibid., pp. 123–124.

88. Ibid., p. 123; Axinn and Levin, *Social Welfare*, pp. 287–288.

89. Langenbach, "Modern and Traditionalist Issue Groups," pp. 75–81.

90. Eitzen, *In Conflict and Order*, pp. 222–223.

91. William N. Eskridge, Jr., *Gaylaw: Challenging the Apartheid of the Closet* (Cambridge, MA: Harvard University Press, 1999), p. 104.

92. Ibid., pp. 232–233.

93. Reagan alluded to gays when he jokingly remarked that Muammar Gadhafi should be sent to San Francisco because he wears robes, and an assistant trivialized both gays and AIDS by suggesting that Gadhafi be infected with AIDS.

94. Elizabeth Neus, "Epidemic Now a Part of Mainstream America," New Jersey *Courier–Post* (July 23, 1995), p. A5.

95. Ibid.

12

The Reactionary Vision

Biting the Conservative Bullet

The elections of Ronald Reagan and George Bush were the emerging tip of a reactionary iceberg. Faced with a downward-spiraling economy, Reagan promised to eliminate the proliferation of government regulations that "strangled private enterprise" and to balance the budget regardless of who had to "bite the bullet." Bush followed his lead. The ideas were not new: Nixon had begun to limit social spending and institute fiscal change, along with privatization and federalized block grants. Nevertheless, until the Reagan administration, although questions about the process of social responsibility to the poor were raised, most politicians did not advocate its end. However, powered by belief in supply-side economics and unduly influenced by corporate America and a monied and media-wise Religious Right, Reagan began the dismantling of the fallback subsistence programs of the Social Security Acts of 1935. His legitimation was simple: He believed that America was ordained by God to carry out traditional morality and work values no matter the cost. As a spokesperson of the Moral Majority, Jerry Falwell stated the aim simply:

> America's commitment to individualist values, hard work, and the acquisition of property and wealth is divinely inspired.[1]

A clearer statement demonstrating the synergy of religion, economics, and politics would be difficult to find.

Reagan's *domestic* social policies constituted a return to pre–Civil War ideology, as in the Pierce veto of Dix's Ten-Million-Acre Bill. His *tax* policies led us back to pre-1932 supply-side economics, or government support to the wealthy that would "trickle down" to the poor. His *international* policies included a rabid fear of the Soviet threat. Moynihan says,

> the United States government was . . . in the throes of a consummate obsession with an expansion of communism—*which was not happening* . . . all this in the cause of fighting a cold war that was over![2]

Given these policies, Reagan's goals were to balance the budget without cutting military preparedness and to eliminate social programs except for a safety net for the "truly needy." His safety net program was two-tiered: Those covered by social insurance—workers—would keep most benefits, and the nonworking poor would see programs substantially cut to encourage their return to the workforce or workfare.

Winifred Bell says that Reagan's election heralded a return to

> old-fashioned virtues of economic individualism, unfettered private enterprise, and a very limited role for government. . . . [Social programs were] vigorously attacked for their overwhelming cost, depressing effect on savings and private investments, and as ill-conceived liberal efforts.[3]

Reagan had far-reaching support among conservatives, the elite, and fundamentalist religious groups. The political Far Right supported less federal government, free enterprise, and traditional sex roles: men supporting their families and women homemaking and rearing children. The Religious Right, a conglomeration of fundamentalist and evangelist groups, supported political action to enforce morality and assumed the role of watchdog of public morality. According to Midgley, its vision

> extols traditional values, the virtue of the family and local community, statutory sanction over moral behavior, capitalist economic ideals, and a rigorous antiwelfarism rooted in a traditional antagonism to state intervention in social affairs.[4]

Patriarchal values dominated its perspective on women and the Protestant work ethic provided an intense focus on men as family wage earners.

Three morality-based issues permeated Reagan's policies. First was the sanctity of the nuclear family and the maintenance of its traditional male/female roles and statuses. This ideology ignored the fact that two adults working full-time at minimum wages remained in poverty, or that the number of female-headed families was growing exponentially. The second was the morality of income-producing labor at any wage, and its converse, nonwork, as immorality. The third was less precise: superpatriotism and religious belief in the God-ordained future of America. Protection of the "American way of life," and "making the world safe for democracy" rationalized hostility toward other nations, increased war production, and fostered a "dare you to cross this line" attitude.

Reaganomics: The Conservative Political Economy

Reaganomics was, basically, a belief in supply-side economics: High production would keep a large supply of goods on the market, people would continue to buy, and buying more would produce more jobs, producing more money to buy more goods. An upward-spiraling economy would, through taxes on the greater volume of sales and increased income, move revenue upward to the government, and government investments in corporations via business tax breaks, subsidies, and contracts would add more productivity, leading again to higher employment and more consumerism.

Aside from the human problems of losses of jobs and income, Reaganomics had several fatal errors. First, in a recessionary economy with reduced employment causing limited income, fewer people could buy the increased goods, and those with money did not need more basic production items. Second, the 1981–1983 recession was not a "natural economic cycle" (therefore self-limiting), but a deliberate Reagan decision to trade unemployment for lower inflation rates. (Economists say that an unemployment increase of at least a million for two years will reduce inflation by a single percentage point.) According to Levitan and Johnson this

> precipitated a deep recession which brought the highest jobless rates since the 1930s and transformed the marginal income losses of rising prices into the total income losses of forced idleness. His sweeping tax and spending reductions further skewed income distribution in favor of the wealthy, slashing federal benefits for low-income Americans while significantly reducing the tax liability of the rich.[5]

It was estimated that from 1980 to 1984 there was a net transfer of income of $25 billion to the richest fifth of the population.[6]

Third, high production induces buying if prices are lowered through competition. However, the Reagan agenda maintained high prices to garner more taxes from higher income. Fourth, government corporate investments led to increases in production technology that eliminated jobs and moved jobs to foreign countries. Finally, government spending increased while revenue was cut by tax breaks for the wealthy and for corporations. Moynihan says,

> President Reagan . . . never understood the onset of fiscal instability. His first budget director David A. Stockman . . . did in time see what he/they had done. He pleaded for new revenues. Was greeted with amiable incomprehension. He would write of this as "a willful act of ignorance and grotesque irresponsibility."[7]

Reaganomics bore great similarity to pre-1929 economics. The saving grace for the 1980s was safety net programs going back to Roosevelt, such as bank insurance, federally supported mortgages, and social programs. These Reagan duly set about to destroy, leaving a decimated economy.

In 1980 the national population of about 235 million produced a gross national product of $2,631.7 billion, increasing by 1985 to $3,915.9 billion. Polarization of incomes grew with each year of the Reagan and Bush administrations as the rich grew richer, the poor grew poorer, and the middle class shrank. Those at the top remained there: The richest 2 percent controlled

- 30 percent of all financial assets
- 50 percent of all stocks in private hands
- 71 percent of all tax-free bonds
- 20 percent of all real estate
- 39 percent of taxable bonds.

The wealthiest 6 percent of families owned 57 percent of all the nation's wealth and the top 16 percent owned 75 percent.[8]

The Reagan and Bush administrations virtually abolished corporate income taxes and drastically reduced personal income taxes for the rich. During his first year in office, Reagan slashed business taxes by an estimated $169 billion and, in the next six years, reduced individual taxes by $500 billion.[9] By 1984, families earning over $100,000 had net gains exceeding $20,000, while from 1980 to 1984, taxes of the poorest one-fifth of Americans rose by 22.7 percent—a net loss of $240.[10] From 1977 to 1988, the bottom 80 percent of families in the United States lost income while the top 5 percent gained 49.8 percent.[11] The poor paid higher net federal income taxes in 1990 than in 1980. According to Piven and Cloward, the reorganized federal tax structure

> promote[d] a massive upward redistribution of income. New investment and depreciation write-offs favor[ed] large corporations over small businesses; 80 percent of the benefits [went] to the 1,700 largest corporations (which have generated only 4 percent of all new employment over the past twenty years) . . . [with losses] estimated [at] $750 billion in federal revenue.[12]

The federal debt increased four and a half times over the Reagan administration,[13] and when Reagan left office the deficit was $1 trillion.[14]

Between 1978 and 1984, poverty rose by 41 percent for white families and 25 percent for African Americans.[15] By 1982, more than 9 million more families had fallen below the official poverty line ($7,450 in 1980), with a 5.5 million increase just from 1980,[16] and in 1983, 35.5 million people (7.3 million families) were in poverty, an increase of 38 percent from 1978.[17] Between 1968 and 1984, African American income rose from 73.2 percent of white income to 84.8 percent, but by 1982 it had returned to 55.3 percent of white income, virtually the same as in 1960.[18]

Capital gains taxes were cut from 33 to 28 percent to benefit the wealthy during the Bush administration.[19] Although Bush had promised "Read my lips: No new taxes," Reagan-established structures led to unprecedented budget deficits. Karger says,

Throughout the late 1980s, Congress and the Reagan, then Bush administrations, postponed the day when the budget would have to be reconciled with the Gramm Rudman Hollings Deficit Reduction Act. . . . [F]acing a huge revenue shortfall in 1990, the Congress and the President [Bush] . . . created . . . a deficit reduction bill.[20]

The bill included reductions in entitlement programs and defense spending, increases in user fees for government services, tax increases (especially "sin" taxes on alcohol, liquor, and luxury items such as boats), and reduced interest payments on the national debt.[21] However, the deficit at the end of Bush's administration was $4.6 trillion,[22] rising a billion dollars a day.

The New Federalism

Reagan's New Federalism was Nixon's block grant program warmed over. It represented a reversal from societal responsibility to societal disregard for the poor and became the guideline not only for the Reagan/Bush era but for the Republican-dominated Congress of 1994, with its excessively punitive "Contract with America." Reagan's New Federalism had two facets: reprivatization of services for the poor by private charities and churches; and the assumption by state governments of Aid to Families of Dependent Children, Supplemental Security Income, and food stamps, while the federal government took full responsibility for Medicaid. The former paralleled pre-1935 aid to the poor and the latter substituted local/state for federal standards.

Privatization

Privatization—federal funding of services to private for-profit agencies such as hospitals, nursing homes, day care centers, drug rehabilitation centers, and even prisons—was intended to save money through competition. In fact, competition often eliminated services to the poor because financially secure agencies could lobby for and receive higher funding. Agencies with low- or no-fee bases could not afford lobbyists or could not compete. The result was poorer services for the poor and higher client rates for public agencies. Palmer and Sawhill say,

> The dismantling of the public sector social service delivery system [was] defended as a way to obtain cheaper, more effective, more flexible and efficient, and more innovative services [through contracting out]. . . . [F]ew of these benefits have been realized. . . . Contracted out services were no cheaper than those performed by the public service agency . . . and were more difficult . . . to monitor.[23]

The concept of privatization is not new to social welfare, for social work began in service to the poor through private agencies. However, making profit from the poor dates much earlier: to asylums, poorhouses, institutions, and orphanages. Profit-making agencies can afford to lobby for contracts and set their own client profiles, while public agencies serving the poor have fewer dollars to serve an ever-increasing poverty population. Privatization is instrumental in the polarization of social services. Hospitals are an example: Those that have privatized can select low-need, low-risk consumers, whereas public hospitals must fill the gaps in health care among the poor, whose problems are often more costly and extreme.

Privatization is, in fact, a step backward from public and social responsibility because when there is no access to care, a socially moral government has an obligation to provide. Finally, privatization abrogates the application of broad-based standards and regulations that prevent discrimination or abuse. Given that abuse and discrimination have occurred throughout our past when government standards were not enforced, we should not have allowed that to happen again.

Bush followed the conservative move to privatization of social services and expanded services for corporations and the wealthy. His "kinder, gentler nation" did not address the growing numbers of the poor, increasing homelessness, higher school dropout rates, and decreased employment, particularly among minority groups. His attention focused much more intently on international rather than domestic efforts, and the deterioration begun with Reagan expanded.

New Federalism: Returning Programs to States

Reagan's proposed tradeoff—federal payment for Medicaid while states assumed responsibility for AFDC, SSI, and Food Stamps—was turned down by Congress, though Congress severely cut funding for those programs. Legislation that led to cuts included the Omnibus Budget Reconciliation Act (OBRA) of 1981, the Tax Equity and Fiscal Responsibility Act of 1982, the Agriculture and Food Act of 1982 (which provided new eligibility restrictions and spending cuts for food stamps), the Deficit Reduction Act of 1984, the Gramm–Rudman–Hollings Act (GRH) of 1986, and the Family Support Act (FSA) of 1988. Program cuts and losses of revenue were compounded with each new bill under the pretense that money was being retargeted to the needier:

> In fact . . . in no entitlement programs were real (inflation-adjusted) benefits increased . . . when eligibility levels were reduced . . . benefits declined nearly a fifth, from 88 percent of the official poverty threshold in 1970 to 71 percent in 1981.[24]

Under the New Federalism, all social welfare programs lost an average of 7 percent during Reagan's first three years, but

> cutbacks totaled 29 percent in child nutrition; 13 percent in welfare and food stamps; 17 percent in compensatory education; and 60 percent in employment and training programs. Spending for means-tested programs dropped from 13.3 percent of total federal expenses in 1980 to 11.1 percent in 1983, though universal programs [social insurance] rose from 40.8 to 42.9 percent.[25]

Approximately 400,000 to 500,000 families whose adult members worked were put off AFDC, losing extra benefits such as food stamps and Medicaid in the process, and another 300,000 families suffered severe cuts in benefits. States were no longer required to give cost-of-living increases for SSI. Almost half of all people with disabilities lost Old Age, Survivors, and Disability Insurance (OASDI) because of presumed "malingering." Other programs important to the poor were cut: Among them, Legal Services lost most of its funding, planned construction of public housing and veterans' hospitals was reduced, Vietnam veteran counseling centers were eliminated, and the Comprehensive Education and Training Act (CETA) program was abolished.

Of all programs devastated by Reaganomics, children's programs were hit hardest. The average number of children on AFDC per 100 children in poverty dropped dramatically from 71.8 percent in 1979 to only 52.5 percent in 1982, despite the increase of about 1 million children in poverty.[26] Low birth weight, prenatal death, and prematurity increased, especially among children of color, ranking the United States eleventh in infant mortality. According to the Children's Defense Fund,

> In 1984, the Reagan cuts imposed on poor children [saved] the federal government a million dollars an hour . . . [to] offset new Reagan increases: $9 million an hour on defense, $1 million more on tax breaks for corporations; $10 million more an hour on tax breaks for the wealthy; $2 million more an hour on interest on the national debt, to which we add $23 million an hour.[27]

All told, domestic spending for human resources was cut by $101.1 billion, of which $65.4 billion came from programs that provided benefits to poor families.[28]

Omnibus Budget Reconciliation Acts (OBRAs), now an accepted part of our fiscal culture, are intended to balance the national budget by equal funding cuts across all programs. However, certain programs are "more equal" than others; that is, some programs such as defense were given funding breaks and exemptions from the first OBRA (1981), so later cuts were not as drastic. On the other hand, because the deficits abetted by such exemptions had to be made up, other programs—usually social programs—were cut enormously at the beginning, and, even though protected and/or exempted from further OBRA cuts, were crippled.

The Omnibus Budget Reconciliation Acts of 1981 and 1982 reduced federal matching costs for Medicaid, set new eligibility and income limits on many social programs, and gave Reagan about half the cuts he proposed in income maintenance programs of SSI, Food Stamps, and AFDC. OBRA consolidated more than ninety categorical programs into four blocks, with a 20 to 25 percent reduction in federal funding for each. Block grants fostered competition among agencies for scarcer resources, a strategy that left them fighting for existence rather than serving their clients. Moreover, because private enterprise could compete for the grants, the for-profit service industry burgeoned, particularly in child care, nursing homes, and for-profit hospitals.

OBRA also capped Title XX, the social services amendment, at $2.7 billion, replacing it with the Social Services Block Grant and eliminating federal regulations and state matching requirements earmarked for the poor. Because states no longer had to match funds, many reduced programs by up to 50 percent of previous funding. A study in 1982 showed that only about a fourth of federal cuts were replaced in employment, job training, compensatory education, health, and social services programs. In fact, some states reaped savings on the cutbacks because they no longer had to pay the 25 percent matching costs.[29] States reported significant increases in mental health problems as programs were reduced at the same time unemployment increased: More than thirty-eight states detailed increases in severe child abuse and molestation, suicides, and broken marriages. In 1983 thirty-two states reported less child care than in 1981, with the total expenses for such programs dropping by 14 percent.[30]

The Gramm–Rudman–Hollings Act (GRH) of 1986 was intended to make "fair" across-the-board cuts to end the federal deficit by 1991. It exempted some key health and income maintenance programs and made modified cuts in others, but these programs had already been cut massively by earlier Reagan bills. Protected programs—that is, those given modified cuts—included OASDI, AFDC, Child Nutrition, Food Stamps, Medicaid, SSI, Veterans' Compensation and Veterans' Pensions, the Women, Infants, and Children Nutrition program, Medicare, federal input into state unemployment benefits, the Social Services Block Grant, and health programs for migrants, veterans, Native Americans, and communities.

Unprotected programs cut across the board by GRH included Head Start; general revenue sharing; rural development; ESEA grants; training, employment, and rehabilitation services; low-income energy assistance; special services to elderly and other groups; health research; housing assistance; and consumer/occupational health and safety programs. Most administrative costs (in Medicare, for example) were not exempt, so that even if benefits remained intact, administrative cuts ensured delays or cutbacks in worker-intensive services. In 1987 federal spending for education, employment and training, and social services was reduced by $827 million, Medicare administration by $74 million, low-income energy assistance by $81 million (29 percent), and $104 million was taken from nonexempt programs such as child support enforcement. New units of housing were reduced by 2,500–4,000 from the 97,000 authorized in 1986, and Legal Services, already drastically cut, lost another $13 million.[31]

Defense did not suffer, although supposedly it bore half of the GRH cuts. Because it had more funds to begin with, the remainder was still extremely high. Also, President Reagan had wide discretion on defense and exempted virtually all military personnel accounts and the entire Strategic Defense Initiative ("Star Wars"). Finally, in a clever sleight-of-hand, half the savings from cost-of-living adjustments and pensions were credited to defense on the basis that many of those affected were government employees such as retired military and civilian defense department personnel and civil service retirees. However, most of the pensions cut were governmental only by a stretch of the imagination: longshoremen's and harborworkers' compensation benefits or black lung disability benefits, for example.[32] In all, in 1986 the defense budget was still roughly double 1980 levels (an estimated $268 billion).

Though intended to end the deficit, GRH failed because 60 percent of the deficit ($131 billion out of $217 billion) stemmed from tax policies that granted more tax breaks than the budget could afford. GRH neither broadened the tax base nor brought in more revenues. Supporting a triple-failsafe defense system, with enormous cost overrides and without increased taxes, was another unrecoverable waste. Finally, the enormous tax breaks given to the rich and allowed to multinational corporations, with little if any reinvestment in the government, continued to drain revenue from the nation.

Pruning the Programs

Although statistics, demonstration projects, and successful social programs proved beneficial both to recipients and to society, the nation entered a cutting frenzy under Reagan, focused on programs traditionally serving disadvantaged groups: people of minorities, the aged, women, and blue-collar workers.

Old Age, Survivors, Disability, and Health Insurance

Changes to OASDI began in 1981 and continued throughout the Reagan/Bush era: postponement of cost-of-living adjustments (COLAs) for six months, increased deductions and optional premiums for Medicare A and B, taxes on one-half of all Social Security benefits for people whose incomes exceeded $25,000 ($32,000 for couples, raised by Bush to $34,000 and $44,000, respectively), raises in amounts subject to taxes, and decreases in future benefit levels to 70 percent for retirement before age 67.[33] Resident aliens became subject to the same withholding taxes as U.S. citizens, and nonresidents paid a 30 percent tax on half of all earnings.[34] By the Bush administration, the amount of payroll taxes charged to both employers and employees was 7.65 percent each (the self-employed paid 15.3 percent for FICA). Of each of these dollars 73 cents went to OASI, 8 cents to the Disability Insurance (DI) program, and 19 cents to the Health Insurance (HI or Medicare) program.[35]

Whereas the taxable wage base for OASI in 1990 was $51,300, it increased yearly (to $61,200 by 1995). All wages up to $125,000 could be taxed for Medicare and by 1994 HI tax was applied to all earnings. By 1994, retired people age sixty-two to sixty-five could earn $8,040 and those age sixty-five to sixty-nine could earn up to $11,060 without penalty (one dollar of every two earned, no limit after age seventy).[36] Older people not on OASDI could buy into Medicare's Part A by paying premiums, in 1994 $245 a month, and into optional Part B (Supplemental Medical Insurance or SMI) for $46.10 per month (1995). In an attempt to limit Medicare costs, the Reagan administration developed diagnostic related group categories (DRGs). Under DRGs, health care providers were paid a set amount for all patients admitted with certain categories of ailment. Additional ailments at the time of admission were not paid for, and when the "reasonable costs" for the category had been paid, the patient had to be released. Often, seriously ill patients were sent home to care for themselves, or to nursing homes not set up to provide intensive medical care.

By 1992, 132 million workers, along with their employers, paid Social Security taxes, and 42.6 million beneficiaries received $24.5 billion per month.[37] Of these, 37.2 million received OASI benefits and 5.5 million were on disability allotments. About 30.2 million (70.8 percent) received benefits based on work records and 12.4 million (29.2 percent) got spousal or dependent supplements. Of this latter group, 5.5 million were widowed and surviving parents, 3.3 million were spouses, and 3.6 million were children under the age of nineteen.[38] By 1995, the monthly benefit for a single retired worker was $98, and for worker and spouse it was $170.[39] In 1992 the average *private* pension was $599 per month, versus $1,205 for federal military retirees and $1,423 for federal civilian retirees; roughly three-fourths of federal retirees also qualify for Social Security. The average age of military retirement is forty-two for enlistees and forty-six for officers, meaning that "a typical military pensioner spends more years collecting benefits (thirty-five) than earning them (twenty-two)."[40]

During the Reagan administration, people with disabilities suffered disproportionately under presumptions that they did not have true disabilities. Disability reviews, beginning in 1980, increased termination from the programs fourfold. Sixty percent of those cut off won reinstatement, and although the government saved 10 percent while they were in appeal, costs for reinstatement were between $27 million and $69 million. Claimants were required to use federally appointed doctors who, it was discovered, overbilled and marked up lab fees by 300–400 percent. Of the thousands of doctors hired, 108 actually did 22 percent of all the exams and earned an average of $348,672. Six doctors earned more than $1 million each, and one received $3 million for one year.[41] Congress later enacted legislation more cautious in disqualifying beneficiaries with disabilities.

Unemployment Insurance and the New Poor

Beginning in 1979, the unemployment rate began to climb, by May 1980, the national unemployment was 7.8 percent. White unemployment was 5.8 percent, African American unemployment 11.8 percent, and Hispanic unemployment 8.9 percent. Unemployment for all teenagers was 19.2 percent, but for minority youth, it was nearly 60 percent. A total of 12 million people lost their jobs, but according to Ehrenreich, the actual number of unemployed reached more than 35 million, or 23.9 percent of the working population.[42] Six and a half million workers could find only part-time employment and 1.8 million were "discouraged workers," people no longer on the official unemployment rolls.[43]

In a time of increasing unemployment, the unemployment insurance program itself came under attack. Whereas in 1975 over 75 percent of all unemployed workers were covered, by 1980 that number had dropped to 50 percent and by 1988 to a record low of 31.5 percent.[44] In 1978, with 7.6 million people unemployed, unemployment insurance benefits were $31 billion. However, in 1982, with 10 million unemployed, less than $24 billion was paid out,[45] although payments rose to $30 billion in 1983 as unemployment increased.[46] Because the Reagan administration reduced the number of weeks of unemployment insurance available, unemployed people were more quickly forced into marginal jobs or onto public assistance. Of the officially unemployed—those registered with unemployment insurance offices—nearly 60 percent received no unemployment benefits, and payments averaged only 46 percent of before-tax earnings.[47] However, much like OASDI, unemployment insurance is a good investment and does not contribute to the federal deficit, generally taking in more than is paid out.[48]

The primary labor force employs people permanently, at reasonable wages and with fringe benefits, and entitles them to Social Security programs. The secondary labor force includes people working at marginal jobs or in part-time or low-paying jobs. Businesses employing people from the secondary labor force are usually small and highly competitive (such as fast-food chains) and hire for less than full-time at low wages, firing their employees before they qualify for fringe benefits or for OASDHI. Over one-third of all jobs were in the secondary sector in the 1980s, and they were predominantly held by women, young people, and people of color.[49]

Reform legislation in the Reagan administration, in addition to forcing many regular workers into the secondary labor market, threw thousands more into it through cuts in AFDC, SSI, and OASDI and by ending CETA in 1983. CETA had employed 400,000 poverty-level workers through public and private nonprofit agencies, but Reagan replaced it with the Job Training Partnership Act (JTPA), subsidizing the private sector to retrain the adult unemployed and to train disadvantaged youth to have marketable skills. JTPA was another "trickle down" program, but it served fewer people than CETA and people less disadvantaged, "creaming" its JTPA workers to ensure program success.

Even in full-time covered work, workers' control over their employment continued to wane rapidly. Many in the forty-to-sixty age group found themselves unemployed after years on the job, at a time when their earnings should have been highest and would have led to future higher Social Security benefits (impoverishing their families in the present and reducing their retirement security). Companies used government tax breaks and investments to "retool" and roboticize factories and jobs disappeared. "Job skidding" occurred, in which the newly unemployed found jobs, but at salaries significantly lower than former earnings; for example, an electronics job typically paid 61 percent of a factory job. Between 1979 and 1984, an estimated 11.5 million people lost their jobs through plant closings, job relocations, and technical innovations.[50]

Unemployment implied a moral judgment against workers because they could not fulfill the major societal role of family support. This took an emotional toll, keeping them quiet about job changes and cutbacks. It also helped to destroy unions and their fight for workers. Abramovitz says,

Reagan signaled the end of the post-war labor/management pact in 1981 when he fired over 11,000 striking air traffic controllers ... combined with antilabor appointments to the national Labor Relations Board, implicitly granted employers permission to revive long-shunned antiunion practices: decertifying unions, outsourcing production, and hiring permanent replacements for striking workers.[51]

Farmers constituted another group of the new poor. According to Devine and Wright,

The rate of farm poverty dropped dramatically from more than 50% in 1959 to about 11% in 1990. ... This ... does not reflect a major turnaround in the economics of the family farm so much as a continuous replacement of small-scale, economically marginal family farming operations by large-scale agribusiness enterprises. In fact the size of the farm population shrank from more than 15 million in 1959 to less than 5 million in 1990.[52]

While small farms died, the government supported large agribusiness by refusing to put a $500,000 lid per farmer on government subsidies. Some large farmers collected as much as $20 million in government support in 1986.[53] As in the past, the support of agribusiness and new technology forced small farmers off their farms, out of ownership positions, and into whatever labor they could find.

Public Assistance Programs

Supplemental Security Income began in 1974 and by 1985 served over 4 million people (rising to 4.5 million by 1993). More than 60 percent had disabilities, over 33 percent were aged, and the remaining were blind. SSI grants totaled $929.5 million, including both state and federal shares, and the average yearly grant was $2,709 by 1985. SSI for blind people was relatively higher, at $3,300 per year, whereas the grant for people with disabilities was $3,117 and for the aged $1,960. The average monthly SSI payment was $225.09.[54]

Under the Bush administration (1989), countable resources to determine eligibility were limited to $2,000 for individuals and $3,000 for couples, and available income had to be less than the maximum state SSI payment. The first $65 and half of all additional earnings were disregarded to encourage work. Costs in 1991 were $3.9 billion. By 1993, the average monthly grant was $221 for the aged, $351 for blind people, and $361 for people with disabilities. At that time, 58 percent of all SSI recipients were women, and women made up 74 percent of all aged recipients, 57 percent of all blind recipients, and 55 percent of all recipients with disabilities. From the time SSI began in 1974 until 1993, the number of recipients increased from 3,216,000 to 5,984,000.[55]

The Reagan/Bush procedures for SSI were identical to AFDC (discussed next), including retroactive and windfall payments, workfare, and loss of causal or inconsequential earnings such as blood donations.

Aid to Families of Dependent Children (AFDC), always the most stigmatized program, received Reagan's harshest cuts. Antiwelfarism took on an even stronger "moralistic" stance against women (and their "fatherless" children). Before Reagan, AFDC served approximately 3.7 million families (about 11 million people), with grants totaling about $14 billion. Of these families, 88 percent were headed by women. AFDC supported 51.7 percent of poor white families and 43.9 percent of poor African American families. Seven million children, of whom 3 million were under age six, received AFDC grants.[56] During the Reagan administration, the average grant was $1,264.40 per child per year (compared with foster care at $3,753.69 per child per year and $16,712.55 per year for institutionalization).[57] The number of families on AFDC fell by over 300,000 from 1981 to 1982, even though those years constituted the most severe recession since 1929. By 1983, the poverty rate had increased to 15.3 percent, up from 11.7 percent in 1979.[58] AFDC benefits in 1990 were $18.5 billion and by 1992 were $22 billion, with the federal government paying about 55 percent of costs of benefits.[59]

Through OBRA and GRH cuts, cash benefits to over 10.3 million people were cut by 15 percent,[60] based on new assumptions about income:

1. *Assumed income* meant that eligibility workers could assume income, received or not, from stepfathers, court-ordered support from absent parents, Earned Income Tax Credits (EITC) (prorated and deducted from grants each month), and "windfalls"—gifts, insurance benefits, small inheritances (also prorated and deducted).

2. *Allowable assets* were reduced to $1,000 except for a home and a reasonably priced car, one burial plot, one funeral agreement, and marketable real estate (exempt for six months, when repayment from proceeds was expected).

3. Persons above *eligibility caps* were ineligible: in 1981, caps were set at 150 percent of state need levels and increased in 1984 to 185 percent of state need levels.

4. *Age limits for children,* lowered to age sixteen under Reagan, were restored by Bush to age eighteen.

5. Eligibility and benefits were determined on *retrospective budgeting* of the previous month's income, prorated at AFDC levels and expected to last as long as AFDC grants even if the client had no money.

6. *New work provisions* eliminated the $30 and a third disregard on earnings, placing an effective 100 percent tax on wages. Previously, people on public assistance could keep the first $30 and another 30 percent of what they earned each month by working. Now there was no benefit incentive to work. Those who lost jobs could not reapply for a year, and work costs were standardized regardless of real costs of transportation, tax deductions, meals, union dues, and so on: $75 for full-time and $50 for part-time work, $160 a month for each child's care.

7. *Other regulations* included reporting of casual income, such as tips or blood donations; immigrants' sponsors income counted as applicant's income for three years; deduction of some vendor payments such as food stamps; preg-

nancy care moved from first to third trimester; pregnant women were expected to work until the sixth month; state option for emergency AFDC could be provided while applications were being processed.

8. AFDC for the Unemployed Parent (AFDC-UP) was allowed at state option.

The results of the $30-and-a-third disregard reduction immediately eliminated many working women from AFDC with less than a month's notice. Also, depending on state regulations, they lost Medicaid and food stamp benefits.

Forty percent of all AFDC recipients who left the program had incomes below poverty levels for at least the following year, according to a study by Zinn and Sarri. A quarter of their respondents said they had run out of food at least seven times in the year after having lost benefits, and half at least once. A major problem was the loss of Medicaid: Poor people are not healthy people, and in this sample, typical of the poor, one in seven had serious chronic illnesses such as cancer, diabetes, epilepsy, hypertension, sickle cell anemia, and arthritis/rheumatism.[61]

The Family Support Act (FSA) of 1988

In 1988 Reagan legislation changed the *structure* of AFDC as the previously discussed laws had changed the *processes*. No longer a program aimed at supporting children and women's roles in the home (however punitive the regulations), AFDC now became a work ethic program in which women and men were required to "pay back" their welfare grants by working or participating in activities oriented to future work (education and training). This most significant change removed from poor women—at least those on public assistance—all assumed roles as mothers, replacing them with worker roles formerly applied only to men.

FSA 1988 embodied the sexual morality and work ethic values of the Religious Right. It aimed first to decrease AFDC rolls by changing recipient behaviors and second to intensify pressure on clients, their families, and state/local agencies to get off the welfare rolls into work. The law included provisions for education, training, and employment, including subsidies for expenses, child care provisions and transitional support as families moved from welfare to work, and child support enforcement provisions. It required states to implement AFDC for Unemployed Parents (AFDC-UP) by October 1990, and every single parent (with children over age three or one, at state discretion) or at least one parent in intact families had to participate in work or training programs. There were exemptions: those caring for children under age three or without good day care; the ill, incapacitated, or elderly or those caring for such; people working, attending school, or in the second or third trimester of pregnancy; and those for whom states could not provide Job Opportunity and Basic Skills (JOBS) programs, the Community Work Experience Program (CWEP), or on-the-job training (OJT).

The new idea of "case management" developed under FSA 1988 as welfare workers developed contracts with recipients for their future careers. Those who refused contracts or work programs could lose AFDC eligibility.

Recipients who volunteered for JOBS, which replaced WIN, got first chance at the program. JOBS was capped at $600 million in 1989, based on states' previous WIN costs and Medicaid federal matching rates. Child care costs were outside the cap, reimbursed at federal Medicaid matching rates, and states were required to provide day care for every AFDC recipient in the JOBS program. JOBS included basic and remedial education, job skills training, job readiness programs, job search, and job development and placement services, or, at state discretion, school, vocational, technical training, or JTPA programs.

CWEP was the fallback program, requiring recipients to work off their grants. CWEP-eligible people who worked received the same grants as exempt people or those for whom no work was available; in other words, they worked for nothing. "Workfare," sometimes called "slavefare," was justified on grounds such as the need to learn a skill, get off welfare, and get into employment, as well as the notion that no one should get "something for nothing."

Child Support Enforcement Provisions revised the Child Support Enforcement Amendment of 1984, tightening up Title IV.D. (Notice to Law Enforcement Officials, or NOLEO). FSA 1988 instituted the Commission on Interstate Child Support to revise the Uniform Reciprocal Enforcement of Support Act, which traces and returns nonpaying parents across state lines and allows immediate wage withholding of delinquent support. It instituted processes for collection of support from absent parents through written warnings, reports to credit agencies, garnishment of wages, civil and criminal charges, seizure of federal and state income tax refunds, property liens, seizure and sale of property, and bond-posting by the absent parent. FSA produced a particularly important change: It required judges and other officials to establish statewide standards for amounts and collection of child support. Former discretionary awards were no longer legal. Periodic review and adjustment of child support grants were required every three years in AFDC cases. FSA required states to set up 50 percent paternity establishment quotas, to increase by 3 percent every year after 1991, the federal government to pay up to 90 percent of the lab costs. "Paternity establishment quotas" meant that the welfare departments had to establish a certain number of named fathers for each child per year. Fifty dollars of any recovered support was disregarded for grant levels and Medicaid continued for four months for children losing AFDC because of increased child support payments. Despite the intent of FSA, support collection remained low.

Other provisions of FSA 1988 stipulated that minor children who were pregnant or mothers must live with a state-appointed adult such as a parent, legal guardian, foster parent, or other adult relative. An important provision, used extensively by Bush, was the waiver of AFDC regulations to establish demonstration programs. Some states cut benefits if a child did not attend school, froze benefits if the client had another child while on welfare, restricted access to general assistance, paid to have the contraceptive Norplant embedded, encouraged marriage by paying higher benefits to married couples, paid recipients to move to higher-benefit states, or required school attendance or even marriage for unwed mothers on AFDC.

FSA 1988, despite its punitive intentions and results, explicitly acknowledged that states could no longer overlook child care needs. It also beefed up child support mechanisms, required statewide standards for child support, and established AFDC-UP for intact families. In retrospect, although none of these positives worked well, primarily because of lack of state resources, they constituted substantive changes in AFDC legislation. Unfortunately, the moral issues they involved became more important than the substance, and morality became the guideline for what was to follow in the 1990s.

Basic Needs Programs

Reaganomics and Nutrition

The AFDC program provided more food on a regular basis than most poor people would otherwise have had, and the cuts it underwent threw millions into hunger. Beyond that, a major target of Reaganomics cuts was nutrition programs: food stamps, school meals, and nutrition for women and children.

Food Stamps.   By 1982, almost 8 million people of the 22 million receiving food stamps lost their eligibility under the Reagan cutbacks. Fifty-four percent were children under age eighteen, and 78 percent were unable to work because of age, disability, or dependent care. New eligibility regulations totally excluded strikers and temporarily unemployed workers and eliminated more than 200,000 students, leaving an estimated 50,000 students still eligible. These cuts "saved" the government an estimated $7 billion but took their toll in human well-being. Households receiving food stamps had an average income of $3,900, and 90 percent of food stamp recipients are below the official poverty line. With food stamps, households bought 50 percent more food than they would otherwise.

Almost 70 percent of food stamp families were headed by women. In 1980 the average monthly food stamp allowance per person was $34.34, or about 44 cents a meal. Even if this amount—an average of $1,638—were added to a family's annual income, it would still fall about $960 below the poverty threshold.[62] Half of food stamp spending goes to retail food markets and 36 percent to the American farmer, probably over $2 billion in 1981.[63] In 1988, after much damage had already been done, Congress passed the Hunger Prevention Act, which increased food stamp allotments, increased access to food stamps for the homeless (who had been denied because they did not have addresses), and allotted federal funds for outreach to the hungry. Food stamps were also made available, at state discretion, at banks or post offices or through the mail.[64]

School Lunch Program.   The government's largest child nutrition effort, the school lunch program, suffered Reagan cuts of 30 percent, dropping 3 million children. In 1982, despite the cuts, it still served 23.6 million children at a cost of $2.9 billion. However, prices were raised, thereby eliminating many children marginally able to buy lunches, and the quantity and quality of the lunches was lowered dramatically. Lekachman says,

> In the new order, pickle relish and catsup count as vegetables, jam masquerades as a serving of fruit, cookies and cakes define themselves as bread, and the egg in the cake substitutes for meat. A hearty lunch for an adolescent might be two slices of cheese, one-fourth of a cup of grape juice, one cupcake, a cup of whole milk (four, not eight ounces), and a quarter cup of canned peaches.[65]

Until 1981 the goal of this program was to provide one-third of a child's daily nutritional needs, and the Department of Agriculture concluded that poor children got one-third to one-half of their daily nutrition from school lunches.

In response to public outrage, the administration withdrew the changes in school lunch standards, but they crept back as school lunch sizes decreased and costs increased. The school breakfast program, a supplemental program usually carried out by community groups or agencies with surplus commodities, some federal funding, and private donations, now reached only about one-third of eligible children, while the summer lunch program reached only 16 percent.

The Women, Infants, and Children Nutrition Program (WIC).   WIC also suffered a 30 percent reduction. It had been available, at the option of state departments of public welfare and local charitable agencies, to provide supplementary food grants for women during pregnancy and children to age four. All monies except for administration costs came from the federal government, and the only regulation, aside from means-tested eligibility, was that a local agency administer the program. There were numerous counties throughout the nation that refused to include WIC programs in their social offerings, thereby limiting the use of WIC in any case. Nationally, only 2.4 million—fewer than half of those eligible—received WIC food (valued at an average of $378 per year) in 1983.

Yet even that small amount markedly reduced the incidence of low birth weight, with results in savings for long-term care estimated at three dollars for every dollar spent. The cost of WIC was about a dollar a day per recipient. The Center for Disease Control found that WIC reduced anemia in infants and helped to prevent retarded physical growth, susceptibility to contagious diseases, and mental retardation. The nutrition WIC provided was estimated to save $20,000 to $40,000 each in remedial care for low-birth-weight infants, $1,400 a week for hospitalization for undernourished children, and between $0.5 million and $1 million over a lifetime for children requiring institutional care for retardation.[66]

Hunger is an ever-present problem for millions in the United States today. It is not only a statistic: it is real and painful. In a recent book, a woman confides,

I keep praying I can have the will to save some of my food so I can divide it up and make it last. . . . On Friday, I held over two peas from the lunch. I ate one pea on Saturday morning. Then I got into bed with the taste of food in my mouth and I waited as long as I could. Later on in the day I ate the other pea.

When there are bones I keep them . . . I am almost ashamed to tell you, but these days I boil the bones till they're soft and then I eat them. Today there were no bones.[67]

Reaganomics and Health Care

Public health care programs include Medicare, Medicaid, temporary disability insurance, worker's compensation, general hospital and medical care, armed forces and dependents care, school health, other public health activities, veterans' hospital and medical care, medical vocational rehabilitation, and OEO health and medical care. In addition, many private agencies provided health care: nursing homes, the Visiting Nurses Association, extended care homes, and so on. Public funds paid $144,204,000 for health care in 1983, with another $202,921,000[68] in private care. Federal costs of health care in 1991 were $204.1 billion, while state and local care was 79.1 billion.[69]

Under OBRA, Medicare and Medicaid underwent significant changes, and four block grants replaced a variety of programs. Block grants included Alcohol, Drug Abuse, and Community Mental Health; Preventive Health Services; Community Mental Health Centers; and Maternal and Child Health Services.

Medicare.   In 1984, at the same time Social Security cost-of-living increases were cut, the Medicare deductible rose to $400 from $356, and recipients had to pay everything over $100 (up from $89) per day from the 61st to 90th day and everything above $200 a day, up from $178, for lifetime reserve days. The basic premium rose from $14.60 to $17.90 per month (an increase of 15.5 percent) as of January 1, 1987. Medicare payments to hospitals were frozen for all of 1986, and physicians' payments were frozen through March 1986. As a result, the elderly got less care or had to pay more from their own income for medical services.[70] Medicare provided services for 30.5 million people during the Reagan years, with costs of $63.1 billion that rose another $10 billion the next year, the first year of the Bush administration, 1989.

Medicaid.   Along with the raising of Medicaid eligibility limits, cutting many poor people off Medicaid, the program itself underwent structural changes and funding cuts. After Reagan took office, all states cut back on matching funds, in turn allowing massive federal cutbacks. As eligibility for AFDC and SSI was cut, so was eligibility for Medicaid, and 700,000 children were thrown off. State options were reduced: Children in poor non-AFDC families who had been covered until age eighteen (twenty-one if still in school) were only covered to age five. A report from the Congressional Budget Office in 1983 estimated costs for Medicaid for three years at $520 million—about half the estimate of Defense Department annual waste from inefficient spare parts procurement.[71] In addition, OBRA made changes in Medicaid that enhanced states' abilities to limit benefits and deregulated prices for many services.[72]

Maternal and Child Health Program.   The Maternal and Child Health Program, Title V of the Social Security Act, suffered a 47 percent cutback when it was placed into an OBRA block grant even though there was an 84 percent increase in demand related to high unemployment. The grant collapsed seven programs into one: Basic Maternity and Infant and Child Health Care, Crippled Children's Services, services for children with disabilities on Supplemental Security Income, lead-poisoning prevention, sudden infant death syndrome, genetic screening and hemophilia treatment services, and adolescent pregnancy programs.

The funding cuts were particularly devastating for pregnant women. Maternal and Child Health Services block grant programs served 17 million children and pregnant women in 1981. After OBRA, there was a severe reduction in prenatal care and an increase of death rates for all infants between 1981 and 1982. The death rate of infants in Washington, D.C., for example, exceeded that in Cuba and Jamaica.[73] In Florida alone, only 38 percent of 65,000 pregnant low-income women got comprehensive prenatal care, and in Michigan 10,000 of 140,000 delivering mothers had fewer than five of twelve recommended prenatal visits after OBRA.[74]

Babies whose mothers receive no prenatal care are three times more likely to suffer low birth weight and greater risks of birth defects and death. According to Raymond Wheeler,

> We can document decreases in illness, in infant and maternal deaths, in premature births, and in the incidence of iron deficiency anemia and retarded growth among children of the poor . . . these reductions in illness and death have accrued most significantly by women, blacks, and American Indians, and in the ten states with the highest incidence of poverty and malnutrition.[75]

The U.S. infant mortality rank fell from sixth place to a tie for last place among the twenty industrialized nations as nearly 40,000 of the 3.6 million babies born in 1984 died before their first birthday. African American babies suffered twice the toll of white babies.[76]

Such cuts make no ethical or even financial sense, because the cost of care for low-birth-weight or damaged babies is astronomical. States have studied the cost–benefit ratio of health maintenance programs and have generally found that, in the long run, they save money. A Texas study found, for example, that the state saved eight dollars in avoided medical costs for every dollar spent on preventive services, and a North Dakota analysis demonstrated a drop of one-third in Medicaid costs for children who received preventive health care.[77] A $10 cost to immunize against all childhood diseases can save $500,000 to $1 million dollars for children with mental retardation caused by measles. The Center for Disease Control showed that $180 million for measles vaccination saved $1.3 billion in medical care and long-term services for deafness, blindness, and mental retardation.[78] All children up to one year, along with poor pregnant women, could have been covered for about $120 million—roughly the cost of 100 MX missiles and a third of what the federal government spent in 1982 for inspection of animal care facilities to ensure humane treatment.[79]

Alcohol and Drug Abuse Block Grant.   In October 1986, Reagan launched a massive new war on drugs, after having taken away 46 percent of drug funding via block grants. His program was to distribute $100 million to state-run alcohol and drug abuse treatment centers, but this did not recoup losses from cuts already made, such as the 25 percent cut in state treatment programs in 1982, through OBRA. The block grant consolidated many programs dealing with drug abuse, alcoholism, rehabilitation, and mental health concerns surrounding substance abuse. The resulting system, the Alcohol, Drug Abuse, Mental Health Administration (ADAMHA), became a program in progress, however, constantly changing and consolidating more programs into its block grant.

A most controversial part of the Reagan war on drugs was the establishment of urine testing for drug detection for federal employees as part of job eligibility. The General Accounting Office (GAO) noted that such testing (for federal employees) is vague, ineffective, and potentially unconstitutional (Fourth Amendment protection against unreasonable search and seizure), with unmeasurable benefits and high costs, yet it has entered society, and nationwide drug testing is not uncommon. A black market in clean urine samples developed to evade drug use detection, and to overcome this, many businesses require a witness to watch the urine sample being taken.

Housing in the 1980s

According to Rubin and colleagues, in 1970

> there were two low-income housing units . . . for each low-income renter household (income below $5000). By 1983, that situation was reversed . . . two low-income renter households for each low-income unit . . . [and] of the 2 million renters with incomes less than $3000 per year, 86 percent paid more than 60 percent of their incomes for rent.[80]

By 1985 there were 4 million fewer housing units available than renter households needing them.[81] From 1983 to 1987, the number of poor households increased by 300,000 to 7.5 million, yet, even taking inflation into account, the number of units that rented for less than $300 declined by nearly 1 million, in great part lost to disrepair and abandonment. After 1981, the number of new federally assisted housing units being constructed dropped from more than 200,000 to approximately 25,000.[82]

Housing policy under Reagan had two foci. For upper-income groups, tax policies underwrote housing costs through income tax deductions of property taxes and mortgage interest. In fact, these deductions cost the Treasury more in two years, during the Reagan administration, than did the total outlay for subsidized housing over the last half-century.[83] On the other hand, there was an "open market" policy for the poor—in other words, they took their chances on finding housing they could afford. Although Reagan officially endorsed housing allowances, federal subsidy programs for rent were reduced and funds for the maintenance of public housing were cut. During the Reagan years, the budget of the Department of Housing and Urban Development was slashed by 76 percent.[84] Under Gramm–Rudman–Hollings, the Farmers' Home Administration reduced direct loans for rural housing in 1987 to $2 billion, or $91 million less than in 1986 and $1.2 billion (37 percent) less than in 1985.[85]

Cutbacks in housing meant, of course, more homelessness. By 1987 the Department of Health and Human Services estimated that 3 million people were homeless,[86] of whom children were the fastest-growing group.[87] Many of the homeless were former mental patients with little awareness of their rights, although a great number also were those pushed out of work, off the farms, and into the cities by unemployment and consequent loss of their homes. To bring attention to their plight, in 1984 advocacy groups erected tent cities to shelter the homeless (reminiscent of Hooverville) across from Reagan's White House. An estimated five to ten thousand homeless people in Washington, D.C., fasted until President Reagan agreed to renovate a deserted government building into a model home for the homeless.

Reagan later reneged because the cost estimate was $5 to $10 million. The GAO then developed a lower-cost shelter—four huge barrack-like rooms—grossly unlike the model shelter promised. When homeless advocacy groups protested, the government ordered the homeless once more into the streets.[88] Although shelter was later provided, this demonstrated clearly—in ways that statistics hidden in charts and books could not—the reluctance of the government to provide for those obviously unable to provide for themselves.

The answer to homelessness is to provide homes that people with low incomes can afford. However, the nation seems uninterested in increasing the number of low-cost housing units; rather, short-term shelter has been the response to need. In 1986, $80 million was appropriated for transitional housing, and in 1987 Congress passed an emergency homeless bill—the Urgent Relief for the Homeless Act—of $500 million providing for sleeping rooms and shelters.[89] In 1988, $100 million was authorized, but Congress appropriated only $65 billion, of which $20 million was for transitional housing.[90]

Bush took limited leadership in the housing dilemma. Expenditures for HUD in 1990 were $22.8 billion, although only $1.6 billion was targeted for low-income housing programs.[91] He pursued home ownership (Cranston–Gonzalez National Affordable Housing Act) rather than shelter housing, and in 1991 Jack Kemp, Secretary of HUD, developed the Home Ownership and Opportunity for People Everywhere (HOPE) initiative, committing $3.1 billion over two years for the purpose of selling public housing units to tenant management groups.[92] This was as much political as altruistic: One intention was surely to divest the government of ownership, maintenance costs, and overall responsibility for public housing.[93] Despite the growing need, the number of families assisted by HUD, 3.1 million in 1980, grew to only 4.4 million by 1991.[94]

Education and Training

One of Reagan's first acts of office in 1981 was to rescind $440 million in funding for Title I of the Elementary and Secondary Education Act (ESEA). This program, developed especially to serve disadvantaged and handicapped children, had provided compensatory education to minorities and the poor, funding for bilingual education for Hispanic children, and extra services for Native American and African American children. More than half the children ESEA served before 1981 were children from minority groups: 29 percent African American, 21 percent Hispanic, and 4 percent other groups. New policies subsumed the Emergency School Assistance Act, intended to help schools desegregate, into the new block grant system, which was then cut by 35.3 percent (about $269 million), and desegregation funds were virtually eliminated. Although Head Start continued, the number of children it reached was drastically reduced.

In higher education, Basic Education Opportunity Grants (BEOGs), legislated in 1972, had been a major source of financing for disadvantaged youth bound for college. Among those it served, 70 percent were from low-income households (below $12,000 annual income) and 57 percent were minority students. OBRA severely cut BEOGs (renamed Pell grants), and all college grants, loans, and work–study support became more difficult to get and more costly as loan interest rates rose sharply. Financial aid offices were required to assume that parents would contribute $750 toward students' costs whether or not that money was actually available. Despite the cuts, Pell grants in 1983 provided $2.8 billion to needy students, and for 1984, $4 billion was appropriated for all student aid programs.[95]

Federally guaranteed loans and work–study employment reached 9 million students in 1983, attesting to the level of need even with reductions in funding. However, a great many young people were shunted away from higher education. Bell says that keeping certain people—the poor and minorities—out of school will create an educationally segregated elite and make more people available for the labor market. She adds,

> This is a good illustration of how selective programs can be manipulated to keep poor people poor and to nip aspirations in the bud.[96]

Many young people formerly supported by grants and loans dropped out of school to help their families. Enrollment of African American students dropped rapidly: In 1980 about 11 percent of college graduates were African Americans, but in the 1984–1985 school year the number declined to 8.8 percent. Although a few top-ranked African American colleges graduated record numbers, dropout rates at predominantly white schools were abysmal. In graduate and professional schools, African American enrollment declined by 11.9 percent between 1980 and 1984, and the percentage of African American faculty and administration, never very large, decreased by 4.3 percent.[97] According to a study by the College Board, federal aid to postsecondary students dropped from $22.2 billion to $20.7 billion in constant dollars after 1980, with the 1988 budget calling for another $2 billion in cuts.[98]

Civil Rights Under Reagan and Bush

The attack on social programs from 1980 forward was paired with an attack on civil rights. Administration policies clearly demonstrated that programs for empowerment or human rights were to be underfunded or withdrawn. Reagan, and later Bush, called for an end to quotas, even though they had never been part of the affirmative action program, and began to talk about the "angry white male" as undergoing "reverse discrimination." Budgets for civil rights enforcement agencies were slashed and civil rights opponents were appointed to the Civil Rights Commission and the Supreme Court. In 1990 Bush vetoed civil rights legislation that might have mitigated such actions and in 1991 appointed conservative Clarence Thomas, an outspoken critic of affirmative action even though he benefited from it, as Supreme Court Justice.

To recapitulate, the civil rights gained in the two decades preceding the Reagan years included

- The Civil Rights Act of 1957, which established the Justice Department's Civil Rights Division to sue for voting rights
- The Civil Rights Act of 1964, which barred discrimination in public schools, facilities, employment, and federally financed activities
- The Voting Rights Act of 1965, which broadened guarantees of the right to vote
- The Civil Rights Act of 1968, which forbade housing discrimination
- The Educational Amendment of 1972, which made it illegal to discriminate on the basis of sex in schools receiving federal support
- The Rehabilitation Act of 1973, which barred discrimination against people with disabilities
- The Civil Rights for Institutionalized Persons Act of 1980, which gave civil rights protection to prisoners, the mentally ill, and other institutionalized people.[99]

Attacks on civil rights through the courts opened the way to charges of "reverse discrimination" and quota-setting. Although the intent of affirmative action was to redress centuries of institutional inequities, majority people thrust away the historical focus and centered on immediate present effects of affirmative action for individuals. For example, in *Bakke v. Regents of the University of California* in 1978, Bakke charged reverse discrimination and quota-setting because he was denied admission even though his grades were higher than those of people admitted to slots reserved for minority people. The Supreme Court ruled in favor of Bakke, but upheld the university's right to reserve slots for minority students. This decision opened the way for other such court battles and accelerated the trend away from social equity for nonmajority people.

Reagan's personal support for institutional discrimination was clear: He filed a "friend of the Court" brief against a 1983 Supreme Court decision that upheld a Boston decision to fire 700 white workers rather than more recently hired minority workers. The basis for the Court's decision was past discrimination in hiring. The Supreme Court rejected, by close margins, Reagan's argument to limit affirmative action claims to actual victims of past bias. For example, when the Cleveland fire department claimed promotions should not follow racial lines, the Court voted that half of promotions be reserved for qualified minority candidates; in sheetworkers' unions in New York and New Jersey, it provided that nonwhite membership had to be doubled to 29.3 percent by August 1987. Although Reagan encouraged voluntary compliance with fair employment and antidiscriminatory rules, he continued to argue against federal or court intervention in businesses to ensure remedial action. His position rejected class action suits, quotas, numerical affirmative action goals or timetables, and compensation for past discrimination.

Civil rights battles for gays began in earnest in the 1980s and made slow progress, based on First Amendment freedom of speech rights and Civil Rights Act Title VII, which federally prohibits sex discrimination in the workplace. The Reagan administration, enforced by the Moral Majority, validated a moralistic approach to homosexuality even at Supreme Court levels, where antigay Chief Justice Warren Burger held sway. According to Eskridge,

> By treating sex as dirty conduct rather than expression and "homosexuals" as presumptive sodomites rather than citizens, the Burger Court did what it could to preserve the remnants of the 'closet.' "Don't ask, don't tell" sums up the Burger Court philosophy. . . . While the Court did not require antigay policies, it permitted states to choose such options.[100]

At first courts circumvented the First Amendment, ruling that homosexuality is conduct—often criminal conduct—rather than speech. On this basis, suppression of gay "subculture"—bars, social gatherings, literature, mailings, and so forth—could not be termed "speech." Gay-bashing, although an assault crime, was not deemed a hate crime. Civil Rights Title VII was for a time bypassed by determining that the rights of "deviants" *should* be controlled. In 1979, the Ninth Court of Appeals ruled (*De Santis v. Pacific Telephone and Telegraph*) against sexual harassment claims (brought by an openly effeminate man, a gay man, and a Lesbian couple) because—splitting numerous hairs to make the case—they were discriminated against not for their *sex*, as prohibited by Title VII, but by their *sexual orientation*.[101]

Since that time, however, courts and the Equal Employment Opportunity Commission (EEOC) have reinterpreted Title VII to make gender *stereotypes* irrelevant to job decisions and to protect workers against sexualized harassment and treatment, though as of 1995, gay and bisexual men still earned 11 to 27 percent less than straight men.[102] About a third of all states have adopted Equal Rights Amendments, and gays have fought and won inclusion in most, and since 1981 an increasing number of states and cities have adopted laws affirmatively protecting gay people against private discrimination and violence. In the area of marriage and family, gays have not fared as well: When homosexuality becomes an issue in divorce, gays are usually denied custody; adoption of children by gays is usually denied; and gay marriage is almost universally forbidden.

Funding for civil rights action declined 9 percent from 1981 to 1983, and the budgets for the Equal Employment Opportunity Commission (EEOC) and the Office of Federal Contract Compliance Programs (OFCCP) were reduced 10 and 24 percent, respectively. EEOC staff was cut by 12 percent and OFCCP staff dropped by 34 percent.[103] As a result, the number of employment discrimination cases brought by the EEOC and the Justice Department declined by half during Reagan's tenure, although the number of complaints increased by nearly 50 percent. Cases with "no cause" findings (not guilty of discrimination) increased by a third. OFCCP complaints against government contractors for discrimination in hiring dropped from fifty-three in 1980 to eighteen in 1983, with only five in 1982 (see Table 12.1).[104]

In the Department of Health and Human Services, thirty violations by recipients of federal funds were put on hold rather than pursued.[105] Between 1980 and 1983, there was a 25 percent drop in support for enforcement activities such as class action suits against employers and government contractors.[106] There was little action against civil rights violations in prisons and mental hospitals. In housing, only six fair-housing suits were filed during Reagan's first thirty months in office, compared to forty-six for Carter in the same time period.

TABLE 12.1   *OFCCP Enforcement Activities*

Activity	1960	1981	1982	1983
Complaint investigations	1,726	2,136	2,589	2,375
Compliance reviews	2,627	3,135	3,081	4,295
Complaints filed	53	15	5	18
Debarments	5	1	0	0
Back pay awarded (millions)	$9.3	$5.1	$2.1	$3.6
Recipients	4,336	4,336	1,133	1,758

Source: Taken from Lynn C. Burbridge, "The Impact of Changes in Policy on the Federal Equal Employment Opportunity Effort," Washington, D.C.: The Urban Institute, November 1983, Table 3. From Table 6.5 "OFCCP Enforcement Activities, FY1980–FY1983." Reported in John L. Palmer and Isabel V. Sawhill, eds., *Reagan Record: An Assessment of America's Changing Domestic Priorities.* Ballinger Publishing, 1985, p. 205.

In education, Reagan even argued against the long-fought battle for bus-ing to end school desegregation, although the Supreme Court upheld busing in October 1986. In Washington state, when citizens filed a referendum against busing, the Justice Department held that the referendum was racially moti-vated and therefore unconstitutional, but when Reagan took office this stance was reversed.[107] Moreover, under his tenure, the Justice Department filed only one school desegregation case and delayed release of findings in eighty-six investigations. The number of such investigations by the Department of Edu-cation dropped from 10.4 percent in February 1981 to 4.4 percent in January 1982.

In addition to stonewalling efforts *for* civil rights, Reagan supported actions *against* such rights. For example, his administration exempted 300 small colleges from laws barring sex and race discrimination and tried to grant tax exemptions to larger schools practicing discrimination. In one such instance, the Justice De-partment tried to withdraw a suit from the Supreme Court that would have denied tax-exempt status to the Goldsboro Christian Schools for racial discrimination, and Bob Jones University, which forbade interracial dating and housing. The Supreme Court ruled against the Justice Department in these in-stances.

The Civil Rights Commission, investigating Reagan's own record of em-ployment, claimed it evidenced sexism and racism:

> [T]hrough the first two years of the Reagan administration, appointments were 8 percent female and 8 percent minority (4 percent black); Carter's appointments were 12 percent female and 17 percent minority (12 percent black).[108]

Rather than respond to the commission's charges, Reagan fired three of its six members and tried to fire two others. He then created a new eight-member com-mission with members whose civil rights views matched his own.[109]

Some gains were made despite the administration's tacit approval of insti-tutional racism, primarily because of the increased education and political action of people of color in earlier decades. The number of elected officials of African de-scent at all levels of government rose from 1,472 in 1970 to 5,606 in 1983, and num-bers of African American and Hispanic mayors increased, to 248 and 47, respectively.[110] Nevertheless, the move toward civil rights slowed considerably with increasing conservatism in the nation and Reagan's personal involvement in discrimination.

Under the Bush administration, a new kind of civil rights became available: the American Disabilities Act (ADA) protects the rights of people with physical, emotional, or mental impairments that limit "one or more major life activities." It

- Requires employers to reasonably accommodate qualified applicants or em-ployees with disabilities (unless there is a hardship)
- Prohibits state and local governments from discriminating in any program, benefit, policy, or activity

- Requires government agencies with fifty or more employees to identify and change physical and programmatic barriers
- Requires that physical barriers in public facilities be removed, or alternative methods provided
- Prohibits discrimination in public accommodations, although private clubs and religious organizations are exempt
- Requires new transit systems to be accessible and older ones to have one car per train accessible
- Requires special transportation for people with disabilities who cannot use public transportation
- Requires the provision of speech, vision, or hearing equipment to allow equal participation in accommodations or services
- Requires telephone companies to offer telephone relay services to people with disabilities, although they must buy their own equipment.

Importantly, ADA allows people with AIDS-related disabilities to claim disability, making them eligible for the many programs heretofore denied them.

The Costs of Social Welfare

Estimating Poverty

Some people believe that vendor payments—food stamps, housing subsidies, and Medicaid—should be counted when estimating the poverty rate. However, such calculations are an illusion: Payments actually go to the service provider, not the poor.

> Thus, at market value, an AFDC mother with two children . . . "received" an additional $1287 in 1979 because she was covered by Medicaid . . . of course she did not receive a dime. . . . Poor people receive medical services, not income; the latter goes to providers.[111]

In 1982, then, the poverty rate was "reduced" from 11 percent to 9.4 percent because a family of four receiving Medicaid coverage had $547 "released" (or available) to spend on goods other than medical care—an extra $45.58 per month. However, without the vendor payments the person would either not get the services or take the money needed to pay for them out of food money. It is not really "received" money. Besides, as Ehrenreich says,

> [T]he question of whether 20 million or 34 million or 50 million Americans are "poor" is surely an indecent one; the lowest of these figures is a national scandal. . . . No matter how poverty is measured, the decline in poverty that began in the sixties slowed and then stopped in the seventies; since 1978, the numbers below the poverty level have steadily risen.[112]

How Much Did Welfare Cost in the Reagan Era?

In 1980 all social programs constituted only 18.7 percent of the gross national product. All means-tested cash transfers came to $30.1 billion, increasing to $39.9 billion in October 1985, and OASDI payments were $252.7 billion in 1980 and $388.6 billion in 1985. Health and medical care cost $3.9 billion, veterans' benefits $2.6 billion, and education $141.2 billion.[113] Although public assistance (AFDC and SSI) made up only 2.7 percent of the total GNP in 1980, it actually decreased in 1983.[114]

By 1984, OASDI and Medicare constituted 35 percent of all social welfare expenditures, at about $220 billion, whereas all costs of public assistance totaled $80 billion. As a comparison, AFDC cost about $8 billion, and the interest on the national debt cost $111 billion.[115]

Individual taxpayers are misled into thinking social welfare programs, particularly public assistance, take the biggest bite from our tax dollars, but in fact the per capita tax cost we each paid for public assistance was about $30.16 per month during the Reagan years. This was more than in earlier years: In 1960, per capita cost was about $1.87 per month, in 1970 about $6.60, and in 1980 $26.01. However, that cost is minuscule compared to other costs, both public and private.[116] (See Table 12.2.)

Under Bush, although expenditures for social programs seemed to expand, the Reagan cuts had slashed many programs beyond repair. What was left was almost the bare minimum, subject to inflation and future cuts even in entitlement programs. Table 12.3 shows social program costs in the middle of the Bush administration.[117]

The International Element

By the end of his tenure, Reagan had moved away from his warlike stance toward the Soviet Union and overt interference in the internal affairs of nations such as the Dominican Republic. Bush moved even further. Anticipating world economic

TABLE 12.2 *Total and Per Capita Social Welfare Expenditures (1983 dollars)*

Total (millions)		Per Capita (dollars)			
Year	Amount	Total	Social Insurance	Public Assistance	Health
1960	$ 52,106.30	$ 265.42	$ 105.35	$ 22.46	$ 35.01
1970	145,483.90	689.90	261.75	79.26	121.32
1980	492,070.10	2,139.38	995.06	312.91	438.92
1983	640,026.30	2,698.72	1,387.79	361.91	608.05

Source: U.S. Department of Health and Human Services, Social Security Administration, Office of Policy. "Monthly Benefit Statistics, February 1986," p. 18.

TABLE 12.3 *Social Welfare Expenditures Under Public Programs, 1991 (billions, current dollars)*

	Total	Federal	State/Local	Percentage of Federal	Per Capita
OASI	$ 564	$454	$111	67%	$2,196
Public assistance	180	113	67	80	705
Health	69	30	40	63	271
Veterans	33	32	1	43	126
Education	277	19	258	98	1,083
Housing	22	19	3	7	84
Other	20	10	10	87	77
All health and medical	315	213	103	50	1,234
Total	$1,165	$677	$490	58%	$4,542

Source: U.S. Bureau of the Census, *Statistical Abstracts of the United States: 1994* (114th Ed.), Table 572, p. 370.

leadership for the United States, he proposed a "New World Order" in which stability depended not on a balance of war power but on cooperation and the "beneficent intervention" of the United States.[118] He envisioned a *Pax Americana*, with the United States setting standards for economic cooperation and becoming the watchdog of world peace. His view of America as the world's peacekeeper became evident in the Gulf War against Saddam Hussein, the Grenada invasion to "save" American students allegedly held there against their will, and in drug wars in Panama. His support of rich Kuwaitis and their oil was economic rather than altruistic, although publicity focused on Saddam Hussein as a worldwide threat. The assault on Grenada seemed to have little meaning except for muscle-flexing, however, and the invasion of Panama appeared to be an interference in the domestic affairs of another nation, although justified as politically necessary. The arrest and trial of General Manuel Noriega, erstwhile President of Panama, on drug import charges, was a strange step, calling into question both the right to interfere in other nations and, because there was some evidence Noriega was employed by the CIA, the whole issue of covert activity.

Nevertheless, by the time Bush left office, America's isolationist perspective had disappeared on the federal level, although it was still present in the minds of workers displaced in the job market by foreign labor. The nation was well under way in becoming wedded to transnational corporate control of the global economy.

Conclusion: Past Ideology in a Postindustrial World

There is no doubt that the Reagan and Bush administrations made deep inroads on social welfare in the United States. Reagan, with a few strokes of his pen, set back human and civil rights for decades, or perhaps four centuries, depending on one's perspective:

The president clearly did seek to turn back the social policy clock. . . . Given his way, the president would have eradicated most of the hallmarks of the Great Society and would have shrunk the social insurance programs to a scope more nearly approximating their New Deal origins. On the civil rights front the president would have scrapped the federal government's role as a "commanding general" in the war for equal opportunity . . . broad goals, quotas, and timetables would have been replaced by individual disciplinary action according to rather narrowly interpreted rules.[119]

These reactionary administrations redefined those who disagree with traditionalism as malcontents, deviants, and the un-American. Levitan and Johnson say,

The inequities and hardships imposed by the Reagan administration's economic and social policies cannot be construed as merely a response to the demands of an angry public. Reagan social welfare policies, founded on right-wing ideology, have never been ratified by the voting public, and they deviate sharply from the American commitment to opportunity and compassion.[120]

Reagan's ostensible attack on big government, Ehrenreich argues, was

an attack on the idea that government can or should protect people against the power of corporations, landlords, and merchants. The attack on "entitlement" programs is an assault on the idea that economic well-being is a political right. The attack on the . . . legal services program, on affirmative action programs, on laws regulating corporate behavior is an attack on the laws and institutions that enable people to express their rights.[121]

That Reagan only led this attack, and that millions of Americans followed in this battle against justice, is an even more terrifying statement about the state of our society. The Bush years solidified what Reagan began simply by not dealing adequately with domestic issues. This set the stage for a society whose politicians believe cutbacks in social programs and laissez-faire civil rights are the appropriate way of conducting a county. Even democratic President Clinton did not search for a way out of the morass. Rather, despite his rhetoric, he took his cues from the legacy of the Reagan/Bush years: workfare, time-limited public assistance, and personal responsibility for failure (although he seemed to understand the institutional causes and repercussions of this approach). The moral degradation of society appears likely to continue well into the next century.

Study Questions

1. What was the Moral Majority/Christian Right? What was its impact on women? On the poor?

2. What was Reaganomics? What were its effects on the poor, the aged, people with disabilities, and women and their children?

3. What people became the "new poor"? What factors/events led to the creation of the "new poor"?

4. What happened to civil rights under Reagan and Bush? What might that portend for the future?

5. Describe internationalism and the New World Order under Bush. Discuss what it has to do with today's world.

Notes

1. James Midgley, "New Christian Right, Social Policy, and the Welfare State," *Journal of Sociology and Social Welfare*, Vol. 17, no. 2 (June 1990), p. 97.

2. Daniel P. Moynihan, *Pandaemonium: Ethnicity in International Politics* (New York: Oxford University Press, 1993), p. 46.

3. Winifred Bell, *Contemporary Social Welfare* (New York: Macmillan, 1983), pp. 42–43.

4. Midgley, "New Christian Right," p. 94.

5. Sar A. Levitan and Clifford M. Johnson, *Beyond the Safety Net* (Cambridge, MA: Ballinger Publishing, 1984), p. 150.

6. Center on Budget and Policy Priorities, "Analysis of Poverty in 1987" (Washington, D.C.: Center on Budget and Policy Priorities, 1988), pp. 3–6.

7. David A. Stockman, *The Triumph of Politics: Why the Reagan Revolution Failed* (New York: Harper & Row, 1986), p. 373. Cited in Moynihan, *Pandaemonium*, p. 17.

8. Ralph Dolgoff and Donald Feldstein, *Understanding Social Welfare*, 2nd ed. (New York: Longman Press, 1984), p. 144; U.S. Bureau of the Census reports. Cited in *Chicago Tribune*, July 19, 1986, pp. 1–2.

9. Levitan and Johnson, *Beyond the Safety Net*, p. 151.

10. Ibid.

11. James M. Fendrich, Mamie Miller, and Tim Nichel, "It's the Budget, Stupid: A Policy Analysis of Clinton's First Budget," *Journal of Sociology and Social Welfare*, Vol. 21, no. 4 (Dec. 1994), p. 7.

12. Frances Fox Piven and Richard Cloward, *The New Class War: Reagan's Attack on the Welfare State and Its Consequences* (New York: Pantheon Books, 1982), p. 7.

13. Diana DiNitto, *Social Welfare: Politics and Public Policy*, 4th ed. (Needham, MA: Allyn & Bacon, 1995), pp. 57, 60.

14. Fendrich, Miller, and Nichel, "It's the Budget, Stupid," p. 18.

15. U.S. Bureau of the Census reports. Cited in *Chicago Tribune*, July 19, 1986, pp. 1–2.

16. Jule M. Sugarman, Gary D. Bass, Nancy Amidei, David Plocher, Shannon Ferguson, and Julie Quiroz, *OMB Watch: A Citizen's Guide to Gramm–Rudman–Hollings* (Washington, D.C.: Focus Project, Inc., 1986); United Way of Indiana, "Capital Steps" (Indianapolis: United Way of Indiana, n.d.).

17. Levitan and Johnson, *Beyond the Safety Net*, p. 150.

18. John L. Palmer and Isabel V. Sawhill (eds.), *Reagan Record: An Assessment of America's Changing Domestic Priorities* (Cambridge, MA: Ballinger Publishing, 1985), p. 222.

19. Mark Robert Rank, *Living on the Edge* (New York: Columbia University Press, 1994), p. 20.

20. Howard J. Karger, "Income Maintenance Programs and the Reagan Domestic Agenda," *Journal of Sociology and Social Welfare*, Vol. 19, no. 1 (March 1992), p. 57.

21. Ibid.

22. Fendrich, Miller, and Nichel, "It's the Budget, Stupid," p. 18.

23. Palmer and Sawhill, *Reagan Record*, p. 217.

24. Ibid., p. 193 and footnote, p. 193.

25. Levitan and Johnson, *Beyond the Safety Net*, p. 152.

26. Children's Defense Fund, "American Children in Poverty" (Washington, D.C.: CDF, 1984), p. 3.

27. Ibid., p. x.

28. Fendrich, Miller, and Nichel, "It's the Budget, Stupid," p. 18.

29. Levitan and Johnson, *Beyond the Safety Net,* p. 151.

30. Palmer and Sawhill, *Reagan Record,* p. 31.

31. From the Democratic Study Group, U.S. House of Representatives, James L. Oberstar, chairman, "Special Report: Gramm–Rudman—the Cutting Begins" (Washington, D.C.: U.S. House of Representatives, Jan. 1986), no. 99-26, p. 20; Children's Defense Fund, "American Children," p. 3.

32. Sugarman, Bass, Amidei, Plocher, Ferguson, and Quiroz, *OMB Watch,* p. 23.

33. Francis X. Russo and George Willis, *Human Services in America* (Englewood Cliffs, NJ: Prentice Hall, 1986), p. 245.

34. "Current Operating Statistics," *Social Security Bulletin* (Washington, D.C.: U.S. Government Printing Office), Sept. 1984, p. 3.

35. DiNitto, *Social Welfare,* p. 111.

36. Ibid., p. 110.

37. Ibid., p. 107.

38. Julie Rovner, "Ending the Greatest Terror of Life," *AARP Bulletin,* Special Report (1995), p. 12.

39. Ibid.

40. Neil Howe and Richard Jackson, "The Most Unfair Noncut of All: Federal Pensions," *Christian Science Monitor* (July 21, 1995), p. 18.

41. "Panel: Welfare Exams Wasted Millions," *Lafayette (Indiana) Journal and Courier* (Oct. 30, 1986), p. 1.

42. John Ehrenreich, *The Altruistic Imagination: A History of Social Work and Social Policy in the United States* (Ithaca, NY: Cornell University Press, 1985), p. 217.

43. Levitan and Johnson, *Beyond the Safety Net,* p. 40.

44. Howard J. Karger, "Income Maintenance Programs," p. 51.

45. Children's Defense Fund, "American Children," pp. 27–28.

46. Levitan and Johnson, *Beyond the Safety Net,* p. 132.

47. Michael Harrington, *The New American Poverty* (New York: Holt, Rinehart, & Winston, 1984), p. 42.

48. Daniel P. Moynihan, "The Case Against Entitlement Cuts," *Modern Maturity* (Nov.–Dec. 1994), pp. 13–14.

49. Howard Stanback, "Attacking Poverty with Economic Policy," in Alan Gartner, Colin Greer, and Frank Reismann (eds.), *Beyond Reagan: Alternatives for the Eighties* (New York: Harper & Row, 1984), pp. 57–73, esp. p. 62.

50. "Change in America," *Chronicle of Higher Education,* Vol. 32, no. 3 (Sept. 17, 1986), p. 1.

51. Mimi Abramovitz, "The Reagan Legacy: Undoing Class, Race, and Gender Accords," *Journal of Sociology and Social Welfare,* Vol. 19, no. 1 (March 1992), p. 102.

52. Joel A. Devine and James D. Wright, *The Greatest of Evils: Urban Poverty and the American Underclass* (New York: Aldine de Gruyter, 1993), p. 63.

53. *Lafayette (Indiana) Journal and Courier,* Oct. 2, 1986, p. 37.

54. "Current Operating Statistics," *Social Security Bulletin,* Vol. 49, no. 2 (Feb. 1986), Table M-20, p. 42, and Table M-23, p. 44.

55. U.S. Bureau of the Census, Population Reports, *Social Benefits,* from Internet.

56. Piven and Cloward, *New Class War,* pp. 3–4.

57. Ibid.

58. Nancy Rose, "Gender, Race, and the Welfare State: Government Work Programs from the 1930s to the Present," *Feminist Studies,* Vol. 19, no. 2 (Summer 1993), p. 334.

59. DiNitto, *Social Welfare,* p. 187.

60. Tom Joe, "The Case for Income Support," in Alan Gartner, Colin Greer, and Frank Reismann (eds.), *Beyond Reagan: Alternatives for the Eighties* (New York: Harper & Row, 1984), pp. 81–90.

61. Deborah K. Zinn and Rosemary Sarri, "Turning Back the Clock on Public Welfare," *Signs: Journal of Women in Culture and Society,* Vol. 10, no. 2. (Winter 1984), pp. 355–370, esp. p. 357.

62. Bell, *Contemporary Social Welfare,* p. 105.

63. Barbara Howell and Leon Howell, "Food Stamps: Stories and Statistics," *Christian Century* (Jan. 23–30), p. 728.

64. DiNitto, *Social Welfare,* p. 212.

65. Robert Lekachman, *Greed Is Not Enough: Reaganomics* (New York: Pantheon Books, 1982), p. 85.

66. Children's Defense Fund, "American Children," p. 33.

67. Loretta Schwartz-Nobel, *Starving in the Shadow of Plenty* (New York: G.P. Putnam's Sons, 1983). A review in *Lafayette (Indiana) Journal and Courier* (Oct. 27, 1983), p. C-3.

68. "Current Operating Statistics" (Feb. 1986), p. 21.

69. DiNitto, *Social Welfare,* p. 258.

70. "Current Operating Statistics," *Social Security Bulletin,* Vol. 46 (April 1983), p. 70.

71. Children's Defense Fund, "American Children," p. viii.

72. Terri Combs-Orme and Bernard Guyer, "American's Health Care System, the Reagan Legacy," *Journal of Sociology and Social Welfare,* Vol. 19, no. 1 (March 1992), pp. 3–88.

73. Children's Defense Fund, "American Children," pp. 1–4.

74. Ibid., p. 6.

75. Wheeler, in Howell and Howell, "Food Stamps," p. 730.

76. "Reducing the Infant Mortality Rate," *Lafayette (Indiana) Journal and Courier* (Feb. 4, 1987), p. C-4.

77. Levitan and Johnson, *Beyond the Safety Net,* p. 115.

78. Children's Defense Fund, "American Children," p. 33.

79. Ibid.

80. Beth Rubin, James D. Wright, and Joel A. Devine, "Unhousing the Urban Poor: The Reagan Legacy," *Journal of Sociology and Social Welfare,* Vol. 19, no. 1 (March 1992), p. 142.

81. Ibid., p. 129.

82. Elizabeth A. Mulroy and Terry S. Love, "Housing Affordability, Stress and Single Mothers: Pathway to Homelessness," *Journal of Sociology and Social Welfare,* Vol. 19, no. 3 (Sept. 1992), pp. 55–56.

83. C. Dolbeare from a paper prepared for the Policy Conference on Assisting the Homeless, U.S. Advisory Commission on Intergovernmental Relations (Nov. 1988), p. 39. Quoted in Rubin, Wright, and Devine, "Unhousing the Urban Poor," p. 136.

84. Ibid.

85. Democratic Study Group, "Gramm Rudman—The Cutting Begins," pp. A18–A19.

86. Mulroy and Love, "Housing Affordability," p. 60.

87. "HUD Defends Accuracy of Count: Group Rebuts Report on Homeless," *Kansas City Times* (Aug. 16, 1984), p. 5.

88. Jack Anderson and Dale van Atta, "Model Shelter or Workhouse?" *Washington Post* (July 21, 1985), p. 2.

89. Rubin, Wright, and Devine, "Unhousing the Urban Poor."

90. Anderson and van Atta, "Model Shelter or Workhouse?," p. 2.

91. Rubin, Wright, and Devine, "Unhousing the Urban Poor," p. 112.

92. Alice K. Johnson and Michael Sherraden, "Asset Based Social Welfare Policy: Homeownership for the Poor," *Journal of Sociology and Social Welfare,* Vol. 19, no. 3 (Sept. 1994), p. 78.

93. Ibid., p. 74.

94. Rubin, Wright, and Devine, "Unhousing the Urban Poor," p. 116.

95. Levitan and Johnson, *Beyond the Safety Net,* p. 128.

96. Bell, *Contemporary Social Welfare,* p. 131.

97. Levitan and Johnson, *Beyond the Safety Net,* p. 128.

98. "Education," *Newsweek on Campus* (Feb. 1987), pp. 10–18.

99. Michael Wines, "At Issue: Civil Rights," *National Journal* (March 27, 1982), p. 539.

100. William N. Eskridge, Jr. *Gaylaw: Challenging the Apartheid of the Closet* (Cambridge, MA: Harvard University Press, 1999), p. 146–147.

101. Ibid., p. 235.

102. M. V. Lee Badgett, "The Wage Effects of Sexual Orientation Discrimination," *Industrial and Labor Relations Review,* Vol. 48, p. 726. Reported in Eskridge, *Gaylaw,* p. 234.

103. Palmer and Sawhill, *Reagan Record,* p. 208.

104. Lynn C. Burbridge, "The Impact of Changes in Policy on the Federal Equal Employment Opportunity Effort" (Washington, D.C.: The Urban Institute, Nov. 1983), Table 3. From Table 6.5, "OFCCP Enforcement Activities, FY 1980–1983." Cited in Palmer and Sawhill, *Reagan Record,* p. 205.

105. Palmer and Sawhill, *Reagan Record,* p. 539.

106. Joe R. Feagin, *Racial and Ethnic Relations,* 2d ed. (Englewood Cliffs, NJ: Prentice Hall, 1984), p. 240.

107. Wines, "At Issue," pp. 536–541.

108. Palmer and Sawhill, *Reagan Record,* p. 208.

109. Levitan and Johnson, *Beyond the Safety Net,* p. 128.

110. Ibid., p. 109.

111. Leonard Beeghly, "Illusion and Reality in the Measurement of Poverty," *Social Problems,* Vol. 31, no. 3 (Feb. 1984), pp. 324–333, esp. p. 329.

112. Ehrenreich, *Altruistic Imagination,* p. 222.

113. "Current Operating Statistics" (Feb. 1986), p. 20.

114. Ibid., Table 3, p. 17.

115. United Way of Indiana, "Capital Steps," p. 1.

116. "Current Operating Statistics" (Feb. 1986), p. 18.

117. U.S. Bureau of the Census, *Statistical Abstracts 1994,* Government Expenditures for Health Services and Supplies, millions of dollars, 1990 and 1991, Table 154, p. 113.

118. Ray Mosely, *Chicago Tribune* (May 24, 1992), section 4, page 3. Quoted in Moynihan, *Pandaemonium,* p. 18.

119. Palmer and Sawhill, *Reagan Record,* pp. 214–215.

120. Levitan and Johnson, *Beyond the Safety Net,* p. 157.

121. Ehrenreich, *Altruistic Imagination,* p. 185.

13

The Synergistic Cycle

The New Synergy of Values

From colonization onward, although it was not a smooth progression, the United States moved toward social morality in provision for the disadvantaged and equal rights for all. Until 1995. Suddenly, we found the nation reverting to moral and political stances of earliest colonial days: "less eligibility" for the poor, women, children, and the unemployed; an emerging hatred for women public dependents; and a powerful moral elite controlling the processes of government.

The radical reactionary turn of the Republican-led 104th Congress should not have surprised us. Cycles of history demonstrate that when the troika of economics, politics, and religion synchronize, social revolution is upon us. Patterns laid during World War II fell into place: the United States became first in world trade; transnational corporations began a new global economy; the International Monetary Fund (IMF) and the World Bank were established to bring developing countries into the international economy; and new international alliances began to dictate the internal social and economic policies of the world's nations. In the United States, symptoms included

- Growing international economic and political power for the nation's economic elite
- Loss of well-paying jobs to the international labor market, along with computerization, robotization, and jobs and finances easily moved around the world
- A religious fundamentalist coalition powered by its interconnections with the politics of the Far Right.

Across two decades and six political administrations, the scope of massive changes was almost invisible, but the signs were certainly there. Beginning with

406

Nixon and solidified throughout the presidencies of Reagan and Bush were increasing privatization of programs; decreasing federal attention to poverty, civil rights, and income equity; and burgeoning support of the wealthy and transnational corporations. Looking at the glitches—problems easily solved, given a new administration—we ignored the compounded reactionary legislation juggernauting its way toward the 1990s.

We focused instead on the peccadilloes of individual presidents—the Nixon crimes, the Reagan ineptitude, the Bush image-seeking—rather than the clear and oft-spoken intent to reverse the nation's trend toward citizen empowerment in favor of increasing benefits to the elite.

In addition, we tacitly agreed that corporate executives, because they made profits, were "corporate statesmen" who could make government policies. Appointed to national posts, they applied profit making to national and international enterprises, and they gained political and economic access to the world economy. Transnational corporations blossomed, emerging into a global economy with loyalty to no one nation. The flow of industries, money, and jobs across the world quickened until a shadow government of corporate leaders controlled not only the American political economy, but that of most nations.

The consequent internationalization of the American economy resulted in dismantling of both the labor force and social programs, expanding the principle of less eligibility to the international arena. On the domestic level, privatization and defederalization of social programs ensured control by vested interests at state levels, where it is easier than at federal levels. Karger says,

> economic strength translates into political power . . . corporations can blackmail local and state governments by threatening plant closures, relocating operations offshore, and laying off large numbers of workers.[1]

Moreover, state control meant reductions in federal standards, requirements, and safeguards, resulting in loss of long-time citizen protections.

Another trend was more frightening: legislative actions and concepts portending a slow genocide for "socially indigestible" people such as women and their dependent children, the aged, people with disabilities, and people belonging to minority groups. There were already increases in poor health, poor nutrition, disease, homelessness, and crime that, if continued, would automatically reduce our "unwanteds," along with their "problems" and costs to society. Devine and Wright note,

> In the highly segmented and technically sophisticated labor market . . . the unskilled cease to function as an industrial reserve army. Instead, they [become] a dependent surplus population [with] . . . ever-increasing expenditures necessary to contain [it].[2]

"Containing" the poor is expensive, but redefining them as "deviants" or "underclass" absolves society of guilt. As the Reformation justified mercantilism, the work ethic and Puritan morality intimated religious approval of "weeding out." Macarov says,

> the manner in which poverty is viewed as deviance, and refusal to work is considered the cause, dates back to the Puritan's dictum that those who will not work should not be permitted to eat . . . an attitude not conspicuously absent from the public mind today.[3]

Indeed, that particular instruction came long before the time of the Puritans, in St. Paul's letter to the Thessalonians (2 Thessalonians 3:10). It was more recently expressed in the Communist Manifesto (1848) and the writings of Lenin, Trotsky, and Stalin. Thayer says,

> Considering the identical roots of the communist and capitalist versions of the starvation principle, there have been relatively few conceptual and operational differences. All joblessness is considered voluntary. . . .[4]

and,

> Today's popular concept of "dependency" reflects the old fear that food will "spoil" the jobless. . . . Individuals who work for a living are, by definition, "dependent" upon their employers for whatever standard of living they seek to maintain. Only those with huge inherited wealth can be labeled "independent." Yet the unholy alliance of classical economics and ancient religion has easily withstood more than a half-century of data collection and public policies that recognized unemployment as involuntary and compulsory.[5]

The election of President Bill Clinton in 1992 seemed a mandate for reform of the Reagan/Bush legacy of enormous deficit and corporate power; increasing unemployment, crime and poverty; and the growing polarization of rich and poor. He came to office with three major promises: a crime bill, health care reform, and welfare reform. New anticrime legislation was easy because a bipartisan Congress was already calling for reform, but the National Health Insurance bill failed because of opposition from the increasingly powerful health insurance lobby (and backlash against Hillary Rodham Clinton, who led its development).

Faced with a recalcitrant Congress answerable both to a politically powerful Religious Right and economically forceful transnational corporations, Clinton chose politics over principles and backed away from other promises. First to go was his promise to end discrimination against gays in the military, though as Commander in Chief of the Armed Forces he could have ordered it. However, his major retreat was in welfare reform. Despite his protestations of care for children, this politically driven president, concerned with upcoming elections, after two vetoes signed the Personal Responsibility and Work Opportunity Reconciliation Acts (PRWORA, 1996) with its pernicious welfare reform bill titled Temporary Assistance to Needy Families (TANF). To the dismay of those who trusted him, he fulfilled his promise to "end welfare as we know it" by ending sixty years of the citizen entitlements established in the Social Security Acts of 1935.

The Clinton presidency ended with a reduced national debt and an economic surplus. George W. Bush, elected President under a cloud of questions about the election's validity, continued policies that disenfranchised the poor and benefited the rich, and within months the surplus disappeared into a new recession. Suddenly, on September 11, 2001, attacks on the World Trade Center and the Pentagon eclipsed all domestic policies, and the war on world terrorism began.

Economic Context of the 1990s

The Reagan tax structure that sent the country spiraling into deficits could not be reversed because Omnibus Budget Reconciliation Acts (OBRAs) and deficit reduction bills had become part of the legislative structure. Clinton was able to curtail their effects to some extent: When he entered office in 1992, the Gross Federal Debt—the sum of debt held by the public and debt the government owes itself—was $4.2 trillion, mounting at a rate of $1 billion a day. In 1993, Clinton and the Congress enacted a five-year deficit reduction package of spending cuts and higher revenues, designed to cut the accumulated deficits from 1994 to 1998 by about $500 billion. By 1995, the rate of growth had slowed to about $800 million a day ($9,600 per second).[6]

Though at the end of 1997 the Gross Federal Debt was $5.4 trillion,[7] by 1998, under the historic 1997 Balanced Budget Act (BBA), the federal budget had a surplus of $69 billion and the federal debt was reduced by over $50 billion.[8] The BBA provided for $247 billion in savings over five years, extended Medicare's solvency for at least ten years, provided the largest investment in higher education since the G.I. Bill in 1945, and created a $500-per-child tax credit for about 27 million working families.[9]

As Clinton set about repairing the budget, he cut thousands from the government workforce, changed the military procurement system to avoid purchase of overpriced goods, and reduced excessive budgets in federal bureaus.[10] He also raised the tax rate for corporations over $10 million by 1 percent (to 35 percent)[11] and closed more than seventy military bases.

Revenues for 2000 came from individual income tax (48%), social security payroll taxes (34%), corporate income taxes (10%), other taxes (4%), and excise taxes (4%).[12] If we compare the amount from individual and corporate taxes and from 1994 to 2000, we can see that Clinton's major gain was in increasing corporate taxes a little while decreasing "other" and excise taxes. Individual income and social security taxes have risen, perhaps because of the recovering economy under Clinton. Federal revenues are shown in Table 13.1, projected ex-

TABLE 13.1   *Revenues by Source (in billions of dollars)*

	Actual				Estimate	
Source of Revenues	*1998*	*1999*	*2000*	*2001*	*2002*	*2003*
Individual income taxes	$ 829	$ 879	$ 952	$ 995	$1,026	$1,066
Corporate income taxes	189	185	192	195	196	200
Payroll taxes (social ins.)	572	612	650	682	712	742
Excise taxes	58	70	68	77	80	81
Estate and gift taxes	24	28	30	32	35	36
Customs duties	18	18	21	21	23	24
Miscellaneous receipts	33	35	43	40	41	43
Total	**$1,723**	**$1,827**	**$1,956**	**$2,042**	**$2,113**	**$2,192**

Source: Taken from Table 2-1, "Revenues by Source—Summary," *A Citizen's Guide to the Federal Budget: Budget FY 2000,* p. 5; and Table 2-1, "Revenues by Source—Summary," *A Citizen's Guide to the Federal Budget: FY 2001,* p. 4. Available: http://w3.access.gpo.gov/usbudget/fy2000/guide02,04.

penditures are shown in Table 13.2. The surplus for 1999 was $124 billion, with surpluses for fiscal years 2000 and 2001 projected at $148 billion and $160 billion, respectively.[13] However, concurrent with the election of George W. Bush in 2000 came a drastic change: the economy began to slide, reaching recession stage in March 2001.

The Decline of Social Responsibility: Welfare as We Knew It

The "Contract with America"

Before the 104th Congress, the political pendulum swung to the Far Right, which, in concert with the increasingly powerful Religious Right, created a "Contract with America." The ten-item document was signed by 237 Republican candidates and dedicated to a new moral America (with a balanced budget). In the context of the "Contract," blame for the national deficit was laid not to faulty tax structure or unwise fiscal planning. Rather, it was defined as lack of "personal responsibility" of public dependents, primarily women. With the disintegration of the USSR, our Cold War enemy had disappeared, so we chose a new one for a Colder War: women disattached from men and "choosing" to increase an unneeded surplus labor force.

The 104th Congress, sworn in midway into the Clinton term (January 1995), was the first Republican-controlled Congress in forty years. Its "Contract with America," ranging from a balanced budget to the reestablishment of Reagan's "Star Wars" initiative, overtly promised to end social programs and give tax breaks to the wealthy—in other words, to take welfare from the poor and give it

TABLE 13.2 *Selected Government Expenditures, 1998–2001 (in billions of dollars)*

Function	1998	1999	2000	2001
Military	$ 256	$ 275	$ 291	$ 291
International and domestic	117	139	154	149
Education, training, employment	55	56	63	68
Health	131	141	154	167
Medicare	193	190	203	221
Income security	233	238	251	260
Social Security	379	390	407	426
Veteran's benefits and services	42	43	47	46
Justice, government, net interest, offsetting receipts.	232	232	220	207
Total	**$1,638**	**$1,714**	**$1,790**	**$1,893**

Source: Taken from Table 2-3, "Total Spending by Function," *Citizen's Guide to the Federal Budget: Budget FY 2000,* p. 10; and Table 2-3, "Total Spending by Function," *Citizen's Guide to the Federal Budget: Budget FY 2001,* p. 9. Available: http://w3.access.gpo.gov/usbudget/fy2000 and fy2001/guide02,04.

to the rich. The "Contract" led the way to the most overtly anti-woman, anti-poor legislation ever passed in the United States.

Whereas previously our sexist, racist, and classist values were mostly unwritten, legislation based on the "Contract" placed them squarely within the legislative structure of American polity. It undermined most programs of the Social Security Acts of 1935, which for sixty years had provided a safety net against catastrophe. "Welfare reform" became "recipient reform" as Congress capped spending, set up even harsher work requirements, and block-granted programs to defederalize them. The savings, supporters claimed, would be applied to the federal deficit. The direction was clear: Take away welfare as we *know* it and substitute welfare as we had only *guessed* it—support for the wealthy through tax breaks and investments in corporate structures.

The budget-balancing cuts, seven times those of Reagan's first Congress, were far from even-handed. Although means-tested programs were only 25 percent of entitlements, they faced 45 to 62 percent of the cuts. All other programs lost about 1 percent of their funds, but low-income programs lost 13 percent.[14] Cuts or cutbacks included elimination of the summer jobs program, which served about 600,000 poor youth between ages fourteen and nineteen; five HUD programs, which provided temporary shelter and social services for some 600,000 homeless people (slashed by 40 percent); the federal education program for disadvantaged elementary school students, reduced by one-sixth (more than $1 billion); and Legal Services, cut by almost one-third and proposed for elimination.[15]

The attack on the poor began in the first hundred days of the 104th Congress. With new political power, it reiterated the elements of the Nixon/Reagan/Bush proposals:

• Privatization: opening public programs to private competition

- Defederalization: moving power from federal to state governments
- Welfare for the wealthy and corporate entities.

In many cases, Congress instituted cuts by denying allocations before legislation was even considered. Casualties of this maneuver included the Environmental Protection Agency, National Labor Relations Board, Occupational Safety and Health Administration, Department of Commerce, Arts and Humanities Endowments, Federal Election Commission, Legal Services Corporation, and Economic Development Agency.[16]

Restructuring Public Assistance

In 1994 the average number of AFDC households was 4,768,572, with 3,931,624 adult female recipients, 503,007 adult male recipients, and 9 million children (67.7 percent).[17] Of those children, 60 percent were no more than five years old. Only 13 percent were above the age of eleven, indicating that most AFDC mothers stay on welfare only as long as their children are very young. Although African American children were only about 15 percent of the nation's population, they made up a little over a third of the AFDC population, reflecting institutional discrimination and racism.

AFDC benefits in 1994 cost the federal government $22.3 billion, rising from $18.5 in 1990. On the average, AFDC grants throughout the states were about 38 percent of the federal poverty line, ranging from a high of 77 percent in Alaska to 13 percent in Mississippi.[18] The maximum monthly grant in 1995 was $388, or about 38 percent of the federal poverty line.[19] AFDC cost about 1 percent of the federal budget and about 2 percent of state budgets[20] (all federal assistance cost about 2.5 percent of the federal budget).

The average number of people in an AFDC household in 1994 was 2.9 people (1.9 children):[21] the fertility rate of recipients is less than that in the general population.[22] About 8 percent of welfare mothers were under the age of twenty, with only 1 percent under age eighteen, and 32.7 were ages thirty to thirty-nine.[23] The average AFDC mother was twenty-nine years old, with four years of work experience. Only 26 percent of recipients relied solely on the grant. The rest had some combination of family support, employment, and AFDC.[24] About 50 percent left within two years, with 85 percent off the rolls after eight years. Although a persistent myth claims that most AFDC recipients are African Americans, the number of African Americans on AFDC declined during the last five years, from about 45 percent to about 37 percent. In 1994, 39 percent of AFDC recipients were white, Hispanics made up 18 percent, and Native Americans made up 1 percent. In general, about 9 percent received public housing subsidies, 14 percent rent subsidies, and 87 percent received food stamps.[25]

Welfare to Work: Losing the Safety Net

With the passage of the Personal Responsibility and Work Opportunity Reconciliation Act of 1996 and its welfare reform bill Temporary Assistance to Needy Families (TANF), the 104th Congress and President Clinton absolved society of its burden of poor, homeless, hungry people. As we once turned our backs on the colonial poor, letting them die in the wilderness, we now turned our backs on the poor, guiltless as we threw them into the streets, because by law, their lives were *their own* responsibility.

The 104th Congress established the Administration for Children and Families (ACF) in the Department of Health and Human Services (HHS) to oversee TANF. It also eliminated AFDC and parts of SSI, and the Food Stamp program at the national level, merging them into public assistance block grants and capping the federal share at reduced funding. Capped programs also included housing (HUD and Section 8, public housing, Native American housing, rural loans, rental, repair, farm labor housing) and work programs and training programs under the Family Support Act's JOBS program. The combination of caps and block grants meant an overall reduction in state and federal funding, an elimination of categories of service, and a removal of federal obligations and standards. Because states could use block grants as they chose, some programs were dropped entirely and the money spent at state discretion. Reagan federalism come to fruition, these new regulations destabilized the whole pattern of social morality.

Block-granted food programs received about $59 billion less over four years, replacing the Food Stamp Act (1977), Child Nutrition Act (1966), National School Lunch Act, Emergency Food Assistance Act (1983), Hunger Prevention Act (1988), Commodity Distribution Act of 1987 (although commodities might still be distributed), and the WIC program (one of the truly successful nutrition programs of our time).[26] The Child Protection Block Grant, set to replace foster care, adoption programs, and family preservation and support systems, was vetoed by President Clinton in February 1996. However, the nation's governors met and passed a resolution allowing states to opt for a capped entitlement grant for foster care, adoption, and independent living funds that could then be transferred to other activities, as each state chose.[27]

The Child Care Block Grant consolidated six programs for public assistance: the Child Care and Development Block Grant, AFDC Child Care services, Transitional Child Care services, the At-Risk Child Care program, the Dependent Care Block Grant, and the Child Development Association Scholarship program. Funding for this block grant was cut by more than $350 million the first year and $2.5 billion over the next five years. An estimated 370,000 children would lose child care assistance by the year 2000 and states could divert up to 20 percent ($400 million) of the grant to other services or eliminate them altogether, because matching requirements were ended.[28]

More established block grants underwent massive cuts. Compared with 1982 levels, Community Services grants lost 49 percent, Title XX Social Services lost 28 percent, Preventive Health programs lost 7 percent, and Educational Block Grants lost 53 percent (in inflation-adjusted dollars).[29] Education was hard-hit. Clinton's new Goals 2000 program remained unfunded. The Elementary and Secondary Education Act (ESEA) was slashed $1.1 billion, a 17 percent drop from 1995, although it had helped more than 90 percent of the nation's school districts to upgrade schools in poverty areas and provided funds for bilingual education, which had been virtually eliminated. Because of raised loan eligibility, an estimated 300,000 young people were priced out of college loan programs, and the program to eliminate private banks as student loan providers ended. Head Start was slashed by $137 million, to serve 48,000 fewer children in 1996. School Improvement Programs lost $486 million, the program for Safe and Drug Free Schools lost $266 million, Summer Youth Employment lost $871 million, and Low Income Energy Assistance lost $1 billion.[30]

HUD lost $6.4 billion, almost a fourth of its budget, meaning that tenants would pay an average of $83 a month more for subsidized housing even though public assistance was cut by $800 million. Family planning clinics lost $193 million in the face of a drive against out-of-wedlock parenthood.[31] All programs for aliens, except refugees and those over age seventy-five, were cut except for medical emergencies (though later some were restored). All told, domestic spending for human resources was cut by $101.1 billion, of which $65.4 billion came from programs that provided cash or in-kind benefits to families.[32]

The Structure of TANF

TANF is a comprehensive (and bipartisan) plan to rid the United States of responsibility for the poor by demanding work for a time-limited period. TANF replaced AFDC programs and the Job Opportunity and Basic Skills (JOBS) program of Reagan's Family Support Act (1988) and ended all entitlements to public assistance. Monies equivalent to each state's fiscal year (FY) 1994 allotment for these programs, along with monies gleaned from other program cutbacks, are given to states as block grants, totaling $16.5 billion each year through FY 2002. For economically troubled states, TANF has a $2 billion federal matching contingency fund; and its Rainy Day Loan Fund has $1.7 billion to loan to states on a revolving basis. It also has a "performance" bonus of $1 billion over five years for program attainment (if states cut more recipients per year from the rolls than their quota, they get more money); and an "illegitimacy reduction" bonus fund of $20 million a year from 1999–2002 to be divided each year among the five states with the greatest success in reducing out-of-wedlock births without increasing abortions.

Along with the conservatism that swept PRWORA through Congress was the strong belief—common in the late 1880s and part of our public assistance heritage—that local administration served to better control the poor. "Devolution" is, therefore, a prominent aspect of TANF: Administration first devolved to states, territories, and tribes; then to counties, and at times even to cities, communities, or organizations. Each state, territory, or tribe determines its own eligibility and benefit levels, and each must spend 80 percent of their fiscal year 1994 spending (called "maintenance of effort" or MOE) or be penalized dollar for dollar. MOEs are reduced to 75 percent if states meet work quotas: 25 percent of caseloads either working or off the rolls by FY 1997 and 50 percent by 2002. Program administration can cost no more than 15 percent of the block grant, and at state discretion, up to 30 percent of the block can be transferred to the Child Care and Development Block Grant (CCDBG), with 10 percent available to the Social Services Block Grant which provides services to children and families with income up to 200 percent of poverty.

Block grant monies can be used for any plan that furthers TANF purposes, allowing, within state guidelines, local entities such as counties or community entities to administer new or old programs (including entrepreneurship in such activities as creating enterprise zones). With devolution, counties (or other entities) submit their plans and "partner" with the state, setting goals for developing job placements, job training programs, and educational arrangements. In this past century we have seen public assistance come full circle: local to state to federal (1900–1935) and, at the end of the century, from federal to state to counties and smaller local entities.

With the advent of TANF, state public assistance rolls have, of course, diminished drastically. By 1999, 2.4 million families received cash assistance, a 52 percent reduction from the early 1994 level of 5 million. Federal and state expenditures for cash assistance benefits in fiscal year 1999 totaled $12.4 billion, or $10.6 billion less than in fiscal year 1994. Since PRWORA specified that funding remain at 1994 funding levels, available federal funding has not dropped. The annual TANF allocation is $16,500 million, and supplemental grants in 1999 totaled another $161 million.[33]

States may accumulate unspent TANF funds, and 1997 and 1998 showed low levels of expenditures, probably due to uncertainty about allowed flexibility. Final regulations were released in 1999, and since then most states have spent more. With caseloads and cash benefits both reduced, they invest in a wide range of services such as transportation, child care, job training, substance abuse treatment, and so on. TANF outlays since FY 1998 were, in millions of dollars:

Year	Amount
1998	$13,284
1999	$14,161
2000	$15,464
2001	$18,583

The 2001 expenditure of $18,583 indicates use of previous years funds for current costs.[34]

Basically, TANF requires that, within a twenty-four-month period of cash aid, adult recipients engage in either work preparation, work training, or education (with some restrictions); or in employment to take them off public assistance rolls. Whether or not they find work, after twenty-four months their TANF grants end for them and their children. States may re-admit clients after a time they (the states) set, but recipients can only receive grants for a maximum of sixty months (lifetime limit). In addition, states have the option to give noncash aid or vendor payments after TANF grants end and may exempt up to 20 percent of their caseload from the twenty-four-month rule.

At the federal level, TANF has various rules and exemptions: employment and training may be TANF subsidized or not; job search and job skills training count only up to six weeks before counting for the twenty-four-month limit begins; vocational training puts off the time count for only twelve months. Allowable work activities include subsidized or nonsubsidized work in the public or private sector, community work experience, on-the-job training, satisfactory attendance at secondary school, and provision of child care services to other TANF recipients. Teenage mothers must live with parents or responsible adults and be engaged in high school or GED education to receive aid; convicted felons and known drug abusers may be denied cash aid, though their children will receive grants. States must provide child care if they demand work, and they cannot penalize mothers for nonwork if child care is unavailable.

Single parents must be in work-related activity for twenty hours each week the first year and must be in that activity for thirty hours per week by 2002. Two-parent families must work thirty-five hours per week. Each TANF client must sign an Individual Responsibility Plan (IRP) agreeing to send children to school; immunize them; cooperate with child support enforcement in determining paternity; give to TANF any support payments they receive (up to their TANF grant level); and engage in education, training, and job placement services as required by the state.

TANF cut Medicaid, SSI, and food stamps for illegal and legal aliens. However, the Balanced Budget Act of 1997 restored aid to legal aliens, though at lower rates.

States have great latitude in designing their welfare-to-work programs. For example, some states penalize parents if children are absent from school, some require teenage mothers to marry the fathers of their children, some waive time limits or residency requirements in cases of family violence, and so on. Some allow two-year post-secondary education to count as training. Some states impose family caps, refusing to increase grants for children born while mothers are recipients. (Studies of the family cap in New Jersey indicate little connection between fewer children and the cap, probably in part because the increase is so low (about $67). However, the number of abortions rose.)

Privatization of welfare functions can also be part of state plans. As an example, Florida contracted with Lockheed-Martin IMS to provide all welfare functions, from eligibility determination to job training and placement, in three Florida counties. Lockheed had already won contracts to provide limited services to TANF clients in twenty-one Florida counties.[35]

Support from Absent Parents.   Support from absent parents is an ongoing issue. In 1990 absent fathers paid only $14 billion of the $48 billion they owed, and in 1995, despite new enforcement attempts, they paid only $15 billion of their $45 to $50 billion obligations. In 1992 the average amount collected by support agencies (Title IV-D) per year was $3,258 for non-AFDC families and $2,695 for AFDC families. In FY 2000 the ACF paid states $3,222,732,000 for Child Support Enforcement; in FY 2001 it was increased to $3,683,800,000.[36]

Generally, although George Bush's administration strengthened collection measures across state lines, making nonpayment a federal crime, less than 18 percent of overdue support payments were collected. In 1995 courts ordered 57 percent of absent parents to pay support, but only 19 percent of those support orders were collected.[37] Under the Bush law, the penalty for nonsupporters was six months in prison for the first offense and up to two years for subsequent convictions if more than $5,000 was owed. The government filed more than seventy-five cases and investigated another 500, with about twenty convictions up to 1995. However, on appeal the Supreme Court ruled that this denied the rights of state jurisdiction, declaring the law unconstitutional in July 1995.

Child support was a Clinton administration priority, and provisions included in PRWORA 1996 resulted in record child support collections by 1997: A record $13 billion was collected, an increase of $5 billion, or 63 percent, since 1992.[38] Clinton directed the Treasury Department to offset child support debts against most federal payments, such as income tax returns (in 1996 a record $1.1 billion was seized); ordered federal agencies to deny loans, loan guarantees, or loan insurance to people delinquent on child support payments; implemented a program to track nonpayers across state lines (Federal Case Registry and National Directory of New Hires: 90,000 delinquent parents found by 1998); proposed regulations refusing public assistance to women not complying with paternity establishment requirements; and required federal job hires to comply with child support enforcement. By 1998, resources for child support enforcement were increased by 53 percent, and the 1999 Clinton budget allocated $3.2 billion to support enforcement programs, a 19 percent increase over FY 1998.[39]

Jail sentences remain the most popular penalties for nonsupport at state levels. Other penalties at both state and federal levels include garnishment of wages, seizing of income tax refunds and property, and revoking of drivers', professional, and trade licenses. DNA and blood testing can be used to determine paternity, and a Parent Locator System based on social security numbers was established. There is also a more stringent Interstate Enforcement Agreement.

Child Care.   Given the welfare-to-work imperative, funding adequate child care is a major problem in carrying out TANF's work requirements. Thirteen million children, including 6 million infants and toddlers,[40] were already in child care before TANF. Work requirements meant that the children of the estimated 3 million TANF recipients soon to enter the labor force would need child care. However, good child care is scarce: Responsible parents would not want their children in most. In 1995 six of every seven centers gave mediocre to poor care and one in eight jeopardized children's safety and development. Eighty percent of states require no credentials or training for child care staff, and in 1997 only 6 percent of child care centers were accredited by the National Association for the Education of Young Children. Home care is little better: In 1994 one in three homes providing care could have conceivably hindered children's development. Forty percent of placements for infants and children under age three had care poor enough to endanger their health, safety, and development.[41]

Expenses for child care can be astronomical. Families earning less than $14,400 spend 25 percent of their income for child care, and annual costs are $4,000 to $8,000 for preschoolers and $5,000 to $12,000 for infants.[42] Some help is available: In the late 1980s, the Act for Better Child Care passed Congress, developing into the Child Care and Development Block Grant (CCDBG), with about $3 billion in funding per year. Also, in 1997 about 800,000 children were in free Head Start programs.

States may supply additional funds and, as previously noted, 30 percent of TANF grants may be assigned to a state's CCDBG. TANF also can provide another $600 million for day care if states match the amount. In addition, the Child and Dependent Care Tax Credit (CDCC) of $2.8 billion a year is available to working families who make enough money to have tax liabilities, and about half of all states offer state tax credits. Still, the number of families waiting for child care subsidies in 1997 ranged from 6,000 in Kentucky to 21,000 in Florida and 37,000 in Texas.[43] Though TANF requires child care, half of all states do not guarantee it. Yet, without such assistance, families cannot be required to work.

Under the CCDBG in FY 1997, states served an average 1,247,856 children per month. Still, nearly 9 million more children were eligible for support despite expenditures of $4.2 billion, an increase of 35 percent over FY 1996. Generally, parents receive certificates or vouchers from their states' CCDBG to pay child care providers in care centers or family day care, or caregivers in the family's home. Some states reimburse providers directly through contracts in addition to offering certificates to families. In 1997 states spent almost $98 million on improving the quality of child care services—teacher training programs, health and safety improvements—about the required 4 percent of their block grants.[44] In FY 2000 the federal CCDBG awarded $1,182,672,000 to states and $1,199,868,000 in 2001. For FY 2002, $2,299,987,000 was proposed.[45]

Another question, of course, concerns society's right to deprive children of parental love and support. Without a qualm, TANF sends to work the only parent in one-parent families and tries to place children in inadequate, often dangerous child care situations. We know that the Israeli kibbutz experience resulted in children who often could not form emotional attachments. Is this what we really want? As Thayer says,

> This . . . approach [destroys] the tradition that full-time parenting, by rich or poor, is socially useful. Welfare reform obviously seeks to separate poor single mothers from children, either during the work day or forever. The costs of child care will probably justify shoving welfare children into assembly-line and profit-making orphanages . . . [or] foster homes. . . .[46]

What is our real goal in this effort?

Certainly TANF saves money for the government and for taxpayers. But consider that public assistance costs only 1 percent of the federal budget anyway.

A change in federal priorities, say at the corporation level, could easily make up for 1 percent. Of course, money is not really the issue, nor is it the reason for TANF. Those can only be found in our societal values.

The Place of Values in TANF

Throughout history, a surplus worker population threatening traditional patriarchal beliefs has led to concerted attacks on women, their sexuality, and their production of children. This appeared in early conquest and colonization from 6000 B.C. forward, the "witch" burnings of the fourteenth century, America's colonization, and the rape and murder of women in tribal wars of the 1990s in Serbia and Bosnia, for example, and the Hutus and Tutsis in Africa. In America it took the guise of a "Contract," taking food from children to punish their mothers for sexuality—the bearing of children either out of wedlock or as public dependents. Note the misogynistic wording of the Personal Responsibility Act's mission statement (H.R. 4). The intent of Congress is

> To restore the American family, reduce illegitimacy, control welfare spending, and reduce welfare dependence.[47]

"Restoring the family" means a forced return to monogamous marriage for women, "reducing illegitimacy" places the responsibility for the conception of children solely on women, "control welfare spending" threatens the withholding of subsistence to women and children, and "reducing welfare dependency," given stringent but inauthentic work requirements (because no jobs are available), indicates that it does not matter whether women cannot find means of support: After two years of public assistance, they and their children will be "thrown away."

The Religious Right helped to define the act, demonstrating its intimate connection with the political economy of oppression. The act's two major thrusts were Puritan (sexual) morality for women and the work ethic for adult recipients, most of whom are women. As Ehrenreich says,

> [T]he welfare mother makes an ideal scapegoat for the imagined sins of womankind in general. She's officially manless, in defiance of the patriarchal norm.[48]

The first thrust of TANF is that women on public assistance (particularly unwed teen mothers) do not take "personal responsibility" for having children, becoming public dependents, and, by extension, creating and maintaining the massive federal deficit. This hyperbole is used to promote the ideas of both the government's decreasing social responsibility to the poor and its increased financing of welfare for the wealthy. Furthermore, the loss of public support for children is also their mothers' fault: Because they do not take "personal responsibility" for their sexual activities in producing children, they become "personally responsible" when their children go cold and hungry. Moreover, their lack of "responsibility" saddles the "moral" (working, married) public with a monstrous budget deficit, so that the public pays for their "sins."

There are strange conceptual gaps here, one of the first being that the cost of AFDC, at about 1.5 percent of the federal budget ($22.3 billion of $1.5 trillion) was hardly enough to send the government into bankruptcy. However, an even stranger gap in the mission is that there is little mention of the "personal responsibility" of men in impregnating women, becoming fathers, and supporting their families (except that paternity must be proved before women can receive public assistance). Conception is not parthenogenic: Men share the responsibility by half.

Another hiatus in thinking is to deny the complicity of adult men in teenage pregnancy. In fact, the fathers of most children born to teenage mothers—at least 51 percent—are generally over the age of twenty-one. Moreover, many such pregnancies are not chosen by teenagers: Girls under the age of eighteen are the victims of about half of the nation's rapes each year, and as many as 65 percent were victims of sexual abuse in their childhoods. Teenagers who have out-of-wedlock pregnancies, on the average, were less than ten years old at the time of the first abuse, and the offending male was twenty-seven.[49]

The solutions Congress offered were, not strangely, patriarchal in nature and oriented to control by men, relatives, or other authorities. First, unwed teenagers were refused grants unless they married (either the fathers or men who would adopt—it appeared that any man would do). Next, they were required to live with parents or other adults, ignoring the fact that about 65 percent of unwed teens do remain with adults. Ancillary services for housing would be denied. New monies provided for "special homes" where unwed pregnant teens would receive "close supervision" to keep them moral, and for adoptions, foster care, and orphanages to take their children from them to placements more conducive to raising children with good middle-class values.

TANF is clearly punitive. Fear of losing their children has been a control mechanism for women public dependents for centuries. Its bases are punishment of women and control of the upbringing of children to be "moral" adults. We are willing to pay a great deal to ensure this: The annual cost in 1994 for one child receiving AFDC was $2,664, whereas foster care was $4,800 and residential group care, the nearest thing we have to orphanages for nondelinquent children, cost $36,500. Van Bierna says,

> If even a quarter of an estimated 1 million children who would be cut loose under Gingrich's plan ended up in orphanages, the additional cost to the public would be more than $8 billion.[50]

(Newt Gingrich was Speaker of the House of Representatives when he proposed that dependent children be placed in orphanages.)

Congress's "solutions" actually hark back centuries: girls being "married off," relatives taking responsibility for "wayward" girls, institutions for the "sexually immoral" who became pregnant (penitentiaries or almshouses), orphanages or fostering-out of children to teach them to live like "moral" people, and, of course, denial of subsistence to women with dependent children. Intentions are clear: Women need to be controlled from their first onset of sexuality and the penalty for being "uncontrolled" may be starvation and homelessness. Although we do not say "death," as with women the colonial fathers drove into the forest to die, we "out of sight, out of mind" such women—what happens to them is their "personal responsibility," not ours.

Women do not have babies to access the minuscule amount they could receive from public assistance (in New Jersey, $67 a month, for example). Therefore, to believe that ending public assistance will end out-of-wedlock pregnancy—especially because most unwed mothers do not receive public assistance—is extremely naïve. Or, perhaps, it is not naïve at all to incite the public in order to hide what is really happening. At best, denying assistance to poor families will send them into less legal channels to support their children or, before that happens, it will increase abortions. At worst, it will starve children, send them into the streets to die or be killed, or increase their alienation and hostility to the affluent society that has denied them the rights of citizenship. More than that, it will demonstrate to us all that social morality no longer has a place in the United States.

The second thrust of TANF is the issue of work. According to TANF, it "is the intent of Congress to help, cajole, lure, or force adults off welfare and into paid employment": in other words, to *require* them to accept jobs or lose their eligibility for assistance. To accomplish this, Congress placed a two-year one-time and five-year lifetime limit on receiving assistance, cut job subsidies and job training after two years, and required job participation and day care placement for children over age one. Given the reduction of jobs and wages in our economy, expecting women to support themselves totally after two years is simply another sleight-of-hand to ease the public conscience. Obviously, work, work training, and workfare are meant to punish, reform, and control rather than to provide legitimate routes off the welfare rolls. Moreover, as in other such programs, those most likely to find jobs anyway are "creamed," leaving a hard core of people with few skills and no support—social Darwinism at its best.

We know from past experiences—from the 1960s forward—that job training programs are ineffective and enormously expensive. An example from Texas: In 1994 $1.6 billion was spent on workforce training, half of which was paid for by the state. However, in a program where a thousand employees helped recipients in jobs and job training, only thirty-one recipients actually got training, a ratio of more than thirty workers for each recipient trained. The General Accounting Office reported that the federal government spent more than $25 billion per year on 154 work assistance or development programs administered by fourteen agencies—an average of $156 million for each agency.[51]

It is unrealistic to believe that two years of job training can address the problems of poverty in the United States. Training and retraining, particularly when funds for those tasks are cut to the bone, will not replace jobs destroyed because of new technologies or those moved to other countries. The fact is that we have a surplus worker population that, in general, will be limited to much lower income than what they earned over the past fifty years. Nor can we rely on the growing number of service jobs, because they do not produce enough income to take people from poverty. It is time to look at work in a different light—*productivity beyond income*—because no matter how heavily we flagellate those who cannot find work, they cannot find what does not exist.

Our society needs new definitions for work. The idea of income-producing labor as a moral stance grew from the needs of a ruling elite from about the fourteenth century. This has both blocked our perception on the importance of other productivity, such as raising children, and served to maintain a compliant workforce to further benefit that elite. As William Raspberry says,

> It is no longer necessary for everybody to work to produce the things we need, [nor] to look at open-ended economic growth as the main solution to our social ills . . . [nor] to think of full employment as an achievable (or even desirable) goal. . . . [According to Jeremy Rifkin, we need] a full-fledged debate on how to have productivity gains so that everybody is better off . . . [a new] social good.[52]

Our expectations of income-producing work for every person is anachronistic and serves to punish people, demoralizing them into alienation and apathy until they believe in and act on their "sins." However, we continue to demand workfare for the poor even though their work is unneeded and unavailable.

According to a recent study by the Center for Study of Policy Attitudes, Americans in general still believe it is the responsibility of the government to care for the poor. Eighty-four percent said that society has a moral obligation to help the poor and 85 percent said the government should create jobs for those who want to work. Ninety-two percent felt that a reduction in poverty would be a good investment and 73 percent said it would reduce racial tension and crime. In addition, 58 percent said the wealthy should pay more to finance care for the poor.[53] If the public believes this and our government still misrepresents the problems and refuses aid to the poor, what has happened to our American dream?

Does TANF Work?

From the standpoint of numbers off public assistance rolls, TANF is certainly a success. The recipient caseload declined by 53 percent from August 1996 to June 2000,[54] when it constituted only 2.1 percent of the U.S. population, down from 5.5 percent in 1993.[55] Steadily decreasing during the first year of the millennium, the number on public assistance rolls in June 2000 was 5,780,543 individuals, down to 5,382,063 in June 2001.[56] However, social responsibility demands more: that former recipients' (leavers') incomes be high enough to lift their families from poverty.

There is no doubt that, on the wings of a burgeoning economy at the end of the century, overall poverty declined, including the poverty of AFDC or TANF families. Both inflation and unemployment were low in 1999, at 2.2 percent and 4.4 percent, respectively, and the country had attained a budget surplus of about 2 percent of GDP. According to Sheldon Danziger,

The favorable economic conditions led to increased employer demand for workers and welfare reform mandated increased labor supply from single mothers. As a result, the labor force participation rate of single mothers increased and welfare case loads decreased substantially in a period of only a few years.[57]

However, an important *caveat* in the welfare-to-work debate is the analysis of data concerning the poor and TANF clients. These two groups differ greatly, but many interpretations of census data treat them as the same. For example, in an article entitled "How Welfare to Work Worked," author Gene Koretz cites an Urban Institute Study noting that, between 1994 and early in 2001,

> . . .the share of single moms with jobs soared from 59 percent to 74 percent—reducing joblessness for this group from 13 percent to less than 8 percent. . . . and that the median wage of single working mothers rose by nearly 14 percent to $10 an hour.[58]

This equates women on public assistance with all single working mothers, an obvious error that seems to justify TANF's meanness to these poorest of the poor. In fact, the income of the very poor—generally 20 percent of female-headed families with children—actually fell during the early years of welfare reform. While their earnings and overall incomes rose between 1993 and 1995, from 1995 to 1997 they began to decline. Two million families, or 6 million people, lost an average of $580, even with food stamps, housing subsidies, the Earned Income Tax Credit, and earned income. Among the poorest 10 percent, incomes fell about $810, or by one seventh.[59]

Some loss was due to an apparent lack of knowledge by the poor about eligibility for food stamps, emergency cash, or Medicaid—services of which caseworkers should have kept clients informed. While between 1995 and 1997 the number of people living in poverty fell 3 percent, the number receiving food stamps dropped 17 percent; in 1995 food stamps aided 88 percent of poor children, but by 1998 only 70 percent received them. In 1995, 57 percent of poor children received cash assistance, but by 1988, that was down to about 40 percent. In constant 1999 dollars, median welfare benefits decreased considerably from 1972, when their value was $11,400. In 1979 median benefits were $7,690, in 1989 $6,030, and by 1999 only $4,289.[60] Fewer than one-third of leavers received food stamps—about 30 percent—and only about a third of former recipient adults reported having Medicaid coverage.[61]

Census Bureau data and those from studies conducted on post-TANF families differ in interpretation. By 2000, for the seventh year in a row, poverty was down, the poverty rate for African American and Hispanic households was the lowest ever, and the overall child poverty rate was lower than since 1976, at 16.2 percent,[62] still very high among industrialized nations, and not including EITC, food stamps, and other noncash benefits. An index including the latter benefits placed child poverty at around 10 percent.[63] While some conclude that this data indicates the success of welfare-to-work plans, state-specific studies and one national study found that many welfare leavers remained poverty-stricken because of low-wage jobs. In the national study, 29 percent of a representative sample of leavers who worked in 1997 earned hourly wages below $5.75, less than $1.00 per hour above the federal minimum of $4.75, and state-specific studies found that many received much less than this.[64] Leavers who had been off welfare for some time earned no more than recent leavers, suggesting wages remain static over time.[65]

An August 2001 study by the Center on Budget and Policy Priorities belies the common assumption that as families move from welfare to work increased earnings automatically translate into reduced poverty. Families headed by working single mothers in the late 1990s earned more money because of the strong economy, EITC benefits, child care, and TANF supplements, but their increased earnings were fully offset by the decline in government safety net programs. While some families benefited, many were pushed far deeper into poverty. The poverty rate for families headed by single working mothers stagnated between 1995 and 1999 at 19.4 percent, after government benefits and taxes were taken into account. In 1995, this group, including many TANF leavers, fell a total of $5 billion below the poverty line after government benefits, and by 1999, their rate fell $6.3 billion below poverty, about $1,505 for each person.[66]

By 2001, hourly wages (in 1999 dollars) among leavers averaged $7.15, representing annual earnings of $16,320 if people could work at least thirty-five hours per week. However, only 68 percent of former recipients worked a full workweek; about one-quarter worked at night or on irregular schedules, making child care arrangements more difficult; and health and other personal difficulties precluded many from regular work. Danziger says that,

> . . . despite the large caseload reduction, the national poverty rate has fallen rather little. Many who have left welfare for work remain poor. . . . [E]conomic hardship remains high, because, given their human capital and personal characteristics, many former, as well as current, welfare recipients have limited earnings prospects in a labor market that increasingly demands higher skills.[67]
>
> . . . About one-third of . . . leavers say . . . they did not have enough to eat in the past year [and] [m]ore than half . . . worried that their food would run out before they got money to buy more. . . . About half . . . report that food did not last or they did not have money for food at some time in the past year, either often or sometimes.[68]

Institutional racism remains a factor: three of five TANF families are members of minority races or ethnic groups. African American families comprise 37 percent and Hispanic families make up 23 percent.[69] In addition, 75 percent of the people on TANF are children.

Class action suits are beginning to challenge TANF. The most questionable rules are time limits and the rights of legal aliens. Many challengeable issues are based on federal and state statutes such as Title VI of the Civil Rights Act, the Americans with Disabilities Act, and laws affecting workers, such as minimum and prevailing wage laws and laws protecting workers' health and safety. In a study of 100 cases, 77 percent were won: Grounds for litigation included civil liberties questions of denial of assistance for drug-related felonies, the two- and five-year time limits on eligibility, and the exclusion of legal aliens from aid.

At the state level, violations included forcing high school students to leave school for workfare; paid and unpaid work assignments that do not protect health and safety; treating TANF recipients differently from other workers or dependent populations; family cap provisions; and reduced benefits for recipients moving from other states. Required community work is forced volunteerism, especially when such work involves religious organizations, and teenage residency requirements are also in question.[70]

Other Safety Net Programs

The new millennium began with a new President—George W. Bush—a conservative Congress, a federal surplus, and a booming economy, with the poverty rate equaling the record low of the early 1970s at 11.3 percent. New census figures showed that, in a population of 281,421,906, about 31.1 million people were poor in 2000, 1.1. million fewer than in 1999. At 22.1 percent, African Americans set a record low rate, as did female-householder families at 24.7 percent. Poverty rates for other groups were as follows: people sixty-five years and over, 10.2 percent; Asian and Pacific Islanders, 10.8 percent; Hispanics, 21.2 percent; white non-Hispanics 7.5 percent; and married-couple families 4.7 percent. African Americans remained disproportionately poor, though the differences narrowed significantly: in 1993, their poverty rate was 23.2 percentage points higher than that for white non-Hispanics, but by 2000 the difference had narrowed to 14.6 percentage points.[71] Median income in 2000 for people in the United States was $41,800; median income by race is shown in the following list.

Group	*Median Income 2000*[72]
White	$43,800
White non-Hispanic	$45,500
African American	$28,700
Native American, Alaskan Native	$31,800
Asian/Pacific Islanders	$52,600
Hispanic of any race	$31,700

The ratio of women's earnings to men remained unchanged at 73.1 percent.[73] The poverty threshold for a family of four in 2000 was $17,603,[74] and the gap between incomes of rich and poor remained wide (see Table 3.3). Moreover, the plight of those not included in the general boom perhaps worsened because of program cutbacks or stingy financial support. PRWORA's policies weakened many programs other than public assistance cash transfers, the last resort for the poor.

TABLE 13.3   *Measures of Household Income Inequality*

Quintile	Share	Cumulative 2000 Share
Lowest	3.6%	3.6%
Second	8.9	12.5
Third	14.9	27.4
Fourth	23.0	50.4
Highest	49.7	100.0
Top 5%	21.96	

Source: Taken from U.S. Census Bureau, Current Population Survey, March 2000 and 2001, available: http://www.census.gov/hhcs/www.img/incpov00/fig12.html.

Supplemental Security Income

Since the 1970s, SSI has provided supplemental income to people who were aged and disabled. The program continued to grow during both Bush and Clinton terms, with people with disabilities the largest number of recipients. By 1994 there was a backlog of 700,000 eligibility applications for people with disabilities; although those with more obvious disabilities, such as AIDS, were accepted before formal decisions. Of those on SSI in 1993, about 86,000 were blind, 1.5 million were aged, and 4.5 million had disabilities. Children were the fastest-growing group, of whom the largest segment were those with developmental disabilities (44 percent).[75]

Unfortunately, new legislation fell most severely on children with disabilities. PRWORA tightened SSI eligibility by eliminating functional disabilities, so that only the more restrictive medical diagnoses could be used. Those most likely to lose benefits were children with multiple impairments, where none is severe enough to meet medical disability requirements but in combination create disablement. From 20 to 50 percent of children with mood disorders, pulmonary tuberculosis, mental retardation, burns, intercranial injuries, schizophrenia, and arthritis could lose benefits. Disability reviews are required every three years, and the Congressional Budget Office estimates that by 2002, more than 315,000 low-income children who would have qualified under previous laws will be denied SSI.[76]

SSI was also denied to illegal aliens and legal aliens until they became citizens or had worked in the United States for at least ten years. The 1997 Balanced Budget Reconciliation Act, however, restored benefits to noncitizens who were receiving assistance as of August 22, 1996.

In 1999, 6.5 million individuals received SSI payments totaling $6,274,019, with federal input of $4,115,152 and states supplementing with $2,441,482. Of these, 1.3 million were over age sixty-five, 79,291 were blind, and 5.2 million were disabled, with 847,063 children under age eighteen. Average monthly payments were $368, with about $289 a month for older persons ($642 for a couple); $402 for blind people; and $388 for those with disabilities. The average grant for children was $450.[77] In 2000, 6.3 million people received $30.8 billion in federal SSI payments, with average monthly benefits ranging from $254 for people over age sixty-five to $445 for blind and disabled children. In 2002, 6.4 million are estimated to be eligible.[78]

Earned Income Tax Credits (EITCs) and Child and Dependent Care Credits (CDCCs)

In 1975 President Ford signed Earned Income Tax Credits (EITC) into law, creating a refundable income tax credit for low-income workers. President George Bush added new credits for health care and for parents with newborn children, and Clinton expanded the program substantially in 1993, giving a tax cut to 15 million workers and including poor workers without children, making work the only prerequisite for reverse income tax grants. By 1995, about 20 million low-wage workers received tax credits of $500 per child, averaging about $25 a week. In that same year, however, the House Ways and Means Committee's Republican majority moved to save $23 billion over seven years by reducing or eliminating EITC benefits for two-thirds of the working poor, including all childless workers. This excluded more than 4 million people with incomes of $350 to $450 a month, increased the tax burden on more than 14 million low- and middle-income taxpayers (those with two or more children lost an average of $305 per year) and expanded eligibility to families with incomes up to $100,000. EITC cost about $28 billion in 1995, and all but $1.5 billion went to families making less than $2,500 a month.[79]

By 1997, Clinton secured a $500 per child tax credit for 27 million families, including 13 million children from families with incomes below $30,000.[80] Credits ranged from 7 cents to 40 cents per dollar earned, phasing out when earnings reached $500–$600 a week. In 1997 federal spending for EITC was about $27 billion, $10 billion more than federal cash welfare payments.[81] A significant marriage penalty applied to EITC when two-parent income overshot eligibility levels; although two single-parent families could access EITC, an intact family with the same number of children could not.

A third of American children live in an estimated 12.2 million low- and moderate-income families with incomes too low to pay income tax. While this was problematic in the decade before the election of George W. Bush, his 2001 tax plan did not alleviate it. According to the plan, 31.5 percent of all families, 80 percent of them with workers, would receive no EITC grants. While a third of all children were excluded, more than half of African American and Hispanic children were. George W. Bush's plan doubled the benefits, with 48 percent going to the top 20 percent of all families, including for the first time those with incomes in the $110,000 to $200,000 range. Only 3 percent of the benefits would accrue to the bottom 40 percent of families.[82] Since its beginning in 1975, the number of taxpayers claiming EITC has increased from approximately 6.2 million claiming $1.25 billion to 19.4 million claiming $30 billion in 1998.[83]

The Child and Dependent Care Credit (CDCC), managed by the Treasury Department, is another tax benefit for workers with children or adult dependents. If families do not earn enough to pay taxes, however, they cannot claim CDCCs. People with incomes up to $110,000 can benefit, with credits up to $500 per person given dependent care. To qualify for full benefits, family income has to exceed $30,000. As of 2000, the credit was expanded to those making up to $59,000, at a cost of $5 billion over 5 years. Under certain circumstances, both CDCC and EITC credits may be available to families.[84]

Social Insurance

Old Age, Survivors, and Disability Insurance (OASDI).

Before Clinton entered office, incremental changes within OASDI had placed limits and some cutbacks on retirement, disability, and health care aspects of OASDI. Outlays for the program under Clinton were $66 billion (nearly four times the annual cost of AFDC), expected to grow another $17 billion before the year 2000.[85] To justify its attack on the program, Congress accelerated its charges that Social Security—especially Medicare—would bankrupt the nation. In fact, OASDI (without Medicare) continues to run a surplus: Since 1937, $4.3 trillion has been paid into OASDI and $3.9 trillion paid out in benefits. Less than 1 percent has been spent on administrative costs, making it the least expensive and most productive income transfer program in the United States.[86] In 1995 its surplus was $60 billion, expected to rise to $100 billion by 1999 and nearly $3 trillion by 2020.[87] This predicts solvency for at least the next thirty-five years.

We need to understand the myth that OASDI will bankrupt the government. As FICA funds come into the trust fund, surplus revenues must be placed in special-issue government securities, which may be borrowed by the government to use as it needs and pay back with interest. OASDI is *not* part of the national operating budget (although Medicare [HI] is), but is like a bank, which the borrowers (government) may bankrupt through profligate spending and a refusal to pay back. The problem, then, is that the government wants to renege, causing the trust fund to bankrupt, not the other way around. As Moynihan says,

> Clearly, Social Security is not causing the budget deficit. In fact, surplus Social Security revenues are invested . . . and in this way actually help [repay] the deficit.[88]

Under Bush in 1990, Congress removed OASDI from the Gramm–Rudman–Hollings federal deficit calculations, but in practice it is still included in the "unified budget." This enabled part of the deficit (the government debt to the trust fund) to be hidden and part to be blamed on OASDI recipients.

This victim-blaming meant that Social Security itself came under attack by Congress after 1994. While the program itself still has strong support among the "over-age-fifty" lobby, particularly represented by the American Association of Retired Persons (AARP), increments through Cost of Living Adjustments (COLAs) continued to be cut. Though COLAs are intended to keep pace with cost of living expenses, in 1999 the COLA was only 1.3 percent, equal to the first COLA in 1975. Beginning in January 1999, Social Security payments climbed, on the average, from $770 to $780 per month. The highest pension for those retiring was $1,373, and the most retirees could earn without losing benefits was $15,500.[89]

In April 2000, the Senior Citizen's Freedom to Work Act was enacted, eliminating the earnings test for people over age sixty-five. It set earnings limits for persons through age sixty-nine at $17,000 in 2000, $25,000 in 2001, and $30,000 in 2002. Benefits are withheld at the rate of $1 for every $3 of earnings above these exempt amounts.[90] In December 2000, nearly 39 million people (excluding those on disability) received OASI payments, at an average monthly benefit of $787.80. Men's average benefit was $951.50, whereas women's was $729.80. Benefits for white workers averaged $807.60, whereas those for African Americans was $652.70.[91]

Disabled persons receiving OASDI supplements totaled 6,675,280 in December 2000, with an average monthly benefit of $649. Benefits for white disabled persons averaged $677 and those for African American disabled persons averaged $588. Men's average benefit was $883, whereas women's was $661.[92] Eligibility for Disability Insurance (DI) is based on an SSA-appointed doctor's assessment of client capability to work and whether that person is engaged in significant gainful employment. Since 1999, a person is considered gainfully employed by earning $700 a month. Earnings below $300 automatically qualify the recipient, and between $300 and $700 require that, before eligibility is granted, work-related circumstances and client capability to perform the work must be considered. Increases in significant gainful earnings are pegged to increases in the national average wage index and were not affected by the 1999 change.[93]

Since the Reagan years there has been debate on raising the retirement age for Social Security benefits. Smith says,

> There is no mistaking an increase in the retirement age for anything other than a benefit cut . . . [it] means reduced lifetime benefits for all beneficiaries and lower monthly amounts for those who begin to receive benefits before attaining the new, higher retirement age.[94]

In 1999, 36 percent of retired workers and spouses received half their income from Social Security, and 35 percent relied on it for 50 to 89 percent of their support. The remainder—29 percent—depended on Social Security for nearly all their income—90 to 100 percent.[95] For middle-income retirees, Social Security provides 66 percent of their income and for those in the bottom 40 percent, 87 percent of income.[96]

The question of partially privatizing Social Security arose in the conservative 1990s. Supported by Presidents Bush, Clinton, and G. W. Bush, partial privatization means that people would put part of their F.I.C.A. taxes into individual retirement accounts of their own choice. Because benefits from private accounts are related to contribution size and return on investment, lower-earning workers have less to invest or put at risk, according to Marcia Greenberger, co-president of the National Women's Law Center.[97] This would be a harmful situation for older women, since any change taking away retirement-income guarantees leaves them at risk. As it stands, Social Security

> . . . offers lifetime guaranteed benefits, higher returns for low-earning workers, cost-of-living adjustments and spousal benefits for widows and divorced women . . . [and] is just too risky . . . because, on average, women earn less money and live longer than men.[98]

Social Security is not gender-neutral, though it was intended to be, and has already built-in inequities such as a reduction in spousal benefits when widowed, retirement income geared to spouse's benefits, and so on. Because hiring practices and wage decisions are patriarchal in nature, women generally draw smaller retirement benefits than do men. They work for fewer years because of child-rearing responsibilities and at lower wages because high-paying jobs are generally denied them (74 cents to men's dollar). Women also outlive men, so they live on smaller benefits for a longer period of time. In 1999 Social Security was the only source of income for 2.5 million women—26 percent of all older women who are single—automatically consigning them to live below the poverty level,[99] whatever that might be at the time.

Nutrition Programs: Food Stamps, WIC, and Child Nutrition

Food and nutrition programs remained remarkably stable over the decade leading into the new millennium. The Food Stamp Program, extended in 1990 with the Mickey Leland Memorial Domestic Hunger Relief Act, was reauthorized through 1995. By 1992, the federal cost for food stamps was $22.5 billion, with participation at 27 million, more than 10 percent of the U.S. population. More people became eligible by instituting disregards of child support, educational aid, income earned by school children, excess shelter costs (above state AFDC level), income tax refunds, a $131 income disregard (in most states), and disregards for all but $135 of recipient-paid medical expenses.[100]

PRWORA 1996 had a significant effect in reducing participation: In 1995 there were 26.6 million participants, but by 1999, only 18.2 million; in 2000, 17.2 million, and in 2001, 17.3 million.[101] Over the three years, federal benefits averaged about $15.5 billion and provided an average benefit per person of $73.25 per month.[102] The Children's Defense Fund noted that

> The food stamp program . . . is absorbing more than half of *all* the spending reductions made by the law, amounting to well over $20 billion in cuts over six years.[103]

By 2001, many states had completed the transfer from actual paper stamps to electronic debit cards, and some—Indiana, for example—include cash assistance. The cards look and function much like those used for automatic teller machines and are updated monthly electronically, so that recipients do not have to come in to get stamps or wait for checks in the mail. The cards save money in printing, shipping, and administrative costs, and, more importantly, relieve clients of problems of accessing their benefits and loss of self-esteem at groceries and other vendors.

In 1994 the WIC program served 5.4 million participants at a federal cost of $2.6 billion, reaching 60 percent of those eligible. Reauthorized in 1995, it was allotted nearly $3.5 billion, an increase of $260 million, but received no incremental funding through 1998. The Clinton and G. W. Bush administrations supported modest increases: In 1999, 2000, and 2001 the number of participants remained at about 7.2 million, at a cost of about $3.8 to 4.1 million.[104]

PRWORA 1996 ended expansion of school breakfast programs and the Summer Food Service Program, but their use remained stable. From 1999 through 2001, on an average day, the breakfast program served 5.7 million children, with 83.3 percent of all breakfasts served free, at a federal cost in 2001 of $1,443.9 million. The School Lunch Program, which received no significant cuts, increased by 5 percent from 1994 to 1997,[105] but in 1999, 2000, and 2001 continued to serve about 1.3 million children, at a cost in 2001 of $5,603.4 million.[106] About 57 percent of those lunches are free, and children pay a varying rate for the rest. Commodities distribution suffered a cutback with the 1988 Omnibus reforms, from $1,075 million in 1988 to $730.5 million in 1989 and a low of $406.7 in 1996, but has grown incrementally since then, with an expenditure in 2001 of $703.6.[107]

Malnutrition presents significant problems in growing children, among them adverse learning effects, iron deficiency anemia, stunted growth, and nagging hunger that endangers full participation in our society. In addition, poor nutrition among pregnant women often results in low birth weight, high infant mortality (7.6 deaths per 1,000 live births overall, 15.1 among African American children),[108] and children unable to fulfill their physical and mental potentials. Perhaps this is yet another evidence of the "starvation principle" of social Darwinism—if we don't need them, don't feed them.

Housing and Homelessness

Although both Bush and Clinton made home ownership the key to their housing policies, the supply of low-rent housing decreased (by 900,000 units from 1993 to 1995) while need increased by 24 percent.[109] In 1992 Clinton reauthorized the Stewart B. McKinney Assistance Act for the Homeless. As we know, homelessness is no longer a problem just for poor adults, some of whom are mentally ill. In 1997 families with children represented 36 percent of those in homeless shelters, and

> Children who are homeless or constantly moving from one dilapidated place to another suffer numerous serious and long-lasting consequences: poor health, missed school, and emotional damage.[110]

Clinton doubled the amount for Housing and Urban Development (HUD) Section 8 housing to $2 billion. The Home Investment Partnerships Program (HOPE) accelerated—private investors taking over public housing under tenant boards—and the 1995 "National Home Ownership" policy set up partnerships between HUD and private groups such as the American Bankers Association and Fannie Mae, but only to disseminate information about credit access. For 1999, there was an increase of 103,000 Section 8 vouchers in the FY 1999 budget, of which 50,000 went to TANF families and 34,000 to the homeless.[111]

In 1996 about 1 million HUD-assisted families received some income from AFDC/TANF: 260,000 in public housing, 80,000 with Section 8 housing vouchers and certificates, and 250,000 in project based Section 8 housing. One quarter of all TANF families lived in assisted housing, paying about 30 percent of their incomes in rent, and more than 5.3 million households had "worst case housing needs"—lived in substandard housing or paid over 50 percent of their income in rent.[112] Yet Congress (from 1995 on) required that public housing authorities delay reissuance of the approximately 1.4 million HUD Section 8 vouchers and certificates, reducing the annual supply by about 40,000.

In 1997 Congress *prohibited* public housing authorities from lowering tenant rents in response to loss of income from TANF (to protect housing authorities from loss of revenue),[113] meaning that people with reduced grants from TANF and those put off TANF, with problems of low-wage and irregular employment, probably were unable to pay their rents and were evicted. Many landlords refused to rent to TANF recipients. While the nonpoor continue to benefit from mortgage interest tax deductions, which are the primary mechanism to promote home ownership—in 1995, rebates amounted to $83.3 billion.[114]

Finally, racism increased in the housing market. The Association of Community Organizations for Reform Now (ACORN) reported that, based on data filed with HUD by lenders in thirty-five cities, 33 percent of African Americans were refused mortgages in 1997, up from 25 percent in 1955, while rejections for Hispanics rose from 22 to 28 percent in the same period. Minorities received a lower share of conventional mortgages and a higher percentage of government mortgages.[115]

Homelessness remains an urgent problem for America. Though it is difficult to assess the numbers of homeless or near-homeless, the U.S. Census Bureau, in a sample of 170,706 people in emergency and transitional shelters, reported that 61 percent of the homeless sample was male and 25.7 percent were children—22,465 boys and 21,422 girls. Of the sample, 40.8 percent were white and 40.4 percent were African American.[116] A survey by the U.S. Conference of Mayors in December 2001 found that requests for emergency shelter assistance increased an average of 13 percent in the twenty-seven cities surveyed.[117] National estimates of homelessness have found that, over the past decade, shelter capacity in some cities may have doubled. A 1999 study estimated that 700,000 people a night, or 2 million a year were homeless, and shelters are often filled to capacity: In 1998, 26 percent of all requests for emergency shelter went unmet.[118] Twenty-three percent of homeless people are veterans.[119]

Programs extending aid to the homeless are available, but insufficient to meet the need for permanent housing. In FY 2000 Homeless Assistance grants were funded at $1.02 billion; the Housing Certificate Fund at $11,376 billion, with renewals totaling another $10,346 million; and the Emergency Food and Shelter Program at $110 million. HUD also funded Community Development Block Grants at $4.8 billion; Rural Housing and Economic Development at $25 million; Elderly Housing (Section 202) at $710 million; and Disabled Housing (Section 811) at $201 million.[120] President G. W. Bush asked for modest increases in all programs, which seemed unlikely to be passed by the House Ways and Means Committee.

Health Care in America

When President Clinton entered office, he had a clear mandate to design a national health insurance program. He delegated its development to Hillary Rodham Clinton, who led a bipartisan committee representing both public and private interests. The most radical opposition came from health insurers: Their power had grown in the Reagan/Bush era through privatization of managed care. Privatized managed care with government sponsorship actually began when diagnostic related groups (DRGs) were created by private insurers involved in Medicare and Medicaid programs (purchase of services at state option). To save money, DRGs defined the hospital stays of patients under their programs, substituting fiscal for medical decision making.

By the time the Rodham Clinton Health Security Act came to Congress in September 1993, private insurers were already providing for one quarter of all Medicaid recipients and more than half of all AFDC recipients. By June 1994, all but eight states had Medicaid managed care programs in at least some communities. Rodham Clinton's proposal was in fact managed care, but it was defeated as privatized managed care became the course of health care in the United States.

Managed care is based on contracts between health insurance companies and health providers to coordinate medical services and cut costs, often through Health Maintenance Organizations (HMOs) and Preferred Provider Options (PPOs). It became part of the government health care process under Reagan's privatization plans, with contracts for Medicare and Medicaid. DRGs were designed to contain costs. Medicare utilizes managed care DRGs for its patients and offers a variety of Medicare Plus plans. Medicaid recipients are in most cases required to seek medical care at designated HMOs.

Though some believe managed care coordinates services and cuts costs, resulting in better utilization of health care, others believe it is a threat to quality care and ". . . a bureaucratic system that . . . forces doctors to place saving money before saving lives. . . ."[121] In fact, a study among physicians found that 57 percent of respondents felt "pressured to limit referrals," and that this often compromised patient care.[122] The vocabulary of managed care includes "trade secrets," which impose gag orders on physicians about contracts; bonuses, offered for limiting care and referrals to specialists; "medical necessity," a catch phrase allowing insurers rather than physicians to determine medical care; "capitation rates," a limit to the number of patients seen; and of course "case management," in which insurers rather than medical personnel decide the care needed. With all this, health services in the United States have become oriented to profits for the insurers (and for some physicians) at the cost of good medical care.

Case management arrived in the social work vocabulary at about the same time, probably in response to severe program cutbacks. It overlapped managed care in mental health delivery systems, which often required health insurance contracts, but spread throughout public and private agencies. Generally, "case managers," a new category of worker, coordinated services for all client needs, viewing them as "whole persons" rather than cases. However, case management is still a cost-containment mechanism: Often case managers need little or no social work training and, as the "first line" clients meet, are often gatekeepers for their own agencies and for referrals to other agencies.

National Health Insurance died quickly after its defeat during the Clinton administration. Though health measures depending on privatized care were later passed, none had the scope of a national insurance. As early as 1993, the Vaccines for Children (VFC) program provided free vaccines to doctors and other established agencies to immunize uninsured children and those covered by Medicaid. States used their own funds to extend the program so that more children could be vaccinated. The program extended immunization clinic hours and created registries to identify children who were not completely immunized. By 1996, 78 percent of all children were fully immunized, up from 55 percent in 1992, and vaccine-preventable disease declined to all-time lows at less than one-seventh their levels in the mid-1980s.[123]

In addition, Clinton's administration was successful in creating the State Children's Health Insurance Program (SCHIP) under the Health Care Financing Administration (HCFA) Title XXI as part of the Balanced Budget Act (BBA) of 1997. SCHIP provided $48 billion over ten years to cover other medical services for noninsured, non-Medicaid children in families with income less than 200 percent of the poverty line. Each state had great flexibility in developing its own plan: extending Medicaid or producing new plans financed by matching Medicaid rates; requiring cost-sharing by parents; block grants; covering children for twelve months after family income increases or eligibility is lost for other reasons; and so on. "Presumptive eligibility" provided coverage to new applicants for SCHIP,[124] and by the end of the Clinton administration, more than 3.3 million children were enrolled in SCHIP.[125]

Appropriations for SCHIP declined by $1.125 billion after the election of George W. Bush. Fiscal year appropriations were:

Year	*Appropriation*[126]
FY 1998	$4,295,000,000
FY 1999–2001	$4,275,000,000
FY 2002–2004	$3,150,000,000
FY 2005–2006	$4,050,000,000

Yet in the late 1990s, 14 percent of American's children still had no public or private health insurance.[127]

Spending for health care topped $1.2 trillion in 1999, up 5.6 percent from 1998, but continuing a six-year trend of growth below 6 percent. Between 1993 and 1999, because of the shift to managed care, impacts of the Balanced Budget Act (BBA) changes, and growth in the national economy, health spending declined minimally from 1993 to 1999 (13.4 percent to 13.0 percent of GDP).[128]

Medicare

Whereas the privatization of health care was already well under way in Medicaid and nursing home care, Medicare had been considered untouchable. Nevertheless, it proved irresistible and Congress attacked it for a cost of $270 billion over seven years (funding in 1994 was $160 billion). The cuts were tied to increased premiums for the 37 million beneficiaries; new medical Individual Retirement Accounts (IRAs), with $3,000 out-of-pocket spending required; and an end to federal caps on health provider fees, set in 1995 at 115 percent of Medicare-approved amounts (a successful maneuver to gain the support of the American Medical Association). In addition, annual government-sponsored "health fairs" were required so that private health care insurers could market their own "Medicare Plus" programs. This meant that private health care programs would receive Medicare funding and would also have federal support to market private "Medigap" programs.

The rationale for cutting Medicare was that the nation should not burden its children with future taxes. However, tax breaks for the wealthy of about $245 billion were also proposed—repeal of the corporate alternative minimum tax ($22.5 billion over seven years), increased write-offs and deductions ($47.8 billion), and capital gains tax breaks indexed to inflation ($78.6 billion). That provided the wealthy up to $290 billion at a loss of about $629 billion to the poor. If we add in Medicaid cuts ($192 billion) to the $270 billion taken from Medicare, about half the roughly $1 trillion in reduced spending Congress wanted—$452 billion—came from these medical programs. As House Minority Leader Richard Gephardt said, "It doesn't take Einstein to figure it out, just drop the tax cuts and we don't need to cut Medicare."[129]

The powerful American Association of Retired Persons (AARP) fought against the destruction of Medicare, but retaliation from Congress was swift. It launched an investigation of AARP (which represents 33 million members) and charged it with using monies inappropriately or illegally. In addition, it attacked social agencies that came to the defense of the poor in support of Medicare with the Istook amendment to the appropriations bill funding the Departments of Labor, Health and Human Services, and Education. The amendment prohibited "individuals and nonprofits from receiving federal grants if more than 5 percent of their [own] private and non-federal funds are used for advocacy." This effectively muzzled many nonprofit groups and charities. However, there were no such restrictions placed on other groups receiving federal funding; for example, Lockheed and Intel together received more than $54 million from the federal government in 1994 but could use any nonfederal funds to lobby without restriction.[130]

In 1970 there were 20.5 million Medicare recipients at a cost of $7.1 billion, but by 1994 there were 36.9 million enrollees, costing $1,644.5 billion, or more than twenty times as much. The value of the trust fund in 1970 was $32 billion and in 1994 $132.8 billion.[131] In 2001 the deductible for Medicare Part A was $792 per benefit period, and the premium for optional Part B Supplemental Medical Insurance was $54 per month, with a $100 deductible.[132] At the same time, Medicare covered only 53 percent of the average senior's annual medical expenses. Preventive care services remained insufficient to help seniors remain healthy. Routine annual physicals, vision tests, and hearing aids were not covered, and the program continued its fee-for-service cost-sharing structure, often leaving clients with high costs. The gap between tax and premium receipts and Medicare's expenditures was $51 billion in 2000.[133] Medicare spending was only 0.1 percent of GDP in 1998 and 1.0 percent in 1999, well below the average of 9.2 percent for 1993–1997. Medicare spending represented 17.6 percent of every dollar spent on health care in 1999, falling from a peak of 19.3 percent of national health expenditures in 1996–1997.[134] Actual Medicare expenditures in 2000 were $197.1 billion, and estimated outlays for 2001 and 2002 were $219.3 billion and $229.9 billion, respectively.[135]

Medicaid

Medicaid payments to vendors in 1993 were $70.2 billion for care of aged and blind people and those with disabilities (8.9 million), $13.6 billion for AFDC adults (7.5 million), $16.5 billion for children under age twenty-one (16.3 million), and unknown and "other" recipients (.7 million) at $1.4 billion. Total expenditures were $101.7 billion, serving 33.4 million people.[136]

In 1994 Medicaid provided care for more than 35 million people at a cost to federal and state governments of more than $158 billion, up from $125 billion in 1993 (federal cost about 57 percent). Nearly two-thirds of Medicaid patients were people with low incomes, mostly receiving public assistance. The program paid for one-third of all births in the United States, more than a quarter of all emergency room visits, and 37 to 50 percent of long-term care of the approximately 1.5 million people in nursing homes—the elderly and young with disabilities, including people with AIDS, of whom 69 percent rely on Medicaid—at an annual average cost of $38,000 each, about $104 a day. Fifty percent of Medicaid clients were children, but they took only 18.5 percent of its costs. Aged Medicaid clients (11.5 percent) took 28.4 percent of costs and those with disabilities nearly 39 percent. Each elderly patient cost $9,862 on average, whereas Medicaid paid $9,226 for each client with disabilities and $1,360 for each child.[137]

Medicaid was funded at $90 billion in 1995, and cuts were to be at $182 over seven years. The program was merged into block grants without matching state fund requirements, which portended not only a loss of federal funds but a 30 percent loss in state funds.[138] Eligibility rules became more stringent, so that of 22 million children covered by Medicaid, about 4.4 million would be dropped, with no provision for new health coverage.[139] NASW says,

> One in three births is funded by Medicaid. One in four children currently depends on Medicaid for . . . health care coverage. . . . Reduced access of children to preventive and primary care will translate into serious long-term health consequences for our nation's youth. Reduced access to care will also influence immunization rates, which in turn will influence the incidence of preventable, communicable diseases.[140]

Privatization of care for Medicaid-covered children came even before the 104th Congress demonstrated a lack of concern about mandated programs, and it increased with loss of federal standards. For example, although children are entitled to Early and Periodic Screening, Diagnosis, and Treatment (EPSDT), privately managed contracts did not guarantee it. In a study examining thirty-three contracts (in twenty-three states and Washington, D.C.), 82 percent did not require it. Although 59 percent of the contracts required *plans* for EPSDT, only twelve contracts specified that immunizations were required, eight gave providers the option of giving immunizations, and three referred children to public health departments.[141]

Besides children, the elderly and disabled clients of Medicaid are also at risk. In 1995 Medicaid paid about 70 percent of the costs of nursing home care for 1.5 million residents (total cost about $57 billion a year). The Medicaid cut of at least $192 million meant that with reduced federal and state funding, 350,000 nursing home residents lost coverage, along with 1.4 million people with disabilities.

The Balanced Budget Act of 1997 allowed states to force most Medicaid patients to enroll in managed care entities: Managed care organizations (MCOs) and primary care case managers (PCCMs)—physicians, group practices, physician assistants, or nurse practitioners—would serve them. States must give clients a choice of at least two, and providers are required to give patients information on rights and responsibilities, covered services, benefits available outside the managed care entity, and so on. There are also grievance and appeal procedures.[142]

Medicaid spending has continued to increase significantly despite SCHIP. While spending in 1997 was $146.1 billion, by 1999 it had reached $182 billion, and spending is projected to reach $240 billion by 2002.[143] The total number of recipients in 1995 was 36,282,000 and in 1999, 40,649,000, with expenditures of $120.1 billion and $142.32 million respectively.[144] The Medicaid share of total health spending, without SCHIP funding, was 15.4 percent in 1999.[145]

Social Issues

The Clinton Stimulus Package (1993) produced a $16.3 billion fund, of which $8.3 billion was to be spent in 1993, the remainder in future years. It provided nearly $6.5 billion in tax incentives, particularly an investment tax credit for small businesses through Empowerment/Enterprise Zones, put 100,000 new officers on the streets through the Omnibus Crime Bill, increased spending on transportation, accelerated the Home Investment Partnerships program (similar to HOPE, the George Bush bill), and provided funds for environmental cleanups. In addition, he increased the time limit for unemployment compensation and provided $4 billion for extended unemployment compensation.[146]

Major stimulus package programs included the Enterprise and Empowerment Zone program and the Omnibus Crime Bill. The purpose of the former was to put money into blighted or disadvantaged areas. In 1993, funded at $3.5 billion, it set up nine empowerment zones (six urban, three rural) and ninety-five enterprise zones. Each urban empowerment zone received a $100 million block grant for social services such as child development and drug treatment, and each rural zone got $40 million. Enterprise zones received up to $3 million for social services. Business owners received tax deductions for each zone-area resident employed, up to $3,000 (20 percent of the first $15,000 of employees' salaries or wages), and some training expenses. There are now thirty-one Empowerment Zones and ninety-five Enterprise Communities, leveraging over $10 billion in new private sector investment.

There is no doubt that areas and people benefited from the program, through better schools, more social services, and more small businesses, but perhaps direct investment into families rather than another layer of infrastructure would have produced more lasting effects. Latent functions, aside from the political, include

- Provision of tax havens to make more money for the already moneyed
- Pacification of those who are overtly served,[147] encouraging conformity
- Creation of jobs for social workers
- Conflict issues of poverty—classism, racism, and sexism—converted to "social problems" that imply solutions
- Crediting the powerful for their concern for the nonpowerful.[148]

Crime Control

The Clinton Omnibus Crime Control Act of 1994, approved quickly by Congress, allowed for $30 billion to be spent over six years, with $5.4 billion for prevention programs, $7.9 billion for new prison construction, and $8.8 billion for increased police forces. It also instituted the "three strikes and you're out" plan for habitual criminals: life imprisonment after three convictions. The bill applied the death penalty to over fifty new crimes, although it specified that jurors were not required to impose the death penalty and that it could not be imposed on the incompetent, people with mental retardation, or children under age nineteen. Adding to the Brady Gun Control bill, the act also banned at least 150 brands of semiautomatic weapons.

Unfortunately, the latent functions of this "lock-em-up" program intensified action against people who were poor or from minority groups. The bill grew out of not only fear of increased crime, but also from the Reagan war on drugs, which ghettoized neighborhoods in poverty, closing them off for further crime and police action. Disproportionate reporting and apprehension of suspects, along with more convictions and more severe punishment for crimes committed by African Americans and other minorities, are a given in the United States. Heightened efforts to stop the drug business by making more arrests and giving longer sentences made this bill another weapon not only against crime but also against the urban poor.

In the seven years between 1991–1998, violent crime dropped by 25 percent, yet prisons and jails held 1,860,520 inmates, or one in every 147 adult Americans (Russia's prisons hold one in 146 citizens). Despite falling crime rates, the prison population may reach 2 million in 2001[149] (one-quarter of the world's prisoners).[150] The growth of the prison population was responsible for only about 25 percent of the drop in the crime rate. The rest came from changes in the crack cocaine markets, greater efforts by police to get guns off the streets, and the strength of the economy. In turn, the growth of the prison population came from longer sentences for violent and drug-related crimes, more mandatory minimum sentences, and more difficulty in obtaining parole.[151] Almost one in three African American men in their twenties was under some form of criminal supervision on any given day in 1995, and by 1999, 46 percent of all inmates serving a year or more were African Americans. Hispanics constituted 18 percent of the prison population and whites 33 percent.[152]

Most current illicit drug users are white—an estimated 9.9 million, or 72 percent of all users, whereas 2 million are African American (15 percent) and 1.4 million are Hispanic (10 percent). Yet African Americans constitute 36.8 percent of those arrested for drug violations and constitute over 42 percent of those in federal prisons and 58 percent of those in state prisons.[153] Among persons convicted of drug felonies, 32 percent of white defendants received prison sentences whereas the rate for African Americans was 46 percent. The rate of imprisonment for African American women (for all offenses) is more than eight times that for white women, and Hispanic women's rate of imprisonment is nearly four times that of white women.[154]

Social costs of pursuing a hard line on criminal justice are inestimable, especially given the racist nature of prosecution. People convicted of felonies lose their right to vote, and so can no longer participate in governance. Harsh guidelines such as "three strikes, you're out" means that a disproportionate number of young African American and Hispanic men are likely to be imprisoned for life for drug-related offenses, virtually warehousing them into old age.[155] Aside from the cost of maintaining enough prison space for these men, their imprisonment means an end to any kind of family or fatherhood, poorer lives for their spouses and children, and higher social costs for the ensuing poverty of their families.

Education

In 1994 Clinton reauthorized Head Start, with a funding increase of $210 million, and $8 billion in educational service grants for disadvantaged children was earmarked for 1995. Clinton's Goals 2000: Educate America Act would have provided $5 billion over five years to schools that created plans for school reform and raised academic achievement, with $400 million earmarked for 1995, but it remained unfunded. His School to Work Opportunities program established job training programs, apprenticeships, and vocational education systems for young people not going to college, with a $125 million appropriation for 1995.[156]

To aid the college-bound, he designed the National Community and Service Trust Act—Americorps (1993)—which enabled prospective students to volunteer two years of community service in exchange for $9,450 for tuition or student loans and a living allowance of at least $7,400 for 1,700 hours of service. The program also provided health and child care benefits. Volunteers could serve in educational, public health and safety, environmental, or social welfare positions before, during, or after college. A direct federal student loan demonstration program was also enacted, but as a compromise with banks it was phased in to provide 60 percent of all new loans by the 1998–1999 academic year.[157]

Clinton also created College Tax Credits, the largest single investment in higher education since the 1940s. Called the Hope Scholarship, it provides a $1,500 tax credit for the first two years of college. The $1,000 Lifetime Learning Tax Credit reimburses families for 20 percent of their tuition and fees (up to $5,000 per family) for college, graduate study, or job training. Student financial aid doubled during the Clinton administration: Over 3.8 million students received Pell Grants of up to a maximum of $3,750 in 2001. The 1997 Balanced Budget Act also created Education IRAs: For each child under age eighteen, families may invest $500 a year tax-free if used for college expenses.[158] In addition, the expanded 21st Century Community Learning Centers program provided after-school centers serving approximately 400,000 children, and funding increased from $40 million in FY 1998 to $200 million in FY 1999, with an expected increase to $600 million in 2001.[159] In fall 1999, 30,000 new teachers were hired under Clinton's seven-year plan to hire 100,000 teachers to reduce class size. Further, the 1996 Telecommunications Act provided Internet service to almost 47,000 schools and libraries by E-Rate (education rate).[160] In January 2002, G. W. Bush signed into law a $26 billion education bill.

Employment and Jobs

From the 1950s to the 1990s the country lost about half its manufacturing jobs as automation and robotization replaced human work. This major loss of good-paying jobs was exacerbated by the loss of 1 million more lost manufacturing jobs between 1990 and 1995. An additional 6 million workers went to part-time employment. In 1994, despite 3 million new jobs created, poverty rose from 11 percent to 15 percent and real wages fell by 2.3 percent. About three-quarters of the 2.8 million "long-tenured" workers who lost full-time jobs in 1991 and 1992 had found new employment by 1994, but fewer than a third were employed in full-time jobs that paid equal or higher wages.[161]

In 1994 the minimum wage approached a forty-year low in constant dollars, with nearly 20 percent of full-time workers earning less than the poverty level. Moreover, they lost benefits: Those with employer-paid pension funds declined by 25 percent, and an estimated 43.4 million lost health insurance (up 1 million since 1993). Meanwhile, corporate profits were at a forty-five year high, and chief executives, who in 1972 made forty times the average pay of workers, made 140 times as much in the 1990s. (For example, Michael Eisner, the head of Disney, made an estimated $78,000 an hour in 1995.[162]) Only about 11 percent of the labor force was unionized, although, hoping to gain clout with size, the three largest industrial unions—United Auto Workers, United Steelworkers of America, and International Association of Machinists—decided to merge. This created a 2-million member union second in size only to the National Education Association.[163]

The minimum wage was raised in 1997 to $5.15 per hour, yet on that wage a family of three was still below the poverty line. In 1998, despite a booming economy and without the addition of many former TANF recipients, unemployment was rising. In the week of November 6, the number of people filing for unemployment compensation jumped by 12,000 people to a seasonally adjusted 321,000 recorded unemployed.[164]

In 1992, 10 million workers were unemployed, but economic growth under Clinton created a more vibrant economy. More than 22.5 million jobs were created, of which 92 percent were in the private sector. By 1995, unemployment was at 7 percent, but by 2000 it was 4.0 percent. Unemployment for African Americans fell from 14.2 percent in 1992 to 7.3 percent in October 2000, and unemployment for Hispanics fell from 11.8 percent in 1992 to 5 percent in October 2000.[165]

However, coincidentally with the election of President George W. Bush, the boom that pushed us into the new millennium suddenly died. By March 2001, unemployment had begun to rise: Between November 2000 and November 2001, the number of unemployed workers rose by 2.5 million—from 5.7 million to 8.2 million.[166] Factory employment fell by 163,000 in August 2001, bringing the total number of manufacturing jobs lost since July 2000 to 1.2 million. The services industry, where most Americans work, lost 221,000 jobs between November 2000 and November 2001. The 330,000 payroll jobs lost in November 2001 came on the heels of a loss of 468,000 jobs in October, the biggest one month loss in twenty-one years.[167]

From January through August 2001, there were 1.2 million layoffs, exceeding the year-end total for 2000 by 83 percent. Since August 2000, the jobless rate for workers age forty-five and older has jumped 23.5 percent, to 1,478,000, while that for workers age twenty-five to forty-five rose 20.7 percent.[168] In November

2001, 2.4 million workers had been unemployed fifteen weeks or longer, an increase of 16 percent from October, and 1.2 million workers were out of work for twenty-seven weeks or longer, an increase of 32 percent from October, the largest one month increase since these data began in 1948. Unemployment benefits expire after twenty-six weeks, and the number of workers without benefits was, in November 2001, at the highest level in ten years.[169] In January 2002, G. W. Bush extended these benefits for another 13 weeks.

Affirmative Action and Civil Rights

The Reagan civil rights and affirmative action reversals were based on the idea that protecting the civil rights of some defined groups could entail a kind of discrimination against other groups and was thus forbidden by the equal protection clause (Fourteenth Amendment) of the Constitution. This theme permeated the Bush presidency. In 1989 the Supreme Court (in *City of Richmond v. J.A. Croson Co.*) ruled that states could not give preference to minority-owned firms in awarding contracts (although federal set-aside programs were exempt). In another case (*Wards Cove Packing v. Antonio*), people claiming discrimination had to produce proof that an employer intended to discriminate against employees. Congress, aware of the political uproar such reversals brought, brought new legislation for restoration of civil rights, but Bush vetoed the first bill (1990) and rejected a 1991 compromise. However, legislation was finally developed to reverse some such decisions (including the *Wards Packing Company* case). (The bill also allowed punitive and compensatory damages for sexual discrimination cases and "cases of discrimination against people with disabilities and members of religious groups,"[170] the latter leading to the Americans with Disabilities Act.)

During the 1990s, the Supreme Court continued the path set for it in the Reagan–Bush years, reinterpreting laws concerning affirmative action and civil rights in an increasingly restrictive manner. With the appointment of Clarence Thomas by President Bush, the Court's work became driven by a core of conservatives chosen from Reagan onward: Chief Justice William Rehnquist, Justices Antonin Scalia and Clarence Thomas, and frequent allies Anthony Kennedy and Sandra Day O'Connor. A number of affirmative action cases came before this court. In a five-to-four vote, it stopped short of striking down a program to help minority-owned businesses win federal construction projects. ADARAND corporation, in Colorado, lost on a bid for federal road construction to higher- bidding Mountain Gravel, a minority-owed business. The Supreme Court sent the case back to the Appeals Court for closer study, but warned that "racial classifications must serve a compelling government interest and must be narrowly tailored to further that interest."[171] This narrowing of definition meant more restriction in awards, jeopardizing programs under which federal agencies award more than $10 billion a year in contracts to minority-owned firms. In fact, the interpretation led the Pentagon to end most awards to minority contractors.

Another important case dealt with the redrawing of voting districts to include minority representation. The Voting Rights Act of 1965 had outlawed gerrymandering that denied voting rights to people of minority groups, and amendments in 1982 went a step further, allowing redistricting to ensure African American representation. Separate charges were brought by Louisiana and Georgia that the creation of African American majority districts violated the rights of white voters to a color-blind society.[172] The Court, voting in July 1995 with a five-to-four majority, said that when race is the predominant factor in a districting plan, aggrieved white voters could file suit and force the lines to be withdrawn.

During the Clinton administration, funding and staffing for six major civil rights agencies dropped 10 percent, according to the U.S. Commission on Civil Rights, despite a doubling of complaints and cases at some agencies. Most showed marked declines both in number of investigations and number of complaints closed since 1994. The Department of Education Office of Civil Rights, for example, closed 282 fewer cases in 1999 than in 1994, although the number of complaints received over the period rose by 1,326. At this agency, 144 reviews were initiated in 1994 as opposed to seventy-six in 1999. Also, from 1994 to 2000, staffing fell from 821 to 707. In 1998 the Clinton administration sought a substantial increase in funding, but funding grew only moderately for two agencies and declined for the other four, probably due to Clinton's lack of attention to them because of scandal and impeachment problems.[173] President G. W. Bush has supported affirmative action that considers minority-owned firms as disadvantaged in securing government contracts.

President Clinton's stand on civil rights for gays was demonstrated when, under pressure from the Pentagon and Religious Right conservatives, he reneged on his promise to change the "don't ask, don't tell" policy on gays in military services. Military discharges of gays rose in 2000 by 17 percent to the highest total in recent years. In all, 1,212 members of the Armed Services were discharged during FY 2000, compared with 1,034 the year before and 1,145 in 1998. Of the total, 106 were cases in which military members stated their homosexuality. The others were discharged for homosexual acts.[174]

Though many states and cities passed Equal Rights laws that included gays in their protection, the conservative 104th Congress, encouraged by the Religious Right, passed the Defense of Marriage Act (DOMA, 1996) to deny federal recognition of same-sex marriages recognized by states. This effectively denied same-sex couples such basic considerations as

> . . . bereavement or sick leave to take care of a partner or partner's child; pension or Social Security continuation when a partner dies; the ability to keep a jointly owned home if a partner goes on Medicaid, dies, or becomes sick; joint tax returns and exemptions for primary relationships on estate taxes; veteran's discounts on medical care, education, and home loans; immigration and residency for partners from other countries.[175]

DOMA also violates the Full Faith and Credit Clause of Article IV of the Constitution, which provides that the court judgments of one state shall be recognized as valid in other states.[176]

Many states and cities now have laws protecting gays from discrimination and defining gay-bashing as a hate crime. Yet in 2000, all states except Hawaii and Vermont refused marriage licenses to gays, nineteen states still criminalized sodomy, and six states criminalized same-sex sodomy, leaving doors open for prosecution. For lesbian or gay parents, child custody is almost always denied when former spouses object, and three states officially prohibit gays from adopting children, and the prohibition is *de facto* in most others. Informally, many states and communities refuse employment to gays applying for civil positions, such as those in teaching or police work. However, the Supreme Court decision in *Oncale v. Sundowner Offshore Services* (1998) allowed claims for harassment by someone of the same sex, and this could reopen the issue for lower federal courts. Moreover, the Department of Education and the Seventh Circuit Court of Appeals decided that an educational institution's failure to provide relief to gay students harassed by homophobic classmates is sex discrimination.[177]

Private Charity

In the 1990s President George Bush validated Reagan's efforts to decrease federal social programs by calling on private individuals and agencies to become "a thousand points of light" to help their neighbors at the local level in times of hardship. Begging the question as to how many points of light can lift the darkness of poverty and despair, this rationalization for lack of social responsibility continued into the new millennium. Though we Americans believe we are charitable—and we may be, to people we know—we rarely generalize altruism across barriers of economic class and race. In part this is because of social values such as the work ethic and social Darwinism; another part is that we think we pay enough in taxes and charitable contributions so that, if people are poor, it is their own fault.

Whereas the government's retreat from social responsibility is patent, how does private charity look today? It is a fact that many charitable organizations are highly funded by the government. For example, the government provides 96 percent of funding for Volunteers of America, 80 percent for United Cerebral Palsy, 78 percent for CARE, 65 percent for Catholic Charities, and 51 percent for settlement housing and neighborhood centers.[178] Moreover, most of what we call nonprofits have little to do with aiding those in need. They are thousands of educational, health care, arts and cultural, religious, research, civic, and membership organizations. They own a trillion dollars in assets and account for 10 percent of America's gross domestic profits.[179] In 2000 a total of $203.5 billion was donated to charities and other nonprofits, up 6.6 percent over the 1999 figure.[180] However, little of that was earmarked for the poor or our neighbors fallen on hard times.

Expecting that church-affiliated agencies would help their local poor, PRWORA 1996 included the "charitable choice" option, meant to allow programs otherwise disqualified as religious-oriented to access TANF funds. Later, Congress extended that concept to federal drug treatment and community development programs. Yet almost two-thirds of states report no requests for such funding. While thirty-one states and Washington, D.C., awarded no government welfare contracts to religious groups, fourteen states reported sporadic use of the program, and five states—Arkansas, Indiana, Missouri, Ohio, and Texas—embraced it, spending hundreds of thousands or even millions of dollars.[181]

The idea of corporate charity, that corporations are obligated to advance the welfare of the nation, arose in the 1970s. As it works out, however, the main thrust of corporate charity is "cause-related marketing," in which corporations can expand their markets by supporting worthy aims."[182] By supporting orchestras, symphonies, and museums, they reach upscale consumers without the high cost of advertising broadly. Wagner says

> For example, SCM Company, which sponsors museum exhibitions, admits that it would cost $51 million per year on advertising for five years to reach the customers it now does on $200,000 a year.[183]

American corporate giving was $11.02 billion in 1999, about 1.3 percent of pretax income and a jump of 14.2 percent over the previous year. Business owners have learned that "good corporate citizenship polishes a good name.[184]

According to Wagner, charity today is rarely concerned with the social change of structures that impact our most vulnerable citizens. For example, the concern with homelessness in the late 1970s was not oriented to the need for good jobs, the housing crisis, or the need to improve and restore social benefits. Rather, defined as an issue of sympathy by social service, mental health, and church leaders, it created a whole new industry: shelters and soup kitchens, mental health and substance abuse counseling aimed specifically at street people, "Hands Across America" rallies, and Second Harvest food collections.[185]

Charities have a great deal of money. The ten largest U.S. charities, ranked by total income, are: Lutheran Charities, $3.7 billion; National Council of YMCAs, $3.6 billion; Salvation Army, $2.7 billion; United Jewish Community, $2.4 billion; American Red Cross, $2.4 billion; Catholic Charities $2.33 billion; Good Will Industries, $1.65 billion; Boys and Girls Clubs, $800 million; American Cancer Society, $666.9 million; and Planned Parenthood, $660 million. Executive officers are extremely well-paid in salary and benefits: The highest paid CEO works for the Girl Scouts of America at $648,790; the lowest paid works for Lutheran Services at $91,467.[186] A redistribution of some of the wealth owned by charities to our most vulnerable citizens would probably provide enough points of light to end poverty in America.

Welfare for the Wealthy and Corporate Welfare

Capital Assets and Tax Cuts

To carry out their plan to expand benefits to the wealthy, Congress in 1995 again altered the tax structure for families with capital assets. Among the benefits was a new 50 percent exclusion from taxation for the sale of real estate, securities, and other assets, effectively lowering capital gains tax rates from a range of 15–28 percent to 7.5–19.8 percent. In addition, capital gains were indexed to inflation. The corporate rate on capital gains dropped from 35 to 28 percent. Earnings from retirement accounts were no longer taxed, and exemptions on estate taxes would increase over six years to $750,000, with the exemption on family-owned farms and businesses increased to $1.5 million before taxes.

The Republican budget plus tax cuts redistributed wealth from the poor to the richest 1 percent of American families. Each received almost $19,000 a year in tax breaks, often more than a poor family earns in a year. The Treasury Department estimated that nearly 84 percent of Republican tax breaks would go to families making more than $50,000 per year—52 percent for those who earned more than $100,000 annually. Tax breaks for the richest 1 percent totaled about $21 billion, or 42 percent more than the total tax relief for all families earning less than $50,000 a year (more than 61 percent of American families). For the richest 5 percent, cuts amounted to $37 billion—"almost as large as the total of income and health coverage cuts hitting all families with children."[187] Those earning from $50,000 to $75,000 got a tax decrease of 4.2 percent, but those earning from $10,000 to $20,000 paid 2.2 percent more taxes, and those earning under $10,000 paid 9.6 percent more.[188]

As social welfarists, we watched many Clinton efforts with approval, such as educational tax credits and the increase in EITC, which grew from $815 billion in 1993 to $22.6 billion in 1999 and extended tax credits to 6 million additional low-income citizens.[189] However, the Balanced Budget Act of 1997 primarily benefited the wealthy. While the middle 20 percent of families got a tax break of $153 a year, the top 20 percent received more than $1,000 each and the richest 1 percent $16,157. The bottom 40 percent actually get nothing, and because of higher excise taxes, the bottom 20 percent saw a rise in amounts paid to the government. Though EITC gave tax credits to those with incomes less than $110,000 a year, only 2.4 percent of children in the poorest one-fifth bracket qualifies for EITC. In addition, though the education tax credit gives tax reductions to those with incomes up to $100,000, low-income children are not as likely to attend college, so nearly one-half of education credits go to the wealthy.[190]

Cuts in corporate, capital gains, and estate taxes provided about one-half of total tax relief nearly exclusively to the super-rich. In 1998 the top tax bracket for capital gains—sale of stocks, bonds, and similar assets—was 20 percent, down from 28 percent; the minimum corporate tax was eliminated; and the estate tax exemption was raised from $600,000 to $1 million. These breaks gave the richest 5 percent of families 83 percent of the benefits from the three cuts.[191] Those with incomes over $200,000 received an average tax break of $16,372 a year, while those in the $40,000 to $50,000 bracket received $1.[192] There was also a major increase in the tax deductibility of contributions to Individual Retirement Accounts. Moreover, since the national debt is owed to wealthy investors through Treasury bonds, the $247 billion paid in interest went primarily to them.[193]

A 2001 Congressional Budget study indicates that the average after-tax income of the richest 1 percent of Americans grew by $414,000 between 1979 and 1997, or about 157 percent. Average after-tax income for the poorest 20 percent of Americans fell by $100, while middle income families gained $3,400. Those in the highest 1 percent paid an average tax of 37.3 percent on income in 1979, reduced to 32.7 percent in 2001, and their share of national income after taxes nearly doubled between 1979 and 1997. The top 1 percent, in other words, had as much after-tax income as nearly 100 million Americans with the lowest incomes, or 20 percent had as much income as the other 80 percent.[194] In the 1999 tax bill, when cuts go into full effect, 59 percent of the benefits go to the wealthiest 10 percent of households. The top fifth of households get 78.5 percent of the tax cuts, while the bottom 60 percent receive an average tax cut of $166. Fully one-third of all capital gains income goes to taxpayers whose annual capital gains income exceeds $1 million.[195]

In June 2001 President G. W. Bush and the Congress passed a new tax bill benefiting the wealthy. Among the benefits were an expansion of education IRAs that raised the $500 per year limit to $2,000 for those with incomes up to $220,000 and an increase in allowable contributions of IRAs: $3,000 a year in 2002 and $5,000 in 2008. Though his administration also used some of the fast disappearing surplus to give many Americans a $300 to $600 instant tax rebate, about 35 million of the poorest—those without income or who earn too little to pay income tax—received nothing, and the rebates are taxable for the 2001 tax year as income.[196] His tax cuts further widened the income gap between the wealthiest Americans and the rest of us. Once the law is fully in effect, the top 1 percent will receive an average tax cut of more than $46,000, compared to an average tax cut of $600 for the middle fifth and less than $70 for the bottom fifth.[197] It was likely that the $1.35 trillion tax cut passed in the spring of 2001 was the major reason for the vanishing surplus left by the Clinton administration, in addition to the September 11 attack and subsequent war.[198]

Corporate Welfare

According to a *Time* magazine study,

> During one of the most robust economic periods in our nation's history [beginning in 1997], the Federal Government has shelled out $125 billion in corporate welfare, equivalent to all the income tax paid by 60 million individuals and families.[199]

The government supports the corporate system in myriad ways:

- Direct legislation
- Tax breaks and subsidies
- Interest write-offs for corporate debt
- Provision of infrastructure demanded by corporations
- The maintenance of a public assistance system
- Direct purchases of goods and services.

Direct legislation benefiting corporations is demonstrated by the preservation of the $110 million Market Protection Program, which protects such corporations as McDonald's, Pillsbury, and Ernest & Julio Gallo from competition.[200] Congress even allows corporations to define its laws: For example, the Environmental Protection Agency's Clean Water Act was revised to ease antipollution requirements and allow more incursion into such natural resources as forests and wetlands. Ivins says,

> lobbyists for the Chemical Manufacturers Association and International Paper . . . [literally rewrote] the Clean Water Act. . . . Under the Republican revision, 70 percent of the marshlands now protected will once more be open to exploitation.[201]

The 104th Congress's emphasis on laissez-faire corporate behavior was another aspect: By reducing funding to the Department of Occupational Health and Safety (OSHA), it enabled corporations to ignore costly health and safety requirements. In addition, despite antitrust and antimonopoly laws, Congress ignored massive corporate mergers.

In 1994 the Office of Management and Budget found $51 billion in direct subsidies to industries and $53 billion in corporate tax breaks. A 1995 report showed that corporate subsidies to 129 private industries totaled $87 billion, ranging from export promotional funds for giant food companies to transportation and interest-rate subsidies for manufacturing and utilities and the underwriting of defense industry worker recreation programs.[202] Although Congress cut billions in social programs in 1995, it reduced corporate tax breaks only by about $1.5 billion.[203]

Interest write-offs for corporate debt, the preservation of infrastructure to meet corporate demands, and the maintenance of public assistance for corporate benefit are perhaps not quite so obvious. Because of quick corporate mergers and capital turnaround, corporations borrow high-interest corporate loans, on which much interest is lost, costing the government millions in revenue. Increased corporate debt necessitates immediately increased profits, so corporations rid themselves of the least profitable elements—workers—or go to part-time no-fringe-benefit workers. Loss of wages and benefits leads to greater use of public assistance programs, so the government actually subsidizes the downsizing of corporations. Karger says, the government tacitly assumes the social costs of corporate competition in the new global economy. . . . [B]y allowing corporations to create a floating labor force, the government agrees to mortgage its future . . . [because] an unstable labor market means fewer tax revenues.[204]

At the same time, under threat of loss of corporations, the government invests in new roads, advanced communications systems, and public facilities. This further plunges the government into deficit spending and the reduction of social programs.[205]

Corporate lobbying is not the only way to gain support from Congress. Financial support paid to election funds, while its influence is denied by the recipients, is worthy of note. For example, the American financial industry contributed to the reelection of almost every member of the House and Senate Banking committees—the fifty-one members of the House Banking Committee received at least $4.6 million in 1991–1993, with even more contributions in 1995. At one fund-raiser in 1995, the Republican party received $11 million from wealthy individuals and corporations. Is it coincidental that the 104th Congress under Republican leadership has given huge tax breaks to many of America's largest corporations?[206]

Between 1991 and 2001, forty-one companies contributed a total of $150 million to federal candidates and parties through cash contributions to political action committees (PACs), individual contributions from executives and their families, and unlimited "soft money" contributions—perks, favors, and gifts.[207] Primary targets are members of the House Ways and Means and Senate Finance Committees, who, since 1991, have collected $9.7 million from top tax-avoiding companies.[208] From 1989 through June 2001, energy industries contributed $209 million to political campaigns though they already pay the lowest corporate tax rate in America (5.7 percent in 1998). Five accounting firms whose job is to find corporate tax loopholes contributed $29 million, and industries benefiting from special research and experimentation (R&E) credits—primarily pharmaceutical and computer industries—donated $148 million.[209] In the 2000 election cycle, corporate donations included:

Corporation	Amount[210]
AT&T	$4.3 million
Microsoft	$3.4 million
Citigroup Inc.	$3.1 million
Verizon	$2.7 million
Goldman Sachs Group	$2.6 million
United Parcel	$2.5 million[210]

In his first budget (2001), G. W. Bush promised to end breaks to big business, yet powerful agribusiness companies and farmers got combined tax breaks of $800 million, and federal subsidies for the sugar industry cost consumers about

$1.4 billion in higher prices. His budget left intact a $478 million Agriculture Department program to boost overseas sales of U.S. crops, the subsidy for ethanol fuels was $800 million, market-access programs increased from $86 million to $92 million, and timber subsidies amounted to $500 million to cut trees on federal property.[211]

Tax loopholes and corporate-pricing schemes also contribute to corporate welfare. In 1998, using legal tax dodges around the 1986 tax law, twenty-four large companies received income tax refunds. Write-offs for stock options, depreciation, and other tax breaks gave refunds of $186.8 million to Chevron, whose 1998 profit was $708 million; MCI Worldcom, with profits of $2,742.2 million, received $112.6 million; Pepsico, with $1,583 million in profits, was refunded $302 million; and Pfizer, with profits of $1,197.6 million, got back $197.2 million.[212] Multinationals also avoided $45 billion in taxes in 2000 by artificially fixing prices in overseas trade, overpricing goods sold in the United States, and underpricing goods purchased. Examples of overpricing goods coming into the country include $5,655 for a toothbrush or $5,000 for a flashlight; and examples of underpricing include $1.58 for a ton of soybeans, $528 for a bulldozer, and 82 cents for a prefabricated metal building.[213]

One of the biggest beneficiaries of corporate welfare is the war industry, through the military–industrial complex—interlocking memberships in corporate boards, the military, and politicians. Congress began to reconstruct Reagan's antimissile defense system ("Star Wars") against attack from "rogue" governments such as Iraq and Korea or "accidental actions" by Russia and China.[214] To accomplish this, the House Appropriations Committee, which had stripped social programs of more than $10 billion for fiscal year 1996, found an extra $7 billion beyond the $258 billion requested by the president for the Defense Department. It targeted the money for projects neither requested nor planned by the Pentagon. Of the $7 billion, more than $4.1 billion (81 percent) was intended for arms contractors in states represented by senators and representatives sitting on either Armed Services or Defense Appropriations Committees.[215]

For "Star Wars," where $70.7 billion was spent under Reagan (more than double the $32.6 billion the government claimed was spent), Congress added another $625 million to the $3 billion President Clinton requested for 1996.[216] The Cold War was over, the plan would violate arms agreements from 1973 to the latest START accords, and nuclear arms production had ended in 1992, yet Congress persisted in its costly and scientifically improbable "Star Wars" plan. Corporations lobbied heavily for the new funds and succeeded: For example, Northrup Grumman Corporation received $493 million to keep factories open for the sole production of the B-2 (Stealth) bomber ($2 billion each), even though it is similar to other military aircraft.[217] Four Aegis cruisers—two more than requested by the Navy—were commissioned for the home states of William S. Cohn of Maine, Republican chairman of the Armed Services Seapower Subcommittee, and the GOP majority whip, Trent Lott, of Mississippi.[218] To the military construction budget ($106 billion), Congress added $346 billion for forty-four unsolicited projects.[219]

Though at first wary of the Strategic Defense Initiative (Star Wars), Clinton bowed to pressure from the Pentagon and a coalition of "true believers" and arms manufacturers—companies such as Lockheed Martin, Raytheon, Boeing, and TRW, who have spent more than $35 million on lobbying and $6.9 million in campaign contributions since 1997.[220] The "Contract with America" of the 104th Congress called for a national missile defense system, and its proponents gained enough support to develop a modified plan, the National Missile Defense (NMD). Scaled back from Reagan's Star Wars because of the end of the Cold War, NMD aimed to defend the United States from accidental missile launches from Russia or China, or from attack by "rogue states" such as Iraq or North Korea.[221]

NMD research and development was funded at $3 to $5 billion per year until summer 1998, when a congressional panel chaired by Donald Rumsfeld asserted that the risk of attack by a rogue state was much higher than previously predicted. His report, along with missile tests by Iran and North Korea, led Clinton in January 1999 to more than double NMD funding to $10.5 billion over the next six years. A bill declaring it government policy to deploy the system as soon as possible was passed in June 1999. In his final year in office, President Clinton added an additional $2.2 billion to NMD funding, bringing the total over the next five years to $12.7 billion.[221] On coming into office, G. W. Bush promoted NMD even more vigorously, calling for an overhaul of U.S. defense strategy, with the defense screen at its core. Strangely, in a grim vision of the future, during the Clinton administration, Robert Walpole, a national intelligence officer for strategic and nuclear programs stated that

> . . . in the coming years, U.S. territory is probably more likely to be attacked with weapons of mass destruction from nonmissile delivery means (most likely from nonstate entities) than by missiles.[222]

Nonmissile delivery is anything from a suitcase to a truck bomb or other low-tech "delivery vehicle"—methods least effectively deterred by the NMD system.[223] On September 11, 2001, when terrorists struck America, NMD became peripheral to defense.

In 1998 national defense cost $268 billion and in 1999 $274 billion. By 2000, expenditures had grown to $294 billion, with estimated expenses in 2001 of $299.1 billion. The budget called for $319.1 billion (16 percent of the national budget) in 2002,[224] but surely will increase because of September 11, 2001.

Globalization, the International Economy, and American Social Welfare

On September 11, 2001, the people of the United States experienced globalization as we had never expected. The tragic attacks on the World Trade Center and the Pentagon—symbols of our economic and military power—shocked us to awareness that the technologies of international trade brought with them the dangers of nations without barriers, a world without walls. Who would have guessed that our full-blown awareness of the "New World Order" would come not through our prowess in transnational profitmaking, but through the anguish of terrorist attacks?

Globalization—the interlocking of all systems of ecology and human society throughout the world—is the natural outcome of free market capitalist expansion. International economic pacts on trade and financing dictate every nation's economic policies, including those of social welfare. Although America's economic and political leaders have global economic interests, they remain isolationist with regards to the by-products of their profit making: environmental pollution, poverty, health crises, crime, and war. With the end of the Cold War in the Reagan era, what corporate leaders saw as a *fait accomplis* since World War II—the "New World Order"—became a fact of international policy.

Because any nation's social programs depend on government spending, and because our nation's economic well-being is powered by transnational corporations, we need to understand that corporations determine the thrust of social welfare. Corporations are legal entities without concern for the common good except as it affects their goal, and notwithstanding the good and decent people who staff them, profit is that goal. Workers are the costliest parts of production, and it makes sense that cheaper labor means more profit.

From that perspective, we can more easily understand the withdrawal of help for workers and for the secondary labor force comprised most often of women and minorities. They are just not needed, and will not be as long as technology and low wages in developing countries keep production high. Requiring work or earned income for programs such as TANF is an unrealistic demand: good-paying jobs are not available. Low-paying service jobs leave workers even deeper in poverty and despair. At the end, they and their children—the potential next generation of workers—can simply disappear. Though not a planned strategy, the idea is simple enough: If we don't need them, why feed them?

On the other hand, corporations do feed the government. In 1994 the top 500 U.S. corporations produced 63 percent of the Gross National Product.[224] For that, the government pays corporate welfare handsomely: depending on who tallies the statistics, from $85 billion to $125 billion annually in government subsidies. However, we unknowingly pay a much higher cost. Transnational corporations have stepped outside the national scope to form their own trade agreements, and although nations may sign the treaties, they are written by transnational corporations. The North American Free Trade Agreement (NAFTA), for example, took an estimated 395,000 jobs from the United States to Mexico, where workers earn about $5.00 a day as compared to the U.S. minimum wage of $5.15 per hour, or compared more strikingly with the production worker wage of $17.70 per hour.[225]

Money is not the primary cost, however. The loss of our social morality, the loss of people productive in ways other than income, the loss of the environment to the wastemaking of the corporations—these cannot be recouped. The American poor, women, people of color, and other "unwanted" groups represent a conceptual microcosm of what is happening in the rest of the world. Ignoring the needs of individual nations or the purpose of the United Nations as a global over-seer, transnational corporations have formed their own worldwide trade organizations to foster profits, and they are recolonizing the peoples of the world to their own purposes.

The Organization for Economic Cooperation and Development (OECD) is composed of nations in the Northern Hemisphere. Ninety percent of all transnationals are based in the Northern Hemisphere, more than half from five nations: France, Germany, the Netherlands, Japan, and the United States. Their organizations include the World Trade Organization, the World Bank, and the International Monetary Fund (IMF), which carry out and support trade agreements such as the General Agreement on Tariffs and Trade (GATT), which has been called a corporate "bill of rights." The European Economic Community (EEC), thought at first to be a union of nations, protects European trade, while NAFTA protects North American trade. They are not in competition: They protect their corporations from government infringement on profit. General Motors and Ford exceed the combined Gross Domestic Product (GDP) of all sub-Saharan Africa, and fifty-one of the largest 100 world economies are corporations. Transnationals hold 90 percent of all technology and product patents in the world, and handle 70 percent of all trade.[226]

The World Bank and the IMF were intended to aid the Southern nations in economic development. However, when such nations do not meet service payments on those loans, the financial institutions step in to tell them what social programs they must abolish and what and how much they must produce for export. Formerly self-supporting nations, now in debt, must import food and other necessities. Their social programs, including education, health, employment benefits, and public assistance, have been slashed. In 1992 the interest paid on those debts exceeded $160 million—more than two and a half times the size of all foreign aid.[227]

In 2000 the World Bank and the IMF forgave some $34 billion in loans to their twenty-two poorest nation debtors, ostensibly to help them develop programs to help their poor. Just the service on their probably unpayable debts cripple many such developing nations. For example, Zambia owes the World Bank and the IMF nearly twice its annual gross national product—$5.5 billion—and pays $168 million a year on debt service. Therefore, it supports education at only $70 million and health at $76 million. Somewhat less than half of these nations' debts were forgiven, and that depended on conditions that they continue economic, social, and governance reforms.[228]

Transnationals, either directly or indirectly through such mechanisms as the World Bank and IMF, command 80 percent of all land cultivated for export crops.[229] While fostering an expanding international trade system, more than half the earth's population—over 3.5 billion people—are too poor to buy those goods. A fifth of the population of the Southern Hemisphere goes hungry every night, a quarter lacks access to even a basic necessity like safe drinking water, and a third—more than 1 billion people, 70 percent of them women—live in a state of abject poverty.[230]

The seeming all-encompassing power of the transnational corporations include the Multilateral Agreement on Investments (MAI), which gave them a kind of "citizen power" within nations to:

1. Open all sectors of a nation's economy to foreign companies
2. Require states and localities to treat foreign companies the same as local companies
3. Make it unnecessary to hire locally or pay local wages
4. Allow investors to directly challenge laws and seek monetary damages in international courts.[231]

The MAI

> would accelerate economic globalization by severely restricting the ability of national and local governments to regulate corporate investment, including social, economic, and environmental goals. It would give investors and corporations unprecedented legal standing to directly sue governments in international courts for breaking the agreements' rules.[232]

Today, the world is rife with new or proposed economic agreements. The European OECD put into effect its euro currency system on January 1, 2002. Mexico, El Salvador, Guatemala, and Honduras signed an economic accord in June 2001 to promote tourism, trade, education and antidisaster planning and to improve road, rail, air, and sea links. Mexico also has free trade agreements with Costa Rica and Nicaragua and is negotiating with Panama and Belize,[233] in addition to its NAFTA agreement. The thirty-four Western Hemisphere nations, excluding Cuba, plan to create the world's largest free-trade zone (Free Trade Area of the Americas, FTAA) by 2005, to stretch from the Arctic to the tip of South America.[234] In Africa, thirty-five countries ratified a pact for an Organization of African Unity (OAU), which intends to set up an African Central Bank, a court of justice, a single currency, and a parliament.[235]

These agreements represent *economic* rather than national or global interests or concerns. Representatives of the G-8 nations—United States, Japan, Germany, France, Britain, Italy, Canada, and Russia—meet regularly to plan for economic corporate growth. Social issues are usually given short shrift, although in 2001, G-8 did create a health fund of $1.88 billion to help poor nations fight AIDS.[236] Usually, though, when global issues conflict with profit, nations and world organizations tend to be less charitable. For example, the 1997 Kyoto Protocol, intended to reduce greenhouse gas emissions to the 1990 level, was rejected by G. W. Bush despite its acceptance by 178 other nations and despite power plant emissions in the United States exceeding those of 146 other nations combined.[237] His reason: Energy production would be harmed. Other U.S. actions against ecological problems include cutting aid for global warming to Third World countries (reduced by $41 million from 2000's $165 million);[238] revocation of EPA reductions on arsenic in drinking water from 50 to 10 parts per million (lumber and mining industries lobby); and plans to allow mining and oil drilling in the Alaskan Arctic National Wildlife Refuge.[239] Corporations have their own reasons for denying help with social issues. Becker notes that

> Profit-oriented companies will not invest the half-billion dollars and more required to research and develop effective drugs for major diseases if they cannot price them sufficiently high to recoup their investments.[240]

While present-day agreements on antiterrorism have visibly united the world, economic treaties previous to September 11 already had united the political economy of the world through transnational corporations. The terrorist attacks on America were a logical aftermath of terrorist attacks elsewhere that gained little international attention or retaliation: America has become the *symbol* of transnational corporate power over the nations of the world and of homogenization, forced and otherwise, of people and of cultures.

Conclusion: Futureword

The 104th Congress and Presidents Bush, Clinton, and G. W. Bush legitimized control by the wealthy in the legislative, judicial, and administrative branches of government, undercutting the promises of the nation for equal opportunity and equal treatment under the law. In addition, they have reinvested patriarchy—control of women, children, and workers—with a new "morality" that defies humankind's vision of social morality.

We know how to end poverty. Guaranteed annual incomes such as SSI and EITC, even if only a toe in the door, would move people beyond scratching for existence in America. The mechanisms are there, through Social Security and the Internal Revenue Service. What we lack is the moral foresight to accomplish it. We have taken another road, forcing the burdens of harsh values on the already overburdened poor while we pay homage to the rich. Our social aim today is not to end poverty but to make profits, and the targets of society's largesse are not the poor but the rich.

This has set new patterns into society, patterns that divide us and set us against one another. They include rivalries among the poor and near-poor, growing dissension between white and nonwhite people, the polarization of income, and a tacit approval of violence on both private and political levels. This new "tribalism" is often based on race and demonstrates itself in local militia groups, the rise of hate groups such as the Aryan nation, the bombing in Oklahoma City, and increasingly violent federal retaliation against dissidents such as the Branch Davidians at Waco or the siege at Ruby Ridge. Gil says,

> History reveals that societal violence . . . can be traced to the use of coercive measures concerning the organization of work and the exchange and distribution of products of work. . . . Coercive measures became institutionalized . . . [which justify] established, inegalitarian conditions of life and work.[241]

We have created a "Third-World citizenry" within the United States, a neocolonization of our disadvantaged.[242] With wage labor controlled, a segment of our population walled off in urban ghettos killing one another and being killed in "drug wars," and social programs limited, proscribed, and deteriorated, a small group of moneyed elite nevertheless continues to increase profits and reap rewards in the destruction of lives.

Social welfare does not exist in a vacuum. It is a product of the "moral state," influenced by and dependent on the political economy of the nation. Therefore, its policies are fundamentally political and responsive to the requirements of the few who hold economic power. Although altruism and its connection with spirituality have existed from earliest times, rarely has altruism—or love—been enough to institute or maintain policies and programs that did not offer advantages to the elite. Social programs usually occurred because they helped to control economic production or civil activism. On the other hand, the presence of social reformers, including social workers, has brought constant altruistic pressure to change social control to socially moral treatment.

We are now at a moral and professional crossroad, with the conservative elite muscling out the poor. We have new challenges to recognize. One is the legitimation of racism and sexism under the guise of "personal responsibility" that sets up people for problems, blame, and punishment to accomplish the ends of the elite. We are involved in that social control and must find ways to turn its pernicious aspects away from the vulnerable. We must also understand the place work and Puritan morality have in our society. They are *values* rather than facts of life and, given the intent of those who legislate for us, have turned us full circle to the hatred of those who, for whatever reason, differ from the "norm." Another, perhaps greater challenge is the international one. Transnational corporations, by and large, control nations and their political economies—including the United States—and, by extension, their citizenry. We must understand the implications of the global arena on our work at more local levels.

Like those citizens in the United States whose lives are Third World in nature, we have neglected to understand the impact of corporate power and arrogance on the Third World nations themselves. In retrospect, we should not have been so surprised at the heartbreaking attack on America, since America is the symbol, warranted or not, of inequality among people and their lives and work across the world. Nor can we predict the impact of the war against international terrorism on social welfare within the United States, except that it will be costly. This is not a war about nations or governments; rather, though we may refuse to recognize it, this war is about world economics, the decline of national cultures, and the ease of use of technologies to destroy instead of construct—factors that, in fact, war has always been about.

Some of us see social evolution as linear, progressing from past to future, and we often picture our historical cycles as a wheel rolling ever onward. However, looking at social welfare from the perspective of the synergy of politics, economics, and religion, we might better perceive a wheel spinning on its axis rather than its rim. It does not go forward; it remains ever in motion but grinds our lives ever finer. And while it grinds out our social evolution, our moral evolution stays at the hub of the wheel, unchanged and unchanging in past and perhaps future millennia.

We see a powerful elite making decisions about those without power—the poor, women, children, workers, and "outgroups"—those who are different in terms of religion, ethnicity, or a myriad value designations that "they" are not as good (moral, fit, intelligent, whatever) as "us." In this sense, "welfare" has nothing to do with the common good. It is a tactic, a strategy, playing on the needs of certain groups, promising them aid in their desperation in return for their conformity to oppressive systems. Its purpose is to reify systems of power and maintain control for the betterment or profit of those in power. Only the arena is different: from small tribal societies in 6000 B.C. to the world economic political system today. The winners are the same: those who redefine all kinds of morality to fit their own world views. The losers are the same: those who, for whatever reasons, are shunted from power. And the spoils remain the same: increasing accumulations of wealth and power beyond all reasonable world reality.

We began this journey through the history of social welfare by talking about love. Yet, through much of the book, our topics have seemed far from the idea of love and very much about social control of our society's vulnerable groups. For women, it has meant giving only enough to eke out their lives if they are dependent on public resources. For the poor, welfare has meant providing benefits to quell their revolt against inequities. For people who are "different," whether in appearance, religion, or other characteristics, it has meant depriving them of equality in human rights so that they can be exploited. Racism in America has complicated and augmented exploitation of each of our oppressed groups.

From the time humankind began, four species characteristics have existed: curiosity, the use of tools (including use of people as tools), greed, and altruism. The first three have led us into a new global society, very often at the cost of the fourth. But we do not have to continue on that path: We can choose love instead. It is unconditional love for humanity in all its colors, forms, and features that inspires the best part of social welfare, and we must not become blind to that vision. Love is not enough to change the world, but it is surely the best place to begin. And there is still time.

Study Questions

1. Explain the synergistic cycle of social welfare.
2. Explain why the "Contract with America" and TANF ended American social responsibility.

3. What it the "devolution of public assistance"? Give examples at each political level.

4. What new or revised policies under Presidents Bush, Clinton, and G. W. Bush provided welfare for the wealthy?

5. What policies in the same period of time supplied corporate welfare?

6. What were the three most important social welfare acts in the Clinton administration? Explain why you believe each was important.

7. What is the significance for social welfare of the emerging economic accords among nations?

Notes

1. Howard J. Karger, "Income Maintenance Programs and the Reagan Domestic Agenda," *Journal of Sociology and Social Work*, Vol. 19, no. 1 (March 1992), p. 51.

2. Joel A. Devine and James D. Wright, *The Greatest of Evils: Urban Poverty and the American Underclass* (New York: Aldine de Gruyter, 1993), p. 80.

3. David Macarov, *Work and Welfare: The Unholy Alliance* (Beverly Hills, CA: Sage Publications, 1980), p. 201.

4. Frederick C. Thayer (1997, Fall). "The Holy War on Surplus Americans: Soviet Dogma, Old-Time Religion, and Classical Economics," *Social Policy* (Fall 1997), pp. 8–18. p. 13.

5. Thayer, "Holy War," p. 17.

6. Beth Belton, "National Debt Expected to Hit $5 Trillion," New Jersey *Courier–Post* (Aug. 28, 1995), p. 6D.

7. U.S. Office of Management and Budget 2000, *A Citizen's Guide to the Federal Budget: Budget of the United States Government FY 2000*. Available: http://w3.access.gpo.gov/usbudget/fy2000/guide02.html, p. 4.

8. U.S. Office of Management and Budget 2000, *A Citizen's Guide to the Federal Budget: Budget of the United States Government FY 2000*. Available: http://w3.access.gpo.gov/usbudget/fy2000/guide04.html, p. 1.

9. Ibid., p. 7

10. Children's Defense Fund, *CDF Reports* (Washington, D.C.: CDF, Dec. 1994), pp. 4–5.

11. Diana DiNitto, *Social Welfare: Politics and Public Policy*, 4th ed. (Needham, MA: Allyn & Bacon, 1995), p. 60.

12. U.S. Office of Management and Budget 2000, *A Citizen's Guide to the Federal Budget: Budget of the United States Government FY 2000*. Available: http://w3.access.gpo.gov/usbudget/fy2000/guide02.html, p. 4.

13. U.S. Office of Management and Budget 2001, *A Citizen's Guide to the Federal Budget: Budget of the United States Government FY 2001*. Available: http://w3.access.gpo.gov/usbudget/fy2001/guide02.html, p. 9.

14. David S. Broder, "States Will Only Compound Federal Losses Affecting Poor," New Jersey *Courier–Post* (Oct. 2, 1995), p. 5A.

15. Ibid.

16. Sam Walker, "200 Day Drive by GOP Slices Federal Programs," *Christian Science Monitor* (Aug. 7, 1995), pp. 1, 15.

17. U.S. Department of Health and Human Services Administration, Office of Family Assistance, "AFDC Information Memo," to replace first four pages of "Characteristics and Financial Circumstances of AFDC Recipients FY 92." Mimeographed memo Dec. 12, 1994, no. ACF 1M-94–7.

18. Children's Defense Fund, *Welfare Reform Briefing Book* (Washington, D.C.: CDF, Jan. 1995), Table 1, p. 1.

19. Ibid.

20. Children's Defense Fund, *CDF Reports* (March 1995), p. 8.

21. U.S. Department of Health and Human Services, "Aid to Families with Dependent Children (AFDC) Information Memo no. ACF 1M-94–7" (mimeograph). Dec. 12, 1994, p. 1.

22. Mark Robert Rank, *Living on the Edge: The Realities of Welfare in America* (New York: Columbia University Press, 1994), p. 23.

23. Gannett News Service, "Facts About Welfare," New Jersey *Courier–Post* (Jan. 8, 1995), p. 9A.

24. Rank, *Living on the Edge,* pp. 116–118.

25. Children's Defense Fund, *CDF Reports* (Jan. 1995), pp. 4–5.

26. Children's Defense Fund "Contract with America Unfair to Children," *CDF Reports* Vol. 16, no. 2 (Washington, D.C.: CDF, Jan. 1995), p. 2.

27. Ron Jackson, NASW Government Relations, Action Network for Social Education and Research, "Child Welfare and Training Programs (Title IV-E and IV-B)." E-mail transmitted Feb. 12, 1996.

28. Children's Defense Fund, *CDF Reports,* Vol. 16, no. 4 (Washington, D.C.: CDF, March 1995), p. 4.

29. Children's Defense Fund, *Welfare Reform Briefing Book* (Washington, D.C.: CDF, June 1995), p. 11.

30. Children's Defense Fund, *CDF Reports,* Vol. 16, no. 10 (Washington, D.C.: CDF, Sept. 1995), p. 2.

31. Steven V. Roberts, Dorian Friedman, and Kalia Hetter, "Reform by 1000 Cuts," *U.S. News and World Report* (July 31, 1995), pp. 22–24.

32. James M. Fendrich, Mamie Miller, and Tim Nichel, "It's the Budget, Stupid: A Policy Analysis of Clinton's First Budget," *Journal of Sociology and Social Welfare,* Vol. 21, no. 4 (Dec. 1994), p. 18.

33. Ed Lazere, "Welfare Balances After Three Years of TANF Block Grants," Center on Budget and Policy Priorities. Available: http://www.cbpp.org/1-12-2000wel.html, pp. 1, 21.

34. Zoe Euberger, "TANF Expenditures Increased in the Last Fiscal Year," Center on Budget and Policy Priorities. Available: http://www.cbpp.org/11-1-01wel.html.

35. Ruth E. Murphy, e-mail correspondence to welfarem-L@american.edu, March 13, 1998.

36. Administration for Children and Families. Office of Legislative Affairs and Budget, "All-Purpose Table: Fiscal Years 2000–2003." Available: http://www.acf.dhhs.gov/programs/olab/budget/apt02.htm, p. 5.

37. Children's Defense Fund, *State of America's Children: 1998* (Washington, D.C.: CDF, 1998), Table B5, "Child Support Enforcement 1995," p. 112.

38. Department of Health and Human Services, Administration for Children and Families Office of Child Support Enforcement, "Child Support Enforcement: A Clinton Administration Priority." Available: http://www/acf.dhhs.gov/programs/scs/fct/980317b.html, p. 1.

39. Ibid., pp. 3–4.

40. Children's Defense Fund, *State of America's Children: 1998,* pp. 39–40.

41. Ibid., p. 41.

42. Ibid., pp. 30–32.

43. Ibid.

44. U.S. Department of Health and Human Services, Administration for Children and Families, *HHS Fact Sheet.* Available http://www.acf.dhhs.gov/news/press/1998/cc/fund.html, p. 2.

45. U.S. Department of Health and Human Services, Administration for Children and Families, Office of Legislative Affairs and Budget, "All-Purpose Table: Fiscal Years 2000–2002," p. 2.

46. Thayer, "Holy War," p. 13.

47. 104th Congress, 1st session (January 4, 1995), H.R. 4 (Washington, D.C.: U.S. Government Printing Office, 1995), p. 1.

48. Barbara Ehrenreich, "Real Babies, Illegitimate Debates," *Time* (Aug. 2, 1994), p. 90.

49. Joseph P. Shapiro and Andrea R. Wright, "Sins of the Fathers," *U.S. News and World Report* (Aug. 14, 1995), pp. 51–52.

50. David Van Bierna, "The Storm Over Orphanages," *Time* (Dec. 12, 1994), pp. 58–62.

51. Robert Bryce, "Texas Stamps a New Brand on Job Training Programs," *Christian Science Monitor* (Sept. 19, 1995), p. 3.

52. Jeremy Rifkin, *End of Work*. Cited in William Raspberry, "End of Work," New Jersey *Courier–Post* (June 13, 1995), p. 9A.

53. Sonya Ross, "Poll: Americans Still Want to Fight Poverty," New Jersey *Courier–Post* (Dec. 8, 1994), p. 11A.

54. U.S. Department of Health and Human Services, Administration for Children and Families. "Statistics: Change in TANF Caseloads Since Enactment of New Welfare Law." Available: http://www.acf.dhhs.gov/news/stats/aug-dec.html, p. 1.

55. Ibid.

56. Ibid., and ACF Statistics Chart, "Temporary Assistance for Needy Families October 2000–June 2001." Available: http://www.acf.dhhs.gov/news/stats/recipients.html, p. 2.

57. Sheldon Danziger, "After Welfare Reform and an Economic Boom: Why Is Child Poverty Still so Much Higher in the U.S. than in Europe?" Paper presented at the 8th International Research Seminar of the Foundation for International Studies on Social Securities, "Support for Children and Their Parents," Sigtuna, Sweden, June 2001, p. 1.

58. Gene Koretz, "Economic Trends: How Welfare to Work Worked," *Business Week* (September 24, 2001), p. 28.

59. Danziger, "After Welfare Reform and an Economic Boom," p. 1.

60. Ibid., p. 18, Table 1-1.

61. Center on Budget and Policy Priorities, "Average Incomes of Very Poor Families Fell During Early Years of the Welfare Reform, Study Finds," Aug. 22, 1999. Available: http://www.cbpp.org/8-22-99wel.html, pp. 1–2.

62. Ron Haskins, "Welfare Reform: A Mother's Work," *Washington Post* online. Available: http://www.washingtonpost.com/wp-dyn/articles/A18589-2001N0v.12.html, p.1.

63. Ibid.

64. Center on Budget and Policy Priorities, "Testimony of Ed Lazere Before the House Committee on Education and the Workforce, Oct. 7, 1999." Available: http://www.cbpp.org/10-7-99wel.html, p. 1.

65. Pamela LoPrest, "How Are Families That Left Welfare Doing? A Comparison of Early and Recent Welfare Leavers," Urban Institute, April 2001. Available: http://www.newfederalism.urban.org/html/series_b/b36/b36.html, p. 5.

66. Center on Budget and Policy Priorities, "Poverty Rate Among Working Single-Mother Families Remained Stagnant in Late 1990s Despite Strong Economy," Aug. 16, 2001. Available: http://www.cbpp.org/8-16-01wel-pr.html, pp. 1–2.

67. Danziger, "After Welfare Reform and an Economic Boom," pp. 13–14.

68. Ibid., p. 18, Table 1-1.

69. "TANF Fact Sheet" (1998). Department of Health and Human Services. Available: http:www.acf.dhhs.gov/news/caseload.htm, p. 1.

70. Daniel Weisman, "Litigation Strategies and 'Welfare Reform'." Paper presented at Baccalaureate Program Directors Meeting, Albuquerque, NM, October 5–9, 1998.

71. U.S. Census Bureau, "Poverty: 2000 Highlights," March 2001 Supplement to the Current Population Survey (CPS), A Sample Survey of Approximately 50,000 Households Nationwide. Available: http://www.census.gov/hhcs/poverty00.html, p. 1 of 2.

72. U.S. Census Bureau, Current Population Survey, March 2001. "Three-Year Average Median Household Income and Poverty Rate by Race and Hispanic Origin: 1998–2000." Available: http://www.census.gov/hhcs/www/img/incpov00/fig08.html.

73. U.S. Census Bureau, Current Population Survey, March 1961 to 2001. "Women's-to-Men's Median Earnings Rations: 1960 to 2000. Available http://www.censjs.gov/hhcs/www/img/incpov00/fig11.

74. Daniel H. Weinberg, "Press Briefing on 2000 Income and Poverty Estimates." U.S. Census Bureau, Income and Poverty Press Briefing. September 25, 2001. Available: http://www .census.gov/hhcs/income/income00/prs01asc.html, 7.2.

75. DiNitto, *Social Welfare*, p. 137.

76. "NASW Summary of Provisions, PRWORA 1996," *Government Relations Update* (Washington, D.C.: NASW, August 7, 1996).

77. Social Security Bulletin: Annual Statistical Supplement 2000. SSI Summary. Table 7.A1. "Number of Persons Receiving Federally Administered Payments Total Amount and Average Monthly Amount, by Source of Payment, Category, and Age, December 1999," Couples SSI income from SSI Summary Table 7.A2, p. 263.

78. Office of Management and Budget, "Income Security," Table 14-1. "Federal Resources in Support of Income Security. Available: http://www.whiteehouse.gov/omb/budge/ fy2002/bud14.html, p. 3 of 7.

79. Children's Defense Fund, *CDF Reports* (Washington, D.C.: CDF, July 1995), p. 2.

80. Danziger, "After Welfare Reform and an Economic Boom," p. 20, endnote 4.

81. United States Embassy, Japan, "Fact Sheet: President Clinton on Economic Accomplishments," released January 9, 2001. Available: http://usembassy.state.gov/japan/www .je132.htm.

82. Isaac Shapiro, Allen Dupree, and James Sly, "An Estimated 12 Million Low- and Moderate-Income Families—with 24 Million Children—Would Not Benefit from Bush Tax Plan," Center on Budget and Policy Priorities, February 7, 2001. Available: www.treas.gov/tigta/ reports/2000401fr.html.

83. Ibid.

84. Jami Curley and Michael Sherraden, *Policy Report: The History and Status of Children's Allowances: Policy Background for Children's Savings Accounts* (St. Louis, MO: Center for Social Development, Washington University in St. Louis, 1998), p. 13.

85. *AARP Bulletin*, Vol. 36, no. 6 (June 1995), p. 13.

86. Daniel P. Moynihan, "The Case Against Entitlement Cuts," *Modern Maturity* (Nov.–Dec. 1994), pp. 13–14.

87. Ibid.

88. Ibid.

89. "The Federal Budget Dollar: Where Does It Come From?" *Citizen's Guide to the Federal Budget*. Budget of the United States Government FY 1999. Office of the President (Washington, D.C.: Government Printing Office, 1998).

90. "OASDI Current-Pay Benefits: Summary," *Social Security Bulletin Annual Statistical Supplement 2001*. Table 5.A1, "Number and average monthly benefit, by type of benefit, race, age, and sex" (Washington, D.C., December 2000), p. 159.

91. "The Federal Budge Dollar: Where Does It Come From?" *Citizen's Guide to the Federal Budget*. Budget of the United States Government FY 1999. Office of the President (Washington, D.C.: Government Printing Office, 1999).

92. "OASDI Current-Pay Benefits: Summary," pp. 159–162.

93. Social Security Bulletin: Annual Statistical Supplement 2000, p. 2.

94. David A. Smith, "Later Retirement: A 'Disaster' for Many," *AARP Bulletin* (Nov. 1998), Vol. 39, no. 11, p. 29.

95. Ibid., p. 12.

96. Ibid., p. 29.

97. Stan Hinden, "Raw Deal for Women?" *AARP Bulletin*, Vol. 42, no. 8 (September 2001), p. 18.

98. Stan Hinden, ibid., pp. 18–19.

99. Ibid., p. 19.

100. Diana DiNitto, *Social Welfare: Politics and Public Policy,* 4th ed. (Needham, MA: Allyn & Bacon, 1995), pp. 214–216.

101. U.S. Department of Agriculture, Food and Nutrition Services, "FSS Summary, December 2001." Available: http://www.fns.usda.gov/pd/fssummar.htm, pp. 1–2.

102. U.S. Department of Agriculture, Food and Nutrition Services, "FSS Summary, December, 21, 2001." Available: http://www.fns.usda.gov/pd/fsmonthly.htm, p. 1.

103. Children's Defense Fund, *State of America's Children: 1998*, p. 53.

104. U.S. Department of Agriculture, Food and Nutrition Services, "Overview: December 2001." Available: http://fns.usda.gov/pd/Overview.htm.

105. DiNitto, *Social Welfare*, p. 61.

106. U.S. Department of Agriculture, Food and Nutrition Services, "FSS Summary, December 21, 2001," pp. 1–2.

107. U.S. Department of Agriculture, Food and Nutrition Services, "Cost of Food Distribution Programs December 21, 2001." Available: http://www.fns.usda.gov/pe/fd$sum.htm, pp. 1–2.

108. Children's Defense Fund, *State of America's Children: 1998*, p. 33.

109. Barbara Sard and Jennifer Daskal, "Housing and Welfare Reform: Some Background Information," Center on Budget and Policy Priorities, Washington, D.C. (Feb. 12, 1998), p. 7.

110. Children's Defense Fund, *State of America's Children: 1998*, p. 16.

111. Ibid., p. 1.

112. Children's Defense Fund, *State of America's Children: 1998*, p. 17.

113. Sard and Daskal, "Housing and Welfare Reform," p. 8, fn. 3.

114. Edward Scanlon, "Homeownership and Its Impacts: Implications for Housing Policy for Low-Income Families," Working Paper 96–2 (1996), Center for Social Development, Washington University, St. Louis, MO, p. 9.

115. "Mortgages May Be Difficult for Minorities to Obtain," Davenport, IA: *Quad City Times* (Nov. 15, 1998), p. 5B.

116. U.S. Census Bureau, Census 2000 Special Reports, "Emergency and Transitional Shelter Population: 2000," unpublished tabulations. Available: http://census.gov/prod/2001pubs/censr01-2.pdf, pp. 6, 15.

117. "Hunger and Homelessness Up Sharply in Major U.S. Cities," *Conference of Mayors' Twenty-seven City Survey*, released December 12, 2001. Available: usmayor.org.

118. National Coalition for the Homeless, "How Many People Experience Homelessness?" *NCH Fact Sheet #2* (February 1999). Available: http://nch.ari.net/numbers.htm, pp. 2–3.

119. U.S. Department of Housing and Urban Development. "Homelessness: Programs and the People They Serve: An Overview of Homeless Clients: Demographic Characteristics." Available: http://www.huduserorg/publications/homeless/homelessness/ch_2b.htm, p. 5.

120. National Coalition for Homelessness "2001 Budget and Homelessness" (June 30, 2000). Available: http://nch.ari.net/fy2001.htm, p.2.

121. Children's Defense Fund, *CDF Reports* (Washington, D.C.: CDF, July 1995), p. 2.

122. Jami Curley and Michael Sherraden, *Policy Report: The History and Status of Children's Allowances: Policy Background for Children's Savings Accounts* (St. Louis, MO: Center for Social Development, Washington University in St. Louis, 1998), p. 13.

123. Children's Defense Fund, *The State of America's Children: 1998*, p. 24.

124. Ibid., pp. 26–30.

125. Donna E. Shalala, Secretary of Health and Human Services, HCFA Press Office, "HHS Approves First SCHIP Waivers," January 18, 2001.

126. U.S. Department of Health and Human Services. "State Children's Health Insurance Program: Final allotments to States, the District of Columbia, and U.S. Territories and Commonwealth for Fiscal Year 2002," *Federal Register*, V. 66, no. 208 (10-26-2001), p. 54247.

127. Danziger, "After Welfare Reform and an Economic Boom," p. 3.

128. Health Care Financing Administration, "Highlights: National Health Expenditures 1999." Available: http://www.hcfa.gov/stats/nhe-oact/hilites.htm, p. 1.

129. Norm Brewer, "Several Thorny Issues Still Await Congress," New Jersey *Courier–Post* (Oct. 1, 1995), p. 15A.

130. Johnathan S. Landay, editorial in *Christian Science Monitor* (July 28, 1995), p. 20.

131. *U.S. News and World Report* (July 3, 1995), p. 13. A Report from Health Care Financing Administration, Congressional Research Service, based on *Statistical Abstracts*, 1994.

132. George W. Bush, *Welcome to the White House*, "Modernize and Reform Medicare, 2001." Available: http://www.whitehouse.gov/infocus/medicare.htm, p. 1.

133. Ibid.

134. Health Care Financing Administration, "Highlights," p. 1.

135. Office of Management and Budget, Table S-13, "Outlay Total by Function." Available: http://www.whitehouse.gov/omb/budget/fy2002/budiv_13.htm, p. 1 of 2.

136. U.S. Bureau of the Census, *Statistical Abstracts of the United States* (Washington, D.C.: U.S. Government Printing Office, 1994), Table 16.2, "Medicaid Recipients (thousands) and Payments (millions), 1980 and 1982," p. 116.

137. Children's Defense Fund, *CDF Reports*, Vol. 16, no. 9 (Aug. 1995), p. 7; report from Health Care Financing Administration, Division of Medicaid Statistics, p. 7.

138. Children's Defense Fund, *CDF Reports* (July 1995), p. 1.

139. Health Care Financing Administration, Congressional Research Service, *Statistical Abstracts of the United States: 1994.* Reported in *U.S. News and World Report* (July 3, 1995), p. 13.

140. National Association of Social Workers, *NASW Newsletter,* mimeograph (Spring 1995), p. 3.

141. Children's Defense Fund, *CDF Reports,* Vol. 16, no. 5 (Washington, D.C.: CDF, April 1995), p. 1.

142. Children's Defense Fund, *The State of America's Children: 1998,* pp. 30–32.

143. *Statistical Abstracts of the United States,* Sec. 3 Health and Nutrition, Table 159, "National Health Expenditures by Source of Payment, 1990 to 1997, and Projections, 1999 to 2002." Available: http://www.census.gov/prod/2001pubs/statab/sec03.pdf, p. 7.

144. Ibid., Table 172, "Medicaid Recipients and Payments 1990–1999," p. 11.

145. Health Care Financing Administration, "Highlights," p. 1.

146. Fendrich, Miller, and Nichel, "It's the Budget, Stupid," p. 7.

147. Frances Fox Piven and Richard Cloward, *Regulating the Poor* (New York: Random House, 1971).

148. Remember again the James Rule Treatise (*Insight and Social Betterment: Applied Social Science)* on the ways in which social conflicts, which have no solutions that will maintain the state of power of the few over the many, are redefined as social problems, implying that the powerful elite are working on solutions to immediate needs. This also reinforces the status of social workers as agents of social control even though they are working at social treatment.

149. David Ho, "U.S. Prison Population Rising: Incarceration Rate May Top Russia as Highest in World," ABCNEWS.com, Washington, D.C., April 20, 2000. Available: http://my.abcnews .go.com/PRINTERFRIENDLY?...section/us/DailyNews/prisons000420.htm.

150. Alan Eisner, "Analysis: Huge U.S. Prison Population Social Cost Mounts" (Reuters) (Washington, D.C., January 2001). Available: http://www.mapinc.org/drugnews/v01/ n136/a02.html.

151. Ho, "U.S. Prison Population Rising."

152. Eisner, "Analysis."

153. Allen J. Beck and Christopher J. Mumola, "Prisoners in 1998," Substance Abuse and Mental Health Services Administration, "National Household Survey on Drug Abuse: Summary Report 1998" (Rockville, MD, 1999), p. 13; Bureau of Justice Statistics, *Sourcebook of Criminal Justice Statistics 1998* (Washington, D.C.: US Department of Justice, August 1999), p. 343. Available: http://www.lindesmith.org/news/DailyNews/2million_inmates.html.

154. Amnesty International, "Not Part of My Sentence: Violations of the Human Rights of Women in Custody" (Washington, D.C.: Amnesty International, March 1999), p. 1.

155. P. Thomas, "Study Suggests Black Male Prison Rate Impinges on Political Process," *The Washington Post* (January 30, 1997), p. A3.

156. Children's Defense Fund, *CDF Reports* (Dec. 1994), pp. 4–5.

157. Ibid.

158. United States Embassy, Japan, "Fact Sheet," pp. 7, 8.

159. William Waldman, "Clinton Administration FY 2000 Budget Proposal—Complete Summary," American Public Human Services Association (February 1999). Available: http:///www.aphasa.org/hotnews/00budget.htm.

160. "Clinton–Gore Administration Accomplishments: Progress by the Numbers," p. 2.

161. Robert Kilborn, Jr., "Seeking New Jobs after the Pink Slip," *Christian Science Monitor* (July 17, 1995), p. 1.

162. Molly Ivins, "Workers', Futures Hang on Result of Race for AFL-CIO Leadership," New Jersey *Courier–Post* (Sept. 4, 1995), p. 7A.

163. *U.S. News and World Report* (Aug. 7, 1995), p. 12.

164. "Unemployment Benefit Claims Rise to 4-Month High," Davenport, Iowa: *Quad City Times* (Nov. 13, 1998), p. 9A.

165. U.S. Embassy, Japan, "Fact Sheet," p. 1.

166. Center on Budget and Policy Priorities. "Increase in Number of Unemployed Over Past 12 Months Was Largest in Nearly 20 Years" (Washington, D.C., December 7, 2001), p. 1.

167. "Jobless Rate Reaches 5.7%," *Layfayette Journal and Courier* (December 8, 2001), p. A1.

168. Trish Nicholson, "50-Plus Workers Hit by Cutbacks," *The Nation,* AARP (Washington, D.C., October 2001), pp. 1, 24.

169. Center on Budget and Policy Priorities. "Increase in Number of Unemployed," p. 1.

170. DiNitto, *Social Welfare,* p. 376.

171. Justice Sandra Day O'Connor, writing for the majority, reported by Larry G. Gerber, "H-Net List for 'Putting the State Back in,'" AP story on ADARAND decision "High Court Delivers Strong Blow to Affirmative Action," Internet, July 1995.

172. Barbara Reynolds, "Let's Not Lose This Right," New Jersey *Courier–Post* (June 22, 1995), p. 9A.

173. Clarence Lusane, "Decline in Funding for Civil-Rights Agencies Is Cause for Concern," Progressive Media Project. Available: http://www.progressive.org/pmpbvc10.htm. The six agencies were: Department of Education Office of Civil Rights; U.S. Equal Employment Opportunity Commission; Department of Labor Office of Federal Contract Compliance Programs; Department of Justice Civil Rights Division; Department of Health and Human Services Office of Civil Rights; and Department of Housing and Urban Development Office of Fair Housing and Equal Opportunity.

174. "Military Discharges of Gays Up in 2000," *Quad City Times* (Davenport, IA), June 2, 2001, p. A1.

175. Partners Task Force for Gay and Lesbian Couples, "Defense of Marriage Act: Description and the Bill's Text." (2000). Available: http://www.buddybuddy.com/doma.htm.

176. Ibid.

177. William N. Eskridge, Jr., *Gaylaw: Challenging the Apartheid of the Closet* (Cambridge, MA: Harvard University Press, 1999), p. 232.

178. David Wagner, *What's Love Got to Do With It? A Critical Look at American Charity* (New York: The New Press, 2000), p. 131.

179. Ibid., p. 119.

180. "Sweet Charity," *U.S. News and World Report* (June 4, 2001), p. 10.

181. "Most State Welfare Programs Pass on Charitable Choice," *Quad-City Times* (Davenport, IA), March 20, 2001, p. A4.

182. Wagner, *What's Love Got to Do With It,* p. 105.

183. Wagner, *What's Love Got to Do With It,* p. 112.

184. Guy Halverson, "Giving by Firms Registers Big Jump," *Christian Science Monitor* (December 4, 2000), p. 19.

185. Wagner, *What's Love Got to Do With It,* pp. 112–113.

186. "The 50 Largest US Charities Ranked by Total Income," *Christian Science Monitor* (December 4, 2000), p. 16.

187. Molly Ivins, "GOP Just Keeps on Marching to Wrong (and Rich) Drummer," New Jersey *Courier–Post* (October 23, 1995), p. 3A.

188. All figures from Dave Skidmore, "Lawmakers Propose $500 Child Credit," New Jersey *Courier–Post* (October 23, 1995), p. 3A.

189. Bruce S. Jansson, *The Sixteen-Trillion Dollar Mistake* (New York: Columbia University Press, 2001), pp. 297, 309, 345.

190. John Miller, Citizens for Tax Justice, "Clinton and Congress Feed the Wealthy," *Dollars and Sense: What's Left in Economics* (Nov.–Dec. 1997). Available: http://www.dollarsandsense.org/issues/nov97/tax.html.

191. Ibid.

192. "Tax Cuts for the Rich," *International Workers Bulletin* (May 19, 1997). Available: http://www.wsws.org/prblic_html/iwb5-19taxcts.htm.

193. "Tax Cut Bonanza for the Wealthy." *International Workers Bulletin* (May 19, 1997), Available: http://www.wsws.org/pblic_html/8wb5-1919lead.htm.

194. Center on Budget and Policy Priorities, "Pathbreaking CBO Study Shows Dramatic Increases in both 1980s and 1990s in Income Gaps Between the Very Wealthy and Other Americans. (May 31, 2001). Available http://www.centeronbudget.org/5-31-01tax-pr.htm.

195. Iris J. Lav and Robert Greenstein, "Tax Bill Contains Only Modest Benefits for Middle Class Despite Its High Cost," Center on Budget and Policy Priorities (August 20, 1999). Available: http://www.cbpp.org/8-20-99tax.htm.

196. "Surprise Goodies from Uncle Sam," *U.S. News and World Report* (June 11, 2001), pp. 44–45.

197. Center on Budget and Policy Priorities, "Pathbreaking CBO Study."

198. Susan Roth, "Daschle: Tax Cut Hurt the Nation," *Lafayette Journal and Courier* (Lafayette, IN) (January 5, 2002), p. A.3.

199. "Corporate Welfare: A Special Report," *Time* (Nov. 9, 1998), p. 38.

200. David Espo, "Senate Votes Give to the Rich, Then Takes Away from the Poor," New Jersey *Courier–Post* (Oct. 14, 1995), p. 1A.

201. Molly Ivins, "Watt's Back: So Are (Ugh!) His Policies," New Jersey *Courier–Post* (March 27, 1995), p. 5A.

202. David Broder, "Best Way to Cut U.S. Budget: Attack on Corporate Welfare," New Jersey *Courier–Post* (May 24, 1995), p. 9A.

203. Mortimer B. Zuckerman, "The GOP Needs Some Education," *U.S. News and World Report* (Sept. 11, 1995), pp. 62, 74.

204. Karger, "Income Maintenance," pp. 9–11.

205. Ibid., p. 8.

206. Bernard Sanders, "And Now for Some Meaningful Hearings," *Christian Science Monitor* (Aug. 17, 1995), p. 19.

207. Citizens for Tax Justice, "Buy Now, Pay Later: How Generous Corporate Campaign Donors Save Billions in Taxes." Available: http://www.ctj.org/html/camptax.htm, p. 1.

208. Ibid., p. 2.

209. Ibid.

210. "Fat Cat Campaign Donors: Who They Are; What They Give," *Christian Science Monitor* (October 20, 2000), p. 24.

211. Ibid.

212. David R. Francis, "More Firms Find Tax Loopholes," *Christian Science Monitor* (October 20, 2000), pp. 1, 4.

213. Curt Anderson, "Senator: Corporate Pricing Schemes Cost U.S. $45 Billion," *Lafayette Journal and Courier* (Lafayette, IN) (November 22, 2001), p. A.3.

214. Johnathan Landay, "Congress, Clinton Battle over Antimissile System," *Christian Science Monitor* (Aug. 3, 1995), p. 3.

215. Johnathan Landay, "Pet Pork Projects Slip into GOP Defense Budget," *Christian Science Monitor* (Aug. 4, 1995), p. 3.

216. Johnathan Landay, "Pentagon Hit for Hiding Spending on 'Star Wars,'" *Christian Science Monitor* (Sept. 5, 1995), p. 3.

217. Johnathan Landay, "Political Futures, Jobs Hang on Defense Budget Choices," *Christian Science Monitor* (Sept. 12, 1995), p. 3.

218. Zuckerman, "The GOP Needs Some Education," p. 74.

219. Landay, "Pet Pork Projects," p. 3.

220. William D. Hartung and Michelle Ciarroca, "Star Wars Revisited: Still Dangerous, Costly, and Unworkable," *Foreign Policy in Focus*, Vol. 4, no. 24 (September 1999, revised April 2000). Available; http://www.foreignpolicy-infocus.org/briefs/vol4/v4n24star.html.

221. Ibid.

222. Ibid.

223. Ibid.

224. Office of Management and Budget, Budget of the United States Government, FY 2003, "Table 2-3. Total Spending by Function." Available: http://www.whitehouse.gov/omb/budget/fy2002/guide02/htm, p. 11. Accessed 12/27/01.

225. NAFTA Index, "Public Citizen: Global Trade Watch." Available: http://www.citizen.org/pctrade/naftaindex.htm.

226. Joshua Karliner, *The Corporate Planet* (San Francisco: Sierra Club Books, 1997), p. 5.

227. Ibid., p. 25.

228. Mike Crawley, "Rich Nations Grant Poorest Twenty-Two a Checkbook Reprieve," *Christian Science Monitor* (December 26, 2000), p. 7.

229. Karliner, *Corporate Planet*, p. 17.

230. Ibid., p. 22.

231. Friends of the Earth U.S., "OECD Multilateral Agreement on Investment: Fact Sheet." (Feb. 19, 1997). Available: http://www.igc.org/trac/feature/planet/maii_foe.html.

232. Karliner, *Corporate Planet*, p. 10.

233. "Central America Joins Mexico," *Quad-City Times* (Davenport, IA) (June 17, 2001), p. A9.

234. Geri Smith, with Elisabeth Malkin, Jonathan Wheatley, Paul Magnusson, Michael Arndt, and bureau reports, "The Free Trade Area of the Americas," *Business Week* (April 23, 2001), p. 62.

235. "Official: Thirty-five Countries Ratify African Pact," *Quad-City Times* (Davenport, IA), (April 8, 2002), p. A3.

236. "Leaders Create Health Fund at Summit to Combat AIDS," *Quad-City Times* (Davenport, IA) (July 21, 2001), p. A1.

237. David Gergen, "Warming to the Task," *U.S. News and World Report* (June 25, 2001), p. 76.

238. "Bush Wants to Cut Global Warming Aid to Third World," *Quad-City Times* (Davenport, IA) (July 7, 2001), p. A12.

239. "EPA to Revoke Rule on Arsenic in Water," *Quad-City Times* (Davenport, IA) (March 21, 2001), p. A13; Katharine Q. Seelye, "U.S. Quietly Reversing Clinton-Era Green Rules," *Indianapolis Star* (November 11, 2001), p. A4.

240. Earnest Becker. *The Denial of Death*. (New York, The Free Press, 1973), p. 57.

241. David G. Gil, "Work, Violence, Injustice, and War," *Journal of Sociology and Social Welfare*, Vol. 16, no. 1 (March 1989), pp. 41, 43.

242. Thanks to Glayds Robinson, MSW from Temple University.

Bibliography

AARP Bulletin, Vol. 36, no. 6 (June 1995).

Abbott, Edith. *Women in Industry: A Study of American Economic History.* New York: Arno Press, 1910, pp. 48–62.

Abbott, Edith. *Some American Pioneers in Social Welfare.* Chicago: University of Chicago Press, 1937.

Abramovitz, Mimi. "The Conservative Program Is a Women's Issue." *Journal of Sociology and Social Welfare,* Vol. 9, no. 3 (Sept. 1982), pp. 399–424.

Abramovitz, Mimi. "The Reagan Legacy: Undoing Class, Race, and Gender Accords." *Journal of Sociology and Social Welfare,* Vol. 19, no. 1 (March 1992), pp. 91–110.

Adams, Gordon. "Restructuring the National Defense Policy." In Alan Gartner, Colin Greer, and Frank Reismann, eds., *Beyond Reagan: Alternatives for the Eighties.* New York: Harper & Row, 1984.

Addams, Jane. *A Centennial Reader.* New York: Macmillan, 1964.

Aguirre, Lydia R. "The Meaning of the Chicano Movement." *Social Casework,* Vol. 55 (1971).

American Correctional Association report in the *Lafayette (Indiana) Journal and Courier,* Sept. 12, 1986, p. A7.

Amnesty International. "Not Part of My Sentence: Violations of the Human Rights of Women in Custody." Washington, D.C.: Amnesty International, March 1999.

Anderson, Charles. *Toward a New Sociology,* 2nd ed. Homewood, IL: Dorsey Press, 1974.

Anderson, Curt. "Senator: Corporate Pricing Schemes Cost U.S. $45 Billion." *Lafayette Journal and Courier* (Lafayette, IN), November 22, 2001, p. A3.

Anderson, Jack, and Dale van Atta. "Model Shelter or Workhouse?" *Washington Post,* July 21, 1985.

Anderson, Joseph. *Social Work Methods and Processes.* Belmont, CA: Wadsworth Publishing, 1981.

Arendt, Hannah. *On Revolution.* New York: Viking, 1963.

Aronowitz, Stanley. "Labor Is the Key," in Alan Gartner, Colin Greer, and Frank Reismann, eds., *Beyond Reagan: Alternatives for the Eighties.* New York: Harper & Row, 1984.

"Avoiding a Medical Catastrophe." *Lafayette (Indiana) Journal and Courier,* Oct. 30, 1986, p. A7.

Axinn, June, and Herman Levin. *Social Welfare: A History of the American Response to Need,* 2nd ed. New York: Harper & Row, 1982.

Badgett, M. V. Lee. "The Wage Effects of Sexual Orientation Discrimination." *Industrial and Labor Relations Review,* Vol. 48, p. 726.

Baigent, Michael, Richard Leigh, and Henry Lincoln. *Holy Blood, Holy Grail.* New York: Dell Publishing, 1982.

Barber, Elizabeth Wayland. *Women's Work: The First 20,000 Years.* New York: W.W. Norton and Co., 1994.

Baron, Salo W. A. *Social and Religious History of the Jews. Vol. 1: To the Beginning of the Christian Era.* New York: Columbia University Press, 1962.

Barrera, M., C. Munoz, and C. Ornelas. "The Barrio as an Internal Colony." In Harlan Hahn, editor, *Urban Affairs Annual Review,* Vol. 6. Beverly Hills, CA: Sage Publications, 1972.

Barrett, Richard J. "Lords of the Global Economy." *The Nation,* Dec. 19, 1994.

Beck, Allen J., and Christopher J. Mumola. "Prisoners in 1998," Substance Abuse and Mental Health Services Administration. "National Household Survey on Drug Abuse: Summary Report 1998. Rockville, MD, 1999.

Becker, Earnest. *The Denial of Death.* New York: Free Press, 1973.

Beeghly, Leonard. "Illusion and Reality in the Measurement of Poverty." *Social Problems,* Vol. 31, no. 3 (Feb. 1984), pp. 324–337.

Beers, Clifford. *A Mind That Found Itself.* Garden City, NY: Doubleday, 1935.

Bel, Leachman, and Alvin Schorr. *Public Policy and Income Distribution.* New York: New York University Center for Studies in Income Maintenance Policy, 1974.

Bell, Winifred. *Aid to Dependent Children.* New York: Columbia University Press, 1965.

Bell, Winifred. *Contemporary Social Welfare.* New York: Macmillan, 1983.

Belton, Beth. "National Debt Expected to Hit $5 Trillion." New Jersey *Courier–Post,* Aug. 28, 1995, p. 6D.

Benford, Gregory. "A Scientist's Notebook: Sex, Gender and Fantasy." *Fantasy and Science Fiction* (Sept. 1995), pp. 112–120.

Bennett, Lerone, Jr. *Before the Mayflower: A History of the Negro in America 1619–1964.* Chicago: Johnson Publishing Company, 1966.

Berch, Bettina. *The Endless Day: The Political Economy of Women and Work.* New York: Harcourt Brace Jovanovich, 1982.

Berry, Benjamin D. "Black Power and Straight White Males." In Glenn R. Bucher, ed., *Straight/White/Male.* Philadelphia: Fortress Press, 1976.

Bianchi, Eugene C., and Rosemary Radford Ruether, eds. *From Machismo to Mutuality: Essays on Sexism and Woman–Man Liberation.* New York: Paulist Press, 1976.

Blacker, C. P., ed. *Problem Families.* London: Eugenics Society, 1947.

Bloch, Marc. *Feudal Society: The Growth of Ties of Independence,* Vol. 1, translated by L. A. Maryont. Chicago: University of Chicago Press, 1964.

Bonacich, Edna. "Racism in Advanced Capitalist Society: Comments on William J. Wilson's *The Truly Disadvantaged.*" *Journal of Sociology and Social Welfare,* Vol. 16, no. 4 (Dec. 1989), pp. 41–55.

Booth, Sally Smith. *The Women of '76.* New York: Hastings House, 1973.

Braun, Peter. "Crime, Capitalism, and Black America." *Philadelphia New Observer,* Sept. 6, 1995.

Bremmer, Robert H. *From the Depths.* New York: New York University Press.

Bremner, Walter, ed. *Children and Youth in America: A Documentary History.* New York: Arno Press, 1969. Originally published in 1914.

Brewer, Norm. "Several Thorny Issues Still Await Congress." New Jersey *Courier–Post,* Oct. 1, 1995, p. 15A.

Brill, Naomi. *Teamwork: Working Together in the Human Services.* New York: J.B. Lippincott, 1976.

Brockway, Zebulon. *Fifty Years of Prison Service,* pp. 397–398. Discussed in Anthony M. Platt, *The Child Savers: The Invention of Delinquency,* 2d ed. Chicago: University of Chicago Press, 1977.

Broder, David S. "Best Way to Cut U.S. Budget: Attack on Corporate Welfare." New Jersey *Courier–Post,* May 24, 1995, p. 9A.

Broder, David S. "States Will Only Compound Federal Losses Affecting Poor." New Jersey *Courier–Post,* Oct. 2, 1995, p. 5A.

Broverman, I. K., D. M. Broverman, F. E. Clarkson, P. S. Rosenkrantz, and S. R. Vogel. "Sex Role Stereotypes and Clinical Judgments of Mental Health." *Journal of Counseling and Clinical Psychology,* Vol. 34 (1975), pp. 1–7.

Brown, Josephine Chapman. *Public Relief,* 1929–39. New York: Henry Holt, 1940.

Brown, Prudence. *Women, Children, and Poverty in America.* New York: Ford Foundation, Jan. 1985.

Bruere, Robert W. "The Good Samaritan, Inc." *Harper's Monthly Magazine,* Vol. 120 (August 1910).

Bryce, Robert. "Texas Stamps a New Brand on Job Training Programs." *Christian Science Monitor,* Sept. 19, 1995, p. 3.

Bucher, Glenn R., ed. *Straight/White/Male.* Philadelphia: Fortress Press, 1976.

Burbridge, Lynn C. "The Impact of Changes in Policy on the Federal Equal Employment Opportunity Effort." Washington, D.C.: The Urban Institute, Nov. 1983.

Bureau of Justice Statistics report in the *Lafayette (Indiana) Journal and Courier,* July 26, 1986, p. A4.

Burtless, Gary. "Can the Labor Market Absorb Three Million Welfare Recipients?" *Focus,* Vol. 19, no. 3 (Summer/Fall 1998). University of Wisconsin Institute for Research on Poverty, pp. 1–6.

Bush, George W. *Welcome to the White House.* "Modernize and Reform Medicare, 2001." Available: http://www.whitehouse.gov/infocus/medicare.htm.

Butterfield, Fox. "More Blacks in Their 20s Have Trouble with the Law." *New York Times* Sentencing Project, n.d.

Capra, Fritjof. *The Tao of Physics: An Exploration of the Parallels Between Modern Physics and Eastern Mysticism.* Berkeley, CA: Shambhala Publications, 1975.

Cass, Connie. "Study: 32 Percent of Young Black Men Serving Sentence." New Jersey *Courier–Post,* Oct. 5, 1995, p. 5A.

Celente, Gerald. "Middle Class Still Losing Members." New Jersey *Courier–Post,* July 6, 1995, p. 13A.

Center on Budget and Policy Priorities. "Analysis of Poverty in 1987." Washington, D.C.: U.S. Government Printing Office, 1988.

Center on Budget and Policy Priorities. "Average Incomes of Very Poor Families Fell during Early Years of the Welfare Reform, Study Finds." Washington, D.C.: U.S. Government Printing Office, 1999. Available: http://www.cbpp.org/8-22-99wel.html.

Center on Budget and Policy Priorities. "Increase in Number of Unemployed Over Past 12 Months Was Largest in Nearly 20 Years." Washington, D.C.: U.S. Government Printing Office, 2001.

Center on Budget and Policy Priorities. "Pathbreaking CBO Study Shows Dramatic Increases in both 1980s and 1990s in Income Gaps Between the Very Wealthy and Other Americans." Washington, D.C.: U.S. Government Printing Office, 2001. Available: http://www.centeronbudget.org/5-31-01tax-pr.htm.

Center on Budget and Policy Priorities. "Poverty Rate Among Working Single-Mother Families Remained Stagnant in Late 1990s Despite Strong Economy." Washington, D.C.: U.S. Government Printing Office, 2001. Available: http://www.cbpp.org/8-16-01wel-pr.html.

Center on Budget and Policy Priorities. "Testimony of Ed Lazere before the House Committee on Education and the Workforce, October 7, 1999." Available: http://www.cbpp.org/10-7-99wel.html.

Chafe, William H. "Eleanor Roosevelt." In Linda K. Kerber and Jane DeHart Mathews, editors, *Women's America.* New York: Oxford University Press, 1982.

"Change in America." *Chronicle of Higher Education,* Vol. 32, no. 3 (Sept. 17, 1986), p. 1.

Chen, Jack. *The Chinese in America.* San Francisco: Harper & Row, 1980.

Children's Defense Fund. "American Children in Poverty." Washington, D.C.: CDF, 1984.

Children's Defense Fund. *CDF Reports.* Washington, D.C.: CDF, Sept. 1994, Nov., 1994, Dec. 1994, Jan. 1995, March 1995, April 1995, July 1995, Aug. 1995, and Sept. 1995.

Children's Defense Fund. "Every Child Deserves a Fair Start." Washington, D.C.: November 3, 2001. Available: Wyiwyg:///52/http://www.childrensdefense.org/fairstart-faqs.htm.

Children's Defense Fund. *The State of America's Children Yearbook 1995.* Washington, D.C.: CDF, 1995.

Children's Defense Fund. *Welfare Reform Briefing Book.* Washington, D.C.: CDF, Jan. 1995.

"Choices," Vol. 3. Forest Hills, N.Y.: Women's Medical Center, Summer/Fall 1984. From "Feminization of Poverty," a series of hearings held in New York in June 1984, by Gail S. Shaffer, Secretary of State, New York State, and Ronnie Eldridge, Director, New York State Women's Division.

Chrissinger, Marlene Sonju. "Factors Affecting Employment of Welfare Mothers." *Social Work,* Vol. 25 (Jan. 1980), pp. 52–56.

Citizens for Tax Justice. "Buy Now, Pay Later: How Generous Corporate Campaign Donors Save Billions in Taxes." Available: http://www.ctj.org/html/camptax.htm.

Clark, Ramsey. *Crime in America: Observations on its Nature, Causes, Prevention, and Control.* New York: Simon & Schuster, 1970.

Cohn, D'Vera. "Women's Mental Health Studied." *Chicago Tribune,* Jan. 13, 1986.

Coll, Blanche D. *Perspectives in Public Welfare: A History,* U.S. Department of Health, Education, and Welfare Social Rehabilitation Service 91969. Washington, D.C.: U.S. Government Printing Office, 1971.

Coll, Blanche. "Public Assistance in the United States: Colonial to 1860." In E. W. Martin, editor, *Comparative Development in Social Welfare.* London: Allen and Unwin, 1972.

Combs-Orme, Terri, and Bernard Guyer. "American's Health Care System, the Reagan Legacy." *Journal of Sociology and Social Welfare,* Vol. 19, no. 1 (March 1992), pp. 3–88.

Committee on Ways and Means, U.S. House of Representatives. "Overview of Entitlement Programs, 1993 Green Book." Washington, D.C.: U.S. Government Printing Office, 1993, p. 776.

Compton, Beulah R. *Introduction to Social Welfare and Social Work: Structure, Function, and Process.* Homewood, IL: The Dorsey Press, 1980.

Congressional Record S6180, May 23, 1968.

Connelly, Mark Thomas. "Prostitution, Venereal Disease, and American Medicine." In Judith Walzer Leavitt, editor, *Women and Health in America.* Madison: University of Wisconsin Press, 1984.

Conover, Pamela Johnson, and Virginia Gray. *Feminism and the New Right: Conflict over the American Family.* New York: Praeger, 1983.

Constantatelos, D. *Byzantine Philanthropy and Social Welfare.* New Brunswick, NJ: Rutgers University Press, 1968.

Corning, Peter. *The Synergistic Hypothesis: A Theory of Progressive Evolution.* New York: McGraw-Hill, 1983.

Coulton, G. G. *The Medieval Scene.* Cambridge, MA: Cambridge University Press, 1930.

Council on Social Work Education. *Statistics on Social Work Education in the United States: 1983.* New York: Council on Social Work Education, 1984.

Cousins, Norman. "Will Women Lose Their Jobs?" *Current History and Forum,* Vol. 41 (Sept. 1939), p. 14.

Coward, Rosalind. *Patriarchal Precedents: Sexuality and Social Relations.* London: Routledge and Kegan Paul, 1983.

Crampton, Helen M., and Kenneth Kaiser. *Social Welfare: Institution and Process.* New York: Random House, 1970.

Crawley, Mike. "Rich Nations Grant Poorest Twenty-two a Checkbook Reprieve." *Christian Science Monitor,* December 26, 2000, p. 7.

Curley, Jami, and Michael Sherraden. *Policy Report: The History and Status of Children's Allowances: Policy Background for Children's Savings Accounts.* St. Louis, MO: Center for Social Development, Washington University in St. Louis, 1998.

"Current Operating Statistics." *Social Security Bulletin,* Washington, D.C.: U.S. Government Printing Office: Vol. 46, no. 4, April 1983, p. 70; Vol. 46, no. 7, July 1983; Vol. 47, no. 9, Sept. 1984; Vol. 49, no. 2, Feb. 1986, Table m-20, p. 42 and Table M-23, p. 44.

Daly, Mary. *Gyn/Ecology: The MetaEthics of Feminism.* Boston: Beacon Press, 1978.

Danziger, Sheldon. "After Welfare Reform and an Economic Boom: Why Is Child Poverty Still so Much Higher in the U.S. than in Europe?" Paper presented at the 8th International Research Seminar of the Foundation for International Studies on Social Securities, "Support for Children and their Parents." Sigtuna, Sweden, June 2001.

Danziger, Sheldon. Speech at Ball State University, Muncie, IN, Oct. 6, 1986.

Darenkamp, Angela, John McClymer, Mary Moynihan, and Arlene Vadum. *Images of Women in American Popular Culture.* New York: Harcourt Brace Jovanovich, 1985.

Davies, James C. "Toward a Theory of Revolution." *American Sociological Review,* Vol. 27 (Feb. 1962).

Davis, Angela. *Women, Race, and Class.* New York: Random House, 1983.

Davis, Kingsley, and Wilbert E. Moore. "Some Principles of Stratification." *American Sociological Review,* Vol. 10 (1945).

Day, Peter. *Social Work and Social Control.* London: Tavistock Publications, 1981.

Day, Phyllis J. "Sex Role Stereotypes and Public Assistance." *Social Service Review* (March 1979), pp. 106–115.

Day, Phyllis J. "Values Clarification Through Science Fiction." *Journal of Sociology and Social Welfare,* Vol. 7, no. 6 (Nov. 1980).

Day, Phyllis J. "Social Welfare: Context for Social Control." *Journal of Sociology and Social Welfare,* Vol. 8, no. 1 (March 1981).

Day, Phyllis J., Harry J. Macy, and Eugene Jackson. *Social Working: Exercises in Generalist Practice.* Englewood Cliffs, NJ: Prentice Hall, 1983.

Day, Phyllis J., Harry J. Macy, and Eugene Jackson. "A Simultaneity Model of Social Work Practice." *Journal of Social Work Education,* Vol. 20, no. 2 (Spring 1984), pp. 17–24.

Day, Phyllis J. "The New Poor in America: Isolationism in an International Political Economy." *Social Work: Journal of the National Association of Social Workers,* Vol. 34, no. 3 (1989), pp. 227–233.

Degler, Carl N. "What Ought to Be and What Was: Women's Sexuality in the 19th Century." In Judith Walzer Leavitt, editor, *Women and Health in America.* Madison, WI: University of Wisconsin Press, 1984.

Democratic Study Group, U.S. House of Representatives, James L. Oberstar, chair. "Special Report: Gramm Rudman—The Cutting Begins." Washington, D.C.: U.S. House of Representatives, Jan. 1986, no. 99-26.20.

De Riencourt, Amaury. *Sex and Power in History.* New York: Dell, 1974.

Devine, Joel A., and James D. Wright. *The Greatest of Evils: Urban Poverty and the American Underclass.* New York: Aldine de Gruyter, 1993.

DiNitto, Diana. *Social Welfare: Politics and Public Policy,* 4th ed. Needham, MA: Allyn & Bacon, 1995.

Dobelstein, Andrew W. *Politics, Economics, and Public Welfare.* Englewood Cliffs, NJ: Prentice Hall, 1980.

Dobyns, Henry F. "Estimating Aboriginal American Population." *Current Anthropology* (Oct. 1966), pp. 395–416.

Dolgoff, Ralph, and Donald Feldstein. *Understanding Social Welfare,* 2d ed. New York: Longman Press, 1984.

Doyle, Wilma, Leonard Z. Breen, and Robert Eichhorn. *Synopsis of the Older Americans Act, Revised.* West Lafayette, IN: Department of Sociology and Anthropology, Purdue University, 1976.

Drout, John A., and Dixon R. Fox. *The Completion of Independence.* New York: Macmillan, 1944.

Dunn, Finley Peter. "The Carnegie Libraries." In Gail Kennedy, editor, *Democracy and the Gospel of Wealth,* Boston: D.C. Heath, 1949.

Dye, Nancy Schrom. "Mary Breckinridge, The Frontier Nursing Service, and the Introduction of Nurse-Midwifery in the United States." In Judith Walzer Leavitt, editor, *Women and Health in America.* Madison, WI: University of Wisconsin Press, 1984.

Dye, Thomas R., and L. Harmon Zeigler. *The Irony of Democracy.* Belmont, CA: Wadsworth Publishing, 1970.

"Education," *Newsweek on Campus* (Feb. 1987), pp. 10–18.

Ehrenreich, Barbara. "Real Babies, Illegitimate Debates," *Time* (Aug. 2, 1994), p. 90.

Ehrenreich, Barbara, and Deirdre English. *Complaints and Disorders: The Sexual Politics of Sickness.* New York: The Feminist Press, Glass Mountain Pamphlet #2, 1973.

Ehrenreich, John. *The Altruistic Imagination: A History of Social Work and Social Policy in the United States.* Ithaca, NY: Cornell University Press, 1985.

Eisner, Alan. "Analysis: Huge U.S. Prison Population Social Cost Mounts," Reuters, January 2001. Available: http://www.mapinc.org/drugnews.v01/n136/a02.html.

Eitzen, D. Stanley. *In Conflict and Order: Understanding Society,* 3d ed. Needham, MA: Allyn & Bacon, 1985.

Elkins, Stanley. *Slavery,* 2d ed. Chicago: University of Chicago Press, 1968.

Equiano, Olaudah. "The Interesting Narrative of Olaudah Equiano." In Thomas R. Frazier, editor, *Afro-American History: Primary Sources.* New York: Harcourt, Brace, and World, 1970.

Eskridge, William N., Jr. *Gaylaw: Challenging the Apartheid of the Closet.* Cambridge, MA: Harvard University Press, 1999.

Esping-Anderson, Gosta, Martin Rein, and Lee Rainwater, editors. *Stagnation and Renewal in Social Policy.* New York: M.E. Sharpe, 1986.

Espo, David. "Senate Votes Give to the Rich, Then Take Away from the Poor." New Jersey *Courier–Post* (Sept. 20, 1995), p. 1A.

Euberger, Zoe. "TANF Expenditures Increased in the Last Fiscal Year." Center on Budget and Policy Priorities. Available: http://www.cpbb.org/11-1-01wel.html.

Executive Office of the President. "Budget of the U.S. Government FY 1995." Washington, D.C.: U.S. Government Printing Office, 1994.

Fanon, Franz. *Black Skin, White Masks,* trans. by Charles L. Markmann. New York: Grove Press, 1967.

Feagin, Joe R. *Racial and Ethnic Relations,* 2d ed. Englewood Cliffs, NJ: Prentice Hall, 1984.

Feagin, Joe R. *Racial and Ethnic Relations,* 3d ed. Englewood Cliffs, NJ: Prentice Hall, 1989.

Fendrich, James M., Mamie Miller, and Tim Nichel. "It's the Budget, Stupid: A Policy Analysis of Clinton's First Budget." *Journal of Sociology and Social Welfare,* Vol. 21, no. 4 (Dec. 1994), pp. 5–29.

Fine, Sidney. *Laissez-Faire and the General Welfare State.* Ann Arbor: University of Michigan Press, 1964.

Foner, Philip S. *History of the Labor Movement in the United States.* New York: International Publishers, 1947.

Fournier, Ron. "Bentsen/Reich Split on Tax Credits." New Jersey *Courier–Post* (Nov. 28, 1994), p. 2A.

Francis, David R. "More Firms Find Tax Loopholes." *Christian Science Monitor* (October 20, 2000), p. A3.

Friedlander, Walter A., and Robert Z. Apte. *Introduction to Social Welfare,* 4th ed. Englewood Cliffs, NJ: Prentice Hall, 1955.

Friedlander, Walter A., and Robert Z. Apte. *Introduction to Social Welfare,* 5th ed. Englewood Cliffs, NJ: Prentice Hall, 1961.

Friedlander, Walter A., and Robert Z. Apte. *Introduction to Social Welfare,* 9th ed. Englewood Cliffs, NJ: Prentice Hall, 1974.

Friedman, Dorian. "The Flawed Premise of Welfare Reform." *U.S. News and World Report* (Sept. 11, 1995), p. 32.

Friends of the Earth U.S. "OECD Multilateral Agreement on Investment: Fact Sheet," February 19, 1997. Available: http://www.igc.org/trac/feature/planet/mai_foe.html.

Galper, Jeffrey. *Social Work Practice: A Radical Perspective.* Englewood Cliffs, NJ: Prentice Hall, 1980.

Gannett News Service. "Facts About Welfare." New Jersey *Courier–Post* (Jan. 1, 1995), p. 9A.

Gartner, Alan, Colin Greer, and Frank Reismann, editors. *Beyond Reagan: Alternatives for the Eighties.* New York: Harper & Row, 1984.

Gerber, Larry G. "H-Net List for 'Putting the State Back In,'" AP story on ADARAND decision, "High Court Delivers Strong Blow to Affirmative Action," Internet, July 1995.

Gergen, David. "Warming to the Task." *U.S. News and World Report* (June 25, 2001), p. A-1.

Gettleman, Marvin B. "Charity and Social Classes in the U.S., 1874–1900." *American Journal of Economics and Sociology,* Vol. 22 (April–July 1963), pp. 313–329. Reported in Jeffrey Galper, *Social Work Practice: A Radical Perspective.* Englewood Cliffs, NJ: Prentice Hall, 1974.

Giacomo, Carol. "Sterilization Count Higher Than Expected." *Hartford (Connecticut) Courant* (Oct. 13, 1980), pp. A10, A12.

Gies, Frances, and Joseph Gies. *Women in the Middle Ages.* New York: Barnes and Noble, 1978.

Gies, Frances, and Joseph Gies. *Cathedral, Forge and Waterwheel: Technology and Invention in the Middle Ages.* New York: HarperCollins, 1994.

Gil, David G. "Work, Violence, Injustice, and War." *Journal of Sociology and Social Welfare,* Vol. 16, no. 1 (March 1989), pp. 39–53.

Gilbert, Neil, and Harry Specht. *Dimensions of Social Welfare Policy.* Englewood Cliffs, NJ: Prentice Hall, 1974.

Gilbert, Neil, and Harry Specht. *The Emergence of Social Welfare and Social Work,* 2d ed. Itasca, IL: F.E. Peacock Publishers, 1981.

Ginger, Ray. "Women at Hull House." In Linda K. Kerber and Jane DeHart Mathews, editors, *Women's America.* New York: Oxford University Press, 1982.

Ginsbert, Leon. *Understanding Social Problems: Policies and Programs,* 2d ed. Columbia, SC: University of South Carolina Press, 1996.

Glass, Justine. *Witchcraft: The Sixth Sense.* North Hollywood, CA: Wilshire Book Co., 1973.

Goroff, Norman. "Humanism and Social Work: Paradoxes, Problems, and Promises" (mimeograph). West Hartford: University of Connecticut School of Social Work, 1977.

Gough, Kathleen. "The Origin of the Family." In Rayna Reiter, editor, *Toward an Anthropology of Women.* New York: Monthly Review Press, 1975.

Greenwood, Ernest. "Attributes of a Profession" and "Attributes of a Profession Revisited." In Neil Gilbert and Harry Specht, editors, *The Emergence of Social Welfare and Social Work,* 2d ed. Itasca, IL: F.E. Peacock Publishers, 1981.

Grob, Gerald N. (advisory ed.). "Maryland Report on Almshouses." In *The State and Public Welfare in Nineteenth-Century America.* New York: Arno Press, 1976.

Gruber, Katherine. *Encyclopedia of Associations.* Detroit: Gale Research, 1981.

Gugliotta, Guy. "The Minimum Wage Culture." *Washington Post National Weekly Edition* (Oct. 3–9, 1995), p. 6.

Hall, Raymond. *Black Separatism and Social Reality: Rhetoric and Reason.* New York: Pergamon, 1978.

Halverson, Guy. "Giving by Firms Registers Big Jump." *Christian Science Monitor* (December 4, 2000), p. 4.

Handel, Gerald. *Social Welfare in Western Society.* New York: Random House, 1982.

Handler, Joel P. *Reforming the Poor.* New York: Basic Books, 1972.

Harrington, Michael. *The New American Poverty.* New York: Holt, Rinehart and Winston, 1984.

Harris, Marvin. *Patterns of Race.* New York: W.W. Norton and Company, 1964.

Hartung, William D., and Michelle Ciarroca. "Star Wars Revisited: Still Dangerous, Costly, and Unworkable." *Foreign Policy in Focus,* Vol. 4, no. 24 (September 1999, revised April 2000). Available: http://www.foreignpolicy-infocus.org/briefs/vol4/v4n24star.html.

Haskins, Ron. "Welfare Reform: A Mother's Work." *Washington Post* (November 12, 2001). Available: http://www.washingtonpost.com/wp-dyn/articles/A18589-2001Nov.12.html.

Health Care Financing Administration. "Highlights: National Health Expenditures 1999," Available: http://www.hcfa.gov/stats/nhe-oact/hilites.htm.

Heffernan, Joseph. *Introduction to Social Welfare Policy.* Itasca, IL: F.E. Peacock Publishers, 1979.

Higginbotham, A. and A. Leon, Jr. *In the Matter of Color: Race and the American Legal Process; The Colonial Period.* New York: Oxford University Press, 1978.

Higginbotham, A. Leon, Jr. *Shades of Freedom: Racial Politics and Presumptions of the American Legal Process.* New York: Oxford University Press, 1996.

Hinden, Stan. "Raw Deal for Women?" *AARP Bulletin,* Vol. 42, no. 8. (September 2001), pp. 18–20.

Ho, David. "U.S. Prison Population Rising: Incarceration Rate May Top Russia as Highest in World," *ABCNews.com.* (April 2000). Available: http://www.my.abcnews.go.com/

PRINTERFRIENDLY?: . . . sections/us/ DailyNews/prisons000420.htm.

Howe, Neil, and Richard Jackson. "The Most Unfair Noncut of All: Federal Pensions." *Christian Science Monitor* (July 21, 1995), p. 18.

Howell, Barbara, and Leon Howell. "Food Stamps: Stories and Statistics." *Christian Century* (Jan. 23–30, 1983): p. 18.

Hraba, Joseph. *American Ethnicity.* Itasca, IL: F.E. Peacock Publishers, 1979.

"HUD Defends Accuracy of Count: Group Rebuts Report on Homeless." *Kansas City Times* (Aug. 16, 1984), p. 5.

"Hunger and Homelessness Up Sharply in Major U.S. Cities." *Conference of Mayors' Twenty-seven-City Survey* (December 12, 2001). Available: http://nch.ari.net/numbers.htm.

Hunter, Mary Ski, and Dennis Saleeby. "Spirit and Substance: Beginnings in the Education of Radical Social Workers." *Journal of Education for Social Work,* Vol. 13, no. 2 (Spring 1977), pp. 60–70.

Hutchinson Family Encyclopedia. Available: http://195.152.156.15/encyclopedia/88/M0003688.htm.

Hymowitz, Carole, and Michaele Weissman. A *History of Women in America.* New York: Bantam, 1980.

Irons, Peter. "The Return of the 'Yellow Peril.'" *The Nation* (Oct. 19, 1985), p. 316.

Ivins, Molly. "Watt's Back; So Are (Ugh) His Policies." New Jersey *Courier–Post* (March 27, 1995), p. 5A.

Ivins, Molly. "Infamous 100 Days: Let's Recap." New Jersey *Courier–Post* (April 10, 1995), p. 5A.

Ivins, Molly. "Workers' Futures Hang on Result of Race for AFL–CIO Leadership." New Jersey *Courier–Post* (Sept. 4, 1995), p. 7A.

Ivins, Molly. "GOP Just Keeps on Marching to Wrong (and Rich) Drummer." New Jersey *Courier–Post* (Oct. 23, 1995), p. 5A.

Jackson, Eugene, Harry J. Macy, and Phyllis J. Day. "A Simultaneity Model for Social Work Education." *Journal of Social Work Education,* Vol. 20, no. 2 (Spring 1984), pp. 17–24.

Jacobs, William Jay. *Women in American History.* Encino, CA: Glencoe Publishing, 1976.

Jansson, Bruce S. *The Sixteen-Trillion Dollar Mistake.* New York: Columbia University Press, 2001.

Joe, Tom. "The Case for Income Support." In Alan Gartner, Colin Greer, and Frank Reismann, editors, *Beyond Reagan: Alternatives for the Eighties.* New York: Harper & Row, 1984, pp. 81–90.

Johnson, Alice K., and Michael Sherraden. "Asset Based Social Welfare Policy: Homeownership for the Poor." *Journal of Sociology and Social Welfare,* Vol. 19, no. 3 (Sept. 1994), pp. 65–83.

Johnson, Michael P. "Smothered Slave Infants: Were Slave Mothers at Fault?" In Linda K. Kerber and Jane DeHart Mathews, editors, *Women's America.* New York: Oxford University Press, 1982.

Jones, Mother. *The Autobiography of Mother Jones,* 3d ed. Chicago: Charles H. Kerr, 1977.

Kahn, Alfred J. *Social Policy and Social Services.* New York: Random House, 1973.

Karger, Howard J. "Income Maintenance Programs and the Reagan Domestic Agenda." *Journal of Sociology and Social Work,* Vol. 19, no. 1 (March 1992), pp. 45–62.

Karliner, Joshua. *The Corporate Planet.* San Francisco: Sierra Club Books, 1997.

Katz, Michael B. *Poverty and Policy in American History.* New York: Academic Press, 1983.

Kellogg, Kate. "The Far-Right Fringe." *Michigan Today* (June 1987).

Kerber, Linda K., and Jane DeHart Mathews, editors. *Women's America.* New York: Oxford University Press, 1982.

Kern, Stephen. *The Culture of Time and Space: 1880–1918.* Cambridge, MA: Harvard University Press, 1983.

Kessler-Harris, Alice. *Out to Work: A History of Wage-Earning Women in the United States.* New York: Oxford University Press, 1982.

Kessler-Harris, Alice. "Where Are the Organized Women Workers?" In Linda K. Kerber and Jane DeHart Mathews, editors, *Women's America.* New York: Oxford University Press, 1982.

Kilborn, Robert Jr. "Seeking New Jobs After the Pink Slip." *Christian Science Monitor* (July 17, 1995), p. 1.

Klaits, Joseph. *Servants of Satan: The Age of the Witch Hunts.* Bloomington: Indiana University Press, 1985.

Knox, John Knox, editor. "First Blast of the Trumpet Against the Monstrous Regiment of Women." In Carolyn Merchant, *The Death of Nature: Women, Ecology, and the Scientific Revolution.* San Francisco: Harper & Row, 1980.

Koretz, Gene. "Economic Trends: How Welfare to Work Worked." *Business Week* (September 24, 2001), p. 10.

Landay, Johnathan S. "Study Reveals U.S. Has Spent $4 Trillion on Nukes Since '45." *Christian Science Monitor* (July 12, 1995), p. 3.

Landay, Johnathan S. Editorial in *Christian Science Monitor* (July 28, 1995), p. 20.

Landay, Johnathan S. "Congress, Clinton Battle over Antimissile System." *Christian Science Monitor* (Aug. 3, 1995), p. 3.

Landay, Johnathan S. "Pet Pork Projects Slip into GOP Defense Budget." *Christian Science Monitor* (Aug. 4, 1995), p. 3.

Landay, Johnathan S. "Pentagon Hit for Hiding Spending on 'Star Wars.'" *Christian Science Monitor* (Sept. 5, 1995), p. 3.

Landay, Johnathan S. "Political Futures, Jobs Hang on Defense Budget Choices." *Christian Science Monitor* (Sept. 12, 1995), p. 3.

Langenbach, Lisa. "Modernist and Traditionalist Issue Groups in the American Party System: An Examination of the Realigning Potential of Cultural Issues in Changing Cleavage Structures," unpublished doctoral dissertation, Purdue University, West Lafayette, Indiana, Aug. 1986.

Lav, Iris J., and Robert Greenstein. "Tax Bill Contains Only Modest Benefits for Middle Class Despite Its High Cost." Center on Budget and Policy Priorities (August 20, 1999). Available: http://www.cbpp.org/8-20-99tax.htm.

Lazere, Ed. "Welfare Balances After Three Years of TANF Block Grants." Center on Budget and Policy Priorities (January 12, 2000). Available http://www.cbpp.org/1-12-2000wel.html.

Leavitt, Judith Walzer, editor. *Women and Health in America.* Madison: University of Wisconsin Press, 1984.

Lekachman, Robert. *Greed Is Not Enough: Reaganomics.* New York: Pantheon, 1982.

Levitan, Sar A., and Clifford M. Johnson. *Beyond the Safety Net.* Cambridge, MA: Ballinger, 1984.

Levitan, Sar, Martin Rein, and David Marwick. *Work and Welfare Go Together.* Baltimore: Johns Hopkins University Press, 1972.

Loewe, Michael. *Everyday Life in Early Imperial China.* New York: Harper & Row, 1968.

Lopez, Robert S. *Commercial Revolution of the Middle Ages 950–1350.* Cambridge: Cambridge University Press, 1976.

LoPrest, Pamela. "How Are Families That Left Welfare Doing? A Comparison of Early and Recent Welfare Leavers." Urban Institute (April 2001). Available: http://www.newfederalism.urban.org/html/series-b/b36/b36.html.

Lugard, Lady Flora Louisa. *Tropical Dependency.* London, 1911.

Lusane, Clarence. "Decline in Funding for Civil-Rights Agencies Is Cause for Concern." Progressive Media Project. Available: http:www.progressive.org/pmpbvc10.htm.

Macarov, David. *The Design of Social Welfare.* New York: Holt, Rinehart & Winston, 1978.

Macarov, David. *Work and Welfare: The Unholy Alliance.* Beverly Hills, CA: Sage, 1980.

Macfarlane, Alan. *Witchcraft in Tudor and Stuart England.* New York: Harper & Row, 1970.

Macy, Harry, Phyllis J. Day, and Eugene Jackson. "Continuum of Social Work Education" (mimeograph). Paper presented at Indiana Association for Social Work Education Annual Meeting, Indianapolis, April 1989.

Mandell, Betty Reid. "Welfare and Totalitarianism: Part I. Theoretical Issues." *Social Work* (Jan. 1971):

Manning, Seaton W. "The Tragedy of the Ten-Million-Acre Bill" *Social Service Review,* Vol. 36 (March 1962), pp. 44–50.

Marotta, Toby. *The Politics of Homosexuality.* Boston: Houghton Mifflin, 1981.

Mason, Jan, John S. Wodarski, and T.M. Jim Parham. "Work and Welfare: A Reevaluation of AFDC." *Social Work* (May–June 1985), pp. 197–202.

Mathews, Jane DeHart. "The New Feminism and the Dynamics of Social Change." In Linda K. Kerber and Jane DeHart Mathews, editors, *Women's America.* New York: Oxford University Press, 1982.

McHenry, Robert, editor. *Famous American Women: A Biographical Dictionary from Colonial Times to the Present.* New York: Dover Publications, 1980.

McMaster, John B. *A History of the People of the United States.* New York: D. Appleton, 1895.

Mencher, Samuel. *From Poor Law to Poverty Programs.* Pittsburgh: University of Pittsburgh Press, 1967.

Merchant, Carolyn. *The Death of Nature: Women, Ecology, and the Scientific Revolution.* San Francisco: Harper & Row, 1980.

Midgley, James. "New Christian Right, Social Policy, and the Welfare State." *Journal of Sociology and Social Welfare,* Vol. 17, no. 2 (June 1990), pp. 89–106.

Miller, Dorothy C. "AFDC: Mapping a Strategy for Tomorrow." *Social Service Review* (Dec. 1983).

Miller, John. "Clinton and Congress Feed the Wealthy." *Dollars and Sense: What's Left in Economics* (Nov.–Dec. 1997). Available: http://www.dollarsandsense.org/issues/nov97/tax.html.

Mills, Kim I. "Fewer Americans Found to Be Living in Poverty." New Jersey *Courier–Post* (Oct. 6, 1995), p. A7.

Miringoff, Marc L., and Sandra Opdycke. *American Social Welfare: Reassessment and Reform.* Englewood Cliffs, NJ: Prentice Hall, 1986.

Mohr, James C. "Patterns of Abortion and the Response of American Physicians, 1790–1930." In Judith Walzer Leavitt, editor, *Women and Health in America*. Madison: University of Wisconsin Press, 1984.

Morgan, Ted. *Wilderness at Dawn: The Settling of the North American Continent*. New York: Simon & Schuster, 1993.

Morris, Robert. *Social Policy of the American Welfare State*. New York: Harper & Row, 1979.

Morris, Robert. *Rethinking Social Welfare*. New York: Longman, 1986.

Moynihan, Daniel P. *Pandaemonium: Ethnicity in International Politics*. New York: Oxford University Press, 1993.

Moynihan, Daniel P. "The Case Against Entitlement Cuts." *Modern Maturity* (Nov.–Dec. 1994), pp. 13–14.

Muller, Herbert J. *Freedom in the Western World: From the Dark Ages to the Rise of Democracy*. New York: Harper & Row, 1963.

Mulroy, Elizabeth A., and Terry S. Love. "Housing Affordability, Stress and Single Mothers: Pathway to Homelessness." *Journal of Sociology and Social Welfare*, Vol. 19, no. 3 (Sept. 1992), pp. 51–63.

NAFTA Index. "Public Citizen: Global Trade Watch." Available: http://www.citizen.org/pctrade/naftaindex.htm.

National Association of Social Workers. *Encyclopedia of Social Work*, Vol II. New York: NASW, 1977.

National Association of Social Workers. *NASW Newsletter* (Spring 1995).

National Coalition for Homelessness. "2001 Budget and Homelessness." (June 30, 2000). Available: http://nch.ari.net/fy2001.htm.

National Coalition for the Homeless. "How Many People Experience Homelessness?" *NCH Fact Sheet #2* (February 1999). Available: http://nch.ari.net/numbers.htm.

Neus, Elizabeth. "Epidemic Now a Part of Mainstream America." New Jersey *Courier–Post* (July 23, 1995), p. A5.

Neus, Elizabeth. "New Light Shines on TB Cases." New Jersey *Courier–Post* (July 23, 1995), p. 8A.

Newman, Pauline. "Triangle Shirt Waist Fire." In Linda K. Kerber and Jane DeHart Mathews, editors, *Women's America*. New York: Oxford University Press, 1982.

Nichols, Roy Franklin. *Franklin Pierce*. Philadelphia: University of Pennsylvania Press, 1958.

Nicholson, Trish. "50-plus Workers Hit by Cutbacks." *The Nation*. AARP (October 2001), pp. 1, 24.

"OASDI Current-Pay Benefits: Summary." *Social Security Bulletin Annual Statistical Supplement 2001* (December 2000).

Office of Management and Budget. Table S-13, "Outlay Totals by Function." Available: http://www.whitehouse.gov/omb/budget/fy2002/budiv_13.htm.

Office of Management and Budget. Table 14.1, "Federal Resources in Support of Income Security," Available: http://www.whitehouse.gov/omb/budge/fy2002/bud14.html.

Orlin, Malinda B. "State Welfare Reforms: Typology and Analysis." *Journal of Sociology and Social Welfare*, Vol. 21, no. 4 (Dec. 1994), pp. 29–40.

Palmer, John L., and Isabel V. Sawhill, editors. *Reagan Record: An Assessment of America's Changing Domestic Priorities*. Cambridge, MA: Ballinger, 1985.

"Panel: Welfare Exams Wasted Millions." *Lafayette (Indiana) Journal and Courier* (Oct. 30, 1986), p. 1.

Partners Task Force for Gay and Lesbian Couples. "Defense of Marriage Act: Description and the Bill's Text." (2000). Available: http://www.buddybuddy.com/doma.htm.

Pearce, Diana. "Farewell to Alms." Center for National Policy Review, Catholic University Law School. Presented at the Annual Meeting of the American Sociological Association, San Francisco, Sept. 1982.

Pearsall, Richard. "Gap Growing Between the Rich and the Poor." New Jersey *Courier–Post* (June 19, 1995), p. B1.

Peattie, Lisa, and Martin Rein. *Women's Claims: A Study in Political Economy*. New York: Oxford University Press, 1983.

Petrie, W. Flinders. *Social Life in Ancient Egypt*. London: Constable and Co., 1923.

Piven, Frances Fox, and Richard Cloward. *Regulating the Poor*. New York: Random House, 1971.

Piven, Frances Fox, and Richard Cloward. *The New Class War: Reagan's Attack on the Welfare State and Its Consequences*. New York: Pantheon, 1982.

Platt, Anthony M. *The Child Savers: The Invention of Delinquency*, 2d ed. Chicago: University of Chicago Press, 1977.

Pomeroy, Sarah B. *Goddesses, Whores, Wives, and Slaves: Women in Classical Antiquity*. New York: Schlocken Books, 1975.

Rainwater, Lee, editor. *Social Problems and Public Policy*. Chicago: Aldine, 1974.

Rank, Mark Robert. *Living on the Edge: The Realities of Welfare in America.* New York: Columbia University Press, 1994.

Raspberry, William. "End of Work." New Jersey *Courier–Post* (June 13, 1995), p. 9A.

"Reducing the Infant Mortality Rate." *Lafayette (Indiana) Journal and Courier* (Feb. 4, 1987), p. C-4.

Reed, James. "Doctors, Birth Control, and Social Values, 1830–1970." In Judith Walzer Leavitt, editor, *Women and Health in America.* Madison: University of Wisconsin Press, 1984.

Reiter, Rayna R., editor. *Toward an Anthropology of Women.* New York: Monthly Review Press, 1975.

Reynolds, Barbara. "Let's Not Lose This Right." New Jersey *Courier–Post* (June 22, 1995), p. 9A.

Riemer, Eleanor S. "Women, Dowries, and Capital Investment in Thirteenth-Century Siena." In Marion A. Kaplan, editor, *The Marriage Bargain.* New York: Haworth Press, 1985.

Roberts, Steven V., Dorian Friedman, and Kalia Hetter. "Reform by 1000 Cuts." *U.S. News and World Report* (July 31, 1995), pp. 22–24.

Romasco, Albert U. *The Poverty of Abundance— Hoover, the Nation, and Depression.* New York: Oxford University Press, 1965.

Rose, Nancy. "Gender, Race, and the Welfare State: Government Work Programs from the 1930s to the Present." *Feminist Studies,* Vol. 19, no. 2 (Summer 1993), pp. 317–342.

Ross, Sonya. "Poll: Americans Still Want to Fight Poverty." New Jersey *Courier–Post* (Dec. 8, 1994), p. 11A.

Roth, Susan. "Daschle: Tax Cut Hurt the Nation." *Lafayette Journal and Courier* (January 5, 2002), p. A1.

Rovner, Julie. "Ending the Greatest Terror of Life." *AARP Bulletin,* Special Report (1995), p. 12.

Rubin, Beth, James D. Wright, and Joel A. Devine. "Unhousing the Urban Poor: The Reagan Legacy." *Journal of Sociology and Social Welfare,* Vol. 19, no. 1 (March 1992), pp. 111–147.

Rubin, James H. "Study: Race Still Factor in Mortgage Denials." New Jersey *Courier–Post* (July 19, 1995), p. 12D.

Rule, James B. *Insight and Social Betterment: Applied Social Science.* New York: Oxford Press, 1978.

Russo, Francis X., and George Willis. *Human Services in America.* Englewood Cliffs, NJ: Prentice Hall, 1986.

Ryan, William O. *Blaming the Victim.* New York: Pantheon Books, 1971.

Saggs, H. W. F. *Everyday Life in Babylonia and Assyria,* 2d ed. New York: G.P. Putnam's Sons, 1967.

Sanders, Bernard. "Clinton Must Go to the People." *The Nation* (June 21, 1995), p. 865.

Sanders, Bernard. "And Now for Some Meaningful Hearings." *Christian Science Monitor* (Aug. 17, 1995), p. 19.

Sard, Barbara, and Jennifer Daskal (Feb. 12, 1998). "Housing and Welfare Reform: Some Background Information." Washington, D.C.: Center on Budget and Policy Priorities (February 12, 1998).

Sarri, Rosemary. *Under Lock and Key.* Ann Arbor: National Assessment of Juvenile Delinquency, 1974.

Sarri, Rosemary, Elisabeth Cramer, and Virginia du Riváge. "Highlights: Socio-Economic Status of Women in Michigan and the United States." Ann Arbor: The University of Michigan Institute for Social Research and the School of Social Work, 1983.

Sauer, Carl A. *Seventeenth Century in North America.* Berkeley, CA: Turtle Island Foundation, 1980.

Saville, J. "The Welfare State: An Historical Approach." In E. Butterworth and R. Hobman, editors, *Social Welfare in Modern Britain.* Glasgow: Fontana-Collins, 1975.

Scanlon, Edward. "Homeownership and Its Impacts: Implications for Housing Policy for Low-Income Families," Working Paper 96-2, Center for Social Development, Washington University, St. Louis, MO, 1996.

Schmid, Randolph E. "Poverty in America Tops 39 Million." New Jersey *Courier–Post* (Oct. 7, 1994), p. 3A.

Schneider, Herbert W., editor. *Adam Smith's Moral and Political Philosophy.* New York: Hafner, 1948.

Schwartz-Nobel, Loretta. *Starving in the Shadow of Plenty.* New York: G.P. Putnam's Sons, 1983.

Seelye, Katharine Q. "U.S. Quietly Reversing Clinton-Era Green Rules." *Indianapolis Star* (November 11, 2001), p. A4.

Seller, Maxine. *Immigrant Women.* Philadelphia: Temple University Press, 1984.

Shalala, Donna E., Secretary of Health and Human Services. "HHS Approves First SCHIP Waivers." HCFA Press Office (January 18, 2001).

Shapiro, Isaac, Allen Dupree, and James Sly. "An Estimated 12 Million Low- and Moderate-Income

Families—with 24 million children—Would not Benefit from the Bush Tax Plan." Center on Budget and Policy Priorities (February 7, 2001).

Shapiro, Joseph P., and Andrea R. Wright. "Signs of the Fathers." *U.S. News and World Report* (Aug. 14, 1995), pp. 51–52.

Shea, Mary. "The Ideology of Mental Health and the Emergence of the Therapeutic Liberal State: The American Mental Hygiene Movement, 1900–1930." Ph.D. dissertation, University of Illinois at Champaign-Urbana, 1980.

Sherwood, Robert E. *Roosevelt and Hopkins.* New York: Harper & Row, 1948.

Sinclair, A. *The Emancipation of the American Woman.* New York, 1966.

Skidmore, Dave. "Lawmakers Propose $500 Child Credit." New Jersey *Courier–Post* (Oct. 14, 1995), p. 3A.

Slocum, Sally. "Woman the Gatherer: Male Bias in Anthropology." In Rayna Reiter, editor, *Toward an Anthropology of Women.* New York: Monthly Review Press, 1975.

Smith, Adam. *The Wealth of Nations.* New York: Modern Library, 1937.

Smith, David A. "Later Retirement: A 'Disaster' for Many." *AARP Bulletin* (Nov. 1998), pp. 2–3.

Smith, Geri, with Elisabeth Malkin, Jonathan Wheatley, Paul Magnusson, and Michael Arndt. "The Free Trade Area of the Americas." *Business Week* (April 23, 2001), p. 62.

Sniffen, Michael J. "Justice Department Moves to Save Federal Child-Support Law." New Jersey *Courier–Post* (Aug. 29, 1995), p. 16A.

Social Security Bulletin, Vol. 46, no. 7 (July 1983).

Social Security Bulletin, Vol. 49, no. 2 (Feb. 1986).

"Social Welfare Expenditures 1963–1983." *Social Security Bulletin,* Vol. 49, no. 2 (Feb. 1986), p. 20.

Southern, Richard W. *The Making of the Middle Ages.* New York: Dell Publishing, 1982.

Spaeth, Linda E. "More Than Her 'Thirds': Wives and Widows in Colonial Virginia." In Linda Spaeth and Alison Duncan Hirsch, editors, *Women, Family, and Community in Colonial America: Two Perspectives.* New York: Haworth Press, 1983.

Spender, Dale. *There's Always Been a Women's Movement This Century.* Boston: Pandora Press, 1983.

Sprenger, J. *Malleus Maleficarum,* trans by M. Summers. New York: B. Blom, 1970.

Sprull, Julia Cherry. "Housewives and Their Helpers." In Linda K. Kerber and Jane DeHart

Mathews, editors, *Women's America.* New York: Oxford University Press, 1982.

Stanback, Howard. "Attacking Poverty with Economic Policy." In Alan Gartner, Colin Greer, and Frank Reismann, editors, *Beyond Reagan: Alternatives for the Eighties.* New York: Harper & Row, 1984.

"State AFDC Activity: Program Financial Identifiers, AFDC Need Standards and Typical Payment Amounts" (July 1, 1993), copyrighted by H-State Internet.

Statistical Abstracts of the United States. "Sec. 3 Health and Nutrition." Available: http://www.census.gov/prod/2001pubs/statab/sec03.pdf.

Stevens, Doris. *Jailed for Freedom.* New York: Boni and Liveright, 1920.

Stockman, David A. *The Triumph of Politics: Why the Reagan Revolution Failed.* New York: Harper & Row, 1986.

Stone, Merlin. *When God Was a Woman.* New York: Harcourt Brace Jovanovich, 1976.

Strayer, Joseph R., and Dana C. Munro. *The Middle Ages 395–1500.* New York: Appleton-Century Crofts, 1970.

Sugarman, Jule M., Gary D. Bass, Nancy Amidei, David Plocher, Shannon Ferguson, and Julie Quiroz. *OMB Watch: A Citizen's Guide to Gramm–Rudman–Hollings.* Washington, D.C.: Focus Project, Inc., 1986.

Thayer, Frederick C. "The Holy War on Surplus Americans: Soviet Dogma, Old-Time Religion, and Classical Economics." *Social Policy* (Fall 1997), pp. 8–18.

Thomas, Keith. *Religion and the Decline of Magic.* London: Weidenfeld and Nicolson, 1971.

Thomas, P. "Study Suggests Black Male Prison Rate Impinges on Political Process." *The Washington Post* (January 30, 1997), p. A3.

Timms, Noel. *Social Work.* London: Routledge and Kegan Paul, 1973.

Tobias, Sheila, and Lisa Anderson. "Rosie the Riveter: Demobilization and the Female Labor Force." In Linda K. Kerber and Jane DeHart Mathews, editors, *Women's America.* New York: Oxford University Press, 1982.

Torrey, E. Fuller, and Sidney M. Wolfe. *Care of the Seriously Mentally Ill: A Rating of State Programs.* Washington, D.C.: Public Citizen Health Research Group, 1986.

Trattner, Walter. "The Background." In Neil Gilbert and Harry Specht, editors, *Emergence of Social Welfare and Social Work,* 2d ed. Itasca, IL: F.E. Peacock Publishers, 1981.

Treisman, Eric. "The Last Treaty." *Harper's Magazine* (Feb. 1975), pp. 37–39.

Tropman, John E., Alan Gordon, and Phyllis J. Day. "Welfare Codebook," unpublished manuscript developed 1971, based on data from *Statistical Abstracts of the United States 1971*. Washington, D.C.: U.S. Government Printing Office, 1972, p. 312; and *County and City Data Book 1964*. Washington, D.C.: U.S. Government Printing Office, 1960.

Tumin, Melvin. "Some Principles of Stratification: A Critical Analysis." *American Sociological Review*, Vol. 10, no. 4 (1953), p. 380.

United States Embassy Japan. "Fact Sheet: President Clinton on Economic Accomplishments" (January 9, 2001). Available: http://www.usembassy.state.gov/japan/www.je132.htm.

United Way of Indiana. "Capital Steps." Indianapolis: United Way of Indiana, n.d.

U.S. Bureau of the Census, *Census 2000*. U.S. Department of Commerce, Economics and Statistics Administration. *Profiles of General Demographic Characteristics 2000*.

U.S. Bureau of the Census, *Census 2000 Special Reports*. "Emergency and Transitional Shelter Population: 2000." Available: http://census.gov/prod/2001pubs/censr01-2.pdf.

U.S. Bureau of the Census, *CPS Reports. "Poverty in the United States: 2000."*

U.S. Bureau of the Census, *Current Population Survey, March 2000 and 2001*. "Measures of Household Income Inequality." Available: http://www.census.gov.hhes/www/img/incpov00fig12.

U.S. Bureau of the Census, *Current Population Survey*. "Poverty 2000. Poverty Thresholds in 2000, by Size of Family and Number of Related Children Under 18 Years." Available: http://www.census.gov.

U.S. Bureau of the Census. *Money Income and Poverty Status of Families and Persons in the United States: 1982*, CPR series P-60, no. 140.

U.S. Bureau of the Census. "Summary of General Characteristics of Persons, 1990." Washington, D.C.: U.S. Government Printing Office, 1992.

U.S. Bureau of the Census, Economics and Statistics Administration. *Statistical Abstracts of the United States: 1994* (114th ed.). Washington, D.C.: U.S. Government Printing Office, 1994.

U.S. Bureau of the Census. *Current Benefit Statistics*. Washington, D.C.: U.S. Government Printing Office, 1995. Retrieved from the Internet Aug. 14, 1995.

U.S. Department of Agriculture, Food and Nutrition Services. "Cost of Food Distribution Programs December 21, 2001" Available: http://www.fns.usda.gov/pe/fd$sum.htm.

U.S. Department of Agriculture, Food and Nutrition Services. "FSS Summary, December 21, 2001." Available: http://www.fns.usda.gov/pd/fssummar.htm.

U.S. Department of Agriculture, Food and Nutrition Services. "Overview: December 2001." Available: http://fns.usda.gov/pd/Overview.htm.

U.S. Department of Health and Human Services, Administration for Children and Families, Office of Legislative Affairs and Budget. *HHS Fact Sheet*. Available: http://www.acf.dhhs.gov/news/press/1998/cc/fund.html.

U.S. Department of Health and Human Services, Administration for Children and Families. "Statistics: Change in TANF Caseloads Since Enactment of New Welfare Law." Available: http://www.acf.dhhs.gov/news/stats/recipients.html.

U.S. Department of Health and Human Services Administration, Office of Family Assistance. "AFDC Information Memo No. ACF 1M-94-7" (mimeograph). Dec. 12, 1994.

U.S. Department of Health and Human Services. "State Children's Health Insurance Program: Final Allotments to States, the District of Columbia, and U.S. Territories and Commonwealth for Fiscal Year 2002." *Federal Register*, Vol. 66, no. 208 (10-26-2001).

U.S. Department of Housing and Urban Development. "Homelessness: Programs and the People They Serve: An Overview of Homeless Clients: Demographic Characteristics." Available: http://www.huduserorg/publications/homeless/homelessness/ch_2b.htm.

U.S. News and World Report (July 3, 1995), from Heath Care Financing Administration, Congressional Research Service, p. 13.

U.S. News and World Report (Aug. 7, 1995), p. 12.

U.S. Office of Management and Budget 1999. *A Citizen's Guide to the Federal Budget: Budget of the United States Government FY 1999*, "Federal Budget Dollar: Where Does It Come From," Washington, D.C.: Government Printing Office.

U.S. Office of Management and Budget 2000. *A Citizen's Guide to the Federal Budget: Budget of the United States Government FY 2000*. Available: http://w3.acess.gpo.gov/usbudget/fy2000/guide02.htm.

U.S. Office of Management and Budget 2001. *A Citizen's Guide to the Federal Budget: Budget of the United States Government FY 2001.* Available: http://w3.access.gpo.gov/usbudget/fy2001/guide02.htm.

"U.S. Official: AIDS Epidemic Could Be Contained This Decade." New Jersey *Courier–Post* (Aug. 8, 1995), p. 38.

Van Bierna, David. "The Storm Over Orphanages." *Time* (Dec. 12, 1994), pp. 58–62.

Wagner, David. *The New Temperance: The America Obsession with Sin and Vice.* Boulder, CO: Westview Press, 1997.

Wagner, David. *What's Love Got to Do with It? A Critical Look at American Charity.* New York: New Press, 2000.

Waldman, William. "Clinton Administration FY 2000 Budget Proposal–Complete Summary." American Public Human Services Association (February 1999). Available: http://www.aphasa.org/hotnews/00budget.htm.

Walker, Sam. "200 Day Drive by GOP Slices Federal Programs." *Christian Science Monitor* (Aug. 7, 1995), pp. 1, 15.

Watson, Frank Dekker. *The Charity Organization Movement in the United States.* New York: Arno Press and *The New York Times*, 1971, originally printed by Macmillan, 1922.

Weber, Max. *Ancient Judaism.* New York: Free Press, 1952.

Weber, Max. *Protestant Ethic and the Spirit of Capitalism.* New York: Scribner, 1976.

Webster's New Collegiate Dictionary. Springfield, MA: Merriam-Webster, 1980.

Weisman, Daniel. "Litigation Strategies and 'Welfare Reform.'" Paper presented at Baccalaureate Program Directors Meeting, Albuquerque, NM, October 5–9, 1998.

Whitmire, Richard. "Older Men Linked to Nation's Teenage Pregnancy Problem." New Jersey *Courier–Post* (July 30, 1995), p. 7A.

Wietzman, Leonore J. "Legal Regulation of Marriage: Tradition and Change." *California Law Review,* Vol. 62 (1974), p. 1187.

Wildavsky, Aaron. *Speaking Truth to Power: The Art and Craft of Policy Analysis.* Boston: Little, Brown, 1979.

Wilensky, Harold L., and C. N. Lebeaux. *Industrial Society and Social Welfare.* New York: Free Press, 1965.

Williams, Eric. *Capitalism and Slavery.* New York: G.P. Putnam's Sons, 1966.

Wilson, William J. *The Truly Disadvantaged.* Chicago: University of Chicago Press, 1987.

Wines, Michael. "At Issue: Civil Rights." *National Journal* (March 27, 1982).

Wooden, Kenneth. *Crying in the Playtime of Others.* New York: McGraw-Hill, 1976.

Yates, J. V. N. "Report of the Secretary of State in 1824 on the Relief and Settlement of the Poor," reprinted in the *34th Annual Report of the State Board of Charities of the State of New York, 1900,* Vol. 1, pp. 939–963.

Zastrow, Charles. *Introduction to Social Welfare Institutions: Social Problems, Services, and Current Issues.* Homewood, IL: The Dorsey Press, 1982.

Zastrow, Charles. *The Practice of Social Work.* Homewood, IL: The Dorsey Press, 1985.

Zinn, Deborah K., and Rosemary Sarri. "Turning Back the Clock on Public Welfare." *Signs: Journal of Women in Culture and Society,* Vol. 10, no. 2 (Winter 1984), pp. 355–370.

Zuckerman, Mortimer B. "The GOP Needs Some Education." *U.S. News and World Report* (Sept. 11, 1995), p. 74.

Index

Abbott, Edith, 189, 218
Abbott, Grace, 218, 249, 258
Able-bodied poor, 107–108
Abortion, 259, 260, 323, 365–367
   contraception and, 209–211, 366
   1800s and, 209
   Harris v. McRae, and Medicaid, 366
   Hyde Human Life Amendment to
      Medicaid, 366
   Medicaid and, 323
   1970s and, 366
   Progressive Era and, 259–260
   TANF and, 416
   War on Poverty and, 323
Abramovitz, Bessie, 243
Abramovitz, Mimi, 382–383
Academy for Female Education, 172
Access services, 46
Acquired Immune Deficiency Syndrome
   (AIDS), 368
   G-8 nations and, 454
Act for Punishment of Sturdy
   Vagabonds and Beggars, 103
Act to Regulate the Treatment and
   Control of Dependent,
   Neglected, and Delinquent
   Children (1899), 221
Adams, Abigail, 146
Adams, Gordon, 407
Adams, John B., 146, 147
Adams, John Quincy, and Native
   Americans, 177
Adams, Samuel, 147
Addams, Jane, 216–217, 221, 239, 251,
   255
Adler, Felix, 246
Administration on Aging, 335
Administration for Children and
   Families, (AFC), 413
Adoption
   Children's Aid Societies and, 221
Affirmative action, 442–444.
Africa, 57–58
   empires in, 285
   social welfare during 6000–3000 B.C.,
      57–58
African Americans. *See also* Civil rights
   AFDC, TANF and, 412, 424
   assumption of African American infe-
      riority, 151–152
   bias in criminal justice system and,
      355–356
   busing, 363

chain gangs after Civil War, 206
civil rights and, 363
Civil War soldiers, 194–195
children and orphanages, 219–220
colonial mutual aid societies of , 141
Constitution and three-fifths rule, 179
drug abuse and, 439
education and, 358
emancipation and, 204–207
employment in 1970s and, 363
free, 179, 183
Great Depression and, 269, 275
housing discrimination against, 432
institutional racism and, 18
leaders among, 238–240, 326, 397
Legal Principles of African-American
   Inferiority, 151–152
migration following Civil War, 237,
   200–201
1970s and, 363–364
oppression in early 20th century,
   237–238
post-Civil War, 204–207
post-Revolutionary War, 178, 179–182
post-World War I, 338
poverty among, 16–17
protests during 1960s, 320–322
Reagan administration and,
slavery and. *See* Slavery
*Swann v. Charlotte-Mecklenburg Board
   of Education*, 363
vocational training and, 293
voter registration, 293, 325–326
women's clubs, 208
World War I and, 237
World War II and, 293, 291–292
African Empires, 85
Aged and aging
   Clinton and, 428–430
   American Association of Retired
      Persons (AARP), 428, 435
   Area Agencies on Aging, 336
   programs for, under Kennedy and
      Johnson, 335–336.
   Progressive era and, 252–255
   protective services for, 333
   social insurance for, 281–282, 283,
      346–348
Ageism
   institutional, 20–21
   poverty and, 20
   stereotype, 20
Agriculture

Department of , 198
new technologies in Iron Age, 88–89
Agricultural Adjustment Act (1939),
   274–275, 292
Agricultural and Food Act (under Food
   Stamps, 1982), 377
Aid to Dependent Children (ADC), 278,
   283, 284–285
   racism in, 285
Aid to Families of Dependent Children
   (AFDC), 42, 284–285, 286,
   384–385.
   Assistance Payments Administration
      (APA), 332
   Child Support Enforcement
      Amendment (to AFDC, 1984),
      386
   containment and, 310–312
   Eisenhower years and, 310–311
   elimination of program by TANF, 413
   Faubus, Governor Orval, and cut-
      backs, 311
   Kennedy-Johnson years and, 330–331
   King v. King and substitute parent
      policies, 312
   midnight raids and, 312
   1970s and, 349–351
   post-World War II African Americans'
      northward migration and, 312
   Reagan income regulations, 384–385
   Reaganomics and Family Support Act
      (1988), 383–385, 385–387
   Shapiro v. Thompson ends residency
      requirements, 312
   Social Services Amendment capped,
      379
   split in services in 1970s, 333
   substitute parent policies and 311, 312
   suitable home policies and, 311,
      312
   Talmadge Amendments to AFDC
      (1971), 350
   Women's sexuality and, 311–312
   Work Incentive Program (WIN) and,
      333–334
   unemployed parents program
      (AFDC-UP), 385
Aid to the Blind (AB), 252–253, 277,
   283–284,286
Aid to the Permanently and Totally
   Disabled (AD), 252–253,
   277,283–284, 286. *See also* Old
   Age, Survivors, and Disability

Income (OASDI); Supplemental
    Security Income
Alamo, myth of, 184–185. *See also*
    Hispanic Americans
Alaric the Great (King of Visigoths), 76
Alcohol, Drug Abuse, and Mental
    Health Administration
    (ADAMHA), 391
Alianza Federal de Mercedes (1963), 316
Allen, Richard, 183
Allotment Act (Dawes Act, 1887), 203
Almshouses
    children and, 220
    descriptions of, 165–166
    disabled people in, 168–169
    House of Carpenters and, 141
    impotent poor in, 105–106
    immigrants and, 154–155
    mentally ill in, 166
    post-Revolutionary War, 163–165, 190
    Tudor England and, 105–106
    women in, 166
Amalgamated Clothing Workers of
    America, 243
American Anti-Slavery Society, 183, 186
American Association of Charities, 261
American Association of Hospital Social
    Workers, 262
American Association of Medical Social
    Workers, 298
American Association of Psychiatric
    Social Workers, 262, 298
American Association of Retired Persons
    (AARP), 428, 435
American Association of Schools of
    Social Work (later CSWE), 298
American Association of Social Workers,
    261, 262
American Colonization Society, 183
American Dream, 300–301
American Federation of Labor (AFL),
    200, 201
American Ideal, values and, 11–12
American Indian Movement (AIM), 358
American Indians. *See* Native Americans
American Social Service Association, 223
American Temperance Society, 162
American Women's Suffrage
    Association, 187–188
Americans with Disabilities Act of 1990,
    22, 397–398, 424
Americas, settlement of, 119–149
    in Columbus's time, 122
    English in, 128–130
    first immigration to, 121, 123
    French in, 123–125
    indigenous peoples of, 120–123
    slavery in, 142–145
    social welfare in, 135–141, 146
    Spanish in, 125–127
    women in, 132–135
Americorps (National Community and
    Service Trust Act, 1993), 440
Amidei, Nancy, 402, 403, 467
Anderson, Charles, 467

Anderson, Jack, 404, 467
Anderson, Joseph, 467
Anderson, Curt, 465
Anderson, Lisa, 304, 467
Anderson, Marion, 276
Anthony, Susan B., 186, 187, 218, 255
Apprenticeship, 140
Apte, Robert Z., 31, 52, 116, 118, 151, 229,
    471
Army Medical Corps, Civil War, 195
Army of the James, 195
Arendt, Hannah, 51
Arndt, Michael, 466
Arnold, Benedict, 147
Aronowitz, Stanley, 467
Aryan Nation, 352, 364.
Asian Americans, 18, 360–364. *See also*
    Chinese Americans, Japanese
    Americans
    Asian American social workers, 345
    Asian exclusion, legislation regarding,
        235–236
    immigration, 201–202
    institutional racism and, 18
Askia (King of Songhay), 85
Association for Improving the Condition
    of the Poor (AICP), 162–163, 241
    Friendly Visitors of, 161
Association for the Study of Community
    Organization, 299
Association of American Indian Social
    Workers, 345
Association of Community
    Organizations for Reform
    (ACORN), 432
Association of Group Workers, 299
Association of Professional Schools of
    Social Work, 261
Asoka, Prince of India, 67
Augustine, St., 74
Augustus, John, 175
Axinn, June, 151, 227, 228, 229, 230, 263,
    264, 265,302, 302, 303, 304, 305,
    340, 346, 369, 370, 402, 403

Baigent, Michael, 81, 116, 467
Bailly, Sylvain, 102
Balanced Budget Acts under Clinton, 446
Batu Khan (Mongol conqueror), 85
Baker, Ella, and SCLC, 314
Bakke v. Regents of University of California,
    reverse discrimination, 394
Balanced Budget Act (1997), 409, 416,
    434, 435, 437
Barber, Elizabeth Wayland, 55, 79, 467
Barnett, Ida B. Wells, 239–240
Barnett, Canon Samuel, 113, 216
Baron Salo W., 467
Barrera, M., 341, 467
Barrett, Kate Harwood Walker, 215–216
Barrett, Richard J., 26, 467
Barry, Marion, 363
Barton, Clara, and Red Cross, 195
Basic Education Opportunity Grants
    (BEOGs), 393

Bass, Gary D., 402, 403
Batu Khan (Mongolian Emperor), 85
Beard, Marry Ritter, 256
Beck, Allen J., 463
Becker, Ernest, 455
Beecher, Catharine, 172
Beeghly, Leonard, 405, 467
Beers, Clifford, 250
Bel, Leachman, 467
Bell, Winifred, 248, 265, 276, 340, 342,
    373, 393, 402, 403, 438, 458, 467
Belton, Beth, 21–22,
Benford, Gregory, 21–22, 467
Benizet, Anthony, 172
Bennett, Lerone, Jr., 79, 80, 115, 150, 151,
    152, 205, 206, 228, 229, 263, 340,
    341, 467
Bentham, Jeremy, 110
Berch Bettina, 29, 200, 467
Bernard, Thomas, 112
Berry, Benjamin D., 467
Bethune-Cookman College, 239
Bethune, Mary McLeod, 239, 292
Bianchi, Eugene C., 467
Bilingual education, 361.
Bismarck, Otto von, and social insurance
    in Germany, 276
Black Codes, 202–207
Black Death, 93–94, 98–99
Black Muslims, 313, 321
Black Panthers, 321–322
Black Power, 321
Blacker, C.P., 467
Blackwell, Elizabeth, 168–169, 172, 186,
    195
Blackwell, Emily, 169, 172, 186
Blackwell, Henry, 186
Blatch, Harriet Stanton, 243
Blind people,
    aid to, 277, 283–284
    care for, 172–173
    during 1800s, 172–173
    Progressive Era aid, 252
Bloch, Marc, 81, 467
Bloomingdale Asylum, 169
Blundell, Bryan, 145
Bonacich, Edna, 7
Bond, Thomas, 167
Bonding out, 131. *See* Indenture
Booth, Ballington, 215, 216
Booth, Evangeline Cory, 215–216
Booth, Maud Ballington, 215–216
Booth, Sally Smith, 152, 467
Booth-Tucker, Emma, 215
Booth, William, 215
Boss Tweed and welfare corruption, 223
Boston Education Commission, 196
Boston Episcopal Society, 141
Boukman, and rebellion, 182
Boyd, Belle, 194
Boys Clubs, 162–163
Brace, Charles Loring, 220
Bradley, Tom, 363
Brady Gun Control Bill, 439
Brandeis, Louis, 231

Braun, Peter, 467
Breckinridge, Mary, 249
Breen, Leonard Z., 342
Bremmer, Robert H., 467
Bremner, Walter, 147, 467
Brent, Margaret, 133
Brill, Naomi, 27, 467
Brimner, Andrew, 326
Brockway, Zebulon, 173, 174, 191, 467
Broder, David S., 458, 461, 467
Broverman, D.M., 467
Broverman, I. K., 467
Brown, H.. Rap., 321
Brown, John, 179
Brown, Josephine Chapman, 467
Brown, Prudence, 28, 467
Brown v. Topeka Board of Education, 313
Bruere, Robert W., 190, 467
Bryce, Robert, 460, 467
Bucher, Glenn R., 467
Burbridge, Lynn C., 405, 467
Bureau of Indian Affairs, 117, 203, 293
Bureaus of Social Aid, 286
Burger, Chief Justice Warren, 396
Burke, Edmond, 145
Burns, Lucy, 256
Burtless, Gary, 467
Bush, George administration, 280, 283,
        372, 375–376, 377. *See also*
        Reagan-Bush years.
    Americans with Disabilities Act
        (1990), 397, 442
    civil rights under, 394–398
    deficit and, 375
    Drug war, Manuel Noriega and, 400
    housing under, 391–393, 407
    isolationist perspective disappears,
        400
    international affairs under, 399–400
    New World Order and, 400
    program cuts and, 380
    Supplemental Security Income (SSI)
        and, 383
Bush, George W. administration, 408,
        417, 462
    affirmative action and, 443
    Children's Health Insurance Program,
        (CHIP), 434–435
    corporate charities and, 444
    cost-of-living adjustments and, 428
    Earned Income Tax Credits (EITC)
        and, 427
    education and, 440
    employment under, 441–442
    poverty rates and, 425–426
Busing, 363
Butterfield, Fox, 465, 467
Byrne, Ethel, 260
Byzantine Church (Eastern Church) and
        Empire, 74, 75–76, 82

Cady-Stanton, Elizabeth. *See* Stanton,
        Elizabeth Cady.
Calvin, John, 98, 100
Calvinism and work ethic, 99–102

Campos, Pedro Albizu, 316–317
Capitalism,
    American value of, 7–8
    as social institution, 29
    emergence of, 109–110
    laissez-faire capitalism, 153
    Protestant work ethic and, 7–8
Capra, Fritjof, 468
Carey, Matthew, 160
Carmichael, Stokely, 321, 322
Carter, Jimmy, 345, 346.
    Civil rights and (1970s), 356–369
    public assistance, transfer of adult
        categories to OASDI (1971), 346
    social programs in, 346–356
Cartier, French explorer, 123
Cary, John, 145
Case management, 386, 434
Casework, 308. *See* Social casework
Caste system, Indian, 67
Catholic Charities, 41, 89–91
in 1800s, 159
Catt, Carrie Chapman, 255–256
Celente, Gerald, 469
Chadwick, Edwin, 113
Chafe, William H., 303, 469
Chalmers, Reverend Thomas, 102
Chaney, James, 321
Charity, *See also* Philanthropy
    beginnings of, 78–79
    Civil War and, 195–196
    control and, foundations of, 4
    corporate, 444, 445
    early Christianity and, 75–76
    feudal Church and, 89–91
    Judaism, early, and, 5–6, 64–65
    private welfare and, 91–92
    Personal Responsibility and Work
        Opportunity Reconciliation Act
        (PRWORA) and, 411–412, 416
    private and for-profit charities,
        162–163, 444–445
    private interest agencies after Civil
        War, 162–163, 215–216
    Reagan-Bush, and, 444
    ten largest charities, 445
Charity Organization Society (COS), 49,
        192, 211–213, 270
    friendly visitors and, 161, 213–214
    outdoor relief and, 213
    police and, 214
    private welfare and, 91–92
Charlemagne (Emperor of West), 85
Chavez, Cesar, 316
Chen, Jack, 198, 228, 341 , 469
Chicago Women's Bindery Union, 217
Chicago School of Civics and
        Philanthropy, Graduate School
        of Social Services
        Administration, 225
Chicano Liberation Front, 316
Child Abuse and Treatment Act (1974),
        355–356
Child and Dependent Care Credits
        (CDCCs), 417–418, 427, 429

Child and maternal health, 248–249
    Keating Owens Bill and, 247
Child Care Block Grant, programs ended
        under, 413–418
    AFDC Child Care Services, 413
    At-Risk Child Care Program, 413
    Child Care and Development Block
        Grant, 413
    Child Development Associate
        Scholarship Program, 413
    Dependent Care Block Grant, 413
    Transitional Child Care Services, 413
Child care during Clinton administra-
        tion, 352–353, 417–419
Child Guidance Clinics, 251
Child labor, 140, 156–157, 245–247
    child-saving and, 218–221
    in colonies, 139–140
    in factories, 156–157
    juvenile justice and, 221
    Keating-Owens bill and, 247
    Progressive Era, 246–247
    Walsh-Healy Act (1936), 273
Child-saving, 49, 218, 219–221
    and juvenile justice, 221
    orphan trains, 220
Child support and dependency pro-
        grams, 86, 350–351, 386, 416–418
    absent parents (TANF), 416–417
    Child Support Enforcement
        Amendment (1984), 386
    Clinton administration and, 416–418
    Notice to Law Enforcement Officials
        (NOLEO), 350–351, 386
    Reagan administration and, 386
Child Welfare Act (1980), 355
Children
    colonial era, 139–140
    Clinton administration child care,
        417–418
    Clinton administration health care,
        434–435
    dependent, 106–107, 130, 139–140
    disabled, during 1800s, 172–173
    feudalism and, 106–107
    institutionalization of, in Kennedy
        years, 330
    Iron Age, 69
    Kennedy-Johnson era and,
        333–334
    malnutrition and, 431
    maternal and child health and, 45,
        248–249, 390–391
    in 1970s, 350–351
    orphan trains, 220
    poor, 16–17
    post-Civil War period, 219–221
    Progressive era and, 245–249
    Reagan years and, 378
    school lunch program and, 388,
        340–341
    sexually transmitted diseases and, 258
    slave children, 181
    White House Conference on, 246
Children's Aid Society, 220, 221

Children's Bureau (1912), 246, 248, 249, 285, 286
Children's Defense Fund, 378
Children's Health Insurance Program (CHIP, SCHIP), 434–435, 437
China, social welfare in Iron Age, 65–66
Chinese Americans,
    activist groups in 1960s, 318
    benefit societies, 317–318
    discrimination against, 201
    institutional racism and , 18
    labor exclusion, 202
    mutual aid societies, 202
    in 1940s and 1950s, 317
    in 1970s, 360–361
Chinese immigrants
    anti-Chinese Unions, 201
    anti-Chinese riots, 202
    Exclusion Acts (1882, 1892, 1904), 202
    repeal of (1943), 202
    Geary Act (1892) requires identification papers, 202
    immigration after Civil War, 201–202
    McCreary amendment of Geary Act (1893), 202
    mutual aid societies, 202
    immigration after Revolutionary War, 178–179
    shanghaiing for labor, 179
    1970s and, 360–361
    1940s and 1950s, 317
Chisholm, Shirley, 363
Christianity
    beginnings of, 74–76
    Byzantine Church and, 75–76
    early charity, 75–76
    feudalism and, 77–78
    Roman Church and, 74–75
Ciarroca, 466, 472
City of Richmond v. J.A. Croson Co., 442
Civilian Conservation Corps (CCC), 271, 272, 275
Civil rights
    ADARAND corporation, 442
    African Americans and redistricting, 443
    Americans with Disabilities Act and, 442
    Burger, Chief Justice Warren, and gays, 395
    Bush, George administration and, 394–398, 442
    Bush, George W. administration and, 443
    City of Richmond v. J.A. Croson Co., 442
    Clinton administration and, 442–444
    Constitution, amendments to, 442
    equal protection clause of Constitution (14th amendment), 442
    first civil rights movement, 153–154
    gays and. *See* Gay people
    Johnson administration and, 325–326, 336–338

Kennedy administration and, 318–319, 320–329
1970s and, 356–369
Oncale v. Sundowner Offshore Services(1998), 444
protest and, 320–325
Reagan-Bush years and, 394–398
reverse discrimination and, 394
sexual discrimination and, 442
social work profession and, 336–338
struggle for, 312–315
Truman-Eisenhower administration (1940s-1950s) and, 306–307, 312–318
Voting Rights Act (1965), 443
Wards Cove Packing v. Antonio, 442
Civil Rights Act (1964), 320–321, 394–395, 424
Civil Rights Commission, 381, 383, 394, 397
    Reagan and, 377
    Clinton and, 443
Civil War, 193–197
    charity in, 195–196
    political economy following, 197–198
    pre-Civil War period, 153–188
Clark, Ramsey, 355–356
Classism, 12–17
    poverty and welfare and, 12–16
    stratification and wealth and, 12–13
Cleaver, Eldridge 322
Clerc, Laurent, 172
Client-in-situation, 47–48
Clinton administration
    Balanced Budget Act and, 446
    capital assets and, 446–447
    Children's Health Insurance Programs (CHIP), 434–435
    Earned Income Tax Credit (EITC) and, 446
    economy under, 409–410
    educational programs of, 440
        Head Start, 440
        Goals 2000: Educate America, 440
        School to Work Opportunities, 440
        National Community and Service Trust Act (Americorps), 440
        $1000 Lifetime Learning Tax Credit, 440
        Hope Scholarships: College Tax Credit, 440
        Pell grants, 440
        education IRAs, 440
        Telecommunications Act (1996), 440
    employment and jobs, 440–442
    Empowerment and Enterprise Zones, 438
    health care under, 408, 433–437
    Health Security Act, 434
    Home Investment Partnerships (HOME), 438
    gays and, 443

military-industrial complex and, 450
multinational and corporate welfare and, 450
National Missile Defense system, 451
Omnibus Crime Control Act (1994), 438–440
    racism and classism in, 439
    social costs of, 439–440
    three strikes and out policy, 438–439
    program cuts under, 411–412
    SSI under, 426–427
    Strategic Defense Initiative (SDI, Star Wars) and, 451
    tax cuts and corporate welfare, 435, 446–447
    Vaccines for Children (1993), 434
Clinton, Hillary Rodham, 408, 433–434
Clothilde, Queen of Feudal France, 78
Cloth-making, 55, 87–89, 92–93
Clovis (King of France), 78
Cloward, Richard, 37, 193, 227, 228, 302, 342, 370, 375, 402, 403, 463, 469
Cohn, William S., 450
COINTELPRO. *See* Nixon administration
Coit, Stanton, 216
Coll, Blanche D., 117, 154, 164, 189, 190, 227, 228, 229, 248, 263, 264, 265, 469
College Settlement, 216
Collier, John, 292
Colonies
    colonial women in, 132–136
    English in, 128–130
    French in, 123–125
    indentured servants in, 132–133
    Protestants in, 127–128
    revolution in,146–147
    slavery in, 142–145
    social welfare in, 135–141
    Spanish in, 125–127
Columbus, Christopher, and Taino Native Americans, 125
Combs-Orme, Terri, 404–469
Commercial revolution, Middle Ages, 98
Committee on Economic Security, 277
Commission on Interstate Child Support (Reagan), 386
Commons, John R, 253, 254
Communism in Great Depression, 271
Community Action Agencies (CAAs), 453
Community Action Programs (CAPs), 328–329, 337
Community Facilities Act (1941) (Lanham Act), 295
Community mental health programs and Economic Opportunity Act, 328
Community Work Experience Program (CWEP), 386
Comprehensive Education and Training Act (CETA), 353, 382
Compton, Beulah R., 97, 150, 151, 189, 190, 228, 229, 263, 264, 265, 303, 304, 327, 328, 329, 469

Comstock Act (1873), 210, 260
Conference on Charities and
    Corrections, 261
Conflict perspectives on social welfare,
    37–40
    conflict theory, 37
    Marxian perspective, 38
    socialism and socialist feminist, 38
    radical feminist, 38
Congressional Union for Women's
    Suffrage, 256
Congress of Industrial Organization
    (CIO), 273
Congress of Racial Equality (CORE,
    1942), 293–294, 313, 321
Connelly, Mark Thomas, 229, 265, 469
Connor, Bull, 313, 314, 318–319, 321
Conover, Pamela Johnson, 228, 469
Conquistadores, 125
Constantalelos, D., 81, 469
Contraception
    Comstock Act, 210, 260
    1800s and, 210–211
    family planning programs in the
        1980s, 365–367
    Goldman, Emma and, 260–261
    PRWORA and, 419–421
    Progressive era and, 260–261
    Sanger, Margaret and, 260–261.
Contract with America
    104th Congress and, 406, 410–412
    public assistance under, 412
    PRWORA and, 412, 413
Cooper, Anna J., 208
Cornish, Samuel E., 183
Coronado, Francisco Vasquez de, 126
Corporate bill of rights and GATT, 453
Corporate statesmen, 292, 407
    Nixon and, 344
    Clinton and, 446–451
Corporate welfare, 447–451
    G. Bush and, 375–376
    G. W. Bush and, 447, 449–450
    capital assets and tax cuts, 446–447
    corporate lobbying and, 449
    Clinton administration, 446–451
    elections, re-elections and, 449
    Environmental Protection Agency
        and, 448
    government support of, 448
    Market Protection Program, 448
    military-industrial complex and, 450
    multinational and corporate welfare,
        450
    National Missile Defense system and
        Star Wars and (Strategic
        Defense Initiative SDI), 450, 451
    Nixon and, 344
    OSHA and, 448
    pricing schemes and, 450
    profit through public assistance, 223
    Reagan and, 375, 380
    subsidies and, 450
Corporations
    definition of, 452

    Progressive Era and, 232
    top 500 corporations, 452
Cortes, Hernando, 126
Cortina, Juan, 185
Corvee, New World, 58, 121
Cost-of-living adjustment (COLA), 344,
    346, 379, 380, 428–429, 430
    G.W. Bush and, 428
    payments in 2000 and, 429
    Reagan and, 379
Cotton gin invented, 154
Cotton culture, 154,180–185
Coulton, G.G., 90, 116, 470
Council of Energy Resources (CERT),
    359, *See also* Native Americans
Council on Social Work Education
    (CSWE, 1946), 261, 299
    Baccalaureate programs and, 345
Counseling: Personal social services,
    45–46. *See also* Casework
Cousins, Norman, 290
Coward, Rosalind, 56
Cramer, Elizabeth, 26
Crampton, Helen M., 470
Crandall, Prudence, 172
Cranston-Gonzales National Affordable
    Housing Act, 392
Crawley, Mike, 466
Crime and criminal justice system
    adult, 173–174
    African Americans and justice system,
        355–356
    Brady Gun Control Bill, 439
    drug abuse and, 439
    1800s and, 174–175
    jails and prisons in 1980s, 356
    juvenile. *See* Juvenile justice system
    Juvenile Protection and Adult
        Corrections Act (1974), 355–256
    1970s and, 355–356
    Omnibus Crime Control Act (Clinton,
        1994), 438–440
    poverty as, 96–98
    Progressive Era and, 255
Crittenton, Charles, 215
Crittenton Services, 215–216
Cromwell, Oliver, 128
Cubans, during 1970s, 362–363
Cult of True Womanhood, 207–211
Curley, Jami, 461, 470
Curtis, Charles, 357
Custodial services and care, 45

Daly, Mary, 80, 117, 470
Danziger, Sheldon, 422–423, 424, 460
Darenkamp, Angela, 240, 264, 470
Dark and Middle Ages, 82–97
    Black Death during, 93–94
    feudalism during, 86–87, 91–95
    Islam during, 83–85
    mercantilism during, 98
    poverty as crime during, 96–97
    private welfare during, 91–92
    Roman Church during, 76–78, 82–83,
        89–91,

    scientific revolution of, 87–89
    witchcraze during, 93–96
Daskal, Jennifer, 462, 470
Daughters of Bilitis, 325
Daughters of Liberty, 147–148
Daughters of the King , 125
Davies, James, 341, 470
Davis, Angela, 182, 206, 219, 227, 228,
    263, 264, 352, 470
Davis, Kingsley, 25, 470
Dawes Act (Allotment Act,1887), 203
Dawson, Molly, 275
Day care, 44
    Clinton administration and, 404,
        417–418
    21st Century Community Learning
        Centers and Children (day- and
        after-school care), 404
    cost of day care, 418
    day care centers and quality, 417–418
    financing, 44
    Head Start, 418
    Lanham Act (Community Facilities
        Act, 1941), 292, 295
Day, Peter, 31–32, 49, 50–51, 52, 304, 470
Day, Phyllis J., 25, 342, 470
Deaf, care for during 1800s, 172–173
Debs, Eugene V., 232, 234
Decretum, 91
Defense of Marriage Act (DOMA),
    443–444
Deficit Reduction Act (1984), 377
DeForest, Robert, 246
Degler, Carl N., 228, 470
De Paul, St. Vincent, 72, 102
Deinstitutionalization of mentally ill,
    308–309, 392
Democratic egalitarianism, 6
Denison, Edward, 113
De Ovando, Nicolas, and slavery, 454
Department of Health and Human
    Services (HHS), 332, 282, 346,
    396
Department of Health, Education and
    Welfare (DHEW), 282–285, 300,
    332, 329
Dependent Pension Act (1890), 197
Depression
    of 1837, 157
    of 1873–187 and 1893–1898, 159, 198
    Great Depression of 1929, 267–271
    Progressive era and, 240, 241
De Riencourt, Amaury, 80, 81, 115, 116,
    117, 151, 470
De Schweinitz, 117, 118
DeSantis v. Pacific Telephone and Telegraph
    91979) and gays, 367
De Soto, Hernando, 126
Dessalines, Jean-Jacques, 190
De Trevino, Juan,
Deutsch, Albert, 190
Developmental disabilities and pro-
    grams, 172–173
    Eisenhower administration and,
        309

Kennedy-Johnson administrations and, 334–335
Devine, Edward T., 246
Devine, Joel A., 25, 383, 403, 404, 405, 407, 458, 470
Devolution under TANF, 414
Diagnostic related groups (DRGs), 380–381, 433. *See* Medicare
DiNitto, Diana, 402, 403, 404, 458, 461, 462, 470
Disabled people.
    aid to, 172–173
    cutbacks under Reagan-Bush administrations, 380–381
    discrimination against, 22–23
    during 1800s, 172–173
    Post-Great Depression aid for, 283–284
    Progressive Era aid for, 252
Discrimination, 12–13
    ageism and, 20–21
    classism and poverty and, 14–17
    heterosexism and, 21–22
    institutional, 17–24
    otherism and, 22–23
    racism and, 17–19
    sexism and, 19–20
    socioeconomic, 14–17
Disraeli, Benjamin, 112
Dix, Dorothea, 22, 170–171, 195, 372
Dixon, Robert Layton, 260
Dobelstein, Andrew W., 194, 303, 304, 369, 470
Dobyns Henry F., 150, 470
Dolbeare, C., 404
Dolgoff, Ralph, 26, 52, 59–60, 64–65, 80, 115, 116, 117, 151, 230, 304, 369, 470
Douglass, Frederick, 59, 64–65, 183, 186, 187
Doyle, Wilma, 342, 470
Draft Law of 1863, 194
Draft riot (18630, 220
Dred Scott decision, 143, 183, 186
Drout, John A., 189, 471
Drug abuse, 391.
    African Americans and, 439
    Alcohol, Drug Abuse, and Mental Health Administration, 391
    mental health and, 298
    Prohibition and, 298
    Reagan and, 391
Dubois, William Edward Burkhardt, (W.E.B.), 238–239
Dunn, Finley Peter, 471
Dupree, Alan, 461
Du Rivage, Virginia, 26
Dutch East India Company, 128, 129
Dye, Nancy Schrom, 265, 471
Dye, Thomas R., 14, 25, 148, 152, 153, 189, 191, 220, 227, 302, 303, 313, 340, 341, 342, 471

Dyer, Mary, 135

Earned Income Tax Credit (EITC, 1975), 423, 424, 427–428, 446
Eastman, Crystal, 254–255, 256
Economic trade agreements among nations, 454–455
Economic Opportunity Act (EOA)(1964), 326–329
    costs of, 338
    maximum feasible participation in, 339
Economics
    demand-side economics,269
    supply-side economics, 268
Economy. *See also* Political economy
    Clinton administration, 409–410
    Corporate statesmen and, 300
    Eisenhower and, 308
    Johnson, Lyndon B. and, 308–309
    during Middle Ages, 98
    polarization of income, 13–14
    post-Civil War, 197–200
    post-World War II, 297–298
    Shadow government and, 301
    social institution, as, 28–29
Eddy, Thomas, 173, 189
Education, 43–45, 140
    Basic Opportunity Education Grants (BEOGs), *See* Pell grants
    bilingual, 361
    Bush, G.W. administration, 477
    Clinton administration and, 440. *See also* Clinton administration education programs
    colonial, 140
    Contract with America and. *See* TANF, Work and Training Programs
    Education for All Handicapped Children Act, added to ESEA, 354
    Elementary and Secondary Education Act (ESEA), 354, 393
    expansion during Progressive Era, 244–245
    Johnson-O Malley Act (1924), 240
    in Kennedy-Johnson years, 354
    Morrill Act (Land Grant Colleges established), 171
    Reagan administration, 393–394
    segregation and, 312–314
    Smith-Hughes Act (1917), 245
    social workers, of, 261–262
    World War II and G.I. Bill, 300–301
Educational discrimination, race and women, 19
Educational, Recreational, and Rehabilitative Services, 43–45
Edwards, Johnathan, 141
Egalitarianism, democracy and, 6–7
    following Revolutionary War, 153–154
Egypt, social welfare during 6000–3000 B.C. in, 58–59

Ehrenreich, Barbara, 190, 460, 471
Ehrenreich, John, 263, 264, 265, 266, 287, 299, 302, 303, 304, 369, 327, 328, 381, 398, 401, 403, 405, 471
Eichhorn, Robert, 345, 471
Eisenhower, Dwight D., 276, 306–308
    armed forces exclusion of gays, 324–325
    expansion of AFDC, 310–311
    new opportunities for non-white minorities and, 306
Eisner, Allen, 463
Eisner, Michael, 441
Eitzen, D. Stanley, 370, 371, 471
Elders, Jocelyn, and AIDS, 368
Elementary and Secondary Education Act (ESEA), 354, 393
Elizabeth I (Queen of England),103
Elizabethan Poor Laws (1601), 104–105, 138–140, 354, 283, 393
Elkins, Stanley, 471
Elmira Reformatory, 174
Emancipation, 204–207
Emancipation Proclamation, 195
Employment
    G.W. Bush and, 352
    Clinton administration and, 440–442
    early 20th century and, 240–243
    Great Depression and, 268–269
    post-Civil War, 198–200
    post-Revolutionary War, 156–158
    Reagan-Bush administrations and, 381–383
Empowerment and enterprise zones, under Clinton, 438
Enclosure movement., 89, 112
Engels, Friedrich, 111
England
    American Revolution and, 146
    capitalism in, 109–110
    feudalism in, 85–87
    Industrial revolution in, 109–114
    New World colonization by, 128–130
    poverty in Tudor period, 113–114
    Tudor England, 103–109
English, Deirdre, 190, 471
Equal Employment Opportunity Commission (EEOC), 320, 323
    Reagan administration and, 396
    Nixon and, 345
    1970s and, 356
Equal Rights Amendment (ERA), 365–367
Equiano, Olaudah, 152, 471
Eskridge, William J., Jr., 324, 464, 395
Esping-Anderson, Gosta, 303, 471
Espo, David, 465, 471
Euberger, Zoe, 459
Eugenics movement, Eugenics Society, 233, 348
Europe
    barbarian invasions of, 76–77, 78
    in 500 B.C.–300 A.D., 69
    feudalism in, 82–87

labor control in, 96–98
European invasions in New World, 123–130
  English invasion, 128–130
  French invasions, 123–124
  Protestants in, 127–128
  Spanish invasions, 125–127
Evers, Medgar, 319
Ezekial, Raphael, 364

Fabian Society, 113–114, 211
Factory Act (1833), 107
Fair Employment Practices Commission (FEPC), 276, 294
  defeated, 312
  riots of 1943, 294
Falwell, Jerry, 372
Families
  slave, 181
  as social institution, 30
Family Assistance Plan (FAP, Nixon), 346
Family planning. *See* Contraception
Family responsibility
  in colonies, 137–138
  under TANF, 416–418, 419–421
Family Services of America, 220, 215, 261
  child support, 386
  teenage pregnancy, 386–387
  work and sexual morality and, 385
Family Support Act (FSA, Reagan, 1988), 377, 383–385, 385–387, 412–414
Family Welfare Association of America, 261, 270
Fanon, Franz, 471
Far Right, 368, 373, 406. *See* Moral Majority, Religious Right
Farm Credit Administration (1935), 275
Farmer, James, 312
Fathers, absent
  Notice to Law Enforcement Officials (NOLEO), 386
  TANF and, 416–417
Faubus, Governnor Orval
  AFDC cutbacks in Arkansas, suitable homes policy and, 311
  Little Rock riots, 312
Feagin, Joe R., 26, 150, 151, 191, 228, 303, 304, 341, 342, 359, 370, 381, 405, 471
Federal Case Registry and National Directory of New Hires, 417
Federal Deposit Insurance Corporation (FDIC), 274
Federal Employment Act (1906), 254
Federal Emergency Relief Act (FERA), 271, 272–275, 292
Federal Hosing Authority, 274
Federalism, New, 376–380
Feldstein, Donald, 26, 52, 59–60, 64–65, 80, 116, 117, 151, 230, 304, 402, 469, 470
Feminist welfarist perspective, 39
Fendrich, James M., 402, 459, 463, 471
Ferdinand (Archduke of Austria), 233
Ferguson, Shannon, 402

Feudalism, 76, 92–95, 82–114
  agricultural technology in, 87–89
  dissolution of, 92–96
  European societies and, 86–87
  guilds and, 92
  political economy of,
  rise of, 85
  Roman Church and, 89–91
  Roman, 76
  social welfare during, 87–88,
  society in Europe, 86–87
Filipino Americans, during 1970s, 360
Fine, Sidney, 229, 447
Fined Jean, 216
Firmin, Thomas, 108
Fisher, Dr. John, 173
Fleming, Alexander, 258
Fleming, Arthur, 312
Flexner, Dr. Abraham, 259
Florence Crittenton Mission, Homes, 215–216
Flower, Lucy, 218
Flynn, Elizabeth Gurley, 243
Folks, Homer, 174
Follett, Mary, 299
Foner, Philip S., 190, 447
Food programs. *See* Nutrition programs
Food Stamp Program, 334, 353, 387
  elimination of program, 413
Ford, Gerald, 344, 346, 428
For-profit service industry, 378
  privatization and, 376–377
Forrest, General Nathan Bedford, 195
Fort Pillow Massacre, 195
Foster Grandparents Program, 336
Fox, Dixon, 71
Francis, David, 465
Franklin, Benjamin, 141,147, 149, 172
Free Trade Area of the Americas, 454
Freedmen's Bureau, 192, 196–197
Freedom rides, 314
Freedpersons before emancipation, 204–207
Freud, Sigmund, 287–288
French in New World, 123–124
Friedan, Betty, 322, 323
Friendly Visitors, 161, 213–214, 224–225
Friedlander, Walter A., 31, 52, 116, 118, 151, 229, 471
Friedman, Dorian, 459, 471
Friends Almshouse, 141
Frontier Nursing Society, 249
Functionalism
  manifest and latent functions, 33
  social welfare and, 33
Funds to Parents Act (Illinois, 1911), 247–248

G-8 Nations, 454
Gadhafi, Muhamar, 371
Gadsden Purchase (1853), 184
Gallaudet, Thomas, 172
Galper, Jeffrey, 175–176, 278, 304, 305, 471

Gandhi, Mahatma, and non-violent tactics, 313
Gannett, Deborah Simpson, 147, 186
Garrison, William Lloyd, 182, 186
Gartner, Allan, 471
Garvey, Amy Jacques, 29
Garvey, Marcus Moziah, 234, 239
Gault decision and *parens patriae*, 326
Gay people.
  ADARAND Corporation and, 442
  Americans with Disabilities act and, 442
  anti-gay laws in 1930s, 1940s, 324
  Bush, G.W. administration and, 443
  civil rights and, 367, 395–396
  Clinton and, 408, 443
  Daughters of Bilitis and, 325
  Defense of Marriage Act (DOMA, 1996), 443–444
  DeSantis v. Pacific Telephone and Telegraph (1979), 367, 395–396
  Eisenhower and armed forces exclusion of, 324–325
  Equal protection clause (14th amendment), 442
  Gay Activist Alliance, 325
  gay liberation and, 324, 325, 367–368
  heterosexism and, 21–22, 24–25
  Hoover, J. Edgar and blacklisting, 324–325
  Kameny, Frank and Mattachine of Washington Society, 325
  Koch, Ed, and, 367
  Lambda Fund, 367
  legal rights and , 444
  Mattachine Society, 325
  mental illness stigma and, 324
  Milk, Harvey, 367
  Moscone, George, 367
  National Gay and Lesbian Task Force, 367
  Oncale v. Sundowner Offshore Services (1998), 444
  104th Congress and civil rights for gays, 443
  Reagan/Bush administration and, 442
  Smith, Howard V. and sex discrimination, 320
  social revolt and, 367
  stereotypes of, 396, 442
  Stonewall Inn riot, 325
Geary Act (1892) and McCreary amendment (1893), 202
General Assistance (GA), 43
General Federation of Women's Clubs, 208
General hospitals during 1800s, 167–169
Genghis Khan (Mongol conqueror), 85
General Agreement on Trade and Tariffs (GATT), 453
Gentlemen's Agreement (1907), 235–236
George III (King of England),
Gephardt, Richard, 435
Gerber, Larry, 472
Gergen, David, 466, 472

Gettleman, Marvin B., 227, 472
Ghost Dance, 203
G.I. Bill, 300, 301
Giacoma, Carol, 371, 472
Gies, Frances, 88, 98, 472
Gies, Joseph, 88, 98, 472
Gil, David G., 458, 472
Gilbert, Neil, and Harry Specht, 27–28,
    51–52, 212, 472
Gilbert, Thomas, 197
Gilman, Charlotte Perkins, 231
Ginger, Ray, 229, 472
Gingrich, Newt, Speaker of House of
    104th Congress, 420
Glass, Justine, 115, 472
Globalization. *See* International econ-
    omy
Gnosticism, 74, 75
Goals 2000: Educate America Act, 440
Golden Triangle, 143
Goldman, Emma, 260–261
Gompers, Samuel, 200, 201, 242, 253
Gonzales, Corky, 316
Goodman, Andrew, 321
Goroff, Norman, 23, 28, 472
Gough, Kathleen, 79, 472
Gramm-Rudman-Hollings (GRH) Deficit
    Reduction Act of 1986, 376, 377,
    379, 380
    Reagan income regulations and,
        384–385
Grand Design, Roosevelt plan
    (1932–1936), 274, 277
    Agricultural Adjustment Act (1933),
        274–275, 292
    National Industrial Development Act,
        272
    National Industrial Recovery Act
        (NIRA), 273, 274
    Reconstruction Finance Corporation
        (RFC), 270
    Social Security Acts (1936) 276–286
    Works Progress Administration
        (WPA), 271
Gray, Virginia, 228, 472
Gray Ladies, 172
Great Awakening, 141
Great Depression, 267–275
    African-Americans and, 269
    economics during, 270
    Eleanor Roosevelt, 273, 275–276
    Emergency Committee on
        Employment, 270
    Hispanic Americans and, 269
    New Deal and, 271–275
    Reconstruction Finance Corporation,
        270
    stock market crash (1929), 268–269
    social revolt during, 270–271
    social security and, 267–275
    temporary relief during, 270
    veterans march on Washington,
        270–271
    women and, 269
Greek city-states, social welfare in, 67–71

Greeley, Horace, 187
Greenberger, Marcia, 429–430
Greenhow, Rose O Neal, 194
Greenstein, Robert, 16, 25, 465
Greenwood, Ernest, 52, 472
Greer, Colin, 472
Gregory of Nyssa, St., 74
Griffiths, Martha, 320
Grimke, Angelina, 185–186
Grimke, Sarah, 185–186
Griscom, John, 173, 189
Grob, Gerald N., 117, 139, 151, 190, 191,
    229, 472
Group homes and Kennedy administra-
    tion, 330
Group work. *See* Social group work
Gruber, Katherine, 371, 472
Guadaloupe Hidalgo, Treaty of, 184
Gugliotta, Guy, 472
Guilds and social welfare, 92
Gurteen, S. Humphreys, 212
Guyer, Bernard, 404, 472

Haig, Alexander, 358
Haiti, slave rebellion in, 182
Hale, Nathan, Jr., 209
Hall, Raymond, 341, 342, 472
Halverson, Guy, 464, 472
Hamilton, Dr. Alice, 218
Hamilton, Gordon, 299
Hammurabi, 59
Handel, Gerald, 81, 87, 104, 115, 117, 132,
    150, 229, 265, 303, 472
Handler, Joel P., 340, 370, 472
Happiness for Women (HOW), 365
Harding, Warren G., 251
Harrington, Michael, 329, 403, 472
Harris, Marvin, 150, 151, 152, 472
Harris, Patricia, 326, 472
Harris v. McRae, Medicaid and abortion,
    366
Harrison, William Henry, 177
Hartley, Robert, 161
Hartung, William D., 466, 472
Haryou: Harlem Youth Opportunity
    Program, 336
Haskins, Ron, 460, 472
Hastie, William, 299
Hastings, Battle of, and Magna Carta, 85
Hatcher, Richard, 363
Hate Groups, 362–363, 455
Hathaway, Jonas, 106, 107
Hawken, Paul, 472
Hayakawa, Samuel, 360
Hayes, Mary Ludwig,
Hayes, Rutherford B., 201, 205–206
Haynes, George Edmund, 239
Head Start, 354, 418, 440
Health care
    children and, 417–418, 434
    Clinton administration and, 433–437
    Health Maintenance Organizations
        (HMOs), 433
    insurance programs and, 45, 280,
        331–332, 389, 416–417

Keating Owens Bill and, 247
Kennedy-Johnson era and, 331–332
maternal and child health and,
    248–249, 390–391
Medicaid and leavers, 423
medical care and general hospitals,
    167–168
Progressive era, 168–169, 248–249
psychiatric care, 169–171, 249–251
Reagan-Bush era, 389–391
Rodham-Clinton proposal, 433–439
women and medical (gynecological)
    care in 1800s, 167–168
women, by and for, 167–168, 254,
    257–261
Health insurance, 254
Health Maintenance Organizations
    (HMOs), 433
Heffernan, Joseph, 303, 348, 369, 472
Helms, Jesse, 368
Henry III, 85
Henry VIII, 99, 101, 103
Henry Street Settlement, 216
Hernstein, Richard, and African
    American intelligence stereo-
    types, 343
Heterosexism, 21–22
Hetter, Kalia, 459, 472
Hibbens, Anne, 135
Hickok, Lorena, 275
Higgenbotham, A. Leon, Jr., 142–143,
    151–152, 472
    assumption of African American infe-
        riority, 151–152
Hill, Octavia Butler, 113
Hill, T. Arnold, 294
Hinden, Stan, 461, 472
Hirabayashi, Gordon, 360
Hispanic Americans, 184–185
    Alianza Federal de Mercedes (1963),
        316
    Brown Berets, 316
    Campos, Pedro Albizu, 316–317
    Chicano Moratorium Committee, 316
    civil rights and, 315
    Great Depression and, 269
    guest workers and Reagan, 362
    immigration and, 236–237
    Immigration and Naturalization
        Service (INS, 1929), 236
    institutional racism, 18
    labor and, 361–362
    La Raza Unida, 316
    Mexican American immigration cap
        (1965), 361
    Mexican American Legal Defense and
        Educational Fund, 316
    Mexican American Political
        Association, 316
    Mexican Americans and poverty, 361
    National Farm Workers Association,
        316
    National Reclamation Act (1902) and,
        185
    1940s to 1960s, 315–316

1970s and, 361–363
Operation Bootstrap, 317
Political Association of Spanish-
   Speaking Organizations, 316
post-Revolutionary war,
Puerto Ricans, 237, 315–318, 361–363
repatriation and, 236
Texas Rangers (1800s) and, 184
Tijerina, Reies, 316
United Farm Workers Organization
   Committee (1966), 316
Young Lords, 317, 322
Hitler, Adolf, 288
Ho, David, 463, 472
Hollis, Florence, 299
Home Investment Partnerships Program,
   432
Homelessness, 392–393, 431–433
   children and, 431
   Emergency Food and Shelter
      Program, 433
   Homeless Assistance Grants, 433
   numbers of, 432
   racism and, 432
   Stewart B. McKinney Assistance Act
      for the Homeless, 431
   Urgent Relief for the Homeless Act
      (1987), 392
Home Owners Loan Corporation, 274
Home Investment Partnerships (HOME),
   438
Home Relief Employees Association, 286
Homestead Acts
   of 1862, 178
   of 1864, 197
   of 1902, 185
Homophobia, 21–22. See Heterosexism
Homosexuality, 11, 24–25, 367
   AIDS and, 368
   Gay liberation and, 324
   in Greece, 69
   witchcraze and, 94
Holy Roman Empire, 82–83
Hoover, Herbert, 268, 270
Hooverville, 270, 392
Hopewell Indians, 120
Hopkins, Harry, 271, 272, 274, 277, 279,
   283, 304, 305
Hopper, Isaac, 175
Hospitals
   as first social welfare, 90–91
   Civil War period and,
   1800s and mental hospitals, 169–171
   general hospitals in the 1800s,
      167–169
   psychiatric, 298
House Un-American Activities
   Committee (HUAC, 1947),
   306
House of Carpenters, 141
Houses of Correction, 139. See
   Almshouses, Workhouses
Housing, 431–437
   African Americans and, 432
   Clinton administration and, 431–433

consolidation of housing agencies
   under HUD (1966), 335
Cranston-Gonzales National
   Affordable Housing Act, 392
disabled housing, 433
elderly housing, 433
Federal Housing Authority, 274; up-
   dated 1949, 335
Home Investment Partnerships
   Program, 432, 438
Home Owners Loan Corporation, 274
Home Ownership and Opportunity
   for People Everywhere Act
   (HOPE, 1991), 392
Housing Act (1937), 274
housing certificates, 433
Housing and Urban Development
   (HUD) Section 8 certificates, 438
Kennedy and Johnson administra-
   tions and, 335–336
Personal Responsibility Act
   (PRWORA) and, 413
Reagan-Bush Administration, 391–393
1940s and 1950s, 335
1970s and, 355
1980s and, 392–393
Housing Acts (1937, 1949), 274, 300
Housing and Urban Development
   (HUD), 335, 431–433
   consolidation of housing agencies
      (1966), 335
   established, 392
   increase in Reagan-Bush era, 392
   Section 8 certificates, 432
   TANF and, 432
Houston, Charles Hamilton, 313
Houston, Sam, 185
Howard, John (Sheriff of Bedford), 108
Howe, Julia Ward, 187–188
Howe, Neil, 403, 473
Howe, Dr. Samuel Gridley, 173, 223
Howell, Barbara, 404, 473
Howell, Leon, 404
Hraba, Joseph, 191, 227, 228, 264, 340,
   473
Hull House (est. 1889), 216–217
Humanistic management, 299
Human Life (Hyde) Amendment to
   Medicaid, and abortion, 366
Humphrey, Hubert, 338
Hunger Prevention Act, 287
Hunt, Harriet, 168
Hunter, Mary Ski, 24, 473
Hutchinson, Anne, 134
Hutchinson Family Encyclopedia, 115,
   473
Hyde Amendment to Medicaid (Human
   Life Amendment) and abortion,
   366
Hymowitz, Carole, 150, 151, 156, 189,
   190, 191, 227, 228, 229, 264. 265,
   266, 303, 340, 341, 473

Immigration
   almshouses and, 155

Civil War period and, 200, 201–202
   disease and, 155
   Gentlemen's Agreement and, 235–236
   Immigration Act of 1907, 235
   Immigration Acts (1921, 1924),
      235–236
   immigration and almshouses, 155
   Irish indenture and, 131–132
   mutual aid clubs and, 158
   Oriental Exclusion Act (1880), 235
   Oriental Exclusion Act (1924), 236
   Progressive era and, 234–237
   post-Revolutionary War, 154–155
   to Western hemisphere, 120–123
Impotent poor, in colonies, 138–139
Incan Empire, 123
Income, polarization of, 13–14, 374–375,
   409, 410
Income tax amendment (16th amend-
   ment), 232
Indenture, 130–132
   child, 130
   Newlanders and, 130
   political dissidents and, 130–131
India, caste system of, 66–67
Indian Removal Act (1830), 177–178. See
   also Trail of Tears
Indian Reorganization Act (1934),
   292–293
Indian Trade and Intercourse Act (1834),
   178
Individualism, 6
Industrial Revolution, 109–114, 233
   emergence of capitalism and, 109–114
   New Poor Law, England, and, 111–114
Industrial Workers of the World (IWW,
   Wobblies), 242–243
Inouye, Daniel, 359–360
Inquisition, 90, 94–95
Institutional discrimination, 15–23
   ageist, 21–24
   racist, 17–20
   TANF and, 412, 424
   sexist, 19–20
Institutional perspective on social wel-
   fare, 35–37
Institutionalization, children and, 330
Istook Amendment, 435
Insurance. See also Social insurance
   health, 278, 280, 331
   old age, 208, 309
   public assistance comparison to, 41
   social, 279–282, 309, 346–348
   unemployment, 253–254, 348,
      381–383
Internal Security Act (McCarran Act),
   306
International economy, significance of,
   451–455
   AIDS and G-8 nations, 454
   Bush and, 399–400
   G-8 nations and, 454
   General Agreement on Tariffs and
      Trade (GATT), as corporate Bill
      of Rights, 453

G.W. Bush and Kyoto protocol, 454–455
Clinton and, 450–455
definition of, 452
global economy, 407, 449
International Monetary Fund (IMF) and, 453
Multilateral Agreement on Investments (MAI), 454–455
neocolonization and, 456
New World Order and Bush administration, 452
Nixon and oil crisis, 344
North American Free Trade Agreement (NAFTA), 452
Organization for Economic Cooperation and Development (OECD), 453
Reagan and, 399–400
social welfare and, 452
terrorism and, 451–452
transnational corporations and, 452, 453
World Bank and, 406, 453
world poverty and, 458
International Association for World Peace, 217
International Ladies Garment Workers Union (ILGWU), 240, 242
International Monetary Fund (IMF), 453
Interstate Commerce Act (1887) and monopolies, 198
Irish people, indenture in New World and, 131–132
Iron Age and social welfare, 63–67
Irons, Peter, 27, 360, 371
Isis religion and women, 72
Islam, Dark and Middle Ages , 83–85
Israelite societies, 59–63
Ivins, Molly, 27, 448, 463, 464, 465, 473

Jackson, Andrew, and Indian Removal Act, 177
Jackson, Eugene, 440, 443, 473
Jackson, Reverend Jesse, 363
Jackson, Richard, 403, 473
Jackson, Ron, 459
Jackson State University (Mississippi) students killed, 323
Jacobs, William J. 132, 150, 151, 152, 189, 190, 191, 227, 228, 264, 266, 303, 473,
Jansson, Bruce S., 465, 473
Japanese Americans
  Gentlemen's Agreement (1907), 235–236
  in the United States, 360
  institutional racism and, 18
  internment during World War II, 289–290, 360
  Japanese American Citizens League, 290
  mail order brides and, 236
  Progressive era, discrimination during, 238–239

during 1970s, 359–360
Jeanne d Arc, 95
Jensen, Arthur, and African American intelligence, 313
Jesus Christ, 74–76
Jewish people
  in America, pre-Revolution and 1800s, 159
  immigration, post-Revolutionary era, 201
  Jewish Federation, 286
  witchcraze and, 94
Jim Crow laws, 207–208, 228
Job Corps, 325–327
Job Opportunity and Basic Skills (JOBS), 386, 413, 414
Job Training Partnership Act (JTPA, 1981), 382, 386
Joe, Tom, 404, 473
John (King of England), 85
Johnson, Alice K., 443, 473
Johnson, Andrew, 196
Johnson, Clifford M., 331, 374–401, 402, 403, 404, 405, 474
Johnson, Hugh, 273
Johnson, Lyndon B. administration, 307, 319, 325, 338
  Civil Rights Act (1964), 320
  civil rights and 336–338
  Economic Opportunity Act (1964), 320
  Great Society and, 319–322
  Vietnam War and, 327, 328–329, 338
  Voting Rights Act (1965), 320
  War on Poverty, 320
Johnson, Henry, 237
Johnson, Michael P., 191, 473
Johnson-O'Malley Act (1928) and,240
Joliet, French explorer, 123
Jones, Eugene K., 292
Jones, Mary Harris (Mother Jones), 245–246, 251, 265, 473
Jordan, Barbara, 363
Judaeo-Christian charity values, 5
Judaic social welfare, 64–65
Justinian Code of Laws, 83
Juvenile delinquency
  Elmira Reformatory, 174
  Haryou (Harlem Youth Program), 336
  Juvenile Delinquency and Youth Offenses Control Act, 336
  Juvenile Protection and Adult Corrections Act (1974), 355–256
  Mobilization for Youth, 336
  post World War II, women blamed for, 292, 297, 298
Juvenile justice system
  African Americans and, 355–356
  beginnings of, 223
  during 1800s, 173–174
  during 1970s, 355
  Elmira Reformatory, 174
  Juvenile Delinquency and Youth Offenses Control Act, 336
  Kennedy and, 336

Progressive era and, 255

Kahn, Alfred J., 45, 52, 473
Kameny, Frank, 325
Kansas-Nebraska Homestead Act (1854), 178
Kaplan, Marion A., 117
Kaplan, Saul, 350, 370
Karger, Howard J., 375–376, 402, 403, 407, 448–449, 458, 465, 473
Karliner, Joshua, 466, 473
Kashta, 58
Katz, Michael B., 164, 189, 190, 227, 229, 254, 265, 303, 342, 473
Keating-Owens bill, 247
Kelley, Florence, 217, 239, 246, 247, 254
Kellogg, Kate, 371, 473
Kellogg, Paul, 254
Kemp, Jack, 392
Kennedy John F., and Kennedy administration, 276, 307–309
  AFDC and, 330–331
  assassination, 319
  civil rights and, 307–308, 318–319
  group homes and, 330
  Juvenile Delinquency and Youth Offenses Control Act, 336
  Kennedy Commission on the Status of Women (1961), 276
  schools of social work and, 330
  Social Rehabilitation Services (SRS) and, 330
  Social Service Amendments (1962), 329–330
Kennedy Johnson years
  civil rights in, 307–308
  nutrition programs of, 334
  social programs in, 329–336
  work training and AFDC and, 330
Kennedy, Robert F., 318, 329
Kent State University riots, 343
Kentucky Committee for Mothers and Babies, 249
Kerber, Linda K., 151, 191, 264, 266, 303, 341, 473
Kern, Stephen, 264, 473
Kerr, Florence, 275
Kerr-Mills Bill and health care, 332
Kessler-Harris, Alice, 150, 151, 227, 228, 264, 302, 303, 341, 473
Key, V.O., 198, 227
Kieft, William, 128
Kilborn, Robert, Jr., 463, 473
King, Martin Luther, Jr., 307, 313–314, 338
King v. King and substitute father requirements, 312
King's College Medical School, 167
Klaits, Joseph, 95, 99, 116, 117
Knights of Labor, 200, 201, 245
Knox, John, 101, 117, 473
Koop, C. Everett, 368
Koch, Mayor Ed, and gay liberation, 367
Koretz, Gene, 423, 460, 473
Koromatsu, Fred, 360

Kramer, Samuel N., 80
Ku Klux Klan, 52, 205, 235, 313, 319, 364, 368. *See also* Hate groups
Kyoto Protocol and world economy, 454–455

Labor
    Bureau of Labor Statistics established (1884), 198
    child, 139–140, 156, 219, 246–247, 273
    Clinton and, 440–441
    Depression and, 268–270
    feudal, 92–93, 96–97
    New World, 125
    1990s and, 440–442
    social welfare policy and, 106–107
    post-Civil War period, 198–200, 203, 211
    pre-Civil War period, 151–153
    primary and secondary labor forces, 382
    Progressive era and, 240–243
    Reagan administration and, 381–383
    Sherman Anti-Trust Act (1890), 198
    slave, 181–182
    women, 156–157, 181, 290–292
Labor unions
    anti-Chinese unions, 201
    early trade unions, 158
    Great Depression and, 273
    International Workers of the World (IWW, Wobblies), 245
    in 1990s, 440–442
    post-Civil War period, 200
    pre-Civil War period, 153–154
    Progressive era and, 240–243
    Reagan administration and, 383
    social workers and, 286–287
    women in, 198–199, 241–243
Ladies of Charity, 102
Lambda Defense and Educational Fund, 367
Lamison-White, 25
Lamy, E., 117
Landay, Johnathan S., 462, 465, 466, 474
Langenbach, Lisa, 371, 474
Langston, John Mercer, 183
Lanham Act and day care, 292
La Raza Unida, 316
LaSalle, French explorer, 123
Latent functions, definition, 33
Lathrop, Julia, 217, 225, 246, 249, 251
Laughlin, Harry, 233
Lav, Iris J., 474, 474
Law Enforcement Assistance Administration (LEAA), 344, 355
Law v. Nichols and bilingual education, 361
Lazere, Ed, 459, 474
League of Iroquois, 178
League of Nations, 234
League of Women Voters, 256
Leavitt, Judith Walzer, 228, 265, 474
Leavers from TANF, 423

LeBeaux, C. N., 52
Lee, Porter, 261
Lee, Robert E., 179, 185
Legal Principles of African-American Inferiority, 151–152
Legal Services Organization (LSO), 328
Leigh, Richard, 81, 116
Lekachman, Robert, 404, 474
Lesbians. *See* Gay people
Less eligibility, principle of, 34, 113, 161
Levin, Hermann, 151, 227, 228, 229, 230, 263, 264, 265,302, 302, 303, 304, 305, 340, 346, 369, 370, 402, 403
Levitan, Sar A., 331, 340, 342, 370, 374–401, 474
Lewis, John l., 321
Life necessity services, 41–43
Lincoln, Abraham, 193–195
Lincoln, Henry, 81
Lincoln University, 183
Liuzzo, Viola, 321
Local responsibility in colonies, 136–137
Locke, John, 11
Loewe, Michael, 80, 474
London, Jack, 231
Long, Huey, and Share the Wealth Party, 271
Long, Russell, 370
Lopez, Robert S., 93, 116, 474
LoPresto, Pamela, 460–474
Lott, Trent, 450
Louis XIV, New World and, 125
L Ouverture, Toussaint, 182
Love, Terry S., 404
Lowell, Francis Cabot, 157
Lowell, Josephine Shaw, 213–214, 224
Lowell, Mrs. Charles Russell, 229
Lugard, Flora Louisa, 80, 239
Lusane, Clarence, 466, 474
Luther, Martin, 7, 100
    Protestant Reformation and, 99–100
Lynching, 205, 238, 269, 294
    prohibited by law, 312

Macarov, David, 31, 52, 81, 115, 154, 189, 274, 303, 304, 408, 458
MacDonald, Dwight, 329
Macfarlane, Alan, 95, 117, 474
Macy, Harry J., 27, 474
Madison, James, 148
Magna Carta, 82, 85, 90
Magnusson, Paul, 466
Maimonides, 65
Malcolm X, 313, 321
Malkin, Elisabeth, 466
Malthus, Thomas Robert, 8, 111
Managed care, 433–434, 437
Mandell, Betty Reid, 311–312, 340, 474
Manifest destiny, 176, 233
Manifest functions, definition, 33
Mann, Horace, 171
Manning, Seaton W., 190, 474
Manpower Development and Training Act of 1962 and EOA, 326
Marine Hospitals Service, 167, 222

Marotta, Tony, 341, 474
Marriage. *See also* Women
    in Eisenhower years, 308
    in New World colonies, 132–135
    Protestantism and, 100–101
    values and, 10–11
    women in labor force and, 241–243
Marquette, Father, 123
Marshall, John, 154
Marshall Thurgood, 313, 326
Marwick, David, 331, 340, 342
Marx, Karl, and Marxian perspective on social welfare, 38, 111
Mary Ellen Case (1875), 219
Mary Magdalene, 74
Mary Ellen Case (1875), 219
Mason, Jan, 342, 474
Massachusetts State Charities Board, 165
Maternal and child health programs, 41, 42–43, 248–249, 390–391
Maternal and Child Welfare Act, 285–286
Mathews, Jane DeHart, 151, 264, 266, 291, 303, 341, 474
Matthews, William H., 254
Matsunaga, Spark, 360
Maximum feasible participation, 339
McCarran Act (Internal Security under Truman), 319
McCarthy, Eugene, 323
McCarthy, Joseph
    anti-Chinese actions, 317
    McCarran Act and, 319
    Red Scare and, 287, 306, 307
McClymer, John, 264, 474
McHenry, Robert, 229, 230, 264, 303, 305, 474
McKissick, Floyd B., 321
McMaster, John B., 474
McNeil, J.M., 26
Means testing, 34, 42
Medicaid, 21, 42, 436–437
    children and, 437
    clients of, 436–437
    costs of, 437
    Early and Periodic Screening, Diagnosis, and Treatment and, 437
    expenditures in 1990s, 436
    Johnson administration and, 332, 339
    Harris v. McRae and abortion, 366
    Hyde (Human Life) Amendment and abortion, 366
    public assistance and, 436
    Reaganomics and, 378, 389–390
    TANF leavers and, 423
Medical model, social work and, residual perspective as basis of, 34, 287
Medical social work in Progressive era, 249–251, 282
Medicare, 42, 281, 281, 331, 346–348, 380–381
    Clinton and, 428–430, 435–436
    deductibles and, 436

individual medical retirement accounts and, 435
Johnson administration and, 331, 339
Medigap (supplemental medical) insurance and, 435, 436
numbers of recipients, 436
Reagan administration and, 379, 380, 389
Mencher, Samuel, 101, 117, 189, 190, 264, 303, 474
Mental health, 249–251
community mental health programs and clinics, 298, 328
developmental disabilities and, 334
Eisenhower administration and, 309
Kennedy-Johnson era and, 334–335
Mental Health Act, 334
women and, 298
Mental hospitals
almshouses and, 166
Progressive Era and, 249–250
1800s and, 169–171, 298
Mental hygiene movement, 250–251
Mercantilism, rise of, 98–99
Merchant, Carolyn, 115, 116, 191, 474
Meredith, James H., 318
Merriam Survey (1928), 292
Mesopotamia, social welfare 3000–1200 B.C. in, 58–60
Mexican Americans during 1970s, 361–362. *See also* Hispanic Americans
Meyer, Adolf, 249
Middle East in Iron Age, 6000–1500 B.C.
Middle Passage, 144–145
Midgley, James, 373, 402, 474
Migration
agricultural migration after World War II, 308
African Americans after Civil War, 200–201
Civil War and, 178–179
Native Americans and Trail of Tears, 177–178
Milford Conference (1929), 262
Military industrial complex, 344, 450–451
Milk, Harvey, 367
Mill, John Stuart, 110, 154
Mill work for women and children, 156–158
Miller, Dorothy C., 340, 341, 403, 475
Miller, John, 465, 475
Miller, Mamie, 402, 459, 463
Mills, Kim I., 475
Minier, Maude E., 259
Mink, Patsy Takemoto, 360
Miranda decision and suspects rights, 326
Miringoff, Marc L., 4, 24, 65, 80, 475
Mississippi Freedom Democratic Party and SNCC, 321
Missouri Compromise (1829), 183
Mobilization for Youth (MFY), 336
Model Cities Program, 335
Monopoly capitalism, 29

Mohr, James C., 266, 475
Monroe, James, and Native Americans, 177
Montanism, 74
Montgomery, Alabama, and segregation boycott, 313
Moore, Wilbert E., 25
Moral Majority, 365, 368, 372
More, Hannah, 112
Morgan, John, 167
Morgan, Ted, 191, 475
Morrill Act (Agricultural Colleges), 177
Morris, Robert, 342, 369, 475
Morrow, Prince, 258
Moscone, George, 367
Moseley, Ray, 405
Mosher, Dr. Clelia Duel, 209, 228
Mother's pensions, 207, 247–249. *See also* AFDC, TANF
Funds to Parents Act (Illinois, 1911), 247–248
Mott, Lucretia, 172, 186
Moynihan, Daniel P., 373, 374, 402, 403, 428, 461, 475
Moynihan, Mary, 264, 475
Muller, Herbert J., 115, 475
Mulroy, Elizabeth A., 404, 475
Multilateral Agreement on Investments, (MAI), 454–455
Multinational corporations, 452, 453.
Mumola, Christopher J., 463
Munoz, C., 341, 475
Munro, Dana C., 86, 115, 477
Murphy, Dana C., 86
Murphy, Edgar, Garner, 246
Murphy, Ruth E., 459
Mutual aid societies, 141, 162–163

National Afro-American council, 239
National American Women's Suffrage Association (NAWSA), 255
National Association for the Advancement of Colored People (NAACP), 238–239, 275, 293–294
National Association of School Social Workers, 298
National Association of Social Workers (NASW), 261
ELAN (Educational Legislative Action Network, 1970), 345
PACE (Political Action for Candidate Election, 1978), 345
National Clearinghouse on Aging, 336
National Colored Labor Union, 200
National Committee on the Cause and Cure of War, 256
National Committee for Mental Hygiene, 217, 250
National Community and Service Trust Act (Americorps), 440
National Conference on Charities and Corrections, 241

National Conference on Social Welfare, 223, 277
racism and, 237
takeover by welfare rights groups (1969), 337
National Congress of American Indians (1944), 315
National Consumers League, 217, 275
National Coordinating Committee of Welfare Rights Groups, 337
National Council of Clubs, 208
National Equal Rights League, 239
National Farm Workers Association, 316
National Federation of Day Nurseries (1898), 219
National Federation of Settlements, 270
National Florence Crittenton Mission, 216
National Freedman's Relief Association, 196
National Gay and Lesbian Task Force, 367
National Health Insurance Bill, 408
National Industrial Development Act, 272
National Industrial Recovery Act (NIRA), 273, 292
National Labor Relations Act (Wagner Act) (1938), 273
National Occupational Safety and Health Act (OSHA), 282
National Organization for Women (NOW), 323, 364–365
National Reclamation Act (1902) and Hispanics, 182
National Social Work Exchange (1917), 261
National Urban League, 239, 293
National Welfare Rights Organization (NWRO), 337–338, 349
National Women's Party, 257
National Women's Suffrage Association, 187
National Women's Trade Union League (NWTUL), 242
National Youth Authority (NYA), 293
Native American Church, 240
Native American Reorganization Act, 315
Native Americans
Allotment Act (1887) (Dawes Act), 203
American Indian Movement (AIM), 358
American Indian Policy Review Commission, 357–358
beaver trade pre-colonial era, 124
boarding schools and, 203–204,
Bureau of Indian Affairs, 203, 293
Council of Energy Resources, 359
citizenship granted (1924), 240
civil rights and, 315
claims against U.S. government, 359
employment in 1970s, 358

Europeans in New World and, 123–126
fishing, tribal rights to, 359
Five Nations in the New World, 123
genocide of, 176–178
Ghost Dances and, 203–204
Indian Health Service and health, 357
Indian Removal Act (1830), 177–178
Indian Reorganization Act (Wheeler Howard Act, 1933), 292–293
Indian Trade and Intercourse Act (1834), 178
institutional racism and, 17–18
Kennedy ends termination policy, 315
leaders in, 356–357
Merriam Survey, (1928), 292
migration to cities, 357
New World and, 120–123
1940–1950 and, 350
1970s and, 356–359
Northwest Ordinance and, 176
post-Civil War period, 202–203
post-Revolutionary War and, 175–178
pre-European invasion, 120–123
rebellion, 126–127, Alcatraz (1973), Wounded Knee, Adirondack State Park, 358–359
removal of children from Native American parents, 358
Red Power movement, 315
slavery in post-European invasion era, 123–130, 125–127, 129
wards of U. S. Government, 203
World War II and, 292–293
Wounded Knee, massacre at, 203–204
Nefertari, Queen of Egypt, 58
Negative income tax plans
Carter Better Jobs Program, 346
Child and Dependent Care Credits, 418, 427, 429
Nixon's Family Assistance Program (FAP), 346
Negro Fellowship League, 239
Negro Improvement Association, 239
Neus, Elizabeth, 371, 475
New Careers Program, 328
New Deal, 273–278
New Federalism
Nixon and, 344
program cuts under, 377–378
Reagan and, 376–380
Newlanders, 130
Newman, Pauline, 264, 475
New Poor, 381–382, 383
New Poor Law (England, 1834), 111–112
New Puritanism, 8–9
Newton, Huey, 321–322
New World, 119–150
colonies in, 129–130
disease in, 126
Dutch East India Company and, 128
English in, 128–130
before European invasion, 129–123
European invasion of, 123–130
Native Americans and, 123–125

Protestants and, 127–128
religion and women in, 134–135
women's rights and, 133–134
work of women in colonies, 133
New World Order and Bush administration, 452
New York Association of Federation Workers, 286
New York Charity Organization Society, 224
New York City House of Refuge, 173
New York City Mission Society, 158
New York Female Moral Reform Society, 158
New York General Hospital, 169
New York Infirmary for Women and Children, 168
New York School of Philanthropy (1901), 224
New York School of Social Work (1919), 225
New York State Vocational Institution, 173
Nichel, Tim, 402, 403, 463
Nichols, Roy Franklin, 190, 475
Nicholson, Trish, 464, 475
Nightingale, Florence, 113
Nino, Pedro Alonso, 142
Nixon-Carter-Ford era (1970s)
Child Abuse and Treatment Act (1974), 355
civil rights in, 356–369
public assistance: categories transferred to OASDI (1971), 346
Juvenile Protection and Adult Corrections Act (1974), 355–356
National Clearinghouse on Aging (1973), 336
Older Americans Comprehensive Amendments (1973), 336
Revenue Sharing Act (1972), 351
social programs in, 346–356
social services capped, 351
Nixon, Richard M., 323, 338, 343–344, 346, 407
civil rights and, 345
COINTELPRO: Counter-Intelligence Program, CIA and, 344
Family Assistance Program (FAP), 338
House Un-American Activities Committee (HUAC) and, 306
international affairs and, 344
McCarthyism and, 287, 306, 307, 317
oil crisis and, 344
public assistance and, 345
Talmadge amendments to AFDC (1971), 350
Work Incentive Program (WIN) funnel, 350
Noeggerath, Emil, 210
Norris-LaGuardia Act and unions, 273
North American Free Trade Agreement (NAFTA), 452, 475
Northwest Ordinance of 1787, 176–177

Notice to Law Enforcement Officials (NOLEO) and child support, 386
Nuclear family values, 10–11
Nutrition programs, 430–431
Agricultural and Food Act (1982) and Reagan, 377
block-granted programs, 413
breakfast programs under Clinton and G.W. Bush, 431
children and malnutrition, 431
Food Stamps, 387
and Agricultural and Food Act (1982), 377
Food Stamps and TANF leavers, 423
Kennedy-Johnson programs, 334
Mickey Leland Memorial Domestic Hunger Relief Act (1990), 430
PRWORA and food program reductions, 430
Reaganomics and, 387–389
School Lunch Program (1946), 300, 388, 430–431
Summer Food Services, 431
Surplus commodities program doubled, 334
Women's, Infant's, and Children's Nutrition Program (WIC), 388
under Clinton and G.W. Bush, 431
Nutrition programs ended under TANF, 413
Child Nutrition Act (1966), 413
Commodity Distribution Act (1987), 413
Emergency Food Assistance Act (1983), 413
Emergency Food and Shelter Program, 433
Hunger Prevention Act (1988), 413
School Lunch Act, 413
WIC, 413

Oberlin College, 172
O Connor, Sandra Day, 422, 464
Office of Economic Opportunity (OEO), 328–329. 343–344
Office of Federal Contract Compliance Programs (OFCCP), 345, 396
Old Age and Survivors Insurance (OASI), 42, 280–281
Eisenhower and, 42, 309, 310
financing under Reagan and, 381
transfer to OASDI, 346
Old age assistance, 252–253, 279–281, 283, 286
Old Age Assistance (OAA) Program, Roosevelt's New Deal, 279
Old Age, Survivors, and Disability Insurance (OASDI), 280, 281, 339, 344, 428–430
Reagan and, 380–381
Old Age, Survivors, Disability, and Health Insurance (OASDHI), 41–42, 280, 308, 331, 346–348, 380–381. See also Medicare

Older Americans Act (1965), 335–336
Older Americans Comprehensive
    Amendments (1973), 336
Omnibus Budget Reconciliation Acts
    (OBRA), 377, 378–379
    accepted as fiscal culture, 378
    OBRA (1981), 377
Omnibus Crime Control Act (1994), 438,
    439
Opdycke, Sandra, 4, 65
Open Housing Law (1968), 338
O Reilly, Leonora, 243
Organization for Economic Cooperation
    and Development (OECD), 453
Organization of African Unity (OAU),
    454
Organization of Afro-American Unity
    (OAAU), 321
Oriental Exclusion Acts: 1880, 235–236;
    1924, 236
Ornelas, C., 341, 475
Orphan trains, 220
Orphanage for the Care of Colored
    Children, 219–220
Orphanage movement, 162–163, 219–220
Orshansky, Mollie, 14, 52, 340
O'Sullivan, Mary, 217, 243
Otherism, 22–23
Otis, James, 147
Outdoor relief, 107, 112, 163, 164,
    166–167, 213, 220, 222–223, 283.
    See Poor relief
Ovando, Nicholas de, 125
Owen, Robert, 111
Oxley, Laurance, 292
Ozanam, Frederick, 102
Ozawa v. U.S. (1922), 174–175

Paine, Thomas, 147
Palmer, John L., 376, 402, 403, 405, 475
Palmer , Mitchell, 234
Pan-Indian Society of American Indians,
    240
Parens patriae, 219, 235, 251, 255
Parham, T.M. Jim, 342, 475
Parkhurst, Christabel, 256
Parkhurst, Emmaline, 256
Parks, Rosa, 314
Patriarchal religion
    Chinese, 66
    in Europe, 85–86
    Greek, 67–69
    in India, 67
    Israelite, 62–63
    Protestantism and, 100–101
    Roman, 71–72
Patriarchy
    definition of, 9–10
    values of, 373
Paul, Alice, 256–257
Pearce, Diana, 52, 475
Pearsall, Richard, 25, 475
Peattie, Lisa, 475
Pell grants, 393
Penitentiaries during 1800s, 174–175

Penn, William, 129
Pensions
    for aged, 252–253
    for mothers, 247–249
Perkins, Frances, 271, 273, 275, 277, 278,
    296
Perkins Institute, Massachusetts School
    for the Blind, 173
Perlman, Helen, 300
Persian Empire, 500 B.C.–300 A.D.
Personal Responsibility and Work
    Opportunity Reconciliation Act
    (PRWORA, 1996), 42, 285, 408,
    413–427
    Programs cut under, 413–414
    AFDC and, 413–414
    Child Care Block Grant, 413
    Educational Block Grants and, 414
    Elementary and secondary education
        and, 414
    Family planning clinics, 414
    Head Start and, 414
    Housing and Urban Development
        (HUD) and, 414
    Low income energy assistance and,
        414
    mission statement, 419
    nutrition and, 431
    Preventive Health Program and, 414
    racism, sexism and, 456
    Safe and Drug Free Schools, 414
    Summer Youth Employment, 414
    Title XX Social Services and, 414
Personal social services, 45–46
Petrie, W. Flinders, 80, 475
Philadelphia Anti-Slavery Society, 186
Philadelphia Free African Society and
    mutual aid, 141
Philadelphia Society for Alleviating the
    Miseries of Public Prisons, 174
Philanthropy. *See* Charity
Phillips, Wendell, 187
Piankhy, 58
Pierce, President Franklin, 171
Pitcher, Molly, 147
Piven, Frances Fox, 34, 37, 134, 193, 227,
    229, 302, 342, 356, 370, 375, 402,
    403, 463, 475, 476
Planned Parenthood, 260
Plantations, 180–181
Platt, Anthony M., 191, 475
Plessy v. Ferguson, 206, 313
Plocher, David, 402, 403
Polish Women's Alliance, 162
Political economy
    Bush administration and, 375–376
    Clinton and, 409–410, 446–451
    definition of, 54
    Great Depression years and, 268–276
    Industrial Revolution and, 109–114
    1990s and, 406–410
    1970s and, 343–345
    post-Civil War, 197–198
    pre-Civil War, 153–154
    Progressive era, 231–234

Reagan era and, 372–376
    World War II and, 267–271, 288–294
Polity, as social institution, 29–30, 56
Pomeroy, Sarah B., 60, 80, 475
Poor. *See* Elizabethan Poor Laws
    able-bodied poor (sturdy beggars),
        139
    bonding out, 131
    classification of, 138–140
    dependent children, 140
    impotent poor, 138–139
    Institutionalization movement in
        1800s, 163
    relative responsibility for, 137–138
    selling of the poor, 164
Poor laws
    American, 159–161, 163–167, 283
    colonial, 136–141
    early American, 156
    Egyptian, 58
    Elizabethan (England, 1601), 104, 114,
        163–167, 282
    Gratian's *Decretum* (1140), 91
    New Poor Laws (England, 1834),
        111–114
    relative responsibility, 138
    Social Darwinism and, 212
Poor relief, 43, 108–109, 244
    administration in 1800s, 160
    corruption in 1800s and, 222–223
    defining the poor, 14, 15–17
    colonies and, 136–137
    post-Civil War, 222
    Royal Commission on, 112
    1800s, 160
Pope (Tewa shaman), 127
Population
    growth during early 20th century,
        234–237
    Malthus and, 111
Populism, 211, 216–218
Post-Civil War period, 196–228
    political economy of, 197–200
    social welfare in, 211–225
Poverty, 12–17
    blame for, 5–6, 211–215
    capitalism and, 109–111, 153
    children in,16, 423
    Civil War and, 221–223
    classism and, 12–14
    classification of poor and, 138, 140
    colonial families, 137
    contemporary perception of, 455–457
    crime, poverty as, 96–97, 101
    discrimination and, 12–17
    1800s and, 163–164
    Eisenhower years and, 307–309
    ending poverty and, 455
    estimating rate of, 398
    Greek city-states and, 69–70
    Kennedy-Johnson years and, 343–344
    levels of, 14–15, 16
    neocolonialism and, 456
    new poor and, 381–382, 383
    1990s and, 407–408

poverty line calculation, 340
poverty rates and G.W. Bush adminis-
    tration, 447
Progressive era and, 234, 241
Protestant work ethic and, 78
racism and, 18–19, 423
Reagan-Bush administration and, 375,
    384–385, 387
Rome and, 71
social Darwinism and, 8
statistics on, 15–17,
TANF and, 423, 424
Third-World citizenry and, 456–457
social welfare and, 14–18
women and, 453
Power
    corporate, 456–457
    love and, 1, 457
    polity and, 29–30
    social work and, 24
    values and, 23–24
Pre-Civil War period, 153–188
    civil rights movement during,
        153–154
    immigration and city slums, 154–156
    labor in,156
Prisons, 44
    Clinton administration and, 438–439
    1800s and, 175
    1980s and, 356
    Pennsylvania system of solitary con-
        finement, 175
    Prison Act (1877), 108
    Progressive era, 255
    Prison Reform Act (1877), 108
    Quakers and, 174–175
    Tudor England and, 108
Private charities, 222, 215–216, 444–445
Private philanthropy, 141
    colonial, 141–142
    Dark and Middle Ages and, 91–92
    Civil War era, 211–221
    post-Revolutionary War period,
        158–163
Private interest agencies, 215, 219, 221
Privatization
    Nixon and, 372
    Reagan and, 376–377
    Clinton and, 407, 412, 416,
    Medicaid and, 377–379, 437
    social services and, 429–430
Probation, 175
Professional organizations of social
    workers, 286, 287, 297, 345
Progressive Era, 231–263
    aid to disabled people during,
        252–253
    juvenile and criminal justice during,
        255
    labor and unions during, 240–243
    medical and psychiatric social work
        during, 249–251
    old age assistance during, 252–243
    oppression of African and Native
        Americans during, 237–241

population movements and immigra-
    tion during, 234–236
professionalization of social work
    during, 286–288
prostitution during, 211, 257–258, 259
reforms for children during, 245–249
social welfare in, 243–262
unemployment insurance and work-
    ers compensation during,
    253–254
veterans welfare during, 251–252
women and health during, 257–260
women's suffrage during, 255–256
Prosser, Gabriel, 182
Prostitution, Progressive Era, 259
Protective or custodial services, 45
Protestantism, early
    Lutheranism, Calvinism, and work
        ethic and, 99–100
    in North American colonies, 125–126
    Reformation and, 99–103
    slave status and early Protestantism,
        143
    women under Protestantism, 100–101,
        134
Psychiatric social work
    post-Civil War, 263
    Progressive era, 249–251, 308
    psychiatric hospitals, 298
    psychiatry during 1800s, 169–171
Public assistance, 285, 286
    American Revolution and, 163–166
    Civil War and, 221–224
    Clinton administration and, 412
    early, 221–223
    corporations profit through, 223
    Eisenhower years and, 309–312
    Elizabethan Poor Laws and, 104–109
    Greek City-states and, 67–71
    Kennedy-Johnson years and, 311–312,
        329–334
    Medicaid and, 332
    1970S and, 348–350
    Reagan -Bush administrations and,
        383–385, 386–387
    Social Security Act (1935) and, 42–43,
        282–286, 287
    transfer of adult categories to OASDI
        ((1971), 346
Public education. *See* Education
Public health movement
    beginnings of, 43, 222
    public health services, 251, 257
    venereal disease and, 258
    veterans and, 251–253
    Visiting Nurses Association, 216
    women and, 43, 222
Puerto Ricans. *See* Hispanic Americans

Quakers
    in New World, 129, 141
    Philadelphia and, 174
    prisons and, 174–175
Quincy, Josiah, 163
Quiroz, Julie, 402, 403

Race riots, 320–323
Racism
    African Americans and, 179–183
    Chinese and, 178–179, 202
    Contract with America and, 406,
        410–412
    Eisenhower administration and,
        312–319
    Hispanic Americans and, 184–185
    institutional, 17–19, 175–183, 355–356
    justice systems and, 355–356
    Japanese Americans and, 289–290
    Native Americans and, 176–178
    post-Civil War, 203–207
    poverty and, 15–19
    pre-Civil War, 175–187
    Progressive era and, 235–238
    in 1970s, 356–368
    World War II and, 292–294, 292–294
Radical feminism, 38
Rainwater, Lee, 303, 340, 476
Raleigh, Sir Walter, 129
Randolph, A. Phillip, 293–294
Rank, Mark Robert, 402, 459, 476
Raspberry, William., 422, 460, 476
Ray, Charlotte, E., 208
Reagan, President Ronald, 372–373, 375,
    376, 377, 399, 401
Reagan administration, 338, 372–401, 407
    AFDC and. 384–385
    AIDS and, 368
    affirmative action and, 442
    basic needs programs under, 387–394
    block grants in, 378–379
    Bush/Reagan administration, 407–408
    civil rights in, 394–398, 442
    cost-of-living adjustments and, 379
    cost of welfare in, 399
    corporate income tax and, 375
    defense and, 380–381
    deficit spending, 374–375, 376
    diagnostic related groups (DRGs)
        and, 380–381
    drug abuse programs and, 291
    economy and, 374, 375
    education in, 393–394
    employment and, 381–381
    Family Services of America and,
        386–387
    Graham-Rudman-Hollings AFDC
        cuts, 384–385
    guest workers and, 362
    health care in, 389–391
    housing in, 391–393
    income polarization in, 375
    international affairs under, 379,
        399–400, 407
    Medicaid cuts and, 378
    Medicare and, 380
    Native Americans and, 359
    New Federalism and, 376–380
    nutrition programs and, 387–389
    OASDI and, 380–381
    OASI financing and benefits in,
        381

political economy of, 359, 374–380,
 374, 375
poverty and, 375
privatization in,
program cuts under, 378–379, 380–387
public assistance in, 383–387
Reaganomics, 359, 374–380, 374, 375
Star Wars and, 379
Supplemental Security Income cuts
 under, 378
supply side economics and, 372–375
unemployment Insurance and,
 381–382
Reconstruction, 204–205
Reconstruction Finance Corporation, 270
Recreational services, 45–47
Red Cross, 195, 251, 252, 275
Red Power movement, 315
Red Scare, 231, 234
Red Summer (1919) and African
 Americans, 238, 321
Reed, Ira D., 292
Reed, James, 228, 249, 266, 476
Reformatory movement, 173–174
Rehabilitation services, 45–47
Rehnquist, William, 422
Rein, Martin, 303, 331, 340, 342
Reismann, Frank, 403
Reiter, Rayna R., 79, 476
Religion
colonial, 141
Israelite in Iron Age, 60–63
Native American. See Ghost Dance
patriarchal, 56–57, 60–63
pre-Civil War, 158–159
Protestant reformation and, 98–101
Roman Church, 74–78
as social institution, 30–31
Religious Right, 8, 368, 372, 373, 385, 406,
 419, 443, 463
Religious societies following
 Revolutionary War, 158–159
Residual perspective on social welfare,
 34–35
Retired Senior Citizens Program, 336
Revenue Sharing Act (1972), 351
Revolutionary War, 146–146
egalitarianism following, 151–152
social welfare following, 163–167
women in, 146–147
Reynolds, Barbara, 464, 476
Reynolds, Bertha Capen, 287
Rhoades, Charles J., 292
Ricardo, David, 111
Richmond, Mary E., 224–225
Riemer, Eleanor S., 117, 476
Rifkin, Jeremy, 422, 460
Riots. See Social protests
Robers, Dr. Jane E., 216
Roberts, Albert, 191
Roberts, Needham, 237
Roberts, Steven V., 459, 476
Robinson, Gladys, 456, 466
Robinson, Virginia, 299
Roe v. Wade and abortion rights, 366

Roman Church
Dark and Middle Ages and, 82, 86,
 89–91
early, 74–78
feudalism and, 89–91
Roman Empire, emergence and fall,
 72–74, 85
Romasco, Albert U., 302, 476
Rome, early State and Church, 71–78
conversion of barbarians, 82
rise of Holy Roman Church, 76–78
social welfare and, 71, 78, 89–91
Roosevelt, Eleanor, 273–276, 322
Chair, Kennedy Commission on
 Status of Women (1961), 323
Roosevelt, Franklin D., 243, 270, 271–275,
 277, 289, 292, 293, 294, 303
New Deal of, 271–286
Racism and, 292
Social Security and, 278–286
Roosevelt, Theodore, 235, 246, 254
Rose, Ernestine Potowski, 186
Rose, Nancy, 403, 476
Rosenberg, Ethel, 306–307
Rosenberg, Julius, 306–307
Ross, Sonya, 460, 476
Roth, Susan, 465, 476
Rovner, Julie, 403, 476
Royal Commission on Poor Relief (1832),
 112
Rubin, Beth, 391, 476
Rubin, James H., 26, 404, 476
Rucci v Rucci and women, 322
Ruggles, David, 183
Rule, James B., 37, 52, 463, 476
Rumford, Count (Benjamin Thompson),
 102
Rush, Benjamin, 169–170
Ruskin, John, 113
Russo, Francis X., 369, 370, 403
Russworm, John, 183
Ryan, William O., 52, 476

Sadler, William, 265
Saggs, H.W.F., 80, 476
St. Joseph's College for Women, 172
Saleeby, Dennis, 24
Salvation Army, 41, 162, 215
Sanborn, Franklin B., 224
Sanders, Bernard, 25, 465, 476
Sanger, Margaret, 260–261
Sard, Barbara, 462, 476
Santa Ana and the Alamo, 184
Sarri, Rosemary, 26, 370, 385, 404, 476
Sauer, Carl A., 150, 476
Saville, J., 193, 227, 476
Sawhill, Isabel V., 376, 402, 403, 405
Scalia, Antonin, 422
Scanlon, Edward, 462
Scheider, David, 189
Schmid, Randolph E., 25, 476
Schneider, Herbert, 476
Schneiderman, Rose, 243
School lunch program, 388, 430–431
Schwartz, Martin, 308

Schwartz-Nobel, Loretta, 403, 477
Scherer, Andrew, 321
Scientific revolution, 87–89
Scott v. Macy (1965) and homosexual em-
 ployment, 367
Scudder, Vida, 216
Seale, Bobby, 321–322
Seelye, Katharine Q., 466, 477
Seller, Maxine, 189, 190, 264, 266, 477
Seneca Falls Convention, 186–187
Senior Citizens Freedom to Work Act
 (2000),
Servicemen's Dependent Allowance Act
 (1942), 295
Seton Elizabeth Ann Bailey (Mother), 172
Settlement Act (1662), 108
Settlement House movement, 49, 190,
 216–219, 261
Settlement houses
and neighborhood guilds, 216
and women, 216–217, 228
as radical, 244
Sewell, May Wright, 218
Sexism, institutional, 19–20
Sex roles
socialization, 9–10, 38–39, 373
mental health and, 308–310
Sexuality, women and, 209–211, 257–259,
 333, 419–422
Sexually transmitted diseases
AIDS, 368
1800s and, 210–211
1980s and 1990s and, 368
Progressive era and, 257–259
public health and, 258
Shalala, Donna E., 462, 477
Shapiro, Isaac, 461, 477
Shapiro, Joseph P., 460, 477
Shapiro v. Thompson and AFDC residency
 requirement, 312
Shaw, Anna Howard, 255
Shea, Mary, 265, 477
Shepard-Towner Act (1918), 249, 256
Sherman Anti-Trust Act
of 1890, 198
of 1902, 232
Sherraden, Michael, 404, 461, 462, 477
Sherwood, Robert E., 477
Shockley, William, 348
Sillen, Syndic, 102
Sims, Dr. Marion, 211
Sinclair, A., 191, 477
Sisters of Charity, 103, 172
Skidmore, Dave, 464, 477
Slave Codes, 180, 182–183
Slavery, 179–183
African origins, 144
children's status determined by moth-
 ers status, 143
colonies and, 126, 129, 130, 142, 145
Constitution and, 179
cotton culture and, 180–185
end of, in North, 148
legal bases for, 142
legal killing of, 142

manumission, 142
Middle Passage, 144–145
  slave uprisings during, 145
Native American, 125–126, 129
numbers of, 145
Protestantism, early, and slave status,
  143
Revolutionary War and, 148
sexual relationships with whites, 143
slaves as insurable properties, 145
slave families, 181
slave prices, 179
slave rebellions and, 145, 180, 182–183
slave trade (triangular trade), 143–145
Union Army and, 195
white slavery, 259
work of, 181–182
Slocum, Sally, 79, 477
Sly, James, 461
Smalley, Ruth, 299
Smith, Adam, 110, 117, 477
Smith, David A., 461, 477
Smith, Geri, 466, 477
Smith, Hilda Worthington, 275
Smith-Hughes Act (1917), agricultural and
  industrial schools, 245
Smith, Margaret Chase, 320
Sniffen, Michael J., 477
Social casework, 263, 287–288, 299–300
  emergence of, 244
  functionalist group work, 299–300
  Kennedy programs of education for,
    329–331
  problem-solving model, 300
  psychosocial, 299–300
Social control, 2, 50–51
Social Darwinism, 7, 111, 211–213, 226,
    232–233, 313, 348, 421, 431, 444
Social group work, 43, 287–288, 299
Social institutions, 27–40
  definition of, 27, 51
  economy, 28–29
  family, 30
  perspectives on, 37–40
  polity, 29–30
  religion, 30–31
  social welfare, 31–33
Social Insurance programs
  Clinton and, 428–431
  Depression era, 279–282
  Germany and beginnings of, 276
  1950s and, 41–42, 309
  1970s and, 346–348
  United States, early programs of
    276–283
Social model of social work, institutional
  perspective as basis of, 35–37
Social reform following Revolutionary
  War and 1800s, 159–161
Social protests (rebellions, revolts,
  strikes), 318–319
  African American, 320–322
  American Indian Movement (AIM),
    358
  Alcatraz revolt, 358

Wounded Knee takeover, 358
Birmingham in 1960s, 318–319
Black Power, 321
Corporate revolt during Great
  Depression, 273
Fair Employment Practices
  Commission (FEPC) and, 294
Great Depression protests, 270–271
Kelley's Army (1894), 198
Menominee and tribal fishing rights,
  359
Mohawks in Adirondack State Park,
  358–359
Native American claims against U.S.
  Government, 359
Native American, during 1800s,
  203–204
  slave rebellions, 145, 180, 182–183
Progressive era, and 245
  Pittsburgh Railroad Strike, 245
  Hay Market riot. 245
  Pennsylvania Coal Miners strike.
    245
race riots, 321–323
  women's protests in 1960s, 322–323
  youth protests (1960s), 323–324
Social Security, 277–286
  under Kennedy, 329–334
  public assistance programs of,
    282–285
  social insurance programs of,
    279–282
Social Security Acts (SSA, 1935), 42, 267,
    278–286, 306
  Aid to Dependent Children (ADC),
    278. *See also* Aid to Families of
    Dependent Children
  1962 amendments to (Social Service
    amendments), 45, 329–330
    351
  1967 amendments to, under Johnson,
    332–334
  1978 amendments to, 346–347
  Social services capped, 351
Social stratification, 12–14
Social welfare
  colonial social welfare, 135–141
  conflict perspectives on , 33–40
  costs of, and Reagan, 388–400
  definitions of, 32–33
  Dynasties of China and, 65–66
  early Christianity and , 74–79
  early England and, 105–109
  Greek city-states and, 67–71
  growth of, 243–244
  Holy Roman Empire and, 82–83
  institutional perspective on, 35–37
  international economy and, 452
  post-World War I, 244–245
  Progressive era and, 243–262
  poverty and, 14–17
  residual perspective on, 34–35
  scope of, 40–41
  shift from local to state power,
    163–165

social institution of social welfare,
  31–33
split in services in Great Depression,
  267, 270, 272
tactic of control of poor, 457
values in. *See* Values
wealthy, for the, 446–451
work ethic and, 101–102
World War I, following, 244–245
Social welfare beginnings, 54–58
  in Africa and Egypt during 6000–3000
    B.C., 57–58
  in China's dynasties, 65–66
  early Christianity and, 74–79, 86
  in Greece and city-states, 67–71
  Holy Roman Empire and, 82–83
  in India, 66–67
  in early Roman society, 71–74
  in Iron Age (1200–400 B.C.), 63–67
  in Mesopotamia during 3000–1200
    B.C., 58–60
  prehistory to 6000 B.C., 54–57
  Roman state and church and, 74–78
  Tudor period, 103
Social welfare programs. *See also specific
  programs*
  1800s and, 221–224
  Kennedy and Johnson administra-
    tions and, 329–334
  1950s and, 309–312
  1970s and, 345–348
  Reagan administration and, 399
  social work profession and, 336–338
  World War II reforms and, 297–299,
    300
Social work profession, 46–50
  Asian American Social Workers, 345
  Association of Puerto Rican Social
    Service Workers, 345
  Association of American Indian Social
    Workers, 345
  civil rights and welfare and, 336–338
  emergence of, 49–50
  Kennedy support of, 329–331
  National Association of Black Social
    Workers, 345
  National Association of Social
    Workers (NASW), 261
  professionalization of social work
    and, 193, 224–225, 261–263,
    286–288
  radical social work unions and,
    286–287
  resurgence after World War II,
    297–299
  retreat to conservatism, 345
  socialist perspective on, 38
  split in services, 286
  unionization of, 286–287
Social Work Research Association (1949),
  299
Socialist feminism, 38
Socialist party beginnings, 231–232
Socialist perspective on social welfare,
  38–39

Society for Reformation of Juvenile Delinquents, 173
Society of the House of Carpenters, 141
Society of St. Vincent de Paul, 102
Solomon, Hanna Greenbaum, 218
Southern, Richard W., 115, 477
Southern Christian Leadership Conference (SCLC), 314
Spaeth, Linda E., 134, 150, 151, 477
Specht, Harry, 27, 51–52, 27–28, 212, 472
Speenhamland Act, 109
Spencer, Herbert, 212
Spender, Dale, 264, 477
Sprenger, J., 116, 477
Sprull, Julia Cherry, 151, 477
St. Cyprian, 76
St. Paul, 408
St. Vincent de Paul, 102
Stamp Act, 146
Stanford, Dr. John, 172
Stanton, Alfred, 308
Stanton, Elizabeth Cady, 186–187
Starr, Ellen Gates, 216–217
State Agencies on Aging, 335–333, *See* Older Americans Act (1965), 335
State Boards of Charities, 163–164223–224
Statute of Artificers (1388, 1583), 97, 103
Statute of Laborers (1349), 96–98
Stevens, Doris, 264, 265, 477
Stevens, Thaddeus, 204
Stevenson, Dr. Sarah, 218
Stewart B. McGivney Assistance Act for the Homeless, 431
Still, Dr. Caroline V., 208
Still, Cooper, 208
Stockman, David A., 402, 477
Stone, Hannah, 260
Stone, Lucy, 186, 187–188
Stone, Merlin, 63, 80, 477
Stover, Charles B., 216
Stowe, Harriet Beecher, 172
Strayer, Joseph R., 86, 477
Strikes, 242. *See* Social revolt
Strock, L.F., 150
Structural model of social work institutional perspective as basis of, 35
Student Democratic Society (SDS), 322, 367
Student Non-Violent Coordinating Committee (SNCC), 314, 321, 322
Sturdy beggars, 107–108, 139
Substitute parent policies of AFDC, 284, 311, 312
Sugar trade, 144
Sugarman, Jule M., 402, 403, 477
Suitable home policy in AFDC, 284, 311, 312
Sumerians, 59
Sumner, Charles,204
Sumner, W.G., 51
Supplemental Security Income (SSI), 284, 346, 349, 383, 413, 426–427
cuts in under PRWORA, 426

Reagan-Bush and, 378, 383
Surplus Commodity Program, 334
Supply side economics and Reagan, 372–375
Suttee, 67
Swann v. Charlotte-Mecklenburg Board of Education and segregation, 363
Synergy, ix–x, 1–2, 37, 60, 62, 78, 372, 406, 408, 457

Taharka, 64
Taft, Jessie, 299
Taft, William Howard, 246
Talent Search program, 354
Talmadge amendments to AFDC (1971), 350
Talmud, 64
Talon, Jean, 125
TANF. *See* Temporary Assistance to Needy Families
Tappan, Arthur Lewis, 183
Tax Equity and Fiscal Responsibility Act (1882), 377
Taxes, 29
capital gains and tax structure, 375–376,, 448
income, 231–232, 374–375
tax base for OASDI, 384
Taylor, Frederich, 299
Tecumseh (Shawnee Chief), 177
Temporary Assistance to Needy Families (TANF), 8, 20, 41–42, 44, 285
absent parents and, 416
child support and, 414–417
class action suits against, 424–425
cost of, 418–419
day care and, 417–419
disability and, 426
effectiveness of, 409, 413, 414, 422–425
housing and homelessness and, 431–433
Housing and Urban Development (HUD) and, 432
Istook amendment, 435
institutional discrimination in, 412, 424
leavers of, 422, 423–424
leavers and Medicaid and, 423
Maintenance of Effort (MOE), 415
Medicaid and, 416
morality for women and, 419–422
nutrition programs and, 430–431
Protestant work ethic and, 422–423
single parents and, 416
state programs under TANF, 389–390
structure of, 414–416
success of, 422–425
Supplemental Security Income and, 426
teenage pregnancy and, 365–370, 420–421
time limits and, 416, 421
values and, 419–422
welfare to work program of, 413–419
women's sexuality and, 419–422

work training programs of, 416, 421
Ten-Million-Acre Bill, 171, 372
Tenskwatawa (Shawnee prophet), 177
Terrorism, 409, 451–452, 455, 456
and international economy, 451–452
poverty and, 455–456
Tertullian, 74
Texas Rangers, 184
Thayer, Frederick C., 408, 418, 458, 459, 477
Theodora, 83
Thirds, custom of, 134
Third World citizenry in United States, 456–457
Thomas Aquinas, 88
Thomas, Clarence, 442
Thomas, Keith, 95, 117, 447
Thomas, P. 463, 477
Three-fifths Clause of Constitution, 179, 197
Tijerina, Reies, 316
Tilden, Samuel J., 205
Timms, Noel, 478
Tillmon, Johnnie, 337
Tobias, Sheila, 304, 378
Torrey, E. Fuller, 26, 478
Townsend, Joseph, 271
Townsend movement, 271, 283
Toynbee, Arnold, 114
Toynbee Hall, 114, 21
Trail of Tears, 177–178
Tramps, following Civil War, 199, 222
Transnational corporations, 452–453
Trattner, Walter, 116– 478
Treisman, Eric, 370, 478
Trevino, Juan de, 127
Triangle Shirt Waist Factory, 242–243
Triangular trade, 143–145. *See also* Golden triangle
Tropman, John E., 342, 478
Trotter, William Monroe, 238–239
Troy Female Seminary, 172
Truman, Harry S., 276, 283, 294, 300, 306
civil rights and, 294
McCarran Act and McCarthyism, 319
Trusts, monopolies, and supercorporations, 232
Truth, Sojourner, 187
Tubman, Harriet, 183
Tuckerman, Joseph, 160–161
Tudor England, 103–109
able-bodied poor during, 105–106
almshouses during, 105
dependent children during, 106–107
Elizabethan Poor Laws of 1601 in, 104–105
prisons during, 108
Tumin, Melvin, 25, 478
Turner, Mary, 238
Turner, Nat, 182

Underclass, 15
Unemployment
Clinton and, 440–442
1980s and, 381–382

Great Depression, 268–269
New Poor and, 381–382, 383
post-Revolutionary War, 157
Progressive Era and, 253
State Employment Security
    Commissions, 281
tramps and, 199
Wagner-Rainy Bill, 270
Women and minorities in Great
    Depression, 269, 273
World War II and, 292
Unemployment compensation, 42, 279,
    281–282
Unemployment insurance, 381–383
during 1970s, 348, 381–383
Progressive Era and, 253–254
Reagan-Bush administration and,
    381–382
state Employment Security
    Commissions, 281
Unionization and labor
African Americans and, 294
Civil War and after, 198–200, 203, 211
Great Depression and, 273
1960s and, 307
Norris-LaGuardia Act, 273
post-Revolutionary War, 156–157
Progressive Era, 198–199, 241
social workers unions, 286–287
women and, 198–199, 200, 241–242,
    243
Unions
American Federation of Labor (AFL),
    273
children and, 219, 220
Congress of Industrial Organizations
    (CIO, 1937), 273
in early 1800s, 158
Home Relief Employees Association,
    286
International Ladies Garment Workers
    Union (ILGWU), 240, 242
merger of United Autoworkers,
    United Steelworkers,
    International Association of
    Machinists, 441
National Colored Labor Union, 200
National Education Association, 441
National Women's Trade Union
    League, 242
social Darwinism and, 212
Women and, 198, 199, 291
Working Women's Protective Union,
    200
United Fund, 214, 261
United Nations, 276
United Racist Front, 364
U. S. Constitution, 147–148, 179, 197, 302
Amendments thirteen, fourteen, fif-
    teen, 197
Bill of Rights amendments, 148
as elitist document, 148
income tax amendment (16th amend-
    ment), 232
Seventeenth Amendment, 231

slavery and, 149
three-fifths clause rescinded, 197
U.S. Sanitary Commission, 163, 195,
    214
United Way, 214, 261
Universal Declaration of Human Rights,
    276
Upward Bound, 328
Urban League, 298
Urban renewal, 336, 355
Utilitarianism, 110–111
United Fund, 214

Vaccines for Children (VFC) program,
    434
Vadum, Arlene, 264
Values, 1–26, 411
American Ideal and, 11–12
definition of, 3–4
egalitarianism and individualism and,
    6–7
foundations of, 4
Judaeo-Christian charity values,
    5–6
marriage and nuclear family and,
    10–11
New Puritanism and, 9–10
new synergy of, 406–409, 455–457
patriarchy and, 9–10
power and, 23
Protestant work ethic and capitalism
    and, 7–8
reification of past values, 114
social Darwinism and, 8
TANF and, 419–422
Van Atta, Dale, 404, 478
Van Bierna, David, 420, 460, 479
Van Kleeck, Mary, 287
Verrazano, French explorer, 123
Vesey, Denmark, 182
Veterans
colonial, 136
Civil War, 197
Dependent Pension Act, 197
march on Washington, Great
    Depression, 270–271
mental hygiene movement and, 251
Progressive Era, 251–252
Reagan and, 378
Veteran's Administration (VA), 300
veterans services, 250
veterans welfare, 251–252
Vietnam, 378
World War I and, 251–252, 270–271
World War II and, 295
Veterans Bureau, 251
Vietnam War, 307, 323, 378
Johnson and, 327, 328–329, 338
Visiting Nurses Association (est. 1893),
    216
Visiting teachers, 43
Vives, Juan Luis, 101–102
Vocational Education Act (1965), 327
Vocational rehabilitation and training, 44,
    251, 277

Voluntary agencies, 40–41, 43. *See also*
    Private charity
Volunteer Prison League, 215
Volunteers in Service to America
    (VISTA), 327
Volunteers of America, 41, 215, 162–163
Voting rights, 325
men and, 189
1930s-1940s registration, 293
pre-Civil War, 153
Suffrage Amendment, 257
Voting Rights Act of 1965, 443
women and, 186–187, 257

Wagner Act, National Labor Relations
    Act (1938), 273
Wagner, David, 9, 25, 445, 464, 479
Wagner-Rainey Bill, 270
Wald, Lillian, 216, 246
Waldman, William, 463, 479
Walker, Sam, 458, 479
Walpole, Robert, 451
Walsh-Healy Act (1936) and child labor,
    273
Wards Cove Packing v. Antonio, 442
War industry, corporate welfare and,
    450–451
Warner, Amos G., 214
Warren, Mercy Otis, 149
War on Poverty, 307, 338–339
War Risk Insurance Act, 251
Washington, Booker T., 206–207, 238
Washington, George, 139, 147, 176
Watson, Frank Dekker, 117, 190, 229, 265,
    479
Wayland, Francis, 199
Wealth
American obsession with, 119
capital assets and tax cuts, 446–447
polarization of income and, 446–447
Protestant ethic and
    stratification and, 12–17
Weaver, Robert, 292, 326
Webb, Beatrice, 113
Webb, Sidney, 113
Weber, Max, 99–100, 117, 479
Weinberg, Daniel H., 461
Weisman, Daniel, 460, 479
Weissman, Michaele, 150, 151, 156, 189,
    190, 191, 227, 228, 229, 264, 266,
    303, 340, 341, 473, 479
Weitzman, Leonore, 341, 479
Wesley, John, 112
Wheatley, Jonathan, 466
Wheeler Howard Act (Indian
    Reorganization Act, 1933),
    292–293
White House Conference on Children
    (Child Dependency) (1909), 216,
    246
White, Walter, 264, 293, 313
Whitefield, George, 141
White supremacy groups, 362
Whitmire, Richard, 479
Wilberforce University, 183

Wildavsky, Aaron, 369, 479
Wilensky, Harold L., 52, 479
Wiley, George, 337
Willard, Emma Hart, 172
Willard, Frances, and WCTU, 208
William the Conqueror, 85
Williams, Aubrey, 272
Williams, Eric, 150, 152, 479
Willis, George, 369, 379, 403
Wilson, William J., 15, 25, 479
Wilson, Woodrow, 234, 251
WIN funnel (Work Incentive Program), 350
Wines, Frederick, 174, 223–224
Wines, Michael, 404, 479
Winslow, Rose, 256–257
Winthrop, John, 134, 342
Witchcraze, during Dark and Middle Ages, 94–95
    Inquisition and, 116–117
Witmer, Lightner, 251
Witte, Edwin, 278
Wodarski, John, 134
Women
    almshouses and, 166
    Christianity, early, and , 74, 75
    Cult of True Womanhood and, 207–210
    discrimination against, WWII, 296–297
    early Christianity and, 74, 75
    1800s and, 167–169
    employment and Civil War, 198
    employment during World War II, 290–292
    feudalism and, 85–86, 91
    Great Depression and, 269–288
    health care and, 209–211, 251–260
    in Israelite tribes, 62–63
    institutional sexism and, 19–20
    Iron Age, 66–67, 69
    juvenile delinquency and, 297, 298
    Keating-Owens bill and, 247
    Kennedy-Johnson years and, 322–323
    medical care in 1800s, 167–169
    medical profession and, 168–169, 195, 196
    mental health and, 298–300
    New Deal and, 275–276
    New World colonies and, 132– 136
    patriarchy and, 9–10
    post-Revolutionary War, 156–157
    povertization of, 39, 453
    prehistoric society and, 54–57
    Progressive era and, 240–243
    Protestantism, early, and, 100–101, 134
    Revolutionary War and, 146–147
    Roman Empire and, 69–70, 72, 83
    sexuality and, 209–211, 228
    social insurance and, 280–281
    suffrage and, 153, 187
    TANF and, 419–422
    unions and, 241–243, 296
    Victorian era, 324
    witchcraft and, 134–136
    witchcraze and, 135
    work and, 112, 198–199

workhouses and, 107, 135, 157
    World War II and following, 290–292, 296–297, 298
Women's Bureau, 256
Women's Central Association of Relief, 195–196
Women's Christian Temperance Union (WCTU), 208–209
Women's clubs, 240
Women's, Infants, and Children Nutrition Program (WIC), 286
    Clinton administration and, 413, 430–431
    Reagan administration, 379, 388
Women's Medical College, 168
Women's movements
    1800s and, 185–187
    following Revolutionary war, 185–187
    1870s and, 361–367
    Progressive Era, 255–256
Women's Peace Party, 255–256
Wooden, Kenneth, 370, 479
Woods, Robert, 254
Woodward, Ellen, 275
Woolson, Howard, 258
Work. See also Labor
    colonialism and, 129–135
    Industrial Revolution, 112–114
    industrialism and, 112
    new definition of, 100, 421–422
    poor and, 119
Worcester Asylum, 171
Workers compensation, 253–254, 277, 279, 282
Work ethic, 7–8, 17
    Calvinism and, 99–100
    children and, 219, 220
    mercantilism and, 98–100
    Protestant Reformation and, 101–102
    social Darwinism and, 212
    religious legitimation and, 8, 99–100
    social welfare and, 103–105
    TANF and, 419–422, 423
    wealth and, 119, 143, 154, 188
Work Experience Program (WEP), 44, 327
Workhouses, in Tudor England, 107–108
Work Incentive Program (WIN), 333–334, 350, 386
Work and Training Programs, 421
    Community Work Experience Program (CWEP), 386
    Comprehensive Education and Training Act (CETA), 353, 382
    Job Opportunity Training (JOBS), 44, 413
    Johnson administration Work Study and Work Training, 327
    Kennedy administration, AFDC and, 330–331
    New Careers Program, 328
    Senior Citizens Freedom to Work Act (2000)
    Temporary Assistance to Needy Families (TANF) Work Programs, 413–416, 421

Upward Bound, 328
Work Experience Program (WEP), 327
Work Incentive Program (WIN), 333–334, 350, 386
Workhouse Act (1696), 107
Workhouse test, 107, 113, 135, 157
Working Women's Protective Union, 200
Works Progress Administration (WPA), 271, 274
    African-Americans and, 293
World Bank, 406, 453
World War I, 234–235
    African American migration and, 237
    Archduke Ferdinand and, 233
World War II, 288–297
    economy during, 268, 290
    families in, 291
    internment of Japanese Americans during, 236, 289–294
    minorities during, 288–290
    Native Americans, 293
    resurgence of social work following, 297–300
    servicemen and, 294–295
    Servicemen's Dependent Allowance Act (1942), 295
    social welfare services during and after, 294–295
    women after, discrimination in employment, 296–298
    women's employment during, 290
Worthy and unworthy poor, 7–8, 14, 42, 69–70, 97, 102, 277, 278, 284, 407–408, 419–422, 457
Wounded Knee, massacre at, 203–204
Wovoka (Paiute Messiah), 203
Wright, Andrea R., 460
Wright, Frances, 172
Wright, James D., 25, 383, 403, 404, 407, 458

Yates, John V.N., Report, 159–160, 190, 479
Young, Andrew, 363
Young Lords (Puerto Rican activist group), 317, 322
Young Men's Christian Association (YMCA), 162
Young Women's Christian Association (YWCA), 162
Youth
    Haryou: Harlem Youth Opportunity Program, 336
    Mobilization for Youth (MFY), 336
    National Youth Authority (NYA), 293
    Neighborhood Youth Corps, 293
    protests during 1960s, 323–324

Zakrzewska, Marie, 168, 169
Zastrow, Charles, 26, 52, 479
Zeigler, L. Harmon, 14, 25, 148, 152, 153, 189, 191, 227, 229, 302, 303, 313, 340, 341, 342, 479
Zinn, Deborah K., 385, 471, 404
Zuckerman, Mortimer B., 465, 466, 479